MANAGEMENT
An Integrated Framework

MANAGEMENT
An Integrated Framework

Second Edition

Martin J. Gannon
University of Maryland

LITTLE, BROWN AND COMPANY
Boston / Toronto

Library of Congress Catalog Card No. 81-82312

ISBN 0-316-303348

9 8 7 6 5 4 3 2 1

HAL

Published simultaneously in Canada
by Little, Brown & Company (Canada) Limited

Printed in the United States of America

Photographs on pages 4, 106, 212, 298, and 420 appear courtesy of the Ford Motor Company.

Dedicated to my wife Doris,
with love and appreciation

Preface

Over the years professors of management have taught the basic undergraduate management course from various perspectives. Perhaps the major perspective has been that of the management process school, which argues that the individual manager completes his or her activities in a process that starts with planning and logically leads to organizing, directing, and controlling. However, some writers such as Simon (1976) and Mintzberg (1980) have attacked this perspective as not reflecting what managers actually do. At the same time, some professors began to teach the basic management course by either replacing or supplementing the management process perspective with other perspectives, including the quantitative, systems, and contingency perspectives.

This textbook is built around a contemporary management process perspective that integrates all the other major perspectives or schools in the management field. From this contemporary perspective, there are four organizational dimensions within which managerial activities take place: (1) planning and control, (2) organization design, (3) behavioral processes, and (4) managerial decision making. This organizational framework shows the relationships among these dimensions; managers and students can evaluate individual and organizational performance by examining these relationships. However, an instructor teaching the basic undergraduate course can use this organizational framework flexibly; it is easily adapted to any of the other major perspectives.

As this discussion implies, one of my major objectives in writing this book was to develop and refine this contemporary process approach or integrated organizational framework. But I also sought to accomplish many other objectives.

This book is based on fifteen years of teaching the basic undergraduate management course. Students taking this course usually have limited work experience: they have not been involved much, if at all, in the management of organizations. Thus, I have tried to go well beyond the simple description and analysis of the work of managers. I have tried to convey a sense of what it is like to be part of a functioning organization in today's world.

The first two chapters set the stage by providing an historical overview of the management field. The two major streams of management—the traditional management stream and the behavioral science stream—as well as the schools within each stream are described in detail in these two chapters. Chapter 3 then describes the integrated organizational framework, and three short case studies give students a chance to apply it to real organizations. The organizational framework is then used as the framework for the next three parts of the book: planning and control, organization design, and behavioral processes. Part V focuses on specific organizational issues, including social responsibility, conflict and creativity, and managing change and development. Part VI, Managerial Careers and Orientations, examines the issues of managerial performance and career success and the outlook for management.

Each chapter of this book begins with a set of performance objectives, so that the student can direct and evaluate his or her own study. Discussion questions following each chapter encourage the reader to think beyond the text, to apply the concepts introduced to real or hypothetical situations. Suggestions for additional reading, also at the end of each chapter, indicate sources that can amplify the material.

In this book, there is a conscious attempt to allow the student to experience what it means to be a manager. After almost all chapters, there are critical incidents, short cases to be studied by the student or discussed in class. Longer case studies follow three parts of the book (Parts II, III, and V). Ordinarily, it is difficult to involve students actively in the solution of critical incidents and cases, because of limited classroom space. To overcome this problem, I have developed two experiential exercises, the Case Observational Method and Theoretical Case Analysis (see Appendices A and B). I developed Theoretical Case Analysis so that our organizational framework could be applied to the solution of cases. In addition, experiential exercises follow Parts IV, V, and VI. These include questionnaires on motivation, leadership, and conflict resolution; an exercise on group decision making; and one role playing exercise on the promotion interview.

This textbook also contains a continuous case, describing the history of the Ford Motor Company, before each of the first five parts of the book. Again, the student is exposed to real management problems, and he or she can apply our organizational framework to their solution if desired.

Thus this course can be taught entirely by means of lectures, by a combination of lectures and participatory methods, or entirely by means of participatory methods. My preference is for the second option.

Throughout this book, I have attempted to strike a balance between the presentation of concepts and their illustration. Studies, examples, and case material all have been selected to illustrate a wide variety of organizational environments, including business corporations, government agencies, military organizations, universities, and health care organizations. In addition, I have tried to indicate the increasingly important role of women and minority group members in management.

Professors may not want to attain all of the objectives this book seeks to achieve; the text is structured so that each can choose his or her own approach in teaching the course. In short, the book is set up to be flexible, adaptable to the needs and preferences of various instructors.

A Study Guide, a Test Bank, and an Instructor's Manual are also available. The Test Bank contains over 2200 questions, and it has been computerized. The Instructor's Manual is arranged sequentially by chapters and parts of the book and contains additional lecture material; summaries of topical articles for discussion; answers to discussion questions, critical incidents, and cases; experiential exercises; suggested projects, book reports, and films; and suggested teaching methods and approaches for presenting the course material.

Finally, I would appreciate any feedback you may wish to provide.

To the Student

At the end of the chapters and parts of this textbook, there are a number of critical incidents (short cases) and long cases, some or all of which you may be asked to evaluate, either individually or as a group. The following steps should simplify your task:

1. First skim the case, then read it carefully, taking notes, so that you understand it completely.
2. Identify and list problems. List facts by problem areas from the notes you have taken and from a third reading of the case if desired. Then use these facts to diagnose the causes of each problem.
3. Identify the major problem.
4. Develop alternative solutions to this major problem. First, list all identifiable solutions; then reduce the list only to feasible solutions. Repeat this process for minor problem areas.
5. Evaluate alternatives and select the most feasible solution to the major problem. First, list pros and cons associated with it. Weigh the pros and cons and then select the best alternative. Repeat this process for the solution of minor problems.
6. Defend each of your choices by questioning the workability of the solution selected, listing all possible problems that may arise.

This case format follows closely our treatment of managerial decision making (Chapter 4). If you would like to go beyond this format, you can employ the experiential exercise, Theoretical Case Analysis (see Appendix B). This exercise applies the integrated organizational framework used in this book to the solution of case problems.

About the Author

Martin J. Gannon (Ph.D., Graduate School of Business, Columbia University) is Professor of Management and Organizational Behavior at the College of Business and Management, University of Maryland, College Park, Maryland. He has also served as Acting Associate Dean for Academic Affairs and Chairperson of the Faculty of Organizational Behavior and Industrial Relations within this college, and has received an Outstanding Faculty Award from the MBA Alumni Association at Maryland. He has been awarded a Senior Research Fulbright Fellowship to Germany for the 1981–1982 school year.

Mr. Gannon has written over fifty articles in such journals as the *Academy of Management Journal*, the *Academy of Management Review*, the *California Management Review*, *Business Horizons*, the *Journal of Applied Psychology*, and *Industrial Relations*. In addition, he is the author of *Organizational Behavior* (Little, Brown, 1979) and co-editor of *Readings in Management* (Little, Brown, 1977). He has served as President of the Eastern Academy of Management and as Chairperson of the Personnel/Human Resources Division of the Academy of Management. He has been and is a consultant to a large number of organizations, including the U. S. General Accounting Office, the Upjohn Company, the Chemical Bank of New York, the National Commission for Manpower Policy, and the National Association of Personnel Consultants. Mr. Gannon has been involved in management training programs for the Advanced Executive Programs at Columbia University, Unilever of England, the University of Maryland, and various government agencies.

Acknowledgments

I would like to thank the following individuals for reviewing all or part of this book prior to publication:

Professor John R. Anstey, College of Business Administration, University of Nebraska
Professor Peter Arlow, Department of Management and Marketing, Shippensburg State College
Professor John Bachman, Management Development Programs, College of Business Administration, University of Tennessee
Professor Lloyd Baird, School of Management, Boston University
Professor P. Nick Blanchard, Department of Management, Eastern Michigan University
Professor Stephen J. Carroll, Jr., College of Business and Management, University of Maryland
Professor Richard Cosier, School of Business, Indiana University
Professor Dallas Defee, School of Management, State University of New York at Binghamton
Professor Kirk Downey, College of Business Administration, Oklahoma State University
Professor K. Fatehi, Department of Management, College of Business, Western Illinois University
Dr. James Gatza, American Institute for Property and Underwriters
Professor Lee A. Graf, Department of Management and Marketing, College of Business, Illinois State University
Professor Ronald Greenwood, School of Business Administration, University of Wisconsin
Professor Vincent Luchsinger, College of Business Administration, Texas Tech University

Professor James M. McFillen, College of Administrative Science, Ohio State University

Professor Michael McGinnis, Department of Management and Marketing, Shippensburg State College

Professor Jack Mendleson, Department of Management, Arizona State University

Professor Jan P. Muczyk, Department of Management and Labor, College of Business Administration, Cleveland State University

Professor Paul Thompson, Graduate School of Management, Brigham Young University

Professor Robert Vecchio, Department of Management, College of Business and Administration, University of Notre Dame

Professor Robert Wood, College of Business and Management, University of Maryland

Professor Daniel Wren, Division of Management, College of Business Management, University of Oklahoma

Elizabeth Zubritsky, College of Business and Management, University of Maryland

There are two individuals whom I especially want to cite for their help, Peter Arlow and Michael McGinnis, both Associate Professors at Shippensburg State College in Pennsylvania. These professors wrote the Study Guide to accompany the textbook. Also, Professor Arlow was my co-author for Chapter 16 and Professor McGinnis for Chapters 6 and 7. Their help proved to be invaluable.

I also want to thank my wife Doris and our two children, Marlies and Reid. They have been very patient and helpful and have complained only very mildly about the inconveniences associated with the writing of a book.

In addition, I wish to thank the staff of Little, Brown and Company for providing much-needed assistance and advice – particularly Milton Johnson, my editor; Sue Warne, my book editor; and Nancy Arbuckle, editorial assistant. Although many individuals have been helpful, I must take final responsibility for any errors or omissions.

Contents

PART I AN INTRODUCTION TO MANAGEMENT 3

CONTINUOUS CASE: The Ford Motor Company, 1903–1912 5

1 **Traditional Management 7**

Management in Preindustrial Society **8**
Early Concepts of Management, **9** A Working Definition, **10**

Max Weber and Bureaucracy **10**
Capitalism, **12** Bases of Authority, **12** Bureaucratic Organizations, **13** Other Preconditions, **15**

Henri Fayol and the Management Process School **17**
General Management, **17** Functions of Management, **18** Principles of Management, **20** Fayol's Bridge, **21** Criticisms, **22**

Frederick Taylor and Scientific Management **22**
Worker-Management Relations, **23** Task Management, **23** Taylor's Four Principles, **25** Problems of Application, **26**

The Quantitative School **28**

Summary **29**

Discussion Questions **30**

Critical Incident **30**

Suggested Readings **31**

2 **Management and the Behavioral Sciences 32**

Human Relations **33**
Initial Experiments of the Hawthorne Study, **33** Test Room Experiments, **34** Interviewing Program, **35** Observation Room Study, **36**

Systems Theory **37**
Assumptions, **38** Barnard's Systems Theory, **38** Evaluation, **40**

Human Resources **42**
Argyris's Theory, 42 Theory X and Theory Y, **43**

Contingency Theory **44**
Organic and Mechanistic Structures, **46** Tosi and Carroll's Perspective, **48** Critique, **50**
Summary **51**
Discussion Questions **52**
Critical Incidents **52**
Suggested Readings **54**

3 **Management Within an Organizational Framework 55**

Organizational Dimensions of Management **56**
Planning, **57** Control, **59** Organization Design, **60** Behavioral Processes, **61** Managerial Decision Making, **61**
Relationships Within the Organizational Framework **62**
Impact of Planning and Control, **62** Impact of Design, **64** Impact of Behavioral Processes, **64** Setting for Managerial Decision Making, **64**
Relationships to Management Schools **68**
Traditional Management, **68** Behavioral Science Stream, **69**
Dynamics of the Framework: Three Cases **70**
The New Engineers, **70** U.S. Office of Personnel Management, **74** Branch Banking, **76**
Summary **78**
Discussion Questions **79**
Suggested Readings **80**

4 **Managerial Decision Making 81**

Stages in Decision Making **82**
Stimulus Event, **82** Information Search, **82** Problem Formulation, **83** Evaluation of Alternatives/Choice, **83** Implementation, **84**
Decision Environments **84**
Amount of Uncertainty, **84** Perceived Psychological Conflict, **85** Goals and Policies, **85** Organizational Level, **86** Societal Expectations, **87** Culture, **87**
Decision Strategies **88**
Two General Strategies, **88** Programmed and Nonprogrammed Strategies, **89** Certainty-Uncertainty Strategies, **90**
Suboptimization **91**
Human Limits to Rationality, **91** Biased Information Search, **92** Defective Strategies for Making Decisions, **93**

Improving Decision Making **93**
Normative Models, **93** Problem Factoring, **94** Decision Heuristics, **96** Use of Groups, **97** Groupthink, **98**
Summary **99**
Discussion Questions **100**
Critical Incidents **101**
Suggested Readings **102**

PART II PLANNING AND CONTROL **105**
CONTINUOUS CASE: The Ford Motor Company, 1913–1920 **107**

5 **An Introduction to Planning 110**
The Organizational Planning Process **111**
Defining the Mission: Giant Food, **111** Goals and Strategies, **112** Objectives and Tactics, **113** Policies, Procedures, and Rules, **114** Simultaneous Activities, **115**
Forecasting **115**
Types of Forecasts, **116** A Forecasting Typology, **117** Qualitative Forecasting Techniques, **119** Time Series Analysis and Projection, **120** Mathematical Models, **121**
Planning with Precise and Imprecise Goals **122**
Specifying Goals, **122** Departmental Planning, **124**
Management by Objectives (MBO) **124**
Research on MBO, **126** Limitations, **127** Advantages, **128** The Future of MBO, **129**
Strategic Failures **129**
RCA and IBM, **129** Itel and Lloyd's of London, **130** The Edsel, **131** Duke Tobacco, **131** Chinese Fast-Food Chain, **132**
Summary **133**
Discussion Questions **134**
Critical Incidents **135**
Suggested Readings **136**

6 **Planning Techniques 137**
Break-even Analysis **138**
Costs, **139** Price, **139** Demand, **139**
Capital Budgeting **141**
Linear Programming **142**

Networks 144
Gantt Chart, **144** PERT and CPM, **145**
Probabilistic Models **148**
Expected Value, **148** Waiting Line Analysis (Queuing), **149** Decision Trees, **150** Simulation, **150**
Implications for Managers **152**
Summary **154**
Discussion Questions **155**
Problems **155**
Suggested Readings **157**

7 Techniques for Controlling Organizational Systems 158

The Concept of Control **159**
Feedback and Feedforward Control, **159** Control of Members and Subsystems, **160** Combinations of Control, **161**
Budgetary Control **162**
Types of Budgets, **162** Standard Costs, **162** Responsibility Centers, **163** Zero-based Budgeting, **164**
Inventory and Quality Control **165**
Three Inventory Models, **165** Defining and Monitoring Quality, **167**
Management Information Systems **167**
Computers and Centralization, **168** Designing the MIS, **169** Key Attributes, **170** Networks and MIS, **171** Impact of the Computer, **171**
Additional Control Techniques **172**
Financial Statements, **172** Cybernetic (Machine-controlled) Systems, **173** Attitude Surveys, **173** Management Audit, **174**
Summary **174**
Discussion Questions **175**
Suggested Readings **176**

8 Selection and the Personnel Control Process 177

Selection **178**
Job Search Methods, **178** Tests, **180** Application Blanks, **181** The Hiring Interview, **183**
Job Orientation **184**
Training and Development **185**
Training, **186** Development, **189**
Performance Appraisal **193**
Rating Methods, **193** Additional Issues, **197**

Reward Systems **199**
Motivational Framework, **199** Employee Preferences, **201**
Summary **202**
Discussion Questions **203**
Critical Incidents **204**
Suggested Readings **205**

PART II CASE STUDY: Monitoring the Performance of Bank Tellers **206**

PART III ORGANIZING **211**

CONTINUOUS CASE: The Ford Motor Company, 1921–1929 **213**

9 **Classical and Contemporary Concepts of Organizing 216**

Hierarchy and Specialization **217**
Building the Organization, **217** Bases of Departmentalization, **223** Constructing Guidance Systems, **226**
Barriers to Integration **233**
Voluntary Barriers, **233** Hierarchical Barriers, **234**
Improving Integration **236**
Structural Methods, **236** Personal Methods, **239**
Summary **239**
Discussion Questions **240**
Critical Incidents **241**
Suggested Readings **243**

10 **Alternative Methods of Organizing 244**

Modern Forms of Organization **245**
Federal Decentralization, **245** Project Management, **247** Matrix Organization, **249**
Specialized Forms of Organization **256**
Professional Organizations, **256** Government Organizations, **257** Specialized Service Organizations, **258** Etzioni's Typology, **259**

Economic Forms of Organization **260**
Employee-owned Companies, **260** Conglomerates, **261** Vertical and Horizontal Integration, **261** Ventures, **262** State-backed Corporations, **262** Multinational Corporations, **263**
Summary **264**
Discussion Questions **265**
Critical Incident **266**
Suggested Readings **267**

11 **A Contingency Approach to Organizing 268**
Three Critical Factors **269**
The Blau Study, **269** The Woodward Study, **270** The Lawrence and Lorsch Study, **272** Successful Integrators, **274** The Chandler Study, **275** An Alternative Explanation, **276**
The Information-Processing Synthesis **276**
Five Strategies, **277** Seven Steps for Creating Lateral Relations, **278**
Summary **280**
Discussion Questions **282**
Critical Incident **282**
Suggested Readings **283**

PART III CASE STUDIES: The Overly Successful Bank **284**
State University Medical Center **287**

PART IV **DIRECTING BEHAVIORAL PROCESSES 291**
CONTINUOUS CASE: The Ford Motor Company, 1930–1945 **293**

12 **Interpersonal Communication 298**

Perception **299**
Factors Influencing Perception, **300** Organization of Perception, **302**
Communication Among Individuals **305**
A Basic Model, **305** Barriers to Communication, **306** Communication Networks, **307** Two-Step Flow, **309** Methods of Communication, **310** The Yale Studies, **312**
Interpersonal Communication and Managerial Work **313**
Nature of Managerial Work, **313** Styles, **316**
Summary **318**

Discussion Questions **319**
Critical Incidents **319**
Suggested Readings **321**

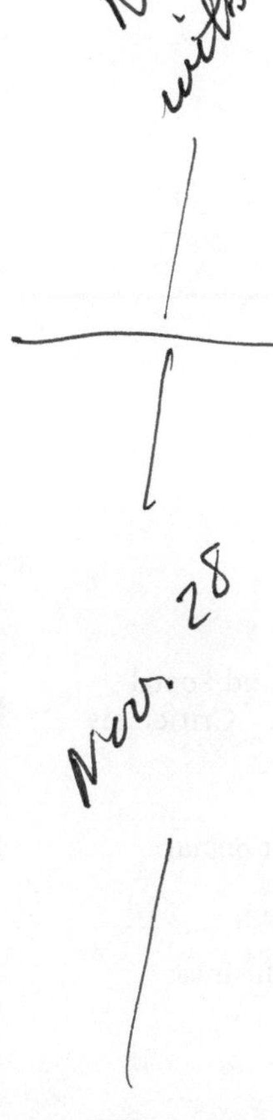

13 Motivation 322

Process Theories **324**
Expectancy Theory, **324** Locke's Goal-setting Theory, **326** Cognitive Dissonance, **327** Adam's Equity Theory, **328**
Content Theories **328**
Maslow's Need Hierarchy, **328** Herzberg's Two-Factor Theory, **331** Job Diagnostic Survey, **334** McClelland's Need Theory, **335**
Conditioning Theories **336**
Additional Concepts, **337** Schedules of Reinforcement, **338** Ratio Schedules, **339** BMod Program and Techniques, **340**
Factors Affecting Job Satisfaction **342**
Occupational and Organizational Level, **343** Design Factors, **344** Labor Market, **345** Orientation to Work, **345** Psychological Characteristics, **346**
Summary **346**
Discussion Questions **347**
Critical Incidents **348**
Suggested Readings **349**

14 Leadership 350

A Profile of Managerial Leadership **351**
Nature of Leadership, **351** Types of Power, **352** Managerial Roles, **352**
Theories of Leadership **356**
Trait Theory, **356** Leader Behavior Theory, **357** Managerial Grid, **358** Leader Effectiveness: Fiedler, **360** Leader Effectiveness: Path Goal, **362** Reciprocal Causation Theory, **364** Vertical Dyadic Theory, **365**
Contingency Factors Influencing Leadership **366**
Influence of Subordinates, **366** Short-Term Versus Long-Term Effects, **366** Personality, **367** Locals and Cosmopolitans, **368** Organizational Position, **370** Type of Industry, **370** Substitutes for Leadership, **372**
Subordinate Participation in Decision Making **373**
Summary **374**
Discussion Questions **376**
Critical Incident **376**
Suggested Readings **377**

15 **Group Behavior 378**

Group Formation and Development **379**
Homans's System Theory, **380** Evolution of Groups, **381** Joining Groups, **381** The Ideal Group, **383**
Types of Groups in Organizations **383**
Primary and Secondary Groups, **383** Problem-solving Groups, **384** Creative Groups, **385**
Factors Influencing Behavior in Groups **386**
Physical Environment, **386** Characteristics of Groups Members, **388** Group Composition, **391** Group Structure, **392**
Contingency View of Groups **395**
Tavistock Coal-mining Study, **395** Industrial Work Groups, **397** Alienation and Work Group Behavior, **399**
Summary **403**
Discussion Questions **404**
Critical Incident **404**
Suggested Readings **406**

PART IV EXPERIENTIAL EXERCISES: Assessing Motivation, Satisfaction, and Congruent Jobs **407**
T-P Leadership Questionnaire: An Assessment of Style **414**

PART V **SPECIFIC ORGANIZATIONAL ISSUES 419**

CONTINUOUS CASE: The Ford Motor Company, 1946 to Present **421**

16 **Social Responsibility in Management 424**

Evolution of Social Responsibility **425**
Earlier Views, **425** Beginning of the Modern Era, **428** CED and Social Responsibility, **429** Current Era of Social Responsibility, **431** Criticisms of Corporations, **431**
Pros and Cons for Social Responsibility **433**
Arguments for Social Responsibility, **433** Arguments Against Social Responsibility, **435** Assessing the Arguments, **436**
Business Ethics **436**
Social Responsibility and Business Ethics, **437** Research on Business Ethics, **437** Remedial Actions for Business Ethics, **439**
Social Audits **441**
Concept, **441** Approaches, **441** Current Status, **441**

Current Issues **442**
Quality of the Environment, **442** Government-Business Relations, **445** Ethics and Managerial Practices, **446**
Summary **447**
Discussion Questions **448**
Critical Incident **448**
Suggested Readings **450**

17 **Managing Conflict and Creativity 451**
Conflict in Organizations **452**
Increased Importance of Conflict, **452** Types of Conflict, **453** Interpersonal Conflict, **453** Interdepartmental Conflict, **455** Zero-Sum Conflict, **456**
A Contingency Approach to Resolving Conflict **458**
Conflict in Matrix Organizations, **458** Methods Used by Chief Executives, **459** Additional Methods, **460**
The Creative Process **462**
Steps in the Creative Process, **462** The Creative Individual, **463** The Creative Organization, **463** The Innovation Process, **464** Sources of Creative Ideas, **465**
Creativity Techniques **466**
Nominal Group Technique, **466** Synectics, **467**
Summary **468**
Discussion Questions **469**
Critical Incidents **469**
Suggested Readings **470**

18 **Managing Change and Development 471**
Managing Task Assignments **472**
Job Enrichment Revisited, **473** Role Negotiation, **474** MAPS, **475**
Managing Technological Change **476**
The Automated Factory, **476** The Automated Office, **477** Telecommunications, **478**
Managing People During Change **479**
Labor Force Reductions, **479** Relocations, **480** Introducing Technological Change, **481** Introducing Inevitable Change, **481**
Managing Structural Changes **482**
Work Processes, **483** Work Scheduling, **483** Shift Work, **484**
Organization Development **485**
Steps in OD, **486** Specific Techniques, **486** General Types of Intervention, **489** Specific Types of Intervention, **490**

Complex Issues Facing OD **492**
Familiarity and Dependency, **493** Time and Measurement, **493** Ethics, **494**
Summary **495**
Discussion Questions **496**
Critical Incident **497**
Suggested Readings **498**

PART V EXPERIENTIAL EXERCISES: Conflict Styles: Organizational Decision Making **499**
Group Decision Making **503**

PART V CASE STUDY: Acme Markets, Inc. **506**

PART VI MANAGERIAL CAREERS AND ORIENTATIONS 509

19 Managerial Performance and Career Success 511

Models of Managerial Success **512**
General Model, **512** Specific Model, **513**
Career Preparation **516**
Past Performance, **516** Academic Training, **517** Having a Unique Feature, **517**
Career Strategies **518**
Job Challenge, **518** Personal Responsibility, **518** Specialist Versus Generalist, **519** The Protégé, **520** Special Factors, **520**
Time Management **520**
Benefits, **521** Priorities, **521** Techniques, **522**
Periodic Assessment **523**
Age-Salary Ratio, **523** The Fast Track, **525** Job Satisfaction, **525**
Entrepreneurial Management **526**
Personal Traits, **526** Manager Versus Entrepreneur, **528** Reasons for Failure, **531**
Summary **533**
Discussion Questions **534**
Critical Incidents **534**
Suggested Readings **535**

20 **The Current and Future State of Management 536**

Changes in the Work Force **537**

White-Collar Work Force, **537** Education, **538** Additional Demographic Changes, **538** Changing Careers, **538**

Changing Expectations of Work **539**

The Humanistic Ethic, **539** Racial Minorities, **541** Women, **542** Part-Time Workers, **542** Two-Career Families, **543** Military and Government Employees, **544**

International Management **544**

Management Styles, **545** Japanese Management, **547** Working Abroad, **549** Investments in Foreign Countries, **550**

Management of Declining Resources **551**

Relative Economic Position of the United States, **551** The Energy Crisis, **551** Limits to Growth, **552**

Complex Role of the Manager **552**

Polyspecialist, **552** Integrator, **553** Manager Pairs, **553** Specialized Managers for Specialized Jobs, **554**

Summary **554**

Discussion Questions **555**

Suggested Readings **556**

PART VI EXPERIENTIAL EXERCISE:
Role Playing: The Promotion Interview 557

Appendix A: The Case Observational Method 562

Appendix B: Theoretical Case Analysis 565

Glossary 568

Bibliography 582

Name Index 609

Subject Index 616

MANAGEMENT
An Integrated Framework

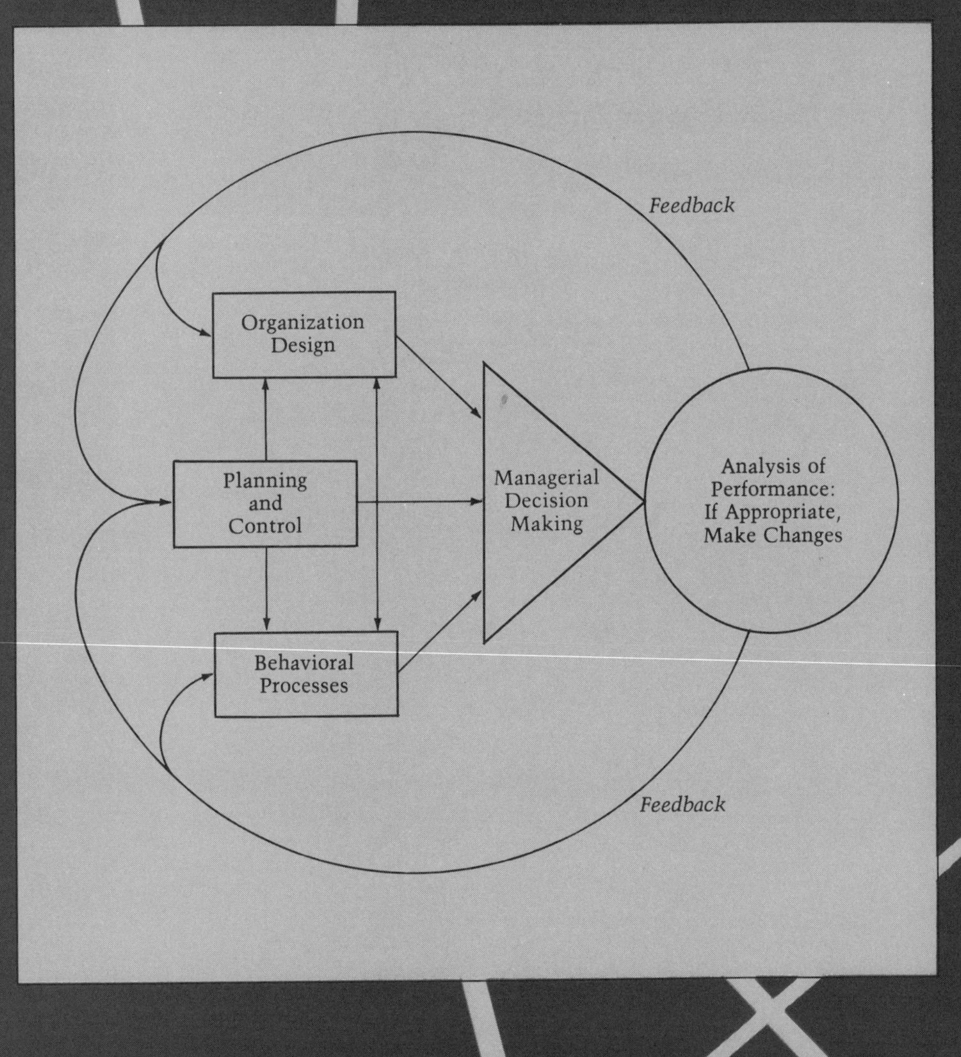
Feedback
Organization Design
Planning and Control
Behavioral Processes
Managerial Decision Making
Analysis of Performance: If Appropriate, Make Changes
Feedback

I AN INTRODUCTION TO MANAGEMENT

Managerial activities are highly diverse, and it is possible to classify them in many different ways. This book takes an organizational perspective: Managerial activities are seen as those that must be performed in order for an organization to function. From this perspective managerial activities fall into four organizational dimensions. *Planning and control,* in combination, constitute the first dimension; they represent the opposite sides of the same coin. The remaining three organizational dimensions are *organization design, behavioral processes,* and *managerial decision making.* We will construct an integrated organizational framework in terms of these dimensions, emphasizing the dynamic relationships among them. All the chapters in this book relate directly to these four organizational dimensions and the resulting organizational framework we will construct using them.

There are two main streams of modern management: the traditional management stream and the behavioral science stream. Chapter 1 contains a historical description of the major schools in the traditional management stream, Chapter 2 of those in the behavioral science stream. In Chapter 3 our integrated organizational framework is described. This framework is based on the integration of the perspectives of the major management schools discussed in Chapters 1 and 2. The final chapter in Part I treats managerial decision making, the only dimension of our organizational framework that is directly influenced by the other three dimensions of planning and control, organization design, and behavioral processes.

THE PARK COMMISSIONERS
HEREBY FORBID ANY ONE FROM
DEPOSITING ANY FILTH, OR RUBBISH
ON THIS BEACH,
UNDER PENALTY OF LAW.
A WRITTEN APPLICATION WILL BE
REQUIRED BY THE PARK COMMISSIONERS
TO ENABLE ANY PERSONS TO ERECT, OR
MAINTAIN ANY BATH HOUSE, OR
OTHER STRUCTURE ON
THIS BEACH.

The Model T

CONTINUOUS CASE

The Ford Motor Company 1903–1912

NOTE: The first five parts of this book open with a continuous case describing the history of the Ford Motor Company. Each section of the case highlights some of the major ideas presented in that particular part. In addition, the instructor can use each section independently, since a short summary of preceding material is given at the beginning of each section of the case.

Henry Ford was a successful engineer and businessman even before he launched the Ford Motor Company in 1903. He had been chief engineer at the Edison Light Company and had been involved in several automotive companies, though these were unsuccessful. It was not until Ford was 40 years old that he, Alexander Malcomson, and James Couzens founded the Ford Motor Company.

Henry Ford was especially ambitious during the company's early years. He developed a distinctive strategic plan that other car manufacturers considered impractical—an inexpensive, all-purpose car (the Model T) that could be purchased by the average citizen. There was considerable opposition within the company management to this position. Because only affluent individuals could purchase the expensive automobiles of the turn of the century, companies generally believed, incorrectly, that only expensive automobiles should be manufactured. At that time it was common for a car to cost $10,000 (about $100,000 in today's dollars). From 1903 until 1909 the Ford Motor Company competed against other auto companies by manufacturing several makes of automobiles that appealed to the affluent customer. However, Henry Ford was hard at work on the Model T, which he began to produce in 1909.

During the early years of the company's history, Henry Ford was fortunate to have the services of James Couzens, who handled the business affairs of the company with unusual skill and success. Hence Ford could concentrate on directing production, a job to his liking. Automobiles were constructed by highly skilled workers. All or most of the parts were custom-made. Henry Ford enjoyed the company of the workers, for they were proud of the cars they produced. Ford maintained a personal relationship with his workers until approximately 1909, when the number of workers had risen to more than 1000.

When the Model T appeared in 1909, it was a great success. The Ford Motor Company soon became the dominating force in the auto industry. However, Ford's labor costs were very high; the workers were highly skilled and therefore well paid. To continue to manufacture the inexpensive Model T, Henry Ford needed to reduce significantly his labor costs.

QUESTIONS: Why did Henry Ford pursue a strategy different from that of other car manufacturers? What approaches could Henry Ford have used to reduce his labor costs?

1 Traditional Management

MANAGEMENT IN PREINDUSTRIAL SOCIETY
MAX WEBER AND BUREAUCRACY
HENRI FAYOL AND THE MANAGEMENT PROCESS SCHOOL
FREDERICK TAYLOR AND SCIENTIFIC MANAGEMENT
THE QUANTITATIVE SCHOOL
SUMMARY
DISCUSSION QUESTIONS
CRITICAL INCIDENT
SUGGESTED READINGS

PERFORMANCE OBJECTIVES

1. To explain why preindustrial society viewed managerial activities in an unfavorable light.
2. To develop a working definition of management.
3. To identify the preconditions that allowed the emergence of a capitalistic, industrial society in which management became a central activity.
4. To describe the major schools in one of the two main streams of modern management, the traditional management stream.

To understand the field of management, one must comprehend the nature of organizations and the forces constraining managerial decision making within them. Most experts agree that *management* can be defined as the activity that attempts to achieve goals with and through people (Wren 1979). It is the general objective of this book to provide the student with a broadened and enriched understanding of the field of management.

The introductory section of this chapter discusses the related concepts of work and management in preindustrial societies; then a working definition of management is presented. The remainder of the chapter provides a historical description of the major schools in the traditional management stream (see Figure 1–1).

MANAGEMENT IN PREINDUSTRIAL SOCIETY

The development of modern management thought and practice can be traced by examining the evolution of societies as they have passed from preindustrial to industrial economic structures. Such an examination also allows us to develop a practical definition of management.

Modern industrial and postindustrial societies have been in existence for only a few hundred years. Before their advent people in preindustrial societies had a standard of living that was very low. Preindustrial societies were biased against the concept of managing organizations effectively and efficiently. Most societies were antibusiness, antiachievement, and even antihuman. Societies were essentially static: Individuals were bound to their stations in life, kings ruled by dictates that could not be questioned, and individuals focused on the supposed pleasures of the afterlife rather than the improvement of their lot on earth. Essentially there were only two social classes in preindustrial societies: a small number of individuals who ruled through force, religion, or related methods, and the large mass of individuals who possessed little freedom or property. Given the rigid and hierarchical nature of organizations developed by preindustrial societies, it is not surprising that management did not evolve as a separate and identifiable field of study. Modern managers attempt to guide organizations so that they grow and prosper, but preindustrial societies simply wanted their organizations to remain static—to retain the status quo.

Preindustrial societies viewed commerce and profit-making activities unfavorably. The dominant view was that work, trade, and commerce were beneath the dignity of the ruling elite. For instance, work in ancient Greece was done by slaves and less-than-respectable citizens. In Greece manual workers and merchants were not allowed to become citizens because the Grecian ruling classes held these individuals in such low esteem.

In short, as the noted management historian Daniel Wren has

FIGURE 1–1
The Two Streams of Modern Management and Their Schools: Historical Development of the Field

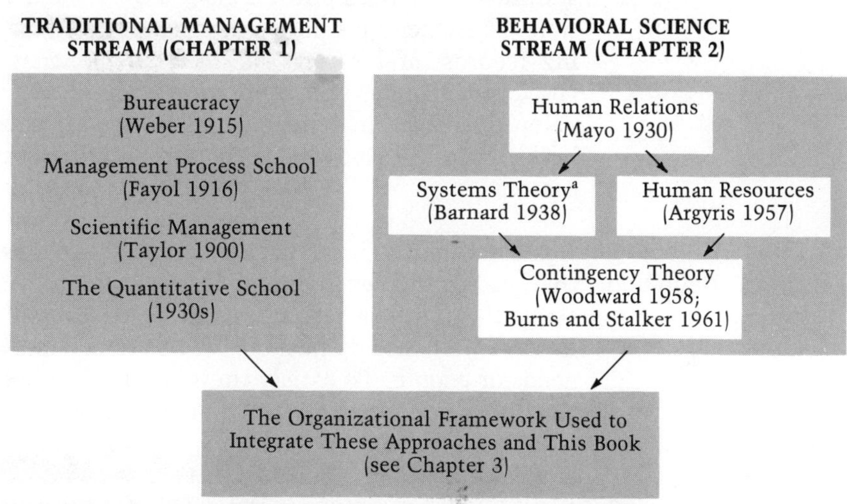

[a] Systems theory is interdisciplinary in nature and was developed through the work of mathematicians, physicists, and behavioral scientists. Hence many systems concepts are part of the structure of both the modern quantitative school and the behavioral science stream of management.

pointed out, two themes dominated in preindustrial society: (1) People had a relatively parochial view of the role that managers could play in organizations, primarily because of the static nature of society; and (2) the prevailing cultures viewed profit-making unfavorably (Wren 1979).

Early Concepts of Management

Some attempts were made to develop management theory in preindustrial society, but they were scattered, and no one tried to integrate effective and efficient managerial practices into a cohesive body of knowledge. For instance, a well-known principle of management is the span of control: A superior can direct the work and activities of only a limited number of subordinates. If the number of subordinates is too large, the superior cannot effectively communicate with them or coordinate their activities. Ancient Egyptians employed this principle by stipulating that each supervisor should direct the work of ten servants. However, few other societies applied this technique.

Advanced managerial practices were to be found in some preindustrial societies. Several Chinese factories around 4000 B.C. utilized specialization of work, written job descriptions, and a hierarchy of authority. Also, in ancient Mesopotamia around 3000 B.C., the temples developed an early concept of a *corporation,* that is, a group of temples operating under the direction of a common body of management. One high priest directed the ceremonial and religious activities, while an administrative high priest managed the secular aspects of the organization. These temples had specialization of labor, clay tablets for keeping records, and a hierarchy of officials that supervised activities. However, while some thoughtful individuals in these societies developed enlightened managerial practices, they did not attempt to build a body of knowledge that could provide guidance for their successors.

A Working Definition

Against this historical background one can determine the conditions that lead to the development of management. As shown in Figure 1–2, general scarcity of resources and hostile outside forces such as a belligerent neighboring nation give rise to economic, social, and political needs of people. To satisfy these needs, people form economic, social, and political organizations. Such organizations require direction, which is provided by managers. Thus *management* can be defined as an activity that performs certain functions in order to acquire, allocate, and utilize human and physical resources to accomplish some goal (Wren 1979).

As we have seen, preindustrial societies developed relatively simple and static organizations that did not satisfy the needs of most individuals. But during the fifteenth and sixteenth centuries, conditions began to change dramatically. Industrialists began to build factories on a grand scale. In these factories, specialization of activities and responsibilities became the norm. As the number of factories increased, people moved from the country to the city to take advantage of the job opportunities provided by them. These and related changes created the need for modern management. In modern organizations management is not only important, it is essential, because managers must provide the direction and leadership that help organizations prosper and grow.

MAX WEBER AND BUREAUCRACY

The transition from preindustrial to industrial society is of obvious importance to the theory and practice of management. In this section we describe the *preconditions* that allowed this transition to occur. These preconditions have been analyzed by Max Weber, a major management theorist in the traditional management stream of modern management (see Figure 1–1).

Until very recently Max Weber was not treated as a member of the traditional stream of management thought. Weber, a sociologist, was only secondarily interested in applied management problems. However, his views are very similar to those of other members of the traditional stream of management thought who were concerned about these applied problems, as will become evident when the works of Max Weber and Henri Fayol are compared. Most importantly, Weber gives us a convincing description of the conditions that encouraged the move from preindustrial to industrial society.

Weber is a major figure in the history of modern social science. His influence was so great that he is generally considered one of the founders of modern sociology. He was a fascinating individual: a distinguished professor, the head of the German Red Cross during World War I, and a tireless worker who sometimes went without sleep for several days. Throughout his busy life he maintained an avid interest in the study of industrial society and its growth.

FIGURE 1–2
People, Management, and Organizations

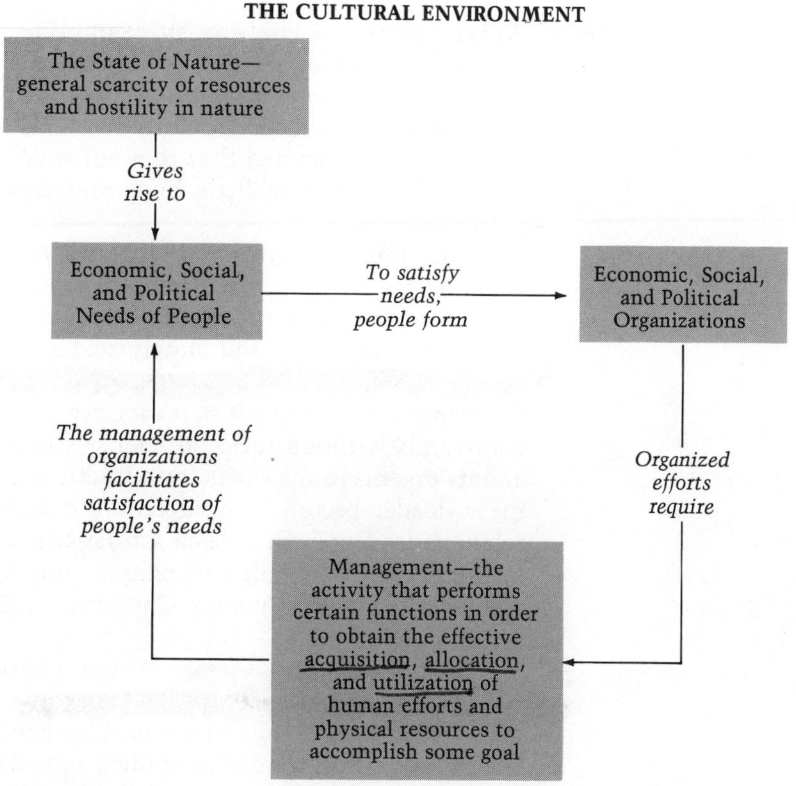

Source: Daniel Wren, *The Evolution of Management Thought,* 2nd ed. (New York: John Wiley, 1979), p. 10. Used by permission.

Capitalism Weber's analytical starting point is unusual in the history of management (Weber 1930, 1947). Unlike others who were concerned with the applied and daily problems that beset organizations and managers, he initially focused his attention on *capitalism.* This form of economic and social organization emphasizes the private ownership of goods, private investment, and a free market that determines prices, production, and the distribution of goods. Modern capitalism arose during the transition from preindustrial to industrial society in Western Europe in the fifteenth and sixteenth centuries.

Weber's initial question was this: What makes modern capitalism so different from earlier forms of economic organization? Capitalism in elementary forms had existed in older societies, such as China in 4000 B.C. But Weber felt that modern capitalism was radically different from those earlier forms. A great amount of economic activity throughout society, thousands of individuals employed by one large organization, complex trade agreements that span several countries—such conditions were not prevalent in earlier capitalistic societies.

Bases of Authority Weber begins his analysis by examining the legitimate or socially acceptable bases of authority that societies employ to guide their individual and organizational activities. In preindustrial societies *traditional* authority dominated: Individuals obeyed the ruling elite because tradition dictated that they must do so. Society was essentially static, and there was little hope and possibly even little desire for major changes.

What brings about major changes? According to Weber the stage is set by a gradual accumulation of technological improvements and the restiveness of younger members of society, so that traditional authority is challenged and slowly undermined. However, a major societal change does not occur until a *charismatic leader* appears. Charisma is a unique gift of leadership that motivates others to follow commands without question. Hence the base of authority in society and its organizations shifts from tradition to charisma, and the charismatic leader becomes the *agent of change.* Weber identifies major religious leaders such as Jesus Christ as prototypical agents of change. Contemporary examples of charismatic leaders include Charles de Gaulle of France, Winston Churchill of England, and Adolf Hitler of Germany.

The charismatic leader, Weber continues, typically lives for only a few years after he initiates change—or if he lives, he is displaced after a short time by some of his key followers. The charismatic leader has little interest in applied organizational problems, and he does not develop an organizational structure through which he can institutionalize the changes he has wrought. While there is great excitement among the followers when the charismatic leader is in charge, there is also great uncertainty, because they cannot predict what will happen. Weber aptly points out that a society is passing through the "shatterzones of history" as long as the charismatic leader governs.

Although the charismatic leader is not concerned about developing an organizational structure through which activities can be systematically completed, his followers are, and they strive to develop an organizational structure that will allow the major changes initiated by the charismatic leader to become permanent. Weber terms this process "the routinization of charisma."

Within this organizational structure a third type of authority emerges: *rational-legal authority.* In a bureaucratic organization a superior possesses this type of authority purely by virtue of the position or office he holds in the hierarchy. Bureaucracy is consequently a unique organizational structure that is radically different from the traditional structures found in preindustrial societies.

Bureaucratic Organizations

The key concept of bureaucracy is *hierarchy,* the ranking of individuals according to the amount of rational-legal authority they can exercise when they are fulfilling the responsibilities of their positions. When an individual comes into the organization, he or she is assigned a particular position. An immediate superior has *power* over this individual—that is, the ability to give commands that he or she must accept. The individual, in turn, has power over his or her own subordinates. Typically an individual reports to only one superior in order to avoid confusion and role conflict, so there is *unity of command* throughout the hierarchy.

The Dominant Structure. Weber was aware that bureaucratic organizations had existed before the fifteenth century—for example, in the Catholic church and the Roman army. However, only in industrial, capitalistic society did bureaucracy become *the* dominant model for business and governmental organizations. In preindustrial societies business and governmental structures were a direct reflection of a society's social structure (as they still are in developing countries). Typically the social class into which one was born determined the type of job one could expect to obtain. But the bureaucratic organization is divorced from society. Relationships become impersonal, with rewards based on efficiency rather than on familial connections. In fact, Weber believed that the emphases on expertise, education, and bureaucracy in business and government would eventually lead to a society in which class distinctions would be blurred.

"I fired them all. 2,437 of them. I'll go it alone."

Additional Characteristics. For employees to feel committed to this impersonal organization, they must view their work not merely as a job but as a career. The hierarchy typically establishes a definite number of positions through which each individual can advance in terms of promotions, pay increases, and greater responsibilities. These rewards are the motivating elements that generate a high degree of efficiency and commitment from organizational members.

Although the nature of the work completed by large organizations may be simple or unskilled, the bureaucracy, to be efficient, requires specialization. Written job descriptions are highly formal; consequently, behavior in the bureaucracy is routinized by implementing them. Job descriptions indicate to the organizational member the tasks he is supposed to accomplish and his minimum level of competence.

In developing job descriptions, the organization makes a significant distinction between line and staff. A *line officer* or employee (for example, a vice-president of production or a production worker) is one whose work contributes directly to the accomplishment of organizational objectives. A *staff officer* or employee (for example, a vice-president of personnel) advises and assists the line officers. For Weber the distinction between line and staff was critical, because the complex nature of the hierarchy in a large organization demands that roles and functions be as clear and simplified as possible.

Another aspect of bureaucracy that Weber considered vital was record keeping. When proper records are kept, the firm is able to generate a moving picture of its historical activities, so that corrective actions can be taken if deviations become evident over time. Weber would have approved of the sophisticated, computerized management information systems that have become popular since World War II; the volume of records that can be handled efficiently with these systems has increased tremendously.

Weber discussed other aspects of bureaucracy, but those just mentioned are the most essential: rational-legal authority, hierarchy, unity of command, career orientation, formal job descriptions and routinization of behavior, distinction between line and staff, record keeping, and impersonality in the sense that the position or office in the hierarchy is independent of a particular individual and is not owned by him. These elements provide the organization with a structure that can be highly productive. Moreover, they were especially well suited to the large-scale economic activities that began in the fifteenth and sixteenth centuries. Even today, although more complex organizational structures appropriate for modern problems have replaced bureaucracy in many instances, its essential features are still important. Admittedly, an excessive amount of bureaucracy can lead to inefficiency; for example, an organization may emphasize record keeping so much that it begins to drown in its own paperwork. Nevertheless, a bureaucracy is vastly superior to an organization in which an individual's status and position are determined by accidents of birth.

Other Preconditions

In addition to bureaucracy, Weber identified several other preconditions of modern capitalism and industrial society. A major precondition was the growth of a *skilled labor force*, enabling a middle class to arise. In the absence of a middle class there would be only a few rich individuals and the masses of the poor, a combination not likely to generate much economic activity. By the fifteenth century a skilled middle class had arisen in Western Europe, trained and protected by the craft guilds, which were the forerunners of modern craft unions.

Another precondition for large-scale capitalism was an appropriate method for keeping track of business transactions. Thus arose *double-entry accounting*, a detailed listing of a firm's assets and liabilities developed by Italian businessmen in the thirteenth century. This system allows firms to plan wisely for the future, because all transactions, both sources of income and expenses, are laid out in detail. Double-entry accounting provides an effective visual representation of what the firm is doing and should be doing to survive.

Just as double-entry accounting was critical, an effective *legal system* was necessary to handle disputes between business firms. The legal system common in fifteenth-century Europe was particularly suitable for capitalism and industrial society, since there was a definite bias in it toward the ownership of private property, the payment of debts, and the punishment of individuals who violated the rights of others.

Weber also identified *ideology,* or a system of beliefs used to justify a particular position, as a key precondition. As emphasized previously, preindustrial society held profit making in low esteem, since its ideological position reinforced the concepts of static society and organizations in which the ruling elite could govern with a minimal amount of opposition. But with the beginning of the Protestant Reformation in Europe, opinion concerning the pursuit of profit began to shift. Protestant theologians argued that worldly success was an outward sign of God's favor; Weber coined the term *Protestant ethic* to describe this fusion of worldly success and religion. The Protestant ethic encouraged the acquisition of material resources, both for individuals and for corporations. A good illustration of this fusion is found in the "Acres of Diamonds" speech that was given at least 4000 times by the Reverend Russell H. Conwell, the first president of Temple University:

> I say you ought to be rich; you have no right to be poor. . . . I must say that you ought to spend some time getting rich. You and I know that there are some things more valuable than money; of course, we do. Ah, yes. . . . Well does the man know who has suffered that there are some things sweeter and holier and more sacred than gold. Nevertheless, the man of common sense also knows that there is not any one of those things that is not greatly enhanced by the use of money. Money is power; money has powers; and for a man to say, "I do not want money," is to say, "I do not wish to do any good to my fellow man." It is absurd thus to talk. It is absurd to disconnect them. This is a wonderfully great life, and you ought to spend your time getting money, because of the power there is in money.
>
> Greatness consists not in holding some office; greatness really consists in doing some great deed with little means, in the accomplishments of vast purposes from the private ranks of life; this is true greatness (*Burr 1917, pp. 414–415*)

Weber identifies the *Protestant theologians,* particularly John Calvin, as a necessary precondition of capitalism and industrial society. These theologians became the agents of change because they argued persuasively against the prevailing view that seeking wealth was unholy. Through their efforts rational-legal authority eventually replaced both traditional and charismatic authority as the legitimate or socially acceptable base upon which society and its newly formed bureaucratic organizations were founded.

In summary, Weber identified bureaucracy as a major precondition of modern capitalism and industrial society. Other major preconditions included double-entry accounting, a mature legal system, the Protestant ethic (the religious justification for making profits), and the Protestant theologians, who became the agents of change that allowed the base of societal authority to shift from tradition to rational legalism.

HENRI FAYOL AND THE MANAGEMENT PROCESS SCHOOL

As we have seen, Max Weber was basically a social theorist who was not concerned about the specific problems of real organizations. Henri Fayol was the opposite, for his theories grew out of his years of experience as a successful businessman in the coal-mining industry in France. Fayol, originally trained as a mining engineer, joined the Commentary-Fourchambault Company in 1860 and spent his entire career with it. Fayol became the managing director of the company, unfortunately at a time when it was facing bankruptcy. Through adroit management he brought the company from the brink of bankruptcy to a healthy financial position. Today this company is part of Le Creusot-Loire, the largest mining and metallurgical group in central France.

In 1916 Fayol published *General and Industrial Management*, which has become a classic in the management field. For many years the basic management course in business schools was based on the ideas developed by Fayol in this book; even today the basic management course relies heavily on these ideas.

General Management

One of the intriguing ideas that Fayol articulated is that management is a *general* discipline similar to other academic disciplines and that it can be learned. In particular, Fayol argued that the successful manager must perform specific functions in a systematic process and follow tested management principles. Fayol believed that these functions and principles are universal in the sense that managers using them will be successful, and that these principles and functions can be taught in a formal fashion. But in 1916 there were only a few business schools in existence, and the traditional academic departments in colleges and universities generally viewed them as less than respectable. Fayol deplored this aversion to management training, given the importance of management in directing society's organizations.

Fayol believed that a manager needs specialized training in a particular business function, such as accounting, early in his career. Specialized training allows the manager to perform work that is critical in the organization. However, as a manager takes on progressively more responsibilities, the importance of the initial specialized training declines and general managerial abilities come into play. According to Fayol, a manager is analogous to the captain of the ship: He provides overall guidance and direction.

Fayol argued that a manager in fulfilling the general role must possess some minimum level of knowledge of the basic activities performed by an organization – technical, commercial, financial, security, accounting, and administrative activities (see Figure 1–3). To perform the role of the general manager effectively, the individual should possess the following characteristics (Fayol 1949, p. 7):

1. Physical qualities: health, vigor, and address.
2. Mental qualities: ability to understand and learn, judgment, mental vigor, and adaptability.
3. Moral qualities: energy, firmness, willingness to accept responsibility, initiative, loyalty, tact, and dignity.
4. General education: general acquaintance with matters not belonging exclusively to the function performed.
5. Special knowledge: that peculiar to the function, be it technical, commercial, financial, or managerial.
6. Experience: knowledge arising from the work itself; that is, the recollection of lessons that one has derived from the work.

Functions of Management

Fayol is rightly regarded as the father of the management process school. He was the first to identify the functions that a manager must perform, in a systematic process or sequence, to be successful in the completion of administrative activities (Figure 1–3). Fayol identified five functions: planning, organizing, commanding, coordinating, and controlling.

According to Fayol, a good plan of action includes the following characteristics:

1. Unity: one overall plan followed by specific plans for each activity.
2. Continuity: both short-range and long-range plans tied together through the overall plan.
3. Flexibility: changing the plan in response to unexpected events.

The second function, *organizing*, involves the structuring of activities and relationships and the selection, training, and evaluation of personnel. *Commanding* includes getting "the optimum return from all employees . . . in the interest of the whole concern" (Fayol 1949, p. 97). Modern writers sometimes use the word *leading* as a synonym for commanding. The fourth function, *coordinating*, was defined as the ability "to harmonize all the activities of a concern so as to facilitate its working, and its success" (Fayol 1949, p. 103). The final function, *controlling*, refers to the ability of "verifying whether everything occurs in conformity with the plan adopted, the instructions issued, and the principles established" (Fayol 1949, p. 107).

According to Fayol, planning is the primary function that a manager performs, since he must complete this activity before any of the other functions come into play. The *management process sequence*, then, logically proceeds from planning to the other functions of organizing, commanding, coordinating, and controlling. Fayol realized that, in practice, managers did not neatly move from one function to another in such a systematic sequence and that they frequently performed two or more functions simultaneously. However, his intent was to describe the essential functions that a manager performs and to show how they are interrelated.

FIGURE 1–3
Fayol's Concept of the Essential Activities in an Enterprise

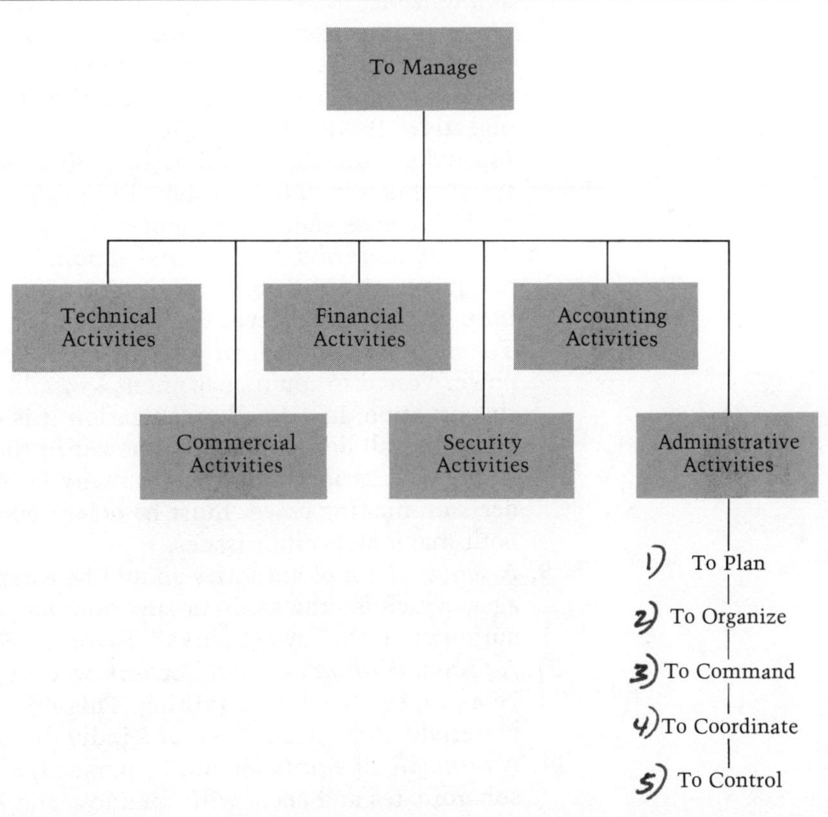

Principles of Management

Fayol also argued that a manager, if he is to perform the management process effectively, must follow fourteen general principles that have been shown to be critical in directing organizations. These principles of management are consequently the *means* by which a manager can effectively guide an organization. We will examine the most important principles in depth in Chapter 9; here we describe them briefly.

1. *Division of work* or specialization of labor should be implemented whenever possible.
2. *Authority,* or "the right to give orders and power to exact obedience," should be vested in the manager (Fayol 1949, p. 21). A good manager should supplement formal authority with personal authority. In addition, authority and responsibility are related; whenever authority is exercised, responsibility arises.
3. *Discipline* should be based on obedience and respect between the managers and the employees.
4. *Unity of command* should be established; a subordinate should receive orders from only one superior in order to avoid confusion and tension.
5. *Unity of direction,* which is directly related to unity of command, should be provided by the manager; there should be "one head and one plan for a group of activities having the same objective" (Fayol 1949, p. 25).
6. *Individual interest* should be *subordinated* to the general interest; this principle is designed to minimize undesirable behavior such as selfishness, ignorance, and excessive ambition.
7. The *remuneration of personnel* should be based on the concept of equity, with the objective of motivating individuals to perform at an optimal level.
8. The *degree of centralization*—the amount of decision-making power vested in top management—should vary according to the situation. In a small organization it is quite possible to centralize all decision-making power in the top manager. In a large organization that includes many levels and individuals, decision-making power must be delegated to lower echelons on both major and minor issues.
9. A *scalar chain* of authority should be established by the manager, which is "the chain of superiors ranging from the ultimate authority to the lowest ranks" (Fayol, 1949, p. 34).
10. A *principle of order* should be followed; that is, there should be a proper place for everything. This principle is applicable to materials, shop cleanliness, and individuals.
11. A *principle of equity* should be pursued; a manager should treat subordinates and peers with kindness and justice.

FIGURE 1–4
Fayol's Bridge
The dotted line from F to G represents a bridge. In a rigid hierarchy F would have to send his message through D, B, A, C, and E. The bridge allows equals in different parts of the hierarchy to communicate directly.

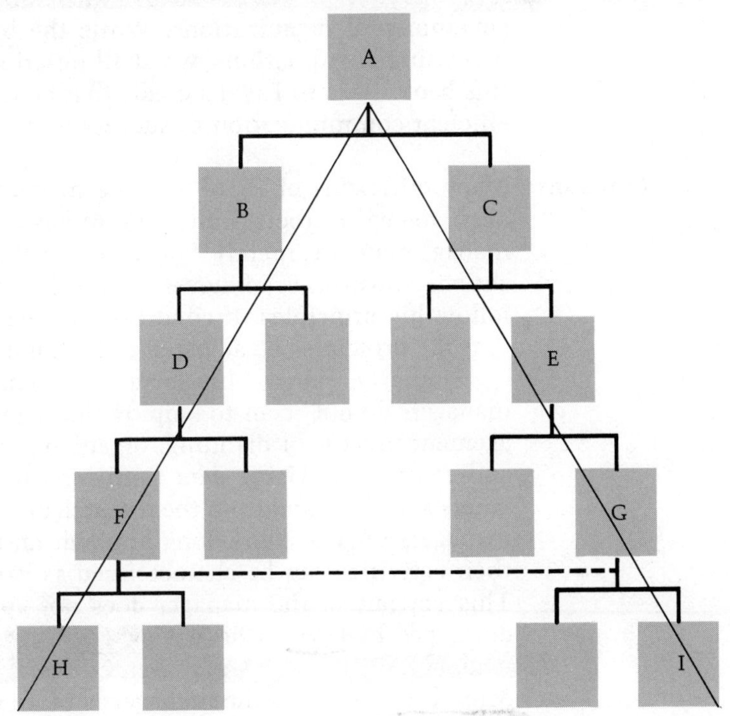

Source: From Henri Fayol, *General and Industrial Management,* trans. Constance Storrs (London: Pitman, 1949), p. 34. Reprinted by permission of Editeur Dunod.

12. *Stability of tenure of personnel* should be emphasized; that is, a manager should provide for orderly personnel planning and suitable replacements as individuals leave the organization.
13. *Initiative* should be invoked in exhorting individuals to display zeal and energy when completing organizational tasks.
14. Finally, an *esprit de corps* should be built by stressing harmony and unity.

Fayol's Bridge Fayol, like Max Weber, realized that bureaucracies tend to become rigid because communications pass through many superiors before plans can be implemented. To eliminate this problem, he proposed that bridges be constructed throughout the hierarchy (see Figure 1–4).

If someone in one part of the hierarchy wants to communicate with equals in other sections, he should do so directly rather than relaying the message to his superiors. If superiors were constantly transmitting the messages of subordinates, they would have trouble completing their own work. Fayol observed that an overly formal pattern of communication is a frequent cause of rigidity in bureaucracies such as governmental organizations. While the bridge was only one way of increasing coordination—we shall describe several other methods in this book—it is to Fayol's credit that he recognized the importance of efficient communication to successful organizations.

Criticisms Many criticisms of Fayol and the management process school have been voiced. Herbert Simon (1976) has argued that the principles of management are merely "proverbs" rather than effective guides to action. However, Fayol never intended that managers should slavishly follow his principles. If conditions change, Fayol would recommend that the principles be adjusted to fit the new circumstances.

Similarly, Henry Mintzberg (1980) has cogently pointed out that managers do not seem to employ the sequential and systematic management process of planning, organizing, commanding, coordinating, and controlling. Using data from his own study of the work of five chief executives and from the research of others, Mintzberg shows that managers tend to work long hours at an unremitting pace, and that their activities can be characterized as varied, fragmented, and brief. This portrait of the manager does not appear to correspond to that developed by Fayol, who viewed the manager as a logical, systematic planner following the management processes sequentially. In fact, Mintzberg feels that the manager is more reactive than proactive: He reacts to problems as they emerge rather than planning so that such problems can be minimized or avoided.

This book views Fayol's and Mintzberg's positions as complementary rather than antagonistic. Managers do plan, and the amount of time spent on planning increases as a manager's organizational level rises (Martin, 1956; Mahoney, Jerdee, and Carroll 1965). They also perform other functions in an organization, such as directing and controlling activities. The organizational framework described in Chapter 3 incorporates the positions of both Fayol and Mintzberg.

FREDERICK TAYLOR AND SCIENTIFIC MANAGEMENT

In the United States at the turn of the twentieth century, another major school in the traditional management stream came into prominence. Termed *scientific management*, it is the application of logical and systematic techniques to work processes.

Frederick Taylor was the chief advocate and spokesman for this school. His father was a prosperous Quaker lawyer and his mother was of Puritan ancestry; owing largely to this background, Taylor developed an intense spirit of inquiry for the truth, a desire to confirm facts scientifically, and an urge to attack the evils of waste and laziness. He was admitted to Harvard College after passing the examinations with honors, but poor health and failing eyesight persuaded him to accept an apprenticeship as a pattern maker and machinist in Philadelphia. It was here that he began his study of the work processes in industry.

Worker-Management Relations

Taylor prospered in his new position, and he immensely enjoyed the companionship of the employees with whom he worked. However, he thought the industrial conditions were highly unfavorable. Many workers "soldiered" on the job, that is, they performed far less work than they could; the managers were inferior in ability and leadership; and there was active hostility between management and the workers.

From Taylor's perspective many of these problems occurred because of the manner in which management treated the workers. Each worker was paid according to the number of units he produced. It was common for management to increase the rate of pay per piece to increase production. When production had increased to a high level, management then cut the rate of pay per piece. Workers needed only one such rate-cutting to realize that their interests were opposed to those of management.

Task Management

In 1878 Taylor moved to Midvale Steel, where he produced some of his major work. His genius lay in his approach to a job: He believed it was possible to determine an optimum way a job should be performed. In essence, he wanted to break a job down into its simplest components, then rebuild the job so that an individual would perform it optimally, or in the "one best way." It was Taylor's intent to identify this best way to perform a particular job. His chief tool was the stopwatch, although he also used other aids, such as a slide rule. Other writers characterized Taylor's approach as "scientific management," but he preferred to identify it as *task management.*

To be sure, other researchers had employed the stopwatch in industrial situations before Taylor. However, they merely measured the time it took a worker to perform a given job. Taylor's approach was unique and normative: There was one best way to perform any given job, and Taylor would discover this way.

To demonstrate the importance of scientific management, Taylor needed an employee who would submit to his instructions completely. The job he selected for study was the handling of pig iron. The pig iron handler bends down, picks up a 92-pound pig of iron, walks a few feet, and then deposits it on the ground or on a pile. Taylor observed that the pig iron handlers averaged about 12.5 tons per day. He also noticed that a particular pig iron handler named Schmidt was performing an adequate job according to that standard, although he was strong enough physically to do much more work. Taylor reasoned that Schmidt was an energetic individual who could be significantly motivated by money:

> "Schmidt, are you a high-priced man?"
>
> "Vell, I don't know what you mean." [Conversation at this point lasts several minutes.]
>
> "Well, if you are a high-priced man, you will do exactly as this man tells you tomorrow, from morning until night. When he tells you to pick up a pig and walk, you pick it up and walk, and when he tells you to sit down and rest, you sit down. You do that right straight through the day. And what's more, no back talk. Do you understand that?"
>
> Schmidt started to work, and all day long, and at regular intervals, was told by the man who stood over him with a watch, "Now pick up a pig and walk. Now sit down and rest. Now walk, now rest. . . ." He worked when he was told to work, and rested when he was told to rest and at half-past five in the afternoon, had his 47½ tons loaded on the car. And he practically never failed to work at this pace and do the task that was set him during the three years the writer was at Bethlehem. (*Taylor 1911, pp. 46–47*)

As this example demonstrates, Taylor employed the stopwatch in a careful manner. To find the best way to perform a job, Taylor believed that it was necessary to monitor the employee constantly.

The Gilbreths and Motion Study. Taylor primarily relied on the stopwatch, since he focused on the amount of time it takes to complete a particular job. Thus he is usually called the father of time study. Two other researchers, Frank and Lillian Gilbreth (1912), emphasized the ideal motions required to perform a job in an optimal fashion. These researchers developed the concept of the *therblig* (*Gilbreth* spelled backward except for the transposition of the *h* and *t* for ease of pronunciation); a therblig is an elemental hand or arm motion. According to the Gilbreths, there are seventeen therbligs. To pinpoint the therbligs suitable for a particular job, the Gilbreths photographed the worker in action and then observed the film in slow motion.

The Gilbreths used motion study successfully in many different situations. In one study they analyzed the work of stonemasons; skilled work with a centuries-long tradition. The Gilbreths noticed that each stonemason soon tired because he had to bend continually to pick up his bricks, which were arranged in a small pile before him. To eliminate wasted motions, the Gilbreths constructed a special adjustable stand for the bricks. Productivity rose 200 percent.

In short, many of the experiments conducted by advocates of scientific management proved highly successful. It was typical for productivity to double, and in some instances it increased by 500 to 600 percent. Needless to say, American industrialists became very interested in this approach.

Resistance to Scientific Management. But there was also a vicious reaction against scientific management. Humanitarian newspaper columnists accused Taylor of treating the human being like a machine, since the scientific management school emphasizes that the worker must submit totally to instructions if the job is to be performed most efficiently. The job is considered constant; the worker is viewed as variable in the sense that his behavior is molded to the job's requirements. Labor unions, too, opposed scientific management, primarily because it would restrict them during collective bargaining. If the employer knows how many units each worker should be able to produce, a union would be hard pressed to justify large wage increases if production is not up to the maximum.

There is some truth in the criticisms leveled against scientific management, although, in retrospect, it is hard to understand the wave of antagonism that greeted this new approach. In a congressional investigation of Taylor in 1913, he openly stated that the individual who would best meet the requirements of scientific management would be someone akin to an ox. This committee was actively hostile to Taylor's work, and he made this unfortunate statement after repeated attempts were made to discredit him. During the congressional testimony he was frequently and rudely interrupted before he could define and explain his position.

Taylor's Four Principles

In his writings Taylor presents a balanced view of scientific management. He believed that a "mental revolution" would have to take place so that management and workers would see that their positions were compatible. He pointed out that as productivity rose, the salaries of both managers and employees would rise. At the same time, he emphasized that managers must avoid such practices as rate cutting, because they lead to employee hostility toward management. Taylor even advocated the concept of a *differential piece rate:* After a worker had manufactured a specified number of units, he would be paid a higher rate per unit for any additional units he produced, and the rate per piece would increase after each succeeding plateau had been reached.

Economic man

To summarize his beliefs, Taylor listed four principles of scientific management (1911, pp. 36–37):

1. Develop a science for each element of a man's work, to replace the old rule-of-thumb method.
2. Scientifically select and then train the worker. (In the past the worker had chosen his own work and trained himself as best he could.)

3. Heartily cooperate with the men to ensure that all the work done is in accordance with the principles of the science developed for the work.
4. Divide the work and the responsibility equally between the management and the workers. The management should take over all work for which it is better fitted than the workmen. (In the past almost all the work and the greater part of the responsibility had been thrown upon the workers.)

Problems of Application

Scientific management has been absorbed in a modified form in industry. The fears of humanitarians and labor unions have proved largely unfounded. But several obstacles have arisen to the approach as Taylor envisioned it.

First, the very foundation of scientific management – the complete cooperation of the workers whose jobs are being measured – is rarely found. Workers know they will be forced to meet new standards and so they slow down when an engineer begins to pace their jobs.

Second, and more importantly, the tools of scientific management are imperfect. Two engineers who examine the same job independently sometimes differ by as much as eighty percent on how much time a worker needs to perform a given job cycle.

Third, as Taylor and his followers knew, the ideal application of scientific management requires violating the principle of unity of command. In Taylor's system an employee would be responsible to several supervisors, each one examining one small part of the employee's job. Taylor termed this type of supervisor a "functional foreman." Although the system can work in selected instances, it is difficult to use in many industrial and nonindustrial situations because of its complexity. As shown in Figure 1–5, eight supervisors would oversee the work of each employee: four supervisors in the planning room concerned with production routing, methods, time and cost, and discipline; and four supervisors on the shop floor focusing on machine speed, worker speed, quality, and maintenance of equipment. Under such conditions conflict is bound to arise.

Fourth, many incompetent consulting firms, calling themselves experts in the implementation of scientific management, came into existence. These firms were primarily interested in making money, and so the task management systems they installed were often hastily conceived and unsystematic. Taylor was discouraged by the emergence of these consulting firms, and he publicly designated only four other individuals as true members of the scientific management school. These were the only individuals he would recommend to managers who wished to install a system of scientific management.

Fifth – and perhaps this problem is the most basic one – the system exhibits internal inconsistency. One of Taylor's essential principles

FIGURE 1–5
Taylor's Functional Foremanship

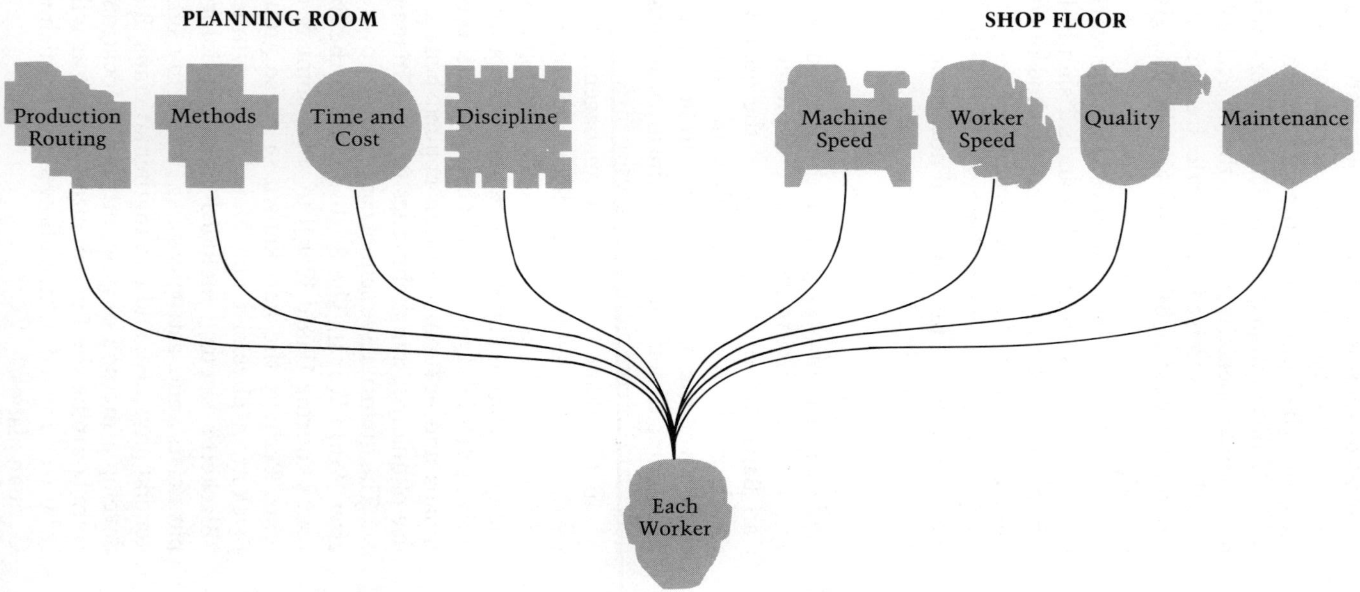

was cooperation. Everyone would benefit financially if the ideal method for performing a given job were found, but discovering it required full cooperation between management and labor. However, once they had pinpointed the ideal method, Taylor vested all power in the hands of management. The worker—who was constantly monitored since specialization was the objective—became a passive individual who exercised very little freedom or responsibility. In this situation a worker might find that he had given up his freedom and gained nothing.

In summary, Taylor believed that the worker level in an organization was critical and that a standard should be established for every job, based on the most efficient method of completing the work. Although he stressed the importance of cooperation between management and labor, the techniques he used essentially rendered the worker a passive entity who did not participate in organizational decisions that directly influenced his job.

THE QUANTITATIVE SCHOOL

Frederick Taylor was one of the first advocates of the quantitative approach in solving management problems. One of his associates, Carl Barth, another proponent of the quantitative approach, created the slide rule. Barth was involved in a series of experiments designed to discover the optimal way to cut steel. The slide rule allowed the researchers to perform quickly the intricate mathematical calculations necessary to complete the experiments.

In the work of scientific management and that of economists writing in the 1890s, we can discern the beginnings of the quantitative school, since the focus was on the development of reasonable, logical, and quantitative arguments, whenever possible. However, the quantitative school did not begin in earnest until the 1930s, when mathematicians and economists of an applied bent started to emphasize the use of quantitative techniques to solve management problems.

The quantitative school came into its own during and immediately after World War II. The English created the first "operations research teams" during World War II to solve some of their management problems. Perhaps the best-known of these groups was led by P. M. S. Blackett, a physicist and Nobel Prize winner. His team, known as "Blackett's circus," included three physiologists, two mathematical physicists, one astrophysicist, one army officer, one surveyor, one general physicist, and two mathematicians. Blackett's team wanted to develop a method of pinpointing the location of German planes that were bombing the English cities almost at will. Through their efforts radar was created, which allowed the English to locate and destroy the German planes.

The first modern computer was also invented during World

War II. Modern computers allow quantitative specialists to attack complicated management problems that previously were difficult if not impossible to address. This school of management uses the quantitative techniques that we will discuss in detail in Chapters 6 and 7. Through the advances made by this school, management practice has been considerably enriched.

SUMMARY

Preindustrial society was essentially static and consisted of two major social classes: a few individuals in the ruling class and the large mass of individuals who possessed little freedom or property. To protect itself, the ruling class discouraged any innovations or changes that would jeopardize its position. Under such static conditions managerial activities designed to make organizations prosper and grow were viewed unfavorably.

Management can be defined as the activity that performs certain functions in order to obtain the effective acquisition, allocation, and utilization of human and physical resources to accomplish some goal. Management became important in the modern industrial, capitalistic society that arose in Europe in the fifteenth and sixteenth centuries.

Max Weber identified several preconditions that allowed industrial society to emerge: a skilled middle class, double-entry accounting, agents of change, the Protestant ethic—that is, the religious ideology justifying profit-making activities—a mature legal system, and bureaucracy. Bureaucracy is a distinctive type of organization based on rational-legal authority, as opposed to traditional or charismatic authority. It is essentially divorced from society: Once in a bureaucracy, the individual's performance is judged not in terms of such spurious measures as familial connections but in terms of ability to complete assigned tasks.

Max Weber founded the bureaucratic school in the traditional stream of modern management. Henri Fayol, whose works were similar to those of Weber, is recognized as the founder of the management process school. According to this school, a successful manager must perform specific functions systematically and follow certain principles, such as the optimum span of control.

Scientific management is another school in the traditional management stream. Its chief spokesman was Frederick Taylor, who argued that each job can be broken down into simple components and then reassembled so that the worker can perform it in the one best way. Time and motion studies are the tools the engineer uses to identify the one best way.

Scientific management represents the beginnings of the quantitative school of management, since it employed sophisticated mathematical approaches in determining the best way to do each job. The quantitative school came into prominence during and immediately after World War II. The importance of this school has increased since World War II; quantitative researchers now rely heavily on the computer for solving the complicated equations that are employed in their analyses. Since the computer industry continues to grow, it is reasonable to expect that the quantitative school will continue to play a central role in modern management theory and practice.

DISCUSSION QUESTIONS

1. Scientific management is still popular, and management uses it when it can measure the work processes in a fairly precise way, primarily in blue-collar work. Do you feel that scientific management is appropriate for white-collar, technical, and professional work? Why? Do you believe that scientific management will increase in importance and use in the United States? Why?
2. The key concept of bureaucracy is hierarchy. Can an organization be truly nonbureaucratic in the sense of having no hierarchy at all?
3. What are some major similarities and differences between scientific management and the management process school?
4. How would you define management? Were managerial activities important in preindustrial societies? Why or why not?
5. How would you define charismatic leadership? Describe three charismatic leaders. Must a successful manager be charismatic? Why or why not?
6. Do you think societies develop particular kinds of organizations that are a direct reflection of the kinds of problems they face? Explain. Would Max Weber agree with your position? Why or why not? Do you feel that bureaucracy is the most appropriate type of organization for our society? Explain.
7. What does Fayol mean by the functions and principles of management? How are they related to one another? Do you agree with Herbert Simon that the principles of management are merely proverbs? Why or why not?

CRITICAL INCIDENT

NOTE: This critical incident can be used by the whole class with the case observational method (see Appendix A) or used for thought and discussion by individual class members.

In this chapter we described Taylor's differential piece rate as a method for motivating employees to be productive. Henry Towne, a contemporary of Taylor's, proposed a gain-sharing plan under which each worker was guraranteed a wage rate plus a 50–50 split of the productivity gain in the worker's department. Towne was opposed to profit sharing for the entire plant, because the gains in one department could be offset by laziness in other departments.

A plantwide system of profit sharing was advocated by Joseph Scanlon. The essential features of the Scanlon plan are a group reward for suggestions, joint committees for discussion and for proposals of labor-saving techniques, and a worker share, on a pro rata basis, in reduced costs, not increased profits.

A different type of motivational scheme was implemented by James Lincoln in the Lincoln Electric Company of Cleveland, Ohio. Lincoln assumed that workers are primarily motivated by recognition of their skills. Under Lincoln's plan management strove to develop their employees to their highest level of ability and then to reward them with a bonus for their contributions to the success of the company. This bonus was in addition to their regular salaries.

Finally, Robert Owens, a nineteenth-century visionary who established a utopian factory community in New Lanark, Scotland, and in New Harmony, Indiana, attempted to motivate employees by moral suasion. One of the prominent techniques he employed was the silent monitor. Owens awarded four types of marks to each superintendent, and each of them then rated their subordinates. These marks were transformed into the color codes of black, blue, yellow, and white in ascending order of merit. Owens mounted a block of wood on each machine, and the four sides were painted according to the code. Each day the appropriate code side of the block was turned to face the aisle. Thus anyone passing the machine could immediately identify the worker's previous day's level of productivity.

QUESTIONS: Do you feel that all these techniques—Taylor's differential piece rate, Towne's gain-sharing plan, the Scanlon plan, the Lincoln plan, and Owens's silent monitor—are effective in raising productivity? Why or why not? What are the strengths and limitations of each of these approaches?

SUGGESTED READINGS

George, Claude. *The History of Management Thought.* 2nd ed. Englewood Cliffs, N.J.: Prentice-Hall, 1972, 223 pages, paperback.

George provides a survey of management thought that spans the spectrum from ancient civilization to modern times.

Wren, Daniel. *The Evolution of Management Thought.* 2nd ed. New York: Wiley, 1979, 598 pages, hardback.

This is a splendid, readable, and interesting book. Quite possibly it is the best history of management currently available. Wren describes management thought as it evolved in both preindustrial and modern societies.

2 Management and the Behavioral Sciences

HUMAN RELATIONS
SYSTEMS THEORY
HUMAN RESOURCES
CONTINGENCY THEORY
SUMMARY
DISCUSSION QUESTIONS
CRITICAL INCIDENTS
SUGGESTED READINGS

PERFORMANCE OBJECTIVES

1. To discuss the major differences between the behavioral science stream of management and the traditional stream of management.
2. To describe the major schools within the behavioral science stream of management.
3. To show how these schools are related to one another.

The traditional stream of modern management was and still is very important. Managers must emphasize such management process activities as planning and organizing if organizations are to be successful. Similarly, scientific management is again becoming popular, not only for blue-collar work but also for technical and professional work, at least in part because of declining levels of productivity in the United States. In addition, the quantitative school, which owes much of its origin to the approaches championed by advocates of scientific management, is of unquestioned relevance both in the business school curriculum and the actual practice of management.

The second major stream, the behavioral science stream, is also central to the practice of modern management. Several surveys of business executives indicate they believe that of all business school courses, those in behavioral science are most relevant when they actually begin working. More importantly, the behavioral science stream complements traditional management. Both students and practicing managers need to understand the major schools in the behavioral science stream and to know how they differ from the major schools in the traditional management stream.

This chapter describes the main schools in the behavioral science stream (see Figure 1–1). Within this branch the major schools are human relations, systems theory, human resources, and contingency theory. Each school will be discussed in turn.

HUMAN RELATIONS

The human relations school helps us to understand the historical factors underlying the development of the field of modern management. It arose as a direct reaction to scientific management and evolved out of a series of studies known as the *Hawthorne study*, carried out at the Hawthorne plant of Western Electric between 1924 and 1932. (For an extended review of these studies, see Roethlisberger and Dickson 1939.) Like Taylor's work, these analyses focused on the operative level. However, as we have noted, the human relations school takes a point of view opposite to that of scientific management.

Initial Experiments of the Hawthorne Study

The first studies completed at Hawthorne were guided by the concepts developed by advocates of scientific management. These studies, directed by researchers from the National Academy of Sciences, focused on the relationship between illumination and individual efficiency.

The researchers analyzed the behavior of two groups of workers. In the control group no changes were made in the illumination of the work environment. In the experimental group, consisting of six workers, illumination was increased, and productivity rose. But some puzzling results began to emerge: Sometimes a *decrease* in lighting resulted in an *increase* in productivity. At one point the investigators selected two workers for intensive study and decreased the illumination from normal to 0.06 of a footcandle, an amount of light approximately equal to that of an ordinary moonlit night. Even then the two workers maintained their previous levels of efficiency. They even stated that they were *less* tired than when working under the normal lights.

The researchers decided that illumination was not the significant variable explaining changes in individual efficiency. Systematically and one by one, they began to vary methods of wage payments, rest periods, length of workday, and length of workweek to ascertain the significant variable that might explain changes in efficiency. All these variables independently seemed to influence the level of efficiency in a positive manner.

The researchers were discouraged because they could not identify the one variable that would lead to increases in productivity. They then decided to eliminate all privileges and to return to the original conditions of work. They expected that the workers would respond negatively and decrease their levels of productivity. The opposite occurred: Efficiency rose. Reinstating the rest pauses and refreshments yielded another increase in output to an all-time high. In short, during these initial studies from 1924 until 1927, individual output rose from an average of 2400 relays per week to 3000 per week per worker.

The Hawthorne researchers eventually explained these puzzling results by proposing that the intrusion of an investigator into the normal working world of employees caused a subtle and perhaps unconscious change in their behavior. In effect, the employees enjoyed being studied, which nullified the negative effects that would normally accompany such changes as a reduction of light in the work area. This phenomenon was eventually dubbed the Hawthorne effect: When human beings are aware of being studied, they may alter their behavior.

Test Room Experiments

In 1927 the test room experiments, which were subsequently analyzed by Elton Mayo and a group of social scientists associated with the Harvard Business School, began at Hawthorne. The researchers analyzed a group of five female workers who were assigned to a special test room so that the normal working environment of the plant would not influence their behavior.

During these experiments the researchers concentrated on two major factors that could reasonably influence productivity:

1. Increased wage incentive: The women worked under a standard group piecework system. Each worker received the same wage, calculated in terms of the average number of units the five-member work group produced. In the small group the women could clearly

see the relationship between the incentive plan and wages. In a large group, such as an entire plant, it is difficult for employees to understand and appreciate the relationship between a group piecework system and productivity.

2. The informal and considerate style of supervision that was exercised in the test room: The researchers theorized that the considerate style of supervision would minimize the employees' fear of management and increase their job satisfaction, thus raising productivity.

In one stage of the experiment the researchers varied only the wage system. Specifically, they set up a group piece-rate incentive system for the five workers that was separate from the plantwide incentive system. Productivity rose twelve percent. The researchers then put a new group of five workers in the test room and paid them under the group piece-rate incentive system that applied to all workers in the plant. However, the researchers did vary one factor: They stressed human relations by using a considerate supervisor who allowed the workers to make many of their own decisions, such as the length of their rest pauses and their workday. Productivity jumped sixteen percent.

On the basis of these results the researchers partially agreed with Taylor that money is important; the change in the wage system appeared to bring about a twelve percent increase in productivity. But they argued that the human relations approach may be more important, since its effect seemingly brought about a sixteen percent increase in productivity. The researchers consequently proposed that any organizational change, such as the use of a considerate supervisor or a new wage system, affects job satisfaction and productivity through employee attitudes. When employees feel an organizational change, such as a new wage system, is being introduced to obtain more work for less money, job satisfaction and productivity will not increase, but when management is genuinely interested in their welfare, they will react positively to an organizational change and increase their rate of productivity.

Interviewing Program

In the next stage of the research Mayo and his associates conducted over two thousand interviews with employees at Hawthorne. Initially each interview was *structured:* The interviewer asked several questions that management and the researchers felt to be important. The time allotted for each interview was approximately 30 minutes. However, the workers wanted to talk about many issues not covered in the structured interview format. The researchers then decided to use an *unstructured* interview format in which the interviewee controlled the pace and subject matter of the interview; the interviewer merely asked general questions and allowed the worker to describe any issues that he felt important. The average time for each interview increased from 30 to 90 minutes.

An intriguing finding emerged. The researchers looked into the complaints of the workers and frequently found them to be different from the facts. For example, one interviewee complained about the low piece rate when his real concern was the payment of medical bills for his wife's illness. Hence the researchers argued that there are two levels of complaints, the *manifest* or *material* content versus the *latent* or *psychological* content of the complaint. The researchers believed that certain complaints must be treated not as facts but as *symptoms* or *indicators* of personal or social situations that the interviewer should address.

As a result of these findings, the researchers introduced supervisory training in the art of unstructured interviewing. They emphasized that supervisors and managers cannot accept on face value all the statements that workers make. Rather, supervisors and managers must uncover the real facts and separate them from the symptoms or indicators of personal and social situations that need to be handled in a humane manner.

Observation Room Study

In the final stage of the Hawthorne study, the researchers centered their attention on the social structure of the work group. To complete this study, they placed an observer in a test room where twenty-three male operatives worked. His job was to observe the behavior of the workers and, at the same time, keep records of their productivity.

Some of the major findings were as follows (Roethlisberger and Dickson 1939):

1. The workers set their own production standard, which was well below what they could have accomplished.
2. There were sizable differences in status among subgroups in the work test room.
3. The workers exercised social control to ensure strict adherence to status differences and the group's level of productivity. This control was harsh, and it included sarcasm, name calling, ostracism, and ridicule. Even minor physical assaults were employed by the group. If an individual did not adhere to the group's mode of behavior, he was "binged" on the arm with a piece of steel.
4. The group had specific ideas about the way a worker should conduct himself. You should not turn out too much work; if you do, you are a "rate buster." You should not turn out too little work; if you do, you are a "chiseler." You should not tell a superior anything to the detriment of a fellow worker; if you do, you are a "squealer." You should not try to act important.

The most important and clear finding in this study is that the informal relations in the work group influence attitudes, which then affect the individual's level of productivity. This informal organization did not correspond to the role descriptions of the bureaucratic or formal organization.[1]

These findings strengthened the conclusions reached in the earlier phases of the Hawthorne study. Specifically, the Hawthorne researchers moved away from the model of *economic man* to that of *social man.* While individuals obviously need a minimum amount of money and material resources (economic man), the influence of the group on individual behavior is of major significance (social man). Earlier writers such as Taylor did identify group norms as relevant in activities such as setting low rates of production. However, the Hawthorne researchers focused on the group as a *social system* in which the behavior of each individual could be understood only by examining his or her relations with others in the group. This idea of the social system was a major building block in the systems theory of management, as we shall soon see.

SYSTEMS THEORY

Throughout the 1930s a series of seminars was held at Harvard to discuss the data derived from the Hawthorne study. Individuals attending these seminars were quite diverse in background and included L. J. Henderson, a physiologist interested in systems theory, and Chester Barnard, an executive who developed a pioneering approach to management that was largely based on systems theory.

During both the actual Hawthorne study and the seminars, it became clear to the researchers that many forces affected the behavior of each worker and work group. For instance, fear of unemployment during the early part of the Depression in 1931 and 1932 influenced the attitudes and behavior of workers. They focused primarily on the extrinsic aspects of their jobs: wages, fringe benefits, and job security. These were so important that they showed little concern for the intrinsic aspects of the job, such as performing interesting and meaningful work. Researchers began to believe that workers and work groups cannot be studied in isolation. Rather, both the systematic and interdependent relationships among work groups and the influence of the external environment should constitute the basis of analysis. In short, the researchers' original interest in one work group as a social unit was broadened to include a study of *systems forces.*

[1] It should be noted that alternative explanations of the Hawthorne results have been offered. For example, Parsons argues that behavior modification or operant reinforcement contingencies, discussed in Chapter 13, explain these findings. See H. M. Parsons, "What Happened at Hawthorne?" *Science,* March 8, 1974, pp. 922–932.

Assumptions

According to the *systems* viewpoint, an organization is a system that consists of subunits or *subsystems* that not only interact with one another but also are heavily dependent upon one another (see Barnard 1938). For this reason it is important to comprehend the nature of the interactions and interdependencies among the subsystems. For example, two subsystems may depend heavily on one another if they must share machinery, personnel, and space. Further, the organization is an *open system* that interacts with its external environment and is heavily dependent on it for its existence. Some of the external environmental forces that affect the organization include the degree of competition in the industry, laws, and social norms. To understand the functioning of an organization within the systems framework, one must pinpoint the specific external environmental forces that affect the subsystems and the interdependencies among them.

Systems theories constitute an interdisciplinary perspective on organizations and behavior, and management researchers and practitioners frequently borrow systems concepts. For example, researchers trained in biology frequently emphasize systems theory. This perspective is consonant with biological research on the symbiotic relationship between organisms. Similarly, physicists tend to view the world from a systems perspective; they frequently focus on fields of force in the universe and the relationships among them.

It is important to emphasize that systems theorists conceptualize the organization as an open system. It interacts with its external environment, is influenced by it, and in turn influences it. The organization receives inputs from the external environment and, through transformation processes (throughputs), produces outputs (see Figure 2–1). The conception of the organization as an open system is one of the most important postulates of systems theory.

However, some organizations do not rely on the external environment as much as other organizations do, and so there are degrees of openness. In subsequent chapters we shall see that this continuum of openness is central to the design of the organization, since the degree of openness is basically equivalent to the degree of environmental uncertainty. It is this variable, environmental uncertainty, that is of major importance in the design of an organization.

Barnard's Systems Theory

Chester Barnard attended Harvard College but left before receiving his degree to take a job with the Bell Telephone Company. He became a very successful business executive, eventually rising to the presidency of Bell Telephone of New Jersey.

Barnard's systems theory was heavily influenced by the writings of the Hawthorne researchers. While at Harvard, he regularly attended the seminars on the Hawthorne study that were directed by Elton Mayo. It was during this time that Barnard began to work on his book *The Functions of the Executive* (1938), which has become a classic.

Cooperative System. Barnard initially focuses on the importance of the external environment in which the organization operates. He begins by defining a cooperative system as "a complex of physical, biological, personal, and social components which are in a specific systematic relationship by reason of the cooperation of two or more persons for at least one definite end" (Barnard 1938, p. 66). A formal organization is just one of the systems in a cooperative system; a formal organization is "a system of consciously coordinated activities or forces of two or more persons" (Barnard 1938, p. 73). From this perspective the cooperative system represents the external environment that influences the formal organization and, in turn, is influenced by it. For example, a company is a formal organization, and it operates in a cooperative system which includes laws, societal norms, competitors, and so forth.

Thus far Barnard is a traditional systems theorist. However, he begins to structure a distinctive theory when he identifies the essential elements of an organization—systems of communication between individuals and groups, motivation or the willingness to serve, and common purpose integrating the efforts of individuals and groups (Barnard 1938, p. 82). Then, in opposition to the Hawthorne researchers who had highlighted the relevance of work group behavior, Barnard stresses the importance of the executive as *the* critical agent who activates the system or organization. The key functions of the executive are to provide a system of communication, to promote the securing of essential efforts, and to formulate and define purpose (Barnard

FIGURE 2–1
The Organization as an Open System

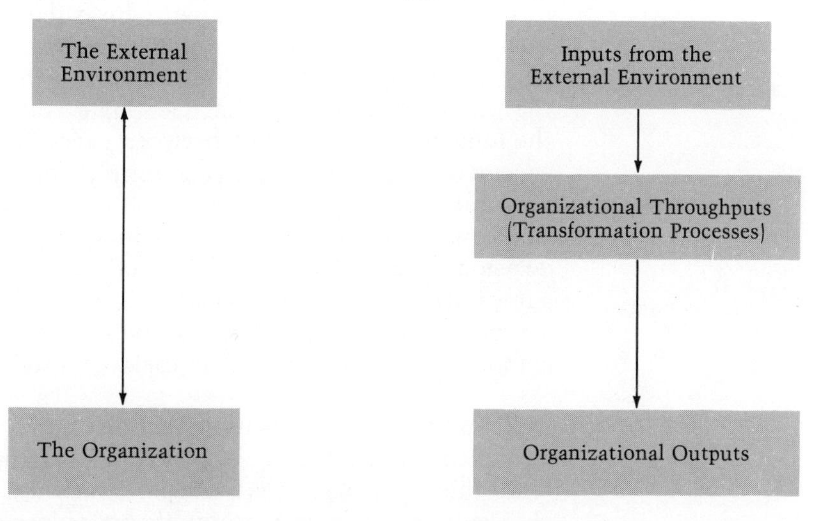

1938, p. 217). These functions correspond exactly to the essential elements of an organization.

Barnard then argues that the executive must meet two conditions if cooperation and financial success are to be attained. First, the executive must emphasize the importance of *effectiveness,* which is the degree to which the common goal or goals are achieved. Second, the executive must be mindful of *efficiency,* which is the satisfaction of individual motives. Thus:

> The test of effectiveness is the accomplishment of a common purpose or purposes; effectiveness can be measured. The test of efficiency is the eliciting of sufficient individual wills to cooperate. *(Barnard 1938, p. 61)*

Other Concepts. Barnard is also noted for developing other management concepts. For instance, he repudiates Max Weber's concept of power, the ability of a superior to give a command to a subordinate that must be accepted. Barnard argues that in the real world power is the ability of a superior to persuade the subordinate to accept a command that he has given. If an executive is constantly autocratic with his subordinates, they will begin to disregard as many of his commands as they can without being punished and will not expend any effort other than that required to perform the job at a satisfactorily minimal level.

Barnard was heavily influenced by the Hawthorne researchers in the area of organization design. These researchers had pointed out the importance of work group behavior in the functioning of an organization. Barnard echoes this approach by arguing that an organization should consist of *units,* each of which should not contain more than ten members. Within such a small unit it is possible for the executive to communicate effectively with his subordinates and to motivate them to accomplish the common goals. When the work of units overlaps, their executives should form an *executive unit* that coordinates the interdependent activities (see Figure 2–2). From this perspective the fundamental difference between executives and employees is that executives are members of two units, an operating unit and an executive unit.

Barnard also developed a distinctive concept of the manager as decision maker. To Barnard, the effective manager focuses only on a few critical factors when faced with a complex problem. By analyzing a problem in this manner, the manager is not overwhelmed by its complexity and can arrive at a satisfactory solution.

Evaluation Systems theory provides us with a distinctive set of perceptual lenses by which we can analyze and evaluate organizations. The use of systems theory is particularly important when a major organizational change is undertaken. Systems theory guides the manager to see that

FIGURE 2–2
Barnard's Unit Concept

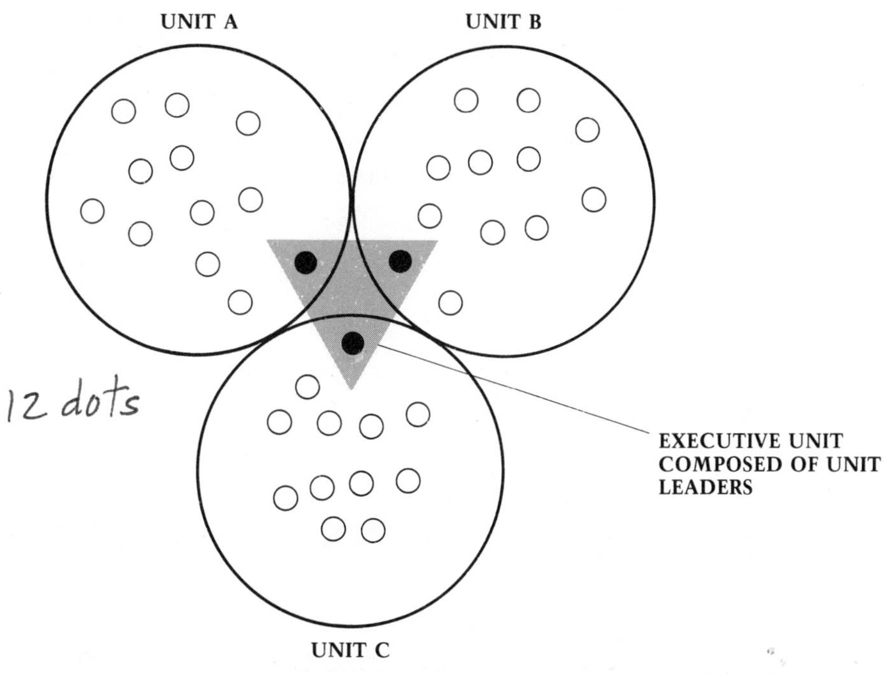

Source: Based on Chester Barnard, *The Functions of the Executive* (Cambridge: Harvard University Press, 1966; originally published in 1938).

changes in one part of the organization frequently bring about changes in other parts of the system. Also, systems theory moves away from the conception of the organization as a closed system that does not interact with its external environment to that of an organization as an open system.

However, systems theory is not without its problems. It is somewhat abstract and hence is difficult for an executive to apply to daily problems. As we shall see in Chapter 3, it is relatively easy to specify a problem in terms of the four organizational dimensions—organization design, planning and control, behavioral processes, and decision making. When a manager faces a problem, he or she can make changes within one or more of these dimensions to solve it. But such specificity is lacking in systems theory.

Also, systems theory does not identify the specific relationships that exist among organizational dimensions. For example, organization design frequently directly affects behavioral processes, but systems theory does not account for this relationship. Similarly, systems theory makes no distinction between types of variables—for instance, the constraint imposed on decision making in our organizational framework by the other three organizational dimensions.

In addition, systems theory rests upon some questionable assumptions. One of its basic propositions is that a change in one subsystem directly affects the other subsystems. While this is certainly valid in some instances, there are many situations in which a subsystem change affects only that particular organizational unit. Further, systems theory has a conservative tinge to it, for it basically maintains that organizations always seek a state of equilibrium.

In summary, systems theory is a valuable addition to the theory and practice of management, and it can be incorporated into our integrated organizational framework.

HUMAN RESOURCES

As was the case with systems theory, the human resources school of management was a direct outgrowth of human relations. This school is not opposed to systems theory; in fact, it reinforces the major tenets. However, human resources is a school important and distinctive in and of itself. This school basically argues that managers frequently create their own problems by vastly underestimating the potential of individuals to assume responsibility.

Argyris's Theory

Chris Argyris was an early theorist in human resources, and his book *Personality and Organization* (1957) has become an important building block in the field of management. In this book Argyris argues that the human relations proponents were basically incorrect. They assumed that management would operate in a rational manner and implement human relations programs that would motivate employees to perform in a superior manner. However, managers frequently behave in an irrational or arational manner. They may construct rigid organizations that stifle the creativity and motivation of employees. Even when using human relations, managers tend to select programs that do not provide an increase in responsibility for employees—for example, additional medical benefits, coffee breaks, and additional holidays. While employees may enjoy these programs, they soon begin to view them as rights rather than privileges. The motivational value of the programs is consequently diminished.

Argyris believes that managers typically construct organizations that are designed to produce childlike behavior among the employees, who are given little, if any, responsibility. In this manner managers create a self-fulfilling prophecy: Because managers see workers behaving in a childlike fashion at work, they assume that the workers are immature. According to Argyris, such childlike activity as engaging in horseplay and deliberately destroying equipment may actually be psychologically healthy for workers in dull and monotonous jobs.

As an alternative, Argyris proposes that management should structure organizations so that workers may achieve their potential and exercise responsibility. Throughout his fruitful professional career Argyris has served as a consultant to many organizations when their managers have attempted to put his ideas into practice (see Argyris 1964 and 1970).

Theory X and Theory Y

Another major theorist in the human resources school is Douglas McGregor. He suggested that managers have developed two distinct philosophies concerning the roles they play in organizations. These two philosophies, which he called Theory X and Theory Y, represent opposite points of view. The approach McGregor felt had traditionally dominated, Theory X, consists of the following propositions:

> The average human being has an inherent dislike of work and will avoid it if he can.
>
> Because of this human characteristic of dislike of work, most people must be coerced, controlled, directed, threatened with punishment to get them to put forth adequate effort toward the achievement of organizational objectives.
>
> The average human being prefers to be directed, wishes to avoid responsibility, has relatively little ambition, wants security above all. *(McGregor 1960, pp. 33–34)*

These propositions suggest that a manager who sees his or her role in terms of Theory X would tend to be autocratic.

What McGregor proposed as an alternative was Theory Y, which rests on an entirely different set of assumptions.

> The expenditure of physical and mental effort in work is as natural as play or rest. . . .
>
> External control and the threat of punishment are not the only means for bringing about effort toward organizational objectives. Man will exercise self-direction and self-control in the service of objectives to which he is committed. . . .
>
> Commitment to objectives is a function of the rewards associated with their achievement. . . .
>
> The average human being learns, under proper conditions, not only to accept but to seek responsibility. . . .
>
> The capacity to exercise a relatively high degree of imagination, ingenuity, and creativity in the solution of organizational problems is widely, not narrowly, distributed in the population.
>
> Under the conditions of modern industrial life, the intellectual potentialities of the average human being are only partially utilized. *(McGregor 1960, pp. 47–48)*

"In case of power failure. We like to think ahead."

Like Argyris, McGregor argues that individuals want to exercise responsibility and that the best way for managers to use the human resources in an organization is to allow them to do so.

Table 2–1 outlines the major differences among traditional management, human relations, and human resources.

CONTINGENCY THEORY

The contingency theory of management arose directly out of systems theory. It accepts the major propositions of systems theory but extends them in several crucial ways. The basic proposition of contingency theory is that there are no universal principles of management that can be applied uncritically. Rather, the decision makers must analyze such key variables as technology and external environmental uncertainty and then take a course of action that is appropriate to that particular situation. It is consequently a *situational* theory of management.

In this section we discuss contingency theory from the perspective of management. In subsequent chapters contingency theory will be discussed from the perspectives of motivation, leadership, conflict, and related areas.

TABLE 2–1
Three Schools of Management

Traditional model	*Human relations model*	*Human resources model*
Assumptions: 1. Work is inherently distasteful to most people. 2. What workers do is less important than what they earn for doing it. 3. Few want or can handle work that requires creativity, self-direction, or self-control.	*Assumptions:* 1. People want to feel useful and important. 2. People desire to belong and to be recognized as individuals. 3. These needs are more important than money in motivating people to work.	*Assumptions:* 1. Work is not inherently distasteful. People want to contribute to meaningful goals they have helped establish. 2. Most people can exercise far more creative, responsible self-direction and self-control than their present jobs demand.
Policies: 1. The manager's basic task is to closely supervise and control subordinates. 2. The manager must break tasks down into simple, repetitive, and easily learned operations. 3. The manager must establish detailed work routines and procedures and enforce these firmly but fairly.	*Policies:* 1. The manager's basic task is to make each worker feel useful and important. 2. The manager should keep subordinates informed and listen to their objections to plans. 3. The manager should allow subordinates to exercise some self-control on routine matters.	*Policies:* 1. The manager's basic task is to make use of untapped human resources. 2. The manager must create an environment in which all members may contribute to the limits of their ability. 3. The manager must encourage full participation on important matters, continually broadening subordinate self-direction and control.
Expectations: 1. People can tolerate work if the pay is decent and the boss is fair. 2. If tasks are simple enough and people are closely controlled, they will produce up to standard.	*Expectations:* 1. Sharing information with subordinates and involving them in routine decisions will satisfy their basic needs to belong and to feel important. 2. Satisfying these needs will improve morale and reduce resistance to formal authority—subordinates will "willingly cooperate."	*Expectations:* 1. Expanding subordinate influence, self-direction, and self-control will lead to direct improvements in operating efficiency. 2. Work satisfaction may improve as a by-product of subordinates making full use of their resources.

Source: From Raymond E. Miles, *Theories of Management.* Copyright © 1975 McGraw-Hill. Used with permission of McGraw-Hill Book Company.

Organic and Mechanistic Structures

One of the fundamental distinctions in the contingency literature is that between organic and mechanistic structures. Two English researchers, Tom Burns and G. M. Stalker (1961), analyzed the organizational structures of twenty industrial firms in the United Kingdom. Their analysis suggested the existence of two major types of organizational structures, mechanistic and organic. Essentially, the *mechanistic* organization is highly bureaucratic, while the *organic*, its opposite, is flexible and responsive. Organizations exist along a continuum extending from mechanistic to organic. In real situations it would be difficult and perhaps impossible to identify an enterprise at one end of this continuum. However, it is possible to pinpoint differences between these two structures and to classify an organization as either more mechanistic or more organic.

In a sense, these two types of organizational structures represent the two major streams of thought in management—the traditional management stream and the behavioral science stream. A mechanistic organization focuses on efficient structure; an organic organization emphasizes the needs of employees within the structure. There are seven important characteristics that differentiate the mechanistic from the organic organization (see Table 2–2). Three of these characteristics—division of labor, hierarchy of authority, and jobs and procedures—represent the traditional focus of the management field. The remaining four—motivation, style of leadership, group relations, and communication—reflect the behavioral processes that we will discuss in Part IV.

In the mechanistic organization, duties and responsibilities are divided by means of functional specialization. Everyone has a specialized role to play, and he or she typically works in a department that primarily or totally includes similar specialists. An example of functional specialization is the automotive assembly line, where workers perform routine jobs in which they are able to exercise only a very small amount of responsibility. In the organic organization the division of labor emphasizes enlarging each worker's job, so that the individual performs a variety of activities, and enriching it, so that he or she also exercises significant responsibility. For example, top management of Volvo in Sweden has enlarged and enriched the work by deemphasizing the assembly line and allowing a work team to be responsible for the production of an entire car.

A second feature that distinguishes mechanistic and organic organizations involves their hierarchy of authority. In the mechanistic organization, authority is clearly defined and centralized. Most individuals in the hierarchy operate in a limited sphere in which their authority is restricted. This feature is logically related to the concept of division of labor: The more specialized the work, the more clearly defined are the relative positions of individuals. In contrast, authority

TABLE 2–2
Characteristics of Organic and Mechanistic Organizations

Characteristics of structure	*Mechanistic organizations*	*Organic organizations*
1. Division of labor	Functional specialization or departmentalization by function	Job enlargement and job enrichment
2. Hierarchy of authority	Clearly defined and centralized	Decentralized and participative
3. Jobs and procedures	Formal and standardized	Flexible
4. Behavioral processes		
a. Motivation	Primarily economic	Both economic and noneconomic
b. Leadership style	Authoritarian	Democratic
c. Group relations	Formal and impersonal	Informal and personal
d. Communication	Vertical and directive	Vertical and lateral, consultative

in the organic organization is decentralized, and individuals in the lower levels can make many decisions without double-checking constantly with their superiors. In addition, most employees are involved in making decisions that directly influence their own work; hence the distinction among workers of various ranks tends to become blurred.

The specification of jobs and procedures used to complete the work is another feature that separates organic from mechanistic organizations. In a mechanistic structure jobs and procedures are formed and standardized. Employees know exactly what procedures to follow in any situation and what tasks are part of their jobs. In the organic organization both jobs and procedures for completing them are very flexible. When a problem occurs, the individuals directly affected attempt to solve it, regardless of the procedures specified in the official job classification system.

In the area of behavioral processes motivation distinguishes mechanistic from organic organizations. To generate commitment from employees, leaders in the mechanistic organization rely primarily on economic motivation: Employees are paid a high wage to keep their productivity high. The organic organization uses both economic and noneconomic factors to motivate employees. While money is still important, other factors such as job enrichment and recognition from superiors for excellent performance are also highlighted.

In the mechanistic organization the style of leadership is highly authoritarian. The leader's word is law, and the subordinate had better obey his or her commands. The opposite situation exists in the organic organization; the leaders tend to be democratic and participative. The leader tries to involve his or her subordinates as much as possible in any decision that will affect their position in the organization.

Mechanistic and organic organizations also differ with respect to interpersonal and group relations. In the mechanistic organization, communication is vertical and directive. That is, the superior gives commands to his or her subordinates (vertical) who are expected to respond to them immediately (directive). In the organic organization, communication is both vertically directive and laterally consultative. Superiors still issue commands to subordinates, but everyone can communicate laterally with his or her equals when problems arise. Such communication is *consultative* because it involves exchanging opinions rather than giving orders.

Tosi and Carroll's Perspective

Henry Tosi and Stephen Carroll have developed a contingency perspective that emphasizes two of the major variables in management theory: technology and market uncertainty, or external environmental uncertainty, as shown in Figure 2-3. They categorize technology as either routine or nonroutine. An organization operates with a routine technology if there are few technological changes that influence the manner in which it produces its final good or service. For example, the technology in the textile industry has not changed significantly in the past hundred years. This routine technology is in marked contrast to that in the picture tube industry. Rapid techno-

FIGURE 2-3
Tosi and Carroll's Contingency Perspective

TECHNOLOGY	MARKET OR EXTERNAL ENVIRONMENT: *Stable*	MARKET OR EXTERNAL ENVIRONMENT: *Volatile*
Routine	Hierarchical, bureaucratic organizations, e.g., banks, insurance companies, government agencies	Market-dominated organizations, e.g., textile industry
Nonroutine	Technologically dominated organizations, e.g., power cable companies	Flexible, dynamic organizations, e.g., aerospace, electronics, small R&D firms

Source: Adapted from Stephen Carroll and Henry Tosi. *Organizational Behavior* (Chicago: St. Clair Press, 1977). Used by permission.

logical changes force firms in this industry to operate with a non-routine or constantly changing technology.

Tosi and Carroll make a similar distinction between stable and volatile market conditions. Environmental uncertainty is very high if a firm operates in a volatile market in which it is difficult to predict changes in market share from year to year. Conversely, a stable market is one in which the organization can reasonably predict its share of the market over an extended number of years.

Four Types of Organizations. Using these distinctions, Tosi and Carroll argue that there are four basic types of organizations. The *hierarchical* or *bureaucratic* organization represents a situation in which the firm operates with a routine technology within the structure of a stable market. Under such conditions it is possible and desirable to employ the bureaucratic form of organization. Many government agencies exist in such an environment. Typically a government agency receives an annual budget that is not determined by competitive and market forces, and its technology is routine. Banks and insurance companies are also illustrative of the hierarchical, bureaucratic organization.

Some organizations are *market-dominated:* The technology used to produce the final good or service is routine, but the market is highly volatile. Fashion stores are in this category; customer whims frequently spell either a major success or a major failure when management introduces a new line of clothes. However, as indicated above, the technology used to produce these clothes is routine.

Some organizations must periodically introduce new and sophisticated technologies, even though their markets are stable. Hence they are *technology-dominated.* In countries such as Taiwan only a few companies make picture tubes, and they service only thirteen or fourteen major clients. The government allows the firms to decide on the relative distribution of market shares, so these organizations can predict their revenues with precision from year to year. While the picture tube companies operate in a stable market environment, nevertheless they must constantly develop new technologies to service the demands of their clients.

Similar situations exist in the United States. For instance, only a few large firms are in the power cable industry, since it requires a large expenditure of capital to underwrite the cost of the technology necessary to produce the final good. Hence the firms in this industry can predict with reasonable assurance their shares of the market from year to year. However, safety standards and performance requirements are constantly changing. Thus firms in this industry must periodically introduce new technology to meet these standards.

Finally, there are *flexible, dynamic* organizations that operate with a nonroutine technology under volatile market conditions. Aerospace companies such as Boeing fit into this category. Frequently technological advances occur that revolutionize the industry. At the same time there is intense competition, especially for the government contracts that are a major part of the industry's market. The loss of one major contract can force an aerospace company to reduce operations and lay off thousands of workers.

Managerial Style. According to Tosi and Carroll, the style of management should be suitable to each of the four types of organizations that they have identified. For example, it is possible to use bureaucratic rules in a government agency but not in a small research and development firm or even in a large aerospace company. In those organizations the engineers and scientists must be allowed to define their own work if they are to create new products.

Tosi and Carroll also argue that a large company may actually include departments representative of one or more of the four basic organizational forms. In a food company the market research department would be market-dominated, since there are frequent changes in consumer tastes that it must monitor. In the same company the production subsystem would be bureaucratic, since the production of food is relatively routine.

Critique Contingency theory has added to our store of knowledge about organizations. It specifies the environmental and technological situations under which organizations operate and argues that the managerial style of decision making should be appropriate to them. As we have seen, it is an outgrowth of systems theory and views these environmental and technological constraints in terms of their influence on the behavior and interdependent nature of subsystems.

However, contingency theory seems to represent a classification system rather than a true theoretical formulation. The basic objective appears to be to classify an organization into one of several types rather than to develop interrelated propositions that can be used to predict behavior. But even given that objective, contingency theory does not take into account the fundamental differences between organizations, even when they can be classified into one type. For instance, General Motors and the Ford Motor Company represent the same type, but their managerial styles are vastly different.

Additionally, contingency theory does not adequately account for change. At one time a government agency may fall into the bureaucratic cell; later, because of some rapid and unexpected changes, the same agency may move into the flexible, dynamic cell. Contingency theory does not directly address how and why such movements occur.

Another problem is that most contingency theorists focus on only a limited number of organizational types. As we have seen, the contingency theories discussed in this chapter examine at best only four organizational types. In the real world the number of organizational types is much larger. Thus contingency theory can make only a gross rather than a fine distinction among organizational types. Because of this limitation, an organization may fit into more than one category.

Contingency theory can be incorporated into our organizational framework, as we shall see in Chapter 3. First, we can identify the organizational type into which a specific organization fits. Within each type we can then apply our organizational framework, focusing on the four fundamental dimensions and the relationships among them.

SUMMARY

The behavioral science stream of management does not replace but, rather, supplements the traditional stream. It includes four major schools: human relations, systems theory, human resources, and contingency theory.

The first major school, human relations, moved away from the concept of economic man to that of social man. According to this school, one must consider the norms and forces acting on an individual in a group setting in order to understand that person's behavior. Hence a group is a social system rather than a mere collection of individuals.

Systems theory evolved out of this conception of a group. It has two major postulates: (1) An organization is an open system that influences its external environment and, in turn, is influenced by it; and (2) an organization consists of several interdependent subsystems that influence one another. Accordingly, an organization cannot be considered as a collection of individual subsystems that exist in a vacuum. Chester Barnard, an early advocate of the doctrines put forth by Elton Mayo and other members of the human relations school, developed important theories for the systems school.

The school of human resources also arose out of the human relations school, and it reinforces the ideas of systems theorists. This school argues that management must learn to conserve and effectively utilize its most valuable resources, namely, its organizational members. To accomplish this task, managers must allow organizational members to exercise responsibility commensurate with their abilities. Major theorists in this school include Chris Argyris and Douglas McGregor.

Contingency theory basically argues for a situational approach to management: Managerial practices should be chosen for their appropriateness to the particular situation. Burns and Stalker demonstrated that there are essentially two kinds of organizational structures: the mechanistic or highly rigid organizational structure and the organic or highly flexible organizational structure. Tosi and Carroll expanded on this distinction between mechanistic and organic structures and developed a four-cell typology of organizations. Their classifications are based on the key variables of technology and environmental uncertainty.

DISCUSSION QUESTIONS

1. How does systems theory differ from contingency theory? What are some similarities?
2. In Chapter 1 we discussed scientific management. What are some of the major differences and similarities between scientific management and human relations?
3. What does a contingency theory of management mean? Does the human relations school represent a contingency viewpoint? Why or why not? How about the human resources school?
4. Scientific management argues for the model of economic man and human relations for social man. What kind of model underlies the human resources school? Why?
5. How does Barnard's theory differ from the human relations approach? What are some similarities?
6. Some writers argue that contingency theory is not a theory per se but only a perspective. What do they mean?

CRITICAL INCIDENTS

NOTE: These critical incidents can be used by the whole class with the case observational method (see Appendix A) or used for thought and discussion by individual class members.

1. During the mid 1960s the American economy was robust. Because of the favorable economic climate, many workers quit their current jobs to obtain ostensibly better positions; it was therefore difficult to obtain reliable workers.

One of the major banks in the United States, headquartered in Manhattan, faced particularly troublesome issues. Some of its employees in its 140 branches were traveling two hours a day on the subway to get to work. Also, since banks pay relatively low salaries, many of its employees were being lured away for higher salaries elsewhere.

For instance, it was quite common for the male employees to quit to become policemen.

Still, the bank had developed many enlightened personnel policies. The employee career ladder consisted of nine separate steps, and middle managers thought that this career ladder should have provided sufficient motivation for the more mature employees to stay at the bank. Hence the managers argued that some variables—such as the robust state of the economy, the travel inconveniences, and the higher-paying occupations against which the bank could not effectively compete—were simply uncontrollable.

However, top management became very concerned as the turnover rate of its new employees reached fifty percent within the first year of employment; it engaged a large consulting firm to survey its 4000 employees and pinpoint the major problems. The consulting firm constructed a detailed questionnaire to examine many job-related issues such as attitudes about pay, supervision, challenging work, and fringe benefits. All the employees completed this questionnaire. The consulting firm then summarized the major findings and published them in an attractive booklet, giving a copy to every employee. In this booklet the consulting firm indicated that management was initiating changes in accordance with the employees' responses and wishes.

QUESTIONS: Do you think Mayo and the Hawthorne researchers would have agreed with the approach used by the Manhattan bank? Why? Do you feel that middle management was correct in assuming that some variables were uncontrollable? Explain. Could the consulting firm have created a Hawthorne effect? Why or why not?

2. The following quotation is taken from an employee manual for one of the largest department stores in Chicago in the year 1857 (Shultz and Coleman 1959, p. 114):

> The employee who is in the habit of smoking Spanish cigars, being shaved at the barber's, going to dances and other places of amusement will surely give his employer reasons to be suspicious of his integrity and honesty.
>
> Each employee must not pay less than five dollars per year to the church and must attend Sunday School regularly.
>
> Men employees are given one evening a week for courting and two if they go to prayer meeting.

QUESTIONS: What kind of design is this organization using, mechanistic or organic? What type or types of organizations in our own society come closest to approximating such an organization? Under what conditions might Tosi and Carroll recommend that such an organization be constructed? Why?

SUGGESTED READINGS

Miles, R. *Theories of Management.* New York: McGraw-Hill, 1975.

Miles is noted for comparing and contrasting the three schools of traditional management, human relations, and human resources. This book provides an excellent summary of his views, which are now widely accepted.

McGregor, D. *The Human Side of Enterprise.* New York: McGraw-Hill, 1960.

McGregor, a major theorist in the human resources school, describes in detail Theory X and Theory Y. See the description in this chapter.

Williams, W. *Mainsprings of Men.* New York: Scribner, 1925.

Although it may be difficult to obtain this book because it was published in 1925, it is well worth reading. Williams was a successful corporation executive who spent a year as a common laborer among men who did not know his background. He was very surprised by the factors that influenced group behavior among common laborers, and he reported them in an interesting fashion in this highly readable book.

3 Management Within an Organizational Framework

ORGANIZATIONAL DIMENSIONS OF MANAGEMENT
RELATIONSHIPS WITHIN THE ORGANIZATIONAL FRAMEWORK
RELATIONSHIPS TO MANAGEMENT SCHOOLS
DYNAMICS OF THE FRAMEWORK: THREE CASES
SUMMARY
DISCUSSION QUESTIONS
SUGGESTED READINGS

PERFORMANCE OBJECTIVES

1. To identify and define the organizational dimensions within which managerial activities take place.
2. Using these dimensions, to construct an organizational framework within which managerial activities can be studied.
3. To understand the dynamics of the organizational framework, that is, how these organizational dimensions directly and indirectly influence one another.
4. To describe how our organizational framework incorporates the main propositions of the major schools of modern management.
5. To illustrate the usefulness of the framework through its application to three case studies.

Managers engage in an extremely large number of activities, many of which do not appear to be logically related. For example, when a visitor walks into a manager's office, he is sometimes overwhelmed by the diversity of activities taking place. The manager may tell a subordinate over the phone to pursue a particular course of action; he may inform his secretary that he cannot attend an important meeting; he may sign some letters; he may interrupt the discussion to talk with another subordinate who needs an immediate answer; and, finally, after 15 minutes he may turn his full attention to the visitor. For centuries practitioners and scholars have attempted to describe the behavior of individuals in organizations in a manner that logically relates such diverse activities.

This chapter describes managerial activities within an organizational framework and illustrates the dynamics of this organizational framework through its application to three case studies. In addition, we discuss how our organizational framework incorporates and integrates the two major streams of management and their major schools, which were examined in Chapters 1 and 2. All the chapters in this book relate directly to our organizational framework.

ORGANIZATIONAL DIMENSIONS OF MANAGEMENT

Managerial activities can be described in terms of four organizational dimensions. Planning and control in combination constitute the first dimension; organization design, the second; behavioral processes, the third; and decision making, the fourth (see Table 3–1). In any organization managerial activities take place within these four dimensions. Thus the perspective of our framework is that of the entire organization rather than that of the individual manager. It is quite common for a manager to be involved in activities within two or even three dimensions simultaneously; however, it is less common for an individual to be involved in activities within all four dimensions at any one moment. For example, an individual manager does not constantly concern himself with the design of the organization, although management in its entirety is vitally interested in this dimension.

This framework includes not only the four basic dimensions within which activities take place but also the relationships among them. As we shall see, a manager's plans for an organization usually involve its design; his or her methods of control influence behavioral processes; and so on. Although some decisions are made in the isolation of the manager's office, their effects are felt much more widely, often in several areas of the organization.

The framework effectively describes the activities that take place in all or most organizations. Once an individual understands the four dimensions and the relationships among them, he or she can then apply a common body of organizational and managerial skills to a

TABLE 3–1
Four Organizational Dimensions

Planning and control
Planning and control in combination constitute the first organizational dimension, as they represent the opposite sides of the same coin. Planning involves the following activities: (1) through environmental forecasting, selecting the basic mission or missions of the organization, the business or businesses the organization is in; (2) developing desired outcomes—long-term goals and short-term objectives—the organization seeks to attain in light of its mission or missions and environmental forecasts; (3) developing means—strategies and tactics—to achieve goals and objectives; (4) updating forecasts periodically to take account of environmental changes; (5) possibly changing missions, goals, and objectives in light of the revised forecasts; and (6) implementing policies, procedures, and rules in light of the missions, strategies, tactics, goals, and objectives. *Control systems* monitor the organization's implementation of its plans and pinpoint significant deviations from plans. In some situations the control system contains an action device that automatically corrects such deviations. In other situations individuals must determine what corrective action is appropriate.

Organization design
The design of an organization establishes its structure, provides a framework for its activities, and delineates lines of authority and responsibility. The appropriate design for a given organization depends on such factors as its technology and the external environment within which it functions.

Behavioral processes
The behavioral processes within an organization—perception and interpersonal communication, motivation, leadership, and group behavior—are the preconditions for interactions and the actual interactions between and among organizational members that enable the organization to move toward its goals.

Managerial decision making
Decision making is a process of choice leading to the selection of one alternative rather than others. More generally, it involves problem-solving activity that comes into play when the manager realizes that a significant gap exists between what is and what should be. Such problem-solving activity begins and ends with an analysis of the performance of organizational members, organizational subsystems, and the entire organization (separately or together). Decision making involves a stimulus event motivating the individual to recognize a significant gap between what is and what should be; information search; problem formulation; evaluation of alternatives/choice; and implementation.

variety of organizations, from business firms to government agencies to charitable institutions, even though some features of each type of organization are unique and require special study.

Planning

Without planning there is no control, for control is the monitoring of plans and the identification of significant deviations from them. Hence planning and control are closely related and, in combination, constitute the first organizational dimension of management. To understand planning, one must understand the organizational planning process. In this section we describe this process.

Even before managers design an organization, they must engage in planning activities. The first step in planning is *environmental*

"People must be spending their money on something, Jackson, and it's your job to find out what that something is!"

forecasting: examining the external environment to determine if there is an environmental niche or a demand for a product or service that is not being met. Using the results of the forecast, the organization attempts to determine its *mission* or *missions*: the business(es) or market(s) the organization is in and those that it is not in.

A good illustration of this first step comes from the Gillette Company, which was started at the turn of the twentieth century by a door-to-door salesman. At that time it was difficult to shave at home because the equipment was so elaborate. Tired of going to the barber frequently for shaves, and interested in starting a new business, Mr. Gillette defined the mission of the Gillette Company as providing comfortable shaves at home.

Once a mission has been defined, it is necessary to construct *long-term goals,* that is, specific ends to be accomplished, usually within a particular number of years. Some goals at Gillette might be to make $1 million in profit by the end of the first five years and to have a profit margin of ten percent by the end of the first five years. Further, it is necessary to develop means to accomplish these goals. These means are called *strategies.* Initially Mr. Gillette emphasized two strategies. First, he created the safety razor, which was consistent with his company's basic mission. This strategy allowed him to market a new product to fill an environmental niche or demand. However, at that time there were no retail outlets through which Mr. Gillette could sell his safety razors. Therefore his second strategy, based on his own experience in sales, was to hire salesmen to sell the safety razors door-to-door.

In addition to long-term goals, the organization must develop *short-term objectives,* frequently stated in terms of one year. For Mr. Gillette these might be to sell 10,000 razors the first year and to have a profit margin of five percent in the first year. And just as it is necessary to develop strategies to accomplish long-term goals, it is necessary to develop *tactics* to accomplish short-term objectives. Strategies and tactics are closely related; they are both means to achieve desired outcomes (goals and objectives). The Gillette Company initially used such tactics as advertising the advantages of shaving at home and the degree of safety associated with the new razor.

As another part of the planning process an organization usually will update its forecasts on a regular basis. Based on the revised forecasts of new inventions, new competitors, or other changes in the environment, the organization may change or enlarge its mission(s). It may also revise its long-term goals, strategies, short-term objectives, and tactics.

To accomplish its missions, goals, and objectives, the organization also develops *policies,* general guides to action that the individuals in the organization follow, although reasonable exceptions are permitted. One policy might be to assume that the customer is always right. At Gillette, management might instruct each door-to-door salesman to return a dissatisfied customer's money. However, a salesman might violate this policy if the same customer always demanded repayment. In organizations, there are policies to cover most kinds of activities, financial, personnel, advertising, and so on.

As a general rule, policies are accompanied by *procedures*: customary ways of handling activities in accordance with established policies. Policies are broad guidelines; procedures are specific and describe the exact *sequence* in which a particular activity can be completed. Procedures, in turn, are subdivided into *rules,* or one stage in a procedure. A procedure can be defined as a series of rules.

In Chapter 5 we shall describe planning in detail. However, for an overview of the organizational planning process, you might refer now to Table 3-1 and Figure 5-1.

Control

Once plans have been stated and implemented, the organization must develop control systems to check continually how well they are being carried out. *Control* can be defined as monitoring plans and pinpointing significant deviations from them. Planning and control are opposite sides of the same coin; without planning, there can be no control. In some situations the control system automatically corrects these deviations; in other situations the manager must determine what corrective action is appropriate.

Like plans, control systems can be either strategic or tactical. *Strategic control* usually guards against a long-term loss of clients or markets. For a business firm the profit statement over a period of years serves as a strategic control mechanism. If profits decline continuously, some major adjustments in either the firm's plans or its means of carrying them out may be necessary. In a religious order the number of applicants over a period of years operates as a similar control mechanism, since the organization's existence would be threatened if only a few individuals wanted to join it. In all organizations there are strategic control systems that run parallel to strategic planning systems.

Tactical control systems are typically specific and short range. A tactical plan to reduce defective parts by twenty percent within one year might be accompanied by a control system that emphasizes close supervisory attention to each employee's work. In addition, management might penalize an employee who produces a significant number of defective parts.

As the discussion thus far suggests, control consists of two separate concepts. The first is the control of the entire organization and its major subsystems. For example, a budget is a control mechanism that monitors deviations from plans on an organizational basis; if an organizational unit exceeds its budget by a significant amount, its management must explain why this deviation has occurred. The second concept is the control of organizational members, for they must perform adequately if plans are to be completed successfully. Control of individuals includes the proper selection of employees, their job orientation and training, and the measurement of their performance. If employees perform adequately, they are usually given rewards such as promotions and salary increases. If they do not perform effectively, they may be given a warning or a demotion, or they may even be fired.

Organization Design

The second of the four dimensions is organization design, the way the organization is constructed. It includes issues such as lines of responsibility, authority, and communication within an organization, all of which are important for creating an effective structure within which organizational activities can take place. A typical design problem is to determine the *optimum span of control:* the proper number of subordinates each manager should supervise.

Even before management designs an organization, the founders must identify overall objectives. Typically this general planning focuses on the establishment of goals, in order of importance. The founders normally scan the external environment so they can understand the impact of outside forces, such as the degree of competition in the industry, existing or proposed governmental regulations, and the rate of technological change that will directly influence the marketability of their products. Thus a certain amount of general planning must precede design; then management must design the organization before anything else can occur.

Organization design includes many activities, such as determining the amount of responsibility that should be placed in each organizational position, constructing a formal system of communication among units, and developing procedures for handling employee grievances. These and similar activities relate directly to the way the organization is constructed.

Behavioral Processes

The third organizational dimension is the behavioral processes in organizations. These are the preconditions for interaction and the actual interaction among organizational members that enable the organization to move toward its goals.

There are four major behavioral processes: perception and interpersonal communication, motivation, leadership, and group behavior. *Perception* is the organization of stimuli or sensations into a meaningful whole. It is a precondition for *interpersonal communication*, or communication among individuals. Hence we treat perception and interpersonal communication together as a distinct behavioral process. *Leadership* is a critical behavioral process, since the superior or manager must direct and coordinate the work of subordinates. The *motivation* of individuals is also critical; if individuals are not motivated to work, the overall efforts and productivity of the organization will suffer. The final behavioral process is *group behavior*. When groups and units are functioning effectively, the probability increases that the tactical and strategic plans of the organization will be accomplished.

Behavioral processes in the organization must be in balance if goals and objectives are to be attained. When they are not working smoothly, organizations suffer negative consequences such as a high rate of employee turnover and a low rate of productivity.

Managerial Decision Making

Managerial decision making is the fourth dimension in our organizational framework. Decision making can be defined as a process of choice leading to the selection of one alternative rather than others. More generally, it is a problem-solving activity that comes into play when the manager realizes that there is a significant gap between what is and what should be (MacCrimmon 1974; Simon 1965).

Decision making is initiated by a *stimulus event,* an event that motivates the individual to perceive a problem. Individuals vary enormously in their responses to a stimulus event; the same stimulus event will lead one individual to perceive a problem and another to perceive nothing. *Information search* is the second stage of decision making. After recognizing the existence of the problem, the individual searches for information about its causes. Using this information, the individual carries out the third stage: *problem formulation.* Here the individual attempts to describe the problem and identify possible causes of it. That is, the individual attempts to organize the information he has gathered into a coherent view of the problem and its possible solutions. In the fourth stage, *evaluation of alternatives/choice,* the individual evaluates the relative attractiveness of the various solutions and selects one of them. The final stage of decision making is the *implementation* of the preferred alternative.

RELATIONSHIPS WITHIN THE ORGANIZATIONAL FRAMEWORK

The relationships among the four dimensions are important. The framework is dynamic, for it incorporates not only the various dimensions but the associations among them, as shown in Figure 3–1. Technically, it is a systems feedback framework. In this section we look at the impact on the organization of each dimension.

Impact of Planning and Control

Planning on all levels influences the other dimensions of an organization. One frequent result of strategic planning is its influence on the design of the organization. For example, when the Ford Motor Company decided to produce the Edsel during the 1950s, the strategic plan was to market a car for affluent buyers who wanted a unique possession. To persuade customers that the Edsel was indeed unique, top managers at Ford changed the company's organizational structure to set up a separate dealership for it. They reasoned that regular dealers could not provide enough personal service because they were selling several models of cars. But since the regular Ford dealers were not allowed to sell Edsels, they became hostile, even to the point of telling customers that the Edsel was an inferior car. Although there were other causes, such as changing customer tastes, this relationship between strategic planning and organization design partially contributed to Ford's decision to curtail production of the Edsel and take a $350 million tax write-off.

Tactical planning also influences the design of the organization, although usually on a smaller scale. When too many tactical plans fail, management may create a new system for delegating authority, restructure work groups and units, or replace people with machines.

Planning also affects the behavioral processes that take place in an organization. When management alters its direction by developing a new strategic plan, individuals are frequently upset because they fear they may be let go or given undesirable assignments. Similarly, if management constantly changes tactical plans, individuals can become annoyed about interruptions in their routines. When individuals become too upset, there may be negative consequences, such as high rates of absenteeism and low rates of productivity.

While control systems run parallel to planning systems, they can independently influence behavioral processes. For example, two companies may want to decrease defective parts by twenty percent within one year, but one of them may buy new machinery to accomplish this tactical plan while the other may tighten up its control of employees by closely monitoring their work. This tight control could easily make the workers uneasy and create difficulties between them and their

FIGURE 3–1

A Framework for the Four Organizational Dimensions Within Which Activities and Behavior Take Place

The perspective is that of the organization rather than the individual. A particular individual may be involved only in activities within two or three dimensions at any given moment; however, management in its entirety is vitally interested in all four dimensions and the relationships among them. All these dimensions are affected by the external environment.

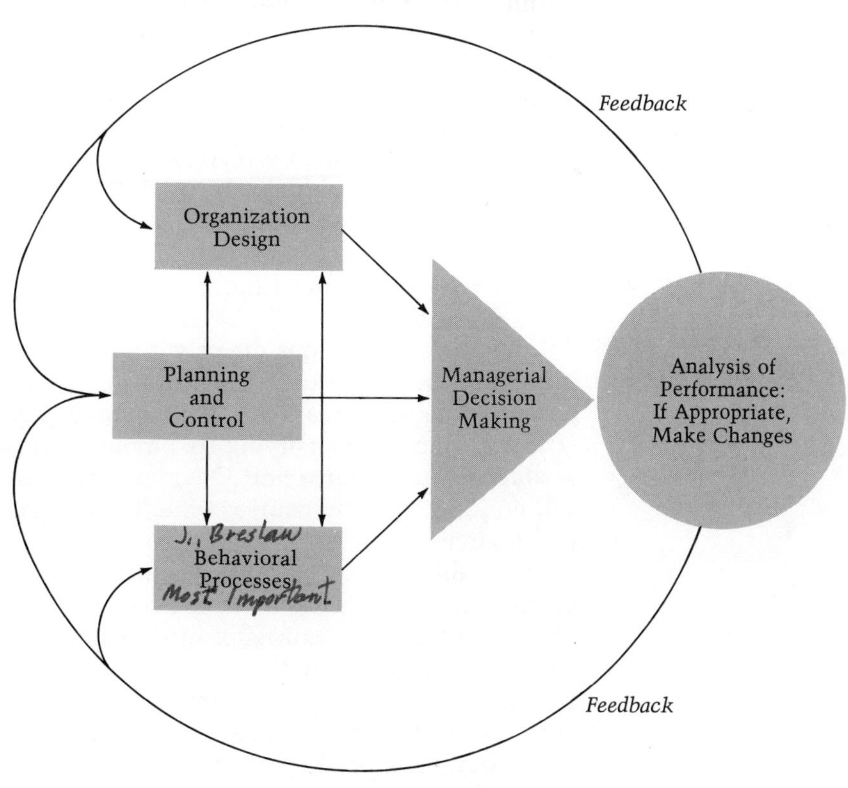

supervisors. And when tight control systems are implemented, the design of the organization normally becomes rigid and highly bureaucratic.

Impact of Design

The design of the organization can affect the behavioral processes that take place within it. For example, management may design an organization so that a subordinate reports to two superiors. This practice can create behavioral problems if the subordinate cannot complete his assignments for both superiors. In this situation the subordinate will probably experience role conflict and a sense of frustration. Or management may decide to save money by routinizing the work and replacing skilled workers with unskilled workers. This design change can dramatically alter behavioral processes, because unskilled workers characteristically have higher rates of turnover and absenteeism, show a much greater amount of friction in work groups, and are less responsive to informal leadership (see Sayles 1958).

Impact of Behavioral Processes

Just as organization design directly influences behavior, so behavioral processes directly influence the formal design of an organization. For example, informal relations frequently emerge in organizations that do not follow the formal design. And in extreme cases the informal relations bear no association whatsoever to the formal design. Joan Woodward (1965), an English researcher, once asked a senior manager for the organization chart of his company, which he gave her. But he also presented her with a second chart listing powerful managers in the company, their actual and real duties and responsibilities, and the degree to which they could influence major decisions. In such situations behavioral processes have a distinct influence on the formal structure of the organization.

Setting for Managerial Decision Making

All the other dimensions directly influence managerial decision making. In essence, the other dimensions provide a setting within which decision making takes place. For example, a company may develop a strategic plan of diversifying its product line, manufacturing several products instead of just one. Obviously managers, as decision makers, can no longer pursue courses of action that relate only to the sale of the original product.

It is difficult to separate planning and decision making when creating the organization. As the founders develop a set of strategic plans, they are also engaging in decision making when they eliminate undesirable alternatives. Later, once the initial plans are put into practice, the plans help to form a setting in which decision making takes place. If the founders or managers determine that changes in the initial plans need to be made, they are involved with the dimension of decision making.

The design of the organization also influences the decision-making scope of management. If a firm invests millions of dollars in new equipment that allows the organization to hire unskilled rather than skilled workers, management cannot even think about using its previous method of production or its former design. Managers must tailor their decisions to make the change to a new organizational structure as smooth as possible. Once the revised structure is functioning, managerial decisions must take it into account; courses of action that would have suited the former design are no longer appropriate.

Behavioral processes, too, critically influence decision making in organizations. When decision makers experience clashes of personality, it is difficult for them to coordinate their efforts. Behavioral problems among employees, such as a high rate of turnover or absenteeism, may even force managers to make decisions they consider relatively unattractive. For example, managers may delay the introduction of a new product when a high turnover rate occurs, for they must train new employees even before the production process can begin.

Analysis of Performance. For the organization to be effective, organizational members and organizational subsystems must perform at a satisfactory or superior level. To evaluate past decisions and gather information for future ones, managers must continually analyze the performance of organizational members, organizational subsystems, and the entire organization (either separately or together). If analysis indicates it is advisable, managers make changes within the dimensions of organization design, planning and control, and behavioral processes.

Analysis of performance is part of decision making. As the previous discussion indicates, decision making is usually a problem-solving activity; *analysis of performance* is the manager's means of determining that there is a problem.

If an organizational subsystem or the entire organization is performing in an unsatisfactory manner, management typically tries to bridge the gap between what is and what should be by undertaking changes within the dimensions of organization design, planning and control, and behavioral processes. For instance, the managers may decide that they must develop a new set of strategic plans if their competitors have taken a substantial amount of business away from their organization. Or they may feel that the planning systems are operating effectively but the control systems are not efficient in signaling deviations from plans. They may determine that the organization is not properly designed. They may even decide that behavioral processes are at fault—the rate of employee turnover may be so high that

FIGURE 3–2
Standards of Performance: Goals of Productive Organizations

TYPES OF ISSUES	PRIMARY FOCUS: *Internal*	PRIMARY FOCUS: *External*
Economic	Internal economic goals, e.g., quality and quantity of production, costs, etc.	External economic goals: e.g., product acceptability in terms of price, quality, etc.
Social	Internal social goals, e.g., job satisfaction and worker health	External social goals: e.g., social responsibility

Source: Adapted from Charles Summer, *Strategic Behavior in Business and Government* (Boston: Little, Brown, 1980), p. 7.

the organization is understaffed and unable to manufacture its products efficiently.

To elaborate on this last point, for example, if an organizational member is not performing satisfactorily, managers typically use negative control techniques, such as a reprimand or a short layoff, to change his or her behavior (see Chapter 8). To reinforce satisfactory performance, managers normally use positive control techniques, such as salary increases and promotions. In some situations managers may try to improve the performance of an organizational member, whether satisfactory or unsatisfactory, by focusing on the dimension of behavioral processes. Sending the individual to a human relations training course or assigning him or her to a work group in which he or she feels comfortable are two such approaches. Managers rarely change the design of the organization to improve the performance of organizational members unless more than a few members are involved.

Even if the performance of the organizational subsystems and the entire organization is effective, managers may decide that the gap between what is and what should be is too wide to insure continued or greater success. Again, analysis may indicate that changes should be made within the dimensions of organization design, planning and control, or behavioral processes. For example, General Motors was very successful in 1920, although the Ford Motor Company dominated the automotive market. The top managers at General Motors could have been content with this success. Instead, they decided to undertake several major changes that led to the company's becoming the unchallenged leader in the industry.

Decision making, including analysis of performance, influences and is influenced by the other three organizational dimensions, as shown in Figure 3-1. Nearly every other activity involves decision making in some way, and it is therefore the focal point in our organizational framework.

A Performance Typology. Charles Summer (1980) has constructed a performance typology for management that is directly related to our organizational framework. As shown in Figure 3-2, managers use four major types of goals or standards to evaluate performance, and these are constructed in terms of two major dimensions: the primary focus, which can be either internal or external to the organization, and the types of issues involved, whether they are economic or social in nature.

Internal economic goals concern such variables as the quantity and quality of production and cost control. External economic goals essentially involve product acceptability, without which an organization could not exist. Both internal and external economic goals reflect the traditional economic concept of the manager as a *profit maximizer.*

However, managers now must also use internal social goals as standards of performance. These social goals reflect both the physical and psychological aspects of health among organizational members. Measures of the physical aspects of health include accident rates and days lost because of illness. Job satisfaction and executive stress are examples of the psychological aspects of health. Frequently managers make use of an attitude survey to assess job satisfaction so that various subsystems in the organization can be compared to one another (see Chapter 10).

In addition, managers are increasingly concerned about external social goals, those categorized under the term *social responsibility*. Today organizations are held accountable for their products; they are forbidden by law to deliberately produce goods that are harmful to the consumer. Organizations must also face problems such as air and noise pollution, racial discrimination, and so forth.

Hence the standards of performance have broadened considerably. Managers can no longer think of themselves merely as profit maximizers. Rather, managers have begun to stress the importance of social goals that are central both to the internal and external operations of the organization (see Chapter 16).

Two other topics relative to Summer's performance typology deserve mention. First, the goals are interdependent in many instances. Achievement of one goal may limit the possibility of achieving another goal. If a company acts in a socially responsible manner by spending millions on noise abatement, it may have to increase the costs of its production. Second, the emphasis on achieving particular goals shifts over time. At one time managers may stress the achievement of external social goals; however, as the profit picture dims, managers may have to focus on internal economic goals. Hence standards of performance are flexible and responsive to changing environmental conditions both within and outside the organization.

RELATIONSHIPS TO MANAGEMENT SCHOOLS

Chapters 1 and 2 describe the major schools in the two major streams of modern management, traditional management and behavioral science. The organizational framework described in this chapter incorporates the main tenets of these major schools.

Traditional Management

In the traditional management stream Max Weber's emphasis on bureaucracy and efficiency are important concepts within our organizational framework. Management represents the achievement of goals with and through organizational members. To complete managerial activities effectively, managers must synchronize activities within the four organizational dimensions of our framework. Managers must divorce the position from the individual and reward subordinates for their performance, if they want to be successful. All these ideas are consistent with Weber's ideas.

Similarly, scientific management's emphasis on the verification of facts through the use of experimentation is compatible with our organizational framework. Managers should use any reasonable techniques at their disposal to solve problems, and these include the quantitative techniques championed by scientific management and subsequent generations of the quantitative school (see Chapters 6 and 7). As technology and business become more complex, the application of quantitative techniques will rise in importance in the areas of management information systems, computerized career planning systems, and control systems.

It is true that our organizational framework is quite different from the management process school, which holds that a successful manager must perform sequentially the functions of planning, organizing, directing, and controlling. But this management process approach views an organization as a closed system; it does not show the relationships among the functions, and it is static rather than dynamic, that is, it does not describe the feedback mechanisms or constraints that come into play in the decision-making process. In contrast, our organizational framework is dynamic in that it shows how the dimensions act on one another, it provides a feedback loop showing how the dimensions *directly* and *indirectly* influence one another, and it assumes that the organization is open to external environmental influences rather than closed to them. Most importantly, our perspective is that of the organization rather than that of the individual manager.

Still, the essential features of the management process school are incorporated into our organizational framework. Planning and control are prominent dimensions within our framework, although, as we just mentioned, the perspective is that of the organization rather than that of the individual manager. The management process function of leading has been expanded into our organizational dimension of behavioral processes, and that of organizing into organization design. However, managerial decision making has been separated from planning to show how the other three organizational dimensions—planning and control, behavioral processes, and organization design—provide a setting for it and in effect influence it.

In short, there are marked differences between the major schools in traditional management and our organizational framework. Nevertheless, the essential features of these schools are compatible with our organizational framework.

Behavioral Science Stream

In the behavioral science stream the human relations school argues against the model of economic man—that is, that the individual is motivated purely or primarily by wages and fringe benefits. Rather, human relations posits that a work group is a social system. The behavior of an individual can be best understood by examining the forces and norms that affect him or her within a group setting. Hence the individual is motivated by social forces over which he or she sometimes has little control. This model is called social man.

Our organizational model does not reject the proposition that the individual is influenced by economic and social forces. Rather, it extends this line of thinking to include all types of variables that are of importance, such as prior learning, the psychological state of the individual, and so forth. Such variables go beyond the economic and social aspects of the work situation and argue for a new model of man, which we might term *complex man*.

The systems school also fits into our organizational framework. If a group is a social system rather than a mere collection of individuals, it takes only one additional step to argue that, first, an organization is an open system that interacts with its external environment, and, second, an organization consists of a series of mutually interdependent subsystems that act on one another. Within such systems the managerial activities described by our organizational framework are performed.

Similarly, the human resources school also is consistent with the basic thrust of our organizational framework. Managers should make decisions that lead to a high level of performance, both of an individual and of an organizational nature. To accomplish this objective, managers must effectively utilize the human resources in an organization, since they constitute the main resources that an organization possesses.

Finally, contingency theory is compatible with our organizational framework. It is quite valid to state that managerial practices that may lead to success in one situation may bring about disaster in another. Thus a manager may successfully alter the design of an organization, since inappropriate behavioral processes may be occurring within the original design. However, the manager must be careful not to alter organization design every time a problem arises, because other dimensions—planning and control or behavioral processes—may be the root of the problem in other situations.

Advocates of the contingency perspective frequently construct a typology of organizations, such as the distinction between mechanistic and organic structures. The basic argument is that managerial practices leading to success in a mechanistic structure are vastly different from those bringing about success in an organic structure. Again, our organizational framework agrees with this stance. However, our framework goes beyond it by arguing that a manager should first identify the type of organization or organizational subunit in which he or she is working. Once the manager identifies the type of organization, he or she should then apply our organizational framework to identify the cause or causes of ineffective performance.

Thus, as was the case with the traditional management stream, the schools in the behavioral science stream are consonant with our organizational framework. Needless to say, there are differences, but these differences are so minor that our organizational framework can integrate the basic premises of the schools within its structure.

DYNAMICS OF THE FRAMEWORK: THREE CASES

In this section we use three case studies to illustrate the dimensions of our organizational framework and the relations among them. Since each case is unique, the framework must be used selectively to analyze the important relationships among dimensions. For example, the relationship between planning and organization design may be critical in one situation; in another setting the relationship between organization design and behavioral processes may be most important. It is appropriate to discuss these cases in class from the perspective of our integrated, organizational framework.

CASE The New Engineers*

The Organic Chemicals Division of a major chemical manufacturer operates a medium-sized plant in a major eastern industrial center. The plant employs about 350 blue-collar workers and about 90 white-collar workers, 30 of whom are graduate engineers. The facility mainly produces organic intermediates and insecticides. Much of the equipment at the plant is old and outdated, but about 25 percent of the processes use modern technology, either continuous or semicontinuous. Under continuous-process production, the worker does not see the material being manufactured, and its flow through the production facilities is automatically controlled by machines. Semicontinuous production operates in the same manner, except that the worker does see some of the material being manufactured.

Entry-level positions for engineers are located in the Process Engineering Section (see Figure 3–3). This section is usually composed of six to eight engineers under the direction of the process superintendent. Each of the engineers reports directly to the process superintendent; there is no distinction between junior-level and senior-level engineering positions. Since there is no management hierarchy in the section, there is little chance for advancement; upward mobility for aspiring engineers generally means moving into the production department at the unit supervisory level.

Description of the Job. The work performed by the engineers in the Process Engineering Section falls into two broad categories, process improvement and new-process start-up.

Process improvement work consists of becoming familiar with unit processes used for production, evaluating the effectiveness of these production methods in light of current technology, experimenting with process changes both in the laboratory and in actual production processes, and making recommendations aimed at increasing yields or improving the profitability of an operation in some other way. Each newly employed engineer is given a few processes to study in any manner he deems appropriate, subject of course to any limitations imposed by the unit supervisor whose process he is studying. These limitations are sometimes substantial, since unit supervisors are concerned with production schedules and are often reluctant to permit experimentation that might interfere with their schedules. The troubleshooting aspect of these assignments requires the engineers to apply the knowledge they have acquired during process study to actual production problems when production department personnel are unable or too busy to work on processing breakdowns. The engineers are free to work at their own pace; they are seldom under any pressure to produce immediate results. Since the engineer's role is often rather undefined and effectiveness is rather difficult to evaluate, there is no formal performance appraisal program. Consequently, there is no significant link between performance and pay. Information about progress on various projects is generally transmitted upward through informal conversations or infrequent staff meetings. In summary, then, the process engineers are free to approach problems as they see fit and are limited mostly by their creativity, their ability to sell their ideas to unit supervisors, and budgetary constraints.

FIGURE 3–3

Schematic Diagram of Organization Structure

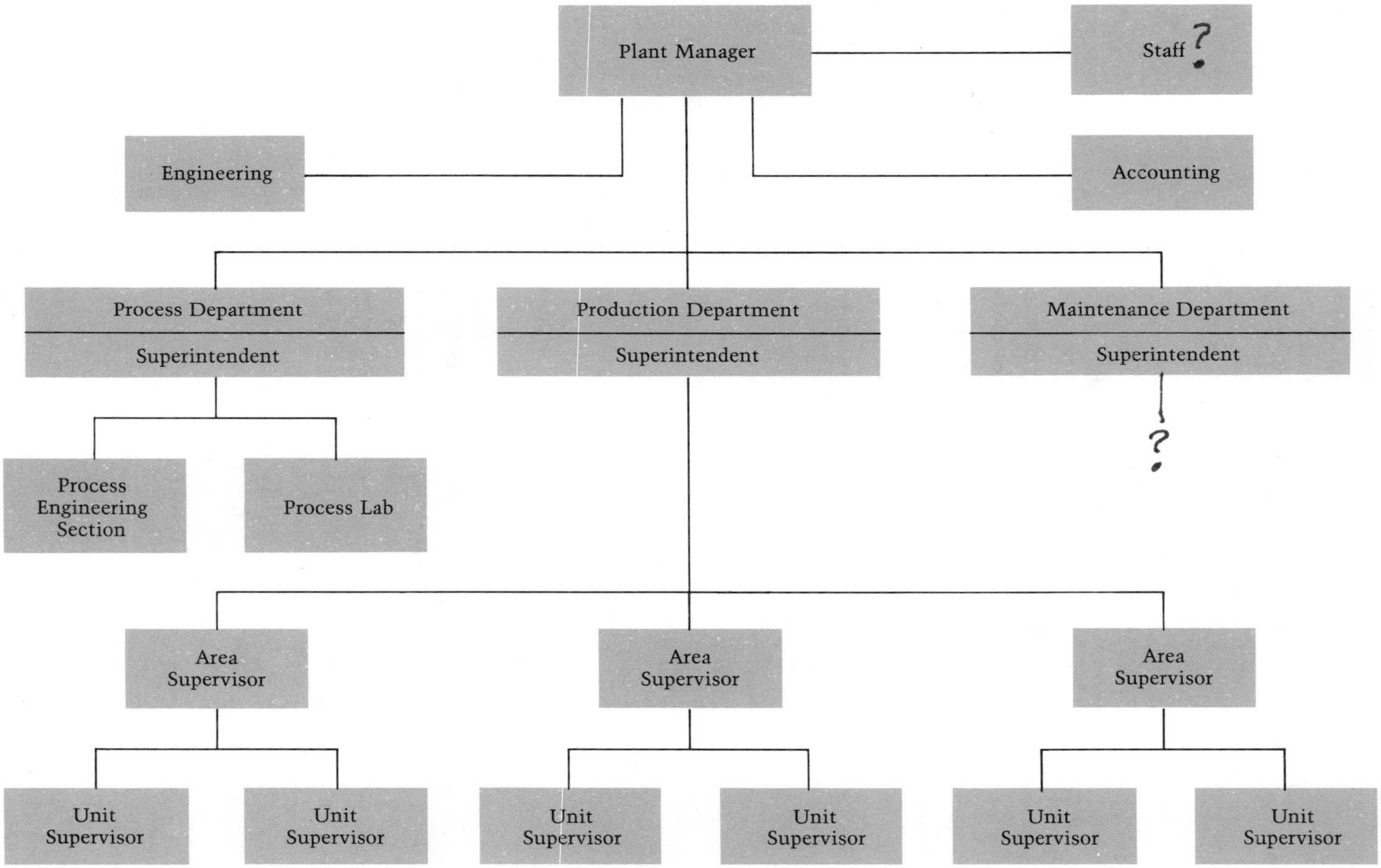

Plant Manager

Staff

Engineering

Accounting

Process Department
Superintendent

Production Department
Superintendent

Maintenance Department
Superintendent

Process Engineering Section

Process Lab

Area Supervisor

Area Supervisor

Area Supervisor

Unit Supervisor

Unit Supervisor

Unit Supervisor

Unit Supervisor

Unit Supervisor

Unit Supervisor

Process engineers assigned to new-process start-ups are essentially on loan to the production department until the new process has reached the desired level of capacity and operational regularity. During the start-up period one or two process engineers are assigned as shift supervisors on the evening and night shifts and are responsible for correcting operating problems and instructing the operating personnel in the procedure to be followed. While serving in this capacity, the process engineer reports to the unit supervisor in charge of the process.

Problems. This setting seems to be ideal for recently graduated chemical engineers who want to get some hands-on experience and learn the workings of the chemical industry. However, it proved to be difficult for this organization to assimilate new engineers into its structure as productive employees. During one six-month period the company hired four recent college graduates into the Process Engineering Section; within two years all four had left the organization. The four all had the skills necessary to practice in the engineering profession and performed reasonably well when assigned to start-up projects, but they did not generate many ideas for process improvement, and their overall productivity level was considered inadequate by management. Management's opinion of the poor performance of these four engineers was not unfounded or attributable to the ambiguous nature of the process engineer's job, and it might best be substantiated by the following examples:

1. Engineer B, the second to enter the section, had a keen interest in the stock market and had inherited some money, which he invested. When he found that he was not held accountable for his time at the plant, he began to spend as much as four hours a day performing technical analyses of security issues in which he was interested.
2. Engineer C, the third of the four to be hired, was near the top of his graduating class at a large state university, had worked for one year in a similar position, and probably had the best technical background and training of the four. He also was not held accountable for any results. This engineer spent nearly all his time in the library or his office reading technical journals and solving scientific and mathematical brainteasers.

The situation eventually became intolerable to upper management, so they demoted the process superintendent to a position in the production department and replaced him with an engineer from outside the company. By the time this change was made, one of the four engineers had been fired, one had resigned, and the other two were actively searching for new jobs, which they both found within six months.

QUESTIONS: Suppose you are hired to examine this situation and introduce major changes that would eliminate these problems. What kinds of changes would you make? How would you go about introducing them? How is planning related to control in this case? Are behavioral processes or organization design more important in explaining the behavior of these engineers?

CASE
U.S. Office of Personnel Management

In the last decades of the nineteenth century political corruption was rampant in the United States. This period was characterized by the famous phrase "the spoils system." For appointment to government jobs competence was not nearly as important as knowing an influential politician.

To combat this problem, President Chester Arthur established the U.S. Civil Service Commission in 1883. Its basic mission was to protect the merit system. For many years the commission compiled an enviable record in the area of merit hiring and promotion. To accomplish its mission, the commission relied heavily on on-site evaluations of federal agencies and carefully scrutinized all job applicants for federal employment.

In recent years, however, many federal managers have complained that the commission seriously and negatively influenced their work. Sometimes federal managers would wait as long as one year before the commission would give them permission to hire a particular individual. By the time permission had been granted, the job applicant had obtained work in the private sector. Additionally, the civil service laws and regulations made it very difficult to demote or fire an incompetent individual. The commission's lengthy appeals process involved several levels of appeals.

It was true that many of the problems facing the commission occurred because of its relatively small size. It included only about 6000 employees, and they were charged with overseeing the hiring and promotion practices of a federal work force of approximately 2.2 million workers. Still, the commission was attempting to complete a mission that contained within it some fundamental conflicts.

Clear Goals. While the commission's basic mission was clear, the goals it was supposed to accomplish in completing it were never clearly spelled out. The commission was designed to be apolitical. To that end, the president in power appointed three commissioners to head it, two from the dominant political party in power and one from the party out of power. However, politics was always a problem for the commission. It was not uncommon for the political party in power to attempt to manipulate and violate the merit system in order to gain regular federal jobs for unqualified individuals.

More importantly, the commission could never decide whether it was a management agency or an employee agency. For many years commission managers heatedly debated whether they were policemen who should strictly and actively enforce the merit system by protecting employees or consultants who should help agency managers to accomplish their own distinctive goals.

By comparison, the U.S. Office of Management and the Budget (OMB), also a relatively small agency, never experienced such difficulty. Its director is appointed by the president. The appointment is strictly a political appointment, and the president can remove the director whenever he so desires. Hence OMB is definitely a management agency, and it essentially fulfills the role of consultant to the president.

Civil Service Reform. When Jimmy Carter was campaigning for president, he promised to undertake civil service reform. Such promises had been made by other presidents, but the promises were never fulfilled, in large part because of political opposition. However, President Carter was very successful in putting into law many major civil service reforms.

The Civil Service Reform Act of 1978 abolished the commission and replaced it with two new organizations. The first organization, the Merit System Protection Board, which has approximately 300 employees on its staff, acts as a guardian against merit system abuses and is empowered to protect "whistle-blowers" (employees who expose incompetence or corruption) from reprisals by their agency superiors. However, one of the interesting aspects of the Reform Act is its streamlining of employee appeal procedures. As indicated above, when the commission was in existence, the appeals procedure was very lengthy. Consequently, agency managers experienced great difficulty in demoting or firing incompetent employees. Because of the streamlining of procedures, the appeals process is much shorter and shifts the burden of proof away from the agency to the employee.

The Reform Act also created the U.S. Office of Personnel Management (OPM), whose main function is to manage the personnel systems of the federal workforce; it has approximately 6000 employees. Thus this new agency is about the same size as the old commission. However, its organizational design clearly makes it a management-oriented agency similar to the Office of Management and Budget. The president appoints one director for OPM, who reports directly to him and serves at his discretion.

OPM has resolved, to some extent, the dilemma of the policeman versus consultant role. It is not an employee-oriented agency interested in employee advocacy or the active protection of employee rights, which is now the mission of the Merit System Protection

Board. OPM is charged with enforcing *compliance* with the law rather than protecting the merit system per se. At this time OPM provides agency managers with much more discretion in shaping systems to their differing needs than did the commission. It is quite clear that the Carter administration wanted to limit OPM regulation of federal agencies, and the Reform Act basically supports this stance.

Still, conflict between the two roles of policeman and consultant may emerge in OPM in the future. As actual experiences under the new Reform Act increase, it is quite possible that serious flaws will become visible. OPM still contains a major unit, Agency Compliance and Evaluation with approximately 400 specialists, that evaluates agency compliance with the law. This is now OPM's basic mission, rather than protection of the merit system per se. But since this unit consists of experienced evaluators, it is quite possible that a new administration might seek to expand OPM's role. Hence OPM may again shift toward the policeman role. At the present time, however, OPM is attempting to maintain a delicate and appropriate balance between the two roles of consultant and policeman, with the emphasis being placed on the consultant role.

QUESTIONS: How did the external environment help to influence the creation of OPM? Describe the relationships among the four dimensions of our organizational framework at OPM. Which are the most important relationships? Do you feel OPM has resolved the conflict between the roles of policeman and consultant? Why or why not?

CASE Branch Banking

The banking industry has typically been very conservative, partly because societies cannot tolerate a free-wheeling but unstable banking system. When banks are unstable, an entire country's future becomes perilous. For this reason many regulations are placed on banking operations.

Between 1945 and 1969 the United States experienced its longest period of prosperity. During this time some bank managements decided to shed some of their conservatism. For instance, management of a New York bank developed a strategic plan to increase its customers by offering a larger variety of services rather than just a few specialized services (cashing checks, putting money into savings accounts, and making loans). Management wanted the bank to increase in size and keep pace with the growing prosperity in the United States.

Typically, a consumer selects a bank in terms of convenience—he or she frequents a branch close to home or place of work. For the average consumer banks are interchangeable, since they all basically provide the same services.

This case study focuses on a large bank in New York City that operated 20 branches in 1958. By 1970 the branch-banking system had grown to 180.

To attract new customers, the bank started to provide specific services not available elsewhere. New customers received gifts; tellers provided specialized services such as the sale of baseball and football tickets; and interest rates on savings accounts were placed at the highest level the law would permit. One of the bank's most interesting ploys was to eliminate the distinction between checking and savings accounts. A customer who kept a minimum balance in a checking account would receive interest on it and therefore not need to open a savings account. Another important plan created preferred customers: If a customer used the bank extensively over a period of three years, he or she then would receive some special services free of charge, such as a free safe deposit box, and the bank would back his or her checks to a limit of $500 if there was not enough money in the account to cover them.

Because of these strategic and tactical plans, the branch-banking system expanded at a spectacular rate. However, the control of organizational subsystems became troublesome. As the number of checks increased, it became difficult to process them efficiently. Many monthly statements were in error or sent out late, and the bank spent a lot of money on computer equipment to handle this problem.

Control of individuals also proved problematic. When the branches were small, tellers could process the work efficiently but pleasantly. When trade increased, branch management encouraged tellers to work faster. Inevitably they began to make mistakes and could not account for some of the money. A conflict occurred between speed and accuracy, and, at the time of this writing, management has not developed a final solution to the problem.

The bank's success also created problems in its design. When the system contained only 20 branches, their efforts could be coordinated from headquarters. By the time the system had increased to 80 branches, they had to be grouped into regions. In effect, a new level in the organization was created.

Before the regions were established, problems could be solved throughout the bank on an informal basis. Such solutions are difficult within the regional structure, for management at the headquarters level coordinates the efforts of branches and regions with a series of policies and rules that regulate everyone's activity. Hence the authority of the branch managers has been severely restricted.

The success of the plans and the new design of the organization also created behavioral problems in the system. When the branches were small in size, employees felt a loyalty to them. The employees personally knew all their customers and treated them in a pleasant manner. In the new system impatient customers who wait in long lines for service become merely numbers to managers and employees. Turnover of employees and managers increased dramatically.

Within this setting, the managers or decision makers confront new and difficult problems. Previously, employees and managers had been trained informally; this procedure is no longer possible. Additionally, the complaints of irate customers have become bothersome; in some branches the branch managers spend as much as ten hours a week handling them. Although the bank continues to grow, top management has started to wonder about the optimum size of the system; some managers argue that the optimum level has already been passed.

In short, the spectacular success of this branch-banking system has been accompanied by many problems, several of which are extremely difficult to solve. This system has evolved from a small organization that operated informally into a giant that necessarily is somewhat impersonal. All decisions made within this new structure are heavily influenced by the changes that have occurred within the dimensions of planning and control, organization design, and behavioral processes.

QUESTIONS: What do you see as the major planning problems in this branch-banking system? How might they be solved?

SUMMARY

This chapter has described an integrated organizational framework within which managerial activities take place. The framework consists of four organizational dimensions: planning and control, organization design, behavioral processes, and managerial decision making. The organizational planning process involves environmental forecasting; selecting the basic mission or missions of the organization; developing long-term goals and short-term objectives; developing means (strategies and tactics) to achieve these goals and objectives; possibly changing missions, goals and objectives in light of revised environmental forecasts; and implementing policies, procedures, and rules. Control is the monitoring of plans and the correction of deviations from them. Organization design is the manner in which an organization is structured. Behavioral processes are the preconditions for interactions and the actual interactions between and among organizational members. Decision making involves a stimulus event motivating the individual to recognize that a significant gap exists between what is and what should be; information search; problem formulation; evaluation of alternatives/choice; and implementation.

To incorporate these dynamic relationships, the framework includes a feedback loop that comes into play after a manager has decided that individual or organizational performance is substandard and requires alteration. Thus analysis of performance is an extension of managerial decision making.

We emphasize that the perspective of this integrated framework is that of the organization rather than that of the individual manager. While it is common for a manager to be involved in activities within two and even three dimensions simultaneously, it is less typical for him to perform activities in all four dimensions at the same time.

Charles Summer has developed a performance typology that is consistent with our framework. According to Summer, there are four types of goals or standards that managers use to evaluate performance, and these are constructed in terms of two major dimensions: (1) the primary focus, which can be either internal or external to the organization, and (2) the types of issues involved, whether they are economic or social in nature. Thus the four types of goals or standards of performance are internal and economic, external and economic, internal and social, and external and social.

Our framework incorporates the major ideas of the main schools of thought in modern management. While there are some differences, they are minor in nature, and the framework is sufficiently broad to include these schools comfortably.

DISCUSSION QUESTIONS

1. Think of an organization of which you have been a member—a school or religious group, a club, or a business firm for which you have worked. How would you describe that organization's activities in terms of the framework developed in this chapter? Now describe an ideal organization—or what you consider to be an ideal organization—that is the same type as the one you just described. What are some of the major differences between the actual and ideal organization?
2. The framework proposed in this book applies to business and government organizations. Do you think it also applies to other kinds of organizations such as volunteer groups, friendship groups, work groups, the family, the church, and the school? Why or why not?
3. Do you think it is possible for a single manager to be effective in all four organizational dimensions? Why or why not? Do you think it is possible for an organization to perform effectively if it neglects any one of these dimensions? Explain.
4. Why is it important for the analysis of performance to derive from the interactions among the four dimensions and to link them together by means of a feedback loop?

5. Why is the framework proposed in this chapter dynamic rather than static? How does this framework differ from that proposed by the management process school?
6. How would you rate the effectiveness of your class in terms of the four dimensions of our framework? Explain.
7. This chapter has argued that the organizational framework incorporates the major ideas of the main schools of modern management thought. What are some ideas proposed by these schools that are *not* consistent with this framework?

SUGGESTED READINGS

Barmash, Isadore, ed. *Great Business Disasters.* New York: Ballantine Books, 1973, 302 pages, paperback.

This short and inexpensive paperback contains a series of case studies focused on some of the outstanding business disasters in recent history. The student learns to appreciate management by examining these failures. RCA's $500 million venture into computers, the $350 million Edsel fiasco at Ford, the Penn Central collapse, and other failures are highlighted in an interesting and entertaining fashion. This book is a perennial favorite with students.

Mintzberg, Henry. *The Nature of Managerial Work.* Englewood Cliffs, N.J.: Prentice-Hall, 1980, 217 pages, hardback.

This readable book summarizes the research on the work and activities of managers. The emphasis is on what managers actually do, not on what they should do.

4 Managerial Decision Making

STAGES IN DECISION MAKING
DECISION ENVIRONMENTS
DECISION STRATEGIES
SUBOPTIMIZATION
IMPROVING DECISION MAKING
SUMMARY
DISCUSSION QUESTIONS
CRITICAL INCIDENTS
SUGGESTED READINGS

PERFORMANCE OBJECTIVES

1. To identify the stages of the decision-making process.
2. To describe the decision environments: the conditions or constraints under which decision making occurs.
3. To discuss the various types of decision strategies that individuals employ when engaged in decision making.
4. To identify the factors that create suboptimization or less-than-optimal decisions.
5. To outline and discuss ways to improve decision making.

Managerial decision making is of obvious importance in organizations. Everything else is irrelevant if an organization fails to take courses of action that ensure its continued growth and success. Typically management is responsible for making key decisions, although sometimes nonmanagers may be involved in decision making. In any event, the overall objective is to ensure that the correct decisions are made.

Decision making is a process of choice leading to the selection of one alternative rather than others. More generally, it involves problem-solving activity that comes into play when the manager realizes that a significant gap exists between what is and what should be.

This chapter describes the stages that occur in decision making. Decision environments are then identified as the conditions or constraints under which decision making occurs. Various types of decision strategies are also discussed, as are the factors that help to produce less-than-optimal or suboptimal decisions. Some ways to increase the effectiveness of decisions are then examined.

STAGES IN DECISION MAKING

Decision making typically occurs in stages, although there are times when individuals skip stages or collapse them into a smaller number. In this section we describe these stages.

Stimulus Event

Some event must provide the stimulus that motivates an individual to engage in decision making. This stimulus event may be a performance gap. For example, a student who receives a C on a midterm examination may feel capable of doing A work; hence the gap between actual performance and what the student feels capable of accomplishing is too great. Alternatively, the stimulus event may be an opportunity gap. For instance, a company may be very profitable, but its management may feel that it can become even more profitable if it begins to produce a new line of products.

Individuals vary enormously in their responses to stimulus events. One student receiving a C on an examination may breathe a sigh of relief and satisfaction; another student may decide to discuss the matter with the instructor to see if he or she can improve performance.

In an extended hypothetical example we shall examine the career of John Edmond, a middle manager who has not received a promotion in three years, although recently a middle manager who had joined the company at the same time as John received a major promotion. This stimulus event upsets John, and he begins to worry about it.

Information Search

John starts to search for information about the promotion policies in his company. He discovers that the average length of time between promotions for managers in the organization is two years. Since John has not received a promotion for three years, he concludes that a performance gap in fact exists.

John may extend his information search by talking to his immediate superior, by comparing himself to others in the organization, and by talking to his peers. He may also discuss the matter with his wife, seeing if she has some insight into the problem. Gradually his search should provide him with a rich store of information.

Problem Formulation

Using the information available to him, John can examine several causes for his lack of promotion. These might include the following:

1. The quality of his work has significantly deteriorated in the past two years.
2. His immediate superior does not like him, even though he is performing satisfactorily.
3. He is doing such an outstanding job that his immediate superior does not want to lose him and thus locks him into his present job.
4. The company has no job available into which he can be appropriately promoted.

In light of his information John may formulate the problem in terms of his relationship with his immediate superior, since the other possible causes do not seem reasonable. John eventually decides that the cause of his problem is his poor relationship with his immediate superior, and he believes that this superior has recommended against his promotion.

Evaluation of Alternatives/Choice

At this point John will probably develop alternative solutions to his problem. Some of these solutions could be as follows:

1. Quit immediately and look for work elsewhere.
2. Stay in the organization until he finds another job.
3. Discuss the problem in a nonthreatening manner with his immediate superior and with managers at the upper levels in the organization.
4. Discuss the problem with his immediate superior and upper managers, informing them he will leave if he is not promoted in the near future.

From these possible solutions John may decide to eliminate the alternative of telling his immediate superior and other managers that he will leave unless they promote him. Making such a threat would probably put them on the defensive, so that they might be more inclined to fire than to promote him. Also, John may embarrass himself if he cannot find work elsewhere. Eventually John may decide to approach his immediate superior and other upper-level managers in a nonthreatening manner.

Implementation John would then implement his plan by discussing his situation with his superiors. At the very least, this course of action should provide him with information that will assist him in his decision-making process. John might learn that he has incorrectly identified the cause of his problem and that he is in a dead-end position from which he will never be promoted. Or he might find out that his chances for promotion within a year are excellent.

Using the additional information he obtains from discussing his situation with his superiors, John might then engage in contingency planning. If John discovers he is in a dead-end position, he might begin to search for work elsewhere. However, his contingency approach would involve staying in the organization while searching for a new job, since he might not obtain what he wants and would need his present job, even with its limitations.

This extended example of a manager's dissatisfaction with his rate of promotion includes all the steps that effective decision making usually involves:

1. The stimulus event motivating the individual to perceive either a performance or an opportunity gap.
2. Information search.
3. Problem formulation.
4. Evaluation of alternatives/choice.
5. Implementation.

DECISION ENVIRONMENTS

Decision makers are constrained by the environments in which they operate. In this section we describe the conditions or constraints under which decision making occurs, conditions that include the amount of perceived uncertainty and perceived conflict, organizational goals and policies, organizational level, societal expectations, and culture.

Amount of Uncertainty A major constraint on decision making is the amount of uncertainty an individual perceives, both in the causes he or she believes are leading to the problem and the preferences he or she holds regarding possible outcomes of various actions. James Thompson (1967) argues that decision making always involves these two major dimensions. These dimensions operate even when only one individual is involved in the decision-making process, but their complexity increases as two or more decision makers interact. Although each dimension can take on a range of values, Thompson dichotomizes each of them for discussion purposes. In this section we describe these two dimensions in terms of a group of two or more individuals.

According to Thompson, sometimes the members of a group agree with one another in that they are certain about the cause of a problem. Under such a condition it is relatively easy for the group to take action. Alternatively, members of a group may be uncertain about the causes of a problem. Under this condition many hypotheses are offered, and individuals are split as to what course of action is appropriate. Similarly, if individuals in a group splinter in that they all prefer different outcomes, uncertainty occurs, and it is again difficult for the group to take action. Conversely, a group has a relatively easy time taking action if its members agree with one another in the sense that they are certain as to what outcomes they prefer.

Perceived Psychological Conflict

Irving Janis and Leon Mann (1977) argue that the amount of perceived conflict between the actual and the ideal initiates decision making. From their perspective decision making is psychological in nature: The individual experiences conflict or dissonance, which is triggered by a stimulus. Hence the amount of perceived or psychological conflict is a constraint under which decision making occurs. Janis and Mann's approach to decision making is consistent with our organizational framework, both in their psychological orientation and in their emphasis on the difference between actual and ideal states.

Goals and Policies

Top management normally establishes several goals that it wishes the organization to attain. The organization then develops policies or general guides to action that are designed to help accomplish these goals, and rules and procedures to carry out the policies (see Chapter 5). These related factors impose organizational limits on the kinds of decisions that managers can make.

As an example of this situation consider the bank that wanted to increase its scope of operations (see Chapter 3). The bank accomplished this goal successfully; the number of branches increased from 20 to 180 between 1958 and 1970. The bank's major policy during this period was to attract customers by offering them a wide range of distinctive services. It then established specific rules to accord with this policy. Tellers provided specialized services such as the sale of baseball and football tickets; interest rates on savings accounts were placed at the highest level the law would permit; and long-term and preferred customers received special privileges such as receiving a free safe-deposit box and having unbacked checks honored up to a limit of $500. Branch bank managers, seeing that top management was encouraging growth through these policies and rules, even began to offer their own specialized services within these constraints, such as opening drive-in windows that operated beyond normal business hours, providing a limited amount of financial sponsorship of local community activities, and so forth.

TABLE 4–1
Time Required for Decision Making at Different Managerial Levels

	Highest level			*Lowest level*
Time required for decision	*Works manager*	*Division superintendent*	*Department foreman*	*Shift foreman*
Short (0–2 weeks)	3.3%	54.2%	68.0%	97.7%
Moderate (2 weeks to 1 year)	46.1	41.4	30.4	2.1
Distant (over 1 year)	50.0	4.3	1.5	0.0
Total	99.4%	99.9%	99.9%	99.8%

Source: From N. Martin, "Differential Decisions in the Management of an Industrial Plant," *Journal of Business* 28 (1956): 251. Copyright © 1956 by the University of Chicago Press. Reprinted by permission of the University of Chicago Press.

Organizational Level

Another constraint on a manager's decision-making scope is the level at which he or she is operating in an organization. According to Talcott Parsons (1960), all organizations have three basic levels. The first is the *technical level*, where the actual production of the organization takes place. The *institutional level* consists of the top managers who monitor changes in the external environment and define the overall goals the organization is to pursue. At the *managerial level*, managers coordinate the organization's efforts so that the production process operates efficiently. These managers also work with the top managers at the institutional level to accomplish the overall objectives of the organization.

Usually managers at the technical level confront routine problems such as how many units an individual worker must produce. They work with a high degree of certainty because they generally know both the cause of a problem and the outcome they seek. The amount of certainty is less at the managerial and institutional levels. Examples of decisions at the institutional and managerial levels include how much money should be invested in new equipment, what actions to take in response to government safety regulations, and how to attract workers who are in scarce supply, such as engineers.

As we might expect, managers at different levels in the organization spend different amounts of time on any particular decision. In general, the higher their level in the organization, the more time they spend (see Table 4–1). At the first-line level of supervision, foremen usually face problems that can be solved within two weeks. At the institutional level of the organization, uncertainty forces managers to make decisions that require much more time and thought. Fifty percent of the problems confronting top managers require at least a year before a final decision can be made. These findings confirm the importance of organizational level in the decision-making process.

Societal Expectations Society also imposes conditions upon decision makers. Managers cannot make decisions in a vacuum; rather, they work within an area of *bounded discretion* (Shull, Delbecq, and Cummings 1970). That is, the freedom of managers to make ideal decisions is limited by social norms, rules, and policies within the organization and by legal restrictions and moral and ethical norms.

In modern America the area in which management can make unregulated decisions has narrowed significantly in the past seventy years. President Baer of the Philadelphia and Reading Railroad made the following statement in 1903 in his reply to W. F. Clark, who had urged him "as a Christian gentleman" to make some concessions to his workers who were on strike:

> I see you are evidently biased in your religious views in favor of the right of the working man to control a business in which he has no other interest than to secure fair wages for the work he does. . . . The rights and interests of the laboring man will be protected and cared for, not by the labor agitators, but by the Christian men to whom God in His infinite wisdom has given control of the property interests of the country. *(Harris 1939, pp. 126–127)*

A president of a company would not dare to make a similar statement today. Many restrictions now regulate the kinds of decisions that a president and his or her subordinates can make. In fact, it is currently fashionable for managers to support the concept of social responsibility (see Chapter 16). They now attempt to eliminate negative influences they might exert on society by putting voluntary controls on pollution, hiring underprivileged workers, and supporting cultural activities.

Culture Although frequently overlooked, the culture of a society is a significant constraint upon the actions that decision makers can take. This influence is especially pronounced when managers make decisions.

Japanese managers, for instance, appear to have a style of leadership that is quite different from that of Americans (Haire, Ghiselli, and Porter 1966). In Japan, group decision making is much more important than individual decision making. Typically lower-echelon managers, as a group, analyze a problem and generate alternative solutions to it. After eliminating all but one or two of the alternatives, they present their analysis to the upper-echelon managers, who hold the proper authority to make a decision. The final decision thus is based on the information supplied to the top managers by the lower-echelon managers. This approach reduces the amount of time the upper-echelon managers must spend on a problem. In addition, the lower-echelon managers participate in the major decisions and feel a sense of responsibility because of their involvement.

Japan's managerial style seems to have evolved from the country's unique cultural problems. Japan is very small, and it does not possess abundant natural resources. To overcome these disadvantages, Japanese leaders have traditionally emphasized the belief that all parts of the society—individuals, families, groups, organizations, and the government—are closely intertwined. This attitude dictates not only that decisions be made by a group but that the obligations of Japanese managers extend not only to the firm but to all parts of the society.

DECISION STRATEGIES

There are general and specific strategies that individuals employ, either knowingly or unknowingly, when making decisions. This section is devoted to a discussion of these strategies.

Two General Strategies

We can study decision making in terms of two general strategies that individuals use: the rational comprehensive strategy and the incremental stratcgy. Whcn a manager uses the *rational comprehensive strategy*, he or she examines a large number of alternatives to accomplish a particular goal and from these attempts to choose the most desirable alternative.

Perhaps the best study of the *incremental strategy* has been done by Charles Lindblom (1959), who studied decision making in government agencies and large private organizations. When faced with a problem requiring a change in policy, managers "muddle their way" through the decision process by examining only a very narrow range of alternatives that differ to only a small degree from the existing policy. According to Lindblom, the manager operates in steps: He or she makes a change, interprets the feedback, makes another change, and so forth. Hence the organization moves forward only in small, incremental steps. From Lindblom's perspective, this is a rational approach to decision making, as the organization does not jeopardize its existence when the incremental strategy is employed.

James Quinn (1980) has also studied incremental decision in ten successful multinational corporations. According to Quinn, successful top managers move in a step-by-step fashion toward ends that initially are broadly conceived but then are constantly refined and reshaped as new information appears. Quinn terms this decision-making approach "logical incrementalism"; he feels that it represents a rational approach to decision making, especially when the manager must make decisions under such constraints as a high degree of environmental uncertainty or conflict.

Source: © Ross/Rothco.

"What we need is a brand new idea that has been thoroughly tested."

Programmed and Nonprogrammed Strategies

Managers' strategies also vary in response to the type of problem they are trying to solve. In general, a decision maker faces two types of problems: structured and ill structured (March and Simon 1958). A *structured* problem is one the manager can solve by means of a *programmed decision,* that is, the application of a rule, program, routine, or procedure that he or she has previously used to solve such problems. In some instances a structured problem can be expressed in numbers or in terms of a numerical objective, such as minimizing costs. It is usually easier to deal with a problem that can be quantified than with an abstract problem. For example, a manager in charge of three plants located in three different cities might want to minimize transportation costs. There are standard quantitative techniques he or she can use to solve this problem.

However, not all programmed decisions express a problem numerically. For example, when the turnover rate among keypunch operators in a large company became abnormally high, the top managers sponsored a questionnaire survey of the employees. This survey indicated that the operators were dissatisfied with their working conditions. To solve the turnover problem, top management built a new cafeteria and redecorated the work area. Turnover subsequently declined.

Many problems are *ill structured,* that is, the manager cannot easily apply a standard rule, program, or procedure that he or she has previously used to solve such problems. Rather, he or she must make a *nonprogrammed decision*—a creative response to a new problem.

For instance, if a major customer of a firm quit and began to use the services of a competitor, the manager might respond by trying to win back the customer and preventing other customers from doing the same thing. The decisions he or she would make would probably be nonprogrammed, for judgment rather than a formula would be needed in reacting to the complaints of the former customer. Managers also usually must make nonprogrammed decisions when they decide to expand their organizations, because they cannot predict future conditions with complete certainty.

Certainty-Uncertainty Strategies

As indicated previously, James Thompson (1967) believes that a major constraint on decision making is the amount of uncertainty that a single decision maker or a group of decision makers perceives, both in terms of the causes of the problem and the preferences for various outcomes. As in our previous discussion, we shall treat these two dimensions in terms of a group of decision makers, mindful of the fact that these dimensions are also activated when only one decision maker is involved.

According to Thompson, the perceived uncertainty about the causes leading to a problem and the preferences for various outcomes leads to the use of one of four strategies. If the decision makers agree with one another both about what is causing a particular problem and about what kind of an outcome they desire, the strategy that the group should employ is *computational* or programmed, as discussed above (see Figure 4–1). However, the decision makers may be certain about cause-effect relations but uncertain about the outcomes they prefer, in which case they should employ a strategy of *compromise.* For example, managers may be in agreement that low salaries are leading to a high rate of employee turnover, but they may disagree about the rate of turnover that is desirable if the organization is to be kept viable.

FIGURE 4–1
Decision Processes and Decision Strategies

BELIEFS ABOUT CAUSE-EFFECT RELATIONSHIPS	PREFERENCES REGARDING POSSIBLE OUTCOMES: *Certainty*	*Uncertainty*
Certainty	Computational Strategy	Compromise Strategy
Uncertainty	Judgmental Strategy	Inspirational Strategy

Source: Adapted from James D. Thompson, *Organizations in Action,* p. 134. Copyright © 1967 by McGraw-Hill, Inc. Reprinted by permission of McGraw-Hill Book Company.

If the decision makers are uncertain about cause-effect relations but are certain about their preferences for established outcomes, they should use a *judgmental* strategy. That is, they know what they want but must discover the means to obtain their goals. Finally, the *inspirational* strategy should be employed if the decision makers perceive uncertainty about cause-effect relations and about the outcomes they wish to obtain. This situation is highly volatile, and decision makers would probably attempt to move into one of the other three decision-making molds before taking action.

Thus the computational strategy is equivalent to programmed decision making, and the inspirational strategy is equivalent to nonprogrammed decision making. The other two types—compromise and judgmental strategies—represent intermediate points between programmed and nonprogrammed decision making.

SUBOPTIMIZATION

It is quite common for individuals to choose alternatives that are not the best. In this section we describe two of the major causes of suboptimal decision making: human limits to rationality and biased information search. We also describe some suboptimal decision-making strategies.

Human Limits to Rationality

As our discussion of incrementalism implies, individuals are limited, since it is difficult, if not impossible, to adequately examine a very large number of alternatives before making a decision. Using an actual study of managerial behavior, Herbert Simon (1976) argues that an individual cannot possibly be aware of all the alternatives he or she might pursue, nor all the goals he or she might wish to accomplish. Rather, the manager reduces the complexity of each problem in order to make a decision. Typically the manager will examine only four or five alternatives that are minimally acceptable and choose one of them. That is, the manager *satisfices* rather than *maximizes:* He or she chooses a solution that will be adequate rather than taking additional time and effort to find the best possible solution. In this sense the manager bounds reality by limiting the number of alternatives he or she will examine to make a reasonable decision.

Simon's approach supports the incremental strategy of decision making. Managers frequently approach decision making in a sequential fashion, considering only four or five alternatives: The manager makes his or her decision, interprets the feedback, makes another decision, and so forth. By breaking down the decision-making process into steps, the manager can increase decision-making effectiveness.

Using Simon's perspective on satisficing and nonprogrammed decision making, Peer Soelberg (1967) analyzed the decision process among graduating graduate students at the Massachusetts Institute of Technology who were searching for full-time jobs. He interviewed one group of graduating students over a period of time in 1964, and then he developed definite hypotheses he wished to test. In 1965 he tested these hypotheses by interviewing each of 32 graduating students biweekly for the eight weeks when they were seeking work.

Soelberg found that the students generally stopped searching for new alternatives or jobs long before they were willing to admit to having made this decision. Usually a student had two or more acceptable job offers before he or she ended the search. If the student had obtained a firm job offer from only one organization during the period when he or she wanted to end the job search, he or she tried hard to secure, and usually did obtain, at least one other acceptable offer to have something to compare against the one alternative.

The student also tended to make a decision early in the job search by selecting a favorite alternative, although he or she did not consciously recognize this fact. Even if a student had five or six firm offers, he or she tended to compare only two alternatives before selecting an implicit favorite. If the two were essentially noncomparable, the student typically compared them in terms of only one or two criteria, which simplified the decision process.

The students generally did not experience any uneasy feelings or dissonance afterward about their final decisions unless they had been unable to identify an implicit favorite or had only one firm job offer at the time they announced a decision. In these two instances Soelberg's data suggest a student might subsequently become unhappy with the new job and initiate new search procedures.

Soelberg's research thus generally confirms and extends Herbert Simon's theory of nonprogrammed decision making. The manager typically bounds reality by examining only a few acceptable alternatives and satisfices by selecting one of these minimally acceptable alternatives. Soelberg's research also suggests that a manager should systematically evaluate his or her alternatives as early as possible in the decision process, before unconsciously selecting an implicit favorite. Once the manager has selected this favorite, he or she tends to eliminate all the other acceptable alternatives. And once the manager has announced a decision, he or she will probably not change it or search for new alternatives.

Biased Information Search

Another reason that managers choose alternatives that may not be the best is that they search for information in a biased way. Janis and Mann (1977) discuss this problem in terms of a phenomenon termed *bolstering the alternative.* Even before accumulating the information on which to base a decision, the individual may prefer one alternative to all the others; he or she therefore searches for information that will rationalize this choice. Only information that supports the preferred alternative is considered legitimate and acceptable.

An individual's professional training and identification with a particular department also help to bias the search for information. In one study sales executives tended to view most problems with a sales bias, regardless of their nature, while finance executives perceived the same problems in terms of finance (Dearborn and Simon 1958). Although such biases are bound to exist, it is important to be aware that they can strongly influence our ability to make decisions.

Defective Strategies for Making Decisions

Janis and Mann (1977) have identified four defective strategies that lead managers to choose alternatives that are not the best. Under the first two strategies, *unconflicted adherence* and *unconflicted change*, the individual experiences initial psychological conflict, but then makes an incomplete search for information, inadequately appraises the alternatives, and makes a decision with which he is satisfied. However, the process of decision making is poor. In unconflicted adherence the individual chooses to make no change; in unconflicted change he chooses to change.

Defensive avoidance is the third defective strategy. When the manager employs this strategy, he or she makes a decision after an incomplete information search and an inadequate appraisal of alternatives, but then avoids all stimuli and cues suggesting that the decision is incorrect. Hence it is difficult to reverse a poor decision. The opposite of defensive avoidance is *hypervigilance*, the fourth defective strategy. The manager employing this strategy spends too much time searching for information and appraising alternatives. Hypervigilance occurs because the individual is too anxious and tense. Hypervigilant individuals experience a great amount of difficulty in making decisions.

IMPROVING DECISION MAKING

While suboptimization occurs frequently, it is possible to counteract it and improve the decision-making process. In this section we discuss various ways to improve decision making, including normative models, problem factoring, training, decision heuristics, and the use of groups.

Normative Models

Several prominent *normative* or prescriptive models of decision making describe the manner in which individuals *should* make decisions. Frequently these models consist of a sequence of questions that can be applied to a problem. The decision maker begins by asking a question to which he or she must respond yes or no. Then a branching process begins whereby the yes response leads to a second question and a no response leads to a different second question. The branching process continues until the decision maker arrives at the final decision. Prominent normative models have been developed by Janis and Mann (1977) and Vroom and Yetton (1973). We shall discuss the Vroom and Yetton model in the leadership chapter (Chapter 14), since it focuses on both decision making and style of leadership.

Charles Kepner and Benjamin Tregoe (1965) have developed a normative decision-making model that is quite consistent with our organizational framework. They believe that the problem-solving process involves three separate stages:

1. The identification of a problem, which begins when the individual perceives that there is a significant gap between what is and what should be.
2. An analysis directed at finding the cause of the problem.
3. The choice of a specific corrective action.

The specific steps for solving the problem are as follows:

1. Examine problems in terms of what is and what should be, and then decide to work on some of them and ignore, at least temporarily, others.
2. Implement programmed decision making if the cause of the problem is known and it is possible to apply a rule or procedure to solve it.
3. When the cause is unknown, systematically gather and evaluate the information necessary to pinpoint it. This process will involve the following procedures:
   a. Precisely describe the deviation from what should be by answering these questions: What is it? What is it not? Where is it? Where is it not? When is it? When is it not? What is the extent of the deviation? What is not the extent?
   b. Look for distinctions between the *is* and the *is not* as the questions above are answered.
   c. Focus on changes in developing possible causes. If, for instance, a worker performs in an outstanding manner for several years and then performs poorly, examine changes in his health, marriage, financial stability, and so forth.
   d. Test for cause. For example, discuss the problem with the worker and systematically eliminate causes by asking him directly about their relative importance.

Problem Factoring

As our discussion of incrementalism, satisficing, and normative models suggests, it is important to break down a large problem into smaller parts—that is, to *factor* the problem. In this way the decision maker is not overwhelmed by the problem or the amount of information that is necessary to solve it.

CRITERIA FOR DECISION MAKING

Irving Janis and Leon Mann identify seven criteria that a decision maker should use to the best of his abilities and within his information-processing capabilities. According to Janis and Mann, the decision maker:

1. thoroughly canvasses a wide range of alternative courses of action;
2. surveys the full range of objectives to be fulfilled and the values implicated by the choice;
3. carefully weighs whatever he knows about the costs and risks of negative consequences, as well as the positive consequences, that could flow from each alternative;
4. intensively searches for new information relevant to further evaluation of the alternatives;
5. correctly assimilates and takes account of any new information or expert judgment to which he is exposed, even when the information or judgment does not support the course of action he initially prefers;
6. reexamines the positive and negative consequences of all known alternatives, including those originally regarded as unacceptable, before making a final choice;
7. makes detailed provisions for implementing or executing the chosen course of action, with special attention to contingency plans that might be required if various known risks were to materialize.

One way to factor a problem is to treat it in stages, as the normative models suggest. An alternative procedure is to construct an organization in such a way that its various departments are responsible for small portions of the problem and its solution. Thus the production department would be responsible for producing the product, the marketing department for advertising and promoting it, and the sales department for selling it.

It is also possible to increase a manager's ability to factor a problem by on-the-job training. For instance, a newly hired salesman may feel that he will have difficulty in making sales. But on-the-job training under the watchful eye of an experienced salesman will gradually convince him that there are particular stages in the sales process and specific skills he must master for each stage.

Finally, as our earlier discussion of Japanese management indicates, it is possible to use *completed staff work* to factor a problem. In this situation staff experts analyze a problem, generate alternative solutions to it, and present a written report to top management describing the relative feasibility of each proposed solution.

Decision Heuristics

Although decision making may appear complicated to the uninitiated, the use of a few *decision heuristics,* or rules, will simplify the process enormously. For example, when faced with a problem, the individual can evaluate the alternatives by making a list of the positive and negative aspects associated with each alternative. The individual should *weight* each of these aspects, for some may be more important than others. For instance, one middle manager accepted a job after evaluating its career potential because there was only one negative aspect associated with it. Unfortunately, this negative aspect—living in an undesirable part of the country—was so important that it outweighed all the positive features, and he eventually quit.

Also, to counteract bolstering of the alternative and a biased information search, the individual should ask a colleague to serve as a devil's advocate, that is, someone who will evaluate, objectively and unemotionally, the feasibility of a proposed course of action (Schwenk and Cosier 1980). It is important that the devil's advocate not use emotional arguments, because this approach will only cloud the decision-making process.

Another decision heuristic is to ask: What *must* I do and what would I *prefer* to do? In this way the individual is factoring the problem in terms of priorities. This approach was used by the College of Business and Management at the University of Maryland when it introduced a new master of business administration program. For over a year the various faculty groups in the college discussed, at times heatedly, the specific courses that should be included in the new program. Finally, the faculty groups listed all the *must* courses, after which they discovered that disagreements centered around only three of the eighteen courses.

Similarly, it is helpful to *sequence* the solution, especially in terms of what must be accomplished before any other action is taken. In the College of Business and Management at Maryland there were also heated discussions about the semesters in which various courses should be offered over a four-semester period. The faculty groups finally were able to arrive at a consensus, but only after they had outlined the sequence of required courses. Most of the difficulties disappeared once the sequence had been written down.

Decision making can also be improved if an individual specifies the criteria he or she plans to use to judge the relative attractiveness of various alternatives *before* actually evaluating the alternatives. For example, many individuals buy a house based on first impressions and do not make a systematic analysis of its strengths and weaknesses. Only after signing a contract do they begin to evaluate the newly purchased home systematically. It is much better for the individual to specify precisely what he or she *must* have in a new house *before* beginning to house hunt; this approach will narrow the range of alternatives by eliminating from the start houses that would prove unsatisfactory.

Throughout this chapter we have emphasized that many individuals do not obtain sufficient information to make a good decision. At the very least, the individual should have two alternatives from which he or she can choose; the use of only one alternative generally indicates that the search for information has been incomplete. Similarly, to avoid an incorrect appraisal of alternatives, the individual should guard against making a hasty decision. For example, a job applicant generally should not accept a job immediately after it has been offered, even if the recruiter pressures him or her to do so. Waiting a few days provides perspective, and the individual can adequately appraise alternatives before making the final decision.

Finally, the individual should engage in contingency planning. He or she should develop alternatives to consider should the original decision turn out to be incorrect. Failure to plan on a contingency basis shows defective decision making (Janis and Mann 1977).

Use of Groups Decision making also can be improved by using groups. Although group decision making is not as prominent in the United States as it is in Japan, it is becoming an increasingly popular technique for dealing with complex problems. Since the complexity of the world in which organizations operate is increasing, it is more and more difficult for one manager to make important decisions independently. In fact, this complexity may eventually create a situation in which group decision making is the dominant mode in this country, especially when modern forms of organization are constructed (see Chapter 10).

There are many advantages associated with group decision making. These include the following (Huber 1980; Harrison 1975):

1. A greater sum of knowledge or information is brought to the decision.
2. Participating in decision making increases managers' acceptance of the final choice.
3. Managers involved in making the decision can inform members of their units about the reasons for it. Since more managers are involved, more units increase their understanding of the reasons underlying a decision.
4. A problem is approached in more ways and more alternative solutions are proposed.

FIGURE 4–2

Analysis of Groupthink, Based on Comparisons of High- and Low-Quality Decisions by Policymaking Groups

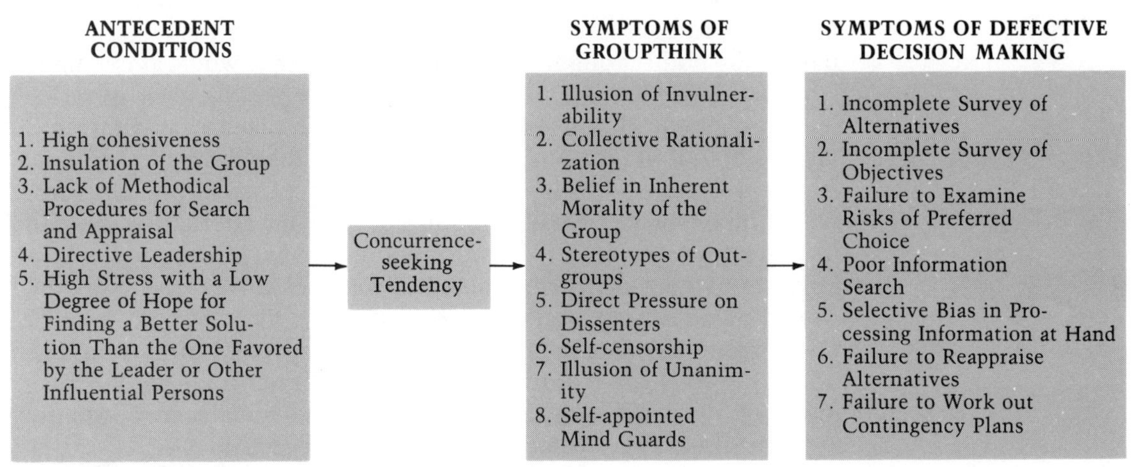

Source: Reprinted with permission of Macmillan Publishing Co., Inc. from Irving Janis and Leon Mann, *Decision Making: A Psychological Analysis of Conflict, Choice and Commitment* (New York: Free Press, 1977), p. 132. Copyright © 1977 by The Free Press, a Division of Macmillan Publishing Co., Inc.

However, group decision making also has some liabilities (Huber 1980; Harrison 1975):

1. Members of the decision-making group may feel pressure to accept the decision supported by the majority.
2. When members of a group reach agreement on a tentative solution, they frequently refuse to look for a better approach.
3. One or a few individuals may dominate the group.
4. Groups tend to use more time than an individual would in arriving at a decision.
5. A group may make a decision that is not consistent with the goals of the organization.
6. Individuals may begin to expect that they will be involved in all decisions and resist subsequent decisions that are appropriately but unilaterally handed down by upper management.
7. The group may not be able to reach a decision, thus delaying progress and leading to ill will among its members.

Groupthink Irving Janis (1972) has analyzed one organizational phenomenon, *groupthink,* that comes into play when a group of managers is trying to make a decision. His work focuses on some well-known decision-making fiascos, such as the Bay of Pigs and the buildup of United States forces in Vietnam during the early 1960s. In retrospect, it is hard to understand how intelligent, experienced, and sophisticated individuals could ever make such decisions—or is it?

From his analysis of good and bad decisions made by policymaking groups, Janis argues that there are antecedent conditions leading to a tendency to seek a concurrence in small decision-making groups (see Figure 4–2). For instance, the group may have a high degree of cohesiveness, it may be insulated from external pressures and information, it may lack procedures for adequately searching for alternative solutions and appraising them, it may be led in a highly directive manner, and it may operate under conditions of stress with little hope of finding a better solution than the one favored by the leader or other influential persons.

Under such conditions groupthink emerges, and it possesses the following characteristics:

Illusion of invulnerability.

Collective rationalization.

Belief in inherent morality of the group.

Stereotypes of out-groups.

Direct pressures on dissenters within the group.

Illusion of unanimity.

Self-appointed mind guards who try to limit other members of the group in their search for alternatives.

According to Janis, defective decision making then occurs, and it is characterized by the four defective strategies described in this chapter: unconflicted adherence, unconflicted change, defensive avoidance, and hypervigilance.

SUMMARY

Decision making is a process of choice leading to the selection of one alternative rather than others. More generally, it involves problem-solving activity that comes into play when the manager realizes that a significant gap exists between what is and what should be.

There are five stages in the decision-making process: the stimulus event indicating that there is a problem; information search; problem formulation; evaluation of alternatives; and implementation of the choice. Many constraints restrict the decision maker's freedom, and they make up the environments in which decisions are made. These constraints include the amount of perceived uncertainty and perceived conflict, organizational goals and policies, organizational level, societal expectations, and culture.

Individuals can employ two general strategies when making decisions. The rational comprehensive strategy is the examination of a large number of alternatives to accomplish a particular goal. From this number the manager chooses the most desirable alternative. In the incremental strategy the manager operates in steps. He or she makes a change, interprets the feedback, makes another change, and so forth.

More specifically, managers employ programmed and nonprogrammed strategies in response to the problems they face. A programmed strategy is used when the manager can solve a problem by the application of a rule, program, routine, or procedure that he or she has previously used to solve such problems. Nonprogrammed strategies are creative responses to unstructured problems that cannot be solved by a set routine. James Thompson has expanded on the distinction between programmed and nonprogrammed strategies. His computational strategy is equivalent to the programmed strategy, and his inspirational strategy to the nonprogrammed strategy. Thompson's remaining two strategies—compromise and judgmental strategies—represent intermediate points between programmed and nonprogrammed strategies.

As we might expect, it is common for individuals to make suboptimal decisions. There are human limits to rationality and, as a consequence, individuals attempt to satisfice rather than maximize. When satisficing, the manager examines only a limited number of alternatives and chooses the most desirable alternative within this limited range of choices. Suboptimal decision making also occurs because of biased information search, which is strengthened by the professional training and departmental identification of the manager.

There are four defective decision-making strategies that are activated because of biased and/or incomplete information search and inadequate appraisal of alternatives. These are unconflicted adherence to the current plan of action, unconflicted change, defensive avoidance, and hypervigilance.

To improve decision making, several writers such as Kepner and Tregoe have proposed normative models that managers should follow. Frequently these models are sequential in nature. Decision making can also be improved by problem factoring, that is, breaking a problem into stages or areas of responsibility. Additionally, decision making can be improved by employing decision heuristics or simple decision rules, such as making a list of the positive and negative features associated with each alternative and weighting them.

DISCUSSION QUESTIONS

1. Overall, do managers use programmed decision-making techniques more frequently than nonprogrammed decision-making techniques? Why or why not?
2. In this chapter we have discussed various constraints or conditions under which decision making occurs. Describe one additional constraint.

3. What are some cultural factors in the United States that influence the kinds of decisions managers can make?
4. Describe some situations in an organization in which group decision making would be more appropriate than individual decision making. Explain.
5. Describe a problem that could be effectively attacked by using a rational comprehensive strategy. Now describe a problem that could be effectively attacked by using an incremental strategy.
6. Describe the decision-making strategy that you plan to use in seeking a job after graduating from college.
7. What is the difference between a performance gap and an opportunity gap?
8. What is meant by *bolstering the alternative?* Describe at least two ways of counteracting it.

CRITICAL INCIDENTS

NOTE: These critical incidents can be used by the whole class with the case observational method (see Appendix A) or used for thought and discussion by individual class members.

1. John Hodges is a young middle manager with a large corporation who works in finance. He has been very successful during his first three years on the job. Recently he was asked to make a major presentation on financial planning to thirty of the company's top regional officers. This presentation is very important to John, for it will expose him to a select group of influential managers who may later offer him a promotion.

John makes a well-prepared presentation, after which he answers some questions from the thirty managers. One of these managers is particularly hostile toward him. He begins his question by asking, "What is your definition of financial planning?"

John has only a few seconds to think of an answer. As he begins to respond to the question, the regional officer says, "Don't give me any of the academic jargon." At this point it looks like the regional officer wants to dominate the discussion and show his superiority over John.

QUESTION: How should John react?

2. At a large state university the granting of promotions and tenure became uncertain as student enrollment started to decline. Members of the various departments were particularly upset because the credentials of their internal candidates for promotion were evaluated by a universitywide oversight committee. However, deans and department chairpersons frequently hired associate and full professors from outside the university, and their credentials were not evaluated by the oversight committee until they had been in residence at the university for one year, at which point it was virtually impossible to refuse tenure to them. Only once in the history of this university was an outside candidate denied tenure after being in residence for one year.

The sociology department recently recommended two internal candidates for promotion. Also, the chairperson of the sociology department, with minimal faculty input, hired a full professor from another university. The tenure and promotion committee convened, since they had to approve this hiring, although its actions were usually symbolic. This committee felt that the promotion policy was inequitable, since it favored outside candidates who did not go through the oversight committee *before* being hired. Some members of the committee wanted to reject the outside candidate, especially since they believed his credentials were slightly inferior to those of the internal candidates. This action would bring the committee into direct conflict with the department chairperson.

QUESTIONS: What actions should the tenure and promotion committee take to minimize conflict but, at the same time, ensure that the internal candidates would be promoted?

SUGGESTED READINGS

Harrison, E. Frank. *The Managerial Decision-Making Process.* Boston: Houghton Mifflin, 1975, 341 pages, hardback.

This is a readable and sophisticated treatment of the decision-making process. Harrison reviews the major research studies and theories in this area.

Huber, George. *Managerial Decision Making.* Glenview, Ill.: Scott, Foresman, 1980, 225 pages, paperback.

This book is a short, well-researched, highly readable introduction to managerial decision making.

Simon, Herbert. *Administrative Behavior.* 3rd ed. New York: Free Press, 1976 (originally published 1947), 364 pages, paperback.

This is a classic study of actual decision making.

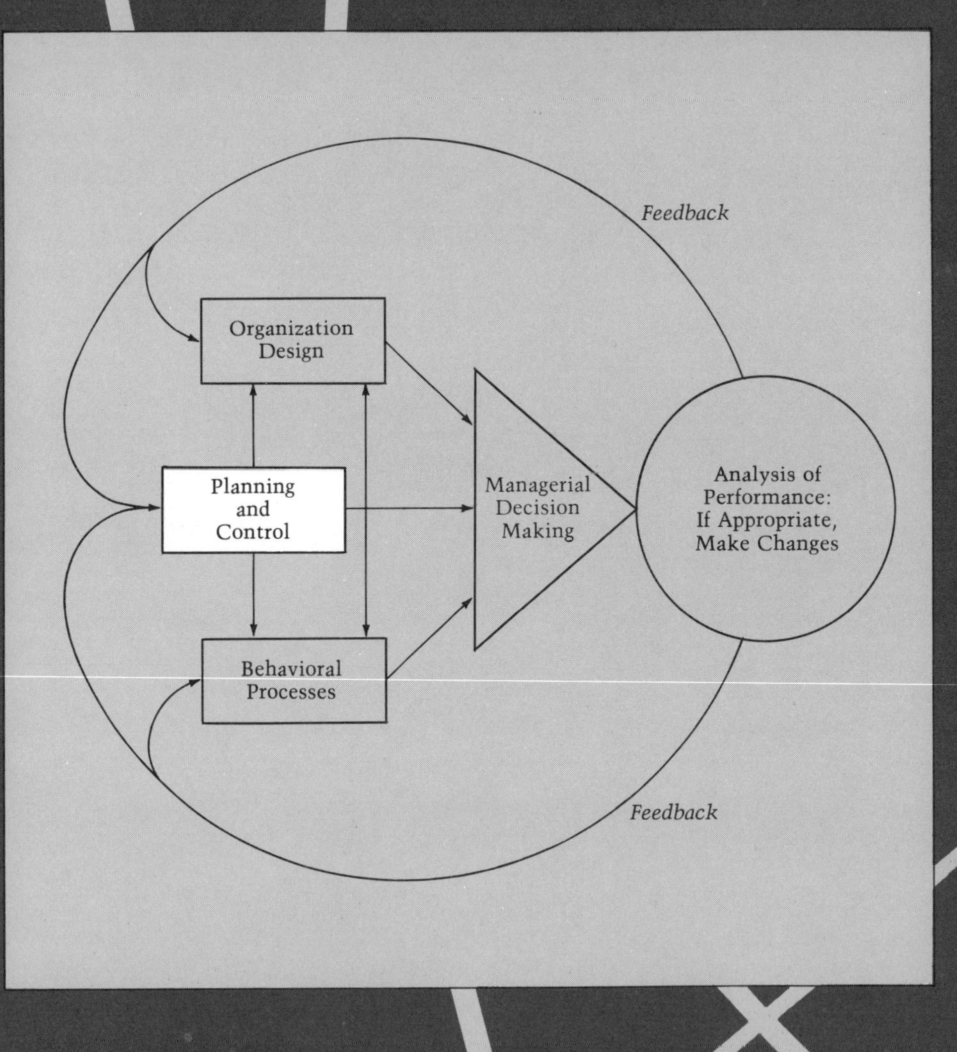
Feedback
Organization Design
Planning and Control
Managerial Decision Making
Analysis of Performance: If Appropriate, Make Changes
Behavioral Processes
Feedback

II PLANNING AND CONTROL

Planning and control in combination constitute one of the four major dimensions of our organizational framework. The planning systems determine what goals the organization and its major subsystems pursue, while the control systems monitor these plans and identify any significant deviations from them. All the organizational subsystems, and their employees and managers, receive guidance from the planning systems. At the same time the control systems monitor the performance of the entire organization, its major subsystems, and employees and managers, so that significant deviations from plans can be pinpointed and corrective action taken. Hence planning and control operate simultaneously and interdependently.

In Chapter 5 planning is defined and the organizational planning process is described in detail. Chapter 6 contains a description of various types of planning techniques. Chapter 7 defines various types of control and examines the control techniques that are employed to monitor organizational subsystems. This part of the book then concludes with a chapter devoted to a discussion of the control of organizational members (Chapter 8).

Magneto assembly line at the Highland Park plant, 1913

CONTINUOUS CASE

The Ford Motor Company 1913–1920

SUMMARY: Unlike the aim of other car manufacturers, Henry Ford's strategic plan was to produce an all-purpose, inexpensive car, the Model T (see Continuous Case, Part I). When this car appeared in 1909, it was a major success. However, to continue to produce an inexpensive car, Henry Ford needed to cut his labor costs.

In 1913 Henry Ford began to redesign his organization with the express purpose of cutting labor costs. He began to routinize the work and use unskilled workers. In 1913 Clarence Avery and William Klann, two of Ford's assistants, created the concept of the conveyor belt, which, in turn, brought about the assembly line and mass production.

However, the unskilled workers at Ford were not happy. By 1913 dissatisfaction among them had resulted in high turnovers—there was a labor turnover of over 380 percent in 1913 alone (Ford with Crowther 1926, p. 161). Undoubtedly mass production accelerated this trend, for no longer could most workers be accorded the status of skilled employees. Moreover, during the summer of 1913, grievances began to crystallize under the leadership of the International Workers of the World (IWW), a Communist-infiltrated union that appealed to immigrants, a large number of whom worked at Ford. Although it was small, this union served as a focal point and outlet for worker hostility. Finally, the country as a whole experienced a minor depression in 1913. Henry Ford decided to combat the rising labor problems.

REVOLUTIONARY PERSONNEL REFORMS

On January 14, 1914, Henry Ford raised the average salary of his workers from $2.34 to $5.00 a day. Almost overnight he became known internationally as a friend and defender of the worker. This action ended his labor problems, at least for the short run, since over 100,000 men immediately lined up for employment outside the Highland Park plant in the freezing January weather.

There were undoubtedly business reasons for the $5 day. An end to high labor turnover was definitely a prime consideration. Ford could acquire workers who were actually energetic in the fulfillment of their obligations. He later admitted that the $5 day was one of the finest cost-cutting moves the company ever made (Ford with Crowther 1922, p. 147).

Even though Henry Ford's motives in introducing the $5 day probably involved business more than charity, the host of other beneficial acts he undertook during this era of benevolence indicated his sincere interest in his workers' welfare. In 1914 a Safety and Health Department was created and immediately began efficient operations. The year 1916 witnessed the opening of the Henry Ford Trade School, an institution in which boys could learn a trade while attending school. The popularity of this school was so great that in 1920 it had 15,000 applicants for 1,500 positions. Acceptance in the school was largely based on need.

A startling policy initiated during this period was the hiring of partially incapacitated workers, ex-criminals, epileptics, and former inmates of mental hospitals. Although no other large company had any policy comparable to this one, Ford was not afraid to take chances by employing such people. Moreover, it was a continuing program; in 1934 approximately twenty percent of the Ford workmen were physically disabled (Federal Trade Commission 1939, p. 639). Such farsightedness was and is highly unusual; even today tradition militates against hiring such workers.

OTHER PERSONNEL REFORMS

Another innovation was the Ford Sociology Department, which advised both management and employees on matters involving employees. This department investigated Ford's workmen to determine their eligibility for the $5 wage. It also counseled the workmen on how they should budget their money to get the best possible bargains for it. Further, the department provided information to them concerning the purchase of houses and other high-priced goods. This department was somewhat paternalistic, even to the extent of secretly visiting the homes of workers in order to ensure that disorderly behavior did not scandalize or harm the company in any way. However, the workers generally liked its activities, for it was a major source of protection for them. As an example of the dangers the workmen sought protection from, after receiving their first $5-a-day paychecks, Ford workmen were besieged at the gates of the Highland Park plant by all types of predatory salesmen (Sward 1948, p. 61).

Under the direction of the Sociology Department, the Ford Motor Company conducted a language school for its workers who were foreign-born. Thus Henry Ford helped in the acculturation of many individuals who otherwise would have found not only the American labor market but also the American society impersonal and almost unapproachable.

Ford also developed an employee profit-sharing system in which employees received extra income if the profits of the company rose. In addition, Ford opened grocery stores for his employees, which in 1919 were selling foodstuffs twenty-five percent below the market prices. This action contrasted rather sharply with the company stores, still in existence, in some coal towns in the United States. Another point of interest is that the *Dearborn Independent,* the newspaper directly owned and controlled by Henry Ford, supported the union in the steel strike of 1919.

Labor, for its part, reciprocated Henry Ford's good will. In 1918 he decided to run for senator from the state of Michigan. Although he lost, one of his most ardent backers was the American Federation of Labor. Apparently the workers felt their interests could be best pursued by this man who identified with them even though he was one of the richest men in the world.

Many analysts are of the opinion that the only major labor reforms in the early part of the twentieth century were those carried out by Henry Ford (Commons 1935; Lippman 1961). Few other companies followed Ford's example; the National Association of Manufacturers even criticized him in their publications. The top managers of other companies considered Henry Ford a maverick and scornfully allowed him to go his own way. Considering this environment, it is remarkable that he introduced so many innovative labor policies.

QUESTIONS: Should Henry Ford change his strategic plan? Did Henry Ford create a sense of rising expectations among his workers? What would happen if he eliminated the labor reforms he had introduced? At the Ford Motor Company, what kind of link existed between planning and organization design?

5 An Introduction to Planning

THE ORGANIZATIONAL PLANNING PROCESS
FORECASTING
PLANNING WITH PRECISE AND IMPRECISE GOALS
MANAGEMENT BY OBJECTIVES (MBO)
STRATEGIC FAILURES
SUMMARY
DISCUSSION QUESTIONS
CRITICAL INCIDENTS
SUGGESTED READINGS

PERFORMANCE OBJECTIVES

1. To explain the importance of planning, especially in terms of an organization's activities and success.
2. To describe various types of forecasting techniques, and to identify in a general way when each type is appropriate for specific situations.
3. To define the organizational planning process and describe its various stages.
4. To discuss the organizational planning process within the context of planning with precise and imprecise goals.
5. To describe a distinctive planning system, Management by Objectives (MBO), which focuses on identifying goals and objectives.
6. To highlight the importance of planning by describing some major strategic failures in organizations.

It seems reasonable to assume that one major factor contributing to organizational success is effective planning; in fact, both observation and research support this assumption. For example, Stanley Thune and Robert House (1970) analyzed the planning function in 36 similar firms in 6 industries. The average performance of companies after formal planning was initiated increased by 38 percent in sales, 64 percent in earnings per share, and 56 percent in stock price. As environmental uncertainty increases, organizations also increase their emphasis on formal planning systems. William Lindsay and Leslie Rue (1980) studied the planning systems of 199 corporations in 15 different industries and discovered that firms tend to adopt more sophisticated planning systems as the complexity and instability of the business environment rise.

This chapter discusses the process that organizations typically follow when the planning system is established correctly. Various types of forecasting techniques are outlined, and a general description is given of the situations in which each type is appropriate. In addition, a comparison is made of organizations that can identify goals precisely and those that cannot. The chapter also describes a distinctive planning system, Management by Objectives (MBO), which focuses specifically on the development of long-term goals and short-term objectives. Finally, the importance of planning is highlighted by describing some major strategic failures.

THE ORGANIZATIONAL PLANNING PROCESS

The process of organizational planning is complicated and involves several related concepts. In this section we use a case study of a successful organization to illustrate the organizational planning process and to define the basic concepts that must be used within this process.

Defining the Mission: Giant Food

Giant Food is a food chain store headquartered in Washington, D.C., and it recently became the largest and most profitable food chain in that area. Much of its success is attributable to the organizational planning process it employs.

For years Giant Food was just another ordinary food chain store. Then its top management began to engage in environmental forecasting and realized that Giant Food needed to develop a unique mission if it was to survive and prosper in the highly competitive food industry. Profit margins in this industry are low—one to two percent of sales—and many firms have experienced lean times and even bankruptcy. Giant Food wanted to avoid these consequences.

Using the environmental forecasts, top management at Giant Food attempted to define the organization's missions. That is, they wished to answer the question, What business or markets is the organization in and what business or markets is it not in? Giant Food then defined its mission in broad terms as a *consumer service* organization supplying a full spectrum of goods and services rather than just food, although the food section of each store is the largest subunit. Within a typical Giant store the following outlets are housed: a pharmacy with full-time pharmacists on duty at all times; a clothing store; a hardware department; a beer and wine section; and a maternity department. Thus the consumer can go to only one Giant outlet to satisfy his or her needs in several areas that have traditionally been scattered throughout a shopping center.

Goals and Strategies

Once a firm such as Giant defines its mission, it must then define its *long-term goals.* Ordinarily top management will define four or five major goals that it seeks to achieve within a relatively long period of time. In Giant's case the goals might involve increasing net income in each of its outlets within five years in the following manner:

Food outlet, 60 percent.

Maternity shop, 30 percent.

Clothing outlet, 40 percent.

Pharmacy, 70 percent.

Hardware outlet, 80 percent.

These goals would be derived from an analysis of the various specialty markets and forecasts of changes in them. Giant might decide that offering a wide variety of foods would help it attract customers away from other food chains, thus increasing net income by 60 percent. Similarly, if a severe recession is forecast for this five-year period, hardware sales should increase substantially (80 percent), since many home owners will begin to fix things themselves rather than replacing them or hiring someone to fix them. Similar forecasting approaches, some of which are admittedly subjective as we will see, would be implemented in the other areas.

There are, of course, many other types of goals that Giant might wish to achieve by the end of five years. These might include decreasing the yearly managerial turnover rate from 35 percent to 20 percent; decreasing the yearly employee turnover rate from 40 percent to 30 percent; reducing the number of items returned by Giant customers by 10 percent; and decreasing the number of customer complaints filed with the complaint department by 30 percent.

Normally an organization will then develop the means to achieve these long-term goals. These means, called *strategies,* are *general* and *overall plans of action* that the organization uses to accomplish its long-term goals and fulfill its missions. In Giant's case the strategy is two-pronged: (1) to sell a wide variety of foods that will appeal to a cross section of customers, including gourmets, and (2) to sell a relatively small number of low- to medium-cost items within each of its specialty areas. Thus the clothing outlet will sell not suits and dresses but undershirts, blouses, and so forth. In this way Giant is not competing directly with the specialty stores in each shopping center. At the same time Giant is able to increase profits by focusing on items that the ordinary food shopper could easily buy, since only small amounts of money are involved.

Objectives and Tactics At this point top management normally focuses on the development of short-term goals, or *objectives,* which are usually expressed on a yearly basis. For the first year Giant might decide that net income should increase by ten percent in the food outlet, five percent in the clothing outlet, and so forth. Top management would then develop tactics to achieve these objectives. *Tactics* are means that the organization employs to achieve its short-term objectives—and, by implication, its long-term goals. Hence tactics are part of the overall strategies that the organization employs.

One tactic that Giant Food recently introduced was to stop marking the price on each item of food. A time study indicated that Giant Food could decrease its labor costs considerably by just listing one price above several of the same food items on the shelves. Management is planning to decrease food prices if this tactic is accepted by the customers.

Another tactic that Giant originally introduced on an experimental basis was to hire Esther Peterson, the first advisor to the president on consumer affairs. Peterson not only helps Giant management but also appears on television explaining to consumers how they can save money. Giant was also one of the first large food chains to introduce unit pricing, another tactic designed to achieve its overall strategy by showing the consumer how to save. Periodically Giant also sponsors special sales, not only in its food outlet but also in its other outlets. Giant uses the tactic of keeping its largest stores open seven days a week for 24 hours each day. And recently Giant discontinued the use of the popular store coupons, which are actually subsidized by Giant customers. The elimination of these coupons has resulted in a decrease in the prices Giant must charge for its products. Thus this tactic indicates to the consumer that Giant is indeed a broad-based consumer service organization (its mission) that is sensitive to the needs of its customers.

As this discussion implies, Giant may change its tactics rather frequently. If special sales for some items do not seem to be successful, Giant will discontinue them. Whatever happens, the firm's objectives must be accomplished, and tactics will be changed to see that they are.

Policies, Procedures, and Rules

All these factors—missions, long-term goals, strategies, and tactics—then become the basis for the policies, procedures, and rules that top management implements to direct day-to-day activities in each store. *Policies* are *general guides* to action that all or most members of an organization must follow. Of course, exceptions to policies are permitted for valid reasons.

There are many types of policies: financial, personnel, marketing, and so forth. For instance, to achieve its goals and objectives, Giant might follow a personnel policy of hiring only part-time workers. Giant might discover that such workers are highly motivated. However, a store manager might deviate from this policy by hiring some full-time employees. Similarly, Giant might follow the policy of advertising only in general-circulation publications, in accordance with its mission of being a broad-based, consumer-service organization.

Typically policies are accompanied by *procedures:* customary methods of handling activities in accordance with established policies. Procedures differ from policies in that they are *specific* rather

FIGURE 5–1
The Organizational Planning Process

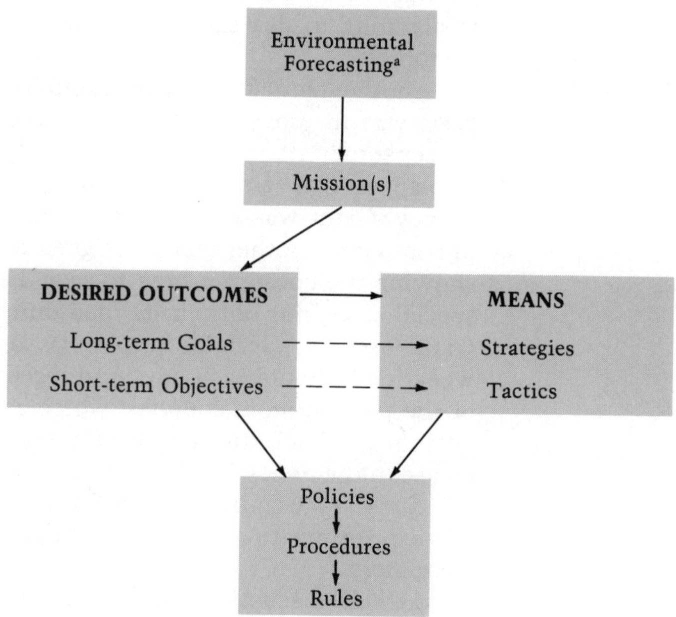

Note: Some of these stages or activities frequently occur simultaneously, such as the development of strategies and tactics.

[a] Forecasting is updated periodically to take account of environmental changes. Using these revised forecasts, the organization may change its mission, goals, or objectives.

than broad guidelines, and they describe the exact sequence in which a particular activity must be completed. For instance, a company might develop a procedure whereby all advertising expenditures must be approved by three different departments in the organization before action can be taken.

Procedures, in turn, are normally subdivided into *rules,* which represent the simplest types of plans. Thus a procedure can be defined as a series of rules. A rule does not allow for any discretion on the part of the individual; he or she must perform a given action in accordance with a given rule. For example, Giant might develop the rule that a manager must complete particular financial forms before he or she can obtain approval for advertising expenditures. However, not every rule is directly related to a procedure or policy. "No smoking," for instance, is a rule not directly related to any procedure.

The organizational planning process we have described in this section is delineated in Figure 5–1.

Simultaneous Activities

It is important to point out that we have described an *ideal* organizational planning process consisting of several discrete stages (see Figure 5–1). However, in many situations the activities within various stages occur simultaneously. For example, the organization may develop long-term goals and short-term objectives at the same time. Nevertheless, a thorough understanding of each step in the organizational planning process increases the probability that managers will lead the organization successfully, both in the short run and in the long run.

FORECASTING

A problem central to planning in any organization is knowing what is likely to happen, both within the organization and in its external environment. In government, for instance, a manager who fails to anticipate events can misallocate resources, attract adverse publicity, and even face removal from office. In the private sector of the economy ineffective forecasting can lead to the selection of incorrect courses of action, unsold inventories, decreased profits, and, in some cases, the financial failure of the firm. While these examples are extreme, they do emphasize the critical role that forecasting plays for both the organization and the individual manager.

Forecasting essentially serves two purposes. The first is to provide a basis for long-range planning. Areas influenced by long-range forecasting include production planning, capital budgeting allocations (the apportioning of large sums of money to various projects), determination of overall personnel requirements, financial planning, and inventory needs. The second purpose concerns short-range scheduling decisions. Areas usually affected by short-range forecasts include production scheduling, manpower needs, and procurement management (the determination of supplies an organization needs to function effectively).

More specifically, the basic purpose of forecasting is to predict future demand for the organization's goods or services. Failure to anticipate trends in demand can have disastrous results. For example, the airline industry was forced to ground several airplanes in 1974 when forecasted passenger traffic did not materialize. Similarly, the recreation vehicle industry underestimated the effect of the energy crisis on demand and found itself swamped with thousands of unsold vans and campers. And the fashion industry underestimated the strength of customer resistance to maxi fashions in the early 1970s; dozens of firms were bankrupted in the resulting downturn.

Types of Forecasts

Forecasts are of three major types. The long-range forecast refers to the long-term planning needs of the organization; the short-range forecast describes the firm's immediate needs; and the rolling forecast combines these two into one comprehensive forecast that is constantly updated as the time of accomplishing an objective approaches and as new information becomes available.

To prepare a *long-range forecast,* managers examine information that has traditionally indicated changes in business and economic conditions in the distant future—for example, the general state of the economy. The *planning horizon*—the period of time a long-range forecast covers—may vary from a few weeks to several years. However, a typical long-range forecast will estimate conditions one to five years into the future. Quantities and product mixes are usually stated in general terms—for example, the number of tennis rackets customers will buy rather than the number within each model. The firm relies heavily on published and public data for its long-range forecasts, since many of the factors that influence long-range forecasts are external to the organization and cannot be controlled directly by it. Some organizations that publish these data are the U.S. Department of Commerce, the U.S. Department of Labor, and the U.S. Department of the Treasury. In short, the long-range forecast is tentative in nature and very sensitive to changes in *external* economic conditions.

The *short-range forecast* is usually more detailed than the long-range forecast. Its planning horizon typically ranges from a few days to a year. The analyst examines recent business and economic conditions to estimate the immediate market demand for the firm's product or service. Both products and quantities that seem likely to meet the demand are specified precisely. A short-range forecast is more dependent on internal data, such as sales in previous years, than on external data. In addition, the short-range forecast is sensitive to short-run changes, such as a strike at a customer's plant, a competitor's sidewalk sale, and even the weather.

Source: © 1973 by Sidney Harris/ *Supervisory Management.*

"Don't we have anyone *who took business administration?"*

The *rolling forecast* integrates the long-range and short-range forecasts into one comprehensive forecast that is continually revised. If goals are not met or if conditions change, management alters its rolling forecast. Because of its flexibility, the rolling forecast accomplishes at least two purposes: It enables management to maintain a long-range overview of its operations and to make adjustments in operating plans within an overall perspective; and it allows management to plan and manage resources rather than constantly react to problems on a daily basis.

In general, the rolling forecast seems to be more useful than either long-range or short-range forecasting alone. It can include most or all of the specific planning techniques described in this chapter. It is flexible and sensitive to economic changes. And it can be used for short-range and long-range planning. The rolling forecast also encourages managers to focus attention constantly on the effectiveness of their planning.

A Forecasting Typology

James Utterback (1979) has constructed a forecasting typology that is useful for managers who need to decide how much effort and money they should invest in forecasting. His work is based on the analyses completed by Robert Duncan (1972).

The Environment. In line with Burns and Stalker's research (see Chapter 2), Utterback assigns a critical role to the degree of external environmental uncertainty facing an organization. There are two key dimensions in the external environment: the *simple-complex* dimension and the *static-dynamic* dimension. A simple environment is one in which the external factors an organization faces are few in number and relatively homogeneous. For instance, the Retirement Division of the U.S. Office of Personnel Management performs only a few major functions: advising government employees on retirement issues and processing checks for retirees. This simple environment is in marked contrast to the complex environment of the Internal Revenue Service, which processes income tax returns, monitors them, prosecutes offenders, and develops policies and procedures for future years.

The static-dynamic dimension focuses on the relative degree of stability in organization-environment relations. As noted earlier, many government agencies are relatively stable within this dimension, for they receive their yearly budgets from Congress and do not experience the intense competition for revenue that exists in the private sector. Aerospace firms reflect the dynamic dimension, since they must be constantly aware of technological advances and must compete intensely with other aerospace firms for government contracts.

Four Types of Forecasts. According to Utterback, when the environment is both simple and static, management does not need to invest in formal forecasting (see Figure 5–2). Expert opinion of managers or other individuals knowledgeable about the problems facing the organization is sufficient. However, when the environment is static but complex, managers must do more than rely on expert opinion. They must be alert for any changes in the environment. Hence they must closely *monitor* changes in the external environment that may affect the organization.

In a simple but dynamic environment managers should employ

FIGURE 5–2
Types of Environment Related to Forecasting Methods

COMPLEXITY	CHANGE: *Static*	CHANGE: *Dynamic*
Simple	No formal methods, expert opinion only	Expert opinion, monitoring, trend extrapolation
Complex	Expert opinion, monitoring	As above and sophisticated quantitative models

Source: From James M. Utterback, "Environmental Analysis and Forecasting," in Dan E. Schendel and Charles W. Hofer, eds., *Strategic Management: A New View of Business Policy and Planning,* p. 139. Copyright © 1979 by Little, Brown and Company (Inc.). Adapted by permission.

expert opinion and close monitoring of the environment. But they also must scrutinize carefully any *trends* that may be occurring and *extrapolate* them into the future. Finally, managers in the complex but dynamic environment must make the greatest investment of effort and money in forecasting. They must rely on expert opinion, monitoring, and trend extrapolation. In addition, managers must develop sophisticated *quantitative models* so that they can refine their predictions.

Qualitative Forecasting Techniques

There are many forecasting techniques. However, John Chambers, Satinder Mullick, and Donald Smith (1971) have pointed out that these techniques can be categorized into three groups: qualitative forecasting methods, time series analysis and projection, and mathematical methods. In this section we describe some qualitative techniques, which primarily involve subjective estimates of the future. Although the estimates may be summarized statistically or mathematically, the original data are subjective in nature, as is the final managerial judgment.

The Delphi Technique. One of the most important qualitative forecasting methods is the *Delphi technique.* Named after a Greek oracle, it predicts long-run technological and market changes that will eventually affect the organization. In this technique the organization polls, at periodic intervals, a small number of experts. For example, an oil company might poll, on a yearly basis, fifty to seventy-five experts in the area of natural resources to assess future energy needs. The organization usually guarantees the experts anonymity to ensure that they will be as candid as possible.

First the experts are asked to complete a questionnaire on which they give numerical estimates of the likelihood of specific technological or market changes occurring within a certain time. In the case of the oil company the experts might be asked if they feel that the United States can develop in the next twenty years a new kind of fuel that is competitive with oil as a source of energy. A summary of this survey is then prepared, usually in terms of some descriptive statistics. For example, eighty percent of the experts may believe that the United States will not develop a new kind of fuel competitive with oil within the next twenty years. The organization returns this summary to the experts, who are allowed to revise their earlier predictions if they wish. A summary is again prepared and sent to the experts, but they are now asked to justify their predictions if their responses deviate significantly from the others. Thus if eighty percent of the experts still believe that the United States will not develop a new kind of fuel competitive with oil in the next twenty years, the remaining twenty percent of the respondents are asked to indicate why they disagree.

The organization then prepares a final summary of the results, which is given to top management.

Panel Consensus. A related forecasting technique is the *panel consensus,* which assumes that several experts can arrive at a better forecast than can one person. These experts meet as a group periodically to discuss the issues and factors they should examine. Management encourages open communication among the experts and deemphasizes secrecy. Unfortunately, social factors may influence the forecast. For example, one individual may convince the others of his position, even though several members of the group feel strongly that he is wrong. Also, research indicates that a group tends to make decisions that are superior to those advocated by the *average* member of the group but inferior to those put forth by the *most informed* member of the group (Harrison, 1975).

As in the case of the Delphi technique, management typically employs the panel consensus to make long-range technological and new-product forecasts. The time required to develop a forecast is at least two weeks and does not necessarily require a computer.

Visionary Forecasts. Our final qualitative method is the *visionary* forecast. It also focuses on long-range and new-product predictions. The visionary forecast emphasizes the use of personal insights and judgments and frequently involves imagining more than one scenario in terms of the kind of society that will exist in the future and the types of products that will be marketable. Visionary forecasts are less systematic and scientific than the other qualitative forecasting techniques. It takes only a week to make a forecast, since only a few experts need be involved. However, the accuracy of these forecasts is poor.

Time Series Analysis and Projection

Time series analysis and projection is the second major category of forecasting techniques. Time series analysis examines past activities and extrapolates statistically and mathematically into the future.

Moving Average. A mathematical technique that management uses for inventory control of low-volume goods is the *moving average.* Each point of a moving average of a time series is the arithmetic or weighted average of several consecutive points of the series. Typically the moving average is based on previous sales. Management selects data points so as to eliminate or reduce the effects of seasonal or irregular changes in demand for the product.

In the short term (up to three months), the accuracy of the moving average varies widely from poor to good. Beyond the short term the accuracy is poor or very poor.

Trend Projections. A related technique is *trend projection.* Managers study actual data from a trend and derive an equation to fit the data. They then project the equation into the future to predict the trend. This technique is appropriate for new-product forecasts.

The accuracy of trend projection is very good in the short term and good beyond it. It requires approximately one day to make a forecast and does not necessarily involve the use of a computer.

Mathematical Models

Mathematical models represent our third group of forecasting techniques. The object in developing such models is to identify the underlying variables or factors that influence and predict the changes that the forecast describes. Unlike qualitative and time series forecasts, mathematical models not only describe the changes but present a systematic explanation of why a change is likely to occur.

Regression Model. The *regression model* specifies several independent variables that, *in combination,* predict changes in a dependent variable, such as sales or return on investment (ROI). For example, sales may be a function of the following variables: state of the economy, time of the year, degree of competition in the industry, amount of capital investment in the last five years, and number of experienced employees. The analysis is based on the coefficient of correlation (r), which is the degree of relationship between each independent variable and sales. *Multiple correlation* shows the degree of relationship between *all* the independent variables *combined together* and sales. The square of the multiple r indicates how much of the variation in sales is explained by variations in all the independent variables when they are combined. For instance, a multiple r of 0.9 indicates that 81 percent (0.9^2) of the variation in sales is predicted by the variations in all the independent variables when they are combined.

An outstanding application of regression is PIMS (Profit Impact of Market Strategies). Originally developed at General Electric, it is now housed in the Strategic Management Institute in Boston. Several large firms contribute data and financial support to PIMS. The most publicized use of the PIMS data is a regression model containing 37 independent variables that predict 80 percent of the variance in return on investment (Anderson and Paine 1978).

Diffusion Index. The *diffusion index* is a refined version of time series analysis. It represents the percentage of a group of economic indicators that are going up or down, with the percentage becoming the index. In essence, the index assumes that this group of indicators is the key influence on economic activity. Thus the model is causal in nature.

There are several widely used diffusion indices. *Business Week*

POOR FORECASTING

The abolishment of pain in surgery is a chimera. It is absurd to go on seeking it today. "Knife" and "pain" are two words in surgery that must forever be associated in the consciousness of the patient. *(Dr. Alfred Velpeau 1839)*

The population of the earth decreases every day, and, if this continues, in another 10 centuries the earth will be nothing but a desert. *(Montesquieu 1743)*

That [the atom bomb] is the biggest fool thing we have ever done. . . . The bomb will never go off, and I speak as an expert in explosives. *(Admiral William D. Leahy to President Truman 1945)*

My figures coincide in fixing 1950 as the year when the world must go to smash. *(Henry Adams 1903)*

What, sir, would make a ship sail against the wind and currents by lighting a bonfire under her decks? I pray you excuse me. I have no time to listen to such nonsense. *(Napoleon to Robert Fulton, inventor of the steam engine)*

The demonstration that no possible combination of known substances, known forms of machinery, and known forms of force can be united in a practical machine by which man shall fly long distances through the air, seems to the writer as complete as it is possible for the demonstration of any physical fact to be. *(Simon Newcomb, astronomer, 1903)*

regularly publishes an index that is used for predicting the state of the entire economy. When firms develop their own diffusion index, they employ it to predict sales by product classes. Accuracy varies from poor to good for predictions of two years or less, and very poor beyond that point. An organization must generally spend at least one month developing an application and making the forecast, and it is not necessary to use a computer in the analysis.

PLANNING WITH PRECISE AND IMPRECISE GOALS

As suggested above, some organizations such as Giant Food can attempt to achieve their missions through specific long-term goals and short-term objectives. However, the mission must be relatively precise, since it provides the guiding light and framework for the development of goals and objectives.

Specifying Goals

Unfortunately, many organizations experience difficulty in defining their mission(s) and, consequently, their long-term goals and short-term objectives. For example, if a rival organization was established to compete directly with Giant Food, its top managers might not be able to arrive at a consensus about the relative emphasis that should be placed on each of the specialty outlets within each store. Similarly, research and development units in large organizations might find it difficult to determine goals and objectives for its scientists and engineers. The objective of requiring each scientist to come up with one new idea every year might force the scientists to deemphasize an important long-term research project. In a university, requiring faculty members to publish at least one article a year may force a faculty member to publish an important research study prematurely, thus turning an excellent study into a mediocre study.

Michael McCaskey (1974) points out that an organization should not specify goals too precisely under the following conditions:

When it is too early to set goals—that is, before an individual or organization has identified its mission(s).

When the external environment in which the organization operates is unstable.

When organizational members cannot build sufficient trust or agreement to decide upon common goals.

McCaskey also points out that there are conditions, representing the converse of the conditions above, under which an organization should stress planning with precise or specific goals.

When at a stage in the life of an organization top management wants to narrow its focus.

When the environment is relatively stable and certain.

When there are severe limits on time or resources.

In short, planning is contingent upon the nature of the external environment. When top management can predict the degree to which it can control the external environment—in Giant Food's case, its net income or market share within each of its specialty areas—planning with precise or specific goals is appropriate. However, if the organization cannot predict the degree to which it can control the external environment, planning with imprecise or diffuse goals, or *directional* planning, should be used; that is, managers decide, as specifically as their information allows, what course to pursue.

According to McCaskey, planning with precise or specific goals is suitable if an organization is mechanistic in design—that is, when there is a high degree of job specialization and when the individual's freedom to exercise responsibility is clearly and strictly delimited. Conversely, directional planning is consistent with an organic organization in which tasks are varied, complex, and relatively ill defined. Thus the contingency theory of designing organizations is paralleled by a contingency theory of planning (see Chapter 2).

Departmental Planning

Frequently we assume that planning takes place only at the top levels of an organization. Planning by top management is of obvious importance and focuses on missions, strategies, and long-term goals. However, much planning also occurs at the middle-management level.

As with top-level planning, middle-level, or *departmental,* planning can be of two types: planning with precise goals and planning with imprecise goals (directional planning). The production department, for example, can typically specify precisely its goals and objectives. However, the research and development department, which must constantly monitor technological changes, might employ directional planning. Thus both types of planning may exist side by side in the same organization, and it is the responsibility of both top and middle management to decide which type is appropriate within specific departments.

Finally, even though our discussion has focused on a dichotomy—planning with precise and imprecise goals—in fact we are analyzing a continuum. At one end are specific, measurable goals that are developed in a rational, analytic fashion. At the other end of the continuum are diffuse, difficult-to-measure goals that managers develop in a predominantly intuitive fashion. Most planning systems fall somewhere in the middle regions of this continuum. A comparison of planning with precise and imprecise goals is shown in Table 5-1.

MANAGEMENT BY OBJECTIVES (MBO)

As indicated in the previous section, both long-term goals and short-term objectives are critical in the organizational planning process. The emphasis on goals and objectives has given rise to the development of a distinctive, organizationwide planning technique called *Management by Objectives* (MBO). In general, MBO involves the establishment and communication of organizational goals, the identification of individual objectives directly related to these goals, and the periodic and final review of performance as it relates to the objectives.

Thus MBO is partly a technique for appraising individual performance; we shall describe this aspect of MBO in Chapter 8 when we discuss performance appraisal. However, MBO is basically a planning technique that involves the following activities:

1. Top management plans proactively rather than reactively, establishing and changing goals so that they are appropriate to the external environment in which the organization operates.

2. Top management provides a small number of long-term goals and short-term objectives that it wishes the organization to accomplish. These top-level goals and objectives are then specified in more detail by the lower organizational levels, in a descending order. Thus the goals and objectives at a lower organizational level become the means for achieving the goals and objectives at the organizational

TABLE 5–1
Planning with Precise and Imprecise Goals

Planning with precise goals	*Planning with imprecise goals (directional planning)*
Characteristics	
1. Specific missions	1. Diffuse missions
2. Specific and measurable goals	2. Diffuse goals that are difficult to measure
3. Rational, analytic	3. Intuitive, using many non-quantifiable elements
4. Focused, narrow perception of task	4. Broad perception of task
5. Lesser need to process novel information	5. Greater need to process novel information
6. More efficient use of energy	6. Possible redundancy, false leads
7. Separate planning and acting phases	7. Planning and acting not separate phases
Contingencies	
1. People prefer well-defined tasks	1. People prefer variety, change, and complexity
2. Relatively stable external environment	2. Relatively unstable external environment
3. Mechanistic organizational structure	3. Organic organizational structure

Source: Adapted from Michael B. McCaskey, "A Contingency Approach to Planning: Planning with Goals and Planning Without Goals," *Academy of Management Journal* 17, no. 2 (June 1974): 290. Used by permission.

level directly above it. Hence there is a cascading effect of top-level goals and objectives, with the result that a means-end chain is established throughout the organization, from the highest to the lowest level. In this sense MBO is an organizationwide planning system, because it directly affects the objectives that each individual in the organization must accomplish in any given time.

3. The top management in the organization is fully committed to the MBO system.

4. The organization emphasizes mutual or participative setting of goals and objectives, involving not only superiors but also their subordinates, whose performance is to be evaluated eventually in terms of the achievement of specific objectives.

5. Managers undertake frequent performance reviews, during which the superior and his or her subordinate identify the degree to which goals and objectives have been achieved and alter them if this course of action seems appropriate.

6. The subordinate is allowed some degree of freedom to develop and use his or her own means to achieve the objectives.

7. The subordinate receives ample rewards, such as salary increases and promotion, for accomplishing objectives.

MBO seems to be a rational planning process that is consistent with our description of the organizational planning process. For this reason it is appealing to management. At the same time there are problems associated with its implementation. In this section we discuss research on MBO, its major advantages and limitations, and its future use in various types of organizations.

Research on MBO

Carroll and Tosi (1973) have summarized the research on MBO (see also Muczyk 1979; Kerr 1972). They point out that this research has focused primarily on three aspects of MBO: the setting of goals, feedback or knowledge of results, and subordinate participation in decision making.

Generally speaking, the setting of goals does appear to improve task performance. However, the goals and objectives should be specific, challenging, and realistic. Otherwise, this practice may result in a decrease in performance. However, keep in mind that there are some tasks for which it is difficult to specify goals and objectives precisely.

Periodically the subordinate should receive feedback about performance in terms of accomplishing his or her objectives. Research indicates that knowledge of results can improve performance. However, the research also suggests that the feedback will be more helpful if it is timely, specific, and relevant to the tasks being completed or the objectives being accomplished.

Carroll and Tosi also examined research on the relationship between subordinate participation in the setting of objectives and productivity. The key moderating variable seems to be whether the individual perceives the participation to be legitimate. If the subordinate feels that pseudoparticipation is being implemented—that is, that the superior is giving the subordinate a chance to speak but not a chance to be involved in the actual setting of objectives—productivity will decline. Thus legitimate participation must include involvement not only in the setting of objectives but also in the selection of the means used to reach them.

Over a five-year period Carroll and Tosi completed an intensive study of MBO as it was implemented in the Black and Decker Manufacturing Company. Many of the results in this study have been confirmed by other researchers analyzing MBO in a large urban community service organization (Straub, Sorensen, and Babcock 1976). Some of the most important findings in the Carroll and Tosi study, which confirm the previous research, were these:

1. As goals increased in perceived clarity, importance, and relevance, subordinate managers were more positive toward the MBO program.
2. As the frequency of performance reviews increased, there was an

increase in favorable attitudes toward MBO, better superior-subordinate relations, and higher accomplishment of goals.

3. The more positively the subordinate viewed the superior, the more likely he or she was to have positive attitudes toward MBO.
4. Superiors seemed to carry out the MBO process more effectively when they perceived top-management support of the program.

However, both research and the actual implementation of MBO programs indicate that this planning system has some serious limitations, which we now examine.

Limitations Even in the Carroll and Tosi study, which concluded that MBO is a useful and important management program, some problems developed during the actual implementation phase (see Table 5–2). The major problem was the excessive formal requirements of the MBO system: the process of completing forms, updating changes, and providing other information to the personnel unit monitoring the MBO program.

And there are many other limitations of MBO. It may be difficult for superiors and subordinates to establish goals jointly and to create an atmosphere in which the subordinate is considered to be a peer of the superior. In many hierarchical organizations the gulf between a superior and his or her subordinates may be too wide to cross. Steven

TABLE 5–2
Problems and Disadvantages Associated with MBO (Black and Decker Study, 48 Managers)

Problem	*Percentage of managers recognizing the problem*
Formal requirements are excessive (completing forms, updating changes, etc.).	43.7
MBO is not used to full potential.	20.8
MBO does not consider different goals for different jobs and levels.	14.5
I never get good feedback.	14.5
I was never really involved in the program.	14.5
It is undesirable to commit oneself to goals formally.	10.5
MBO does not provide information about personal characteristics such as innate ability and motivation.	4.2
There were no real problems.	37.5

Source: Adapted with permission of Macmillan Publishing Co., Inc. from Stephen J. Carroll, Jr., and Henry L. Tosi, Jr., *Management by Objectives* (New York: Macmillan, 1973), p. 26. Copyright © 1973, Macmillan Publishing Co., Inc.

Kerr (1972) doubts whether it is possible for unequals to develop goals jointly:

> The supposition that the superior can comfortably go from "boss-judge" to "friend-helper" and back again is central to MBO. . . . The research literature provides abundant evidence that hierarchical status differences produce some very predictable effects upon interaction patterns, subordinate defensiveness and quantity and quality of communications, which "stack the deck" against joint goals set by unequals. *(Kerr 1972, p. 39)*

In one large and conservative organization that does not like to fire managers openly, this problem has undermined the entire approach. Rather than firing the subordinate outright, the superior will get him to agree to a set of unrealistic objectives that could not possibly be attained. After six months or a year, the superior advises the subordinate to seek work elsewhere. Subordinates in the organization have become wise to this misuse of MBO, and their reactions have considerably weakened its implementation.

Another limitation of MBO relates to organizations that operate in volatile or unstable external environments. Such organizations must manage with imprecise goals (directional planning); MBO, which attempts to develop specific goals and objectives, is usually not appropriate in these situations.

Finally, the proper use of MBO requires that managers understand the MBO approach thoroughly and allot sufficient time to implement it properly. However, many organizations have treated MBO as a panacea that can be put into force almost immediately, without actively involving the lower levels of the organization in its development. For instance, one government agency with 6000 employees created an office of top-level staff planners who outlined 275 goals for the various units in the organizations. The organizational units were not involved in the construction of these goals, and the MBO program failed miserably.

Advantages

The advantages of MBO outweigh the disadvantages. We have already identified one major advantage—namely, that MBO is a rational system that is relatively easy for everyone in the organization to understand. Also, MBO seeks to link actual job performance or the accomplishment of objectives directly to the rewards that individuals receive. Thus MBO is an organizationwide planning system that gives major consideration to the motivation of subordinates.

Further, MBO is a direct aid to managers in performing their jobs. Many organizations fail because their managers really do not know what goals and objectives they are supposed to accomplish; under MBO these goals and objectives are spelled out precisely. And even when an organization must plan without goals (directional planning),

MBO can be used with modifications; managers may at least begin to think within a framework of goals and objectives and specify them whenever possible.

In short, the research does suggest that the proper use of MBO is related to positive changes in attitudes, behavior, and actual job performance. However, organizations must be careful to implement MBO correctly if the system is to be successful.

The Future of MBO

Anthony Raia and Gerard Rossy (1979) have surveyed fifty MBO experts about its future. Three groups were represented: academics, management consultants, and practicing managers with experience in using MBO. The consensus was that, although the use of MBO in the public and not-for-profit sectors will continue to increase significantly over the next twenty years, it will be employed most heavily in the private sector. One possible reason for this prediction is that public and not-for-profit sectors still manage without goals or with diffuse goals to a large extent, thus making some aspects of MBO inappropriate.

The experts also concluded that MBO will be increasingly linked to strategic planning and individual bonuses. This prediction parallels our discussion of the organizational planning process, which, if completed successfully, requires effective development of strategies. And according to the experts, the use of MBO will continue to grow, because the United States will face an increasing shortage of natural resources. In addition, management education will continue to expand, thus making managers more sophisticated and interested in approaches such as MBO.

In short, we can expect MBO to be with us for a long time. Admittedly organizations will need to tailor MBO to their own distinct problems, and different types of MBO systems will develop. But the basic features of MBO that we have described will be used in many organizations in the future.

STRATEGIC FAILURES

As we have seen, strategies represent overall plans of actions that organizations develop in order to accomplish their mission or missions. Very frequently the outcomes of these strategies are spectacular failures. In this section we describe some major strategic failures.

CASE RCA and IBM

In the early 1960s Robert Sarnoff and other top managers at RCA decided to expand their computer operations and compete directly against IBM in the midsize computer market. At that time RCA operated a small but profitable computer business that covered one percent of the midsize market. Sarnoff wanted to expand this percentage to ten, which meant direct competition with IBM.

To accomplish this goal, Sarnoff hired a top executive from IBM to direct a new subsystem at RCA. Other IBM executives and engineers soon followed him. RCA management poured millions of dollars into the effort. RCA was confident that it would be successful and was relying heavily on the knowledge and expertise of the former IBM engineers, who felt they could produce a computer superior to anything that IBM might develop.

Finally RCA announced that its new line of computers was ready and that they were faster and less costly than the comparable models at IBM. However, RCA immediately began to run into difficulty with its long-term customers, who found that the old computers were not compatible with the new and were forced to replace completely their old systems. RCA might have overcome this problem if it had kept a sufficient number of its experienced engineers and computer specialists. However, many of these individuals quit working for RCA when they realized that the newly hired engineers and computer specialists from IBM were receiving more favorable treatment.

A few months after RCA had announced the availability of its new line of computers, IBM also unveiled a competitive line. The IBM computers were faster, less costly, and more flexible than the RCA computers. Because of the trouble it was having with its long-term customers and the increased competition, RCA decided to leave the computer industry entirely and take a tax write-off of $450 million in 1969, the highest tax write-off in the history of American business.

CASE
Itel and Lloyd's of London

IBM also played a key role in the current troubles of two large organizations, Lloyd's of London and Itel Corporation. Lloyd's is a broker for many insurance companies that are willing to underwrite very risky projects. It was founded in the eighteenth century on the basis of an innovative idea: insuring oceangoing ships. Premiums paid by all ships would more than pay for the losses incurred if a few sank, and there was practically no danger that a great number of ships would sink at the same time. Since that time Lloyd's has insured high-risk enterprises in the same manner.

However, in the early 1970s Lloyd's moved away from insuring against disaster and began to insure computer-leasing companies against ordinary business risk. Itel Corporation, founded only in 1967, is involved in all types of leasing activities, particularly computer leasing. Its innovative leasing practices produced spectacular success; in 1977 its revenues approached $1 billion. However, Itel's innovative practices in leasing computers almost bankrupted the company. Ordinarily organizations leasing computers sign a seven-year agreement with the leasing company, but they can cancel the lease after three years. Lloyd's insured Itel and some smaller leasing companies; however, Lloyd's added one major item to its contracts: It agreed to cover the losses of the leasing companies if leasing contracts were canceled after three years.

The computer industry is dynamic, and innovations are constantly coming onto the market. IBM recently shocked the market by introducing new types of computers that are faster and more flexible than their predecessors. Consequently, many companies canceled their leases with the leasing companies after three years so that they could use the new equipment.

The result has been a fiasco for Itel, for smaller leasing companies, and for Lloyd's of London. Under the generous contracts that Lloyd's signed with the leasing companies, it owes over $2 billion to the leasing companies; when the final figures are computed, Lloyd's may actually owe over $4 billion. Lloyd's is contesting the claims of these leasing companies in court, and proceedings may drag on for years. In the meantime, Itel sales have slipped disastrously, companies have canceled Itel computer leases en masse, and the future is bleak: Itel now owns a large inventory of outdated computers and has an insufficient cash flow to continue operating on a greatly reduced basis.

CASE The Edsel

Every car buff in the United States knows about the Edsel, a stylish car the Ford Motor Company manufactured in the late 1950s. Ford had great expectations for the Edsel but eventually took it out of production and declared a pretax loss of $350 million.

Why did this happen? When the prototype of the Edsel was unveiled at a meeting of top managers at Ford in 1952, they stood up and cheered. Such an enthusiastic display never occurred at Ford before or since the introduction of the Edsel. However, the Korean War intervened, and consumer tastes changed dramatically. Small and inexpensive cars became very popular. Ford executives did not closely monitor these changes in tastes; the Edsel was introduced in 1957, and it was simply unsuitable for the changed market. Although other reasons were also important, failure to monitor changes in consumer tastes resulted in a strategic failure at Ford.

CASE Duke Tobacco

James Duke was a successful entrepreneur who founded the Duke Tobacco Company in the late nineteenth century; Duke University is named after him. He made his fortune by procuring long-term leases on machines that allowed mass production of cigarettes. Duke was the only entrepreneur who possessed these machines, and hence he was able to charge considerably less for cigarettes than his competitors, who were forced to produce hand-rolled cigarettes. In addition,

Duke integrated his organization vertically, controlling all aspects of the enterprise from the actual production to the actual sale of cigarettes. These two factors, mass production and vertical integration, became the basis of his considerable success.

Duke decided to manufacture cigars on a mass basis and implement vertical integration once again. He established a chain of United Cigar Stores throughout the United States, some of which are still in existence. However, his strategy with cigars was a dismal failure and almost bankrupted him. Again the reason was customer taste. Cigar smokers are similar to wine drinkers—that is, they have idiosyncratic tastes and do not like bland uniformity. Such idiosyncrasy is not a major factor among cigarette smokers. Unfortunately, consumers generally felt that Duke's cigars were bland, and they simply stopped buying them. Thus a strategic plan that was very successful in one situation proved to be very unsuccessful in another.

CASE
Chinese Fast-Food Chain*

Thus far we have described catastrophic failures involving large firms. However, many small firms also fail because of defects in their strategic plans.

As an example we shall consider a group of Chinese entrepreneurs who decided to open a Chinese fast-food chain in the shopping malls around Washington, D.C. They reasoned that this strategic plan would lead to success, because Chinese food ranks just behind French and Italian food in popularity for non-American food.

The six entrepreneurs were related to one another, and each of them put up $5000 to start the corporation. However, although they published a handsome brochure to attract other investors, they were unable to do so. Investors primarily questioned the wisdom of putting money into a family-run enterprise. Later on these blood relationships caused additional difficulties; some of the owners worked harder than others, but it was difficult to criticize and correct the situation because of the close family ties.

Eventually the six entrepreneurs were able to borrow $70,000 from the bank, giving them a total of $100,000. Initially they had difficulty selling their concept to the owners of the suburban shopping malls, which usually housed a regular Chinese restaurant. Eventually they did open one outlet, and they gradually persuaded other suburban malls to rent space to them. Favorable publicity in a long article about their chain in the style section of the *Washington Post* also helped their cause and attracted many new customers to their outlet.

However, their troubles began when they deviated from their strategic plan—the concept of a Chinese fast-food chain—for the bicentennial of the United States in 1976. Many activities were sched-

*Courtesy of Y. A. Lau.

uled to be held in Washington, D.C. The entrepreneurs spent $30,000 to purchase custom-designed pushcarts in order to sell their food outdoors. At the opening ceremonies on the Fourth of July, sales were brisk. However, the predicted boom in visitors to Washington never materialized, and the entrepreneurs also had difficulty obtaining reliable pushcart salespersons. Eventually they decided to sell the carts but could not find any buyers, primarily because the carts could not be used for any purpose other than selling Chinese fast food. They took a loss of $30,000.

The entrepreneurs estimated that they could have succeeded in completing their strategic plan if they still had $100,000, but they could not succeed with only the remaining $70,000. Creditors started to demand payment, some of the original owners lost interest in the corporation, and eventually it went out of business.

SUMMARY

Planning involves the following activities:

1. Using environmental forecasting to select the basic mission(s) of the organization. That is, what business is the organization in and what is it not in?
2. Developing desired outcomes—long-term goals and short-term objectives—that the organization seeks to attain in light of its mission(s) and environmental forecasts.
3. Developing means—strategies and tactics—to achieve these goals and objectives.
4. Updating forecasts periodically to take account of environmental changes.
5. Possibly changing missions, goals, and objectives in light of these revised forecasts.
6. Implementing policies, procedures, and rules in light of the mission(s), strategies, tactics, long-term goals, and short-term objectives that the organization has selected.

It is possible to outline and describe stages in the organizational planning process. However, stages in this process frequently occur simultaneously.

There are three general types of forecasting methods: qualitative forecasting methods, time series analysis and projection, and mathematical models. Qualitative methods include the Delphi technique, panel consensus, and visionary forecasts. The moving average and trend projection constitute two prominent examples of time series analysis and projection. Important mathematical models are regression and the diffusion index.

As the case studies in the chapter indicate, organizations can experience spectacular strategic failures. To combat the probability of such failure, organizations attempt to forecast the future. However, as Utterback has shown, the amount of time and money an organization should invest in forecasting is largely dependent on two factors in the external environment: the static-dynamic dimension and the simple-complex dimension.

While it would be preferable to plan with specific or precise goals, it is frequently difficult if not impossible to do so. Hence many organizations manage with imprecise or diffuse goals; these goals provide only a sense of direction (directional planning) for individuals and subunits. However, some departments or subunits within the same organization, such as production, may be able to plan with specific goals, while others, such as research and development, may have to rely on directional planning.

An organizationwide planning system based on the concepts of goals and objectives is Management by Objectives (MBO). Under MBO top management specifies a small number of long-term goals and short-term objectives that each succeeding level in the organization specifies more precisely. Thus goals and objectives are linked throughout the organization. Also, if possible, subordinates are involved in the development of the objectives they must accomplish; there are frequent performance reviews; the subordinate is allowed some degree of freedom in selecting the means to attain his or her objectives; and there are sufficient rewards for attaining objectives.

Research generally supports the efficacy of the MBO system. However, there are limitations; sometimes it is difficult to specify goals precisely, and frequently there are excessive reporting requirements. Nevertheless, the advantages seem to outweigh the disadvantages, and expert opinion suggests that the use of MBO will spread.

DISCUSSION QUESTIONS

1. How do goals and objectives differ from one another?
2. Identify an organization that you understand thoroughly. Define its mission or missions, its strategy or strategies, its tactics, its long-term goals, and its short-term objectives.
3. When should an organization plan with imprecise or diffuse goals?
4. What is the relationship between forecasting and the organizational planning process?
5. What are some of the critical factors that an automobile manufacturer will consider in the formulation of a long-range forecast? In a short-range forecast?
6. Can James Utterback's typology help management decide how much time and effort to invest in forecasting? Why or why not?
7. Is the degree of environmental uncertainty facing IBM less or more than that facing other companies in the computer industry? Explain.

CRITICAL INCIDENTS

NOTE: These critical incidents can be used by the whole class with the case observational method (see Appendix A) or used for thought and discussion by individual class members.

1. The state of Indiana faced an alarming problem around 1965. Indiana has one of the nation's largest medical schools in the country in its capital city of Indianapolis. However, the state was experiencing a severe shortage of physicians. The Medical School studied this situation and discovered that more than half of the graduating medical students were leaving the state for internships and residency opportunities. Thus, at least in the medical field, Indiana was suffering a brain drain.

Some leaders in the state began to emphasize the need to build an additional medical school, which experts estimated would cost at least $250 million in 1965 dollars to staff, build, and equip. Other leaders were reluctant to make such an expensive investment, especially since the additional medical school might not solve the problem but exacerbate it. The number of graduating doctors would increase, but the new medical school would not be able to provide many additional internships and residency opportunities, especially in proportion to the number of graduates. Medical students would still seek internships and residency opportunities outside the state.

QUESTIONS: What are some of the options or alternatives the state of Indiana could pursue? Which option do you feel is superior? What do you think the state of Indiana eventually did to solve this planning problem?

2. During the early 1980s domestic automobile sales plummeted as the demand for the larger, fuel-inefficient, domestically produced models collapsed. Capitalizing on the shortage of domestically produced, fuel-efficient models, the market share of imported cars increased to 25.2 percent of total domestic sales during March 1980, from historical levels of 15 to 18 percent.

As the sales of imported models increased during 1979, some domestic producers, some members of Congress, and the United Auto Workers Union began a campaign to persuade foreign automakers to start producing cars in the United States. The Japanese automakers, who had experienced substantial market share increases in the American auto market, were reluctant to commit themselves to manufacturing in the United States because of uncertainty about lower quality levels and higher costs of American plants, excess auto-producing capacity at home, and the possibility of market share erosion in the middle 1980s due to new models expected from General Motors, Ford, and Chrysler. On the other hand, a reluctance to build auto plants in the United States could result in the establishment of barriers to the American domestic markets in the form of import quotas or higher tariffs.

Negotiations have dragged on with the largest Japanese producers, Nissan Motor Company (Datsun) and Toyota Motor Company, who are noncommittal about producing cars in the United States. Meanwhile, the United Auto Workers and certain members of Congress have become more impatient and have begun to press for mandatory import quotas.

QUESTION: What recommendations would you make to the management of Nissan and Toyota?

SUGGESTED READINGS

Sloan, Alfred. *My Years with General Motors.* Ed. J. McDonald and C. Stevens. Garden City, N.Y.: Doubleday, 1963, 472 pages, available in hardback and paperback.

Sloan has written a long but fascinating study of the creation and development of General Motors. This book contains some excellent material on planning.

Summer, Charles. *Strategic Behavior in Business and Government.* Boston: Little, Brown, 1980, 377 pages, paperback.

Summer has written an excellent introduction to strategic planning.

6 Planning Techniques

BREAK-EVEN ANALYSIS
CAPITAL BUDGETING
LINEAR PROGRAMMING
NETWORKS
PROBABILISTIC MODELS
IMPLICATIONS FOR MANAGERS
SUMMARY
DISCUSSION QUESTIONS
PROBLEMS
SUGGESTED READINGS

PERFORMANCE OBJECTIVES

1. To demonstrate how managers apply deterministic planning methods when the input data are certain and probabilistic planing methods when the input data are uncertain.
2. To describe several prominent deterministic and probabilistic planning methods.
3. To show how deterministic planning methods can supplement the use of probabilistic planning methods.
4. To describe the practical implications of the deterministic and probabilistic methods for managers.

To be successful, a manager must understand and control the complex world in which he or she operates. In many situations the manager has recourse to standard decision-making techniques he or she can apply to problems that can be quantified. Although a staff analyst may perform the calculations, the line manager must be sufficiently familiar with the techniques to use the results with confidence. Thus staff analysts and line managers frequently work together. The manager frames the problem in general terms and the analyst develops a statistical-mathematical model of it which he or she can then solve.

In general, there are two kinds of models the manager can employ to solve quantitative problems: deterministic and probabilistic. In the *deterministic* model the law of chance plays no role. A deterministic model applies when all factors involved can be quantified exactly. For instance, the formula profit = revenue minus costs represents a deterministic model since all the factors are quantities that can be determined exactly. The solution determined from this formula is also an exact quantity.

The *probabilistic* model takes account of chance or random factors that exist under conditions of uncertainty or risk. Both data and solutions are expressed as probabilities rather than certainties. For example, automobile insurance companies have developed tables that profile the probability of car accidents for various subgroups of car owners in the population. In probabilistic models factors are quantified, but they are recognized not as exact but as most likely.

This chapter describes several deterministic and probabilistic planning methods that managers employ as aids to their decision making. In addition, the chapter shows how some deterministic planning methods may supplement the use of probabilistic planning methods.

BREAK-EVEN ANALYSIS

Managers want to make money. To do so, they must exceed their *break-even point,* which is the level of operations at which a product's total revenue equals its total production cost. Total revenue depends on the market demand for a particular product, and it varies with the product's price. Total costs vary with the number of units of a product an organization manufactures. Thus the break-even point varies with the number and cost of units produced and the number and price of units sold. The objective of *break-even analysis* is to determine the *optimum* break-even point, that is, the point at which profits will be highest. This is done by considering the costs associated with each level of demand and the demand for a particular product at varying prices.

As suggested by this discussion, break-even analysis involves three steps. First, managers examine the costs of the organization to determine the relationship between cost and volume of output. Second, they determine the number of units that must be sold to cover costs at a specific price per unit. Third, they evaluate the effect of demand on profitability at various prices.

Costs The break-even model depends heavily on the distinction between fixed and variable costs. *Fixed costs (FC)* are relatively stable over time; for example, property taxes and rent essentially stay the same no matter how output changes. *Variable costs (VC)* change with the level of output; for example, the materials and labor used in the production process cost more as more units are produced.

Let us consider the case of Cumberland Industries, a hypothetical firm whose sole product is bronze candleholders. This firm has fixed costs of \$180,000. Its variable costs are \$6 for each candleholder produced. Total costs *(TC)* equal total fixed costs plus total variable costs. For Cumberland Industries total costs for 100,000 units are \$180,000 + \$600,000 (\$6 per unit), or \$780,000.

Price Without knowing the *selling price* of Cumberland Industries' product, we cannot determine the company's *profitability* (or lack thereof). To figure profitability, we must first know total revenue, from which we deduct costs. Let us assume that each bronze candleholder retails for \$25. The retailer pays Cumberland Industries \$15 per unit. Let us also assume that there are no quantity discounts. Consequently, each bronze candleholder generates \$15 revenue for Cumberland Industries. From the \$15 brought in by one candleholder, Cumberland Industries must first pay the \$6 variable cost. The rest of the \$15 must go toward paying off the company's fixed costs, until enough candleholders have been sold to cover all the fixed costs (\$180,000). At that point, the break-even point, *total revenue (TR)* equals total costs, and profits equal zero.

To determine the break-even point, or the *sales volume (Q)* necessary to cover the total and fixed costs, we use the following formula:

$$\begin{aligned} TR &= TFC + TVC \\ \$15(Q) &= \$180{,}000 + \$6(Q) \\ \$9(Q) &= \$180{,}000 \\ Q &= 20{,}000 \text{ bronze candleholders} \end{aligned}$$

This is the break-even point (see Figure 6–1).

Demand Let us now assume that Cumberland Industries is able to sell 25,000 candleholders per year when it charges \$15 per candleholder. At this *demand* level total profit *(TP)* will be the amount left over after fixed and variable costs have been paid.

$$TR = TFC + TVC + TP$$
$$(\$15)(25{,}000) = \$180{,}000 + (\$6)(25{,}000) + TP$$
$$\$375{,}000 = \$180{,}000 + \$150{,}000 + TP$$
$$\$375{,}000 = \$330{,}000 + TP$$
$$\$45{,}000 = TP$$

While the profit of $45,000 is good, it may be possible to generate even more. Market research into the demand for bronze candleholders indicates that annual sales would vary with prices as follows:

Price	$12	$15	$17	$19
Annual Demand	32,000	25,000	21,000	17,000

To determine the price that will maximize profits, we construct a price-demand table, as shown in Table 6–1.

Table 6–1 indicates that Cumberland Industries will reap the highest profits if it charges $17 per bronze candleholder to retailers. Although Cumberland Industries could charge the retailers $19 per candleholder, demand would fall to 17,000, causing a decline in total profits. Hence Cumberland Industries should increase its price per candleholder from $15 to $17 in order to make the highest profits.

In general, break-even analysis provides the decision maker with an overview of the effect of price on profit, which is helpful when he or she attempts to set the price of a product.

FIGURE 6–1
Break-even Chart

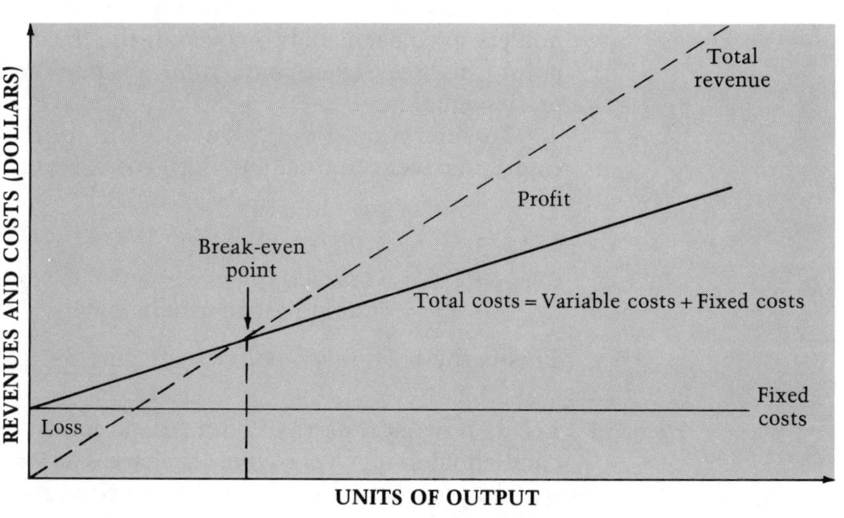

TABLE 6–1
Effect of Price on Demand for Bronze Candleholders

Price	*Demand*	*TFC*	*TVC*	*TC*	*TR*	*TP*
$12	32,000	$180,000	$192,000	$372,000	$384,000	$12,000
15	25,000	180,000	150,000	330,000	375,000	45,000
17	21,000	180,000	126,000	306,000	357,000	51,000
19	17,000	180,000	102,000	282,000	323,000	41,000

However, pricing decisions are influenced by many other factors, including competitive conditions, trade relations, and level of capital investment. The manager must also take these factors into account when he or she sets prices.

CAPITAL BUDGETING

Capital budgeting provides a set of techniques a manager can use to evaluate the relative attractiveness of various projects in which a lump payment is made to generate a stream of earnings over a future period. Examples of capital-budgeting projects include an investment in a new machine that will increase profits by reducing costs, an investment of a sum of money into an advertising campaign to increase sales (and profits), and an investment in research and development that will improve the product and result in increased profits due to higher sales.

Let us consider now the case of Franklin Enterprises, which has $10,000 to invest and three possible ways to invest it. Management can put the $10,000 into new production machinery that will save the company $3,000 per year for the next five years; it can spend the $10,000 on revised package graphics that will increase profits by $4,500 for the first two years and by $2,000 for the following three years; or it can invest in research that will result in product improvements that will increase earnings by $1,000 in the first three years and by $6,000 in the fourth and fifth years. (Obviously these figures are estimates, but we will assume that they are reliable.) All three projects have an economic life of five years.

Several issues confront the decision maker in evaluating the three projects. First, we can see that all three projects require an initial investment of $10,000 and will return $15,000 in additional earnings within five years. Second, we can see that the projects have different rates for their earning flows. Project B generates its highest earnings in the first two years, and project C generates most of its earnings in its last two years. Project A's earnings occur uniformly over the five-year period. Finally, the three projects differ in the time needed to recover the initial investment, which is called the *payback period (P)*.

TABLE 6–2
Payback Method of Capital Budgeting

	A	*B*	*C*
Investment *(I)*	$10,000	$10,000	$10,000
Annual earnings *(E)*	$ 3,000	$ 4,500 1st 2 yr $ 2,000 last 3 yr	$ 1,000 1st 3 yr $ 6,000 last 2 yr
Payback period *($P = I/E$)*	3.33 yr.	2.50 yr	4.17 yr

It can be determined by the formula $P = I/E$, in which P equals the original investment *(I)* divided by the annual increase in earnings *(E)*. The payback periods for the three projects in our example are given in Table 6–2. We can see from Table 6–2 that project B has the shortest payback period. In general, managers prefer the project with the shortest payback period, since they are averse to risk and like to avoid the uncertainty of long-term investments.

LINEAR PROGRAMMING

Linear programming was developed about the time of World War II to solve large-scale allocation and scheduling problems. In recent years the use of linear programming has increased dramatically, in large part because of the availability of computers. In essence, *linear programming* focuses on either maximizing some objective function, such as profits, or minimizing some objective function, such as costs. Linear programming involves the solution of linear equations and is appropriate when the manager must allocate scarce resources to competing projects or objectives. Examples of this type of problem include finding the most advantageous product mix, allocating advertising budgets, and allocating machinery and personnel to various projects.

Suppose that Gray Industries has a division that manufactures two products, a hand lawn mower and a power mower. The hand mower contributes $20 per unit to profit after variable costs have been paid. The power mower contributes $120 per unit to profit after variable costs have been paid. Gray Industries employs two resources in the production of both lawn mowers, assembly time and testing time. The hand mower requires 1 hour of assembly time and 2 hours of testing time per unit of output; the power mower needs 5 hours of assembly time and 2 hours of testing time per unit. A total of 40 man-hours of assembly time and 60 man-hours of testing time are available per day. Gray Industries' objective is to maximize profits. Hence the problem is to determine the number of units of each product that will maximize daily profit.

This simplified problem can be solved without the aid of a computer. However, managers typically face complex situations in which they must allocate scarce resources to several products. In addition, several resources are normally required to produce each of these products. To solve complex problems, the manager can use a standard program, the *Simplex Method,* which is available on most large computers. The Simplex Method also provides other important information such as the value to the firm of additional resources the managers might want to buy, and the effect that changes in product profitability and resource availabilities will have on the ideal product mix.

Managers can also use the *Transportation Model,* a distinctive linear-programming approach for the solution of warehousing problems, allocation problems, demand-supply imbalance, and location analysis problems. A typical problem might involve a manufacturing firm that operates three plants and three distribution centers. The three manufacturing plants are in Atlanta, Boston, and Chicago. The distribution centers are in Kansas City, Louisville, and Minneapolis. Monthly demands, in cases, at each distribution center are 1000, 2000, and 3000 for Kansas City, Louisville, and Minneapolis, respectively. Production capacities in cases per month are 1800, 1900, and 2300 at Atlanta, Boston, and Chicago, respectively. Variable costs per case, including variable manufacturing costs and distribution costs, between each plant and distribution center are shown in Table 6–3. The goal of this firm is to minimize variable costs.

The solution of this problem is beyond the scope of this textbook (methods for solving such problems can be found in standard textbooks on operations research). After obtaining an optimal solution, management can then calculate the total costs per month that would occur if variable costs were minimized.

In some situations it might be feasible to supplement the transportation model with capital budgeting. To meet an expected fifty percent increase in business, the firm described above might evaluate the relative attractiveness of two options: building a new plant in Dayton or expanding the capacity of its Chicago plant. Management would calculate optimal solutions under both options and then would

TABLE 6–3
Variable Costs per Case

	Destinations		
Sources	*Kansas City*	*Louisville*	*Minneapolis*
Atlanta	$ 7.00	$4.00	$6.00
Boston	10.00	5.00	8.00
Chicago	4.50	3.00	5.50

apply a capital-budgeting technique such as the payback method to determine the best investment opportunity.

In summary, linear programming is a powerful tool for managerial decision making. It has two major functions: It establishes optimal operating conditions and pinpoints areas that may need managerial attention, and it identifies the sensitivity of operating variables to changes in conditions. This information allows managers to focus attention on areas sensitive to change, where their input is most important.

NETWORKS

During World War I the United States Army had serious difficulties in planning and controlling the execution of interrelated activities. The army asked Henry Gantt, one of the major figures in the school of scientific management, to attack this problem. His work led to the development of the Gantt chart, which became very popular and is still in use today. It was an early predecessor of PERT and CPM, two important techniques we discuss in this chapter. Techniques discussed in this section are frequently termed *networks,* because they focus on completing a project or task involving interrelated activities.

Gantt Chart

A *Gantt Chart* is a graphic representation of the work flow through the various departments in an organization. It enables the manager to tell at a glance the status of both the projects that are under way and the activities and performance of the operating departments. The Gantt Chart shown in Figure 6.2 represents the work flow in Print-Rite, a custom print shop. The horizontal lines indicate the current

FIGURE 6–2
Gantt Chart for Print-Rite

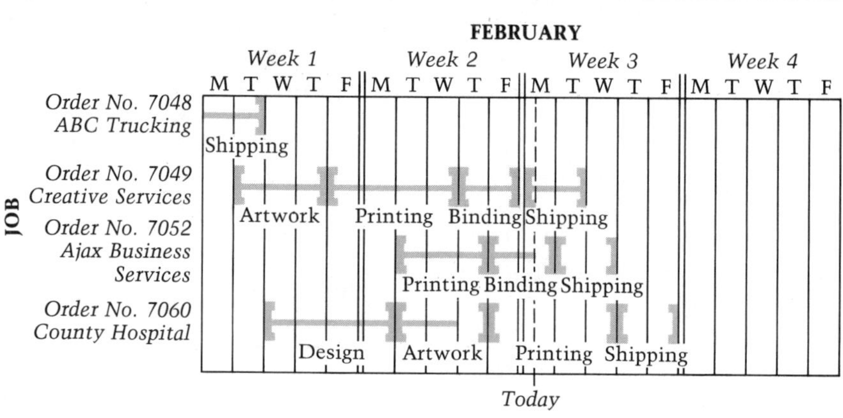

Source: *Changing Times*, July 1974, p. 14. Reprinted with permission from *Changing Times Magazine*, © 1974. Kiplinger Washington Editors, Inc., July 1974.

"You will notice there are ten of us and only eight chairs. Now, since we must cut our staff, here is my plan . . . ."

status of projects and the brackets indicate scheduled dates for a project to be in a certain department. Everything is evaluated in terms of the dotted vertical line, "today." From the Gantt Chart, we see that order No. 7048 was shipped the week before last, because the horizontal line terminates at "shipping." Order No. 7049 was shipped ahead of schedule (the bracket shows that it was scheduled to be shipped tomorrow but the horizontal line shows that it has already been shipped), order No. 7052 is in the binding department and is on schedule and artwork preparation is underway for order No. 7060 but the project is behind schedule. Management should concentrate its attention on order No. 7060 to complete the artwork and get it back on schedule if the shipping date of this coming Friday is to be met.

PERT and CPM

When a project consists of many interrelated steps or activities, PERT (program evaluation and review technique) or CPM (critical path method) may make it easier to plan. Both techniques specify a series of interrelated steps necessary to complete a specific project. They became widely known during the 1960s because PERT was the major planning technique for the Polaris missile program. To build the Polaris missile, management developed an intricate plan that consisted of a series of interrelated steps, some of which could be implemented simultaneously and some of which had to be finished before others could begin.

TABLE 6–4
Milestones for Project 81

Milestone	Description	Expected time (in weeks)	Preceding milestone
A	Formulate product	6	None
B	Create packaging, structural design	4	None
C	Design package graphics	10	B must be completed 4 weeks before graphics are complete
D	Design promotional literature	5	C
E	Modify production equipment	20	A
F	Inform sales force	8	D
G	Procure raw materials	6	A
H	Procure packaging materials	12	C
I	Produce initial inventories	3	E,G,H
J	Inform middlemen	4	F
K	Ship to retailers	1	I,J

These two techniques, PERT and CPM, are very similar to one another. However, there is one major difference, namely, the time estimates used. With CPM the time estimates are certain, while with PERT the time estimates are probabilistic. Because the techniques are otherwise similar, the balance of the discussion focuses on CPM, a deterministic planning model.

In its simplest form CPM consists of laying out or diagramming the flow of activities in a project in order to identify all the possible sequences of steps between the beginning and the end of the project. The longest sequence is the *critical path,* which determines the completion time of the project. Once it is known, managers can focus on those particular activities that are likely to delay the project.

The first step in the CPM process is to identify every significant event that must happen for a project to be completed. After the identification of these events, called *milestones,* management must ascertain the *order* in which they must be completed and the *time* to be allotted to each of them. Each milestone is plotted on a chart so that the managers can pinpoint various possible sequences of milestones and the length of time it will take to complete each sequence. Managers then can calculate the total time that must be allocated for the completion of the entire project.

Let us assume that a roller skate manufacturer is developing a new kind of skateboard, a project tentatively entitled Project 81. The product manager must ensure that Project 81 is completed rapidly so the new skateboard can go on sale well before other companies start introducing competitive models. Information gathered on this project from various corporate subunits has indicated that eleven milestones are critical for producing the new skateboard (see Table 6–4).

The eleven milestones are plotted on a CPM chart in such a way that the project manager can see which ones must be completed before others can be started (see Figure 6–3). It is not necessary for all eleven milestones to be placed one after the other. Usually different parts of the project team will be working on different milestones at the same time. For example, the production department will work on path A-E-I-K and path A-G-I-K, while the marketing department will focus on paths C-H-I-K and C-D-F-J-K. These two departments will be jointly responsible for path B-C-H-I-K.

Comparing the total time for each sequence or path indicates that the entire project will require 30 weeks, for the longest path is A-E-I-K (see Table 6–5). This sequence is called the critical path. Any delay in completing the milestones in the critical path will stall the entire project by the length of the delay. If problems develop so that product formulation (milestone A) requires 10 weeks rather than 6 weeks, the critical path A-E-I-K will increase to 34 weeks (see Tables 6–4 and 6–5).

If the critical path can be shortened significantly, it may no longer be critical. It might be possible to complete production equipment (milestone E) in 2 weeks rather than 20 weeks, so the path A-E-I-K would become 6 + 2 + 3 + 1 or 12, rather than 30. If this occurred, path C-D-F-J-K (27 weeks) would become the critical path.

While CPM and PERT are not panaceas for all projects, they are useful managerial tools in diverse organizational settings. Through CPM and PERT managers can easily discover deviations from the time allotted to each milestone and take appropriate corrective action.

FIGURE 6–3
Project 81 CPM Chart
To determine the critical path for Project 81, one must identify all paths from the beginning to step K. These paths are described in Table 6–4. All times are expressed in weeks.

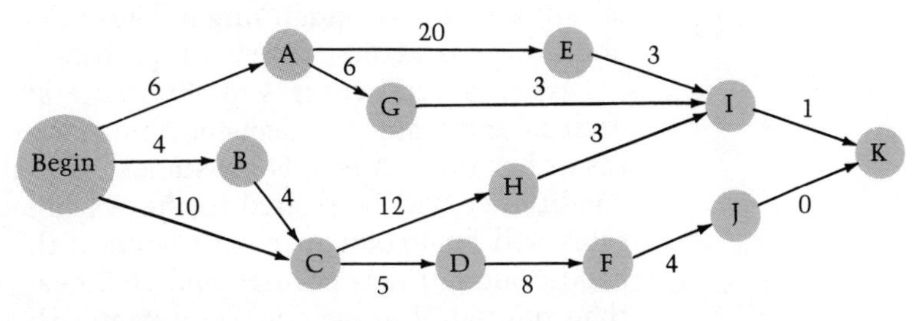

Additional Data needed

TABLE 6–5
Project 81 Paths

Path	*Time (in weeks)*	*Total time*
A-E-I-K	6 + 20 + 3 + 1	30
A-G-I-K	6 + 6 + 3 + 1	16
B-C-H-I-K	4 + 4 + 12 + 3 + 1	24
C-H-I-K	10 + 12 + 3 + 1	26
C-D-F-J-K	10 + 5 + 8 + 4 + 0	27
B-C-D-F-J-K	4 + 4 + 5 + 8 + 4 + 0	25

PROBABILISTIC MODELS

Managers prefer to make predictions that are certain and accurate; for this reason they use deterministic planning models whenever possible. However, the information available to the manager is often less than certain and highly probabilistic. For example, a forecast of next year's sales does involve some objective or certain estimates, but it also includes subjective guesses. To treat all information as precise and certain would inevitably lead managers to poor planning and subsequent unanticipated results. Thus managers must at times use probabilistic models.

In this section we describe some well-known probabilistic planning models. In addition, we show how some probabilistic models can be used in combination with deterministic models.

Expected Value

The expected value model is based on the concept of *probability,* which refers to the likelihood that an event will happen. Probability is expressed as a fraction or percentage. For example, there may be a 30 percent chance, or probability, that it will rain tomorrow. Some probabilities can be established *empirically* by observing some phenomenon over time. For instance, flipping a fair coin several times provides data the individual can use to predict the likelihood of either heads or tails in the future. Most events a manager needs to predict cannot be observed so conveniently, however. In those cases he or she can establish probability by estimating the likelihood of one event on the basis of previous similar ones. For example, from past experience an automobile salesman might figure that a family with six children and a dog has a 0.60 (60 percent) probability of buying a station wagon.

When several courses of action are available and the outcome of each is uncertain, the decision maker can use probabilities to select his or her final choice. For instance, the sales level of a new room air conditioner will be related to the warmness of the summer. Annual sales will be 40,000 air conditioners if the summer is hot, 28,000 air conditioners if it is normal, and 16,000 air conditioners if it is cooler than normal. Past experience indicates that the probability for a very warm summer is 0.3; for a normal summer, 0.5; and for a cool summer, 0.2. These three probabilities add up to 1.0, and there are no significant possibilities besides these three. These conditions are always necessary for use of the expected value technique.

The *expected value* for any event is the income it would produce times its probability. Adding the expected values of all possible events yields *expected sales,* the average level of sales that can be expected over the long run if the given probabilities hold (see Table 6–6). For the air conditioner described above expected sales for the summer are 29,200 air conditioners.

Having calculated expected sales of our air conditioners, we can then proceed with a break-even profitability analysis. Notice that in this situation we use a deterministic planning technique, break-even analysis, with a probabilistic planning technique, expected value.

Let us assume that each air conditioner generates \$250 in revenue (R) when sold by the manufacturer, that fixed costs (FC) are \$2,000,000 per year, and that variable costs (VC) per air conditioner are \$140. We can now calculate expected total profits (TP):

$$\begin{aligned} TR &= TFC + TVC + TP \\ (\$250)(29{,}200) &= \$2{,}000{,}000 + (\$140) \times (29{,}200) + TP \\ \$7{,}300{,}000 &= \$2{,}000{,}000 + \$4{,}088{,}000 + TP \\ \$7{,}300{,}000 &= \$6{,}088{,}000 + TP \\ \$1{,}212{,}000 &= TP \end{aligned}$$

This profitability analysis of air conditioner sales informs the manager that expected sales will be 29,200 units per year with an expected profit per year of \$1,212,000.

Waiting Line Analysis (Queuing)

Waiting line analysis is a technique that originated in the early 1900s. Waiting line analysis focuses on the speed with which units or individuals come into a queue and the speed with which they can be processed. It was developed by A. K. Erlang, a Danish telephone engineer who wanted to estimate the influence of fluctuating demand on

TABLE 6–6
Expected Value Model

Event	*Outcome (unit sales)* ×	*Probability* =	*Expected value of each alternative*
Hot summer	40,000	0.3	12,000 units
Normal summer	28,000	0.5	14,000 units
Cool summer	16,000	0.2	3,200 units
Expected annual sales			29,200 units

Note: The sales of an air conditioner will depend on how hot the summer is. Adding the expected value of each alternative yields expected sales for the summer.

automatic-dial switching equipment. Since World War II management has expanded the use of waiting line analysis to include a variety of problems, such as checkout lines, shipping or receiving docks, and the flow of work throughout an organization.

Let us suppose that the management of a ship-loading facility is faced with three choices because of increased business:

Build a single, low-speed facility in which ships must wait for several hours and sometimes days before being unloaded.

Build two low-speed facilities.

Build a single, high-speed facility in which ships would be unloaded very quickly.

Some of the factors that management must consider in solving this problem are the average arrival rate of ships per week; the average service rate or unloading rate of ships per week; the total number of facilities in the organization; the projected number of ships in the system; and the average waiting time of ships in the system. Many of these factors can be expressed only as probabilities. Hence queuing techniques can be applied to this problem to help the decision maker arrive at a choice.

Decision Trees

Another probabilistic model for planning is the *decision tree.* This technique is appropriate when a series of decisions must be made but the outcome of each is unknown.

As an illustration, let us assume that a toy manufacturer is in the process of deciding whether to market a new product, the Hijack Game. Management estimates that costs over the first three years will be $14 million. Revenues are projected to be either $30 million if competition does not materialize or $10 million if it does. The probability that competition will materialize is estimated to be 0.6, the probability that it will not, 0.4.

Calculating the expected revenue associated with the production of the Hijack Game produces the following results:

$$\text{expected revenue} = (0.4)(30) + (0.6)(10) = 12 + 6 = \$18 \text{ million}$$

As shown in Figure 6–4, the expected profit of not marketing the Hijack Game is zero. However, the expected profit of marketing the product is $4 million ($18 million gross income minus $14 million costs). Management might reasonably decide to manufacture the product on the basis of this information.

Simulation

The complexity of many problems precludes the use of either deterministic or probabilistic models of the type discussed thus far. When faced with complex problems, the analyst may resort to simulation

FIGURE 6–4
Decision Tree for Expected Profit on the Hijack Game

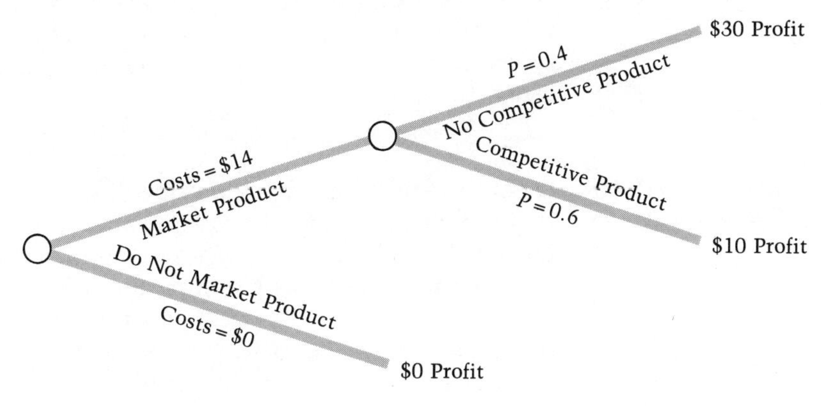

in order to obtain useful information. *Simulation* is a process of building, testing, and operating models of real world phenomena through the use of mathematical relationships that exist among critical factors. Figure 6–5 summarizes simulation methodology. Because large electronic computers have become accessible in recent years, management can now simulate complex situations to determine the best course of action.

The first step in a simulation is to define the problem. An example of such a definition might be this: Evaluate the flow of customer orders from the time they are received until the time the order is shipped and billed.

The second step, construction of the simulation model, requires a specification of all relevant steps, interactions among them, and decision rules that will be used in the process. For example, a relevant variable might be to forward the order to the warehouse. A decision rule might be to obtain credit department approval before forwarding to the warehouse.

In the third step management specifies the values of the variables and parameters or boundaries. In some cases management may assign values to the variables; in other instances management may employ probability distributions for assigning values.

Once management has identified the relevant variables and assigned values to them, the simulation can be completed. The results of one simulation may lead to a refinement of the analysis, and management may then complete additional simulations.

Because of the introduction of large-scale computers in the late

1950s and early 1960s, managers have begun to attack complex problems via simulation, problems that had previously been difficult to solve. For example, simulation has been used in the areas of complicated waiting lines, production processes, physical distribution systems, alternative corporate strategies, and product demand patterns.

IMPLICATIONS FOR MANAGERS

Deterministic methods are a valuable aid to the planning process. But their value to the manager is not limited to the specific answers determined by the method. These planning methods also provide the manager with fresh insights that allow him or her to redirect attention and efforts. For example, the Simplex Method of linear programming may help the manager to better understand the effect that changes in the firm's product mix will have on overall profitability. In another instance the examination of pricing, unit sales volume, and total profitability in break-even analysis should provide the manager with a more sophisticated understanding of pricing decisions.

An additional feature of the deterministic planning methods is that they help the manager to focus on critical issues. For example, capital-budgeting analysis enables the manager to identify the capital projects that are attractive to the firm. With this information, the manager can focus his or her energies on these projects rather than wasting time on what may later prove to be unattractive projects.

However, deterministic methods are suitable only if the input data are known with certainty. While it is often tempting for managers to assume that the world is certain and reliable, this assumption may be dangerous, for both conditions and outcomes are typically uncertain. Thus probabilistic planning models, because they reflect the state of the real world, are a valuable way for the manager to analyze a problem rationally.

In addition, probabilistic models enable the manager to quantify many decisions that otherwise could not be evaluated. The manager can assess the relative impact of several courses of action based on different assumptions, and he or she can redefine probabilities and hence outcomes when conditions change. This flexibility is valuable in actual decision-making situations. For example, a manager might select a risky rather than a conservative approach to a particular problem because its expected value is considerably higher.

However, probabilities should be used cautiously, for there is a chance that the actual outcome may be the least desirable one, regardless of its probability. For this reason a manager should always consider the impact on the organization of the least desirable event. If it would result in bankruptcy, a more cautious approach than the one suggested by quantitative techniques is advisable.

FIGURE 6–5
Simulation Methodology

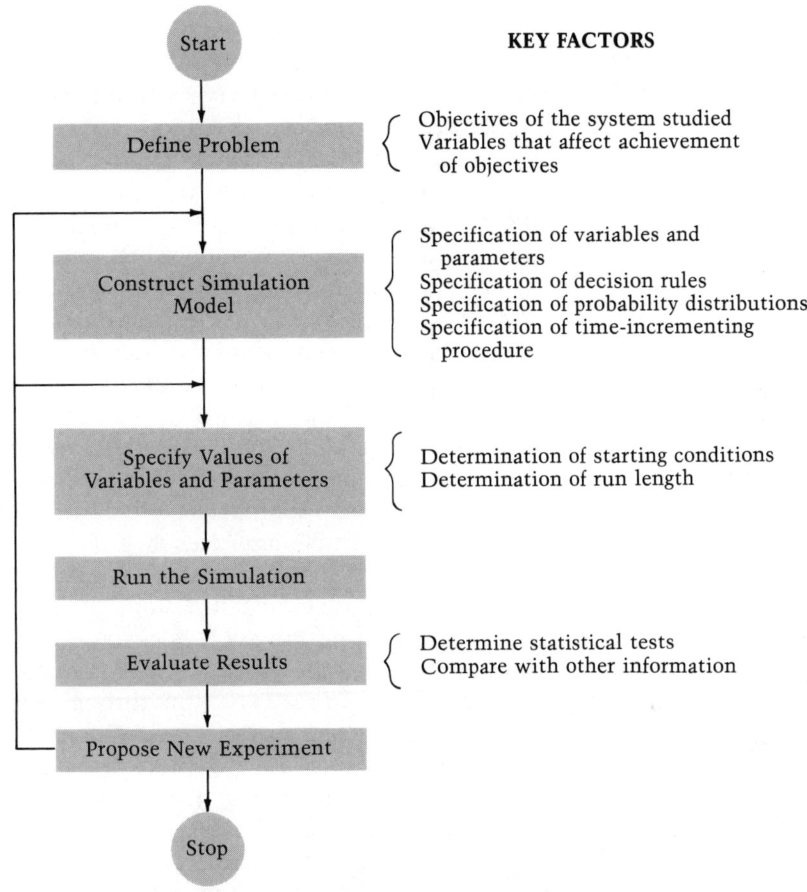

Source: Richard B. Chase and Nicholas J. Aquilano, *Production and Operations Management: A Life Cycle Approach* (Homewood, Ill.: Irwin, 1973), p. 384. © 1973 by Richard D. Irwin, Inc. Used by permission.

Clearly managerial judgment is critical when probabilistic models are employed. While the use of mathematical estimates to represent real events may create the impression that there is one best solution that the manager can determine, it is usually not that simple. In the final analysis probability techniques are not an effective substitute for good judgment but rather an aid to decision making.

Finally, managers do not need to be mathematical geniuses to use the planning techniques discussed in this chapter; most organizations employ staff specialists who can perform the calculations. Nevertheless, the managers must thoroughly understand the basics of these techniques so that they can detect errors in any analysis that is completed under their direction.

SUMMARY

Managers can use quantitative planning techniques if the problem can be expressed in numbers. There are two general types of quantitative models, deterministic and probabilistic. A deterministic model is appropriate when all factors are exact and the law of chance plays no role in the formulation or solution of the problem. The probabilistic model includes chance or random factors.

Three of the major deterministic models are break-even analysis, capital budgeting, and linear programming. In break-even analysis the break-even point is the level at which total revenue equals total costs. The objective of break-even analysis is to determine the optimum break-even point by taking into consideration the costs associated with each level of demand and the way demand changes as price changes. Linear programming is an extension of break-even analysis that is particularly appropriate when an organization manufactures two or more products and uses two or more resources. It guides the organization in allocating scarce resources to the products so as to maximize some objective function, such as profits, or to minimize some objective function such as costs.

In this chapter we also examined Gantt Charts, which are graphic representations of the work flow through the various departments of an organization. The use of Gantt Charts led logically to the development of two sophisticated network planning devices, PERT and CPM. Both techniques describe a series of interrelated steps necessary to complete a specific project. However, CPM is a deterministic planning technique, since the time estimates are certain, while PERT is a probabilistic planning technique.

The expected value method is one of the four probabilistic models we discussed. The expected value of an event is its outcome (such as sales) times its probability of occurrence. With this model managers can determine expected sales by adding together the expected values for various events or outcomes. The other three probabilistic models we examined are decision trees, which managers can use if they must make a series of decisions; waiting line analysis, which focuses on queues in which individuals or projects must be sequentially processed in some systematic manner; and simulation, which is the process of building, testing, and operating models of real world phenomena via mathematical relationships. As this chapter indicates, it is sometimes possible to use a combination of deterministic and probabilistic approaches to solve a problem.

All these planning methods have major implications for managerial work. Probably the most important implication is that they are an aid to managerial decision making, not decision making per se. Managers must learn to use these techniques carefully and systematically, but ultimately it is the acuteness of managerial decision making that propels an organization to success.

DISCUSSION QUESTIONS

1. What are some of the advantages of simulation in comparison to the other analytical techniques discussed in this chapter?
2. How can a deterministic planning technique supplement a probabilistic planning technique? When would it be inappropriate to supplement a probabilistic planning technique with a deterministic planning technique? Why?
3. How are decision trees and the expected value method similar? How are they different?
4. What is the relationship between Gantt Charts and PERT or CPM? How do Gantt Charts differ from them?
5. Discuss some situations in which capital budgeting would be a useful analytical technique.
6. In what way is linear programming an extension of break-even analysis?

PROBLEMS

1. Given the following PERT chart, identify the steps needed to complete the project. (All times are expressed in days.)
   a. Determine all paths and identify the critical path.
   b. What will be the critical path if A–E becomes six days? If D–G becomes ten days?

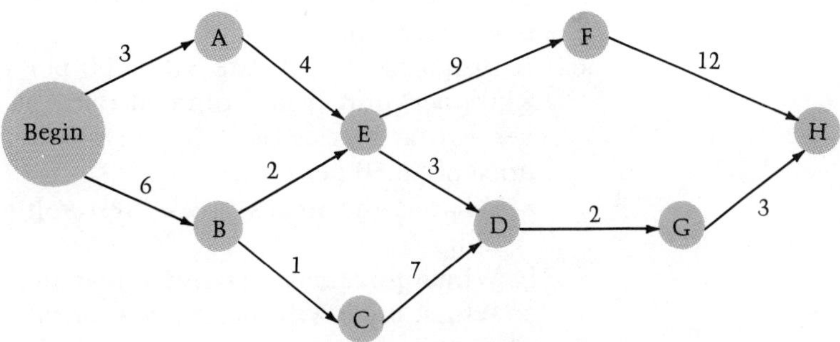

2. You have been assigned a project that has five milestones. The milestones, the expected time to complete each milestone, and the order of completion are given below.
   a. Construct a PERT chart of this project.
   b. What happens to the critical path if milestone D shortens to three weeks?

c. What happens to the critical path if milestone D shortens to four weeks and milestone C increases to five weeks?

Mile-stone	*Expected completion time (in weeks)*	*Preceding milestone*
A	5	None
B	8	None
C	2	A,B
D	10	B
E	3	C,D

3. A manufacturer of electronic calculators has annual fixed costs of $5 million per year. His plant can produce 300,000 major appliances annually. If his variable cost per appliance is $150, how much must he charge to achieve his profit objective of $2.4 million if he can sell only 80 percent of his production capacity? What would his profits be if sales were at 60 percent of capacity? At 100 percent of capacity?
4. For Problem 3 market research indicates that the manufacturer can sell 240,000 major appliances annually at a price of $180 or 300,000 annually at a price of $170. What price should the manufacturer set to maximize profits?
5. Bill McGowan is evaluating a new piece of equipment for his production department. The management of the engineering department estimates the cost to install and debug the equipment is $20,000. From past experience Bill knows that there is a 0.5 probability that the actual cost will be 50 percent higher than the estimate, a 0.4 probability that the cost will equal the estimate, and a 0.1 probability that the cost will be 20 percent lower than the estimate. Find the expected cost of installing and debugging the new equipment.
6. A firm's fixed costs are $100,000 per year and variable costs are $3.00 per unit. It is estimated that the firm can sell 30,000 units per year at a price of $8.00 per unit or 40,000 units per year at a price of $6.50 per unit.
   a. What is the firm's break-even volume at a price of $8.00 per unit?
   b. Which price will maximize revenues?
   c. Which price will maximize profits?
7. The profitabilities and probabilities for a project are given below. What is the expected profit of this project?

Probability	*Profit*
0.25	$8000
0.45	6000
0.30	2000

8. Two alternative strategies are being considered by management for the development of a new product. Conditional profits, probabilities, states of nature, and expected profits for the two alternatives are given below. Management feels that a loss in excess of $5 million would seriously weaken the firm. Which strategy should management choose?

State of nature	*Probability*	*Conditional profits*	
		Strategy A	*Strategy B*
Good sales	0.3	$15,000,000	$10,000,000
Fair sales	0.4	12,000,000	6,000,000
Poor sales	0.3	−8,000,000	−3,000,000

9. Joan Rexford is considering the replacement of her eight-year-old car. She has estimated the average annual cost for the next five years of keeping the old car, buying a used car, and buying a new car.

   If she keeps the old car, there is a 0.5 probability that it will last for five years with an average annual repair bill of $300. There is also a 0.5 chance that the car will deteriorate so much that she will be forced to buy a new car, which will cost $2000 per year in combination with repairs on her old car. There is a 0.7 chance that the cost of the used car will be $700 per year and a 0.3 chance that it will deteriorate and have to be replaced at an average annual cost of $3000 per year. Average annual costs for a new car will be $1200 per year if it causes little trouble (0.5 probability) and $1800 per year (0.5 probability) if it turns out to be a lemon. Which automobile strategy will result in the lowest expected annual cost?

SUGGESTED READINGS

Chase, Richard B., and Aquilano, Nicholas J. *Production and Operations Management: A Life Cycle Approach.* Rev. ed. Homewood, Ill.: Irwin, 1977, hardback.

See especially Chapter 7, "Design of the Scheduling System," and the supplement to Chapter 12, "Critical Path Scheduling."

Miller, David, and Starr, Martin. *The Structure of Human Decisions.* Englewood Cliffs, N.J.: Prentice-Hall, 1967, 177 pages, paperback.

This book contains a very readable introduction to quantitative planning techniques.

7 Techniques for Controlling Organizational Systems

THE CONCEPT OF CONTROL
BUDGETARY CONTROL
INVENTORY AND QUALITY CONTROL
MANAGEMENT INFORMATION SYSTEMS
ADDITIONAL CONTROL TECHNIQUES
SUMMARY
DISCUSSION QUESTIONS
SUGGESTED READINGS

PERFORMANCE OBJECTIVES

1. To define control and to show how it relates to planning.
2. To distinguish between feedback control and feedforward control, and between the control of organizational subsystems and the control of organizational members.
3. To describe some major control techniques designed to monitor organizational systems.

In Chapter 5 we saw how planning is used to direct an organization toward its goals. However, there is always the possibility that an organization will fail to achieve its goals. To eliminate or minimize this possibility, an organization develops control systems. *Control* is the process of monitoring plans and pinpointing significant deviations from them. Hence, as we have stated earlier, planning and control are intimately related.

This chapter defines the concept of control and describes various types of control systems an organization may use. In addition, the chapter discusses some major control techniques that management can employ to monitor organizational systems.

THE CONCEPT OF CONTROL

Control ideally involves four separate but interrelated activities (Porter, Lawler, and Hackman 1975). First, the organization must establish a standard or set of standards against which deviations from plans can be measured. Second, the organization must develop monitoring devices to measure the performance of the individual or system. While one monitoring device may suffice, it is preferable to use two or more so that performance can be measured accurately. Third, the measurements obtained through different monitoring devices are compared to determine whether the current state is close enough to the planned state. Finally, the organization must employ *effectuating* or *action* devices to correct any significant deviations. Sometimes the control system contains an action device that automatically corrects these deviations. In other situations the manager must decide what action is suitable for correcting the deviations.

For example, management might measure the performance of a factory worker by establishing several separate but interrelated standards: he or she is expected to (1) produce 100 units of a particular item per day; (2) have an error rate of 1 unit per 100 units; (3) be late for work an average of one day per month; and (4) be absent from work an average of one day per month. If the employee's performance is substandard in any of these areas, management has recourse to action devices to correct the deviation. In this case appropriate action devices might be counseling sessions, a reprimand, or a short layoff.

Various *types* of control can be exercised by an organization. There are two major distinctions, feedback and feedforward control (Filley, House, and Kerr 1976), and control of organizational members and organizational subsystems (Ouchi and Maguire 1975).

Feedback and Feedforward Control

Feedback control uses information from events that have already occurred to make corrections for the future. When management uses feedback control, an *error* in the system is the signal indicating that corrective action is appropriate. A thermostat represents this kind of control, for it does not correct until the temperature in a room falls below the desired level. Management frequently monitors the performance of factory workers by means of feedback control. Inspectors evaluate the finished goods factory workers produce; if the inspectors determine that the quality of these goods is below a preestablished standard, they return them to the workers, who are then required to redo the job.

Feedforward control anticipates or predicts deviations from standards even before they occur. Hence managers can use action devices to correct deviations before an actual error is spotted. For example, managers might automatically increase their levels of inventories as soon as sales volume rises to some predetermined level, preventing inventories from running out. Feedback control cures problems; feedforward control prevents them.

Organizations employ both types of control. Feedback control is much more common than feedforward control, since feedforward systems are much more difficult to develop. In some situations it is possible to develop an overall system that combines feedback and feedforward control. Feedback control in a factory would occur if managers hire additional workers when more than 3 out of every 100 units prove defective. Simultaneously, however, feedforward control would be employed if managers hire additional workers when sales increase by 10 percent.

Control of Members and Subsystems

Another important distinction involves the difference between control of organizational subsystems and control of organizational members. Managers frequently attempt to control the organization's major subsystems by means of control techniques that are integrated with one another. For example, top management may allocate a specified budget to each of its ten major subdivisions. When a particular subdivision exceeds its budget by a significant amount, that deviation indicates a problem exists.

Top management also needs to control organizational members so that they will perform at a satisfactory or superior level. Top management exercises this control by means of promotions, salary increases, demotions, and so forth.

The control of organizational subsystems is more directly related to planning than is the control of organizational members. If an organization, or any of its major subsystems, is operating ineffectively, the entire planning apparatus and the organization's existence are jeopardized. Such outcomes do not typically occur if only one or a few individuals are functioning ineffectively. Thus management is vitally interested in the control of its financial systems, production systems, and so forth. All these systems are interrelated since a failure in one of them frequently spreads to other areas in the organization.

Source: *New Yorker*, January 2, 1971, p. 17. Drawing by Whitney Darrow, Jr.; © 1971 The New Yorker Magazine, Inc.

"Just listen to all that whirring and buzzing and clicking, and not a single demand for a raise!"

Combinations of Control

Of course, control of organizational subsystems and control of organizational members are not independent of one another. In fact, they influence each other so strongly that a problem with one may be corrected by changing the other. When employees do not perform at a satisfactory level, management frequently changes the control systems that govern the behavior of the entire organization or its major subsystems. Similarly, if a particular subsystem is ineffective, management may combat the problem by tightening its control of organizational members by demoting or firing some individuals. However, these two types of control are more often carried out in different ways.

Ideally organizations would like to use only feedforward control of subsystems and members. They would like to avoid errors, which is possible when feedforward control is employed. However, it is simply not practical to use only feedforward control. For instance, management might not want to make any changes in its control systems until it determines the company's profits (feedback control). At present, most organizations find it both desirable and feasible to use a mixture of feedback and feedforward control in controlling subsystems and members.

This chapter focuses on the control of organizational subsystems. In this discussion of various control techniques, either feedback or feedforward control is specified when possible.

BUDGETARY CONTROL

In this section we describe various types of budgets and focus on the major issues surrounding their use.

Types of Budgets

One typical means of control is through an organization's budget, which is a detailed listing of the resources or money assigned to a particular project or unit. Usually top management approves the various budgets that guide the activities of the major operating divisions of the organization. Budgets normally represent feedback control. If an operating division exceeds its budget, an error is assumed to have occurred and the division must justify the increased expenditures to top management. If the division fails to justify the deviation, top management may take corrective action, such as deciding that the probable profitability of this division is lower than that of other divisions and consequently decreasing the amount of money allocated to it. Or top management may decide to increase the budget of an operating division that has not exceeded its estimates and has been profitable for three consecutive years if it is likely that this trend will continue.

Although top management normally approves a proposed budget, the operating division usually constructs it. Some of the factors the operating division uses to construct a budget include previous and expected sales figures and production costs. Once the budget has been constructed and approved, top management must closely watch its use.

In recent years some companies have employed budgets as feedforward control mechanisms. These companies do not establish one rigid budget that is monitored at the end of a reporting period. Rather, the budget is flexible; it can be changed within a reporting period if economic conditions indicate that a new approach is warranted. Hence errors can be corrected even before they occur. For example, Emerson Electric Company of St. Louis has been highly profitable for several years, at least in part because it has developed a feedforward budget control system. At Emerson there are three budgets: (1) a budget based on the division's reaching its anticipated sales volume, (2) a budget to which a division can retreat if sales slip ten percent below expectations, and (3) a budget to be used if the market collapses completely. This approach to control allows the company to respond quickly to its problems. If plans do not work out successfully, the company can change its direction and budget with a minimum of difficulty.

Standard Costs

To be useful, planning and control techniques such as budgets require reliable data. One data source for both planning and control systems is past experience. Knowing how much something cost in the previous fiscal year is an obvious way of predicting how much it will cost this year. However, these historical costs do not always accurately reflect the current situation. For example, management has found historical costs to be of limited value during the past few years because of the high rate of inflation. In addition, inefficiencies or unique situations that affect historical costs may limit their usefulness as a basis for predictions.

To provide more reliable data for control systems, management frequently constructs a standard cost system, which measures the cost of each component of a product against a preestablished standard. *Standard costs* are estimates of a company's resource requirements for producing its product and each of its components, expressed in dollars. They incorporate past costs, suppliers' estimates, industry data, engineering estimates, and any other available information. Standard costs provide a basis for budgeting and for other control techniques to be discussed in this chapter.

Responsibility Centers

A major problem in organizational control is matching the accountability of the suborganizations with the authority they possess. A classic problem of this type involves the handling of marketing-related product costs. In most companies the production department is responsible for product costs, but marketing has the authority to decide that an attractive but more costly package is needed to meet marketing objectives. Under these conditions intraorganizational conflicts are likely to emerge, because the production department is accountable for costs that are not entirely under its control (in this case, the costliness of the new package). Here the technique of responsibility centers may alleviate the problem.

Responsibility centers are intended to (1) identify the responsibilities of each manager in the company, (2) match the responsibilities and authority of each manager and his or her organization, and (3) design an accounting system that measures the activities for which the manager is responsible. There are various kinds of responsibility centers, such as cost centers, profit centers, and revenue centers, and, as shown below, these various centers are usually linked together. In addition, the underlying concept is the same in all instances—that is, aligning accountability and authority of the subsystems in the organization.

In many firms the conflicts between marketing and production that result from decisions in one affecting the other have largely been eliminated by the use of responsibility centers. A typical solution would be to designate the marketing department as a profit center in which the product is purchased from the production department at standard cost. Marketing then assumes responsibility for inventory levels, sales, and product profitability. The production department is designated as a cost center in which its performance is measured against standard cost. A change in the type of packaging in this situation would result in a new standard cost against which the production department's performance would be evaluated. Marketing's decision to use the more expensive package would be based on its assessment of whether the new package would be worth the higher standard cost. By using responsibility centers, management can minimize the conflicts between production and marketing and can charge the added costs to the department that is causing the cost (in this case, marketing).

Zero-based Budgeting

Zero-based budgeting (ZBB) is a relatively new and innovative approach; it was introduced by Texas Instruments in the late 1960s. When former President Carter was governor of Georgia, he applied this approach to the state government. And when he was president, he introduced it on a wide scale in the federal government system.

ZBB is radically different from the traditional method of budgeting, which relies heavily on the previous year's data. For instance, managers frequently attempt to increase their budgets, and they use the previous year's data as a major source of justification. Under ZBB, managers must start the budgeting process at zero every year, and they must justify any requests they make. Even if under the traditional budgeting procedures managers have always received money to underwrite specific activities, once ZBB is installed, they must explain and justify why such funding should continue.

Thus ZBB attempts to avoid the perpetuation of unnecessary programs. In this respect ZBB is a feedforward control technique. Its application is frequently appropriate in the service and support areas of the firm, such as training and career development, where programs are more likely to be discretionary. That is, management can change such programs easily if cost-benefit analysis indicates that such action is warranted. However, ZBB is less applicable in manufacturing areas, since it is very difficult to change programs and activities on a regular basis owing to the heavy investment in permanent technology.

The ZBB process involves the following: identifying decision packages, ranking decision packages, and setting cutoff points for various programs that management funds. Decision packages consist of alternative plans of action for each activity. Management evaluates the impact of each alternative in terms of the costs and benefits that would be derived from implementing it. It then ranks the decision packages. Final rankings of decision packages are normally the outcome of two or more rounds of voting. However, periods of discussion typically precede the voting to clarify points of disagreement, refine estimates of costs and benefits, and reconsider priorities. The final step is to establish cutoff points for each program. At this point management designates some programs as essential, others as nonessential but helpful if profits or sales justify them, and still others as unjustifiable and inappropriate for funding under any circumstances.

Managers have voiced some serious reservations about ZBB, possibly because it is a relatively new technique. Under ZBB managers must increase the time they spend at meetings, and the amount of paperwork rises. However, these same criticisms apply to other management techniques, such as Management by Objectives (see Chapter 5). Ultimately such problems may be unavoidable in the modern world, for group decision making in management has become much more important than it once was because of the complexity of the problems that managers face.

INVENTORY AND QUALITY CONTROL

Clearly management must utilize budgets in the process of controlling organizational subsystems. But management must also control its levels of *inventories* or *goods in stock*, for otherwise financial resources will be depleted; the amount of money that is tied up in goods should be minimized. At the same time, inventories must be high enough to satisfy customer demand promptly. Thus the management of inventories requires a fine balance between cost control and customer satisfaction.

Management must also control the *quality* of the goods produced. Although management may be very successful in budgeting resources and controlling inventories, it will fail if quality control is deficient. In many instances reliability of quality is as important as the overall level of quality. In fact, a good quality level may be more desirable than sporadic achievement of very high quality that is combined with some average and some very poor quality output.

In this section we discuss the related issues of inventory and quality control.

Three Inventory Models

Three prominent techniques of inventory management, which are closely related to one another, are the Economic Order Quality (EOQ) model, the Economic Order Point (EOP) model, and the Material Requirements Planning (MRP) model.

The EOQ model is based on the management of inventory levels of each individual product or item as usage occurs. In this method a reorder of optimum quantity is placed when inventories of a particular item or product fall to a predetermined level. The EOQ model is useful when management can order the items or products independently of one another. For instance, management in manufacturing firms usually order independently the individual materials they use. That is, there is a unique reorder point and reorder quantity for each item.

In other situations reordering practices are based on placing orders for all items or products simultaneously at certain intervals. This

FIGURE 7–1
Cereal Packaging Line Control

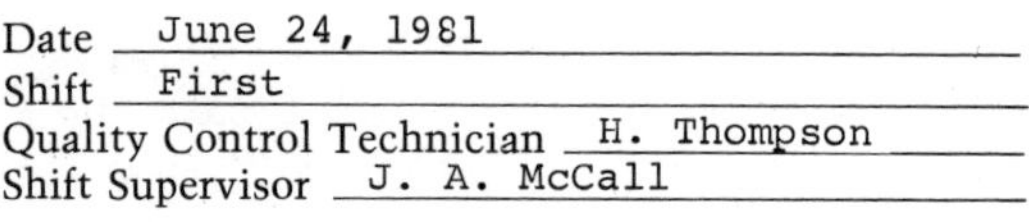
Date June 24, 1981
Shift First
Quality Control Technician H. Thompson
Shift Supervisor J. A. McCall

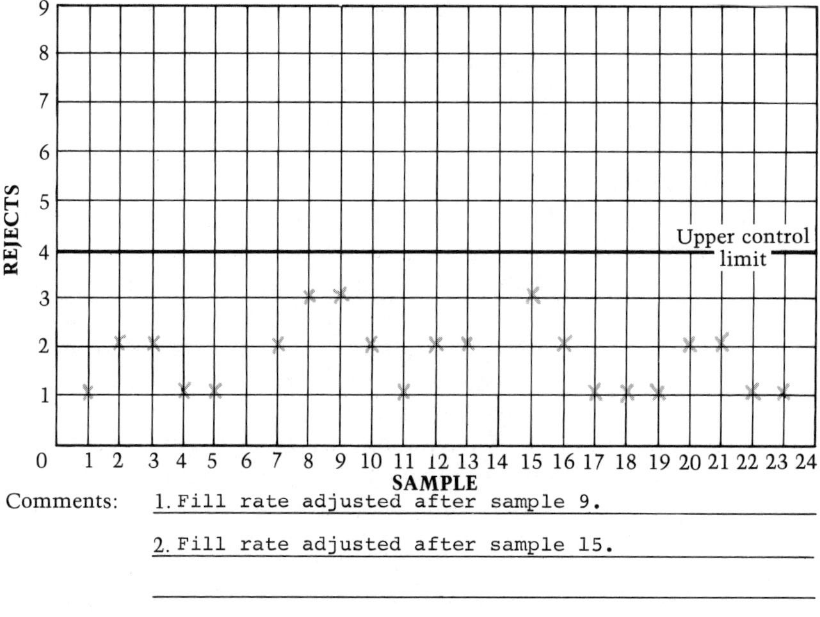

Comments: 1. Fill rate adjusted after sample 9.

2. Fill rate adjusted after sample 15.

Helen J. Thompson
Signature of Quality Control Technician

J. A. McCall
Signature of Shift Supervisor

practice is typical in the retailing industry. Under these conditions the EOP model is appropriate.

The third type of inventory control, MRP, is suitable when there is a commonality among products, that is, when a subcomponent is used in more than one product. The advent of large-scale computers has enabled managers to use MRP on a wide scale, and many products such as automobiles now contain interchangeable parts.

Defining and Monitoring Quality

The term *quality* has different meanings to different people. In this book *quality* refers to the grade and the consistency in characteristics of the product. Grade refers to properties of the product such as smoothness, texture, flavor, color, and size. In some instances management can measure the characteristic to be graded and evaluate performance against a standard. For example, in controlling the amount of breakfast cereal in a 10½-ounce package, management may use a weighing device in the packaging line that rejects any package heavier or lighter than some predetermined limits. With the advent of electronic and other sophisticated technologies, the quality of all output of many production processes may be evaluated. Electronic beams can be used to control the thickness of rolled metal sheets, and continuous monitoring of machine tool parts allows computer adjustments to be made on the process before defective parts are produced.

In other situations the evaluation of quality may be highly subjective. For example, test kitchens in which quality control inspectors taste a baked product are common in a frozen pie plant. In manufacturing processes where the product cannot be continuously monitored or where the testing process destroys the product, management may achieve quality control through statistical sampling.

Another means of monitoring quality is a *control chart,* which is a graph of an operation's quality performance over time. After management has established standards, it can monitor operating performance so that deviations from normal quality levels can be quickly spotted and corrective action can be taken. In the example of the breakfast cereal packaging line, management might employ a control chart to keep track of the number of rejects (either over- or underweight) occurring per 15-minute period. Figure 7–1 demonstrates a control chart for this example. If the number of rejects appears to be increasing, then minor corrective action should be taken. Corrective action may include adjusting the filling equipment or checking the product for consistency. In cases where the number of rejects exceeds the upper control limit, management would shut down the packaging line to find the reason for the rejects and to take corrective action.

MANAGEMENT INFORMATION SYSTEMS

A *management information system* (MIS) is any way of collecting data that will help the manager perform his or her job efficiently. For example, in many organizations each staff group provides the line officer with a separate report on operations in its own area. Thus the personnel department may issue a report that contains information on turnover rates, absenteeism, and lateness; the training department may file a report that lists the dollar amounts spent for training employees and executives; and the engineering department may provide a set of standard and actual costs. The line manager must examine

TABLE 7–1
Strategic Factors in a Management Information System for a Branch-banking System

Financial information	*Performance information*
Percent of change in net income	Amount of money lost because of inefficiency and theft
Percentage of change in dollars for various types of deposits and accounts	
Percent of change in number of various types of customers	
Personnel information	*Customer information*
Percent of change in absenteeism	Complaint letters
Percent of change in employee turnover	Marketing surveys

Note: Data tabulated by branch for one year's performance.

each report independently. However, reports may be combined so that the line manager can analyze related sources of information. Thus the training report could be combined with the personnel report.

As another example, consider a branch-banking system. Management here might construct an MIS with four distinct parts: financial information, personnel information, performance information, and customer information (see Table 7–1). Management would collect information on each branch so that it could compare all the branches on all four dimensions. Ideally, all this information would be housed within a central office, making it easily accessible to top management.

An MIS clearly can become very complicated, for the number of specific factors being measured is often quite large. Therefore, it is up to an individual manager to pinpoint the factors he or she considers most important. Top management usually will use several measures of performance to evaluate the effectiveness of one of its units. At lower levels in an organization managers may need to focus on only a few measures, such as the percentage of change in net income and the rate of employee turnover. And in other instances managers may rely heavily on information that is highly subjective, such as complaint letters, which can serve as a barometer of feelings toward the organization.

Issues that face the manager regarding MIS include its impact on centralization, guidelines on the role of computerized MIS, and the key attributes of an MIS. In this section we address these issues.

Computers and Centralization

In today's world many management information systems are computer-based, which means that a large number of reports can be generated easily. The growth of computerized MISs during the 1970s was phenomenal. For instance, sales of IBM, the largest manufacturer of big computers, increased from $7.5 billion in 1970 to an estimated

$26.0 billion in 1980.[1] Sales of minicomputers and computer services increased even more dramatically. The computer industry is now the third largest industry in the United States, behind the oil and the automotive industries.

Computerized MISs allow management to centralize or decentralize operations as conditions change. If the organization is operating in a stable environment, use of computer technology seems to reinforce centralization, since top management quickly receives computerized information that otherwise would have been filtered through several organizational layers. The computerized information enables top management to direct and control operations more effectively. However, if a firm exists in a dynamic environment, computers appear to reinforce decentralization. In these situations computerized information allows lower levels in the organization to make quick and effective responses to external pressures. In the dynamic environment lower-level managers need sufficient information to assess external pressures without depending on upper management for direction, information, and guidance. Hence computer operations are normally decentralized throughout the organization (Blau, Falbe, McKinley, and Tracy 1976).

Designing the MIS

Design and management of the MIS is a complex issue. A host of questions face the manager. What reports are needed? How much information is needed? What role should MIS play in decision making? The guidelines presented below are useful in the design and management of the MIS.[2]

1. The information system should focus on the needs of the responsibility center, not on the manager, since managers have fairly high turnover rates. Designing the MIS to individual needs of the manager may result in either excessive detail or lack of needed information.

2. Information specialists should avoid both oversystematizing and undersystematizing the MIS. In situations where cause and effect relationships are not well understood (such as in the case of fashion goods), it is better to trust managerial experience and judgment rather than overload managers with low-grade information. On the other hand, when problems are recurring and relationships are well understood, a great deal of information should be developed to support managers.

[1] *Value Line,* August 17, 1979.

[2] These guidelines are adapted from Richard L. Daft and Norman B. MacIntosh, "A New Approach to the Design and Use of Management Information," *California Management Review* XXI, no. 1 (Fall 1978): 82–92.

3. Technologies within an organization vary widely, so a uniform, companywide MIS is headed for trouble. The MIS should be tailored to meet the needs of each responsibility center.

4. Managers should be cautious about transferring information systems from one company to another and from one division to another. An MIS that works well in one company (or division) may be oversystematized or undersystematized for another.

5. Top management work is not well understood, and top managers use an array of hard and soft information. Thus designers of management information systems should consider the complexity of managerial work and develop systems that complement managerial information gained from other sources.

6. Information system design requires a flexible approach. The MIS must fit the technology of the organization and meet management information needs.

Key Attributes There are several key attributes of an MIS (see Henderson and Nutt 1978). Cost is a major consideration. Computers are expensive, and managers must analyze very carefully the benefit-cost ratio before deciding to make a substantial investment. This issue is critical if management wants to decentralize the computer operations, since in this case each facility will receive a separate and costly computer.

The data generated by the computer must also be timely and accurate. Mintzberg (1980) has shown that managers frequently dislike a computerized MIS because the information is dated by the time they receive it. Similarly, managers want accurate data, and they tend to distrust computer-generated information, feeling it may be distorted. For example, in one large bank each branch reported such subjective information as the number of customer contacts it initiated each year, and management then summarized these data in the form of computerized reports. Lower-level managers viewed the reports suspiciously, since they had originally provided the information, which was highly subjective. In fact, lower-level managers joked among themselves that they revised their yearly estimates to ensure that top management would believe them to be exemplary performers.

Accuracy is also a problem if the computer programs are not debugged. Managers have based major decisions on computer-generated information, only to learn subsequently that the computer programs were generating inaccurate information.

A computerized MIS also should provide consistent data and reports. If the computer specialists are constantly changing the format of the reports, line managers can easily become disenchanted, since they must periodically learn anew how to read and understand the outputs.

A computerized MIS should be creative in the sense that it is sufficiently flexible to handle the nonroutine problems that line managers need to solve. If the report formats are so inflexible that line managers cannot change them to meet emerging problems, they will see little value in the MIS. The computer program should also be comprehensive—that is, no key function of management should be omitted. If line managers cannot analyze some of their central problems through this control technique, they are likely to react negatively. Hence it is important for staff specialists to involve line managers in the development of the MIS, for line managers are the basic users of the outputs of the system.

In short, the key attributes of a computerized MIS are cost, timeliness, accuracy, consistency, creativity, and risk of omission (Henderson and Nutt 1978). The usefulness of the MIS will depend primarily on the extent to which the key attributes are satisfied. Large integrated MISs are justified in organizations that operate in simple environments. When the organization's environment is ambiguous and complex, the MIS may be obsolete before it is fully implemented. Under these conditions management may need to make judicious trade-offs among the key attributes to obtain an optimal MIS.

Networks and MIS

There is a close relationship between networks—PERT or CPM (see Chapter 6)—and a computerized MIS. Networks provide top and middle management with valuable information and hence become a major part of any MIS. At the same time both PERT and CPM typically involve use of a computer, since staff specialists can more readily solve the complex equations through its use. Hence networks and MIS, while distinctive control systems in themselves, overlap in the daily activities of both staff and line managers.

Impact of the Computer

Initially, organizations used computers principally in the accounting area, usually for routine work such as employee payrolls and record keeping. Most organizations now use computers for this purpose. For instance, 89 percent of 408 companies, each of whom employed at least 500 individuals, reported that they applied the computer to their payroll operations; 48 percent used it to automate their pension check processing (Morrison 1969). In addition, many companies have extended their computer use to the areas of finance, marketing, and production scheduling.

Nevertheless, organizations have yet to realize the vast potential of the computer. Because of the computer, it is now possible to create a *completely integrated* MIS, linking all major subsystems in the organization (accounting, finance, marketing, production scheduling, and so forth). However, few companies have developed such a system.

Some researchers, in assessing the impact of the computer, have focused attention on its effects on the employees. The computer creates more routine jobs and more skilled jobs, but jobs at the intermediate levels of skill demand are frequently abolished (Bass 1968). For example, the computer has led to the development of the skilled job of programming but also to the unskilled job of pressing bent IBM cards.

Researchers also found that, after the introduction of the computer, supervisors spent more of their time by themselves than they had previously (Whisler 1970). In addition, computer specialists have gained significant informal power because of the importance of the computer for the success of the organization (Whisler 1970; Reif 1968). The computer even affects many of the first-line workers. They communicate less with other employees and their supervisors after the introduction of the computer than they had previously, largely because the routine nature of their responsibilities requires them to produce a standard output within a specific period of time (Whisler 1970).

ADDITIONAL CONTROL TECHNIQUES

Some control techniques do not fit neatly into the categories that we have just described. These include financial statements, cybernetic (machine-controlled) systems, attitude surveys, and the management audit. We discuss these techniques in this section.

Financial Statements

Managers typically use their financial statements as control mechanisms. The *income statement,* which is a detailed listing of sources of revenues and expenses, profiles the financial operations of the organization for a given year. If top managers determine that a particular expense is too high, they can take corrective action. For example, they might decide that salaries are too high and put a freeze on hiring or salary increases.

The *balance sheet* is a detailed listing of the assets an organization owns and the financial liabilities it has incurred. If the organization determines that its financial assets are not sufficient to meet its liabilities, it may need to rectify the situation by selling assets.

Under normal circumstances financial statements represent feedback control. Corrective action is not initiated until after the construction of the income statement or the balance sheet, both of which reflect past activity. Financial statements are important precisely because they are indicative of the organization's overall economic wellbeing. They provide a framework for planning future financial outlays and controlling or correcting past inefficiencies.

Cybernetic (Machine-controlled) Systems

Cybernetic control systems use machines rather than humans to detect deviations and to take corrective action. James Watt, the Scottish inventor, was one of the first managers to implement a cybernetic system in his factory to control operations during the early phase of the Industrial Revolution. Today the use of cybernetic systems is widespread. One of the most familiar cybernetic systems is the thermostat in the home heating and cooling system. The thermostat detects deviations from plan (the temperature setting on the thermostat), takes corrective action (sends a signal to start the heating or cooling system), and terminates the correction (sends a signal to stop the system) when the correct temperature has been restored.

In industrial processes cybernetic systems are widely used to monitor and control continuous-process technologies, such as oil refining. With the advent of the low-cost, widely available electronic computer technology, cybernetic or near-cybernetic systems have been developed in retail inventory control processes, machining processes, and health care processes. Future cybernetic systems will monitor automobile engines to simultaneously optimize fuel economy, emission levels, and performance.

Attitude Surveys

A control mechanism that can be used in any organization, regardless of its size, is the *attitude survey.* An organization might survey its employees by asking them about their working conditions, their supervisors, or any other related aspects of the job. Usually such a survey involves the distribution of a questionnaire, preferably on a yearly or biyearly basis. Management can then pinpoint areas that need improvement by examining attitude changes over time. Thus if eighty percent of the employees in 1980 believed their supervisors were effective, and only thirty percent in 1981 are of the same persuasion, management should examine the reasons for this change of heart.

The U.S. Office of Personnel Management, formerly called the U.S. Civil Service Commission, employs the questionnaire survey when it analyzes the personnel practices of government agencies. The raw data for a unit are converted into percentiles, which compares a specific unit to all other units in the data bank in terms of a 0–100 scale. For example, if the positive percentile response of unit A to the issue of promotions is 10, this response indicates that, in comparison to the other units in the data bank, unit A is more positive about promotions than only 9 out of every 100 units.

While questionnaires are the most common way of measuring employee attitudes for control purposes, personal interviews provide another approach. The major advantages of a questionnaire survey are that much information can be collected in a short time and respondents do not need to identify themselves. The major advantage of the interview is that it provides a wealth of detail. Generally, management is on firm ground in recommending a particular course of action if the questionnaire data and interview data both indicate it is desirable.

Management Audit

The management audit is a control technique that assesses the overall quality of management through the use of several methods such as questionnaires, interviews, and the analysis of hard data elements (turnover, productivity, and so forth). Frequently the management audit focuses on one major operational component of an organization's activity. For example, the U.S. General Accounting Office monitors the financial and accounting practices of government agencies. However, the management audit also can be comprehensive. The American Institute of Management has developed a questionnaire with 301 items that focus attention on the following organizational issues: economic function, corporate structure, strength of earnings, fairness to stockholders, research and development, directorate analysis, fiscal policies, production efficiency, sales vigor, and executive evaluation.

Because of its scope, the management audit is not as precise as most of the other control techniques discussed in this chapter. Still, it can uncover problems that would otherwise go undetected. In general, this technique is effective in identifying extremely poor or extremely good management practices.

SUMMARY

Control is the process of monitoring plans and identifying significant deviations from them. It involves establishing a standard or set of standards, using monitoring devices to measure performance, comparing the measurements of different monitoring devices to be sure the current state of the system is close enough to the ideal state, and using action devices to correct any significant deviations from plans. Managers may use feedback control, which is the correction of an error in a system after it has occurred, or feedforward control, which anticipates deviations from standards or errors before they occur. Usually the most effective form of control involves both feedback and feedforward control to monitor organizational subsystems and organizational members.

In controlling organizational subsystems, management has recourse to several techniques. A budget, which is a detailed listing of the resources assigned to a particular project or unit, is a common control technique that almost all organizations use in one form or another. Management should assign budgets to responsibility centers, which match the accountability of subunits with the authority they possess. Two distinctive budgeting systems are the standard cost system and zero-based budgeting. Under a standard cost system managers evaluate the cost for each component of a product against a preestablished standard. Under ZBB managers must start each budgeting cycle at zero and justify each request they make.

Management must also control its inventories. There are several prominent types of inventory control, including the EOQ model, the EOP model, and the MRP model. Management uses the EOQ model when only one product is involved and the EOP model when more than one product is to be ordered. Management employs MRP when it orders interchangeable components for several products. Further, management must ensure that the quality of its products meets specified minimum standards. Otherwise, customers are likely to become dissatisfied. Sometimes quality control is subjective, such as the tasting of products by food inspectors. However, quality control normally involves a statistical analysis of the goods being produced, and it is based on sampling procedures rather than on a complete survey.

Another major control technique is the management information system (MIS), which is any way of collecting data that will help the manager perform his or her job efficiently. In today's world computerized MISs have become very popular. If an organization exists in a stable external environment, management tends to centralize the computer operations. In a dynamic environment management tends to decentralize the computer operations so that lower-level managers can make quick responses to external pressures. There are several guidelines that management should follow when designing a computerized MIS—for example, focusing on the needs of the responsibility center rather than on the needs of the manager.

Additional techniques designed to control organizational subsystems include financial statements, cybernetic systems, attitude surveys, and the management audit. Although some of these techniques rely on data provided by individuals, their basic thrust is to control organizational subsystems.

DISCUSSION QUESTIONS

1. Why would top management decide *not* to make a heavy capital investment in a computerized MIS? Explain.
2. Does an MIS require the use of a computer? Why or why not?
3. Describe the impact of a computerized MIS on the structure of an organization and the behavior that takes place within it. Does this description confirm any of the relationships in our integrated organizational framework? Explain.

4. Can an excessive emphasis on standard costs ever reduce profits? Why or why not?
5. Describe two situations, one in which feedback control was used successfully in an organization, the other in which feedforward control was implemented successfully.
6. In what ways does the control of organizational members overlap with the control of organizational subsystems? Can these two types of control ever be independent of one another? Why or why not?
7. If planning and control represent opposite sides of the same coin, why are they treated separately? Can planning take place without control? Can control occur without planning? Explain.
8. What are some of the major criticisms of ZBB? Are they valid? Why or why not? Can management eliminate the sources of difficulty leading to these criticisms? Why or why not?
9. What are responsibility centers? How do they help to minimize conflict in organizations?

SUGGESTED READINGS

Chase, Richard B., and Aquilano, Nicholas J. *Production and Operations Management: A Life Cycle Approach.* Rev. ed. Homewood, Ill.: Irwin, 1977, hardback.

See especially Chapter 5, which contains an excellent discussion of the design of quality control systems.

Horngren, Charles T. *Cost Accounting: A Managerial Emphasis.* 4th ed. Englewood Cliffs, N.J.: Prentice-Hall, 1977, hardback.

See especially Chapter 7, which provides a clear and interesting treatment of standard costs.

Tersine, Richard J. *Materials Management and Inventory Systems.* New York: North-Holland, 1976, hardback.

Tersine describes inventory control in a clear and comprehensive manner.

8 Selection and the Personnel Control Process

SELECTION
JOB ORIENTATION
TRAINING AND DEVELOPMENT
PERFORMANCE APPRAISAL
REWARD SYSTEMS
SUMMARY
DISCUSSION QUESTIONS
CRITICAL INCIDENTS
SUGGESTED READINGS

PERFORMANCE OBJECTIVES

1. To describe the process by which the organization controls the behavior of its members.
2. To discuss various techniques that organizations use to select their members and the job orientation that takes place prior to the time that the actual work begins.
3. To show how organizations train their members, and to explain how training differs from development.
4. To describe the various methods that organizations use to appraise the performance of their members.
5. To analyze the relative influence of various reward systems that organizations use.

To increase the probability of success, managers must effectively control the critical activities of the entire organization and its major subsystems, as we have seen in the previous chapters. In addition, management must control the behavior of organizational members so that they will continue to produce at a high level. Although these two types of control overlap, they are sufficiently different that they can be treated separately.

This chapter describes the control of individuals in the context of the personnel process. The process begins with *selection*, the formal and informal screening of applicants so that only qualified individuals are offered positions. *Job orientation*, becoming familiar with both the job and the organization, is the next step in the personnel process. The other major steps in this process—*training and development*, *performance appraisal*, and *reward systems*—are sometimes completed simultaneously. Normally the successful job applicant is enrolled in a training program, after which he or she begins working. Performance appraisal by the individual's superior follows and is typically repeated at set intervals, say, six months or a year. Management then employs a system of rewards that includes both incentives and sanctions to ensure that subsequent performance will be satisfactory. In addition, management typically prepares a developmental program so that the individual can be trained for higher-level jobs systematically.

Admittedly there are deviations from our description of the ideal personnel control process. Still, our description approximates what happens to a successful job applicant and identifies the major aspects of the personnel control process.

SELECTION

Selecting employees and managers is a very difficult task. While there are various techniques that management can use, they are far from perfect. In fact, management should rely on at least two selection techniques, especially as the complexity of the work increases. Some of the important selection techniques include information on job search methods, weighted application blanks, the hiring interview, and tests. Each of these methods is discussed in this section.

Job Search Methods

The methods individuals use to seek work have been shown to be related to an important measure of individual performance, employee turnover. These methods are usually classified as either formal or informal in nature. *Formal methods* include the use of newspaper advertisements and employment agencies; *informal methods* include recommendations by school administrators, recommendations by current employees, just walking into the organization to apply for a job without any knowledge of whether a job opportunity exists (walk-ins), and reemployment of former employees.

"This resumé is one of the most boastful, deceptive pieces of fraud I've ever seen. You're hired."

Three studies have examined the relationship between job search methods and employee turnover among regular, full-time employees, and all have shown similar results (Ullman 1966; Reid 1972; Gannon 1971a). The largest of these studies involved 6390 former employees of Chemical Bank of New York (Gannon 1971a). In this study the turnover rates for the four informal methods of job search listed above were significantly lower within the first year of employment than those for the two formal methods. The turnover rates for the two formal methods within the first year were 39.4 percent and 40.0 percent; for the informal methods the range was 21.3 percent to 28.8 percent. Relationships did not vary over time.

These results are significant since organizations spend a great deal of money selecting and orienting employees to their jobs. If employees leave within the first year, the organization frequently loses a large amount of time and money. In addition, the production process is impeded, for new employees and managers are somewhat inefficient while becoming familiar with their tasks.

However, organizations use newspaper advertisements largely because they cannot recruit enough workers through informal methods.

But management must be careful that such advertisements provide a clear description of the work; that is not always the case (Johnson 1978). For example, some advertisements are written in such a way as to discourage applications from blacks and women. However, this situation may be changing; minority-group members and women have dramatically increased their use of legal action to attack the problem of discrimination (see Figure 8–1), and organizations have become sensitive to that fact.

Tests Management employs a variety of tests as selection devices. These include tests measuring skills, abilities, and psychological characteristics. Federal law requires that these tests possess *validity,* that is, that they actually measure what they purport to measure. If the tests are invalid, many job applicants who could effectively perform the work are unfairly eliminated.

FIGURE 8–1

Growth and Type of Charges Filed with the Equal Employment Opportunity Commission

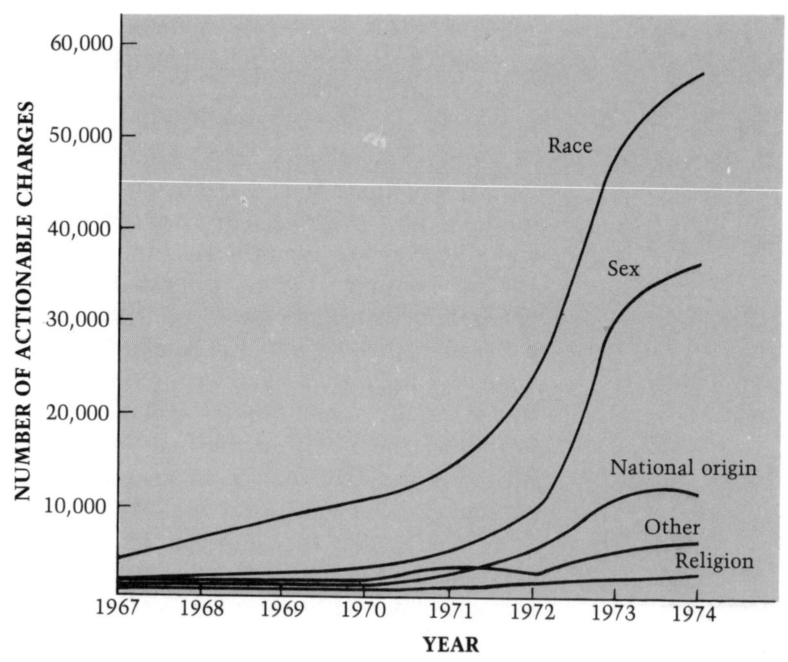

Note: Actionable charges refer to the total of incoming charges minus those rejected for lack of probable jurisdiction.

Source: Equal Employment Opportunity Commission, *Annual Reports* (Washington, D.C.: Government Printing Office, 1967–1974).

Ideally, a test should possess *predictive validity*—that is, later job performance should be related to the test results. To determine this form of validity, management hires a group of applicants without eliminating any of them. At time of hiring these individuals complete the test. After a period of time management relates the test results to actual performance on the job. If the test has predictive validity, those scoring high on it should be successful performers.

When it is difficult to use a test with predictive validity, because of such problems as the need to complete the study quickly, management can rely on tests with *concurrent validity,* comparing two groups of current workers separated into high and low performers. The test is valid if it significantly differentiates these two groups of workers.

Tests should also possess *reliability.* A test is reliable if an individual taking it at two different times receives approximately the same scores, or if individuals similar in background characteristics receive similar scores.

Generally speaking, tests that measure specific abilities, such as typing skills, are highly reliable and valid, since these tests actually measure what the individual will be doing in the organization. However, as the nature of the work becomes complex, tests tend to become less reliable and valid, presumably because they cannot capture the intricacies involved in complex jobs. Nevertheless, many tests have been successfully designed for complex work.

Tests are not magical predictive devices. Rather, management relies on them because it is difficult to measure a person's abilities, skills, and characteristics in any other way. Ideally, management would prefer to obtain an actual measure of job performance, such as that provided by a typing test or a seminar given by a candidate for a professorship. But since this ideal situation cannot always be approximated, management must be especially careful that the organization's tests are both valid and reliable.

Application Blanks

It is generally agreed that the best predictor of future performance is past performance. In fact, some management researchers speak of a life-style of success: Individuals who become successful managers are characterized by a high degree of participation in extracurricular activities in high school and college, assumption of important responsibilities rather early in life, and active participation in religious, charitable, and civic groups (Campbell et al. 1970). For this reason the application blank is important, since it contains information on the individual's past performance. However, research has shown that some of that information, sometimes as much as twenty or twenty-five percent, is distorted or incorrect (Miner 1975). For example, an individual may indicate that he was an undergraduate major in business

TABLE 8–1
Weighting an Application Blank

Education	*Number of workers in low-productivity group* ($n = 100$)	*Number of workers in high-productivity group* ($n = 100$)	*Percentage of workers with this factor in high group*	*Weight on application blank*
Grade school	10	5	33	3
High school incomplete	8	15	65	7
High school graduate	10	20	67	7
College incomplete	20	30	60	6
College graduate	47	25	35	4
Graduate work	5	5	50	5

Note: First, a sample of workers is divided into two groups on the basis of their comparative productivity. Each weight is based on the percentage of workers in the high category, rounded off. The higher the total weighted score for all items—education, previous work experience, age, and so forth—the more desirable is the job applicant.

administration when in fact he has only six credits of accounting on his transcript.

However, assuming that the information on the application blank is valid, management can construct a powerful selection technique, the weighted application blank, from the data. The *weighted application blank* compares the background factors of successful and unsuccessful performers and assigns differential weights to these factors. Then each individual receives a final score that indicates whether he or she should be hired. As in the case of tests, weighted application blanks must possess both validity and reliability.

Management can create a weighted application blank, using either predictive or concurrent validity, by first dividing its workers into two equal groups, one low and one high on some measure of performance or productivity. Management then determines the percentage of workers in a given category—such as twelve years of education—who fall in the high group. For instance, perhaps thirty-three percent of the workers who have only graduated from grade school are in the high group. This percentage is rounded off and becomes a weight. All the other educational categories are similarly weighted (see Table 8–1). The same procedure is used for other background factors, such as marital status, work experience, military service, and grades in school. Management then hires workers who obtain a high score when their application blank is weighted by this procedure. Hence the personnel office increases its likelihood of hiring high performers. In this sense management is exercising feedforward control, for it has excluded individuals from the organization who would probably be poor performers.

The Hiring Interview

One of the most popular and frequently misused selection techniques is the hiring interview. There are many sources of bias that enter into the evaluation of the applicant during the selection interview, including positive evaluation of the candidate because of similarity of backgrounds between the hiring interviewer and the applicant, the attractiveness of the applicant, and even the clothing the applicant wears. If a male applicant is handsome, tall, and well dressed, the probability of successfully obtaining the job increases dramatically (Carroll 1966). In one study a young man applying for a managerial position dressed in two contrasting styles: a nondescript lower-middle-class style and a distinctive and elegant upper-middle-class style. In the nondescript style of dress he was usually rejected for the job—sometimes he could not even obtain an interview. In the elegant style of dress he almost always received a job offer (Steinberg 1975).

As our discussion implies, the initial impression a job candidate creates is of overwhelming importance. In fact, the decision to hire or not to hire is usually made within the first three or four minutes of the interview (Webster 1964). On infrequent occasions the interviewer may change his mind; however, the change tends to be from positive to negative rather than from negative to positive.

Another difficulty with the hiring interview is that in many situations interviewers make unrealistic promises to the applicant, which subsequently lead to a high rate of turnover. In one study 19.1 percent of 304 former salesmen indicated they had quit primarily because they received promises that were never fulfilled (Jolson and Gannon 1972). On the other hand, a realistic job preview during the hiring interview leads the applicant to believe that the interviewer is honest, but it also leads to a higher probability that the applicant will reject the job once it is offered (Reilly, Tenopyr, and Sperling 1979).

Despite these problems, for many jobs, especially those in the upper levels of the organization, it may be necessary to use the hiring interview. One way to improve the validity and reliability of the interview is to train interviewers, both in interviewing techniques and in the actual demands of the job offered. The insurance industry, for example, has developed a three-day workshop designed specifically for training interviewers who hire life insurance agents. This workshop is based on extensive information about the work performed by insurance agents, and the insurance industry has validated the workshop. Thus even though the hiring interview is widely misused, it is possible to eliminate the problems associated with it through careful validation studies.

JOB ORIENTATION

Once hired, a person should be introduced into the organization so that he feels comfortable about the job and the individuals with whom he will be interacting. But for some unknown reason many organizations provide little job orientation. For instance, a questionnaire survey of employees of a federal government agency produced the following answers to the question of how they were oriented to the organization: by fellow employees, 81.2 percent; by their supervisors, 65.2 percent; either "sink or swim," 24.2 percent; by formal orientation sessions, 15.9 percent (Gannon and Paine 1972).

Job orientation programs, sometimes lasting one or two days, are intended not only to help employees to become efficient as quickly as possible but also to give them a positive attitude about the new job and the company. It is to the company's benefit to do this, for some research indicates that individuals who have received job orientation are more satisfied and less likely to quit than those who do not (Marion and Trieb 1969). Even an employee's interest in an organization is influenced by the job orientation he or she receives. Miner and Heaton (1959) discovered that employees who participated in job orientation sessions tended to read company publications more than those who did not.

It is also important for the job orientation program to focus both on informational issues, such as parking regulations, and on the social aspects of the job (Reed-Mendenhall and Willard 1980). A study at Texas Instruments confirms this generalization (Gomersall and Myers 1966). One group of employees was given the traditional orientation associated with their jobs. For two hours they were briefed on such topics as leave policy, work rules, and employee services, after which they began working as trainees. The second group also received this two-hour orientation, but the remainder of the first day of work involved informal discussions with personnel specialists. During these discussions the specialists attempted to relieve the new workers' anxieties, and they emphasized four points:

Your opportunity to succeed is very good.

Disregard "hall talk."

Take the initiative in communication.

Get to know your supervisor.

In the second group actual training time following job orientation was shortened by a half, training costs were lowered to a third of their previous levels, absenteeism and tardiness dropped to a half of the previous norm, waste and rejects were reduced to a fifth of the previous levels, and costs were cut as much as fifteen to thirty percent.

However, if a job orientation program is not well-organized, it is just about useless. During the 1960s Chemical Bank of New York was having difficulty hiring bank tellers, so it overhired. As a result, many of the new employees could not immediately attend the two-week training program. Instead, the bank's management oriented the new employees to the organization by sending them to branches, where they were supposed to observe the work and gain a feel for the organization. However, since the experienced tellers were too busy to bother with the new employees, the new employees just sat idly by and became bored. Most of them quit within a few days. And even if they waited out the orientation, they entered their new jobs with negative feelings.

Job orientation represents the starting point of an organization's attempt to socialize its members (Schein 1961). An organization wishes its members to hold values that are consonant with its goals and objectives and to exhibit behaviors that will help achieve these goals and objectives. But if job orientation and other aspects of organizational socialization are ineffective, the organization will not function efficiently—and in extreme cases it will not function at all.

Like selection, job orientation is a form of feedforward control. The organization eliminates potential problems even before they occur by answering the individual's questions about job duties, allowing the individual to express reservations, and providing a gradual introduction to the work. Job orientation thus can be an effective control technique.

TRAINING AND DEVELOPMENT

Although training and development are closely related, they represent separate entities. Training is job-specific: An individual receives instruction to complete a specific task. Development is career-specific: Management outlines a series of activities and jobs, each successively involving greater responsibility and authority, through which the individual progresses throughout his or her career in the organization. While the developmental plan for a specific employee or manager is subject to change based on such conditions as performance and organizational needs, the objective is to have the individual achieve his or her potential at the same time that the organization's present and future needs are met.

Some organizations discuss training and development needs during performance appraisal interviews. However, many organizations now conduct separate interviews: a performance appraisal interview, during which training needs are discussed, and a developmental career interview, during which developmental needs and programs are highlighted. In the federal government, agencies are now required by law to separate these two interviews.

Training

For training to be effective, behavioral conditions under which it occurs should be favorable. In addition, there are specific training rules and techniques that are related to successful training. In this section we examine these issues; then we describe some actual training programs of well-managed organizations.

Behavioral Conditions. All things being equal, an individual highly *motivated* to learn will do so faster than an individual who is not motivated. To motivate an individual, one must capture his or her attention. Methods of accomplishing this include a pleasant setting in which the training takes place, attention-getting devices and charts, and a brief discussion of the importance of the training activity.

From a practical viewpoint the trainer should attempt to teach an individual new material when he is ready to learn it. Similarly, an organization should provide the kind of training program an employee or manager actually wants to complete, for otherwise the probability that he will actively and successfully participate in it is low.

It is frequently difficult to assess the motivational level of organizational members, especially if there are many of them. Still, the following rule can be reasonably followed: Provide training to the organizational members precisely at the time they express a great desire for it. Desire constitutes the triggering mechanism that typically enhances the learning process.

Knowledge or *feedback* of results is another behavioral determinant of learning (Annett 1968). The more individuals know about their success or lack of it, the more capable they become of altering their behavior to achieve their objectives. Admittedly, learning can occur without feedback. For instance, an individual reading a biology textbook is learning. However, this learning is strengthened if the student receives feedback through periodic examinations. Likewise, an organization can provide feedback in a training program for its employees and managers by testing their skills and abilities. If the training program is very general and does not use feedback of results, it is probable that the employee or manager will not be stimulated by it and will not absorb much information.

Prior learning is also a behavioral condition that can enhance learning. Generally speaking, it is easier for the individual to learn a subject if it is similar to something he already knows. An individual will probably learn psychology more quickly if he has studied sociology rather than mathematics, since there is some overlap between the two fields and many of the stimulus-response combinations are similar. However, there are some situations in which prior learning will inhibit the learning of new material, for example if the individual views new material as contradictory to material he already knows.

Training Rules. An important issue in learning relates to the training rules that are used to enhance it. Several writers have examined this issue in depth (Filley, House, and Kerr 1976; Bass and Vaughan 1966; McCormick and Tiffin 1974; Maier 1973). One conclusion of this research is that *frequent repetition* is generally effective in increasing the rate of learning. This is particularly true for tasks involving much memorization.

For most standard training situations *distributed* or spaced repetitions yield higher performance levels than do *massed* repetitions. Distributed repetitions seem to be effective when the individual is attempting to learn basic concepts in a complex field such as psychology or chemistry. Also, the longer the task, the more effective distributed practice is. However, massed repetitions work well for memorizing and for routine tasks such as typing. And massed repetitions can be effective if there is need for a warm-up period, or when long intervals create a situation in which the individual forgets too much of the material he is trying to learn.

Researchers generally advocate *whole learning* over part learning. The individual first perceives a difficult task by obtaining a general impression of the entire project, and then he or she focuses on its specific parts as the training continues. Whole learning is also helpful to group activities and parts of tasks, for it is easier to comprehend the whole task if the individual sees parts and their relationships rather than their discrete elements.

Recitation or *active repetitions* are generally more effective than passive reading or listening to someone else read. The individual should be actively involved in the learning process. Researchers have also found that *uniqueness* facilitates learning. For example, when an individual is learning a series of nonsense symbols and a solitary number is included in the list, he will remember the number better than any of the nonsense symbols. This finding confirms the fact that attention-getting devices, such as uniqueness, facilitate learning.

Training Techniques. There are several training techniques that can promote different kinds of learning. *Programmed instruction* seems to be particularly effective when the objective is to acquire knowledge. Using programmed instruction, the individual attempts to understand a preliminary set of concepts at his or her own pace and advances only after answering a set of questions on those concepts. If the individual answers some of the questions incorrectly, he or she receives instructions to study additional material on the subject before moving on. Twenty research studies have focused on this technique, and they indicate that immediate learning was at least ten percent higher under programmed instruction in seven comparisons and that there were no practically significant differences in the other instances (Nash, Muczyk, and Vettori 1971).

Similarly, the individual effectively acquires knowledge when he or she attends *lectures.* This method is economically sound, for it provides several individuals simultaneously with a broad array of concepts. However, unless discussion accompanies the lecture, the trainee can easily distort the messages the trainer is seeking to impart. And, in general, there are no significant differences in effectiveness between television courses and conventional lecture courses (Carroll and Tosi 1977).

If the objective of the training is to change attitudes rather than impart knowledge, *discussion* seems to be superior to the lecture. Also, *role playing* can be an effective method for changing attitudes. Research suggests that role playing is particularly helpful if the individuals participating in it must take a point of view opposite to their own and must verbalize this point of view (Janis and Mann 1954). In addition, role playing seems to increase the trainee's effectiveness as a problem solver (Maier and Hoffman 1960). It also can be used to develop the interpersonal skills of individuals.

There are other training methods we have not discussed, such as the film and the case study. At this point we do not have much information on their effectiveness, and so we will not focus on them. However, in Chapter 18 we will examine one such training method, sensitivity training, because it has become very important in the area of organizational development and change.

Effective Training Programs. Lester Digman (1978) has described in detail the effective training programs used in well-managed organizations (see also Newstrom 1980). He surveyed the best-managed companies in the United States as rated by *Dun's Review* for the period 1972–1976. As shown in Table 8–2, organizational size is related to the type of training that well-managed organizations provide at the middle-management and executive managerial levels.

At the executive managerial level, as organizational size increases, companies increase their in-house training, although this is supplemented by guest lectures and some outside-the-company exposure. Also, as organizational size increases, training at the executive managerial level begins to stress not only business strategy but also sensitivity to the relationship between the company's internal structure and the external environment in which is operates.

A similar pattern emerges at the middle-management level in that larger organizations rely primarily on in-house training. However, regardless of size, middle-management training focuses on human relations and conceptual skills.

TABLE 8–2

Types of Training in Well-managed Organizations: Program Type and Level Versus Organization Size

Program level	Organization size: Medium to large, less than 2000 managers	Large, 2000–8000 managers	Very large, over 8000 managers
Executive	Programs largely individualized. Primarily outside the company, some internal on contract, some completely ad hoc. Oriented toward conceptual skills and strategy.	Programs divided between in-house and outside the company. Oriented toward conceptual skills, strategy, and environmental understanding.	Programs largely in-house and centralized, supplemental lectures, some outside company exposure. Oriented toward interface of internal and external environment.
Middle	Programs mixed between in-house (supplemented by lecturers) and outside the company. Oriented toward human and conceptual skills and analytical abilities.	Programs largely in-house, with little outside the company. Conducted on centralized corporate basis. Oriented toward human and decision-making skills, geared to company policy.	Programs predominantly in-house, either corporate- or division-centralized. Orientation is on human, decision-making, and conceptual skills.
Supervisory	Programs on-site in division. Orientation is on basic technical and human skills, geared to company procedures.	Program on-site in division. Orientation is on basic technical and human skills, including company procedures.	Programs on-site in division. Orientation is on basic technical and human skills, including company procedures and policy. Program instructors are centrally trained.

Source: Adapted by permission of the publisher from "How Well-Managed Organizations Develop Their Executives" by Lester Digman, *Organizational Dynamics,* Autumn 1978, © 1978 by AMACOM, a division of American Management Associations, p. 69.

At the supervisory level, organizational size is not important in predicting the types of training programs that well-managed companies use. The program is typically on-site in the division and emphasizes basic technical and human skills geared to company procedures.

Development As indicated previously, training is job-specific, while development is career-specific. In this section we describe various types of career development programs and effective developmental interviews.

Types of Developmental Programs. *Career counseling,* advising the individual about his or her career possibilities and career progression, is the first major type of career developmental program. It can occur at various times, including the employment hiring interview, a career-counseling training program, and the performance appraisal interview.

This counseling is used not only with employees whose potential is high, but also with those who are likely to be demoted.

A *career path* is a series of jobs through which an individual will proceed if performance remains high and organizational positions open up. Sometimes career paths involve *job rotation,* moving an individual through a series of jobs temporarily so that he or she becomes acquainted with the overall activities of major subsystems or the entire organization. Whatever the approach, the use of career paths allows the individual to acquire the necessary experience for future jobs.

Many large organizations now employ a *human resources file,* a computerized inventory of backgrounds and skills that management uses to identify individuals capable of performing the activities in a vacated position. A good example of its use comes from the Carter administration. When President Carter assumed office, he wanted to appoint capable women to high-level government jobs. Since only a small number of women were working in high-level government positions, Carter's personnel specialists were able to obtain computerized printouts of all women working in governmental jobs of GS-15 and above. These printouts, listing such factors as previous work experience and educational background, allowed the personnel specialists to identify women capable of performing high-level government work, many of whom became Assistant Secretaries and Deputy Assistant Secretaries.

Many training programs focus on developmental activities. They address issues such as career management for women and minority group members and refresher courses for midcareer managers. Several organizations even sponsor placement programs for managers who are leaving the organization. In most instances these terminations occur not because of poor performance but because of organizational constraints (Labor Letter, *Wall Street Journal* 1979). In placement programs the company provides not only career counseling but an office and salary for a specified time while the manager seeks a new position.

A distinctive training program with developmental trappings is the *intern program.* Typically a recent graduate is hired as a management trainee, and for one of two years he or she receives specific training, some involving classroom instruction, in the various activities performed by the organization. Intern programs can, in fact, be more helpful for career development than a graduate degree in some fields. The two-year management training program of the Chase Manhattan Bank is so good that managements of other banks hire its graduates. A typical day in this program involves three hours of classroom instruction, four hours of work in a functional area of the bank, two more hours of classroom instruction, and two or three hours of homework. At one point the top management of Chase Manhattan considered eliminating the program—primarily because most of its graduates were lured away by other banks.

Assessment Centers. At present, perhaps the most popular program that can be used for selection or development is the *assessment center.* In recent years over 20,000 companies have created assessment centers to help them evaluate candidates' managerial potential (see Howard 1974; Rice 1979). The concept of an assessment center was drawn from the procedures of the elite Schutzstaffel (SS) guard in Germany during the 1930s. To select the best applicants for this military force, management put the candidates through a series of simulated exercises, group discussion sessions, and extended psychological interviews. Psychologists then evaluated a person's overall potential as an SS officer.

In recent years management has used the assessment center both as a selection technique and a developmental program, for a major objective is to realize a person's full potential within a specific organization. Each center should be tailored to the needs of the organization sponsoring it. But almost all assessment centers involve some exercises that measure the individual's ability to function under pressure. For example, in the in-basket training exercise the individual is informed that he or she is to take the place of the superior, who has been hospitalized. He or she is then assigned to the superior's desk and told to handle all business matters in the in-basket. Usually a telephone is provided with a list of numbers the individual can call as he or she attempts to solve problems. A time limit of three or four hours is fixed so that the individual's ability to function under pressure can be judged.

In the 1950s American Telephone & Telegraph Company (AT&T) developed an assessment center that managerial trainees attended for three and a half days. Psychologists then predicted the probable success of the trainees. The psychologists did not give their results to top management, since that might have created a self-fulfilling prophecy; that is, top management might have advanced the trainees who were rated most likely to succeed. Follow-ups during the past twenty-five years indicate that a person's performance in the AT&T program did to some extent predict his managerial success.

Although the organization gains by using an assessment center, since it improves the chances of selecting effective individuals, the trainee also benefits. Early in the trainee's career he or she is made aware of the chances for success within a *particular* organization. Evaluations of performance in the assessment center are given to each trainee; each learns about his or her strengths and weaknesses; and each obtains a general idea about the probability of succeeding in the organization. If the probability of success is low, the trainee can move to a new organization at a point when he or she is still highly mobile. Or the trainee can change his behavior to improve the chances of success if he decides to stay with the organization. And when assessment centers are employed as development mechanisms that managers may attend during their careers, they find out how well they have overcome their managerial weaknesses.

Successful Development Programs. Jon English and Anthony Marchione (1977) have delineated the conditions that management should observe in constructing an effective development program for organizational members. Foremost is assessing the skills and abilities that the organization requires currently and in the future. Top management's involvement should be encouraged, and participants should be invited to discuss what they feel they want to accomplish in their career development program. In addition, the program should have a practical orientation so that individuals do not feel they are wasting time on theoretical learning that cannot be applied in their careers. There should be continual reinforcement of career objectives during the development interviews, and the career development program of the organization should be periodically evaluated and updated. Under such conditions English and Marchione feel that both organizational and individual developmental needs are effectively met.

Ronald Burke, William Weitzel, and Tamara Weir (1978) have focused on a related issue, the characteristics of successful appraisal and developmental interviews. Their empirical studies have compared successful and unsuccessful interviews, and they indicate that the following characteristics are important if the subordinate is to benefit from the appraisal or developmental interview:

A significant amount of employee participation in the program through joint setting of goals between the superior and subordinate.

A helpful supervisor genuinely interested in the subordinate.

The removal of job problems hampering the employee's performance.

The setting of future performance targets.

The involvement of the subordinate in planning self-developmental activities.

An unthreatening atmosphere.

Additional Issues. It is important to realize that training and developmental needs vary by career stages. For instance, during midcareer the technical skills of many managers and employees become obsolete unless they update their education. Engineers are constantly faced with this problem; technological advances in the United States are so rapid that engineers must receive additional formal schooling at midcareer if they are to maintain their professional skills. Under such conditions the individual should openly express his or her feelings about the well-known midcareer syndrome. Openness about the matter will allow the individual to adjust technically and emotionally and advance comfortably to the next stage of his career.

Finally, there are many hidden issues that demand attention in the career development area. These include encouraging people to assume responsibility for their own careers, overdeveloping individuals or raising expectations when there are few opportunities to advance in an organization, and providing adequate information about career development programs in the organization. And in many cases developmental programs can have a boomerang effect—highly productive individuals may leave the organization if they gradually perceive that the developmental activities in which they are engaged are of great value only in *other* organizations. Consequently, the organization should not provide career-enhancing activities if they can only result in frustration for the subordinate.

PERFORMANCE APPRAISAL

Management must evaluate employees' performance regularly; typically appraisal interviews are held once or twice a year. As we have indicated, it is preferable to separate performance appraisal interviews and career development interviews whenever possible. In this section we describe various methods that management uses to rate performance, and we evaluate their strengths and limitations.

Rating Methods

Several methods currently are used to appraise performance. We shall focus on four well-known methods: traditional trait ratings, global ratings, behaviorally anchored rating scales, and goal-oriented evaluations.

Traditional Trait Ratings. For many years the most popular way of rating an employee was in terms of *traits,* such as perseverance and maturity, that he or she manifested. This technique was used, for example, in 1979 when former President Carter fired several members of his cabinet and appointed Hamilton Jordan as his chief of staff. Jordan then instituted trait rating to evaluate the performance of high-level government executives (see Figure 8–2).

However, this type of rating has fallen into some disrepute. It is very difficult, although not impossible, to measure such traits, as we shall see in Chapter 14. And even if these traits can be measured, superiors and subordinates tend to find this approach unacceptable. When a superior gives a subordinate a poor rating on such traits as

FIGURE 8–2

Jordan's Report Cards

This trait-rating form was used by Hamilton Jordan, former President Carter's chief of staff, to evaluate the performance of high-level government executives.

Office: ____________

Name of Rater: ____________

STAFF EVALUATION

Please answer each of the following questions about this person.

Name: ____________

Salary: ____________

Position: ____________

Duties: ____________

Work Habits

1. On the average when does this person:
   arrive at work ____________
   leave work ____________
2. Pace of Work:
   1 2 3 4 5 6
   slow — fast
3. Level of Effort:
   1 2 3 4 5 6
   below capacity — full capacity
4. Quality of Work:
   1 2 3 4 5 6
   poor — good
5. What is he/she best at? (rank 1–5)
   __conceptualizing
   __planning
   __implementing
   __attending to detail
   __controlling quality
6. Does this person have the skills to do the job he/she was hired to do?
   yes____
   no____
   ?____
7. Would the slot filled by this person be better filled by someone else?
   yes____
   no____
   ?____

Personal Characteristics

8. How confident is this person? (circle one)
   x x x x x x
   self-doubting — confident — cocky
9. How confident are you of this person's judgment?
   1 2 3 4 5 6
   not confident — very confident
10. How mature is this person?
    1 2 3 4 5 6
    immature — mature
11. How flexible is this person?
    1 2 3 4 5 6
    rigid — flexible
12. How stable is this person?
    1 2 3 4 5 6
    erratic — steady
13. How frequently does this person come up with new ideas?
    1 2 3 4 5 6
    seldom — often
14. How open is this person to new ideas?
    1 2 3 4 5 6
    closed — open
15. How bright is this person?
    1 2 3 4 5 6
    average — very bright
16. What are this person's special talents?
    1 ____________
    2 ____________
    3 ____________
17. What is this person's range of information?
    1 2 3 4 5 6
    narrow — broad

Interpersonal Relations

18. How would you characterize this person's impact on other people? (for example, hostile, smooth, aggressive, charming, etc.)
    1 ____________
    2 ____________
    3 ____________
19. How well does this person get along with:

superiors	1	2	3	4	5	6
peers	1	2	3	4	5	6
subordinates	1	2	3	4	5	6
outsiders	1	2	3	4	5	6
	not well					very well

20. In a public setting, how comfortable would you be having this person represent:

you or your office	1	2	3	4	5	6
the president	1	2	3	4	5	6
	uncomfortable					comfortable

21. Rate this person's political skills.
    1 2 3 4 5 6
    naive — savvy

Supervision and Direction

22. To what extent is this person focused on accomplishing
    administration's goals ____%
    personal goals ____%
    100%
23. How capable is this person at working toward implementing a decision with which he/she may not agree?
    1 2 3 4 5 6
    reluctant — eager
24. How well does this person take direction?
    1 2 3 4 5 6
    resists — readily
25. How much supervision does this person need?
    1 2 3 4 5 6
    a lot — little
26. How readily does this person offer to help out by doing that which is not a part of his/her "job"?
    1 2 3 4 5 6
    seldom — often

Summary

27. Can this person assume more responsibility?
    yes____
    no____
    ?____
28. List this person's 3 major strengths and 3 major weaknesses.
    Strengths: 1 ____________
    2 ____________
    3 ____________
    Weaknesses: 1 ____________
    2 ____________
    3 ____________
29. List this person's 3 major accomplishments.
    1 ____________
    2 ____________
    3 ____________
30. List 3 things about this person that have disappointed you.
    1 ____________
    2 ____________
    3 ____________

Source: Hamilton Jordan.

maturity and the ability to interact effectively, he or she must justify the report. But justification is difficult to accomplish, since the ratings are typically subjective. Also, many superiors experience only a limited amount of interaction with subordinates and have little basis for judging such traits as maturity. And many subordinates react negatively if their superior characterizes them as immature and lacking in ambition. Additionally, the relationship between performance and rewards becomes clouded; there is little clarification of job duties; and the atmosphere is not conducive to counseling that is focused on training and career development.

For these and many other reasons, the actual performance appraisal meeting tends to become ritualistic rather than meaningful. The superior completes the required forms and generally rates only a few subordinates as either outstanding or poor; most employees receive average ratings. When the superior calls the subordinate into his office, he shows him the form, asks for any comments, and then requests that the employee sign it. In such situations employees frequently feel that their performance has not been appraised. A phenomenon called the vanishing performance appraisal becomes a reality: The superior will say that he recently conducted a genuine performance appraisal meeting with a subordinate, but the employee cannot even remember that it took place (Hall and Lawler 1969).

Single Global Ratings. A related way of evaluating an employee is to provide a *single global rating* of a subordinate. The superior rates the subordinate in terms of only one item that is general in nature and does not specify aptitudes, traits, or other criteria. Typically the superior will rate the subordinate on a five-point scale extending from excellent to poor on an item such as: "In terms of all of the subordinates that have worked for you in the past five years, how would you rate this employee?"

Many of the problems associated with traditional trait ratings also accompany single global ratings. Some employees react defensively if their ratings are below average or average; the climate of the appraisal meeting does not encourage the manager to provide counseling and development information or to clarify the nature of the job; and the relationship between performance and rewards becomes unclear.

Behaviorally Anchored Rating Scales. As we have seen, one of the major difficulties associated with trait and global ratings is that they are not directly related to the job itself and do not clarify its requirements so that the employee can improve specific aspects of his or her performance. To overcome this problem, researchers have argued that rating scales should be directly tied to the requirements of the job;

that is, the scale should reflect actual instances of ineffective and effective behavior. This scale is termed a *behaviorally anchored rating scale.* For example, Marvin Dunnette and his associates (1968) developed a nine-point behaviorally anchored rating scale for measuring the dimension of handling customer complaints and making adjustments among salespersons in a department store. The most ineffective behavior was described as follows: could be expected to tell a customer who tried to return a shirt bought in Hawaii that a store in the States had no use for a Hawaiian shirt. The most effective behavior was described this way: could be expected to exchange a blouse purchased in a distant town and to impress the customer so much that she would buy three dresses and three pairs of shoes.

This type of scale is generally superior to trait and global ratings. Subordinates will accept criticism more easily if it is tied to actual job behavior; the performance appraisal session provides feedback that can be used for training and career development; the nature of the job is clarified; and the performance-reward relationship becomes clear.

However, constructing a behaviorally anchored rating scale is no easy task. The researcher typically observes workers performing the job and develops a series of descriptions characterizing effective and ineffective performance. He or she then meets with the workers and shows them an early version of the scale. Their criticisms and suggestions are subsequently used as the researcher attempts to refine the scale. This process may take several months and several meetings before it is finalized.

Goal-oriented Appraisal. Thus far we have pictured the performance appraisal process as one way: The superior tells the employee how his traits or behavior deviates from expectations. Even in the best of worlds, this creates some resentment in the highly motivated employee, since he is not allowed to participate in defining his own goals and job.

But as we have seen in Chapter 5, management by objectives (MBO) is one organizationwide planning technique that requires employee participation in setting organizational goals. Also, Edwin Locke's goal-setting theory indicates that individuals will tend to reach hard but attainable goals if such goals are accepted (see Chapter 13). For both techniques the setting of goals can be implemented in the performance appraisal session as a method for evaluating employees.

When this method is used, the performance of a subordinate is evaluated only or primarily in terms of his or her accomplishment of specific objectives. The subordinate participates in setting these objectives and in developing a time frame in which they are to be accom-

TABLE 8–3

Evaluation of Four Approaches to Measuring Performance

	Traditional trait rating	*Single global rating*	*Behaviorally anchored ratings*	*Objectives-oriented evaluation*
Acceptability to superior and subordinate	Poor	Moderate	Good	Good
Counseling and development information	Poor	Poor	Moderate	Good if it includes activities measures
Salary and reward administration	Poor	Moderate to good	Good	Moderate
Motivation based upon goal setting	Poor	Poor	Poor	Good
Clarify nature of job	Poor	Poor	Moderate to good	Good

Source: From Lyman Porter, Edward Lawler, and J. Richard Hackman, *Behavior in Organizations,* p. 332. Copyright © 1975 by McGraw-Hill, Inc. Reprinted by permission of McGraw-Hill Book Company.

plished. Hence the discussion between the superior and the subordinate tends to be objective, unemotional, and helpful.

This approach is usually viewed favorably both by superiors and subordinates, since it focuses only on the attainment of specific goals. Ideally, the employee sees a relationship between effort and performance, and between performance and desired rewards.

However, this approach does not describe the specific behaviors that lead to success on the job. In this way it is inferior to behaviorally anchored rating scales. Ideally, a combination of behaviorally anchored rating scales and goal setting should be used in appraising performance in most situations. As shown in Table 8–3, these two approaches are generally superior to trait and global ratings.

Additional Issues

There are other issues in the appraisal process that require discussion. These include the use of a single criterion, invalid data, measuring activities or results, and frequency of sessions. We discuss these issues below.

Single Criterion. One of the major problems in the measurement of performance revolves around the use of a single criterion or, at best, a few criteria that do not encompass the entire job. For example, management may judge the performance of its first-line superiors primarily in terms of the amount of money they overspend in a given time. Once the supervisors are aware of this situation, they will try to keep within their budgets but often at the expense of manufacturing products of inferior quality. By the time management rectifies the situation, the organization may have lost a large number of clients.

The use of a single criterion tends to make subordinates distrustful of their superiors. And as we have seen in our discussion of scientific management and human relations (Chapters 1 and 2), workers frequently tend to underperform when management is directly observing them. The higher the performance, the more management expects from the workers, frequently without an increase in pay. It is partly for this reason that industrial engineers have difficulty in agreeing among themselves about the time and effort required to perform a particular job.

Invalid Data. Even when behaviorally anchored rating scales or goal-oriented evaluations are used, it is difficult for the manager to free himself from bias. If a superior stereotypes an employee as ineffective, the employee has difficulty changing this perception, even if his actual performance is average or outstanding. However, behaviorally anchored rating scales used in combination with goal-oriented evaluation does minimize this problem.

Activities and Results. It is frequently difficult for a superior to differentiate between a subordinate's activities and their results. For instance, a subordinate may stay late for work every day because he does not organize activities efficiently, but the results of his efforts may be substandard. If at all possible, both activities and results should be measured, and feedback should be given to the subordinate on both issues. Focusing solely on one or the other is detrimental, since it tends to force individuals to concentrate on that which is measured. In such circumstances it is difficult to provide subordinates with training and development counseling. If subordinates see how they are deficient on one or the other dimension or both dimensions, they can begin to change their behavior.

Frequency. It is quite typical to schedule performance appraisal sessions on a regular basis, frequently every six months or year. Jaques (1961) has constructed a measure termed the *time span of discretion* that relates directly to the issue of frequency. This span represents the time it takes for substandard performance to show up. Performance appraisal sessions should ideally be scheduled parallel to this time span. If a superior evaluates a subordinate before it is possible for ineffective performance to appear, he or she has little basis for recommending corrective action. The frequency that should be used must be empirically determined by examining the job requirements and the skills necessary for completing it successfully. At the highest levels of the organization, this span may be three or four years; at the lower levels, three or six months. It is obviously difficult to ascertain the exact time span of discretion for a job, because so many variables need to be considered. Still, management should study each job and try to approximate the time span of discretion so that actual rather than perceived performance is measured.

REWARD SYSTEMS

If the performance appraisal system is operating correctly, management will be able to differentiate between effective and ineffective performers. And individuals whose performance is identified as effective should receive rewards. Hence there is a close relationship between the performance appraisal system and the reward system. In this section we discuss the motivational framework of the reward system and the employee preferences.

Motivational Framework

Allan Nash and Stephen Carroll (1975) have constructed a motivational framework based on the expectancy theory of motivation that relates directly to reward systems. In Chapter 13 we shall examine the expectancy theory in depth; in this chapter we merely summarize it. The major propositions of expectancy theory are as follows: (1) an individual must feel that, when he makes an effort, he will be successful; (2) this successful effort will lead to attaining rewards; and (3) he desires these rewards.

According to Nash and Carroll's framework, an individual who is achievement-oriented tends to respond positively to increased responsibility. Also, if the individual is to perceive a relationship between effort and successful performance, self-esteem is critical. Managers with a low degree of self-esteem tend to lower their efforts, while those with a high degree of self-esteem increase their efforts (Carroll and Tosi 1970). The effort-performance relationship is also affected by a person's ability, the resources the organization makes available to him for the completion of his task, role clarity (the degree to which he understands what he is supposed to accomplish), and the proper design of the work (see Figure 8–3). Thus the motivational framework of a reward system must address the managerial strategies used to promote motivation and the employee's satisfaction with the rewards.

Motivational Strategies. Nash and Carroll describe five prominent strategies that managers frequently use to motivate subordinates. These strategies should strengthen the perceptions that effort leads to successful performance and that successful performance leads to desired rewards. The first strategy, *fear,* is a negative approach and should be avoided if at all possible.

Another approach to motivation is *reciprocity:* What one is given

FIGURE 8–3
The Expectancy Model and the Reward System

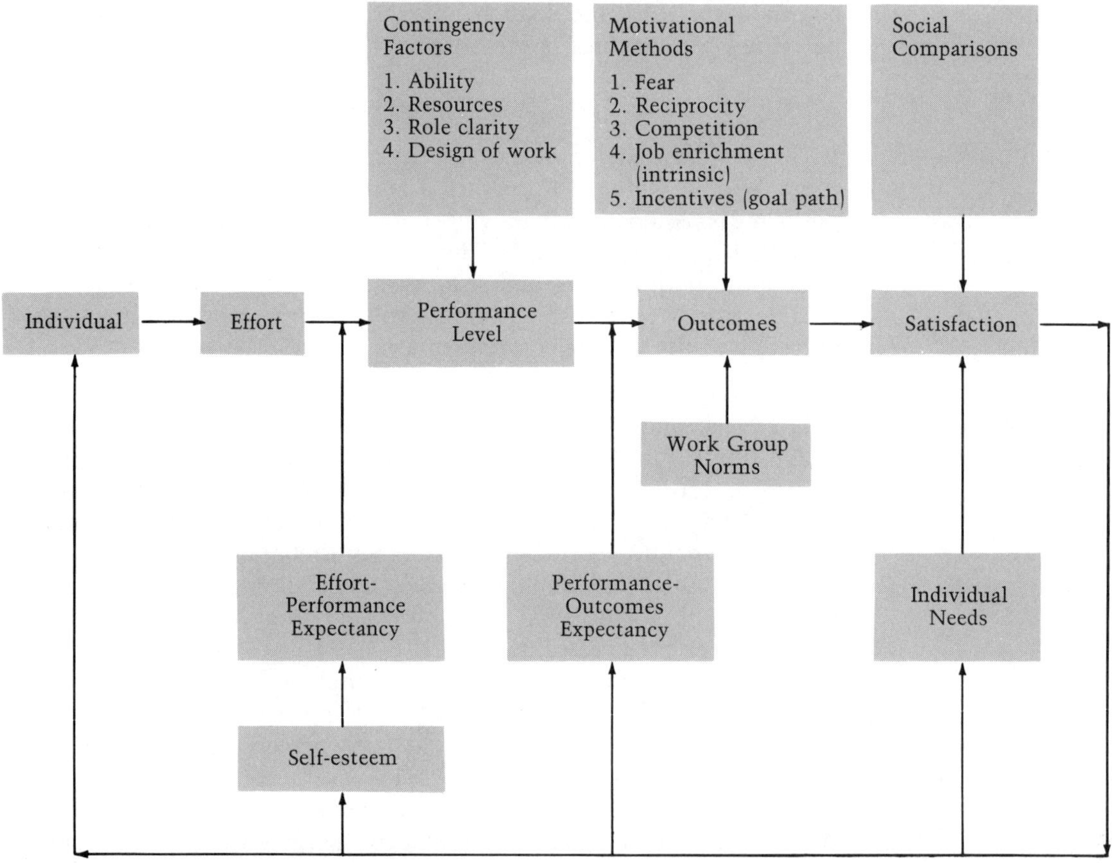

Source: From A. N. Nash and S. J. Carroll, Jr., *The Management of Compensation.* Copyright © 1975 by Wadsworth Publishing Company, Inc. Reprinted by permission of the publisher, Brooks/Cole Publishing Company, Monterey, California 93940.

he shall pay in an equivalent amount. This is the basis of the highly successful organizational intervention termed *role negotiation,* which will be treated in Chapter 18.

Management may also use the strategy of emphasizing *competition.* A considerable body of evidence suggests that individual piece-rate incentive systems are generally related to higher rates of productivity than a reward system offering only regular salaries (Viteles 1953; Vroom 1964). However, only part of this increase can be attributed to the individual incentive system; other contributory factors are improved methods of work typically accompanying the installation of a new incentive system, more efficient organization of the work, and the setting of standards (Nash and Carroll 1975). Also, individual incentive plans create an atmosphere of rivalry and intense competition, which frequently inhibit job satisfaction and lead to an unfavorable organizational climate.

Job *enrichment,* or increasing the individual's job responsibilities, constitutes the fourth common method that can be used to motivate individuals. For individuals who are not highly achievement-oriented, financial incentives seem preferable as a motivating strategy (Atkinson and Reitman 1956).

The final motivational strategy is the *goal path approach:* The organization should establish high performance as the path to the attainment of personal goals. Some research indicates that establishing difficult goals is related to increased effort expenditure *only* among those who believe that successful performance is rewarded (Carroll and Tosi 1970).

In addition to motivational strategies, work group bonds also influence expectancies. Workers may distrust management, thus creating group norms inhibiting productivity (see Chapter 1).

Satisfaction. Whether individuals will be satisfied with the rewards given to them depends on two major factors: their individual needs and social comparisons between the rewards they receive and those received by others doing the same or similar work. If individuals feel they are being treated inequitably in comparison with others, they frequently will decrease input and effort (see Chapter 13). And evidence suggests that when an employee compares his or her compensation to that of others, the closer these other persons are to the employee's own occupation, the more important the comparison is in determining satisfaction (Reynolds 1971). Such evidence confirms the importance of equity in the construction of an organizational reward system.

Employee Preferences

Individuals differ in the kinds of rewards they prefer. Pay, for instance, is very important at the lower levels of an organization. It is usually associated with the satisfaction of basic psychological needs, such as needs for security, status, esteem, and recognition (Lawler 1971). Pay may even be desired as a means of avoiding unpleasant psychological situations. Some research indicates that past experiences may cause an individual to associate inadequate amounts of money with insecurity, with generalized anxiety, and with family discord (Opshal and Dunnette 1966).

Research also suggests that workers generally prefer an adequate guaranteed base for average or adequate performance, and they prefer to see a few individuals receiving merit money for *outstanding* performance rather than having the merit money spread among individuals performing just slightly above average (Beer and Gerry 1968). However, this research then shows that individuals with a high degree of achievement orientation express a lower preference for the guaranteed base in return for the possibility of receiving handsome rewards for outstanding performance.

Many employees prefer increases in some form of supplemental compensation to increases in direct compensation. A highly desired form of supplemental compensation is immediate time off from work in large chunks of several days or weeks (Nealey 1964).

Most studies indicate that workers prefer hourly wages over incentive wage systems (Nash and Carroll 1975). However, once they have had experience with an incentive system, they tend to become more positive about it. And if an incentive plan is used, having the workers participate in its construction increases its acceptability (Lawler and Hackman 1969).

There are many kinds of rewards that organizations can offer, including pay, increased responsibility, fringe benefits, flexible working hours, praise, prizes, annual dinners, office, company car, stock options, a pleasant work environment, trophies and plaques, participation in decision making, recognition, meaningful tasks, and increased variety in the work. While some organizations have instituted innovative and outstanding programs, much more needs to be done; no issue will dominate organizations in the 1980s more than the question of how to revamp incentives to match the new motivations of workers (Yankelovich 1978).

SUMMARY

The personnel process of controlling organizational members involves selection and job orientation, training and development, performance appraisal, and reward systems.

There are several selection techniques for choosing individuals who are qualified, and these include emphasizing the use of informal job search methods, such as contacting school administrators, rather than formal methods, such as newspaper advertisements; testing; and using weighted application blanks. In all cases management should validate the selection technique, that is, ensure that the technique does in fact predict subsequent higher performance among those who score high on the instrument. The hiring interview is also a major selection device. However, many biases enter into the interviewer's evaluation of the candidate, especially if the interviewer has not been well trained. Yet it is possible to validate a workshop that trains interviewers, as has been done in the insurance industry.

While training and development overlap, they are separate issues. We now know a great deal about the behavioral conditions for effective training, the training rules that we should follow, and the techniques that we should use under a variety of circumstances. Lester Digman has studied the training programs of well-managed organizations, and his research indicates that organizational level and size of the organization predict the type of training emphasis.

Several types of career development programs are currently used, and these include career counseling, career paths (a series of positions through which the individual can progress), a human resources file, management internships, and specialized training programs such as midcareer development programs. A popular program that can be employed either for selection or development is the assessment center, which assesses the individual's strengths and limitations through a series of activities such as the in-basket technique and psychological evaluations.

There are several methods for appraising an individual's performance. These include traditional trait ratings, single global ratings, behaviorally anchored rating scales, or goal-oriented appraisal. All these rating methods possess inherent limitations and strengths, as we have seen.

Finally, the expectancy model of motivation can be used to evaluate the effectiveness of an organizational reward system. Managers emphasize many motivational strategies to strengthen the perception that effort leads to successful performance and that successful performance leads to desired rewards. These strategies include fear, reciprocity (obtaining something in return for the reward), competition, job enrichment, or goal path (incentives). Individuals desire different types of rewards, and organizations should structure their reward systems with this idea in mind.

DISCUSSION QUESTIONS

1. Mars, Inc. controls lateness among its employees and managers by providing each of them with a ten percent bonus of the daily salary if they report to work on time. Even the president receives this bonus. What do you think of this approach?
2. How can management control the behavior of employees when they are members of a strong and militant union?
3. How can a nonprofit organization such as the March of Dimes control the behavior of its members, who volunteer to work without pay? How can a church control the behavior of its members?
4. What is the relationship between performance standards and employee training? Between negative control techniques and performance standards?

5. Some organizations combine the performance appraisal interview and the career development interview. When would such a combination be appropriate?
6. What is validity? How is it related to reliability? Why is predictive validity superior to concurrent validity?
7. Hiring interviews are often poor predictors of subsequent performance. How can this problem be eliminated?
8. Under what conditions would a hiring interviewer rely more heavily on a weighted application blank than on the hiring interview in selecting job applicants?

CRITICAL INCIDENTS

NOTE: These critical incidents can be used by the whole class with the case observational method (see Appendix A) or used for thought and discussion by individual class members.

1. It is frequently difficult to compare accurately the performance of employees within a given job category. For instance, the success of salespeople can be measured in terms of three different measures: number of sales, dollar amount of sales, and number of customers who do not reorder. But these measures do not take into account the fact that some sales territories are superior to others.

A similar problem exists among college professors. Their performance is measured in terms of three criteria: teaching, research, and service both within the university and the external community. In one university the psychology department weighted these criteria at salary review time as follows: 5 for research, 3 for teaching, and 2 for service. However, the sociology department decided to use a variable system of weights. For instance, if a particular professor possessed an outstanding service record, a weight of 5 might be assigned to him or her for this dimension.

QUESTIONS: How are the measurement problems of performance similar to one another among salespeople and college professors? What are some ways of eliminating these problems? Do you feel that criteria should be weighted? Why or why not?

2. Office assignments are very important in an organization. When desirable offices become available, individuals frequently fight to obtain them. But large-scale reassignments of offices tend to create uneasiness and uncertainty. Individuals perceive, sometimes correctly, that an assignment to a less desirable office is akin to a demotion and a strong indication that top management is unhappy with their work.

In a psychology department of sixty faculty members within a large university, twenty additional offices became available when the sociology department moved to a new building. Thus it was not possible for every faculty member to move into a more desirable office, but certainly some of them would be able to do so. Immediately, however, problems emerged. Some faculty members with many years of service felt that they deserved priority in office assignments, even if they were not full professors. (The four ranks in this university were full professor, associate professor, assistant professor, and lecturer.) However, some younger faculty members with outstanding publication records did not agree with this stance: They felt that offices should be assigned to the best performers, regardless of rank or seniority. To compound the problem, there was much disagreement about the measurement of outstanding performance. Should it be measured in terms of teaching, scholarly publications, or university and community service?

The department head appointed a task force to solve this problem.

QUESTIONS: How should performance be measured in reallocating these offices? Would you measure performance for salary increases in the same manner? Why or why not? What system should be used to assign offices in an equitable manner?

SUGGESTED READINGS

Miner, John. *The Challenge of Managing.* Philadelphia: Saunders, 1975, paperback, 348 pages.

This short paperback contains research summaries and fascinating case studies focused on managing individuals, especially if performance is substandard.

Schneider, Benjamin. *Staffing Organizations.* Pacific Palisades, Calif.: Goodyear, 1975, paperback, 257 pages.

This short paperback is a succinct introduction to the research on and methods of staffing organizations.

PART II
CASE STUDY

Monitoring the Performance of Bank Tellers

In Chapter 3 we described a large branch-banking system. Most of this system's employees are tellers who provide direct and face-to-face service to the customer in the 180 branch banks. During the middle 1960s this banking system began to experience abnormally high turnover among the tellers; in 1967 forty percent of all tellers left their jobs, including sixty percent of the tellers who had been there less than one year. Since personal and accurate service to the customer is vital in this kind of organization, top management was very concerned about the problem.

Top management had attempted to use feedforward control to minimize employee problems by sending newly hired tellers to a two-week training course, where they learned the ideal way of performing their work. However, once they were working in a branch, the tellers immediately confronted a dilemma—speed versus accuracy. In the training school the instructors stressed that accuracy was more important than speed because of the nature of the work. But since many of the local branches were understaffed, the branch managers and the experienced tellers taught the newly hired tellers shortcuts that enabled them to work faster.

The problem of speed versus accuracy brings into focus another dilemma, that of measuring the tellers' performance. Promotions and pay increases are supposedly related to the size of each teller's dif-

Note: This case can be used by the whole class with the case observational method (see Appendix A) or used for thought and discussion by individual class members.

Source: Martin J. Gannon, "Employee Perceptions of Promotion," *Personnel Journal* 50, no. 3 (March 1971): 215. Reprinted by permission of Personnel Journal Inc., ference account, the amount of money for which he or she cannot account. The difference account, however, is a function of the amount of trade the branch has, managerial practices, and many other factors. Thus one teller may do twice as much work as another teller but have a slightly worse difference account. When an opportunity for promotion arises, the officers tend to turn down the speedy and hard-working teller if his or her difference account is high. Further, while the officers may reward effective tellers with small salary increases and praise, they frequently try to delay their promotions because they process the work so quickly. Hence these tellers are sometimes locked into their jobs purely because they are so efficient.

The bank's management hired a consultant to examine the problem of promotion. This consultant conducted several unstructured interviews with tellers, during which they frequently mentioned six factors they perceived as important in managers' evaluations of their work. Tellers must cooperate with one another: they share the work load by asking customers to step over to their windows when another teller is very busy, by helping each other to balance the books at the end of the day, and by spending time aiding the new tellers. Accuracy in doing the work, as reflected in the difference account, is also a major item, as is speed. Another factor is education: the more education, the better is the chance for promotion. In some branches, getting along well with an influential superior may lead to a promotion. And because they work directly with the public, tellers' good relations with customers are important.

The consultant then asked all 437 tellers in the system to complete a short questionnaire on which they ranked these six items (see Table 1). The tellers felt that two factors were of overwhelming im-

TABLE 1
Rankings by Employees of the Factors Considered Important for Promotion ($N = 437$)

	Most important[a] *(in percentages)*			*Least important (in percentages)*		
	1	2	3	4	5	6
Good relations with customers	6.8	10.3	19.9	19.9	21.0	22.0
Speed in doing work	1.6	11.4	22.0	23.9	22.9	17.2
Recommendation by right person	12.6	17.4	7.1	5.9	17.4	39.8
Cooperation in finishing work	3.6	10.7	23.6	31.1	21.5	9.4
Accuracy in doing work	35.6	32.5	17.8	9.8	3.7	0.5
Education	39.8	17.7	9.6	8.4	13.5	11.1

[a] Percentages calculated by column.

Source: From Martin J. Gannon, "Employee Perceptions of Promotion," *Personnel Journal* 50, no. 3 (March 1971): 215. Reprinted by permission of Personnel Journal, Inc. Copyright March 1971.

portance for promotion—68.1 percent of the tellers ranked accuracy as either first or second and 57.5 percent ranked education as first or second. From the tellers' perspective, speed, or its equivalent, hard work, is not as likely to be rewarded in this system. Helping other employees and managers also is of less significance, as is good relations with customers.

QUESTIONS: How can top management develop a better control system for the performance of tellers? What other factors should top management use to evaluate the performance of tellers? What can the bank do about the dilemma of speed versus accuracy? In what other kinds of jobs would this issue be important?

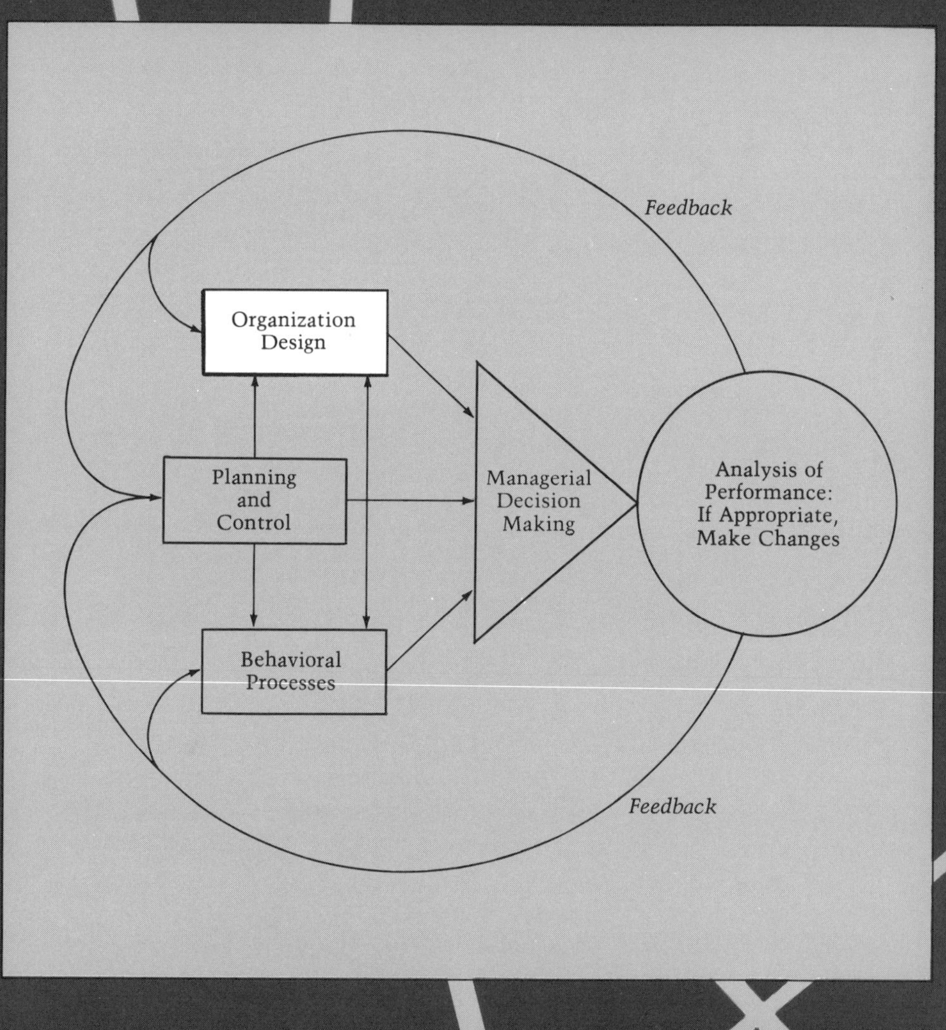
Feedback
Organization
Design
Planning
and
Control
Behavioral
Processes
Managerial
Decision
Making
Analysis of
Performance:
If Appropriate,
Make Changes
Feedback

III ORGANIZING

To operate effectively, management must work within an organization whose design is compatible with the types of tasks to be completed. Until the end of World War I design was a minor managerial issue, for almost all organizations were structured as centralized, rigid hierarchies. In most situations the president and a few key subordinates made all major decisions; most subordinates exercised little responsibility. Only in the past fifty years has management realized the importance of organization design for the attainment of success. Thus in recent years many new designs and approaches have been developed to handle the unique problems that particular organizations face.

Part III examines organization design and the process of organizing. Chapter 9 treats the classical and contemporary concepts of organizing, focusing on the building of the organization, the construction of guidance systems, and the integration of activities and subunits. Chapter 10 describes alternative methods of organizing: modern forms, specialized forms, and economic forms. The final chapter in Part III discusses the situational or contingency approach to organizing.

Model A's on the assembly line at the River Rouge plant

CONTINUOUS CASE

The Ford Motor Company 1921–1929

SUMMARY: Unlike the strategies of other car manufacturers, Henry Ford's strategic plan was to produce an all-purpose, inexpensive car, the Model T. When this car appeared in 1909, it was a major success. However, to continue to produce an inexpensive car, Henry Ford needed to cut his labor costs. He did this by using mass production and hiring unskilled workers, but he then experienced severe labor problems. In 1913 alone there was a 380 percent labor turnover rate. To solve this problem, Ford introduced a series of enlightened personnel practices between 1914 and 1920, including the $5 day, the Safety and Health Department, and the Henry Ford Trade School.

Around 1921 Henry Ford began to emphasize excessive control over the behavior of his workers. His purpose was to keep the price of the Model T at a low level, and to save money, he introduced the *speedup.* Since the assembly line was machine-controlled, the supervisors could easily increase its speed. Now the workers could perform their job cycles in much less time—and without an increase in pay. The supervisors were merciless and drove the workers hard. Discipline was so strict during this period that the workers were not even allowed to talk on the assembly line. One long-term worker managed to avoid this rule by whispering out of the side of his mouth, only to end up with permanent facial distortions in his later years.

How did Ford ensure that strict discipline was maintained? In the late twenties Ford met Harry Bennett, who had underworld connections and had spent some time in jail. Henry Ford took a great liking to him and treated him like a son. Ford asked Bennett to head the Ford Service Police, a 3000-member group that enforced the speedup and other measures of strict discipline within the company. Some workers were physically assaulted by members of this police force, especially those who were involved in any covert union activities.

Because of Ford's emphasis on profits, whatever the cost to his workers, most of the idealistic projects he had initiated in 1914–1920 had premature deaths. Dean Marquis, dynamic head of the Ford Sociology Department, resigned in 1922 when he realized the department was no longer supporting the interests of the workers. With his resignation, Henry Ford closed down the department. The plant foremen were now virtual dictators; they could hire and fire employees with no fear of reprisal. Even the press was stifled; William Brownell, who was editor of the *Ford News* and partial to labor, resigned in 1920 and was replaced by a promanagement spokesman.

However, Ford's treatment of his workers was consistent with his economic philosophy. Ford believed the more money management paid the worker, the more industry's products would be consumed. Industry would benefit, consequently, through the payment of high wages. But though Ford paid workers high wages when they did work, he felt little responsibility to them if they were laid off. He believed workers could always find jobs once industry, after a relapse, began to advance again. Ford thus gave his workers no benefits except high wages, which they could obtain only when the industrialist decided they should work.

Ford's new emphasis on profitability and regimentation of workers was a response to the growth of General Motors at this time. Much of the initial success of General Motors derived from its policies of annual model changes and its appeal to a cross section of buyers. Another important factor was its use of federal decentralization. All the operating units in a company are allowed to make their own decisions and actions throughout a given reporting period, at the end of which top management evaluates their relative performance. Top management may then decide to close down some operating units, renovate others, and increase the budgets of those that have performed in a superior manner (see Chapter 10).

Perhaps the most important advantage of federal decentralization is that it allows a company to respond to its problems flexibly. However, Henry Ford did not opt for designing his company in this manner, at least in part because he clung to his plan of manufacturing an inexpensive, all-purpose, durable car. And now that General Motors was taking customers away from Ford, he knew he had to produce a new car. But his refusal to change his strategic plan eventually led to disaster.

To manufacture his new car, Henry Ford made plans to build the River Rouge, a centralized plant that could produce cars with a minimum of effort. Over 100,000 men could work in this plant, and all the functions necessary for the building of automobiles, from iron ore furnaces to the moving assembly line, were housed there. In the short run the design proved to be effective, for it allowed the company to produce the new car, the Model A, very efficiently and inexpensively. But in the long run the design proved to be a disaster. It was not adaptable to new models, and the entire plant had to be shut down to make alterations.

Production of the Model A began in 1927. While profits were negligible in 1927 and 1928 because of the changeover to the new model, there was a sizable increase in 1929, and in that year the Ford Motor Company outsold General Motors. It appeared as if Henry Ford would regain his position as the leader of the automotive industry, but this was not his destiny—the title was perennially won by General Motors after 1929. Since the River Rouge plant was not adaptable to new models, it was several years—1932, in fact—before Ford introduced another new car. By that time it was too late; General Motors now dominated the industry. Throughout the 1930s the Ford Motor Company consistently lost money.

QUESTIONS: What are some logical explanations for Henry Ford's behavior and decisions? When Ford built the River Rouge plant, what dimensions in our organizational framework was he activating? Was this dimension related to any of the other dimensions? How and why?

9 Classical and Contemporary Concepts of Organizing

HIERARCHY AND SPECIALIZATION
BARRIERS TO INTEGRATION
IMPROVING INTEGRATION
SUMMARY
DISCUSSION QUESTIONS
CRITICAL INCIDENTS
SUGGESTED READINGS

PERFORMANCE OBJECTIVES

1. To show the importance of the hierarchy and specialization within it in the design of organizations.
2. To identify the major factors that management should consider in building organizations, and to describe the guidance systems that organizations use to plan and structure their activities.
3. To identify the main barriers to integrating activities and groups within the hierarchy, and to describe some methods for improving integration.

Management theorists and practitioners have, over the years, developed rather definite ideas about the manner in which organizations should be constructed (see Chapters 1 and 2). As we might expect, much controversy surrounds some of these ideas. Still, an impressive amount of evidence supports many of them, and hence managers can reasonably employ these ideas in constructing their organizations.

Perhaps the most fundamental design concept is that of the hierarchy and the specialization accompanying it. Even if an organization's managers do not wish to create a hierarchy, it tends to arise inevitably. A good illustration of this phenomenon is provided by the experience of some French companies after World War II. These companies attempted to eliminate the hierarchy; they organized purely on the basis of cooperative ownership and shared responsibilities among organizational members, all of whom were considered equals. However, chaos and conflict occurred because organizational members tried to avoid the dull jobs, which tended to predominate. This result forced the members to create a hierarchy and specialize activities within it. If they had not done so, the organizations would probably have become ineffective.

In this chapter we discuss the key issues related to the hierarchy and specialization. We also describe the barriers to integration within the hierarchy and methods for improving integration.

HIERARCHY AND SPECIALIZATION

In this section we focus on some of the major methods of building organizations and the manner in which organizations are departmentalized into distinct subunits. We then examine various ways that management constructs guiding systems for organizations so that they are successfully directed toward the attainment of goals.

Building the Organization

Organizational structures rarely arise spontaneously. Rather, managers make a series of systematic—and sometimes unsystematic—choices about the manner in which the work is to be completed. These choices consequently limit or constrain the activities in the organization. Some of the major issues facing the manager include span of control, tall versus flat structures, unity of command, unity of direction, the scalar principle, and degree of centralization.

Span of Control. One of the classical principles of management is the optimum span of control, or the proper number of subordinates that should report to a superior (see Chapter 1). This principle is still of major interest to managers, since they must periodically decide to set up reporting relationships and modify organizational structures.

Span of control is related directly to the growth of organizations. Henri Fayol, for instance, pointed out that an organization grows *horizontally* as additional workers are added to a particular level of an organization and *vertically* as new levels are created to handle the increased amount of work. He developed a theory of growth on the basis of 15 workers to a foreman and a ratio of 4 foremen/managers to every superior at the next level. Thus an organization grows in a simple geometrical progression whose first term is 15 (workers) and whose common ratio is 4. This approach allows management to keep the number of levels in an organization to a minimum. Thus an organization of 251,658,240 individuals would require only 13 levels of management (Fayol 1916).

It is important to realize that a superior will have great difficulty coordinating the work of subordinates and communicating effectively with them if the span of control is too wide. Although the exact number is difficult to determine, it can be estimated. For example, Joan Woodward studied the relationship between technology and the ideal span of control in one hundred British firms (Woodward 1965). She classified the firms according to three types of technology. A company with *unit* technology spends a great amount of money on labor costs relative to capital investment in equipment; an example might be a custom-made furniture maker. With *mass production* the organization spends a great amount of money on labor but also invests heavily in capital equipment; an example might be an automobile manufacturer. An organization using *process* or *automated technology* does not spend much money on labor costs, but it does invest a large amount of money in capital equipment; an example might be an oil refinery or a chemical plant.

Woodward found that a first-line supervisor had approximately 23 subordinates in a successful unit technology organization; 49 employees in a successful mass production organization; and 13 employees in a successful automated organization. As an organization moved away from its ideal figure, it tended to become unsuccessful. Although Woodward reports that a similar relationship between type of technology and success holds at the upper levels in an organization, she does not mention any specific figures.

There are many other factors that management must consider when determining the span of control. Foremost among them is the level of the organization. At the lower levels, where work is standardized, it is possible to implement a wide span of control. However, the span should gradually narrow as organizational level rises, because the work becomes less standardized and the need for frequent communication with subordinates rises. Additional factors influencing the span of control include the amount of supervisory work performed by managers, the competence of superiors and subordinates, their degree of professionalization, the dissimilarity of activities being supervised, the incidence of new problems within the manager's unit, and the extent to which activities are physically dispersed (Filley, House, and Kerr 1976).

Robert House and John Miner (1969) have investigated the ideal span of control by reviewing the literature on small-group research and other types of behavioral investigations. Like Woodward, they conclude that the type of technology is critical in determining the ideal span of control. Their review suggests that the ideal span of control is likely to be in the range of 5 to 10 under most circumstances. However, they feel that the larger spans, about 8 to 10, are most appropriate at the highest, policymaking levels of an organization, for managers need a large number of different ideas and inputs before they can make decisions that influence the entire system.

In industry, practices vary widely (Dale 1952; Janger 1960; Simonds 1969). Janger (1960) found that the number of key subordinates reporting directly to a company president in 80 large organizations ranged from one to 24. This range is large if, as indicated above, the ideal number at the highest levels of the organization is between 8 and 10. However, it may be that organizations respond to problems by developing spans of control suitable for their distinctive activities.

Tall Versus Flat Structures. As indicated above, managerial decisions concerning the various spans of control in an organization determine the number of levels in an organization. An organization is *tall* if there are many levels; it is *flat* if it has only a few levels. In general, the larger the organization, the taller its structure. And if the spans of control in the organization are narrow, so that only a few subordinates report directly to each superior, the organization tends to be tall.

Some research conducted by Sears, Roebuck and Company suggested that flat structures are preferable to tall structures (Worthy 1950). This research compared Sears department stores that were organized as either flat or tall structures. In the flat structure there were two levels of authority above the salespeople: the store manager and his or her assistant manager, both of whom shared duties and responsibilities, and thirty-two department managers. In the tall structure there were three levels of authority above the salespeople: the department store manager, five or six second-level managers reporting directly to the store manager, and four to six department managers reporting directly to a second-level manager.

A comparative analysis of these two types of department stores indicated that cost and profit figures for the flat structure were more favorable than those for the tall structure. The researchers then conducted follow-up interviews with the store managers. The store managers in the flat structures indicated that they had no choice but to allow their subordinates to exercise a great amount of responsibility, purely because of the large number of subordinates they supervised. This policy increased morale and seemingly led to a rise in the performance of the subordinates, since they were forced to make important decisions. The store managers, because they knew they had to delegate a great amount of responsibility, tended to be careful in selecting, guiding, and training subordinates.

However, other research does not support this study. For example, Carzo and Yanouzas (1969), in an experimental study, showed that groups operating under a tall structure demonstrated significantly higher performance than groups working under the flat structure. These researchers hypothesized that group members could evaluate decisions more frequently and construct an orderly decision process more efficiently under the tall structure than they could under the flat structure.

Research in this area supports the contingency theory of management. That is, managers must examine the critical factors in each situation before deciding whether to construct a tall or flat structure.

Unity of Command. In constructing an organization, management sometimes emphasizes the classical principle of unity of command: A subordinate should receive orders from only one superior. This principle appears sensible, since an individual will tend to experience anxiety and run into conflicting priorities if he reports to two or more superiors who give him conflicting commands. A large-scale study of 725 employees confirms this conclusion (Kahn et al. 1964). Thirty-nine percent of the respondents reported being worried at "some time" that they would not be able to fulfill conflicting demands, and fifteen percent reported that the problem was very serious. Further, individuals experiencing conflicting demands mentioned that their trust in the superiors who imposed the pressure was reduced and that their own effectiveness was impaired.

However, other research suggests that organizations can successfully violate the principle of unity of command in many situations. In fact, certain kinds of organizations operate best with a flexible structure in which there is open and constant violation of unity of command. A common illustration is a firm of research engineers that develops new techniques and products, where an engineer may be working on more than one product at once, each under the direction of a different superior. The work demands that job specifications be flexible, for individuals must respond quickly to external competitive pressures and the internal need of the organization to develop several products.

Unity of Direction. Management also tends to focus on the related classical principle of unity of direction: There is one head and one plan for a group of activities having the same objective. But unlike the case of unity of command, implementing unity of direction appears to be justified in most situations. To develop organizationwide planning systems integrating the activities of diverse individuals and units, management frequently identifies one manager who is ultimately responsible for accomplishing the overall plan (see Chapter 5). There are, of course, situations in which two or more managers are responsible for integration and for accomplishing the overall plan. In these situations the managers are coequals, as in the case of the office of the president, which we discuss later in this chapter.

Scalar Principle. To accomplish its overall goals, management typically constructs the organization by using the *scalar principle;* that is, the hierarchy is arranged in terms of a chain ranging from the ultimate authority to the lowest ranks. Both Weber and Fayol emphasized the importance of this principle. Weber, in particular, stressed that the hierarchy is arranged in terms of various offices detailing specific duties, responsibilities, and rights, all of which are generally incorporated into written job descriptions (see Chapter 1).

However, it is not always desirable to have detailed job descriptions. For example, organizations do not ordinarily use elaborate job descriptions for doctors and professors. The basic assumption that management makes in professional organizations is that trained professionals possess internal standards of excellence, obtained through years of training, and hence they do not require the external pressures that would be generated by rigid job descriptions.

Some organizations do not construct organization charts describing superior-subordinate reporting relationships, although this situation is relatively rare. But even when they do not, there is an implicit use of the scalar principle. Organizational members in these situations do determine whether the head is powerful or weak. If he or she is powerful, there is a tendency for organizational members to develop relationships among themselves and with their head that are comparable to the field of force in physics (Filley, House, and Kerr 1976). Relationships among organizational members are dynamic and dependent upon the whim of the head, who periodically elevates subordinates to positions of prominence while demoting others. Thus rivalry dominates relationships among subordinates.

If the head is not very powerful, there is no organizational chart, and job descriptions are minimal, managers and employees tend to create their own design for the organization. In fact, in some organizations the secretaries assume a disproportionate amount of power, partly because the head is rarely in his or her office (see Mechanic 1962). Alternatively, lower-echelon managers may begin to perform major tasks that the head has not authorized.

However, the most typical pattern is for management to implement the scalar principle, which is fundamental to the concept of hierarchy. Management realizes that a hierarchy will arise spontaneously if it is not explicitly described, so it is to management's advantage to outline the hierarchy it desires. Thus while there may be violations of the scalar principle, it is a major aspect of the design of the organization.

Centralization and Decentralization. When managers build or modify organizational structures, they must identify the degree of centralization they desire. *Centralization* is the extent to which decision-making power is concentrated in the hands of one or a few people or positions. *Decentralization* refers to the power delegated throughout an organization. Centralization and decentralization, although they appear to be opposites, are actually two ends of a continuum. In practice, it is vitually impossible to achieve complete centralization or decentralization.

In a decentralized organization individuals at the lower levels can make some critical decisions without checking with their superiors. Even then, however, the top managers in the organization exercise some control over the kinds of decisions that individuals at the lower echelons can make. In a centralized organization the top managers usually make the strategic decisions, but it is nearly impossible for them to monitor every decision at lower levels.

At the turn of the twentieth century sociologist Robert Michels studied the problem of centralization by examining the organizational structures of political parties in Western Europe, after which he put forth his famous iron law: "Whoever says organization, says oligarchy" (Michels 1915). According to Michels, all organizations tend to become centralized since major decisions are made by a few individuals—an oligarchy. The political parties Michels studied had very different philosophies and objectives (for example, Democrats and Communists), but they all tended to use a highly centralized organizational structure in which only a few individuals decided on courses of action that influenced all the members.

In large organizations Michels's iron law frequently applies, since a few top executives usually make the major overall decisions. But even here it is desirable for the lower echelon managers to make decisions about their own specific problems. If the lower echelon managers constantly referred their problems to the top managers, it would be difficult for the organization to complete its work. Decentralization thus adds considerable flexibility to an organization. For this reason decentralization seems to be appropriate when an organization operates in a highly competitive and constantly changing environment in which executives must respond quickly to the problems that confront them. However, decentralization may create problems if individuals in the lower levels cannot exercise authority responsibly. A

FIGURE 9–1
Departmentalization by Function or Area of Specialization

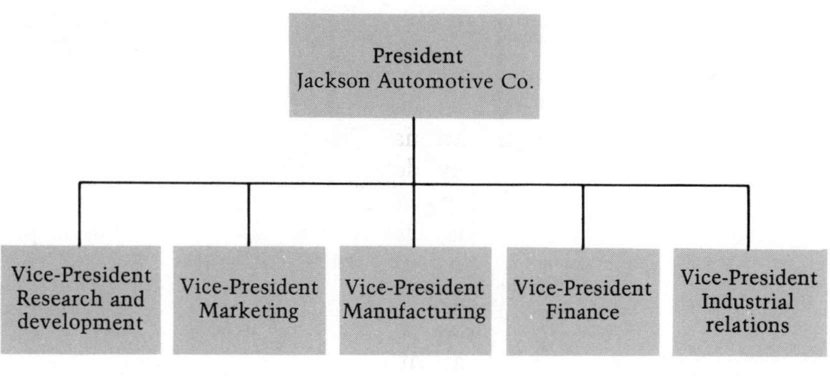

middle manager who exceeds his or her budget by $500,000 may force top managers to cut back on services needed in other parts of the organization.

In short, there is an inevitable tension between centralization and decentralization in an organization. Some large organizations such as Westinghouse have emphasized decentralization at one time and centralization at another. When work is not being accomplished, management may opt for a change in hierarchical relations, and this change frequently involves the degree of centralization.

Bases of Departmentalization

A major issue facing managers when they are building or rebuilding an organization is that of departmentalization, or setting up distinct subunits. Departmentalization allows an organization to divide its work according to the kinds of tasks it faces. Also, it is easier for individuals to identify with a small group or department than with the entire organization.

There are at least four major methods that top managers employ to departmentalize their organizations, by function, by product, by place, and by clientele. And perhaps the two *most* fundamental methods are by function and by product (or purpose or goal).

By Function. Until the twentieth century almost all organizations were structured by function, having separate departments for engineering, personnel, finance, and so forth (see Figure 9–1). This design is appropriate when the organization produces a single product or a few products that can be manufactured in a routine manner and when the organization exists in a stable external environment in which the

FIGURE 9–2

Departmentalization by Product or Goal

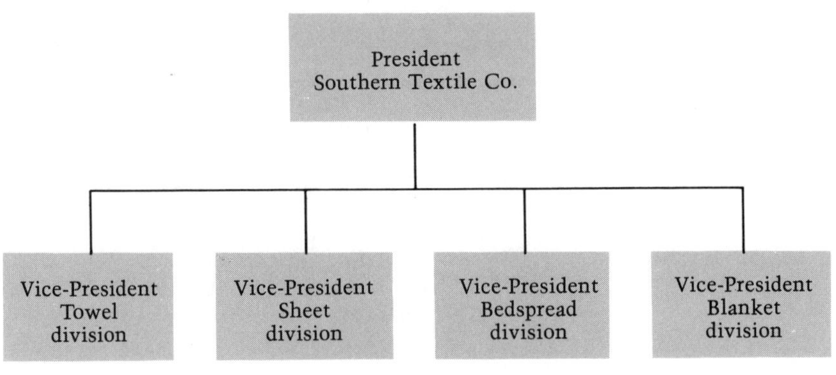

company's market share remains relatively fixed from year to year. Advantages of organization by function include these: (1) All activities are effectively integrated within the hierarchy through top management direction, which focuses on the manufacture of the product(s); and (2) specialists are grouped together in an organizational subunit in which they feel comfortable, since they are interacting with individuals having the same backgrounds and experience.

However, there are many disadvantages associated with this type of departmentalization. Specialists in the various subunits frequently do not understand one another's problems or viewpoints, and hence it is difficult to integrate their activities. Also, as the external environment becomes more volatile or as the firm expands by increasing its product lines, top management frequently experiences difficulty integrating activities, so that efficiency and effectiveness diminish.

By Product. A second major method of departmentalization is by product or goal. Here top management identifies the goals it is seeking to accomplish and assigns many different types of specialists to a department in order to accomplish them. Frequently top management defines these goals in terms of the various products it is producing. For example, as shown in Figure 9–2, the Southern Textile Company would have separate departments for towels, sheets, bedspreads, and blankets. Each department would include such specialists as accountants, personnel managers, market researchers, and so forth.

A major advantage of organization by product is that each department is responsible only for producing its own product, and hence it becomes a subsystem unto itself. Departments do not have to integrate their efforts, except at the top levels of the organization. Also, the organization becomes more flexible: Top management can focus on the problems within each department separately and make changes within a subsystem without influencing the activities of other subsystems.

However, there are some major disadvantages of this form of departmentalization. Specialists in a particular area are no longer housed within the same department, and so they cannot easily share information, ideas, and solutions to problems. In addition, the organization's labor costs tend to rise significantly, since it is necessary to assign specialists within each field to each of the subunits. Since labor costs typically constitute seventy percent or more of total costs, management may decide not to departmentalize by product purely because of the economic burden.

By Place. A third type of departmentalization is by place or region. In this case an organization has a department for each major region in which it is active. Some sales organizations operate in this fashion, as illustrated in Figure 9-3. Since customer preferences may differ from one part of the country to another, having a separate department for each section of the country allows each department to focus on its own special needs and problems.

Usually departmentalization by place is accompanied by a decentralized structure. Each department is allowed to make decisions tailored to the problems within a particular region since the managers at headquarters are so far removed from local customer preferences that they cannot make effective decisions. However, the advantage of decentralization can become a distinct disadvantage if top management is so far removed from activities in any region that it no longer

FIGURE 9-3
Departmentalization by Place

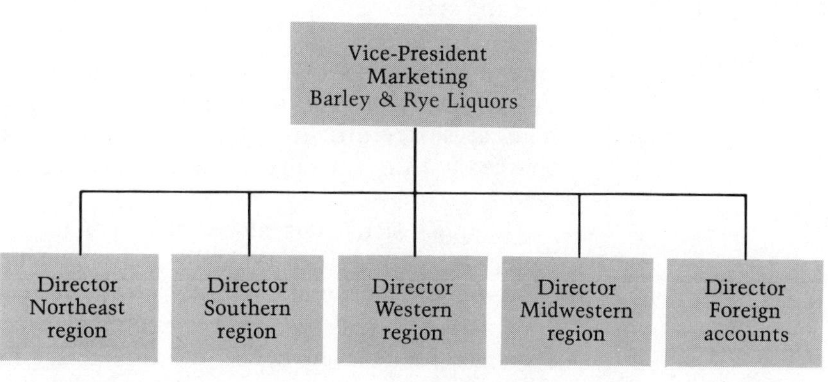

understands its unique problems. In such a case top managers can make incorrect decisions purely because they have a distorted concept of a particular department's work.

By Clientele. The fourth type of departmentalization is by clientele, with each unit serving a different market or market segment. A cosmetics company might use several sales departments, one concerned with the general public, one devoted to wholesale dealers, and another focusing on sales to institutional buyers, like beauty salons (see Figure 9–4).

Departmentalization by clientele allows the firm to cater to the distinct tastes and values of various types of customers. However, this approach may create problems; managers in one department may become blind to market forces acting on the activities of other departments in the organization. Furthermore, it may be difficult to integrate the work and activities of the different departments.

As our discussion indicates, there are both advantages and disadvantages associated with each type of departmentalization. In this sense there is no *ideal* organization. However, there are situations in which one type or two types of departmentalization in combination are clearly superior to others, a topic we will treat in the next chapter.

Constructing Guidance Systems

Organizations also make critical choices about the types of guidance systems that will govern their activities. We shall restrict our discussion of such systems to one major type of organization, the *corporation.* This form of organization can be defined as a group of individuals who obtain a charter granting them, as a body, certain of the legal rights and responsibilities of an individual, which are entirely separate from the rights and responsibilities of the individuals composing the group. Guidance systems in the corporation include stockholders, the board of directors, the chief executive officer (CEO), the office of the president, middle management, first-line supervision, and line and staff.

Stockholders. The owners of a corporation are its stockholders, who invest their money in it in return for stocks that they hope will yield high rates of return. Stockholders elect the board of directors, which is charged with overseeing the activities of the corporation, as explained below.

In most situations stockholders of large companies are passive. Except for voting, they typically do not concern themselves with anything but the value of their stock and the relative rate of return that they can obtain by either keeping or selling it. However, in recent years stockholders have become very active in some corporations. At the annual stockholders' meetings they have demanded that the board be responsive to their demands, such as hiring additional females and

FIGURE 9–4
Departmentalization by Clientele

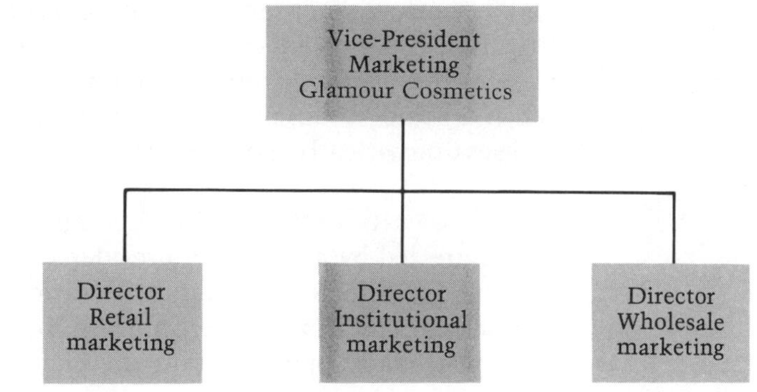

minority group members, selling off unprofitable divisions, and increasing membership on the board to include minority group representatives.

An excellent example of the power of stockholders is provided by SCM Corporation, a $1.75-billion company specializing in typewriters, copying machines, spices, coffee pots, paints and chemicals, and sundry other products. Some dissident stockholders made a serious but unsuccessful attempt to liquidate the company and distribute the proceeds to the stockholders, since they believed that this course of action would yield a higher return than either holding or selling the company stock. While this example of proposed corporate suicide is extreme, it does demonstrate that stockholders represent a potent guidance system in an organization.

Boards of Directors. Most large firms in the private sector operate under the overall guidance of a board of directors. The board typically contains a mixture of inside directors working on a full-time basis for the company and outside directors who do not. Supposedly this mixture provides a balanced and objective view of company activities.

Powers and duties of boards vary widely. However, typically a Board has the power of appointment and removal of the company president if it feels that he or she is performing in an unsatisfactory manner. Similarly, boards are normally charged with the final approval of major projects that the company management wishes to undertake.

The board of directors is elected by the company's stockholders. The company, though, publishes the rules governing membership on the board, frequency of meetings, and rights and responsibilities of the directors. The chairperson of the board is elected by the directors.

In most large corporations the board frequently is passive and allows top management to make the major decisions. Again, however, boards of directors have become very active in recent years, at least in part because their members can be sued. For instance, the threat of litigation has caused some boards to fire the company president and to refuse to approve controversial projects. And as might be expected, when a board assumes an activist stance, its need for information increases dramatically (Boulton 1978).

Chief Executive Officer (CEO). Many organizations in the private sector are led by a company president, who is normally appointed by the board of directors. Under the traditional arrangement the president acts as the chief executive officer (CEO) and is responsible for overseeing the daily operations of the corporation. He or she acts independently; that is, his or her decisions are not subject to approval by

FIGURE 9–5
Advantages of Traditional Arrangement of a Single Top Executive and of Newer Arrangement of the Office of the President

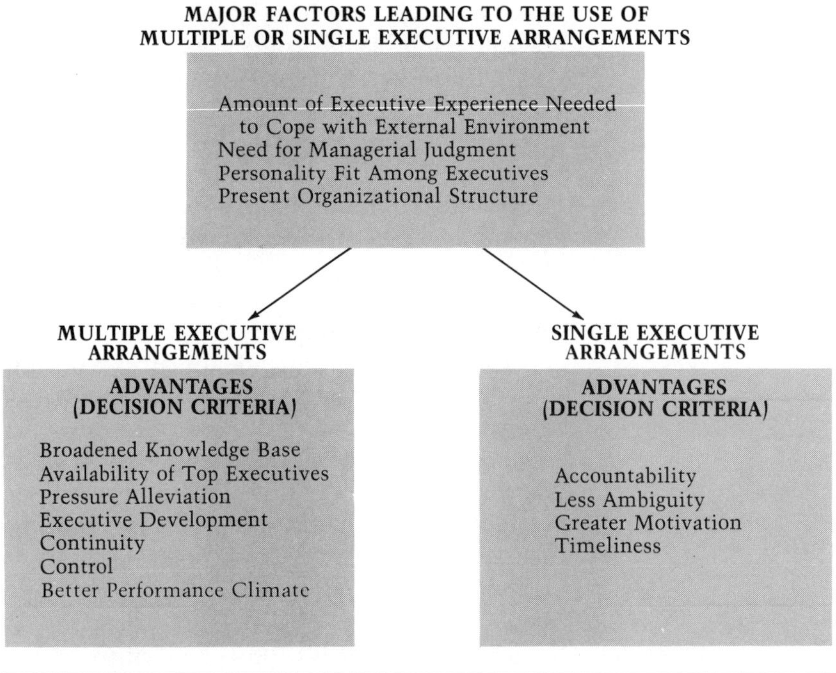

Source: Adapted from Anthony F. Jurkus, "The Multiple Executive Office: Panacea or Selective Cure," *University of Michigan Business Review* XXX, no. 4 (July 1978): 19.

the board unless they involve such critical and well-defined issues as ethical relationships or the allocation of a significant amount of money. Thus the board serves as an oversight committee rather than as an operating unit of the company.

There is, however, an alternative arrangement in which the chairperson of the board becomes the CEO of the company and the president reports directly to him or her. Under this arrangement the chairperson of the board and the board itself are actively involved in the daily activities of the company. Two factors have motivated the board of directors to increase its involvement in company activities in this way: the complexity of modern managerial work and, as suggested above, the threat of litigation. Since these conditions are likely to persist, we can expect corporations to continue to emphasize the use of the chairperson as CEO.

Office of the President. Many large organizations such as Norton Simon have found that they must construct an office of the president to handle the complex activities in which they engage. This office consists of two or more coequal chief executives who divide the work and coordinate their efforts. In the office of the president the chief executives are theoretically equal to one another, although each of them primarily focuses on one major activity, such as overseeing the United States market or the South American market.

Sometimes this guidance system is very successful, especially in cases where one chief executive simply cannot handle the volume of work. But there is an inherent danger in this approach, for the coequal executives may fight among themselves when they apportion areas of responsibilities. Also, one chief executive may become dominant, as RCA and Ford found out when they tried to use an office of the president. Figure 9–5 outlines the major advantages associated with the traditional arrangement of a single top executive and those associated with the newer arrangement of the office of the president.

Middle Management. An important guidance system in an organization is its middle management, which translates the decisions of top management into plans and procedures governing lower-echelon managers, first-line supervisors, and employees. Typically an organization constructs several levels of middle management, such as lower and upper middle management. Most college and university graduates begin their careers as lower middle managers, and some of them are eventually promoted to top management. Hence middle management is a major vehicle for managerial promotions.

While middle managers are definitely part of the management team, their power is often quite limited, especially at the lower levels, and they frequently are locked into routine work. And historically corporations could fire or demote middle managers whenever they desired. The insecurity resulting from this implicit threat has always been an integral part of managerial life. For example, a 1976 survey by the American Management Associations indicated that many middle managers at all levels wished to join a labor union and that they wanted such protection as a grievance system for appealing unfair demotions and terminations. Thus we see that middle managers are caught in the middle, being neither a genuine part of management or of the employee work force. However, currently neither middle managers nor first-line supervisors possess collective-bargaining rights under the National Labor Relations Act, and they formally are considered a part of management. It appears that the role and function of middle management will stay intact, at least for the immediate future.

Despite these disadvantages, middle management can provide one with a satisfying career. Most organizations reward their middle managers handsomely and do offer the possibility of advancement to higher levels.

First-Line Supervision. First-line supervisors direct employees who actually fabricate the final product of the organization. For many generations these supervisors were powerful forces in organizations, because they hired, disciplined, rewarded, and fired employees. Since personnel departments were small or nonexistent, the first-line supervisors completed all the activities now reserved for personnel. But after the turn of the century, many organizations constructed personnel departments and middle management positions, which usurped much of the former power of first-line supervisors.

After World War II first-line supervisors attempted to form their own unions. Top management was shocked at this move; it considered first-line supervisors as managers, not employees desiring unionization. However, both past and current research has shown that first-line supervisors, like middle managers, feel squeezed in the middle, being neither management nor workers. For example, James Driscoll, Daniel Carroll, and Timothy Sprecher (1978) compared the attitudes of first-line supervisors and their managerial superiors in two companies. These researchers concluded that the supervisors possess a relatively sophisticated and modern theory of motivation, roughly equivalent to Theory Y (see Chapter 2). However, these supervisors felt that they had no control over employee rewards, and their managerial superiors indicated that they would not give these supervisors such control. Thus management delegated many tasks to the supervisors but not the necessary authority to carry them out effectively. The first-line supervisors were virtually powerless. Considering these limitations, it is not surprising that many first-line super-

"Lighter, smaller, competitive, fuel-efficient . . . I think Research and Development may have done it again!"

visors resign and return to their former jobs, since the pay there is similar and the frustrations less.

Although these are inherent problems in this guidance system, organizations will continue to use first-line supervisors, since they are needed to direct the actual production of goods.

Line and Staff. In constructing organizations, management typically faces the problem of distinguishing line and staff. As defined in Chapter 1, *line* personnel are those whose work contributes directly to the accomplishment of organizational objectives—for example, a vice-president of production or a worker who actually makes the product the firm sells. *Staff* personnel advise and assist the line personnel. Some common examples of staff employees in large organizations are those in research, personnel, training, and industrial relations. Usually the staff functions are under one jurisdiction or vice-presidency that is separate from that of the line organization.

When an organization is small and uncomplicated, all or most of its members are line personnel. As the organization matures, though, it usually begins to increase its staff personnel because of the complexity of the work; it is simply no longer possible to use only line personnel.

A staff executive can exercise a great amount of authority and responsibility within his or her own department. However, the basic function of staff personnel is to advise and assist line personnel, and hence staff work is normally treated as less important than line work.

For example, top staff officers in some large corporations earn $100,000 or less, but their line counterparts receive nearly $1 million. And in most decision-making situations line officers merely listen to the advice of staff officers and then make their own decisions.

Philip Browne and Robert Golembiewski (1974) studied the differences in perceived images between line and staff in a major branch of a large industrial organization of over 3000 employees. Members of the line personnel perceived their own units as important and powerful, having an outward orientation toward other units in the organization, generating positive feelings, and possessing distinctive dimensions. In contrast, members of the staff personnel perceived their own organizational units as unimportant and impotent, having an inward orientation, producing negative feelings, and possessing few distinctive dimensions. Given the manner in which top management treats staff personnel, as indicated by salary differentials, these findings are not surprising.

However, there are cases in which staff officers are more powerful and important than line personnel. In one medium-sized railroad company, for example, the personnel director wielded enormous influence, since the president usually accepted his recommendations concerning the promotion of both line and staff executives; thus he was able to make many decisions that did not officially fall within the scope of his duties. Similarly, a vice-president of industrial relations wields a great amount of power in an organization that is troubled by labor-management difficulties.

Individuals such as researchers who stay in staff positions for their entire careers generally have different attitudes and orientations from their line counterparts, even though both have the same ultimate interest in the organization's success (Dalton 1950 and 1966; Filley, House, and Kerr 1976). These differences are understandable since staff are usually subordinate to line personnel. If staff personnel also engage in research or professional activities, they tend to be less committed to the organization and to spend more time on outside activities (such as publishing research results in scholarly journals) than do their line counterparts. Friction between line and staff thus seems inevitable. In one large company friction became so intense that management transferred its staff specialists in research and development to a new location, away from the hostility of the production personnel (Woodward 1965).

Top managers have recognized the friction between line and staff and have sometimes established dual ladders of promotion, one for staff and the other for line. However, because staff personnel are usually paid considerably less than their line counterparts, the dual ladder has proved disappointing, and the ambitious staff executive frequently tries to transfer into a line position. For instance, an individual who possesses a master of business administration degree in finance may do financial research for the first few years of his or her career and then transfer to a line position in which he or she actually makes financial decisions that influence production of the organization's final good or service.

BARRIERS TO INTEGRATION

A major problem facing organizations is that of successfully balancing differentiation and integration. *Differentiation* is the process of increasing the number of complex units and differing points of view in the organization as it takes on new and specialized tasks. However, as differentiation increases, integration should also increase. *Integration* is the process of linking together and coordinating the work of interdependent subunits and groups in the organization so that organizational goals are accomplished (Lawrence and Lorsch 1967).

In this section we discuss the barriers to integration. Some of these are voluntary in the sense that top management makes choices that create them; other barriers result inevitably because of the nature of the hierarchy.

Voluntary Barriers

Management may deny that it has voluntarily and consciously decided to create barriers to integration. However, it is clear that managerial decisions do influence the creation of barriers, especially within the areas of organization design and control.

Design Barriers. If management decides to construct a tall organizational structure, information must frequently pass through several levels before it reaches its destination. As the information passes through these levels, it tends to become distorted. Additionally, the amount of time necessary for transmitting information in a tall structure is generally greater than it is in a flat structure. Thus a tall structure creates a barrier to integration.

Similarly, if management decides to violate the principle of unity of command, there is a tendency for integration to break down. Subordinates are confronted with conflicting demands, and they frequently respond in such a way that it becomes difficult to link together the work of interdependent units. An equivalent situation occurs when the span of control is too wide. Communication between the superior and subordinates can easily become distorted and may break down.

Intergration also becomes problematic if top management delegates responsibility but not an equivalent amount of authority, as in the case of first-line supervision. As we have indicated, the first-line supervisors feel isolated, in large part because management voluntarily has designed the organization so as to weaken the integration of these individuals into the mainstream.

Control Systems. Management often creates control systems that eventually weaken integration. A good example is provided by the use of staff. In some organizations top management employs the staff as its eyes and ears—in effect, staff officers and employees are policemen. Under such conditions employees become distrustful of management, and integration is influenced negatively.

Similarly, management may consciously and voluntarily implement close supervision, constantly monitoring the work of first-line employees. When this situation occurs, first-line supervisors and employees tend to become antagonistic toward one another (see Chapter 1).

Hierarchical Barriers

While management may voluntarily make decisions that result in barriers to integration, there are some barriers that seem to arise purely from the nature of the hierarchy. Two of the most important hierarchical barriers are the flow of organizational communication and status differences. Another potential barrier is the company grapevine, which may or may not impede integration. In this section we focus on these three issues.

Organizational Communication. The flow of organizational communication is an important managerial issue, because any breakdown in it can easily cause problems. Horizontal communications among equals or peers tend to predominate at the lower levels of the organization, sometimes because individuals at these levels cover up mistakes so that their superior will be ignorant of them. A. K. Wickesberg (1968) has shown that sixty-seven percent of the communications of lower-echelon managers were horizontal; only thirty-three percent were vertical, that is, between superiors and subordinates. When these conditions exist, communication among organizational levels may break down.

In some situations the flow of organizational communication is interrupted because the channels become overloaded. The manager may be able to solve this problem by delegating some of his or her responsibilities to subordinates. Or the manager might find a way of filtering incoming communication so that only the most important items reach his or her desk. An executive secretary, an assistant, or an entire staff could perform this gatekeeping function for the executive. Similarly, the manager might ask his or her subordinates to complete all the staff work on a project so that his or her function would be merely to approve the final report or product. Whatever method is used, the objective is to reduce the amount of communication that must be channeled through a particular organizational position.

An insightful example of a seemingly inevitable barrier arising because of the nature of organizational communications was provided by the Carter administration. During the early part of his presidency, Carter avoided appointing a chief of staff who would serve as his gatekeeper, partly because President Nixon had been criticized so strongly for using this approach. However, his communication channels became so overloaded that he finally had to appoint Hamilton Jordan as his chief of staff. In this case, and many others, it seems that the hierarchy necessitates the creation of such roles as gatekeeper in order to facilitate the flow of organizational communications.

Status Differences. As our discussion of line and staff indicates, differences in status appear to create inevitable barriers. Research on organizational communications confirms this proposition. The higher the person's status or official rank in the organization, the greater is the distortion in the communications he or she receives (Barlund and Harland 1963; Cohen 1962). In some organizations, when consultants have been hired to solve specific problems, they have been unable to persuade subordinates to talk freely in the presence of their superiors. When, at the request of consultants, the superiors do not attend group sessions, the subordinates tend to be responsive and open about the organizational problems they face. This is especially true of ambitious subordinates: The more ambitious a subordinate is, the more likely he or she is to distort a communication to the superior (Read 1962). This distortion is particularly pronounced when the subordinate distrusts the superior (Maier, Hoffman, and Read 1963; O'Reilly 1978).

The Grapevine. In most organizations there is an informal system of transmitting information known as the grapevine, which is independent of the formal communication system the organization establishes. The grapevine may impede integration if the information it transmits is incorrect or inappropriate. Ralph Rosnow and Allan Kimmel (1979) point out that rumors or inaccurate information tend to be transmitted particularly during times of uncertainty and ambiguity—precisely when management should guard against a grapevine that carries inaccurate information that will only heighten anxiety and impede integration.

Two research studies have confirmed the importance of the grapevine in organizations (Davis 1953; Sutton and Porter 1968). In these studies the researchers deliberately planted a rumor in the organization, and several hours later they passed out a questionnaire about the rumor. In this fashion the researchers were able to find out such things as how many people passed on the rumor and how much distortion had occurred.

An important finding in these two studies is that the grapevine is highly selective. That is, members of the grapevine filter out some information because of its sensitivity. For example, only two of the thirty-one executives who had not been invited to a party given by the president of the company ever learned about it. Further, the grapevine is fast. The news that one executive had become a parent spread to forty-six percent of the members of the organization within three hours (Davis 1953).

However, only about ten percent of the members of the organization were active transmitters on the grapevine. Most members who received information did not pass it on. And some individuals and groups were so divorced from the grapevine that they never received any rumors.

Unfortunately, the information provided by the grapevine is accurate in some situations but inaccurate in others. Robert Hershey (1966) studied 30 items of information transmitted on the grapevine in one organization. Of these 30 items, 16 proved groundless, 9 accurate, and 5 distorted but somewhat accurate. This may be because the greater the quantity of information on the grapevine, the less accurate it is (Rollins and Charters 1965).

IMPROVING INTEGRATION

Even though some of the barriers to integration seem inevitable, there are methods for overcoming them. These methods can be classified as structural or personal. In this section we discuss several methods in both classifications.

Structural Methods

Management frequently uses *structural* methods for improving integration, that is, methods built into the design of the organization or its ongoing, regular operations. Structural methods include linking pins, committees, and task forces.

Linking Pins. Traditional management has always recognized that the hierarchy creates barriers to integration. For example, Fayol argued that bridges should be used throughout the hierarchy to improve communication and integration. Similarly, Barnard felt that organizational units should consist of ten members or less and that executives from interdependent units should form an executive unit that integrates activities (see Chapters 1 and 2).

Building on the concepts of classical management, Rensis Likert (1961, 1967) has suggested that *linking pins* be established within the hierarchy. Each individual designated as a linking pin would be a member of both his or her own work group and another work group whose activities overlap with those of his or her own group. Consequently, the individual would understand the special problems of both units with which he or she is associated. The linking pin would then be charged with the task of integrating the work of the two units. The in-

FIGURE 9–6

Likert's Linking Pins

On the left are traditional organizational structures; on the right are the same structures rearranged according to Likert's linking-pin function. The linking pins (solid circles) are the individuals who provide communication and coordination among groups through membership in more than one work group. Ultimately the entire organization would be linked, both vertically and horizontally, by such individuals.

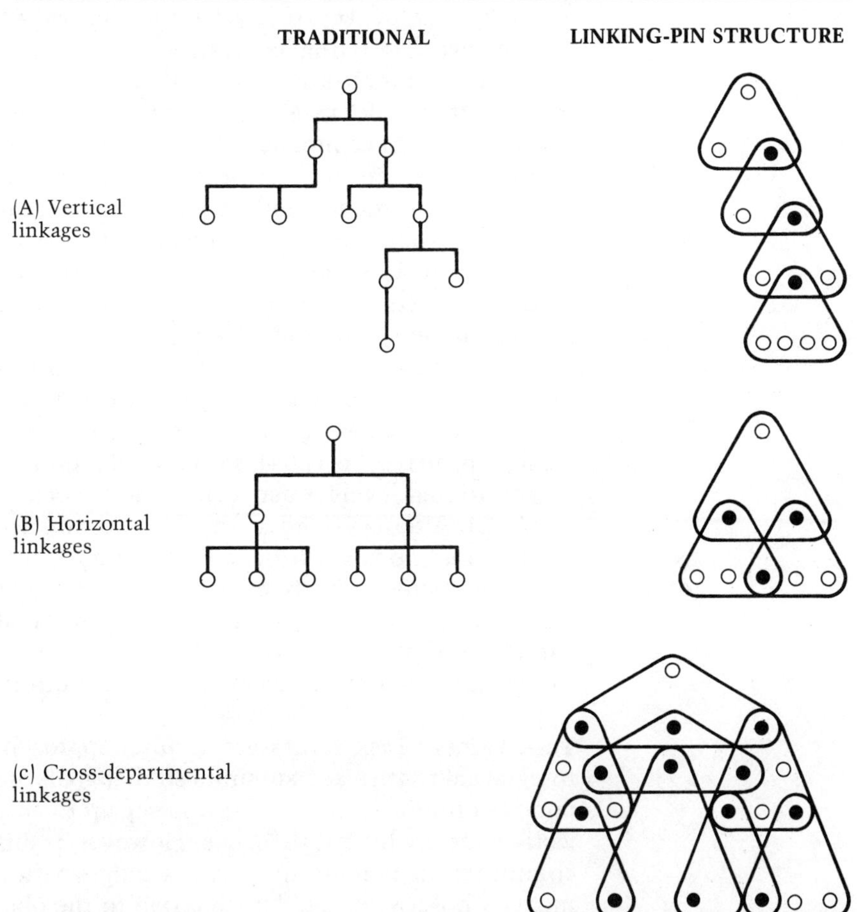

Source: From Raymond Miles, *Theories of Management,* p. 87. Copyright © 1975 by McGraw-Hill, Inc. Linking-pin structure adapted from Rensis Likert, *New Patterns of Management* (New York: McGraw-Hill, 1961). Reprinted by permission of McGraw-Hill Book Company.

tegration of overlapping work should thus become easier, since work groups would be linked together both vertically and horizontally within the traditional hierarchy, as shown in Figure 9–6.

Committees. Another important method for improving integration is the use of committees. One survey of 1,200 firms indicated that 94 percent of firms having more than 10,000 employees and 64 percent of firms having less than 250 employees had *standing committees,* that is, permanent committees formed for a specific purpose (Tillman 1960). For example, many organizations use a finance committee to handle the allocation of resources to various departments. Standing committees are important because they provide a stable structure by which routine or recurring activities can be handled efficiently.

However, standing committees can also slow down activities, since all work that is specific to their jurisdictions must be processed through them. Because the members have full-time jobs in other areas, they often cannot schedule a meeting until they can find a time that does not conflict with their regular work. Even after meetings have been convened, members may fight over minor points in a project proposal, although they may unanimously agree with its thrust. For example, the U.S. Senate operates several standing committees in which members frequently attempt to direct a project so that it benefits the citizens who elect them to office.

Sometimes projects are delayed for years because standing committees create so much red tape. For example, five years may elapse from the time a new course is proposed until it is approved at a university, primarily because so many standing committees at various organizational levels must review the project.

As an alternative to a standing committee, organizations often create an *ad hoc committee,* a temporary committee formed to complete a particular objective, after which it disbands. The use of ad hoc committees allows the organization to respond to problems as they surface, without being weighed down by the excessive red tape that can be generated by too many standing committees.

Task Forces. Task forces are another approach management uses to integrate activities and subunits so that goals are attained. Like a temporary committee, a *task force* is set up to accomplish a specific objective, after which it disbands. However, it differs from a temporary committee in that its members are drawn from the various departments whose work overlaps relative to the objective. For example, if a task force were set up to develop a new method for rating employee performance, some departments that would appoint members are personnel, production, finance, and training. In addition, an individual assigned to a task force works on it for an extended period, sometimes part time but frequently full time. In this sense the task force violates the concept of unity of command, since the individual is responsible to both the head of the task force and his or her regular superior. This violation is especially pronounced if an individual works on the task force only on a part-time basis.

There are many advantages to the task force. Since it includes individuals from various parts of the organization, it benefits from more specialized knowledge than is available in a committee selected from only one department. Also, its members understand the viewpoints of their superiors relative to the objective. In addition, it is much easier to implement a plan that will affect various departments if each is represented in the decision.

However, both task forces and committees can be ineffective if their members are not rewarded for outstanding work. Yet frequently a superior is totally unaware of the work that a subordinate has accomplished. Efforts also can be hampered if a superior assigns the least effective employees to regular work but assigns the most effective employees to critical committees. In these circumstances the routine work may be viewed as a punishment.

Personal Methods

A manager can improve integration through the use of personal interventions. For instance, he can make it clear that he maintains an open-door policy and that he will listen patiently to suggestions, complaints, and even non-work-related problems. And not only will he listen, he will also attempt to solve any significant problems that subordinates identify.

In addition, a manager can actively seek out information in order to improve integration. For example, he or she can conduct informal and unannounced tours of the organization to obtain such information.

SUMMARY

Although management theorists and practitioners disagree about some issues of organizational structure, there is sufficient agreement on several concepts to allow them to be used in the construction of organizations. Perhaps the most fundamental design concept is that of hierarchy and the specialization within it. If management does not prescribe a hierarchy, it tends to arise inevitably. Starting from this initial concept in the building of organizations, management must take into consideration the concept of an optimum span of control (the ideal number of subordinates reporting to a superior), even though it can only be approximated in most instances. Management must also decide on the number of levels that should exist in the hierarchy. As the number of levels increases, an organization becomes taller, a situation that may hinder communication.

Other issues that management confronts in constructing the organization include unity of command (having a subordinate report to only one superior), unity of direction (having one head and one plan for a group of activities that possess one objective), the scalar principle (arranging the hierarchy in terms of a chain, from the ultimate authority to the lowest ranks), and decentralization (the degree to which decision-making power is delegated to lower levels in the organization). Management must also consider departmentalization—setting up distinct subunits. There are four major types of departmentalization: by function, by product, by place, and by clientele.

In building an organization management must also decide on the types of guidance systems that will be used to direct the organization toward its goals. In a corporation the major guidance systems include stockholders, the board of directors, the chief executive officer, the office of the president, middle management, first-line supervision, and line and staff.

A major problem—and perhaps the major design problem—facing organizations is balancing differentiation and integration. Differentiation is the process of increasing the number of complex units and differing points of view within the hierarchy; integration is the process of linking them together so that goals can be accomplished. Management voluntarily creates some barriers to integration, especially in the areas of design and control. However, some barriers arise inevitably because of the nature of the hierarchy, such as those occurring because of status differences or the flow of organizational communication. The grapevine represents another aspect of organizational communication that may (or may not) impede integration.

There are methods for overcoming barriers to integration. Managers may use structural methods, such as linking pins, committees, and task forces. In addition, managers may rely on personal methods, such as an open-door policy and unscheduled visits to actively weed out problems.

DISCUSSION QUESTIONS

1. How is the concept of the linking pin different from those of Fayol's bridge and Barnard's executive unit?
2. What is the CEO? Is the president of a corporation automatically a CEO? How does the concept of the office of the president differ from that of the CEO?
3. How are the following concepts related to one another: span of control, organizational growth, and the degree to which an organization is tall?
4. How do barriers to integration arise in organization? Why?
5. When an organization is very tall, is it highly centralized? Why or why not?
6. Explain why the concept of hierarchy is so important in the area of organization design.
7. Most organizations were departmentalized by function until the beginning of the twentieth century. Why?
8. What is the major difference between a standing committee and a task force?

FIGURE 1
Lines of Authority

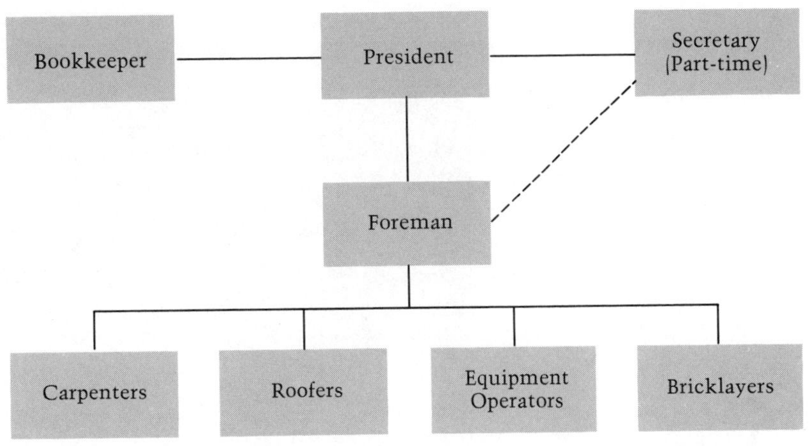

Note: Solid lines indicate formal lines of authority; dotted lines represent underlying lines of authority.

CRITICAL INCIDENTS

NOTE: These critical incidents can be used by the whole class with the case observational method (see Appendix A) or used for thought and discussion by individual class members.

1.* Haines Construction Company is a small, growth-oriented business located in a rural but expanding community in the Middle Atlantic region. The company is owned and operated by Haines, an entrepreneur who started the business eight years ago. He began with himself and an assistant specializing in roofing and home improvement jobs. In recent years the company has grown to include nine blue-collar workers with skills in the areas of roofing, carpentry, bricklaying, and heavy equipment operation. A foreman is in charge of the men when Mr. Haines is not present. There are also two part-time employees on the payroll, a secretary who works three days a week and a bookkeeper who comes in for two days during the last week of the month. The lines of authority are delineated in the organizational chart in Figure 1.

In the past two years Mr. Haines has been interested in expanding the business to the level at which he could incorporate. He felt that incorporating, taking in investors, and diversifying risks would enable him to move from building a few houses a year to building whole communities. However, while profits have grown during the past two

FIGURE 2
Rate of Growth

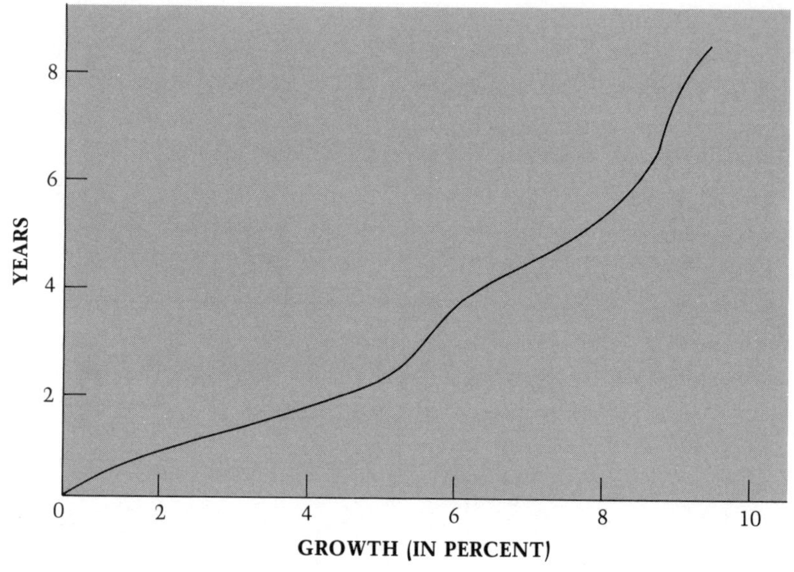

years, retained earnings have not increased to the degree necessary for further expansion, which would enhance the company's chance of attracting large investors. Figure 2 shows the growth rate since the company's inception.

The projects now being undertaken by Haines Construction Company are roofing, additions to houses, building new homes, remodeling, and siding. Usually Mr. Haines is present at the work location, directing the construction. He likes jobs to be done quickly but with a high quality of workmanship that has become his trademark. In addition to working on projects, Mr. Haines talks with possible investors, speculates in real estate, handles all contract negotiations with clients, and bids on large-scale contracts. His working day is typically fourteen hours long.

All the men in the company work on the job currently under construction. Prospective clients call the office and talk to the secretary, who screens the projects and passes the more favorable ones on to Mr. Haines for his approval. If she is not working, there is a twenty-four-hour answering service that she reviews when she comes in.

Because of the pressure to expand, the quality of the work done by Haines Construction has deteriorated slightly. Workers complain of the constant stress to finish jobs quickly and move on. Recently some of the workers have noticed a lack of coordination on the job site. For example, on a house just completed, the foreman had the bulldozer operator grade the site before the basement's exterior walls had been waterproofed with a tar mixture; Haines had told the men not to tar the walls because they were needed for work on another job. Such mishaps have been increasing lately, and Mr. Haines now wonders whether he might have to put off his expansion goals indefinitely.

QUESTIONS: Do you feel Mr. Haines should expand his operations? Why or why not? If he does expand, how should he redesign his organization?

2. The Senate is a critical division of the United States government. Each senator attempts to accomplish two major goals: (1) representing successfully and fairly the citizens from his or her state and fulfilling their needs whenever possible, and (2) being reelected every sixth year. These two goals are separate, but they do overlap.

Most senators organize their offices so as to accomplish these two objectives. The senator represents general management. An administrative assistant coordinates the activities of three distinct subunits, each having its own supervisor who reports to the assistant. The subunits are press relations, constituent services, and legislative relations on Capitol Hill. Most senatorial offices are relatively small, having about twenty-five employees.

QUESTIONS: Do you feel that the structure described above is a good way to organize a senator's office? Why or why not? What kinds of individuals do you think senators tend to hire as their employees? What are some dysfunctional consequences of this form of organization?

SUGGESTED READINGS

Hutchinson, John. *Organizations: Theory and Classical Concepts.* New York: Holt, Rinehart and Winston, 1967, 178 pages, paperback.

Hutchinson briefly reviews some of the major theories of organizations and focuses on many of the concepts highlighted in his part and other parts of the textbook.

Parkinson, C. Northcote. *Parkinson's Law.* Boston: Houghton Mifflin, 1957, 115 pages, paperback.

This book provides a humorous but insightful treatment of problems that occur in hierarchical organizations. Students consistently rate this book as outstanding.

10 Alternative Methods of Organizing

MODERN FORMS OF ORGANIZATION
SPECIALIZED FORMS OF ORGANIZATION
ECONOMIC FORMS OF ORGANIZATION
SUMMARY
DISCUSSION QUESTIONS
CRITICAL INCIDENT
SUGGESTED READINGS

PERFORMANCE OBJECTIVES

1. To explain the importance of two fundamental methods of departmentalization, by function and by goal or product, for the design of modern forms of organization.
2. To describe the similarities and differences among modern forms of organization, which include federal decentralization, project management, and the matrix organization.
3. To show how management employs specialized forms of organization, such as the professional organization, to handle distinctive problems.
4. To describe economic forms of organization, including employee-owned companies, conglomerates, vertical and horizontal integration, ventures, state-backed corporations, and multinational corporations.

As we have seen in the previous chapter, management theorists and practitioners do agree about some of the fundamental approaches that should be implemented in designing organizations. Still, designing an organization is as much art as science: Top managers must consider the relative suitability of alternative methods of organizing for the problems they are facing and the environment in which they exist.

In this chapter we describe some modern methods of organizing, including federal decentralization, project management, and the matrix organization. We also discuss some specialized organizations such as consulting firms and trade associations that typically develop distinctive structures to accomplish their goals. Finally, we conclude the chapter by examining various organization designs that management employs for economic rather than structural reasons.

MODERN FORMS OF ORGANIZATION

Until the turn of the twentieth century most organizations were departmentalized by function or area of specialization, with separate departments for finance, accounting, personnel, and so forth. Since that time many organizations have begun to use several interesting and innovative structures, frequently combining two or more types of departments.

Two fundamental methods of departmentalization are by function and by goal or product or program (see Chapter 9). Modern forms of organization can be understood by examining the various ways of combining these two different methods of departmentalization. In this section we describe some of these combinations.

Federal Decentralization

Some initial attempts to combine the advantages of departmentalization by function and by goal were made by the DuPont company at the turn of the twentieth century. However, it was Alfred Sloan—president of General Motors for forty years, during which time it became the largest and most prosperous corporation in the world—who developed an organizational structure that successfully combined these two forms of departmentalization.

General Motors was founded in 1908 by William Durant, an entrepreneur who bought a large number of companies producing related products in the automotive field. However, he was so unconcerned about the daily organizational activities that he did not even know how many companies General Motors owned in 1920. When the company's financial backers forced Durant out in 1920, it took the accountants several months to identify all the holdings of General Motors. Durant once remarked, supposedly in jest, that he loved to set policies—every time his door opened and closed, he had made and broken another policy. And Durant developed a novel motivational strategy: When Walter Chrysler, his key production manager, constantly complained to him about his lack of attention to details, Durant merely raised Chrysler's salary each time he complained. Chrysler finally reached a salary of $500,000 a year, at which time he quit in disgust and formed his own company.

Alfred Sloan was president and a major stockholder in one of the small companies that Durant bought. An MIT engineering graduate, Sloan recognized the importance of organization design, and he was concerned about the lack of structure at General Motors. In 1919 he wrote a memorandum to Durant outlining a new organization design for the company. Nothing happened. Sloan went to Europe for a vacation, and while there he decided to resign from his position at General Motors. But when he returned, Durant was no longer president; the DuPont family, the major stockholder in General Motors, was in charge. The DuPonts discovered his memorandum among Durant's papers, read it, and decided to implement a new organization design under the direction of Sloan, who was eventually named President. This design was what we now call federal decentralization.

The New Structure. As any good top manager should, Sloan first focused attention on the strategic plans of the company. At that time the Ford Motor Company dominated the automotive industry with the Model T, an all-purpose, reliable, and inexpensive car. Sloan realized that he could not compete directly against Ford. Rather, his strategic plan was to appeal to all kinds of consumers rather than just the solid, middle-class American attracted to the Model T. General Motors developed six lines of cars, which represented the company's tactics. In addition, top management established specific rules that each of the six operating divisions was required to follow. For example, the operating division manufacturing the lowest-priced car had to keep the cost between $450 and $600; the operating division producing the highest-priced car had to stay within the range of $2500 to $3500 (Sloan 1963, p. 67).

Integrating the New Structure. As suggested by this discussion, General Motors was departmentalizing by goal: Each operating division focused on one goal, the production of a specific type of car, such as Buick or Chevrolet. The operating divisions were self-contained; that is, all or most of the capabilities necessary to produce a final product were housed within each division's framework. Top management allowed each unit to operate independently throughout a reporting period, which may have been as long as two or three years. At the end of a reporting period, the Finance Committee of the company examined the relative profitability and problems of the divisions. If necessary, a division would be shut down for months to overhaul its car design and production facilities. Thus top management had increased its ability to respond to external environmental pressures, since it was not necessary to shut down all operations simultaneously.

At the top level of the company, two committees oversaw and integrated all activities: the Finance Committee, whose role was explained above, and the Executive Committee, which focused on strategic planning. The departments at the top level were organized by function, with separate departments for finance, engineering, personnel, and so forth. Also, specialists within each operating division at the lower levels reported to two superiors: the head of the operating division and the vice-presidents of their respective specialties at the top level of the organization. This dual reporting relationship allowed the specialist to maintain his or her identity with other specialists in the area and provided flexibility to top management, which could transfer specialists among the operating divisions as needs dictated (see Figure 10–1).

Various large companies have refined federal decentralization to meet their own unique needs. However, the essential features of federal decentralization are as follows:

Using departmentalization by goal at the operating level and departmentalization by function at the top level of the organization.

Allowing the operating divisions at the lower levels to exercise independence throughout a given reporting period.

Using dual reporting relationships for specialists in order to integrate the operating divisions and the departments at the top level of the company.

Integrating the company through the activities of top-level committees such as a finance committee and an executive committee.

Project Management

Federal decentralization seems to be particularly appropriate when a company is producing a small number of interrelated products in a relatively stable external environment. However, some organizations operate in an unpredictable environment in which it is difficult to schedule work. An outstanding example is the aerospace industry, which relies on government contracts for its survival. Although government contracts bring aerospace firms millions of dollars in revenue, they are awarded irregularly. In addition, the firms must bid against each other for contracts, and hence there is a high degree of competition in this industry, which makes long-range planning difficult. A firm can go through an extended period during which it is not awarded any contracts. In fact, a firm is never entirely certain

FIGURE 10–1
Federal Decentralization

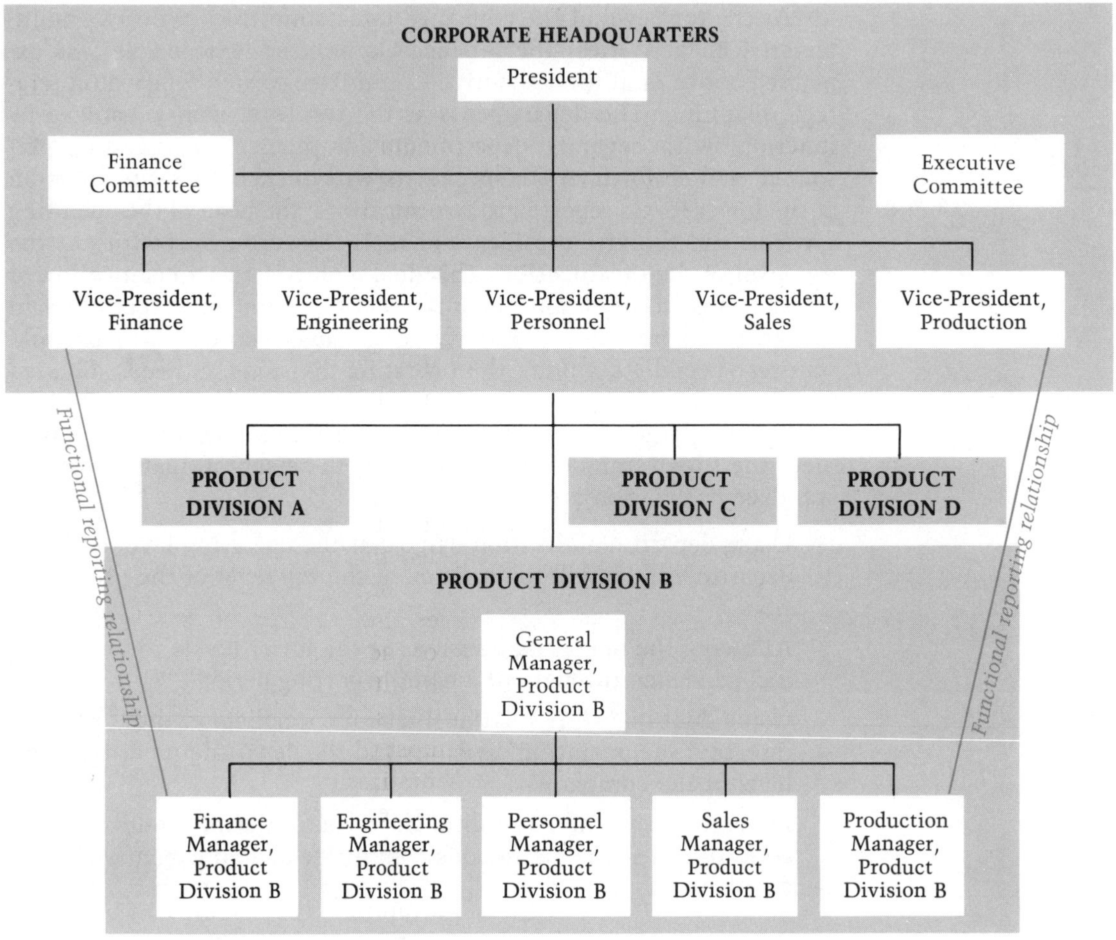

Source: Adapted from David R. Hampton, *Contemporary Management* (New York: McGraw-Hill, 1977), p. 243. Copyright © 1977 by McGraw-Hill Book Company. Used with permission of McGraw-Hill Book Company.

how many contracts it will receive or how much revenue they will generate.

To counteract this problem, some firms use *project management;* that is, each subordinate is responsible to a project manager for the life of a project. When the project is completed, the subordinate is either assigned to another project or let go.

The obvious advantage of this approach is its flexibility, which allows the organization to schedule work in an unpredictable environment. Essentially there is no stable hierarchy of employees who must be paid whether they are needed at the moment or not. Rather, the firm promises to employ the individual only as long as there are projects to which he or she can be assigned. Thus the organization is departmentalized by goal, but the departments are not established on a permanent basis.

As you might expect, there are disadvantages associated with project management. Because the employees know they may be employed only for a short time, they are not particularly loyal. As the final date of the project approaches, many begin to search for work elsewhere, and sometimes their productivity becomes so low that the project fails or falls short of expectations. In addition, the organization can waste a considerable amount of money in start-up time, since new employees must be hired at the beginning of each project. Usually these employees do not operate at peak levels of efficiency for some weeks or months, until they become familiar with the company's operations.

Matrix Organization

To eliminate the problems of project management, executives have devised a modified approach called the matrix organization. In general terms, a *matrix organization* is one in which there is a combination of at least two different types of departmentalization and one in which there is a clear violation of the principle of unit of command, since some subordinates must simultaneously report to superiors in the two different types of departments (see Davis and Lawrence 1977). In this section, we focus on the most popular type of matrix organization, which combines departmentalization by function and by goal (either product or program). However, generalizations made in this description normally apply to all types of matrix organizations.

Within the matrix organization, the product departments that produce the final product or the program departments that are responsible for the achievement of organizational goals are permanent or relatively permanent parts of the system, and they draw on the resources and personnel of the functional departments to handle their different projects (see Figure 10–2). The heads of both the product (program) departments and the functional departments such as engineering and manufacturing report directly to the general manager. And, as this discussion implies, there is little if any difference between a product and program department; they both are goal-oriented. In fact, the literature on matrix management uses these terms interchangeably.

A good example of a matrix organization is publishing. A publishing house hires several product (program) managers who are erroneously called editors, since they do little if any editorial work. For example, a publishing house will have an editor for literature, social science, physical science, and so forth. Each editor and his assistants must in reality be marketing managers who are very familiar with a specific field or market, and they must sign up authors to complete projects within the product or program area. These editors rely heavily on the functional departments of the publishing house at various points during the life of each project. For example, the social science editor does not need to use the art department on a full-time basis, but perhaps only three weeks per year. Thus a negotiation process occurs between each editor and the functional managers.

Until the 1950s management theorists argued that federal decentralization would become the dominant design pattern (Drucker 1946). However, as suggested above, its use is quite limited. Management theorists and practitioners now feel that the matrix organization is the most promising approach for designing organizations and, in fact, probably represents the most common way for structuring modern-day organizations (Sayles 1976; Lawrence, Kolodny, and Davis 1977). A broad spectrum of organizations including hospitals, universities, prisons, publishing houses, engineering firms, consulting firms, and law firms are typically designed as matrix organizations.

Essential Characteristics. Under federal decentralization the president or general manager integrates organizational plans and activities at the highest level of the organization. This individual is a line manager integrating strategic plans and activities *within the hierarchy.* Thus unity of command is achieved, since the company has one plan and one leader for a set of interrelated activities (see Chapter 9).

The general manager in the matrix organization also performs these functions. However, he or she essentially operates *outside the matrix* and attempts to manage the conflicts that arise between the functional and product departments. Hence his or her essential function can be described as the *management of conflict.* In completing this function, the general manager performs three major roles: balancing the power of the functional and product departments, managing the context in which decisions are made, and setting standards and goals (Lawrence, Kolodny, and Davis 1977).

In the matrix organization the managers of the functional departments possess less power than their counterparts in the traditional line organization or in a federally decentralized organization, for they do not have bottom-line responsibility, which rests with the product managers. However, the functional managers are obviously important if the organization is to achieve its goals, and for this reason the general manager must balance power conflicts between the product and functional managers and ensure that the climate in which decisions are made remains harmonious.

FIGURE 10–2

The Matrix Organization

Each product or program manager has budgetary and overall authority over the projects being completed by his or her group (short dotted lines); the functional managers have technical authority over each project (long dotted lines). Thus employees report to their product manager regarding their work on the project and to their functional manager on questions of technical expertise and on routine matters such as salary and employee benefits.

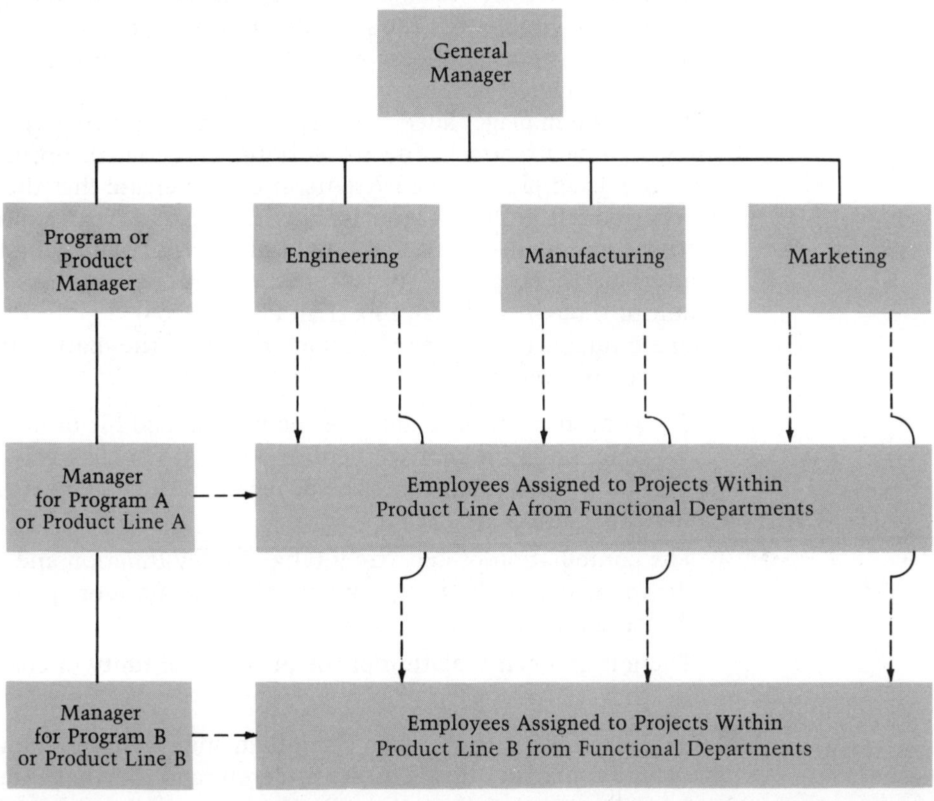

Another important characteristic of the matrix organization is its use of dual lines of authority. The product manager has budgetary and overall responsibility for the successful completion of the projects. However, the functional line managers have technical authority over the projects that each product department must finish. Each project is carried out by a product manager and a group of employees who are lent to the projects by the functional line managers. When the project ends, the employees' superiors in the functional departments assign them to another project. Employees in the matrix organization thus possess more job security than they would have under the pure form of project management.

A major problem with the matrix organization is its open violation of the principle of unity of command, since each subordinate reports to both a functional line superior and a product manager. This violation is extreme if the employee's functional superior assigns him or her to two or three projects simultaneously, since the employee must complete work for several superiors in a limited time. In this situation it is almost inevitable that the subordinate will experience frustration, because he or she must please several superiors, all of whose evaluations can influence pay increases and promotions. For instance, in California one manager sued his employer on the grounds that he experienced a heart attack due to working in a matrix organization. While this example may be extreme, it does indicate that the matrix organization has problems associated with it. And we can expect such negative consequences as a low rate of productivity and a high rate of absenteeism to emerge if it is implemented without a sufficient amount of thought and planning (Kahn et al. 1964).

In summary, the essential characteristics of the matrix organization are as follows:

> The general manager is outside the matrix, and his or her essential function is the management of conflict, which involves balancing power, managing the decision context, and setting standards and goals.
>
> The combination of departmentalization by function and goal is such that the product or program managers are more powerful than the functional managers.
>
> There is an open violation of the principle of unity of command.

Major Causes of Conflict. Hans Thamhain and David Wilemon (1977) have studied matrix organizations in depth, and they have identified seven major causes of conflict. Project managers[1] tend to disagree with the functional managers about schedules because they want to time and sequence their own activities in an optimal manner. And since resources are scarce, the functional managers cannot please all the project managers. Conflict also arises because of project priorities. A project manager frequently disagrees with the functional managers over the sequence of activities and tasks that should be undertaken to achieve successful project completion. Also, the project managers compete with one another for scarce resources and functional line specialists to handle their work.

[1] As suggested previously, project managers in a matrix organization report directly to a product manager. However, sometimes writers use the terms *product manager* and *project manager* interchangeably.

FIGURE 10–3

Relative Frequency of Reported Coping Responses to Conflict by High- and Low-Producing Managers

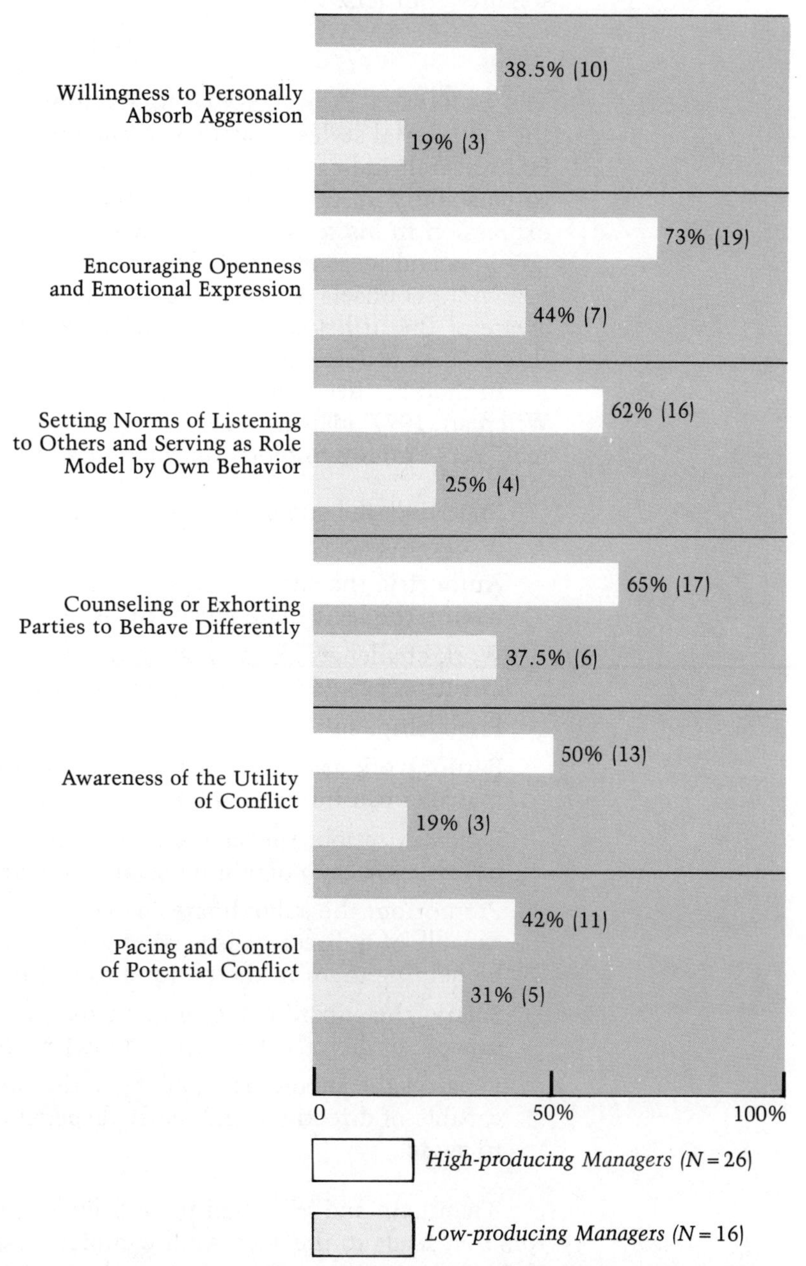

Source: Reprinted from Raymond Hill, "Managing Interpersonal Conflict in Project Teams," *Sloan Management Review* 18, no. 2 (Winter 1977): 57, by permission of the publisher.

Other sources of conflict include manpower resources, technical opinions and the trade-offs that must be made between quality and costs, administrative procedures, costs and cost estimates, and personality conflicts.

The Successful Project Manager. Raymond Hill (1977) has analyzed the managerial styles of successful and unsuccessful project managers. His research indicates that the successful project manager is willing to personally absorb aggression, encourages openness and emotional expression in his relations with subordinates and peers, listens to the opinions and ideas of others, serves as a role model by his or her own behavior, counsels subordinates or peers to behave differently, is aware of the utility of conflict, and paces and controls potential conflict so that it does not become dysfunctional (see Figure 10–3).

In their studies of matrix organizations Hans Thamhain and David Wileman (1977) identified nine major sources of influence that project managers employ to motivate their subordinates.

Expertise: the subordinates perceive the project managers as possessing special knowledge.

Authority: the subordinates perceive the project manager as having the legitimate power to issue orders.

Work challenge: the subordinates enjoy the project and the direction provided by the project manager.

Friendship: subordinates personally like the project manager.

Future work assignments: the subordinates feel that the project manager can influence their future work assignments.

Fund allocation: the subordinates feel that the project manager has the power to obtain budgetary support for the project.

Promotion: the subordinates perceive the manager as being capable of indirectly dispensing valued organizational rewards by helping them in their efforts to be promoted.

Salary: the subordinates perceive the project manager as being capable of directly dispensing monetary rewards.

Penalty: the subordinates perceive the project manager as being capable of directly or indirectly dispensing penalties they want to avoid.

Thamhain and Wilemon then discuss the relationship among factors that leads to the successful completion of a project (Figure 10–4). If the project manager's position or legitimate power in the organization and the intrinsic motivation of his subordinates are high, there is

FIGURE 10–4
Variables of Project Management Effectiveness

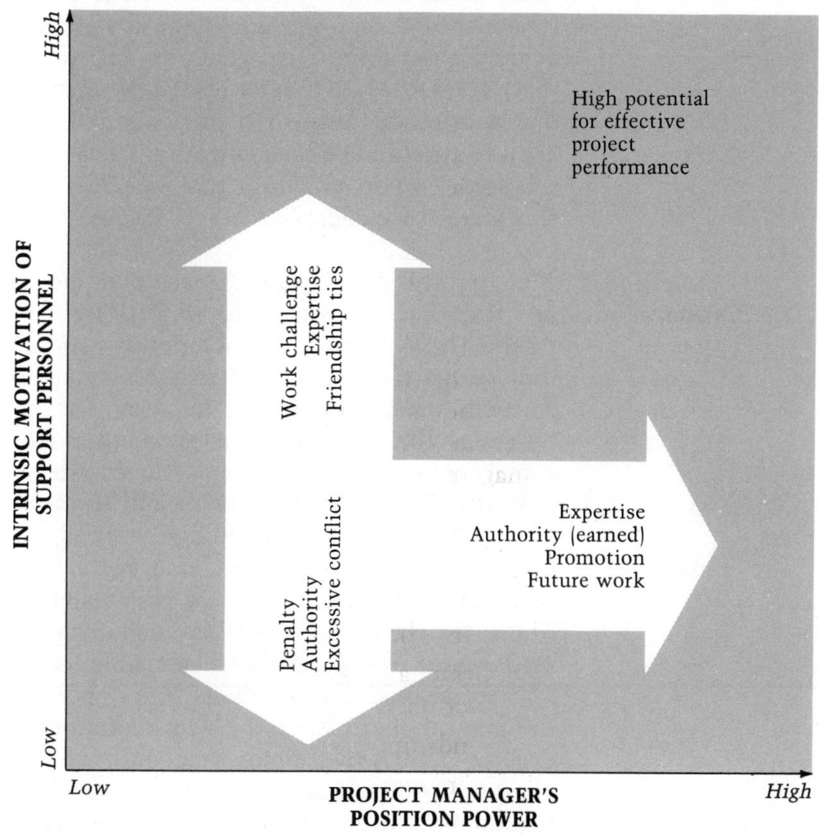

Source: Reprinted from Hans J. Thamhain and David L. Wilemon, "Leadership, Conflict, and Program Management Effectiveness," *Sloan Management Review* 19, no. 1 (Fall 1977): 87 by permission of the publisher. Copyright © 1977 by the Sloan Management Review Association. All rights reserved.

a high potential for effective project performance. The position power of the project manager is high if his or her subordinates perceive that he or she is influential in terms of the following sources of influence: expertise, earned authority, promotion, and future work assignments. Similarly, the intrinsic motivation of the subordinates is high if the project manager can rely heavily on the following sources of influence: challenging work, expertise, and friendship ties. However, intrinsic motivation of subordinates decreases significantly as the project manager begins to rely on the influence of penalties and unearned authority. Finally, intrinsic motivation of subordinates decreases when there is an excessive amount of conflict.

SPECIALIZED FORMS OF ORGANIZATION

Thus far we have examined the general forms of organizational design that modern managers employ to achieve their goals. However, many specialized organizations, such as law firms, trade and professional organizations, and voluntary groups, modify these designs to achieve their distinctive goals. In addition, two organizations seemingly the same, such as two prisons, may be radically different from one another because of their goals and the design they employ to achieve them. Such specialization can be aptly described in terms of a typology of organization that was developed by Amitai Etzioni. In this section we address all these issues.

Professional Organizations

Many professional organizations operate in our society; these include law firms, accounting firms, consulting firms, universities, and hospitals. The dominant characteristic of these organizations is that the professionals (doctors, professors, lawyers) exercise the most control in them and represent line management, since they are responsible for the production of the final good or service in the organization. Conversely, administrators responsible for integration of activities are less powerful than the professionals and represent staff management.

This form of organization is very different from the traditional line organization in which staff management merely advises line managers, who are ultimately responsible for integrating activities. The administrators in a professional organization not only advise line management, they are also responsible for integrating activities.

Professional organizations often operate ineffectively because of the amorphous role of the administrators. The professionals, while experts in their own fields, frequently know little about the management of organizations. Also, in many of these organizations competition among the professionals is keen. For example, to become a partner in a prestigious law firm or accounting firm takes eight or more years, and many never achieve this status. Thus competition inhibits the professionals' ability to integrate activities and goals and compounds the problem of limiting the role of the administrators.

Professional organizations have begun to recognize the deficiencies of their organizational structures and many now employ specialized administrators to integrate activities and goals. An example of the growth of law firm administrators is provided by the Association of Legal Administrators, which formed in 1971 with fewer than 25 members but now has nearly 2000 members and is growing at the rate of 30 per month. Similarly, many universities and colleges now offer graduate degrees in specialized fields of management, such as hospital, prison, or arts management. While these administrators still operate under the direction of the professionals, their intimate knowledge and training in these specialized areas of management have significantly increased their status and power, and professional organizations have correspondingly benefited.

Government Organizations

The influence of the government has increased dramatically in the United States since the turn of the twentieth century. In 1919, 9.0 percent of the American work force was employed by government; by 1975 the percentage was 16.5 (*U.S. Department of Labor* 1975). Most of these workers are employed by state and local governments. Contrary to popular opinion, the size of the federal civilian work force has remained relatively constant at approximately 2 million workers since the end of World War II; approximately 700,000 additional workers are employed by the U.S. Postal Service, which is now a quasi-government organization.

Historically, the major advantage of government employment was job security. Although there have been periodic reductions in force and terminations for ineffective performance, these have been much fewer in number than the terminations in the private sector. Also, because Congress in the 1960s decreed that salaries of federal government workers be comparable to those of private sector workers, total compensation is relatively high in the federal government. In some situations federal workers are paid at a higher rate than their private sector counterparts.

However, the new Civil Service Reform Act of 1978 has streamlined the procedures for demoting and terminating ineffective government workers (see Chapter 3). In addition, the declining level of productivity in the United States, which primarily influences the treatment of workers in the private sector, most probably will have an impact on the governmental work force also as citizens demand a greater return for their taxes.

Most governmental organizations are structured in a bureaucratic manner (Carroll and Tosi 1977). They exist in relatively stable environments in which they can predict reasonable increases in their allotted budgets every year. However, some government organizations such as the Energy Department exist in a highly volatile environment, for political and societal pressures influence the manner in which they complete their work. And while it is rare for legislators to decree the death of an agency, political and societal pressures sometimes do bring about changes. For example, such pressures have caused funding cutbacks in the poverty programs sponsored by the Department of Labor. Similarly, the Department of Education was created when this function was taken away from the Department of Health, Education, and Welfare.

Perhaps the outstanding characteristic of the design of government organizations is the combination of political and career appointees. Political appointees, who have such titles as assistant secretary of labor or assistant secretary of transportation, typically focus on the strategic plans of government agencies, and their tenure is short, since it coincides with that of the party in power. Career appointees report to the political appointees. There is an uneasy relationship between the political and career appointees, mainly because of their respective lengths of tenure in the organization. Many political appointees serve less than a year, which is not even sufficient time for them to learn their jobs thoroughly. Because of the magnitude of this problem, former President Carter asked his political appointees to give him their guarantees that they would serve as long as he needed their service. While this approach will not solve the entire problem, it should make the relationships between political and career appointees more stable.

Specialized Service Organizations

Service organizations do not manufacture a specific product but rather provide a distinctive service or set of services. In 1919, 48.0 percent of the American work force was in the service sector; by 1975 the percentage was 59.2 (*Employment and Earnings* 1975). The spectrum of service organizations encompasses barbershops, hotels, banks, and insurance companies.

It is not possible to identify a typical organizational structure that service organizations employ, because the external environments in which they exist vary from stable to volatile. However, many service organizations such as banks and insurance companies require specialized managerial training. For instance, the Insurance Institute of America sponsors certificate programs for individuals wishing to enter the industry.

As shown by the statistics given above, specialized service organizations are growing, mainly in response to societal needs and

FIGURE 10–5
Etzioni's Types of Organizations

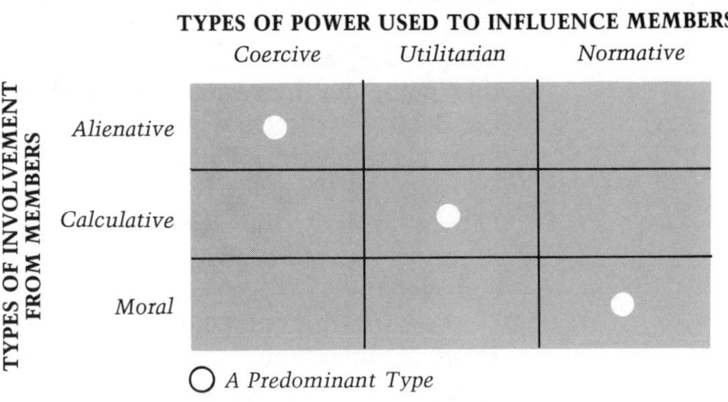

Source: Based, with permission of Macmillan Publishing Co., Inc., on Amitai Etzioni, *A Comparative Analysis of Complex Organizations*, rev. and enlarged ed. (New York: Free Press, 1975), p. 12. Copyright © 1975 by Amitai Etzioni.

pressures. Thus trade associations, which are organizations formed by companies in a particular industry, have increased in number at least in part because of the growth of government. These trade associations lobby legislators on behalf of the organizations that underwrite their budgets. An excellent example of a trade association is the American Trucking Association. Similarly, professional associations such as the American Psychological Association are typically formed and supported by a group of professionals who require such services as annual meetings and the publication of journals. There are now approximately 40,000 trade and professional associations in the United States representing more than 5 million individuals.

Etzioni's Typology

An innovative approach to the design of organizations has been developed by Amitai Etzioni (1975), who classifies organizations by the type of power they use to influence subordinates (see Figure 10–5). Etzioni identifies three types of power. First, an organization can force its members to follow specific courses of action; that is, it can use *coercive power,* as a prison does. Second, the organization can employ *utilitarian power,* in which case a member is not rewarded if he or she does not perform what is expected. Most business firms use utilitarian power. Finally, the organization may use *normative power,* in which case the member obeys mainly because he or she wants to be a part of the organization. Religious orders typically use normative power.

When an organization employs coercive power, members usually react to the organization with hostility, which is an *alienative involvement.* Utilitarian power usually results in a *calculative involvement;* that is, members will leave the organization if they believe they are not benefiting from it. Finally, normative power frequently creates *moral involvement.* In this instance members feel a moral obligation to obey the organization's dictates, since they have joined voluntarily.

Although power and involvement can act independently, in most organizations they are related; thus the three combinations we've just mentioned predominate. Of course, a few organizations combine two or even all three types of power. For example, some labor unions use both utilitarian and normative power to gain compliance from their members.

Etzioni's typology brings into focus the intimate relationship between planning, control, and organization design, as specified by our organizational framework (see Chapter 3). For instance, a mental hospital whose planning system emphasizes the goal of quietly controlling the behavior of patients until they are ready for release is, in reality, a coercively designed organization. Conversely, a mental hospital that seeks to change the behavior of its patients so that they will be cured and will not return once they are released represents a normatively or educatively designed organization. Similar relationships between goals and design can be found in many other types of organizations. And, as suggested above, if an organization is attempting to achieve several goals, it may become a mixed type, such as a utilitarian-normative labor union.

In short, Etzioni's typology demonstrates how goals influence the design of an organization and the types of control systems that superiors employ to monitor the behavior of subordinates. Organizations become specialized in large part because of the nature of the goals they are seeking to attain and the types of relationships that develop between superiors and subordinates because of these goals.

ECONOMIC FORMS OF ORGANIZATION

Modern forms of organizations represent general approaches that managers in many different kinds of situations use to handle their problems. Similarly, specialized forms of organizations come into existence because a company's distinctive problems demand distinctive solutions. In this section we shall see that management may employ other organization designs in order to maximize, at least partially, economic goals. These economic forms of organization affect differentially behavioral processes, managerial decision making, and planning and control systems, the components of our integrated framework (see Chapter 3). Some of the major economic forms of organization are employee-owned companies, vertical and horizontal integration, conglomerates, ventures, state-backed corporations, and multinational corporations (MNCs). In this section we describe these economic forms.

Employee-owned Companies

As we have seen in Chapter 9, stockholders constitute a major guiding system in a corporation. But stockholders typically are divorced from the daily activities of a company; their major interest is return on investment. Hence the actual owners of the company do not make the decisions guiding its destiny; those decisions are made by the company's managers.

However, companies do experience financial difficulties, and one solution to this problem is the *employee-owned company* in which employees purchase the company's stock. Through a novel loan program administered by the federal Economic Department of the Department of Commerce, employee ownership has become increasingly popular and important. One study of three firms indicated that as employee ownership increases, so does job satisfaction (Long 1980). In addition, a recent survey of 75 employee-owned companies indicated that, when compared with a 24-year period before the plan, these companies achieved a 72 percent increase in sales, employed

37 percent more workers, increased pretax profits by 157 percent, and paid 150 percent more in federal income taxes (McCarthy 1979). Presumably these employees feel a personal responsibility for the success of the company, since they are now its owners. Thus it seems that economic performance is enhanced considerably when management and its workers-stockholders combine to increase the efficiency of the company's planning, control, design, and decision-making systems.

Conglomerates

As we have already seen, an organization uses federal decentralization if its operating divisions are producing similar or related products. A *conglomerate,* in contrast, is a combination of two or more companies that produce *unrelated* products. Usually a conglomerate includes a large number of companies, but the essence of this form of economic organization is simply that the firms in it are unrelated.

A major advantage of conglomerates is that they are generally less subject to antitrust regulation than organizations producing only one product or a small number of related products. In addition, a conglomerate is theoretically more flexible than any one of its companies, since its top managers can transfer resources from one enterprise to another when they decide that changes must be made.

The conglomerate does have disadvantages, of course. One problem is that it is difficult for top management to be familiar with the unique characteristics of all the industries under its direction, which can lead to poor decision making. This problem is compounded by the common practice of firing or demoting many of the capable officers when a conglomerate buys a new firm. In addition, effective managers frequently leave voluntarily after a conglomerate purchases a company because the working atmosphere becomes impersonal and insensitive to the firm's special needs. One writer highlighted the impersonal nature of a large conglomerate by titling his book *Welcome to Our Conglomerate—You're Fired* (Barmash 1971).

Vertical and Horizontal Integration

Two additional economic forms of organization are vertical and horizontal integration. *Vertical integration* is the construction of an organization so that it includes all steps in the production process, from the extraction of raw materials through the manufacture of the final product and its sale to the public. A vertically integrated firm thus is not dependent on other organizations at any stage in the production process. This independence can be invaluable; many small firms have gone bankrupt because they could not acquire critical supplies.

If a company attempts to dominate a market at one particular state in the production process, it is tending toward *horizontal integration.* The company is also flirting with the antitrust laws, since its aim is to eliminate or reduce competition at that stage of the production process. A current political issue, for example, is whether laws should be passed to prevent the large oil companies, many of which are already vertically integrated, from becoming horizontally integrated as well by taking on uranium and solar energy interests.

Ventures

To remain viable, companies must develop new products that give them a competitive edge. However, the incentive to develop new products is diminished in a large company, because the scientists and engineers responsible for their development do not own the rights to the products, and they usually benefit only in nominal salary increases. For example, there are documented cases in which a scientist has developed a new product resulting in tens of millions of dollars of profit for the company, but the scientist obtained only a token reward.

To counteract this problem, companies may establish an independent department that seeks out new *ventures.* These venture teams employ project management; that is, the team receives seed money sufficient to cover its expenses for a given period of time, during which it is protected from the rest of the company administratively, financially, spatially, and sometimes legally (Hlavacek and Thompson 1973). Frequently members of the venture team receive a share of the profits resulting from the success of a new product, a situation that increases their motivation.

However, the cost of funding a venture team is sometimes exorbitant, and so two or more companies may band together to form a *joint venture* or joint venture team. Costs of funding the venture team are shared by the companies involved, as are the resulting profits.

State-backed Corporations

In the United States, corporations are relatively free from governmental control and direction, although the situation may be changing. In countries in which the economy is strictly regulated and directed by the government, such as in Germany and Japan, corporations typically receive financial support from the state. These *state-backed corporations* are thus able to compete more effectively in world markets against private corporations that do not receive such support, as is true of most American corporations.

In Germany state-backed corporations operate under a unique organizational structure termed *codetermination.* In this structure the board of directors of each company is tripartite and includes directors from government, the labor unions, and private stockholders.

Because of the intense competition among countries in world markets, we can expect to see an increase in state-backed corporations. For example, Chrysler Corporation, the tenth largest American corporation (employing approximately 350,000 workers), has sought state backing by asking for and receiving a government loan guarantee

"It's not surprising. The production department is in Spain, the warehouse is in Korea, the accounting division is in Bolivia, the Board of Directors is in Canada . . ."

of $1.5 billion dollars. Although Chrysler Corporation is not using codetermination, it recently added Douglas Fraser, the president of the United Automobile Workers of the World, to its board of directors. These two events may portend a move toward codetermination among American corporations.

Multinational Corporations

The multinational corporation (MNC) represents the most powerful economic form of organization that we shall analyze. An MNC, although based in one country for legal purposes, operates divisions in two or more countries. A large MNC such as Exxon has billions of dollars in assets and employs well over a million individuals worldwide. Analysts have pointed out that MNCs are much bigger in assets and company size, as measured by employees, than some medium-sized nations.

The MNCs may represent the most revolutionary worldwide development in the twentieth century, since they are seemingly more powerful than some of the countries in which they operate. But management theorists and practitioners have only recently begun to analyze organization designs that seem to be appropriate for their operations, and most of the companies themselves have given insufficient attention to this problem. General Motors, for instance, considers its huge international division to be of secondary importance; it still emphasizes the importance of its American market (Drucker 1974). In addition, federal decentralization, which has served General Motors' American divisions so well in the past, seems to be inappropriate for handling the worldwide operations of the company.

Whatever the future holds, it is quite clear that state-backed corporations and MNCs, purely because of their vast size, will be a major factor in tomorrow's world. And because of their importance, new organizational designs must be developed to handle the distinctive problems that they face.

SUMMARY

This chapter has examined three different types of organization design: modern forms, specialized forms, and economic forms. Each of these three forms of organization directly or indirectly affects behavioral processes, managerial decision making, and planning and control systems.

Modern forms of organization—federal decentralization, project management, and matrix organization—can be understood within the context of two fundamental types of departmentalization: by function and by goal. Federal decentralization emphasizes departmentalization by goal for the operating units and departmentalization by function at the highest level in the organization. Each specialist in the operating unit has a dual reporting relationship; the specialist reports to the vice-president in charge of his or her department at the highest level of the organization and to the head of his or her operating unit. Throughout a given reporting period the operating units function as independent subsystems. At the end of the reporting period the executive committee and the finance committee (both at the top level of the organization) examine the units' relative profitability and problems. Thus integration at the top level of the organization occurs through the use of the finance and executive committees.

Project management is implemented when a company wishes to complete a single project (an example would be the housing industry). Thus departmentalization is by goal, but the departments are only temporary.

The matrix organization guarantees relative permanence to the departments. And like federal decentralization, the matrix organization, combines departmentalization by project (product) and by function. In addition, in the matrix organization there is an open violation of the principle of unity of command; the general manager's essential function is to manage conflict; and the program or product managers supervising the various projects are more powerful than the functional managers because they have bottom-line responsibility. As several researchers have shown, successful project managers are able to handle conflict and are open and honest in their relations with peers and subordinates.

Specialized forms of organization arise to achieve a company's distinctive goals. Prominent specialized organizations include professional organizations such as law firms, government agencies, and service organizations such as insurance companies and trade associations. Etzioni's typology of organizations shows how companies become specialized: Because of the nature of the goals they are seeking to attain and the types of relationships that develop between superiors and subordinates in light of these goals, organizations take on distinctive structures.

Finally, there are some organization designs that management uses to achieve purely economic objectives. These economic forms of organization include employee-owned companies, conglomerates, vertical and horizontal integration, ventures, state-backed corporations, and multinational corporations.

DISCUSSION QUESTIONS

1. In what types of environment is a matrix organization appropriate? What problems would you expect to emerge when the matrix organization is used? Explain.
2. What are the main differences among the matrix organization, federal decentralization, and conglomerates?
3. What are some of the major sources of influence that a project manager can employ? Outline the profile of a successful project manager. What are the factors that are related to project success in a matrix organization?
4. Is it possible to structure a specialized organization as a matrix organization? Why or why not?
5. According to Etzioni's typology, is it possible to view a specific kind of organization, such as a prison, as representative of more than one type of organization? Explain.
6. What do conglomerates and horizontal integration have in common with one another?
7. Is it possible to describe the majority of American corporations as state-backed? Why or why not?
8. What is codetermination? Does it exist in the United States? Why or why not?

CRITICAL INCIDENT

NOTE: This critical incident can be used by the whole class with the case observational method (see Appendix A) or used for thought and discussion by individual class members.

A major problem with federal decentralization or the multi-divisional form of organization is adequate monitoring, by the corporate level, of activities in the operating units. An excellent illustration of this problem is provided by the Division of Behavioral and Social Sciences of a large state university. The general manager was the provost of this division; his office consisted of 12 professionals, including three assistant provosts. The division included 450 professors in such departments as sociology, anthropology, and psychology and such colleges as business and public management.

The problem revolved around the evaluation of performance. Professors were evaluated in terms of three criteria: research, teaching, and university and public service. However, since it is relatively easy to measure research output in terms of scholarly publications, research became the dominant criterion—and sometimes the only criterion. To provide information on teaching, each faculty member could voluntarily pass out a questionnaire to his or her students, but he or she was in complete control of it and could use the results in whatever way desired. The primary use was at time of promotion, when each candidate usually forwarded the teaching evaluation forms to the provost. Otherwise, the provost's office did not have any information on teaching.

The provost decided that his office should have a better source of information. He felt two critical goals could be accomplished by a new system. First, there would be a more accurate performance appraisal of teaching for salary review and promotion review. Second, the information would help professors improve their teaching.

A task force appointed by the provost suggested that a teaching evaluation and development system be instituted. Professors did not need to participate, but the importance of the information for accomplishing the two goals would be made clear to them. Thus the provost expected almost all faculty members to participate.

Under the new system the provost's office would pass out a questionnaire to students taking courses in the division, and collect and analyze the information. Raw scores on each questionnaire item would be provided, as well as percentiles showing how well each professor scored when compared to all other professors in the division. For example, a percentile score of 60 would indicate that on this item the professor scored better than 59 of the average 100 professors in the division. In addition, a total score would be derived by adding all the questionnaire items together, and this total score would also be converted to a percentile score.

The reaction of the 450 professors was negative. They agreed that some sort of a system was needed, but they felt that only the departments and colleges at the operating level could really evaluate the effectiveness of the teaching in their units. There were too many variables that would be masked by a single score, including size of the class, the quality of the classroom's physical setting, types of courses, and available resources. The provost's office would be so far removed from knowledge of these and other variables that it could not adequately evaluate their impact. Also, while they felt that the provost should receive reliable and valid information, they wanted to maintain control at the operative level. Further, many professors questioned the value of using current students, a large number of whom might not be good judges of teaching performance and course content. And in some cases professors might even inflate grades in order to obtain higher ratings. Finally, they felt that the data might be used only in a negative sense—that is, to deny salary increases and promotions.

QUESTIONS: Do you feel that the provost's two major goals are of equal importance? Why or why not? Should only current students be used as judges? Design a system under which the operating units would control the data, but provide sufficient controls so that the information given the provost would be accurate and desirable in terms of accomplishing the two major goals.

SUGGESTED READINGS

Davis, Stanley, and Lawrence, Paul. *Matrix.* Reading, Mass.: Addison-Wesley, 1977, 235 pages, paperback.

The authors examine the matrix organization in depth. They discuss its evolution, the mature matrix, and matrix pathologies. Case studies are also provided.

Drucker, Peter. "New Templates for Today's Organizations." *Harvard Business Review,* January-February 1974, pp. 45–53.

Drucker briefly and aptly describes traditional and modern forms of organization design.

Parkinson, C. Northcote. *Big Business.* Boston: Little, Brown, 1974, 263 pages, hardback.

Parkinson provides a fascinating description of the rise of the multinational corporations, their relationships with government and labor, and their importance in world markets.

11 A Contingency Approach to Organizing

THREE CRITICAL FACTORS
THE INFORMATION-PROCESSING SYNTHESIS
SUMMARY
DISCUSSION QUESTIONS
CRITICAL INCIDENT
SUGGESTED READINGS

PERFORMANCE OBJECTIVES

1. To distinguish between mechanistic and organic structures.
2. To identify the relationships between the design of an organization and three critical factors—organizational size, technology, and external environmental uncertainty.
3. To outline and discuss the contingency approach to designing organizations, specifically from the perspective of an information-processing synthesis.

Managers must know how to build an organization and construct guiding systems for it, as we have seen in Chapter 9. Similarly, managers must understand the modern approaches that are used to structure organizations (Chapter 10). Still, the manager's knowledge would be deficient if he or she did not comprehend the enormous significance of a contingency (situational) approach to organizing. Thus the objective of this chapter is to describe the contingency approach.

To focus the discussion, we shall utilize the distinction between mechanistic and organic structures or organizations (see Chapter 2). Essentially, the mechanistic organization is highly bureaucratic: It emphasizes the use of a clearly defined and centralized hierarchy in which jobs and procedures are standardized. Conversely, the organic organization employs a decentralized and participative hierarchy of authority in which jobs and procedures are flexible. Organizations exist along a continuum extending from mechanistic to organic. In real situations it would be difficult, if not impossible, to identify an enterprise at one end of this continuum. However, it is possible to identify differences between these two structures and to classify an organization as either more mechanistic or more organic.

In the first part of this chapter we examine research on the major factors that are important in constructing organizations. In the second part of the chapter we examine in detail the contingency approach to organizing.

THREE CRITICAL FACTORS

For the past thirty years management researchers have completed many empirical studies of the factors that seem to influence the type of structure that an organization employs to accomplish its goals. As we might expect, many of these studies have produced contradictory results. However, most researchers agree that there are three critical factors that managers should take into consideration when designing organizations: organizational size, technology, and external environmental uncertainty. In this section we describe a few influential studies in this area and highlight research results that are both consistent across a broad spectrum of empirical studies and important for the structuring of organizations.

The Blau Study

Peter Blau and his associates (1976) focused their attention on factors that managers should consider when structuring organizations. In their study of 110 American manufacturing firms they demonstrate that size, as measured by number of employees, is significantly related to the manner in which an organization is structured. Thus as size increases, the following measures of differentiation also rise: number of organizational levels, organizational divisions, sections within organizational divisions, job titles, and the degree of functional specialization. Blau's research also demonstrates that the degree to which an organization automates or computerizes its activities is also related to the amount of differentiation.

These researchers speculate that size in and of itself may force an organization to develop a more differentiated and automated structure. While many researchers do not agree with Blau on this point, it seems clear that managers must consider the size of an organization when designing or redesigning its structure.

The Woodward Study

In 1965 Joan Woodward and her associates reported the results of a large-scale study of 100 English firms. This study is significant because Woodward was able to identify a relationship among the organizations' technologies, structures, and success. And she found that the distinction between mechanistic and organic structures was important for understanding the relationship.

Woodward classified the 100 firms into three major groups according to type of technology. Under the first type, *unit technology,* the organization spends a great amount of money on labor costs relative to capital investment in equipment (for example, the manufacture of custom-made furniture, which relies heavily on highly skilled workers). The second type of technology is *mass production;* here the organization spends a great amount of money on labor but also invests heavily in capital equipment or machines (for example, the automotive assembly line). The third type of technology is *process* or *automated technology;* here the organization does not spend much money on labor but does invest a large amount in capital equipment (for example, an oil refinery or chemical plant).

Woodward rated each of the 100 firms studied according to an index of success consisting of such traditional measures as net income and percentage increase in market domination. Most successful unit technology firms were found to have an organic structure, and the unsuccessful unit firms generally employed a mechanistic structure (see Figure 11–1). This same relationship occurred in the process firms. However, the trend reversed in mass production firms; most successful companies were organized mechanistically, and the unsuccessful companies organically.

These findings suggest that there is no one best way to organize a company. Rather, the approach that should be taken in designing an organization depends heavily on the technological system that underlies the production process.

Other research has generally confirmed Woodward's original findings (Harvey 1968; Blau et al. 1976). However, another research team in England that intensively analyzed the relationship between technology and organizational structure in forty-one organizations only

FIGURE 11–1

Relationship Among Technology, Organizational Structure, and Success in 100 English Firms

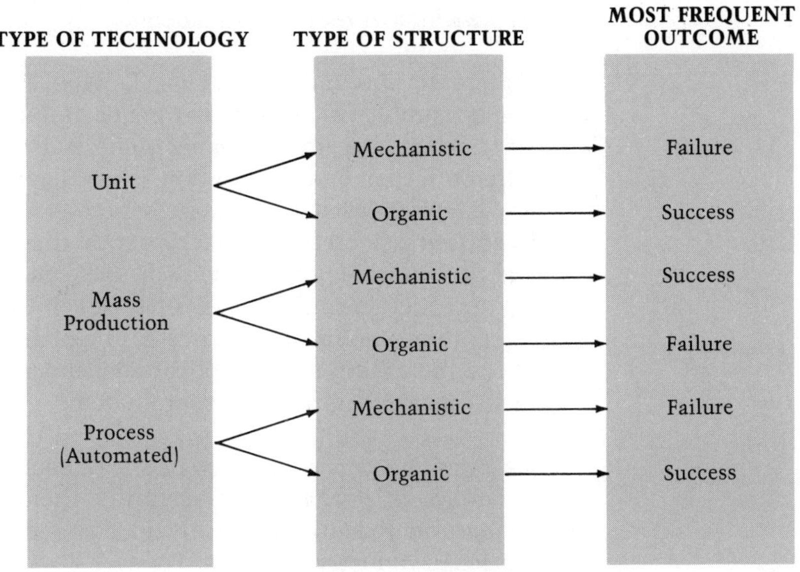

Source: Based on Joan Woodward, *Industrial Organization* (Oxford: Oxford University Press, 1965).

partially confirmed Woodward's original findings (Hickson, Pugh, and Pheysey 1969). These researchers found that size also seems to be a critical factor. If an enterprise is small, technology will directly affect structure, for it dominates the organization. Everything else—sales, marketing, accounting, and so forth—is a minor activity designed mainly to serve the technological requirements of the system. However, in a large organization the influence of technology is weak, for management must stress *all* activities to be successful. And, as was true for Woodward's original study, additional research seemed to confirm these findings (Child and Mansfield 1972), although Blau's large-scale study of 110 American manufacturing firms does not support them. Hence at the present time we must withhold unqualified acceptance of these results.

Even if these findings were found to be valid, though, they do not undermine the importance of technology, at least in a small organization. And in a large organization if management structured activities by breaking the organization into several independent subsystems, then the impact of technology might be expected to increase within each subsystem (Reimann and Inzerilli 1979).

The Lawrence and Lorsch Study

The third major factor that seems to be important in considering the design or redesign of an organization is external environmental uncertainty. A prominent study in this area was completed by two Harvard researchers, Paul Lawrence and Jay Lorsch (1967). In this section we look at their study in detail.

Differentiation and Integration. Lawrence and Lorsch point out that a major problem—perhaps *the* major problem—managers should consider when designing organizations is that of effectively balancing differentiation and integration (see Chapter 9). As an organization grows and faces new challenges from its external environment, differentiation increases. That is, both the number of complex units and the differing points of view in the organization increase as it takes on new and specialized tasks. However, as differentiation increases, integration should also increase proportionately. That is, the work of the increasing number of interdependent subunits and viewpoints in an organization must be coordinated.

Degrees of Certainty. Lawrence and Lorsch selected three types of environment for analysis, defining them by such criteria as the changes in the number of inventions and number of firms within a particular industry over time. For each environment they chose a representative industry for study.

One type of environment reflects a high degree of certainty. It is typified by firms in the container industry, where the technology is stable and sales are relatively predictable over time. Only a few innovations have been introduced into this industry in recent years, and only a few new firms have been created. The dominant problem in a container firm is scheduling, for management does not want to antagonize long-term customers and lose them because of late shipments and inferior products. The dominant subsystem in such an organization is production, since management must ensure that it produces an adequate number of high-quality products to meet the demands of customers.

Within the food industry the environment is moderately certain. Even though innovations do occur and each company's sales figures do change over time, the future is relatively predictable. For instance, General Foods and other large companies in this industry neglected the natural food mania for many years; then they realized their new but small competitors were taking away many of their customers. These large companies have successfully entered this area by producing their own natural foods, many of which have become very popular. The dominant problem in the food industry is rapid change in consumer tastes. Since the companies in this industry basically produce the same commodities, the marketing department is the dominant subsystem in a food company. It must monitor changes in customer tastes and convince the public that its foods are superior to those of its competitors.

Finally, there is the highly uncertain or unpredictable environment, such as that of the plastics industry. Innovations occur rapidly, so a firm's position can change equally rapidly if it does not respond continually to the changing needs of its customers and the new approaches of its competitors. The dominant problem in a plastics company is innovation, and the dominant subsystem is research and development.

Certainty and Structure. Lawrence and Lorsch then compared the organizational structures of the successful firms to the unsuccessful ones within each of the three industries (see Table 11–1). In the container industry, with its highly certain environment, the successful firm used a mechanistic approach. There is a low degree of differentiation in this industry. The firms are not growing in size or complexity. The bureaucratic hierarchy, with its rigid specification of jobs and procedures, is an efficient way to integrate the work of interdependent units. Since innovations are rare, the main worries of top managers are the quality of the goods they produce and the correct scheduling of deliveries so customers do not become dissatisfied. If coordination and communication begin to break down, managers can integrate their interdependent tasks by following bureaucratic rules.

However, the mechanistic organization and its hierarchy proved inadequate in the food industry's moderately certain environment. As the organization grows and adds complex or differentiated subunits, it should solve problems of coordination by relying on *inte-*

TABLE 11–1
Design Strategies: Environmental Uncertainty and Organizational Structure

External environment	*Industry*	*Dominant problem*	*Dominant subsystem*	*Successful organizational structure*	*Degree of differentiation*	*Integrating mechanism*
High degree of certainty	Container	Scheduling	Production	Mechanistic	Low	Hierarchy (rules)
Moderate degree of certainty	Food	Changes in tastes	Marketing	Movement toward organic (integrators)	Moderate	Use of individual integrators
Low degree of certainty	Plastic	Innovation	Research & development (R&D)	Organic	High	Cross-functional teams: the matrix organization

Source: Based on Paul Lawrence and Jay Lorsch, *Organization and Environment.*

grators: individuals charged with coordinating the work of interdependent departments or activities. The integrators cannot be classified as either line or staff personnel. Rather, they have enough authority to ensure that line managers whose tasks are interdependent work together toward the common goals of the organization. Integrators do not make the decisions themselves, but they manage the decision process.

The successful firm in the highly uncertain environment of the plastics industry had further formalized the work of integrators. To ensure that interdependent departments would coordinate their activities and respond quickly to environmental changes, the successful firm established formal departments of integration that both coordinated the work of interdependent units and monitored the external environment for any changes that might influence the firm's competitive position. Thus the successful firm in this industry used a matrix form of organization.

In short, Lawrence and Lorsch have posited a relationship between environmental uncertainty and the successful organizational structure that is appropriate for coping with it. They believe that organizations should move from a mechanistic to an organic structure as the degree of environmental uncertainty increases, for the organic structure is better able to integrate the activities of differentiated and complex units.[1]

Successful Integrators

Using the research completed by Lawrence and Lorsch and others, one can profile the successful integrator (Galbraith 1977). Individuals who would be successful in this role tend to be high in affiliation needs and enjoy interacting with others in the organization. Integrators must be willing to *not* make decisions but, rather, to coordinate the decision contexts. Integrators must be respected by others in the organization, and this respect is based on the integrators' expert knowledge in the uncertainty-absorbing areas confronting the organization. Integrators must be unbiased in their relations with the various subunits whose work must be coordinated. And, as might be expected, integrators must be able to handle effectively the conflict between groups without being absorbed into one of them.

In many ways this profile parallels that of the successful program or product manager in a matrix organization (see pp. 254–255). Thus program managers would probably make effective integrators, given the necessary training. In fact, many matrix organizations have a

[1] Although the concepts underlying the Lawrence and Lorsch study have become important building blocks in the area of organization design, their methodology has been seriously questioned. See Tosi, Aldag, and Storey 1973; Dulz 1977; and Downey and Slocum 1975.

program coordinator who reports directly to the general manager. The program coordinator is an integrator, since he or she must resolve conflicts among the various program managers, who are vying with one another for scarce resources. Hence the matrix organization is integrated *horizontally* through the relationships among the program managers and the functional line managers, and *vertically* through the relationships between the program coordinator and the program managers. Also, the general manager is an integrator, for his or her basic role is the management of conflict (see Chapter 10).

As an example of a successful integrator, consider this individual who recently received his MBA degree. He had spent 20 years in the army as a construction manager (program manager). Because of his work history and newly acquired degree, the Bechtel Corporation, the largest construction company in the world, offered him a very lucrative position as integrator of its geographically dispersed projects in Africa, Europe, and other areas.

The Chandler Study

A second important study of the relationship between external environmental uncertainty and the structure of an organization was undertaken by Alfred Chandler, Jr. (1962). His conclusions were based primarily on a historical analysis of 100 large companies. He also completed a detailed analysis of four companies: DuPont, General Motors, Standard Oil (New Jersey), and Sears, Roebuck. In this study Chandler used historical documents, internal company records, correspondence, and interviews with some of the top managers in each of these four companies.

Chandler's conclusion was that the strategic plans of a company determine the type of organizational structure it should follow. Strategic plans, in turn, depend on the degree of certainty in the organization's environment. A successful organization in an industry that remains relatively stable in markets, raw materials, and production processes should not deviate from its strategic plans and should be structured mechanistically. If, however, environmental changes accelerate in the areas of market demands, availability of raw materials, or the use of new production processes, top management should alter its strategic plans through diversification into new product lines. This strategy of diversification decreases the probability that the organization will fail, since top management has spread its risk by relying on the success of several products. However, diversification should be accompanied by an organic organizational design, since top management must respond quickly to changes in the external environment that directly affect any of its product lines. Top management must meet the competition by allowing individuals and organizational subsystems to respond creatively and responsibly, which would not be feasible in a highly centralized mechanistic organization.

An Alternative Explanation

The studies we have reviewed assume that the three critical factors—organizational size, technology, and external environmental uncertainty—all affect the structure of an organization. Chandler's study is the major exception, for he points out that the strategic decisions top managers make are pivotal: The structure of an organization should be able to handle the environmental uncertainty that the organization faces in light of these decisions.

Using Chandler's work, John Child (1973) has postulated that researchers may have incorrectly reversed the relationships. Child argues that strategic decisions determine the size of an organization, the type of technology that will be used, and even the kind of environment in which the organization decides to operate.

Child's alternative explanation seems logical, since top management obviously makes such major decisions. However, as Blau and his associates have shown, organizational size and automation are closely related to the amount of differentiation in an organization. As size and automation increase, so does differentiation. Thus across a broad spectrum of organizations it seems that the size of the organization and its degree of automation limit the ways in which managers may structure their organizations.

In short, we cannot assume that the three critical factors totally determine the structure of an organization. Similarly, we cannot assume that the strategic decisions of top management totally determine the structure either. Rather there is an *interactive relationship* among strategic decisions, the three critical factors, and organizational structure. Top management initially makes strategic decision concerning the size of an organization, the type of technology that the organization will use, and the nature of the environment in which it will operate. These in turn influence the amount of differentiation and integration that an organization implements. Top management must reconsider organizational structure and the relationship between differentiation and integration when there are significant changes in any or all of the three critical factors.

THE INFORMATION-PROCESSING SYNTHESIS

Jay Galbraith (1973, 1977) has attempted to integrate all the studies concerned with the issues of organizational size, technology, and environmental uncertainty. He begins his analysis by emphasizing the importance of balancing differentiation and integration. As an organization differentiates by adding subunits and specialists to handle growth in business or environmental uncertainty, it must also integrate their activities. To Galbraith, an organization is an *information-processing system.* If differentiation and integration are not in equilibrium, channels of information in the organization do not function effectively, and it is difficult or impossible to coordinate efforts. For

TABLE 11–2

Galbraith's Five Strategies for Processing Information

A. To reduce the need for processing information:
   1. Create slack or additional resources, e.g., increase the number of employees
   2. Create self-contained units
   3. Manage the external environment

B. To increase the capacity for processing information:
   4. Invest in vertical information systems, e.g., computers
   5. Create lateral relations that cut across lines of authority, e.g., the matrix organization

Source: From Jay Galbraith, *Organization Design*, p. 49. Copyright © 1977 by Addison-Wesley Publishing Co., Inc. Adapted by permission.

example, a firm may lose its bid for a major government contract because various departments such as production and finance fail to provide sufficient information to the task force set up to write the contract proposal. Or a firm may not respond adequately to a new competitor because its departments have only a partial understanding of the magnitude of the effort being made by the competitor. In this section we examine Galbraith's information-processing approach to organizing. As we shall see, this approach is a contingency approach to organizational design.

Five Strategies When an organization can no longer process information efficiently, communication and coordination break down. The differentiated subsystems in the organization do not have a sufficient amount of integration so that goals can be attained. To eliminate or minimize this problem of balancing differentiation and integration, the organization must either reduce its need to process information or increase its capacity to do so (see Table 11–2). According to Galbraith, technology and environmental uncertainty must be evaluated in terms of their influence on the processing of information in an organization.

If a firm decides to reduce its need to process information, it can use three strategies to balance differentiation and integration. First, it can increase its use of *slack* or additional resources—employees, materials, or whatever—so as to produce more without actually increasing its previous levels of performance. For example, if a firm is having difficulty meeting its deadlines, it can increase the number of employees or the amount of time it assigns to each project.

Second, the firm can divide its work into *self-contained tasks* so that each work group has available all the resources it needs to perform its jobs. If groups are not interdependent and do not need to work together, the problem of coordination among them and integration of differentiated activities is eliminated or reduced. Thus departmentalization is by task or product. Of course, the costs of either of these strategies may be prohibitive.

Finally, the organization can attempt to *manage the external environment* so that it will be able to decrease the amount of uncertainty it faces and simultaneously reduce its reliance on a high degree of differentiation to handle this uncertainty. For instance, two competitors may form a new organization and assure themselves of a steady stream of clients who would now have difficulty obtaining the same products elsewhere. Hence the organization would require a smaller number of managers and specialists to monitor customer preferences.

If the firm decides to increase its capacity to process information in order to balance differentiation and integration, it has recourse to two strategies. First, it can invest in *vertical information systems* that speed communication and coordination from one hierarchical level to the next. The firm's other alternative for balancing differentiation and integration is to develop *lateral decision processes* that cut across lines of authority. If it opts for this strategy, it is moving from a mechanistic toward an organic structure, allowing workers to communicate with each other and deal with problems directly, without going through superiors. It can also use integrators: people who keep communications open between departments.

Seven Steps for Creating Lateral Relations

If a manager decides to employ the strategy of developing lateral decision processes to create equilibrium between differentiation and integration, he or she has recourse to seven steps that move the organization along the continuum from a mechanistic to an organic structure (Figure 11–2). The manager might implement each step in turn, from the mechanistic to the most organic, until he or she irons out the organization's problems. For example, the manager might stop after step 3 if coordination between individuals and groups improves significantly. Hence the manager determines when the organization has reached the ideal degree of organic structure, one that is appropriate for bringing differentiation and integration into equilibrium.

In the first step, when two departments whose tasks are interdependent are having trouble coordinating their work, managers may reduce the problem by means of *direct contact*. Preferably this contact should be informal and face to face, for the managers should confront the problem directly but in a nonthreatening manner. If this tactic fails, the organization can create a *liaison role* that links two interdependent departments. A liaison is an individual who brings the two departments together to achieve organizational goals. The next

FIGURE 11–2
Galbraith's Strategies for Creating Lateral Relations

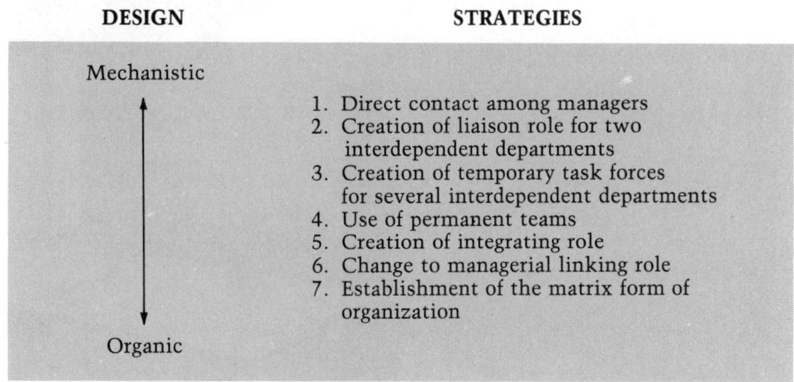

Source: From Jay Galbraith, *Organization Design*, p. 112. Copyright © 1977 by Addison-Wesley Publishing Co., Inc. Adapted by permission.

option is to set up a *temporary task force* to handle coordination among several interdependent departments. Members are usually drawn from all departments that will be affected by any course of action the task force recommends. Once coordination improves significantly, the task force is eliminated.

If this approach fails, the organization can establish *permanent teams* to handle the problem of coordination. As with a task force, members would typically be drawn from all departments whose work must be coordinated. Failure of the team approach would lead to the use of *integrators* charged with coordinating activities, although they would have no authority to make line managers accept their suggestions. If this does not work smoothly, the integrators can be placed in a *managerial linking role,* giving them power to force line managers to coordinate their work. If all these steps fail, the top managers can totally redesign the organization into the *matrix form.*

It is in the matrix organization that the highest degree of differentiation and integration can be attained. This form of organization is particularly appropriate if there is a great amount of external environmental uncertainty. But managers must be careful in constructing matrix organizations. The addition of differentiated activities and subunits creates problems, and it is absolutely essential that managers also develop techniques within the matrix structure that bring about a high degree of integration. Some of these techniques have been discussed in this chapter.

"To my mind, the secret of executive performance is the ability to delegate authority. For instance, nothing *ever reaches this desk."*

The beauty of Galbraith's information-processing approach is that it provides a practicing manager with a set of guidelines to follow in designing or redesigning his or her organization. While more research is necessary to determine how well this approach works in practice, it does integrate and clarify many of the theoretical and practical issues basic to constructing effective and efficient organizations.

SUMMARY

There are two major types of organizational designs, mechanistic and organic. The mechanistic organization is highly bureaucratic and rigid; the organic organization is informal and flexible. These two types represent the endpoints on a continuum; most organizational designs can be described as either "more mechanistic" or "more organic."

Managers should focus on three critical factors when designing or redesigning an organization: organizational size, type of technology, and external environmental uncertainty. In addition, managers should try to balance the degree of differentiation—that is, the specialized subunits and viewpoints—and the degree of integration, which is the process of linking together these specialized subunits and viewpoints.

Blau's research indicates that as organizational size and automation or computerization increase, so does differentiation. Woodward's research indicates that successful organizations using unit or process technology generally employ an organic structure; successful firms using mass production technology usually rely on a mechanistic structure. The research of Lawrence and Lorsch suggests that a successful organization in a highly uncertain environment is one that uses integrators, individuals charged with coordinating the work of interdependent departments or activities.

Alfred Chandler has pointed out that successful organizations develop strategic plans that are appropriate for the external environment in which they operate. Top management then creates an organizational structure that is appropriate for accomplishing these plans. In light of Chandler's research, one can argue that there is an interactive relationship among strategic plans, the three critical factors, and organizational structure.

Jay Galbraith argues that the problem of balancing differentiation and integration is critical for an organization's success. He defines an organization as an information-processing system. Technology and environmental uncertainty directly influence the flow of information in an organization and the balance between differentiation and integration. If the flow of information between individuals and groups whose work is interdependent becomes problematic, the organization can either reduce its need to process information or increase its capacity to do so. If the organization decides to reduce its need to process information, it can create slack (additional) resources, establish self-contained tasks, or manage the uncertainty of the external environment. If the organization opts for increasing its capacity for processing information, it can either invest in vertical information systems or implement lateral decision processes that cut across traditional lines of authority.

For the firm that decides to use lateral decision processes, the distinction between mechanistic and organic organizations becomes important. According to Galbraith, a manager can take seven steps that will move the organization along the continuum from a mechanistic to an organic structure. The manager can use these steps in sequence until he or she determines that the organization has achieved enough coordination to be successful. In sequence, these steps are direct contact between managers; creation of a liaison role to link interdependent departments; use of temporary task forces to coordinate the work of several departments; substitution of permanent teams for task forces; creation of an integrating role whose incumbent does not possess the formal authority to force line managers to work together; use of an officer in a managerial linking role who does have the power to tell line managers how to coordinate their efforts; and, finally, construction of a matrix organization.

DISCUSSION QUESTIONS

1. How is the ideal design for an organization that produces goods likely to differ from that for one that sells a service?
2. Is an organization in the public sector, such as a government agency, less susceptible to the pressures of environmental uncertainty than a privately owned organization? Is a nonprofit organization, such as a church, less susceptible than one run for profit?
3. What do Lawrence and Lorsch mean by an integrator? How might an integrator go about coordinating the work of two or more departments without actually being in charge of them?
4. In defining an organization as an information-processing system, has Jay Galbraith disregarded the issues of type of technology, organizational size, and external environmental uncertainty? Why or why not? Do you think Galbraith's definition applies to all organizations? Explain.
5. Chandler's conclusion is that structure follows strategy. What does this mean? Do you agree with this conclusion? Why or why not?
6. Both human relations and scientific management argued that their respective approaches were the one best way to run an organization (see Chapters 1 and 2). How does Woodward's research agree and disagree with the position that there is one best way to organize and manage?

CRITICAL INCIDENT

NOTE: This critical incident can be used by the whole class with the case observational method (see Appendix A) or used for thought and discussion by individual class members.

Business schools experienced spectacular rates of growth during the 1970s. At one large university, for example, the business school enrolled 2500 students in 1973 and 5500 students in 1978. The university increased the operating budget of the business school proportionately.

This school was organized functionally. There were six separate departments: accounting, finance, organizational behavior, marketing, management science statistics, and general management. Each department had a chair, but he or she did not have budgetary authority. There were fifty-five full-time and forty-five part-time faculty members, distributed in an approximately proportional manner among the six groups. The dean was assisted by an associate dean for academic affairs and an assistant dean for administrative affairs. There were also three directors of undergraduate, MBA, and DBA programs reporting to the dean.

Although the dean spent approximately thirty percent of his time in fund-raising activities, he personally directed the internal operations of the business school and made nearly all the major decisions. While he periodically (but irregularly) scheduled meetings attended by the six chairpersons and his other aides, he primarily relied on them for advice.

The dean was very successful in fund raising and in directing the activities of the business school from 1973 until 1975. However, after 1975 he began to experience difficulties in fulfilling his two major roles. His work load had simply become too heavy. The dean decided to redesign his organization.

QUESTIONS: How would you redesign this organization? Should the dean continue to play two roles, the external and the internal? Should the six chairpersons receive budgetary responsibility so that they can allocate resources and give faculty salary increases, subject to rare vetoes by the dean? Why or why not?

SUGGESTED READINGS

Lawrence, Paul, and Lorsch, Jay. *Organization and Environment: Managing Differentiation and Integration.* Boston: Division of Research, Harvard Graduate School of Business, 1967, 279 pages, hardback.

The authors describe the contingency approach to management. This book provides a good summary of management literature focused on the contingency approach. See the description in this chapter.

Woodward, Joan. *Industrial Organization: Theory and Practice.* New York: Oxford University Press, 1965, 281 pages, hardback.

Woodward describes the relationship between technology, organizational structure, and success. See the description in this chapter. She also provides a series of enlightening case studies.

PART III
CASE STUDIES

The Overly Successful Bank

In Chapter 3 we described a large New York branch-banking network. This bank has been so successful that it has grown from 20 branches in 1958 to its current size of 180 branches. However, its phenomenal success has created many problems, primarily within the dimension of organization design.

There are three major organizational levels in the bank: the main headquarters, 9 regional offices, and 180 branches. Within each of the three levels there are two kinds of officers. *Loan officers* are in charge of lending and financing activities. *Operations officers* handle the personnel activity of the system; they are primarily responsible for the integration and harmony of the work flow. The split between loans and operations is emphasized by the fact that branch loan officers and branch operations officers attend separate regional meetings every two weeks.

Throughout the system the operations officers are subordinate to the loan officers. This subordination is especially pronounced at the branch level: All 180 branch managers are loan officers (see Figure 1). Within each branch loan officers are responsible only to the branch manager. The chief operations officer in each branch oversees the activities of all employees and other operations officers.

The design of the branch-banking system is relatively simple and, at first glance, sensible. However, the design of the system creates problems that impede the decision-making capability of management.

Note: These cases can be used by the whole class with the case observational method (Appendix A) or the theoretical case analysis method (Appendix B), or used for thought and discussion by individual class members.

FIGURE 1
Simplified Organizational Structure of a Typical Branch Bank

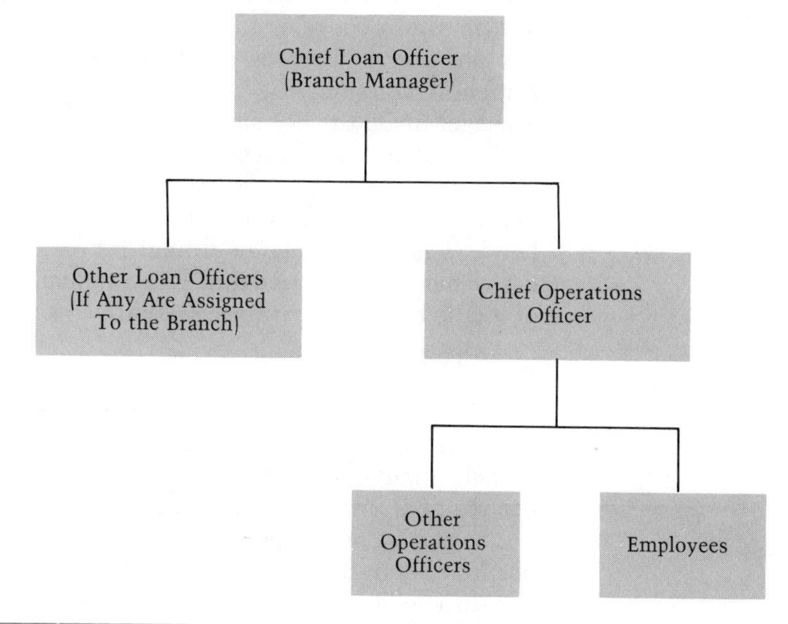

SUBORDINATION OF OPERATIONS OFFICERS

Perhaps the most basic problem in the design of the system is that operations officers are always subordinate to loan officers, regardless of the issues involved. This is true at all levels in the organization: headquarters, region, and branch. Part of the reason for this is the bank's officer training program. When college graduates and MBAs begin to work for the bank, they are sent to a six-month training course that is primarily oriented toward accounting and finance, which are of obvious importance in banking. At the end of the course they receive either a passing or a failing grade. If they pass, they become loan officers; if they fail, they become operations officers. No matter what an operations officer does for the rest of his or her career with the bank, he or she is branded with inferior status because of failure in the training course.

From the perspective of the employees the operations officer is the leader of the branch, for he or she handles all requests for salary increases or promotions. But this position is constantly undermined by the fact that he or she cannot actually grant raises or promotions without the explicit approval of the branch manager. The branch manager is usually far removed from the employees; his or her purpose is generating new business for the branch, not monitoring personnel. If the branch manager decides that a particular employee should not be given a raise or a promotion for budgetary reasons, it is the operations officer who must relay the decision. Further, in order to protect his or her position and status in the branch, the operations officer must somehow convince the employee that he or she and not the branch manager made the decision.

The operations officer faces many other problems. Any aspect of effective performance of a branch is attributed to the branch manager, even if the operations officer's efforts are responsible. On the other hand, it is easy to blame difficulties on the operations officer, since his or her role is so undefined. In a fundamental sense, the operations officer is a nonentity in the system.

BOTTLENECKS

Another major design problem in the system concerns relationships between the three levels in the bank: headquarters, region, and branch. Many decisions made at the branch level can be undercut at the regional or headquarters level. Also, headquarters' decisions may not be carried out properly by the regions and branches. Consequently bottlenecks in the system are frequent.

An excellent example of a bottleneck is provided by the bank's program of salary equalization for tellers. A scarcity of bank tellers in New York had forced the bank to raise the starting salary $15 per week. This increase strained the loyalties of experienced tellers, many of whom now found themselves making less money than the newly hired tellers. To overcome this difficulty, the bank authorized equalization raises for all experienced tellers. But because some regions and branches put through their increases faster than others, several experienced tellers waited for two years or more for the equalization raises. This delay caused discontent and resulted in high turnover among the experienced tellers. Many branches began to receive an unusually large number of customer complaints because of the inexperience of the newly hired tellers.

In short, two major organizational problems in the system are the inferior status of the operations officers and bottlenecks.

QUESTION: Assume that you are a consultant to this bank. What design change would you recommend to solve these two problems?

State University Medical Center

State University Medical Center is located in a small southern city. The center is affiliated with a university in the same town; the university's enrollment is approximately 24,000 students. Along with housing an 800-bed medical-surgical and psychiatric hospital, the medical center includes full teaching and research facilities for a medical school, dental school, nursing school, and other health-related professional schools. Both the state government and the university are extremely proud of the institution, and the people of the central portion of the state consider it a mecca of health care. Despite this success and popularity, as well as generous funding by the state legislature, the medical center faces constant financial difficulties. The teaching hospital, in particular, is unable to break even.

Faced with this general situation, Dr. Patrick Haines, previously the administrator of a large metropolitan hospital and president of a prestigious medical school, has entered the picture. Lured by an excellent salary, favorable climate, and the opportunity to test his abilities with this interesting challenge, Dr. Haines accepted the position of vice-president of health affairs at the university. The position places him in control of the administration of the teaching hospital and the College of Health-related Professions.

As shown in Figure 2, the vice-president of the medical center is accountable for both its management and its budget. While the vice-president has essentially a free hand in internal administrative matters, both the university and the state legislature must approve all long-range plans and budgets. Thus the vice-president must be not

FIGURE 2

Design of State University Medical Center

Solid lines represent formal lines of authority. Dotted lines indicate that the departments within both the hospital and the colleges use the same facilities and services.

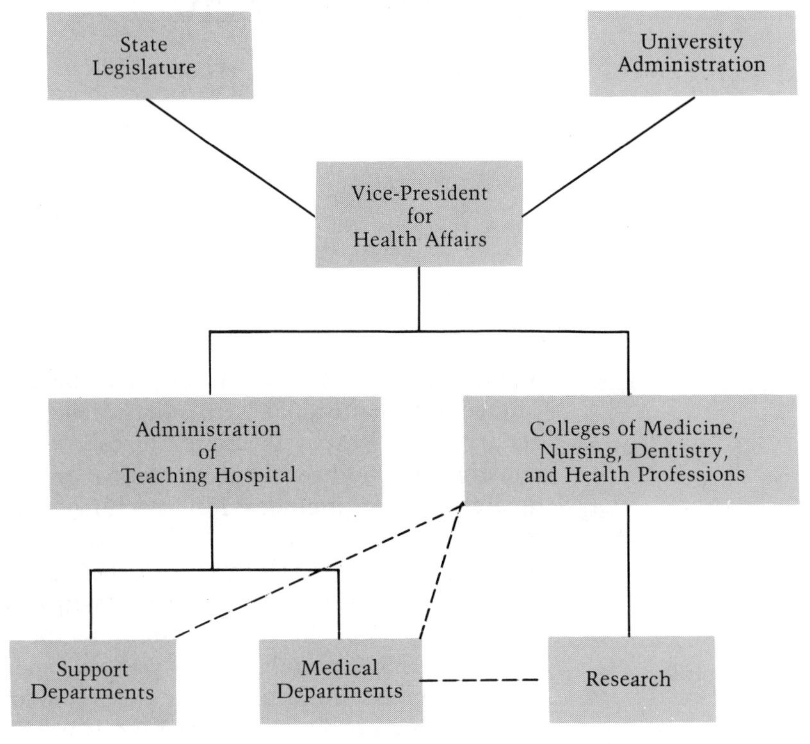

only a manager but a politician. Because the medical center must obtain approval for major programs from both the university and the state legislature, it is subject to their rules, regulations, and priorities. The state legislature favors expenditures for health care, while the university prefers a budget structure supporting teaching and research. Dr. Haines prepared himself for extreme political and financial stress from outside the organization.

At the same time Dr. Haines found internal pressures significant. The educators and health care personnel directly below him in the hierarchy also have conflicting priorities, the former group emphasizing teaching and research and the latter group health care. Second, a sluggish bureaucracy is firmly entrenched in the organization. Most of the important individuals in the organization respect the bureaucracy, since it provides them with the resources they require. However, many individuals within the bureaucracy often foil well-conceived plans because they lack initiative or have no interest in the effective management of the institution.

An example that illustrates both the external and internal problems facing Dr. Haines is the case of the purchasing agent for the medical center. Mr. William Saunders is 55 years old and a retired military officer (something common at the center); he handles the procurement of all items for the hospital, from nuclear radiation equipment to gauze pads. Many of his purchases are dictated by state specifications. However, he frequently buys exactly what every physician orders with no regard for cost. The result is that the budget allocation for purchasing usually runs out after only eight or nine months of the fiscal year, which contributes to the deficit and forces the medical center to borrow supplies from the local municipal hospital. Mr. Saunders neither has attempted to have state specifications changed to obtain cost savings he knows are possible nor has used his influence to persuade physicians and educators to order less expensive items of equal quality. He is not, however, violating any rule or regulation, and he is executing his job properly in terms of the bureaucracy. Dr. Haines soon recognized that Mr. Saunders was not the exception as an employee at the medical center.

QUESTIONS: How would you redesign this organization? What specific problems would you try to eliminate? Construct the organizational chart for the revised structure.

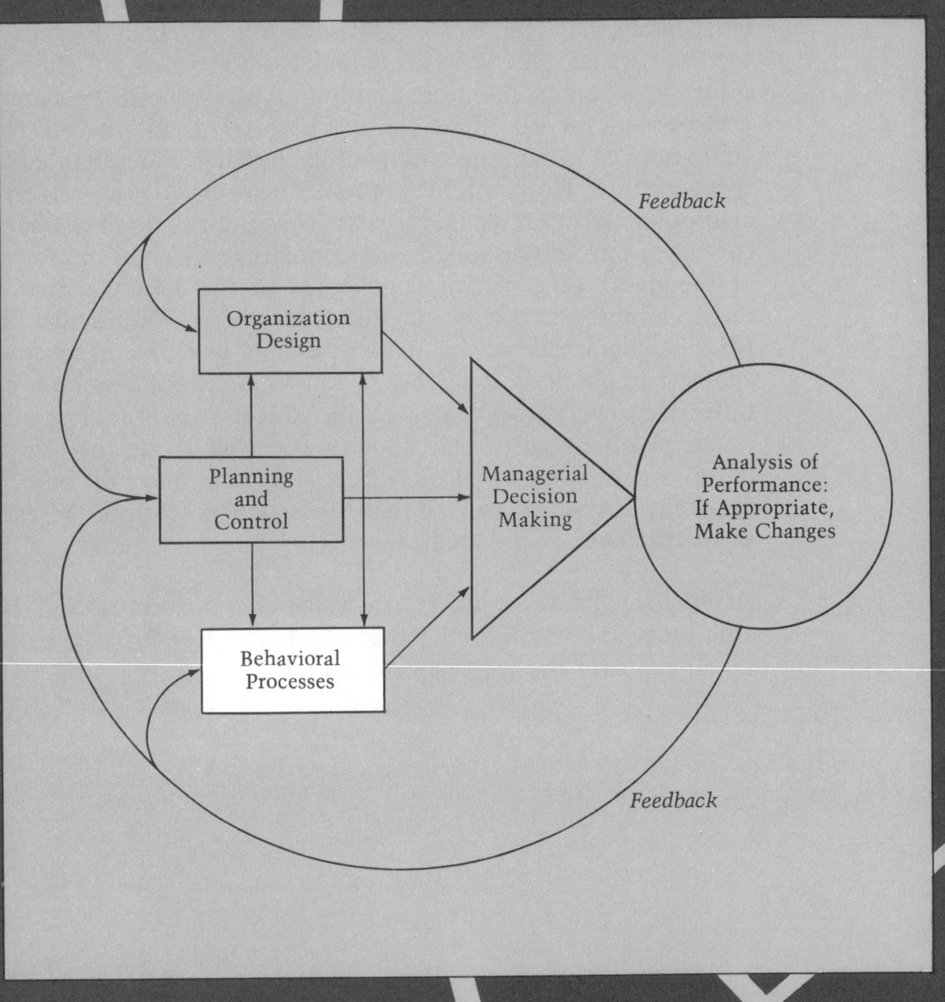
Feedback
Organization Design
Planning and Control
Managerial Decision Making
Analysis of Performance: If Appropriate, Make Changes
Behavioral Processes
Feedback

IV DIRECTING BEHAVIORAL PROCESSES

Even when an organization is designed ideally and its systems of planning and control are excellent, it is quite possible that problems will arise if the behavioral processes are not functioning smoothly. *Behavioral processes* represent the preconditions for interactions and the actual interactions between and among organizational members that enable the organization to move toward its goals.

For example, behavioral processes may be behind the problem of why the production department is so slow at keeping the marketing department informed about new products. Is it because George in production is still mad at Tony in marketing for running into his car in the parking lot? Or is it because the secretary of Tony's assistant cannot send a memo to the secretary of George's assistant without routing it through half a dozen people? Problems that might seem too human and too trivial to worry about have been known to bring a whole organization to a halt.

As our organizational framework of management indicates, behavioral processes directly influence both organization design and managerial decision making. These behavioral processes—perception and interpersonal communication, motivation, leadership, and group behavior—constitute the third essential dimension of the integrated organizational framework proposed in this book. In this part of the book there are four chapters, and each is devoted to one of the four behavioral processes that directly influence organization design and managerial decision making.

The Battle of the Overpass

CONTINUOUS CASE

The Ford Motor Company 1930–1945

SUMMARY: In the previous sections of our continuous case, we have seen that Henry Ford became spectacularly successful because of his strategic plan of manufacturing an all-purpose, inexpensive, and durable car, the Model T. To produce such an inexpensive car on a grand basis, he redesigned his company in 1914 by introducing mass production. In addition, between 1914 and 1920 he instituted many enlightened personnel practices. However, the company's financial status began to change around 1920, primarily because of the success of General Motors. Rather than altering his strategic plan, Henry Ford opted to save money by repudiating his enlightened personnel practices and emphasizing tight control of the workers; this situation was maintained between 1920 and 1929.

Between 1930 and 1945 Henry Ford continued to deemphasize his earlier enlightened personnel practices; his attitude toward our organizational dimension of behavioral processes was certainly negative.

THE HUNGER MARCH

Henry Ford, who was once championed as a hero by American labor, was now viewed as reactionary. In the Great Depression of the 1930s layoffs were inevitable in every industry. But in Detroit resentment was directed against Henry Ford. In March 1932 the Ford Hunger March took place. Only a few hundred individuals participated in it, and their demands were, in terms of present practices, generally reasonable:

> On behalf of the Ford worker as such, the hunger marchers demanded jobs, the right to organize, reduction of speedup, abolition of labor spies, elimination of "graft" in the hiring process, two daily

> 15-minute rest periods on the Ford line, a six-hour day without reduction in pay, an unemployment bonus of $50 per man and free medical treatment for Ford men and their families. *(Sward 1948, p. 233)*

Instead of meeting a sympathetic group of Ford executives who might try to eliminate the unfavorable conditions then in existence, the hunger marchers were greeted by a barrage of bullets from the Dearborn police, who were at that time under the influence of the Ford Motor Company. Four people were killed and over twenty were wounded. There was, of course, a public outcry. Nevertheless, labor conditions at the Ford Motor Company became worse as the 1930s progressed.

LABOR PROBLEMS

In 1933 the Ford Motor Company was again involved in a labor dispute when one of its suppliers, Briggs Company, stopped production because of a strike. The Briggs concern was, through a lease, working in Henry Ford's Highland Park plant. Many of its employees had been working a 14-hour day for 10 cents an hour. They now demanded a 9-hour day and a daily wage of $3.60 for women and $4.00 for men. In other words, they wanted treatment equivalent to that normally practiced at the River Rouge plant. This, however, was not be be. Partially through the support of Henry Ford, the strike was crushed.

In 1933 the National Industrial Recovery Act (NIRA) was passed. Section 7(a) guaranteed the right of employees to organize and bargain collectively through their representatives without interference, restraint, or coercion by employers. Each industry was obliged to draw up a code of rules for its treatment of workers. The automotive industry was able to insert a merit clause into its code whereby it had the right to hire and fire without respect to seniority. But Henry Ford was so opposed to the idea of rights for labor that he would not sign even this watered-down code of rules, although it could in no direct way influence his treatment of workers.

Although NIRA was declared unconstitutional in 1935, labor trouble plagued the Ford Motor Company through 1945. In 1934 there was a strike against speedups at the River Rouge plant; it was quickly stopped. The Ford workers either submitted to conditions then in existence or left. Since people were clamoring for jobs during those years of depression, submission was the usual choice.

Henry Ford, the former friend and defender of the laborer, was gradually becoming the symbol of resistance to policies that would aid workers. Allan Nevins and Frank Hill (1963) cite three major reasons for union opposition to Henry Ford and his company during the 1930s. First, Ford's original liberal wage policy had collapsed. By 1940 Ford workers were being paid less than employees of the other major automotive corporations. Second, Harry Bennett and the Ford Service Police terrorized the Ford workers. Third, the unions were aligned against Henry Ford because of his doctrinaire opposition to any form of labor organization.

The year 1935 was critical for labor in America because in this year the Wagner Act was passed. It established the first national policy of protecting the right of workers to organize and to elect their representatives for collective bargaining. Although it was legally contested, the act was upheld in 1937 by the United States Supreme Court. Under the protection of the Wagner Act, the United Automobile Workers (UAW) began a systematic campaign to organize union shops throughout the automotive industry. By the end of 1937 the entire automotive industry had accepted unions without violence—except the Ford Motor Company.

UNION ORGANIZATION

On May 26, 1937, the UAW began its program to unionize the Ford Motor Company. Under the direction of Walter Reuther, who subsequently became president of the UAW, the union organizers planned to distribute circulars to the Ford workers on their way home from work. It was on a bridge over a road leading to the River Rouge plant that the Battle of the Overpass occurred. Ford Service men were eagerly awaiting the union organizers. When Reuther arrived, he was besieged by press photographers. As his picture was being taken, the Ford Service Police ordered Reuther and the others to leave the bridge. Although they started to comply, the Ford Service men attacked them. Reuther and several others ended up in the hospital with serious injuries. Even the women in the group were beaten and in need of medical care.

Time was running out for the Ford Motor Company. By the end of 1937 all the major automotive companies had submitted to unionization; Henry Ford was the last resister. His tactics were many and varied. Bennett and Ford in 1938 manipulated Homer Martin, the first president of the United Automobile Workers, into private negotiations, which they hoped would neutralize and possibly destroy the UAW. When the executive members of the UAW became aware of these private talks, they impeached Homer Martin and elected R. J. Thomas as president.

Another tactic was the use of the company union or a union not affiliated with any other union. Managers can effectively control a company union, since it has no other allies if it decides to strike. Four company unions were organized at Ford in 1937 and, as expected, they did not help the workers.

A third tactic was used against workers in the Ford plants in

St. Louis, Kansas City, and Richmond and Long Beach in California. In 1937 Henry Ford appeared to reverse his position by granting de facto recognition to the union at these plants. This stance brought the union and its leaders into the open. However, when the plants reopened for fall production, Bennett fired the key union leaders.

Despite Ford's struggles, it was inevitable that the Ford Motor Company would be unionized. By 1941 the UAW once again felt strong enough to unionize the Ford Motor Company. All they needed was a legitimate excuse for a strike. It came on April 2, 1941, when Harry Bennett discharged the eight River Rouge employees who composed the grievance committee at the plant. The workers immediately and spontaneously began to walk off their jobs. Under the leadership of the UAW the workers surrounded the River Rouge plant. They did not dare to stage a sit-down strike in the plant, for the Ford Service men would have the advantage and overpower them. But the workers did deny food and water to the Ford Service men until a contract was signed. On April 11 Henry Ford agreed to recognize the union.

TRANSITIONAL PERIOD

In 1941 the major problem at the Ford Motor Company was the conversion to wartime production. This task was primarily directed by Charles Sorenson, who was Ford's chief line executive for forty years. He was generally regarded as one of the best production men in the automotive business. Although many other executives quit the company because they could not put up with the autocratic manner of Henry Ford, Sorenson had stayed by him both in prosperous and poor times. Nevertheless, after working approximately eighteen hours per day for two years to complete the conversion, Sorenson was fired by Henry Ford. Even in his old age Ford was manifesting the tendency of entrepreneurs to destroy the most loyal subordinates and friends.

Once the Ford Motor Company had made the transition from peacetime to wartime production, it became vital in the operations of the Allied effort. Unfortunately, Henry Ford was becoming senile. By 1943 he was incapable of directing his company. After Ford's death in 1947, Harry Bennett attempted to wrest control of the company away from the Ford family by claiming that a codicil attached to Ford's will named him sole heir. For about a year no one was quite sure who was running the company. At one point John Bugas, director of labor relations, told Bennett he did not believe the codicil existed. Bennett was so angry at this remark that Bugas left the room, fearing, as he later said, that he might be shot in the back by the gun-carrying leader of the Ford Service Police.

Because the operations of the company were so vital to the war effort, the government allowed Henry Ford II to leave military duty to become the active head of the enterprise. Bennett's claims that he was the sole heir to the company proved unfounded, and he was forced to leave. Henry Ford II became president in 1948.

QUESTIONS: What justifications did Henry Ford have for his actions during this period? What are some alternative approaches he might have used?

12 Interpersonal Communication

PERCEPTION
COMMUNICATION AMONG INDIVIDUALS
INTERPERSONAL COMMUNICATION AND MANAGERIAL WORK
SUMMARY
DISCUSSION QUESTIONS
CRITICAL INCIDENTS
SUGGESTED READINGS

PERFORMANCE OBJECTIVES

1. To describe how perception—the selection and organization of sensations or stimuli into a meaningful whole—influences communication among individuals.
2. To examine communication among individuals, including barriers to communication, networks, the two-step flow of communication, and various methods of communication.
3. To explain the importance of interpersonal communication in the completion of managerial work.

Organizations rely heavily on the communications that link the work of individuals and groups. Jay Galbraith believes communication is so important that he has defined an organization as an information-processing system (see Chapter 11). When an organization cannot process its information efficiently, communication becomes distorted or breaks down and members begin to misunderstand one another. In extreme circumstances a breakdown in communication can make it impossible for individuals to work with one another.

Research studies have supported the proposition that communication is very important in an organization. John Hinrichs (1964) analyzed the behavior of 232 managers and professionals in a research organization, all of whom communicated frequently. (Under *communication* Hinrichs included listening, speaking, writing, and reading.) His subjects spent an average of sixty-one percent of their time in communication. The higher the individual's technical and organizational level, the more often he or she communicated with others.

Frequently the concept of communication is examined from four distinct perspectives: intrapersonal, interpersonal, organizational, and technical (Thayer 1968). The *intrapersonal* perspective stresses communication activities within one person, such as neurological and brain processes; the *interpersonal* perspective focuses on the interactions among individuals and within groups; the *organizational* perspective looks at the flow of communications through the various formal or informal organizational channels; and the *technical* perspective centers on the design and operation of management information systems such as the installation of a new computer. We have already examined organizational communication and computers in Chapters 7 and 11. Research on intrapersonal communication is not directly applicable to management. Thus the focus here is on interpersonal communication, since it is one of the four elements within the organizational dimension of behavioral processes, as specified by our organizational framework of management.

The first part of the chapter focuses on *perception*, the manner in which an individual selects and organizes sensations or stimuli into a meaningful whole. Perception strongly influences the manner in which individuals communicate with one another. There is then a discussion of the nature of interpersonal communication, barriers to it, and methods of improving it. Finally, the chapter describes the critical importance of interpersonal communication in the work and activities of managers.

PERCEPTION

It is difficult to describe *all* the factors that influence an individual's perceptions of others. But some of the more important factors are family background, culture, physiology, and self-concept. In this section we discuss these factors, and then we turn our attention to the manner in which the individual organizes his or her perceptions of others.

Factors Influencing Perception

The family is the setting in which the child first learns to perceive the world. And some familial experiences can be so powerful that they become more important than all the other factors influencing perception. If parents disregard a child or show him little love and affection, it is quite probable that he or she will become a somewhat cold and impersonal adult. Such an individual does not interact easily with others. Fortunately, research suggests that such negative familial experiences can be countered if the child is loved by at least one adult, even if this person is outside the family circle (Bronfenbrenner 1977).

The family influences the child's perceptions of the world in many subtle ways. If there is much rivalry among several children in the family, they may begin to act in a similar manner toward those outside this setting. Alternatively, a younger child may feel overwhelmed by the success of an older brother or sister, thus creating a lifelong failure syndrome for the child when he or she interacts with others. These examples suffice to show that the family provides the child with a set of lenses that strategically influences both his or her perception of the world and his or her place in it.

Culture acts as a similar and powerful determinant of perception. Some cultures deemphasize achievement among the young, even in their children's books. Other cultures operate in an opposite manner. As might be expected, the cultures emphasizing achievement at an early age seem to have a disproportionate number of adults who are high achievers (McClelland 1961). Such adults develop a perception that they can achieve difficult tasks.

Many cultures are highly stratified: Birth into one stratum of a society largely determines the child's subsequent social and economic standing. In this setting the child learns at an early age to perceive subtle differences between social classes that are above or below him.

A person's physiology also can be an important determinant of perception. Milton Erickson, a world-renowned hypnotist who has treated approximately 30,000 individuals, has been partially paralyzed most of his life because of a polio attack as a child. This physical loss made him acutely aware of nonverbal forms of expression and also enabled him to perceive the needs and values of others in a very sensitive fashion (Goleman 1977). He, and many others like him who have suffered physiological damage, develop perceptions of the world that are quite different from those of the average person.

An individual's self-concept is also relevant. A person who suffers from a failure syndrome frequently perceives that he or she cannot complete difficult but attainable objectives. If a person is fearful of new events and objects, he or she tends to see any novel situation as threatening. Conversely, individuals who believe they can ac-

FAILURE TO PERCEIVE ACCURATELY?

During one part of the interview an executive said:	*Yet later in the same interview he said:*
The relationship among the executive committee members is "close," "friendly," and based on years of working together.	I do not know how [my peers] feel about me. That's a tough question to answer.
The strength of this company lies in its top people. They are a dedicated, friendly group. We never have the kinds of disagreements and fights that I hear others do.	Yes, the more I think of it, the more I feel this is a major weakness of the company. Management is afraid to hold someone accountable, to say, "You said you would do it. What happened?"
I have an open relationship with my superior.	I have no direct idea how my superior evaluates my work and feels about me.
The group discussions are warm, friendly, not critical.	We trust each other not to upset one another.
We say pretty much what we think.	We are careful not to say anything that will antagonize anyone.
We respect and have faith in each other.	People do not knowingly upset each other, so they are careful in what they say.
The executive committee tackles all issues.	The executive committee tends to spend too much time talking about relatively unimportant issues.
The executive committee makes decisions quickly and effectively.	A big problem of the executive committee is that it takes forever and a day to make important decisions.
The members trust each other.	The members are careful not to say something that may make another member look bad. It may be misinterpreted.
The executive committee makes the major policy decisions.	On many major issues, decisions are really made outside the executive committee meetings. The executive committee convenes to approve a decision and have "holy water" placed on it.

Source: Reprinted by permission of the Harvard Business Review. Exhibit from "Interpersonal Barriers to Decision Making" by Chris Argyris (March-April 1966).

complish great things in life sometimes do the impossible or near-impossible, at least partially because of their self-concepts.

Organization of Perception

Each of us organizes perceptions of reality in a distinctive if not unique fashion. We frequently use perceptual techniques that create biases against some individuals and groups even before meeting them. Some of these techniques are stereotyping, the halo effect, and first impressions.

Biases. An individual tends to develop certain *stereotypes,* generalizations he or she uses to classify people and groups. One researcher has dramatized the importance of stereotypes. In his study managers described pictures of individuals more favorably when they were called managers than when they were designated as union representatives. The group of managers who saw the pictures identified as managers described them in such terms as hardworking, intelligent, and trustworthy. When the pictures were identified as those of labor representatives, another group of managers used such terms as shiftless, lazy, and untrustworthy (Haire 1955).

An excellent study of stereotypes focused on the comparative perceptions of private managers in corporations and public, or governmental, managers (Driscoll, Cowger, and Egan 1979). The private managers believe that they work under extreme time pressures, must exercise a great amount of responsibility, and must respond to many societal and consumer demands that are sometimes unreasonable. Private managers also feel that public managers do not work under these same constraints. Perhaps not surprisingly, the public managers feel that *they* work under extreme time pressures, exercise a great amount of responsibility, and must respond to a large number of unreasonable societal and consumer demands. And the public managers also feel that private managers do not work under these same constraints.

Researchers have also shown that even a hiring interviewer is strongly influenced by the match between the person he or she sees and the type of person he or she has in mind when deciding whether to hire a job applicant (Webster 1964). If the job applicant fits the requirements of the hiring interviewer's stereotype, communication between the two individuals becomes easier, and the applicant has a better chance of obtaining the job.

Even before an individual enters the organization, he or she develops stereotypes that influence the kinds of decisions he or she will eventually make. Some of the most common stereotypes involve people's facial characteristics, race, sex, hair style, dress, and educational background. In a striking study of stereotypes, two researchers provided a description of a factory worker to 179 college students that

PERCEIVING THE UNEXPECTED AND FAMILIAR

With regard to the stimulus, a major determinant is differential intensity. Thus a cannon shot off on a quiet street or sudden silence in the midst of a din gets attention whether or not anyone expects it or wants to hear it. Contrast . . . is one of the most attention-compelling attributes of a stimulus. Thus, a bearded man still gets more attention than a clean-shaven one, and a bearded lady even more.

With regard to expectations, other things being equal, people are more likely to pay attention to aspects of the environment they anticipate than to those they do not, and they are more likely to anticipate things they are familiar with. . . .

Incidentally, the tendency to be more open to some experiences and to shut out others seems to extend, literally, to the pupil of the eye. When looking at interesting or pleasant materials, as compared to neutral ones, the pupil dilates measurably. Conversely, looking at distasteful or disliked materials produces contraction.

Source: Bernard Berelson and Gary Steiner, *Human Behavior* (New York: Harcourt, Brace & World, 1967), p. 148. Reprinted by permission of Harcourt Brace Jovanovich, Inc.

incorporated such elements as works in a factory, reads a newspaper, goes to the movies, average height, cracks jokes, strong, and active. When given this profile, the college students described the factory worker as the "typical American Joe" who is likable, friendly, but not too intelligent. When the researchers merely added the word "intelligent" to the profile, many of the college students refused to accept this concept or deemphasized its importance (Haire and Grunes 1950).[1]

A related phenomenon is the *halo effect,* using one particularly favorable or unfavorable trait to color everything else we know about the person. If a person is friendly, we might easily assume that he or she is also intelligent, kind, and trustworthy.

Personality. Many factors influence perception, but it may be that personality is the most important determinant. Although there are many definitions of personality, it can be succinctly defined as the similarity in the responses an individual makes to different situations (Khandwalla 1977).

[1] For additional empirical studies of sex and age stereotyping, see Rosen and Jerdee 1974, 1976); Schermerhorn, Snelson, and Leader (1975); Bartol and Butterfield (1976); and Bigoness (1976).

FIGURE 12–1
A Model of Interpersonal Communication

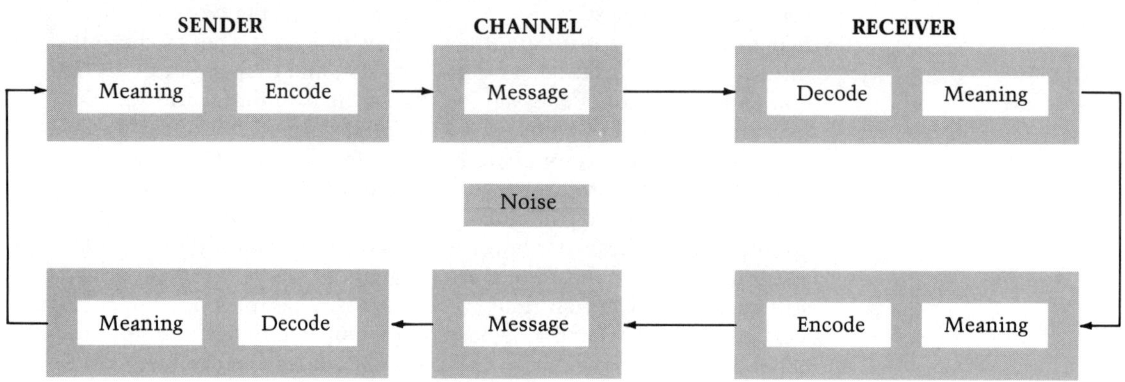

Source: Adapted by permission from C. Shannon and W. Weaver, *The Mathematical Theory of Communication* (Urbana, Ill.: University of Illinois Press, 1949).

In recent years several researchers have focused on various personality types, especially the Machiavellian personality. Jacob Siegel (1973) has shown that Machiavellian individuals are less sensitive to the social needs of others, tend to manipulate others, win more, and are less persuaded by others in face-to-face interactions than non-Machiavellian individuals. Similarly, Gary Gemmill and William Heisler (1972) have demonstrated that Machiavellian individuals are more susceptible to job strain and have a greater desire to control others but are less satisfied with their jobs. These and other studies suggest that an individual's personality influences not only his or her perceptions of reality but also his or her behavior in organizations.

Other Perceptual Techniques. Individuals also rely on other techniques to organize their perceptions. One of these techniques is *projection,* attributing the individual's own feelings to someone else. Murray (1933) graphically showed the operation of this technique in a study involving children. He allowed the first group to play a game called "murder." The second group did not participate. When asked to evaluate photographs, the group that had played "murder" saw more malice and violence than did the other group.

Similarly, the *self-fulfilling prophecy* operates as a perceptual technique that can bias our impressions. This technique allows the individual to make happen what he or she expects to happen. Rosenthal (1966) demonstrated the importance of this technique in a classroom study. He told elementary schoolteachers that one group of students was more intelligent than another group, although there was no significant difference between them. The children whom the teachers thought were more intelligent received considerably better grades than the other students.

Individuals also use *implicit personality theory* as a perceptual technique. We make assumptions about an individual's personality that bias our perceptions. Solomon Asch (1946) highlighted the importance of implicit personality theory by giving two groups of students a written description of a lecturer who would handle their class. One group's description indicated that the lecturer was a cold and impersonal individual; the other group's description stressed that he was warm and outgoing. After the lecturer had met with the class, the group that had received the negative profile rated him as cold and withdrawn; opposite findings emerged in the other group.

COMMUNICATION AMONG INDIVIDUALS

When one person communicates with others, either individually or in a group, there are many barriers that can inhibit or distort the messages he or she is transmitting. One individual may intensely dislike another person and, as a consequence, simply refuse to listen to him or her. Consequently, it is important for a manager to be aware of the barriers to communication and of communication breakdowns. In this section we examine a basic model of interpersonal communication that helps us to understand why communication breakdowns occur. We then describe some research on communication in small groups to illustrate the importance of interpersonal communication in management.

A Basic Model

There are many situations in which individuals fail to communicate effectively with one another. To understand the reasons for such failure, we shall examine a basic model of interpersonal communication developed by Shannon and Weaver (1949); it is shown in Figure 12–1. This model treats only the interpersonal communication between one sender and one receiver, but it obviously can be extended to include many senders and many receivers.

The initial phase of the model begins when the sender wants to transmit a message to the receiver. While the meaning may be clear to the sender, he or she must encode it in such a way that the message actually transmitted is clear to the receiver. The receiver, in turn, must decode the message to obtain a meaning from it that is consistent with the orginal meaning the sender intended. This entire process is disturbed by *noise,* irrelevant information, activity, and emotional nuances that distort the original meaning of the message. The receiver then decodes the message and attributes meaning to it. In turn, the receiver wants to provide feedback to the sender. The meaning of this feedback or message must be encoded by the receiver, and the receiver then transmits it to the sender, who then must decode it and attribute meaning to it. Again, noise can disturb this process.

While the model is simple, it expresses the major problems associated with interpersonal communication. The process of encoding or decoding may be deficient, especially if noise distorts the original meaning or if there is misperception. These deficiencies increase as the number of organizational members rises. As we shall soon see, research in actual organizations strongly indicates that interpersonal communications are far from perfect.

Barriers to Communication

We have already noted some barriers to interpersonal communication, such as stereotyping and the halo effect. Additionally, individuals frequently fail to communicate effectively because they interpret the words they are using quite differently. Tom Burns (1954) reports that a department manager remembered giving instructions or communicating a decision on 165 separate occasions, but the subordinates could

THE ESSENCE OF COMMUNICATION

Almost everything a manager does involves communications, and yet it is only too easy to assume this involved no problems. After all, he has been communicating all his life. . . . But . . .

I thought you wanted me to start the new job after I finished what I was doing.

How did I know he was serious about quitting?

I discount almost everything I hear from those guys in Corporate Communications.

But I was sure you meant London, Ontario.

The steward thinks I am bluffing and won't fire Jones. . . .

The basic problem in communications is that the meaning which is actually received by one person may not be what the other intended to send. . . .

Intent ⟶	Expression ⟶	Impression ⟶	Interpretation
(Motive)	(What is said)	(What is heard)	(Meaning assigned)

Source: George Strauss and Leonard R. Sayles, *Personnel: The Human Problems of Management,* 3rd ed., © 1972, pp. 205–206. Reprinted by permission of Prentice-Hall, Inc., Englewood Cliffs, N.J.

recall only 84 of the cases. In the other instances the communication was received only as information or advice. In another situation a manager may tell a subordinate to finish a particular job "as soon as possible." The manager expects the subordinate to comply with this command immediately. The subordinate, however, may believe the manager wants him or her to complete the task after all other work is finished.

Even symbols can create a barrier. For instance, it is quite common for college seniors looking for work to dress conservatively during hiring interviews, at least in part because they do not want to inhibit communication by wearing clothes or symbols that are too outlandish for the hiring interviewer to accept.

Additionally, the physical setting in which the communication takes place is salient (Steele 1973). If the atmosphere is pleasant, individuals tend to relax and listen more carefully to one another. Similarly, the timing of the communication may affect the message. An individual who is emotionally upset tends to distort the information he or she is transmitting or receiving. Also, if the individual is extremely tired, he or she may not be receptive to communications.

The communication process between individuals can be improved if the sender is sensitive to the needs and values of the receiver. Both the sender and the receiver should be conscious of any symbolic meanings they are attaching to particular words, jargon, or even bodily movement. When possible, face-to-face communication is desirable, since individuals can immediately eliminate any misunderstandings that may arise. To improve communication, people should use simple, clear language.

One specific way to improve communication is to repeat an important message. However, if the repetition is too frequent, the person receiving the message may cease to listen carefully. Managers can supplement repetition with two-way feedback: The receiver rather than the sender can repeat the message. This allows the sender of the message to verify whether it has been correctly received. Studies indicate that two-way communication is less frustrating, more accurate, and produces greater confidence in the correctness of interpretations than one-way communication (Gibb 1964; Leavitt and Mueller 1951).

Communication Networks

In the past thirty years researchers have emphasized the study of communication networks. Essentially a *communication network* is a structured arrangement of a small number of individuals who are allowed to transmit information only in a set and defined pattern. The researchers ask the members of a network under study to solve a specific problem by communicating with one another only through the unrestricted channels of communication. Researchers usually work with four communication networks: the wheel network, the

FIGURE 12–2
Types of Communication Networks

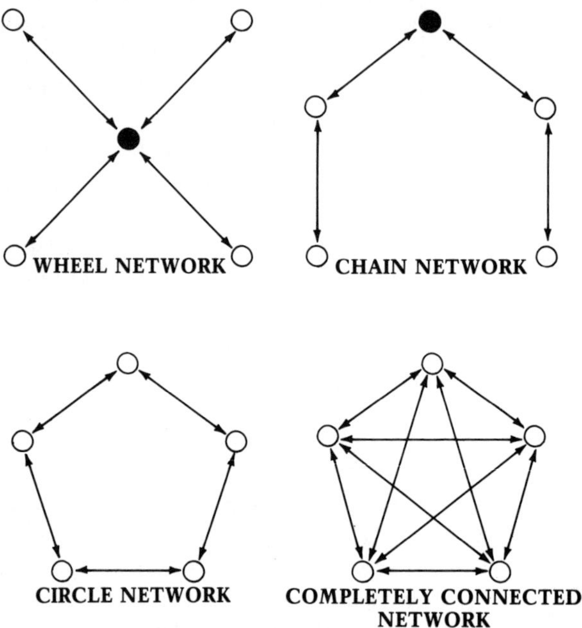

chain network, the circle network, and the completely connected network (see Figure 12–2).

In the *wheel network* one member is at the center and four or more members are each at the end of a spoke. This network is highly centralized, since the members on the spokes can communicate only with the individual at the center and no one else.

In the *chain network* two members serve as endpoints; each can communicate directly only with one other person in the middle. The middle members serve as relay points to the individual in the center. In this situation the center person communicates directly with the two middle members but not the end individuals. Thus the chain network is also centralized but not as much as the wheel network.

The *circle network* is somewhat decentralized, since each individual in it can communicate with the two other individuals next to him. Finally, the *completely connected* (all-channel) *network* is highly decentralized. Each individual in the group can communicate directly with every other individual in the group.

Consequences. The research on highly centralized networks, such as the wheel and the chain, suggests that they are effective in solving routine problems that mainly involve collecting information (Costello and Zalkind 1963). This seems logical, for the individual at the center of the wheel and chain networks is processing and weeding out all the information the group generates, ignoring irrelevant communications. In addition, the leadership position of the central individual in the wheel and chain networks is strong, probably because he or she has the greatest chance to influence the other members of the group. Finally, these groups structure their communication patterns very rapidly, since everyone quickly learns he or she must process information through the individual in the central position.

Decentralized networks, such as the completely connected and the circle, appear to be more appropriate when the group confronts a nonroutine or ambiguous problem. The fact that individuals can communicate directly with each other means they are freer to express opinions and to generate a large number of solutions, many of which may be very creative and innovative. In the decentralized networks there is a higher level of satisfaction among the members of the groups than in centralized networks, probably because individuals are allowed to communicate with one another and to express their own points of view.

Networks in Organizations. These research findings cannot be generalized to an entire organization because of the small number of individuals who participate in a communication network. However, the manager can apply these findings to the behavior of small work groups in his or her own organization. If the work is highly structured so that the members of the group must perform it in a set and routine fashion, the manager is probably dealing with a centralized network. If the manager directs the activities of a group whose work is nonroutine, he or she is probably part of a decentralized network. While all the properties of formal network models may not always exist in actual work groups, there is some evidence that they do occur frequently. For example, unskilled employees who are doing repetitive jobs on the assembly line work in centralized networks, since the pace of the assembly line allows only limited communication among individuals.

Two-Step Flow

A major role of the manager is to persuade subordinates to complete a particular course of action (see Chapter 14). Consequently, it is important for managers to communicate their commands and wishes to subordinates in such a way that those directives will be accepted. Some research has indicated that there is a two-step flow of communication: (1) from the original communicator to the opinion leader in a group, and (2) from the opinion leader to the rest of the group. For example, Elihu Katz and Paul Lazarsfeld (1955) discovered that the average consumer is not directly influenced to purchase products by rele-

"Oh, stop crying, Roseberry! Your job is to come up with imaginative, innovative, and exciting ideas, and my job is to pooh-pooh them."

vant information and advertising. Rather, recognized opinion leaders in the community heavily influence consumers' decisions. When an opinion leader alters his or her outlook, many consumers follow suit. Thus it is important to direct advertising at the opinion leaders.

Managers can apply the two-step flow of information to communications with their subordinates and work groups. As Chapter 2 indicated, there is typically an informal leader in a work group who strongly influences the attitudes and behavior of the other members. Usually an astute manager can pinpoint the informal leaders. The manager can then affect the performance of the group by influencing these informal leaders. For example, if the manager wants to introduce a new program that will require the organization to change some of the job responsibilities of the employees, he or she can first discuss this matter with the informal leaders. If they agree to the new plan, the probability increases that the work groups in the organization will accept it when it is presented to them.

Methods of Communication

There are many methods that can be used to increase the accuracy of communications in organizations so that encoding and decoding problems are minimized. For example, we might strengthen accuracy by combining an oral communication with a written message. Or we might increase accuracy by posting the message on a bulletin board.

Dahle (1954) has studied this issue by focusing on the accuracy of five methods of communication: using only oral messages; using only written messages; combining oral and written communication; placing the message on a bulletin board; and disseminating it by means of the grapevine. As we have already seen, information transmitted on the grapevine is frequently erroneous, at least in part because decoding is hampered when there is too much information being channeled through it (see Chapter 9). And Dahle's studies reinforced this conclusion.

Dahle completed three studies focused on the issue of accuracy: one involving college students enrolled in a public speaking course at Purdue, one using employees of a building materials manufacturing plant, and one involving employees at a single facility of a mail-order chain store. The same information was transmitted by each of the five methods. After a period of time Dahle asked these individuals to recall the original message (recall accuracy).

The results, shown in Table 12–1, are instructive. By far the best way in increasing the accuracy of communication and minimizing decoding problems is to use a combination of oral and written methods. Oral transmission follows closely, but there is then a sharp drop in recall accuracy for the other methods. In all three studies accuracy decreased as follows: oral plus written; oral only; written only; bulletin board; and grapevine only.

Dahle's study highlights the fact that interpersonal communication can be enhanced if it is viewed as a problem of encoding and decoding rather than only as a problem of face-to-face interaction. It is common for an organization facing uncertainty to spawn a grapevine, and it is precisely this uncertainty that makes the grapevine

TABLE 12–1

Mean Accuracy of Recall Scores for Information Transmitted Using Various Media

	College student sample		*Manufacturing employee sample*		*Retail store sample*	
Method of presenting information	*Mean recall score*	*Number*	*Mean recall score*	*Number*	*Mean recall score*	*Number*
Oral and written	6.54	281	7.30	30	7.70	102
Oral only	5.31	161	6.38	13	6.17	94
Written only	4.58	279	4.46	28	4.91	109
Bulletin board	3.52	152			3.72	115
Grapevine only	2.88	157	3.00	13	3.56	108

Source: T. L. Dahle, "An Objective and Comparative Study of Five Methods of Transmitting Information to Business and Industrial Employees," *Speech Monographs* 21 (1954): 24, 26, 27. Used by permission.

such a potent but error-ridden method of transmitting information, at least during a critical period. Under such conditions it would seem logical for management to meet periodically with employees or their representatives to clear up any errors that may be channeled on the grapevine. At the same time, the decision-making group in management might begin to publish and distribute information on the organization's problems via minutes of meetings or company newspapers. This combined approach would help to minimize the inaccuracy of the information channeled on the grapevine.

The Yale Studies

As we have seen, accuracy in decoding interpersonal communications is important. But accuracy is not the only problem in effective communication; it is quite possible that the receiver accurately understands the message but does not want to complete the action requested by it. In fact, this is a major problem in management, persuading the receiver of the message to comply with the command that the manager sends.

A series of studies conducted at Yale University directly address this problem (see Hovland, Janis, and Kelley 1953; Abelson and Karlins 1970). These studies involved an audience; that is, there was only one sender but several receivers. From these studies the researchers were able to derive several generalizations about the major factors that are related to persuading receivers to follow the orders or accept the ideas of the sender.

The Persuader. The sender is not only a transmitter, he or she is also a persuader. The persuasive power of the sender increases if he or she possesses a high degree of credibility, which, in turn, is based on such factors as his or her degree of expertise on the subject and degree of trustworthiness.

Presentation of Issues. To persuade the receiver, the sender must present the issues logically and systematically. If the receiver is generally friendly, the sender should present only one side of the argument. However, if the receiver disagrees with the sender, or if the receiver will hear both sides of the argument at a later date, the sender should present both sides. The sender should also explicitly state his or her conclusions rather than allowing the receiver to draw them on his or her own. Additionally both emotional and factual appeals to the receiver work, but the sender must know when to use them. Sometimes an emotional appeal is superior to a factual appeal, and vice versa. However, the research generally shows a positive relationship between the intensity of fear aroused in the receiver and the degree to which the attitude of the receiver changes. Finally, the sender should simultaneously transmit distractors with the message to decrease resistance to it. An example of a distractor might be this: "As you know, I am in

agreement with many parts of your proposal, and have supported similar proposals in the past, but I am supporting a proposal different from the one you have presented."

The Receiver. While the sender must persuade the receiver to follow a particular course of action, the receiver determines whether the action will be taken. The receiver's level of intelligence determines the effectiveness of some types of appeals. Similarly, the receiver's personality traits influence susceptibility to persuasion. When the receiver's self-esteem is low, the probability of his or her being influenced by the message increases. Also, some receivers are simply easy to persuade. Unfortunately, these receivers are easily persuaded to reject their initial decision when a counterargument is presented.

The Persistence of the Attitude Change. While the sender may initially persuade the receiver, the influence of a persuasive communication tends to wear off. However, as the subtlety or complexity of the message increases, the persistence of the attitude change tends to rise. Also, attitude change is more persistent over time if the receiver actively participates in, rather than passively receives, the communication. And, as we might expect from our discussion of the combined influence of oral and written messages, repeating a communication tends to prolong its influence. Finally, attitude change is affected by a phenomenon termed the *sleeper effect:* The receiver accepts the message and the act demanded by it much more readily at some time after exposure to the communication rather than immediately after exposure to it.

INTERPERSONAL COMMUNICATION AND MANAGERIAL WORK

From a managerial perspective, interpersonal communication is important precisely because the manager is so involved in it as he or she ferrets out information, transmits it, and attempts to persuade others to accept it. In Chapter 1 we briefly reviewed the research of Henry Mintzberg on this subject. In this section we shall elaborate on this description and present a profile of managerial work, especially as it relates to interpersonal communication. We shall also examine a related viewpoint put forth by Alfred Sloan, president of General Motors for forty years. Then we shall discuss additional research on interpersonal communication, including the influence of managerial decision-making styles on interpersonal communication.

Nature of Managerial Work

In 1973 Henry Mintzberg published a major book focused specifically on the nature of managerial work. A major segment of this book describes the studies of other researchers, who have used such techniques as having managers keep diaries of their activities, asking subordinates what their superiors do during the day, and actually following a top-level executive for a period of time to gain firsthand knowledge of what actually transpires. Mintzberg himself based his doctoral dissertation at MIT on firsthand observations of five chief executive officers, each of whom allowed him to accompany them for one week.

Mintzberg has constructed a fascinating profile of managerial work. His research and that of others shows that managers work long hours at an unrelenting pace, at least partly because they must react immediately to the many and diverse problems they face. To solve these problems, managers must constantly communicate with members of their own and other organizations who can provide them with valuable, reliable, and current information.

However, because managers face a variety of problems, their activities and communications tend to be brief. In Mintzberg's own study of five chief executives (1973), half of their activities lasted less than five minutes, and only 10 percent exceeded an hour. Similarly, 56 first-line supervisors averaged 583 separate activities per eight-hour shift, an average of one activity every 48 seconds (Guest 1956). In Rosemary Stewart's study (1967) of 160 British managers, the subjects worked for a half hour or more, without interruption, only about once every two days.

Oral Communication. According to Mintzberg, oral communication is of overwhelming importance to managers. When he studied the activities of five chief executives, he found that 78 percent of their time was spent in oral communication. Stewart (1967), analyzing the activities of 160 British managers, discovered they spent 66 percent

THE IMPORTANCE OF COMMUNICATION

The manager's work is essentially that of communication and his tools are the five basic media—mail, telephone, unscheduled meetings, scheduled meetings, and tours. Managers clearly favor the three verbal media, many spending on the order of 80 percent of their time in verbal contact. Some managers, such as those of staff groups, spend relatively more time alone. But the greatest share of the time of almost all managers is spent in verbal communication. The verbal media are favored because they are the action media, providing current information and rapid feedback. The mail, which moves slowly and contains little "live action" material, receives cursory treatment. Mail processing tends to be treated as a burden.

Source: Henry Mintzberg, *The Nature of Managerial Work* (New York: Harper & Row, 1973), p. 171.

of their time in oral communication. This same pattern of behavior exists at the first-line level of supervision, as indicated by Tom Burns (1954), who reported that the foremen in a study he completed spent 80 percent of their time in oral communication.

One possible reason for this pattern of behavior is that managers want to protect and bolster their power in the organization. A manager often can obtain information orally that many other managers in the organization do not possess. And oral communication is the easiest way to obtain current and live information. Managers frequently disregard information communicated through the mail and in management reports, for much of it is dated and thus of limited use.

As might be expected from this description, Mintzberg also found that managers are strongly oriented to action and dislike reflective activities. This orientation may represent the personal preferences of managers. However, it may also result because managers must respond to many problems every working day that can be handled most efficiently by means of oral communication.

Mintzberg also believes his profile of managerial work holds at all levels of the organization. While managers at different organizational levels obviously perform different activities, they all constantly react to problems and work without letup long hours; they all have activities that are varied, fragmented, and brief; and they all tend to emphasize oral communication.

Research completed by Wickesberg (1968) supports Mintzberg's assertion that his profile of managerial work generally holds at all levels in the organization. Wickesberg asked 91 businessmen to record their communications and the purposes underlying them for one day a week over a five-week period; both managers and nonmanagers were included in the study. Among the managers, 53.5 percent of the communications focused on information, 22.4 percent on instructions, 11.1 percent on problem solving, 6.6 percent on gossip, and 6.2 percent on approval for projects. There was no significant difference between the managers and nonmanagers. For example, 54.2 percent of the communications among nonmanagers was informational.

A Related Viewpoint. Although these studies indicate that managers seem to favor oral communication overwhelmingly, no manager today can be successful by using only this approach, because modern organizations are very complex. For instance, the following departments have been added to most organizations in the past sixty years: personnel, personnel research, management information systems, long-range planning, industrial relations, training, research and development, marketing, marketing research, and public relations. Thus in today's organizations a manager must rely on all these sources of information and channels of communication if he or she is to be successful.

The communication policies of Alfred Sloan serve as a good example of this balanced approach (Sloan 1963). Frequently Sloan is described as the ideal manager, for he was president of General Motors during the period when it became one of the most successful corporations in the world, as it still is. Like other managers, Sloan relied heavily on oral communication. For example, at one time his dealers throughout the country were claiming they were holding too many cars in inventory, even though the reports at headquarters did not agree. Sloan attacked this problem directly by visiting a large number of dealers throughout the country. Both his talks with these dealers and their actual number of cars in stock strongly indicated that General Motors was supplying them with too many cars.

But Sloan also made considerable use of management reports in decision making. He generally prepared himself for meetings or decisions by reading relevant management reports from the many departments of General Motors. In fact, he was so systematic that he frequently wrote memoranda to himself detailing the advantages and disadvantages of various courses of action.

The message from Sloan's autobiography is clear—to be successful in the modern organization, which has become highly complex, a manager must go beyond oral communication. A systematic approach to problems, which emphasizes both oral and other forms of communication, is the one that is most likely to make a manager successful.

Styles It is a truism, and an important one, that individuals possess distinctive decision-making styles. A related truism, and one that is not generally emphasized in the management literature, is that these decision-making styles structure the manner in which the sender encodes the message and the receiver decodes it. James McKenney and Peter Keen (1974) have shed much light on this subject in their studies of nearly 200 MBA students at the Harvard Business School. They emphasized two major dimensions of style: information gathering and information evaluation.

There seem to be two general ways to gather information: preceptive and receptive. A *preceptive* individual approaches a problem in terms of preconceived mental images that he or she uses to order its critical aspects. A *receptive* individual focuses on details and builds up an understanding of the problem without relying on mental images.

Similarly, there are two general ways to evaluate information: systematic and intuitive. *Systematic decision makers* attempt to

FIGURE 12–3

Cognitive Problem-Solving Styles

		INFORMATION EVALUATION	
		Intuitive	*Systematic*
INFORMATION GATHERING	*Preceptive*	Marketing manager, psychologist, historian	Production & logistics manager, statistician, financial analyst
	Receptive	Architect, bond salesman	Auditor, clinical diagnostician

Source: Reprinted by permission of the Harvard Business Review. Exhibit from "How Managers' Minds Work" by James L. McKenney and Peter G. W. Keen (May–June 1974). Copyright © 1974 by the President and Fellows of Harvard College; all rights reserved.

structure a problem in terms of some method that they hope will lead them to a satisfactory solution. *Intuitive individuals* generally use a trial-and-error approach in evaluating information.

McKenney and Keen thus profile four major decision-making styles: preceptive-intuitive, preceptive-systematic, receptive-intuitive, and receptive-systematic (see Figure 12–3). In their studies they were able to classify about three-fourths of the MBA students by means of this four-cell model; only about a fourth could not be so classified, because these individuals tended to move from cell to cell as the nature of the problem changed.

The distinction between information gathering and information evaluation is important. For example, both a classical economist such as Leopold von Mises and a religious leader such as Billy Graham are preceptive, since they rely heavily on preconceived models, one of the economy and the other of religion. However, von Mises is a systematic evaluator of information, while Graham is intuitive.

McKenney and Keen argue that each decision-making style is valuable for different situations, and that intuitive managers should not blindly reject the recommendations of systematic thinkers such as operations research analysts. They also believe that particular decision-making styles are appropriate for different careers. For example, the preceptive-intuitive style is suitable for marketing managers and psychologists (see Figure 12–3).

SUMMARY

Perception strongly influences interpersonal communication. Perception is a process whereby the individual organizes stimuli or sensations into a meaningful whole. Some of the major factors influencing perception are the family, culture, physiology, and self-concept. Also, the individual relies on specific techniques to organize his or her perceptions. One of these is stereotyping, making generalizations to classify people and groups. The halo effect, using a favorable or unfavorable trait to color everything else one knows about the person, also biases perception. Other perceptual techniques are projection, the self-fulfilling prophecy, and implicit personality theory.

A basic model of interpersonal communication indicates that a sender encodes a message and transmits it to a receiver, who then decodes it and assigns meaning to it. The receiver, in turn, provides feedback to the sender by conveying a message that the sender must decode and assign meaning to. There are many barriers to interpersonal communication; for example, words can have different meanings for different people. Managers can avoid breakdowns in communication by using techniques like repetition and feedback and by being sensitive to the needs and values of subordinates. Additionally, managers can supplement the oral message with an identical written message to ensure its accuracy and its transmission.

Admittedly, it is desirable to increase the accuracy of the communication. However, it is also important for the receiver to accept the message and act in accordance with it. The Yale studies indicate that the sender must be a persuader if this outcome is to occur. Related factors that are important are the manner in which the message is presented, the characteristics of the receiver, and the length of time for which the receiver will be persuaded to accept the message.

Research on communication networks, the results of which can reasonably be generalized to small groups in an organization, suggests that centralized structures such as the wheel and the chain are effective in solving routine problems. Decentralized networks such as the completely connected and the circle seem to be appropriate for nonroutine or ambiguous problems. Further, the two-step flow of communication suggests that the manager should identify the informal leaders in his or her work group and persuade them to follow a particular course of action before appealing to other members.

Mintzberg's analysis of managerial work indicates that the activities of executives are varied, fragmented, and brief. In performing these activities, managers rely primarily on oral communication. However, the wise manager also takes full advantage of written forms of communication.

Research suggests that managerial decision-making styles influence the encoding and decoding of messages. James McKenney and Peter Keen have shown that there are two major dimensions of decision-making style: information gathering and information evaluation. There are two general ways to gather information: preceptive, or using preconceived images when gathering information, and receptive, or building up images of the problem without any preconceptions. There are two ways to evaluate information: systematic and intuitive. Using these definitions, the authors then describe four general decision-making styles: preceptive-systematic, preceptive-intuitive, receptive-systematic, and receptive-intuitive. When sending or receiving messages, a manager should be aware of the fact that the other individual in the communication process may be encoding or decoding in a manner radically different from his or her own.

DISCUSSION QUESTIONS

1. Some barriers to interpersonal communications are considered in this chapter. Discuss other barriers to interpersonal communication. What techniques can be employed to avoid or eliminate these barriers?
2. Compare Mintzberg's description of communication with Alfred Sloan's approach. Are they contradictory? Why or why not?
3. Why does it seem logical to generalize research results on networks and the two-step flow only to small groups but not to organizations?
4. How do self-fulfilling prophecies operate in the selection and promotion of employees and managers in an organization? In what other areas in an organization do self-fulfilling prophecies operate? What are some techniques that can be used to minimize the impact of self-fulfilling prophecies?
5. Describe a situation in which a receptive-systematic style of decision making would result in managerial success. Now describe a situation in which a receptive-intuitive style of decision making would result in managerial success.
6. Dahle describes five methods of communications: oral only, written only, oral plus written, the bulletin board, and the grapevine. Describe the relative effectiveness and accuracy of each of these methods. What are some methods that the manager could use to increase accuracy?

CRITICAL INCIDENTS

NOTE: These critical incidents can be used by the whole class with the case observational method (see Appendix A) or used for thought and discussion by individual class members.

1. Janet Turney is an assistant vice-president supervising 100 engineers and scientists in a large research and development (R&D) firm in the Boston area. She has been with the company for fifteen years and in her present position for seven years. During the first four years in her present position, she was relatively successful: she is a highly personable individual who utilizes a receptive-intuitive style of decision making and management. Her subordinates like and trust her.

However, the number of subordinates has increased from 25 to 100 during these seven years, at least in part because Janet was so effective in communicating with and motivating them. During these years Janet tended to operate on a personal basis and deemphasized the importance of organizational structure and bureaucracy. This year Janet's two immediate subordinates in charge of many of the operational details in her unit quit, primarily because the scientists and engineers undercut their authority by going directly to Janet on all matters, major and minor. These two subordinates had urged Janet to implement policies, procedures, and rules that would help to expedite activities, but to no avail.

At the same time a crisis was brewing, since the output of Janet's unit had declined dramatically in the past two years. Many of the scientists and engineers were dissatisfied, and some of the best ones had already quit. The grapevine had grown considerably, but it was transmitting a good deal of incorrect information.

Janet's boss, Ed Bagley, urged her to appoint a disciplinarian as her immediate subordinate to help her run her unit. Bagley himself was somewhat of a Machiavellian manager who could not be trusted. He disliked group meetings and made little effort to involve subordinates in either the generation of ideas or joint decision making. Rather, he dealt with subordinates only on a one-to-one basis, saying one thing to one subordinate and its exact opposite to another. Few subordinates trusted him.

In this crisis Janet turned to a longtime friend, Mike Edwards, who was a highly regarded engineer in her unit, and asked him to become her immediate subordinate and internal administrator. Edwards, who was a receptive-systematic decision maker, really didn't want the job; he was happy in his present position. However, he feared that Ed Bagley wanted Janet to appoint a disciplinarian only as an interim measure; within a few months, after the disciplinarian had become familiar with the unit's operation, Bagley could then fire or demote Janet Turney and put the disciplinarian in her place. Such an administrator would obviously make life miserable for the scientists and engineers in the unit. At the same time, Mike feared that Janet only wanted a pencil pusher as her immediate subordinate rather than a genuine internal administrator of operations. Janet's past behavior was certainly consistent with such an interpretation.

Mike was uncertain about what to do. He liked his job, the unit in which he worked, and Janet. Also, Ed Bagley thought favorably of

Mike and would not oppose his appointment as Janet's internal administrator.

QUESTIONS: How are the communication or decision-making styles of these managers influencing the activities in this subunit? What should Mike do? If he does decide to take the job, Mike feels that there be complete agreement among the three of them before he accepts it, because he does not want to be either a disciplinarian or a pencil pusher. How can he encode or transmit messages to both Janet and Ed about the manner in which he plans to conduct his work?

2.* A large engineering company relied primarily on government contracts for its existence. Recently the Department of Labor found that this company's wage standards for engineering draftsmen did not meet department standards. The Department of Labor directed the company to adjust its standards if it wanted to meet the specifications of the government contracts. The draftsmen expected to receive a sizable bonus because of past inequities. However, management merely added a new set of positions on the career ladder and reclassified most of the employees downward. Management did not allow any of the employees to express their opinions on this course of action. Management actually had much justification for its position, since the costs of its contracts were fixed, and thus the company would have lost a great amount of money if all of the draftsmen had received a bonus.

QUESTIONS: What kind of control problem is this approach creating? How would you have communicated management's decision to the employees?

SUGGESTED READINGS

Fisher, B. Aubrey. *Small Group Decision Making: Communication and the Group Process.* New York: McGraw-Hill, 1974, 264 pages, hardback.

Fisher clearly and effectively summarizes research in the area of communication as it relates to decision making in small groups.

Haney, William. *Communication and Organizational Behavior: Text and Cases.* 3rd ed. Homewood, Ill.: Irwin, 1973, 533 pages, hardback.

Haney develops a distinctive conceptual framework for communication and applies it to a variety of cases.

* Written by Richard H. Kirchmeyer. Copyright © 1977 by Little, Brown and Company (Inc.).

13 Motivation

PROCESS THEORIES
CONTENT THEORIES
CONDITIONING THEORIES
FACTORS AFFECTING JOB SATISFACTION
SUMMARY
DISCUSSION QUESTIONS
CRITICAL INCIDENTS
SUGGESTED READINGS

PERFORMANCE OBJECTIVES

1. To describe how a manager motivates subordinates to behave in a way that will move the organization toward its objectives.
2. To distinguish among three major categories of motivational theories—process theories, content theories, and conditioning theories—and to discuss some useful theories within the broad framework of expectancy theory that are particularly appropriate for explaining work-related activities.
3. To discuss the importance of job satisfaction, the factors that influence it, and its relationship to motivation.

Individuals create organizations to accomplish specific purposes. In turn, the organization attracts other individuals who wish to become members so they can satisfy their needs for money, interesting work, personal recognition, and so forth.

Ideally, the organization should accomplish all its objectives, and its members should satisfy all the needs that have drawn them to it. However, this ideal is rarely attained. For instance, it is ordinarily not feasible to promote every member of the organization, even though almost everyone wants a promotion. For this reason motivation becomes especially important in an organization. *Motivation* basically means an individual's needs, desires, and concepts that cause him or her to act in a particular manner. It is the manager's task to direct individuals so they can satisfy their needs as much as possible while they strive to accomplish the objectives of the organization. To do this, managers utilize motivational theories.

There are several ways to classify motivational theories. Some authors distinguish between process and content theories. *Process theories* describe the actual process an individual experiences as he or she is motivated to pursue a particular course of action. *Content theories* describe the actual factors motivating an individual, such as pay and interesting work. However, sometimes it is possible to classify a particular theory as both process and content, since the distinction between them is not always clear-cut.

Other authors distinguish between needs theories and cognitive theories. *Needs theories* describe the specific needs that an individual possesses that propel him or her to pursue a particular course of action—for example, the desire for interesting work, pay, and fringe benefits. *Cognitive theories* emphasize thoughts as the key internal states motivating an individual. For all practical purposes content theories and needs theories are interchangeable; the same can be said of process and cognitive theories. In this chapter we focus on process and content theories that are directly applicable to work-related activities.

There is also a third general type of motivational theory, conditioning theory. Although *conditioning theory* was originally conceived as a subcategory of learning theory, it is also a subdivision of motivational theory, for it focuses on the cues and stimuli that elicit a particular type of behavior. These three general classes of motivational theory—process, content, and conditioning—are logically related to one another if they are viewed within the context of *expectancy theory,* which is a broad approach to the problem of motivation.

The chapter begins with a discussion of the three general classes of motivational theory. Some practical applications of motivational theory are then highlighted by means of an analysis of types of work and job satisfaction.

PROCESS THEORIES

For many years managers were not very interested in motivation. They generally accepted Frederick Taylor's rather simplistic approach to motivation: Individuals are primarily motivated by economic factors, and they will normally increase their efforts if they receive additional money (see Chapter 1). However, psychologists have demonstrated that motivation is much more complex and important than Taylor believed. Significant process theories of motivation, focused specifically on work-related activities, include expectancy theory, Locke's goal-setting theory, dissonance theory, and equity theory.

Expectancy Theory

Expectancy theory, also called performance-expectation theory and instrumentality theory, is so named because it treats motivation as a function of a person's expectations about the relationships among his or her efforts, the effectiveness of those efforts, and the rewards they obtain (see Vroom 1964). In this sense expectancy theory is a process theory of motivation.

According to this theory, an individual will be motivated to produce at a high level if he perceives that his efforts will result in suc-

FIGURE 13–1

Expectancy Theory

Both the effort-performance linkage and the performance-reward linkage can be expressed in terms of mathematical probabilities, which can be used to predict an individual's or a group's level of motivation.

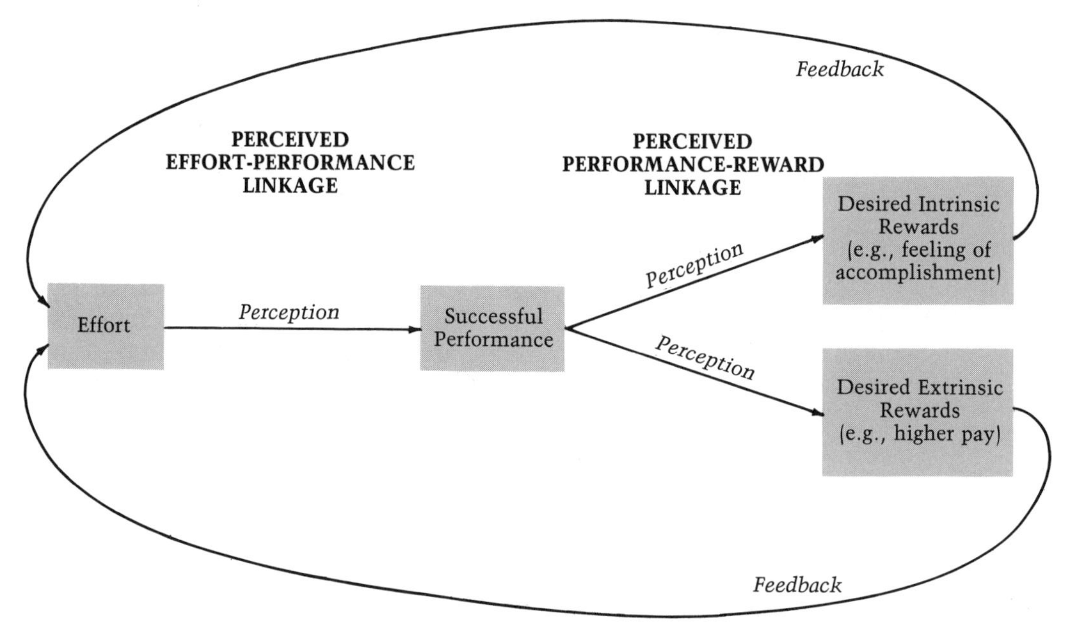

cessful performance. This perceived link between effort and performance is called the *effort-performance linkage* (see Figure 13–1). In addition, the individual must perceive that successful performance will result in rewards. The individual must specify *how much* he desires the various rewards he will obtain if he performs successfully. Thus the second important linkage is between perceived successful performance and desired rewards. For instance, two individuals successfully performing the same job may have differential preferences for money: One may desire it very much, while the other may not.

Desired outcomes can be of two types. First, there are *intrinsic rewards* that relate directly to the nature of the work itself—for example, how interesting and challenging it is. Second, there are *extrinsic rewards* that do not directly relate to the nature of the work—for example, salary increases and working conditions. Because expectancy theory argues that particular outcomes or rewards satisfy specific needs for different individuals, it can also be viewed as a content theory of motivation. However, expectancy theory is first and foremost a process theory of motivation.

Possibly the major advantage of expectancy theory is that the two main linkages can be expressed as probabilities. That is, interviews or a questionnaire survey can be used to measure the strength of employees' expectations that effort will lead to successful performance and successful performance to desired outcomes. From these probabilities management can derive a mathematical equation or function for any individual or work group that should predict the resulting level of motivation.

However, this major advantage is also a disadvantage. It means an employee's attitudes must be translated into exact figures and probabilities before a mathematical equation can be used to predict his or her level of motivation. But given the current state of behavioral science research, it is very difficult to reduce human attitudes to mathematical probabilities in most organizational settings.

Research evidence supports the performance-reward linkage in expectancy theory; that is, individuals do continue to perform at a high level if they obtain intrinsic and extrinsic rewards they desire.[1] For instance, one research study indicated that production workers who were high performers tended to be significantly different from the low performers in that they believed their level of productivity directly affected their attainment of rewards (Georgopoulos, Mahoney, and Jones 1957). However, the linkage between effort and performance has not been clearly established, although some research supports this position (Cummings and Schwab 1973).

[1] In recent years there have been many important studies of expectancy theory. See Sheridan, Slocum, and Min 1975; Sims, Szilagyi, and McKemey 1976; Farr and Joyce 1977; and Mobley and Meglino 1977.

Locke's Goal-setting Theory

In Chapter 5, we described an organizationwide planning technique called management by objectives (MBO). The two major assumptions underlying this technique are that individuals throughout the entire organization should be actively involved in setting goals guiding their activities, and that there be periodic feedback of results. Edwin Locke (1968) has developed a motivational theory that parallels MBO and provides additional support for its use in organizations. Locke (1976) feels that expectancy theory and his *goal-setting theory* are opposed to one another. However, a broad approach to expectancy theory, such as that taken in this book, suggests that Locke's theory can be treated in terms of it.

Locke begins his analysis by arguing that there are two cognitive determinants of behavior: values and intentions (goals). A *value* is something the individual acts to gain or keep. Emotions and desires represent the form that values and value judgments take in the activity of the individual. *Intentions* are goals that individuals seek to attain in order to satisfy their desires or emotions. Even if a goal is not attained, the individual experiences responses when he or she undertakes activity based on them. This, in turn, results in consequences, feedback, and reinforcement. Thus Locke's process model is

Values and value judgments → Emotions or desires → Intentions or goals → Responses or performance → Consequences, feedback, or reinforcement

Although most of Locke's research has taken place in experimental settings rather than in actual organizational situations, he has accumulated an impressive amount of data to support his theory. In particular, he has shown that setting "hard but attainable goals" seems to produce much higher performance than setting easy or moderate goals. In some of his research Locke has shown that even individuals trying for a goal so high they rarely reach it perform better than those who establish relatively easy goals. Also, Gary Latham and Gary Yukl (1975) have shown that there is no difference in performance for groups operating under assigned and participatively set goals. This finding brings into question the need for designing MBO programs that use employee participation in the setting of goals. However, other researchers have found that participation in goal setting is positively related to job satisfaction (Arvey, Dewhirst, and Boling 1976).

Locke's work emphasizes the importance of setting goals in organizations (MBO). Field research in actual organizational settings has supported his theory (Carroll and Tosi 1973; Latham and Kinne 1974; and Kim and Hamner 1976). In some of this research the authors have attempted to place a cost figure on the amount of money an organization would save if it used Locke's goal-setting approach. For example, Latham and Baldes (1975) have analyzed savings in just one small operation at the Weyerhaeuser Corporation that have resulted specifically from implementing Locke's theory, and they show that savings run into hundreds of thousands of dollars.

Like Locke, expectancy theorists argue persuasively that individuals want to achieve goals; that is, effort must be perceived as resulting in successful performance. Also, expectancy theorists posit that rewards or reinforcements must be perceived as following successful performance if the individual is to continue to produce at a high level. Thus Locke's theory can be viewed from the perspective of expectancy theory.

Cognitive Dissonance

Another process theory of motivation has been developed by Leon Festinger (1957), who focuses specifically on the concepts motivating individuals to act in a particular manner. Essentially, the theory of *cognitive dissonance* holds that an individual has difficulty accepting two concepts that contradict each other. To deal with the dissonance between two conflicting ideas, a person will try to modify his or her perception of one of the ideas so it no longer contradicts the other. For example, a college graduate who is looking for a job may be offered two equally attractive positions. After he makes his final selection, he may experience a state of dissonance, since he realizes that he has rejected an excellent opportunity. To reduce this dissonance, he convinces himself that the job he turned down was not as good as the one he took (Vroom 1966). Similarly, when an individual experiences a difference between the actual and desired level of influence in the job situation, dissonance occurs (Hollan and Chesser 1976).

Managers frequently use the techniques of cognitive dissonance in marketing and selling goods. It is common for a salesperson to show a customer a complete line of goods and then encourage him or her to buy the most inexpensive item, even though it is obvious that the customer prefers the medium-priced item. This approach normally offends the customer, who experiences dissonance between the idea of spending money and the idea of being a cheapskate. The customer then frequently attempts to eliminate the dissonance by purchasing the highest-priced item (Zimbardo and Ebbesen 1977).

A manager can motivate employees by using techniques derived from the theory of cognitive dissonance. If an overly confident subordinate is performing slightly below average, the manager might inform him that his performance is very poor rather than moderately poor. The subordinate may increase his level of productivity to eliminate the dissonance between his self-image and the manager's report. However, the manager must be careful in applying dissonance theory, for an undesirable result such as a decrease in productivity might occur.

Expectancy theory relates to cognitive dissonance in that individuals who perceive a dissonant relationship between successful performance and desired rewards will move to reduce the dissonance. For instance, individuals who think their performance is high but their rewards are low may either reduce performance or try to increase rewards. Thus managers should try to prevent dissonance between performance and desired rewards.

Adams's Equity Theory

The link just noted between expectancy theory and dissonance is essentially a description of equity theory, which is a specific form of dissonance theory. According to J. Stacy Adams's *equity theory* (1963, 1965), an individual compares the ratio of his inputs and outcomes to the input-outcome ratio of another individual whom he believes to be comparable to him. Adams has used the following formula to express these ideas:

$$\frac{\text{outcomes}}{\text{individual's own inputs}} = \frac{\text{outcomes}}{\text{comparable individual's inputs}}$$

If the individual does not see a balance in this formula, he will attempt to restore it by working more or less efficiently or by trying to obtain greater rewards. His judgments of balance usually are based on how his situation compares with that of the other individual.

For example, an experienced bank teller probably would feel he or she has been treated unfairly if a newly hired teller is making more money. He or she could respond to this inequity in several ways: complain to the superior, express resentment by showing up late for work or being absent, decrease his or her level of productivity, complain to an outside friend about the situation, call all the experienced tellers together to decide on a course of action that would change the situation, or quit. The selection of alternatives obviously depends on a number of critical factors. For example, the teller will not quit if there are no other available jobs.

CONTENT THEORIES

As we have noted, process theories of motivation essentially describe the manner in which an individual is motivated. In contrast, content theories focus on the specific needs motivating an individual to act in a particular manner. Significant content theories include Maslow's need hierarchy, Herzberg's two-factor theory, and McClelland's need theory.

Maslow's Need Hierarchy

Individuals become members of organizations for a variety of reasons. Many of them seek work primarily because they desire money in order to satisfy their physiological needs for food and shelter. Others, however, may be sufficiently wealthy that they do not work primarily be-

FIGURE 13–2
Maslow's Need Hierarchy

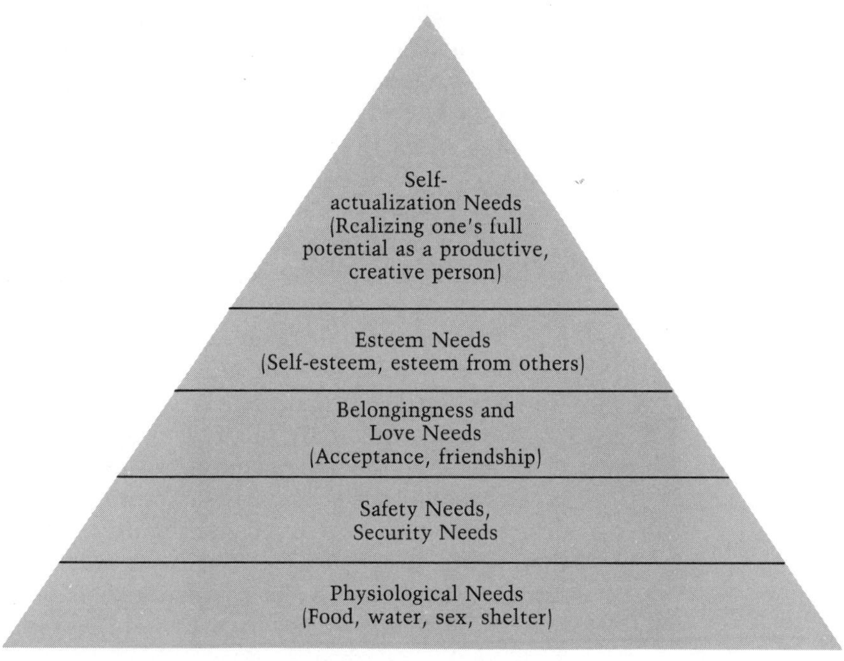

Source: Adapted from A. H. Maslow, "A Theory of Human Motivation," *Psychological Review* 50 (1943): 370–396, American Psychological Association.

cause of the pay they receive. Since an individual does have needs or desires he would like to satisfy, it seems logical that he would focus on some of them before even thinking about the others.

Abraham Maslow (1954) has proposed a content theory of motivation in which *needs* are arranged in a *hierarchy.* According to Maslow, an individual seeks to satisfy these needs in a certain sequence (see Figure 13–2). After the individual's basic and elementary needs are satisfied, he or she turns to higher-order needs. Maslow classifies needs into five types, in ascending order: (1) physiological needs (for example, food and water); (2) safety needs (for example, protection against physical danger and economic disaster); (3) belongingness and love needs; (4) esteem needs (for example, the respect of fellow workers); and (5) self-actualization (for example, realizing one's full potential as a productive and creative person or becoming what one is capable of becoming). As shown in Figure 13–2, physiological needs must be satisfied first, after which safety needs become prominent, and so forth.

Some research supports the idea that an individual must satisfy physiological needs before any of the higher-order needs can be activated, and that he will not be concerned about higher-order needs until he has satisfied security needs (Cofer and Appley 1964; Alderfer 1972). But research does not support the existence of a hierarchy once one moves above the security level (Lawler and Suttle 1972; Rauschenberger, Schmitt, and Hunter 1980). Thus it seems preferable to posit a two-step hierarchy: Physiological and security needs constitute the first step, and the other higher-order needs are the second step.

It is relatively easy for an organization to satisfy the lower-order needs of its employees and managers, especially in an affluent country such as the United States. It is not so easy to satisfy higher-order needs, and yet a survey of 1900 managers indicated they consider the higher-order needs to be more important than the lower-order needs (Porter 1964). These managers also felt that the higher-order needs were less satisfied than the lower-order needs.

The need hierarchy theory can be used to add another dimension to expectancy theory. According to expectancy theory, an individual must believe that successful performance will result in two types of desired rewards—extrinsic and intrinsic. Maslow's theory would say that extrinsic rewards act on lower-order needs; an individual who satisfies them then seeks intrinsic rewards to satisfy his higher-order needs. From this perspective Lyman Porter's conclusion that man-

FIGURE 13–3
Herzberg's Theory of Motivation

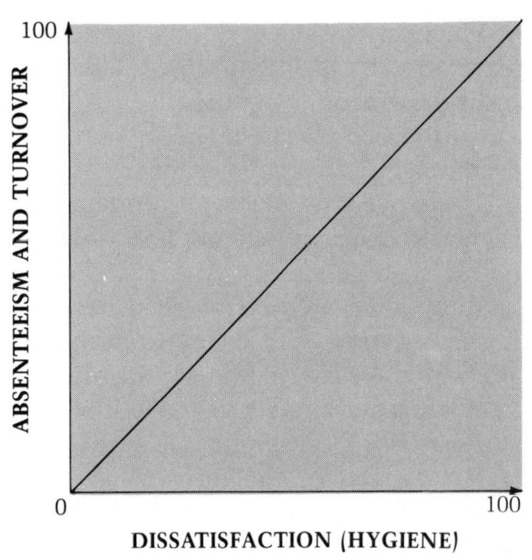

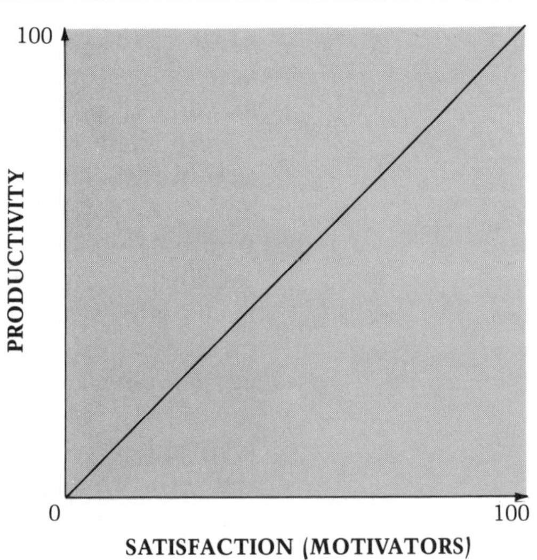

agers feel organizations are more adept at satisfying lower-order than higher-order needs becomes significant to expectancy theory: It is important for management to ensure that successful performance will bring workers intrinsic as well as extrinsic rewards.

Herzberg's Two-Factor Theory

Several years ago Frederick Herzberg and his associates conducted a series of interviews with 200 engineers and accountants, focusing on factors the subjects considered important sources of motivation (Herzberg, Mausner, and Snyderman 1959). Each engineer was asked two questions: (1) Can you describe, in detail, when you felt exceptionally bad about your job? (2) Can you describe, in detail, when you felt exceptionally good about your job?

Hygiene Factors and Motivators. The results of Herzberg's investigation are reminiscent of expectancy theory. When an engineer or accountant described times he felt exceptionally bad about his job, he usually mentioned factors like pay, the technical competence of his supervisor, his relations with other employees, company policies and administration, working conditions, and job security. All these factors can be described as extrinsic; they do not relate directly to the actual work an engineer or accountant performs. These factors are associated more with the *context* of the job than its *content.* Herzberg classified them as *hygiene factors.*

However, when an engineer or accountant described times he felt exceptionally good about the job, he talked about having successfully completed an important task, having been singled out for praise for being effective, having a sense of responsibility for his own or others' work, and getting a promotion. These factors are *intrinsic* because they relate more to the content of the job than to its context. Herzberg termed such factors *motivators,* for they are apparently able to move people to complete their work efficiently.

According to Herzberg, hygiene factors are independent from motivators. Hygiene factors can make a worker dissatisfied, but they do not contribute significantly to his or her sense of satisfaction with a job. Motivators affect the individual's sense of intrinsic satisfaction but not dissatisfaction. According to Herzberg, an individual who becomes too dissatisfied with hygiene factors such as pay or relations with other employees generally will try to escape from the work environment by coming in late, or not at all, and eventually quitting. However, hygiene factors do not significantly influence the individual's level of productivity. Motivators, on the other hand, act directly on the individual's level of productivity, even though they do not tend to affect such factors as lateness, absenteeism, and turnover. Herzberg's theory can be pictured as shown in Figure 13–3.

Herzberg's theory is very similar to Maslow's theory. His dissatisfiers or hygiene factors correspond to the lower-level needs of Maslow's hierarchy (physiological, safety, and security needs). His satisfiers or motivators correspond to Maslow's higher-order needs (belongingness and love needs, esteem needs, and self-actualization needs). However, Herzberg has emphasized work-related items: the work itself, money, supervisory relations, and so on.

Other investigators who have attempted to replicate Herzberg's findings, by means of a questionnaire rather than interviews, have been unable to do so (see Campbell et al. 1970). So researchers are currently revising, trying out, and expanding his theory (see Schneider and Locke 1971). Still, even in its current form Herzberg's theory has important managerial implications for two areas: (1) ranking of job factors and (2) job enlargement and enrichment.

Ranking of Job Factors. As we have seen, individuals can be motivated by many job factors. The most important seem to be the nature of the work itself, pay, promotion, recognition when a job is completed successfully, fringe benefits, working conditions, style of supervision, relationships with co-workers, and the prestige of the company and its top management (Locke 1976). Researchers investigating factors in motivation traditionally have gathered data by asking an employee to rank a list of job factors. Respondents to such a questionnaire normally rank money in the middle (Lawler 1971). From the viewpoint of Herzberg's theory, it would be more appropriate to present the employee with one list of hygiene factors and one list of motivators to rank separately. Other researchers have refined this approach by using three or more general factors.

Job Enlargement and Enrichment. In Herzberg's theory, hygiene factors and motivators are directly linked to the issues of job enlargement and job enrichment (Herzberg 1968). According to Herzberg, *job enlargement* means increasing the number of operations an individual performs in a given job cycle. For example, an employee on an automotive assembly line who performs five distinct operations during his or her job cycle holds a larger job than an employee who performs only four. *Job enrichment,* on the other hand, concerns the amount of responsibility an individual is able to exercise in his or her work environment.

According to Herzberg's theory, job enlargement is related to hygiene factors, for the context of the work rather than its content is involved. Some research on automobile workers supports this theory. Their work is monotonous but less so when an individual is allowed to perform five operations rather than only four or three (Walker and Guest 1952). Hence the tendency to escape from the work environ-

"Let's put it in perspective, coach . . .
The first $12,000 of your salary is for teaching sportsmanship.
The next $50,000 is for winning!"

ment by means of absenteeism or termination should decrease when such a job is enlarged.

Job enrichment involves the content of the work. Because it has to do with motivators, it affects a person's positive feelings about his or her job. For example, a professor can enrich the job of a research assistant by allowing him or her to teach a class periodically. A manager can enrich the job of an engineering draftsman by permitting him to perform work normally reserved for fully qualified engineers. When a job is enriched, the individual assumes responsibilities not previously delegated to him or her.

There does seem to be some empirical support for this idea (see Miner 1973; Filley, House, and Kerr 1976; Ford 1969). In particular, the link between job enrichment and productivity was borne out by a program in which American Telephone and Telegraph (AT&T) Company enriched the shareholder correspondent job in its treasury department. Not only were employees happier, but the company saved $558,000 in the first eighteen-month period after the job was enriched (Ford 1969). Besides decreasing turnover, AT&T's program eliminated

TABLE 13–1
Job Enrichment at AT&T

Projected savings, first 18-month period, after a shareholder correspondent job was enriched in the AT&T treasury department

1. 27 percent drop in turnover: nonsupervisory specialists	$245,000
2. Investigation and file clerks: annual salaries (force reduced from 46 to 24 clerks, 3 management jobs eliminated)	135,000
3. Correspondents' group: salaries (5 management, 4 verifier jobs eliminated)	76,000
4. Stock transfer group: salaries eliminated	40,000
5. Merger of employee stock-pension unit and dividend reconciliation unit: salaries eliminated	100,000
6. Improved productivity (not priced)	?
7. Improved service indexes (not priced)	?
8. Improved tone of exit interviews (not priced)	?
9. Personnel section: job rearrangements (not priced)	?
10. Must offset half the salary of the 6 employees working on job enrichment program part-time	(38,000)
	$558,000

Source: Reprinted, by permission of the publisher, from Robert Ford, *Motivation Through the Work Itself*, p. 44.

salaries of workers performing the duties now transferred to shareholder correspondents. Other benefits to the company were difficult to measure (see Table 13–1).

Job Diagnostic Survey

Other researchers have extended Herzberg's perspective on job enrichment while questioning it at the same time. J. Richard Hackman and Greg Oldham (1975) have developed a questionnaire, the Job Diagnostic Survey, designed to measure the degree to which a job is enriched. They focus on five dimensions of a job:[2]

> Skill variety, or the degree to which a job requires a variety of different skills.
>
> Task identity, or the degree to which a job requires completion of a whole and identifiable piece of work. In other words, the individual does the task from beginning to end with a visible outcome.
>
> Task significance, or the degree to which a job has a substantial impact on the lives or work of other people, whether in the immediate organization or the external environment.

[2] These definitions are taken almost verbatim from Oldham, Hackman, and Pearce (1976). Other researchers are currently assessing the validity of the Job Diagnostic Survey. See Dunham, Aldag, and Brief (1977); Dunham (1976); and Griffin and Chonko (1977).

Autonomy, or the degree to which a job provides substantial freedom, independence, and discretion to the individual in scheduling the work and in determining the procedures used to carry it out.

Feedback, or the degree to which carrying out the activities required by a job results in the individual obtaining direct and clear information about the effectiveness of his or her performance.

Using these definitions, Hackman and Oldham developed the following formula to study the degree to which a job is enriched:

$$\text{motivating potential score} = \left[\frac{\text{skill variety} + \text{task identity} + \text{task significance}}{3}\right] \times \text{autonomy} \times \text{feedback}$$

One consistent finding these researchers report is that job enrichment will be successful *only if* an individual possesses a high need for achievement (Hackman and Lawler 1971; Oldham, Hackman, and Pearce 1976). If individuals are low on this need, management may want to provide training designed to increase it *before* enriching a job. This approach is consistent with the contingency or situational theory of management and organizational behavior.

McClelland's Need Theory

A final and distinctive content theory of motivation has been developed by David McClelland. To measure needs, McClelland used the Thematic Apperception Test (TAT), which consists of a series of ambiguous pictures; individuals are asked to write stories about the characters in the pictures. McClelland has identified three distinct needs that are important for various types of individuals: need for achievement, need for power, and need for affiliation.

In his early work McClelland showed that need for achievement is important for individuals who want to be distinctively recognized and rewarded immediately or almost immediately for their efforts. For example, an entrepreneur frequently starts his own business because he can see almost immediately the results or rewards for his efforts. According to McClelland, this need can be learned. Thus he attempted to instill a high need for achievement into seventy-six managers of small enterprises in India. During this training the managers were taught to create high-achievement fantasies, to examine work in terms of achievement, to internalize the characteristics of high-achieving individuals, and to work together in achievement-oriented groups (McClelland and Winter 1969). Achievement motivation increased significantly after the training program had been completed. Further, the experimental group of managers who had been trained was subsequently more active in an economic sense than members of a control group that did not undergo this training.

In his recent work McClelland has focused on the power need (McClelland 1975; McClelland and Burnham 1976). He argues that successful managers and successful entrepreneurs are motivated differently. The successful manager has a high need for power or influencing people. His or her power need is much greater than his or her need for achievement. However, the manager must control the power need if he or she is to be successful. McClelland argues that the successful manager is also lower than the general population on the affiliation need. Like the entrepreneur, he or she is only minimally motivated by his or her social needs. However, because the successful manager is unlike the entrepreneur in that he or she does not see the immediate results of efforts to influence others, he or she must possess a high degree of emotional maturity. According to McClelland, the two key ingredients of managerial success, especially at the higher levels in an organization, are emotional maturity and a democratic, coaching style.

From the vantage point of expectancy theory, McClelland's approach is significant. Individuals are motivated to succeed, and this motivation stems either from achievement or power needs. Thus it is important for an individual to believe that his or her efforts will result in successful performance and, even more, that successful performance will bring desired rewards. If these two linkages are strong, an individual can be expected to make a significant effort to increase the probability of successful performance.

CONDITIONING THEORIES

Our third broad class of motivational theories is conditioning theory, whereby the researcher applies specific stimuli or sensations to the individual in order to condition or evoke a particular response. The objective is to analyze human beings and animals in terms of their observable behavior. A behaviorist is skeptical of attempts to pinpoint someone's unconscious reason for doing something, or even of attempts to describe someone's mental state. Hence a behaviorist makes no assumptions about internal states, needs, or concepts of the individual that cause him or her to act in a particular manner. For example, most of us think of fear as an emotion. To a behaviorist, fear is a set of physical activities—running from danger, perhaps, or just having sweating palms, a dry throat, and shaking knees.

Within this broad class of theories there are two types of conditioning. Pavlov's work with dogs represents *classical conditioning.* Originally he applied a stimulus—food—to make the dog salivate. Simultaneously, he rang a bell. Pavlov wanted a *new* stimulus—the bell—to bring about a natural or unconditioned response. After a period of time he rang the bell without placing food in front of the dog, and the dog salivated. Thus classical conditioning can be described as the process of causing a new stimulus to bring about a natural or unconditioned response. In this situation the individual is essentially passive and merely reacts to the stimuli that are applied.

Operant conditioning is the second major type of stimulus-response theory. It is directly applicable to *behavior modification programs* currently being implemented in industry, so we will examine these topics in this section. The original premise of operant conditioning is described by the law of effect: Behavior followed by desirable or pleasant consequences will be repeated, while behavior not followed by pleasant consequences will be extinguished (not repeated). There are two basic kinds of learning processes: reflex and operant (voluntary). According to B. F. Skinner (1953), the law of effect can be restated in terms of the basic principle of operant conditioning: Operant or voluntary behavior is a function of its consequences.

Additional Concepts

In classical conditioning the sequence of events leading to a response is independent of the subject's behavior or response. However, in operant conditioning the consequences (rewards or punishments) are made to occur directly as a result of a subject's response or failure to respond. Thus operant conditioning can be defined as the process by which behavior is modified by manipulation of consequences.

A major concept underlying operant conditioning is that of *reinforcer,* which is any consequence of behavior that strengthens the probability of the future occurrence of that behavior, assuming that the reinforcer is available when the desired behavior occurs. Management has recourse to many reinforcers: money, extra time off, praise, fringe benefits, and so forth. However, there is a fundamental difference between a reinforcer and a reward (Mawhinney 1975). Outcomes or rewards of one's behavior possess reinforcing property *only* if they increase the behavior upon which they are made contingent. Rewards, on the other hand, can be simply defined by precedent, tradition, or stereotype. Although we assume that money possesses reinforcing properties, it may well be that some individuals are simply not motivated by it. In such a situation money is a reward but not a reinforcer. If at all possible, management should reward individuals on a differential basis. To this end, some researchers have developed questionnaires that are specifically designed to uncover the wants and desires of organizational members (see Reitz 1971).

For operant conditioning to be successful, the individual must be active and must affect directly the environment. To encourage a behavior that has never occurred, an individual should be rewarded or positively reinforced as he or she gets closer and closer to the correct behavior so that he or she will complete it. Thus both behavior and results are rewarded. Further, most researchers argue that only positive reinforcement should be employed. Admittedly, negative reinforcement, or punishment, motivates an individual immediately after it is administered. However, the individual typically reverts to the undesired pattern of behavior once the negative reinforcement is removed. At the very least, an individual should not be punished when others are present.

Schedules of Reinforcement

There are many ways to arrange the schedule of reinforcements that an individual receives for correct behavior. Classical conditioning uses a continuous reinforcement schedule: Every time a correct response occurs, the individual is rewarded. Operant conditioning emphasizes partial reinforcement schedules in which reinforcement does not occur after every correct behavior. This type of schedule is associated with slower learning but stronger retention of a response (Bass and Vaughn 1966).

There are four basic types of partial reinforcement schedules (Ferster and Skinner 1957; Behling, Schriesheim, and Tolliver 1976). There is, first of all, a distinction between interval and ratio schedules. Under the *interval* or time-based *schedule* the reinforcement is measured in terms of time. The individual is not reinforced until after

THE HARD-CORE UNEMPLOYED: WHY BMod IS APPROPRIATE

Another reality that must be understood in dealing with the hard-core is the strong sense of failure that pervades their lives. Not to do so is to miss a significant building block that goes into the structure of the disadvantaged person and that can help to explain his somewhat puzzling behavior. To the hard-core, arriving at the age of 19, 29, 39, or more and still reading on a 3rd or 4th grade level, with a work history consisting of jobs such as dishwasher and janitor, unable to adequately support a wife, let alone a family, is to have lived with a bitter taste of failure and a deep sense of worthlessness.

If success breeds success, failure breeds failure. Again, the disadvantaged person is conditioned. To fail is his lot. At the same time, trying desperately to hold on to his self-respect, he will resort to a variety of stratagems in order to avoid another failure experience. If this is how he sees the job, he is likely to feel that he can better live with himself by rationalizing quitting than to risk being fired for not measuring up.

Source: National Association of Manufacturers. *Effectively Employing the Hard-Core* (New York: National Association of Manufacturers, 1968), pp. 1–2.

a period of time has elapsed since the last reinforcement. Under the *ratio schedule* the reinforcement is measured in terms of units. The individual is not reinforced until he or she has successfully completed a number of units of work since the last reinforcement. Both interval and ratio schedules can either be fixed or variable.

Interval Schedules. Under the *fixed-interval* schedule a reinforcement is administered only after a regular and specified period of time has passed since the administration of the previous reinforcement. Paychecks given on a monthly basis represent this type of reinforcement scheduling.

Under the *variable-interval schedule,* the reinforcement is administered at some variable interval of time around some average. This approach is appropriate for administering praise, promotions, and supervisory visits. For example, a manager could praise his or her subordinate on an average of once a day but at randomly selected time intervals: once on Monday, twice on Tuesday, and twice on Friday. If the individual is relatively satisfied with his or her situation in the organization, this type of reinforcement is very effective for generating higher rates of response and more stable and consistent performance than are fixed schedules, primarily because of the unpredictable nature of the administration.

This writer once analyzed a situation in one of the country's largest banks in which the use of variable-interval schedules would have been preferable to fixed-interval schedules in granting employee bonuses. This bank was experiencing an abnormally high employee turnover rate of 40 percent per year. However, an examination of quarterly turnover rates indicated that the rate was 20 percent or less for the first three quarters of the year; in the fourth quarter, immediately after Christmas, the turnover rate jumped to 60 percent. The probable culprit was the annual bonus, given regularly to each employee at Christmastime.

Ratio Schedules

As indicated above, ratio schedules are measured in terms of units. The fixed-ratio schedule operates in such a way that a reinforcer is administered only after a fixed number of desired responses takes place. For example, salespeople may receive a commission if their sales exceed a stated objective. Similarly, a piece-rate worker might be given a bonus if he or she produces a specified number of units.

Under the variable-ratio schedule a reinforcer is administered only after a number of desired responses, with the number of desired responses changing around an average from the occurrence of one reinforcer to the next. For example, management might use a 10-to-1 ratio schedule, but the reinforcement would be administered after the 5th, 15th, 7th, and 13th correct behavior. The major advantage of this schedule is its increased level of unpredictability, thus making the situation exciting for the individual. Gambling is an example of this type of scheduling.

Using Schedules in Organizations. It is somewhat difficult to use variable-reinforcement scheduling in industry, especially in the administration of standard pay plans. Because such plans involve large numbers of employees, management prefers to standardize them so that they can be administered easily. However, Richard Beatty and Craig Schneier (1972) have shown that it is possible to combine fixed- and variable-ratio schedules in training hard-core unemployed workers. At the beginning of the training, to increase the speed of correct behaviors, they used a fixed-ratio schedule, for example, rewarding every fifth time. However, once the worker understood the operations of the machine, Beatty and Schneier implemented a variable-ratio schedule that elicited and maintained higher rates of performance (see also Yukl, Wexley, and Seymour 1972).

Some large organizations such as the Black and Decker Corporation have begun to combine fixed-interval and variable-ratio schedules. At Black and Decker the executives receive regular salaries on a monthly basis (fixed-interval reinforcement). However, Black and Decker does not distribute executive bonuses on a yearly basis. Rather, an executive committee meets periodically and determines if a particular manager's performance has been outstanding in terms of some specified unit of measurement used by the committee. This represents variable-ratio scheduling. At Black and Decker it is possible for a manager to receive two bonuses in a six-month period and not receive another one for three years.

BMod Program and Techniques

In organizational settings a behavior modification program (BMod) involves four distinct stages (Hamner and Organ 1978). First, management must define the behavioral aspects of performance and complete a performance audit. Management must then develop and set specific goals, preferably with the participation of the subordinates. Management by objectives, discussed in Chapter 5, can be used in these first two steps of a BMod program (Luthans and White 1971). The third step is to allow the worker to keep a record of his or her own performance. Finally, once the correct behavior occurs, reinforcement should take place.

As this discussion implies, *feedback* is a specific technique that BMod employs. If the individual is performing poorly, he or she should be informed so that the individual can subsequently change his or her behavior. The individual should also be told what is required for obtaining rewards.

It is quite common to transmit feedback in the form of praise.

However, praise can be overused. Paul F. Hammond, manager of systems performance at Emery Air Freight, indicates that the excessive use of praise has dulled its effect in his company and has even made it an irritant (Hamner and Hamner 1976). In using reinforcers, management must ensure that the consequences are equal to the behavior. Rewarding an employee with $100 after he has invented a device leading to savings of millions of dollars will demotivate both him and others in the organization.

Behavior modeling is another common technique in a BMod program. General Electric has used this technique to train over a thousand supervisors (Sorcher and Goldstein 1972). The supervisor is shown a videotape of a model, that is, someone similar to him or her in terms of race, sex, age, and so forth. This model is performing the supervisory activities correctly. Then the supervisor's own activities are videotaped and shown to him or her. Through role playing and reinforcement, the supervisor is taught to make his or her behavior and activities consistent with those of the role model.

Shaping is also a recognized BMod technique. In Beatty and Schneier's work with hard-core unemployed workers, they initially shaped behavior through the use of fixed-ratio schedules and subsequently through the use of variable-ratio schedules. Similarly, it is possible to use the technique of *self-shaping.* For example, salespeople have been taught to meet specified behavioral objectives when interviewing clients, and they can then measure themselves against these objectives when the interview is completed (Morasky 1971).

Contingency contracting is a BMod technique that is popular in some elementary and secondary schools. The teacher and student jointly decide upon the objectives that the student is to attain and the rewards he or she is to receive when they are attained. Such rewards might include extra time off, a school trip, and higher-level work. If the objectives are not attained, the rewards are withheld. Thus the rewards are contingent upon the completion of the contract.

Extent. Craig Schneier (1976) has identified two major periods in the use of BMod programs. From 1969 until 1973 there was some interest in these programs in industry, but management basically focused on types of reinforcement schedules. Since 1973, there has been an explosion of interest in BMod programs, and various types of techniques such as shaping and role modeling have been used. Companies using BMod programs include Michigan Bell Telephone, Questor Corporation, Ford Motor Company, American Can, Upjohn, United Air Lines, Bethlehem Steel, Chase Manhattan Bank, IBM, IT&T, and Westinghouse.

In most instances these companies have reported that their BMod programs are very successful. For example, Emery Air Freight created a BMod program in 1969, and it credits this program with direct savings of over $3 million in the first three years and indirectly with pushing 1973 sales over the $160 million mark (Hamner and Hamner 1976).

Linkages. BMod is linked to many other programs and theories in the field of management. Like BMod, management by objectives emphasizes that goals should be specific and individuals rewarded if they attain them (see Chapter 5). Also, the contingency theory of management highlighted in this book is parallel to BMod: Different individuals require different rewards, and these should be contingent upon the performance of correct behaviors. More importantly, BMod and the expectancy theory of motivation are similar in that they both argue that an individual should be rewarded for his or her efforts and successful performance. BMod is also consistent with job enrichment, that is, granting an employee greater responsibility as soon as he demonstrates he can complete more difficult tasks.

It is quite clear that BMod is a part of organizational literature and practices (Schneier 1976). However, it is arguable that BMod will become a cohesive, empirically based theory of work behavior similar to expectancy theory. At this time it seems that BMod represents only a series of behavior change techniques. Still, BMod is consonant with the other major motivational approaches in the field of management—as illustrated by the fact that it can be incorporated within the expectancy theory of motivation—and it can be used to enhance them.

FACTORS AFFECTING JOB SATISFACTION

Satisfaction is the difference between the amount of some valued outcome a person receives and the amount of that outcome he feels he should receive (Porter, Lawler, and Hackman 1975). Job satisfaction is an important aspect of motivation. As the overall level of job satisfaction increases, absenteeism and turnover significantly decline (Schuh 1967). As expectancy theory suggests, productivity ordinarily is influenced positively by high job satisfaction—someone who finds his or her job rewarding is likely to work harder at it if he or she receives desired rewards. Moreover, job satisfaction affects the organization's productivity, as well as the individual's: It is usually the most competent employees who quit when they are dissatisfied, for it is relatively easy for them to obtain work elsewhere (Likert 1967). Consequently, it is important that managers understand the concept of job satisfaction and the information that major studies in this area have provided about it.

The Survey Research Center of the University of Michigan has been monitoring job satisfaction in the United States by means of a questionnaire that is completed by respondents drawn from a stratified national sample. As shown in Figure 13-4, there was a dramatic decrease in job satisfaction between 1969 and 1977. The Michigan re-

FIGURE 13–4
Decline in Job Satisfaction (1969 = 100)

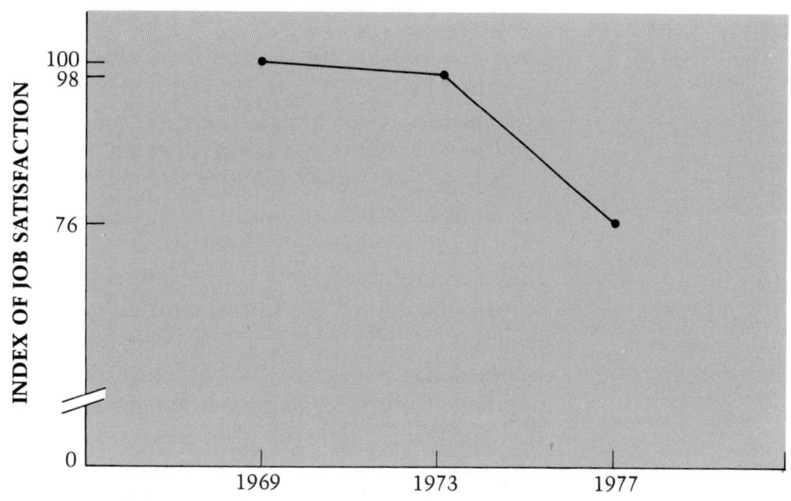

Source: Institute for Social Research Newsletter (University of Michigan) 7, no. 2 (Spring 1979): 10. Used by permission.

searchers used six scales to measure various facets of job satisfaction, and they discovered that significant decreases had taken place on five of the six scales during this period. The decrease was approximately equally distributed among five areas—working conditions or comfort, challenge of the work, financial rewards, adequacy of resources to complete the work, and the potential for promotions—but was absent for the sixth, relations with coworkers. Although we can only speculate, some possible reasons for this decline include a decline in the work ethic and a worsening of economic conditions, especially the recession of 1974.

Occupational and Organizational Level

Perhaps the most important influence on a person's job satisfaction is his or her occupational or organizational level (Locke 1976; Robinson, Athanasiou, and Head 1969). The higher someone's position in his or her field, and specifically in the organization he or she works for, the more satisfied he or she is likely to be. This finding is not surprising, for individuals in the upper organizational levels usually have more freedom and can exercise more responsibility than those in the lower echelons. Also, their pay is higher. However, although organizational level influences job satisfaction, the relationship can work the other way as well: If an individual is very satisfied with his or her work and enthusiastic about it, it is very probable that he or she will be promoted.

A factor related to occupational level is educational level. Much controversy surrounds the relationship between educational level and job satisfaction, for they do not seem to be associated in a linear or direct fashion. However, at least one national survey has indicated that job satisfaction is significantly higher among those who have obtained at least a college degree (Quinn et al. 1974). Since many organizations reserve their higher-echelon managerial jobs for such individuals, this finding seems logical.

In general most workers respond positively when asked: "All in all, how satisfied are you with your job?" Still, other surveys indicate that many workers are dissatisfied with their careers, if not their jobs; they respond negatively to the question: "If you could start over again, would you try to get into a similar type of work?" But workers who respond positively to that question include firm lawyers (85 percent), white-collar workers (43 percent), and unskilled auto workers (16 percent) (Robinson, Athanasiou, and Head 1969). In general the higher the occupational level, the greater is the career satisfaction. These findings again reinforce the fact that there are complex relationships among educational level, occupational level, job satisfaction, and career satisfaction. The higher an individual's educational level—provided that he or she has been trained in a field that is in high demand and suitable for his or her aptitudes and abilities—the greater is the probability of attaining a high occupational position and a high level of job and career satisfaction.

Design Factors

The design of an organization also appears to relate to job satisfaction (see Chapter 11). For instance, the larger the subunit or work group, the lower the satisfaction of those in it (Porter, Lawler, and Hackman 1975, p. 250). Apparently the members of a small subunit can satisfy their social needs, for they are able to interact comfortably both among themselves and with their superior. As the size of the subunit increases, individuals' relationships with their fellow employees seem to become more impersonal (Ingham 1970).

The type of technology an organization uses also influences the job satisfaction of its workers (see Chapter 11). Mass production technology provides the lowest degree of job satisfaction, for the work is narrow and routinized. But when an organization such as an oil refinery uses continuous process production, the employees exercise a great amount of responsibility and are very satisfied.

Another critical organizational design factor is the number of superiors to whom an individual must report. In organizations where the technology demands a mechanistic or rigid structure, job satisfaction is lowest among subordinates who report to more than one superior (Woodward 1965; Gannon and Paine 1974). But where the technology or the work requires an organic or flexible structure, individuals who are subordinate to two or more superiors appear to be more satisfied than those who report to only one. However, someone with multiple superiors may have to deal with conflicting assignments, which can tend to lessen his or her job satisfaction and may make the assignments too burdensome.

Finally, the location of the job appears to be related to job satisfaction. Researchers have compared the job satisfaction of individuals who work at a headquarters office and at regional offices (Paine, Carroll, and Leete 1966). Uniformly, the individuals who work in the field are more satisfied with their jobs, apparently because they have a wider range of responsibility than their counterparts at headquarters.

Labor Market

Another factor that relates to job satisfaction is the state of the labor market. In general, when unemployment is high, workers tend to focus on extrinsic aspects of the job, such as pay and security. When plenty of jobs are available, this focus changes, for individuals are guaranteed many of the extrinsic rewards and are free to concentrate on the intrinsic aspects of their jobs, such as recognition and a feeling of accomplishment (Strauss and Sayles 1972). These findings tend to support the concept of a two-step need hierarchy; individuals must satisfy their lower-order needs before they become concerned about their higher-order needs.

Orientation to Work

Frequently the orientation an individual brings to work affects his or her level of job satisfaction. John Goldthorpe and his associates (1968) analyzed the orientation to work of a sample of factory workers whose fathers had been professionals. Several of these workers had been employed in lower-echelon, white-collar jobs, but they wanted to make

NONECONOMIC MOTIVATION

The evidence concerning noneconomic incentives to work is not restricted to people's reports of their motivations. The existence of "dollar-a-year men" who work with only token economic rewards and entrepreneurs who continue to work after having amassed tremendous fortunes is well known. Furthermore, there is at least anecdotal evidence that people actually do return to work after inheriting large sums of money. [J. A. C.] Brown (1954) mentioned three workers in London factories who won large sums of money from football pools which, if suitably invested, would provide enough income to enable the men to live comfortably for the rest of their lives. In each of the cases, after a short period of leisure, the men returned to work.

Source: Victor Vroom, *Work and Motivation* (New York: Wiley, 1964), pp. 31–32.

more money, so they became factory workers. However, they did not identify with the other workers and generally disliked them. Nor did they socialize with the other workers, either on or off the job. Thus even before coming to work, these workers had developed an orientation that made them dissatisfied with their jobs, which were a far cry from the professional occupations of their fathers.

Psychological Characteristics

We have already seen that psychological characteristics heavily influence the manner in which individuals communicate with one another (Chapter 12). Psychological characteristics are also related to job satisfaction. In particular, one characteristic, the internal-external orientation, seems to be critical. Basically, an *internal orientation* indicates that the individual believes he or she is master of his or her own destiny. An *external orientation* is the exact opposite and suggests that the individual feels that factors outside his or her control critically influence his or her life and activities.

Paul Andrisani and Gilbert Nestel (1976) focused on job satisfaction of 2972 individuals in a national sample and found that internally oriented individuals tend to be more highly satisfied in their work than do externally oriented individuals. In addition, the internals were in the higher-status group of better-paying occupations. Thus this orientation seems to be important not only for job satisfaction but for success (see also Anderson 1977).

SUMMARY

Motivational theory attempts to explain the causes that propel an individual to behave in a particular fashion. Although there is some overlapping, we can categorize motivational theories into three main types: process theories, which attempt to explain the process or manner in which an individual is motivated; content theories, which specify the factors motivating the individual, such as pay and interesting work; and conditioning theories, which stress the relationship between the stimuli applied to the individual and the responses he or she makes to them.

The expectancy theory of motivation is a broad process approach that can incorporate the other major theories. Its main ideas are that an individual must see that his or her efforts result in successful performance and that successful performance results in desired rewards.

Locke's goal-setting theory argues that individuals are motivated to achieve high but attainable goals. Cognitive dissonance theory postulates that the individual seeks to eliminate the conflict between two opposing concepts by changing or discarding one of them. Adams's equity theory holds that an individual is motivated to change his situation if he believes he has been treated unfairly when compared with a peer in the same job. All these theories are basically process theories.

Content theories include Maslow's need hierarchy theory, which assumes that there is at least a two-step hierarchy of needs; an individual must satisfy basic survival needs before he or she can be motivated to higher-level needs. Herzberg's two-factor theory posits two independent dimensions, the extrinsic (hygiene) factors and the intrinsic factors. McClelland's need theory argues that entrepreneurs and other individuals seeking immediate feedback of results are motivated by achievement needs, and successful managers are motivated by power needs.

There are two major types of stimulus-response theories. In classical conditioning the sequence of events leading to a response is independent of the subject's behavior or response. In operant or voluntary conditioning, consequences (rewards or punishments) immediately follow and determine behavior. While classical conditioning uses continuous schedules of reinforcement, operant conditioning emphasizes partial reinforcement.

Behavior modification is the application of operant conditioning in organizational settings. It involves four steps: analyzing the behavioral aspects of performance, developing and setting specific goals, allowing the worker to keep a record of his or her own performance, and reinforcing correct behavior. Both correct behavior leading to success and the actual results should be reinforced. Specific types of BMod techniques include feedback, behavior modeling, shaping, self-shaping, and contingency contracting. Behavior modification is consonant with other major approaches in the field of management, such as the expectancy and goal-setting theories of motivation, MBO, job enrichment, and contingency management.

Job satisfaction is an important aspect of motivation. It is the difference between what an individual wants to obtain from a job and what he or she actually obtains. There are many factors affecting job satisfaction, including the person's occupational or organizational level, the design of the organization, the person's orientation to work, the state of the labor market, and psychological characteristics, especially the belief (or lack of it) that the individual can control his or her own destiny.

DISCUSSION QUESTIONS

1. Are factors such as the design of the organization and work schedules more important in explaining job satisfaction than the types of workers (such as racial minorities)? Why or why not?
2. What is the definition of motivation? Is it possible for managers to disregard motivation completely and still accomplish organizational objectives? Why or why not?
3. What is job satisfaction? How is job satisfaction related to motivation? Why is job satisfaction important for an organization?

4. John Northrup was recently fired from his job. According to the theory of cognitive dissonance, how does he probably feel about his performance in this job? How does he probably feel about the organization? Will these feelings change after he obtains another job?
5. Do you feel employees should be punished in organizational settings? Why or why not? What would the different theories of learning hold about the use of punishment for motivating and training employees?
6. Design a pay program for tellers in a bank that uses all four types of partial reinforcement: fixed interval, variable interval, fixed ratio, and variable ratio.

CRITICAL INCIDENTS

NOTE: These critical incidents can be used by the whole class with the case observational method (see Appendix A) or used for thought and discussion by individual class members.

1. John Bannard is a highly skilled machinist working in a large company in which there is a strong national union. John has been with the company twenty-five years and will retire in another five years. For many years his work had been outstanding, and management presented him with several awards during this time.

However, John's work has deteriorated dramatically in the past two years, and he has become apathetic. He is still meeting minimal standards of performance, so his boss, Thomas Ruddy, cannot discipline or fire him, especially since the union would grieve on John's behalf. Ruddy, of course, is dismayed at the situation. Also, Ruddy has heard through the grapevine that John is openly indicating he will produce only a minimal amount of work and that he is just waiting for his retirement in five years.

QUESTIONS: What should Ruddy do to motivate Bannard? How should he approach Bannard, and what should he say to him? What theory of motivation that we have discussed seems applicable to Bannard's situation?

2. You are the president of a small chemical company. The manager of one of your divisions has recently quit, and you want to replace him with someone with good technical knowledge as well as familiarity with the division. Three employees are possible candidates for the job. Bill Gruziak, a salesman, has been with the company for four years, but his chemistry is rusty. Herman Schultz, one of your best chemists, seems too research-oriented to make a good supervisor. Linda Kelly, the former manager's assistant, is the best qualified for

the job; however, she is young and recently married, and you wonder how likely she is to stick with her career rather than start a family. State law forbids discrimination on the basis of sex, so you must avoid asking Kelly questions such as whether she plans to have children soon. If she doesn't get the job, she could sue.

QUESTIONS: How would you evaluate Kelly's commitment to her work? What other problems would you anticipate if you hire Kelly? How would you handle them? Which candidate would you hire?

SUGGESTED READINGS

Schein, Edgar. *Organizational Psychology.* 3rd ed. Englewood Cliffs, N.J.: Prentice-Hall, 1980, 274 pages, hardback.

Schein's book is a perennial favorite with students, especially if they are unfamiliar with the behavioral aspects of management.

Zimbardo, Philip; Ebbesen, Ebbe; and Maslach, Christina. *Influencing Attitudes and Changing Behavior.* 2nd ed. Reading, Mass.: Addison-Wesley, 1977, paperback, 271 pages.

This book is a lively and well-written introduction to methods, theory, and applications of social control and personal power. It serves as an effective adjunct to an introductory treatment of motivational theory.

14 Leadership

A PROFILE OF MANAGERIAL LEADERSHIP
THEORIES OF LEADERSHIP
CONTINGENCY FACTORS INFLUENCING LEADERSHIP
SUBORDINATE PARTICIPATION IN DECISION MAKING
SUMMARY
DISCUSSION QUESTIONS
CRITICAL INCIDENT
SUGGESTED READINGS

PERFORMANCE OBJECTIVES

1. To discuss the difference between leadership and managerial leadership.
2. To identify the elements of and differences between task-oriented and considerate leadership.
3. To discuss the types of power a leader can use.
4. To present the major theories of leadership and the relationships among them.
5. To discuss the major contingency factors influencing the relationship between leadership style and leader effectiveness.
6. To discuss the relationship between leadership and subordinate participation in decision making.

Without effective management it is difficult for an organization to function. One important role that a manager fulfills in an organization is *leadership:* directing the activities of subordinates. More specifically, managerial leadership encompasses several additional roles, such as developing the organization's planning and control systems, designing an organizational structure appropriate for the tasks undertaken, and acting as a spokesperson for the organization (Mintzberg 1973). Thus effective managerial leadership is a critical factor in the life and success of an organization—and according to Chester Barnard (1938), it is *the* critical factor.

To understand the activities of managers, it is helpful to create a profile of managerial leadership. By means of this profile one can pinpoint the essential differences between managers and nonmanagers. Thus the first part of this chapter develops a profile of managerial leadership. The second part of the chapter focuses specifically on one critical aspect of managerial leadership: directing the activities of subordinates. In this second part a review of the major theories of leadership is presented, with an emphasis on the relationships among them. Then the contingency factors that influence the relationship between leadership style and leader effectiveness are discussed. Finally, the relationship between leadership and subordinate participation in decision making is considered.

A PROFILE OF MANAGERIAL LEADERSHIP

Obviously, many factors are involved in successful managerial leadership. Some factors are difficult to measure; some are even hard to identify. In developing a profile of managerial leadership, we must remember that simply being in a managerial position does not make a person an effective manager. We must consider questions such as these: What assumptions does the manager make about the behavior of subordinates? What is the relationship between these assumptions and the types of power a manager may use to motivate subordinates? Our profile of managerial leadership is based on the idea that a manager does not have a single role but several important roles.

Nature of Leadership

Until approximately 1930 there was not much interest in the idea of leadership, or directing the activities of subordinates, probably because it was not really considered an important and distinctive area of study. A manager was automatically thought to be a leader. The manager did not need any formal training in the area of leadership, for it was assumed that subordinates automatically followed his or her orders. For theorists such as Max Weber, a leader possessed power by virtue of his or her position, and power is the ability to give commands that must be accepted (Weber 1947).

Gradually the importance of leadership was recognized, at least in part because subordinates frequently disobeyed the commands of superiors. In 1938 Chester Barnard proposed a new definition of *leadership:* the ability of a superior to influence the behavior of subordinates and persuade them to follow a particular course of action. In the modern world some subordinates openly defy their leaders or comply halfheartedly with any orders given to them. Thus managers today must view leadership not as a right of office but rather as a skill that can and must be learned in order to motivate subordinates to be productive. However, there are different types of power a leader can employ as he or she attempts to influence subordinates.

Types of Power

According to John R. P. French and Bertram Raven (1959), there are five types of power a superior can use to persuade his or her subordinates to follow a particular course of action. When subordinates obey a superior solely because of his or her position in the organization, the superior is exercising *legitimate power.* Or a superior may influence behavior by *reward power,* persuading subordinates by means such as promotions, salary increases, and interesting assignments. Sometimes subordinates follow the dictates of a leader because of his or her superior knowledge of the matter under discussion. For instance, engineers tend to obey a superior if he or she is more technically capable than they are. This is *expert power.* Further, subordinates occasionally will obey a superior simply because they identify with and like and respect him or her. This is *referent power.* Finally, the leader can force subordinates to follow the course of action outlined for them. If they do not comply, the superior can punish them. In this case the leader is exercising *coercive power.*

Of course, a leader can employ several types of power simultaneously. Engineers may follow the commands of their superior because he or she is technically more capable and because he or she rewards them for outstanding work. Hence both expert power and reward power come into play.

Managerial Roles

The role of the manager is really not a single role at all. Managers perform many functions and play diverse roles in an organization. Several writers have attempted to classify these roles. One of the best-known classifications has been proposed by Henry Mintzberg, who argues that the manager performs three essential types of roles in an organization: interpersonal, informational, and decisional. He then subdivides these three major types of roles into ten distinct roles (see Figure 14–1).

Interpersonal Roles. Interpersonal roles refer to the relationship between the manager and others, both within and outside the organiza-

FIGURE 14–1
Ten Managerial Roles

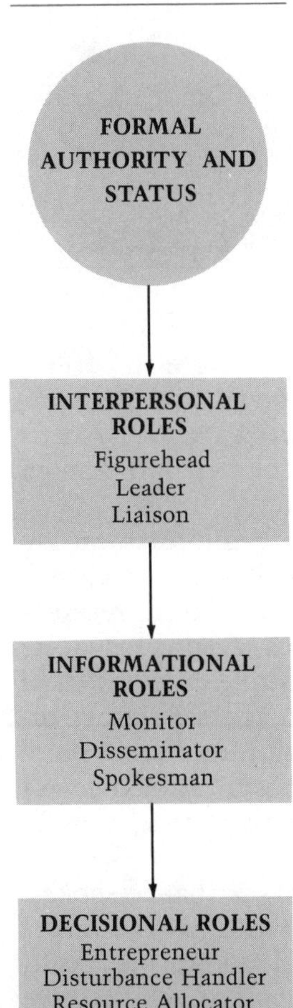

Source: From Henry Mintzberg, *The Nature of Managerial Work* (Englewood Cliffs, N.J.: Prentice-Hall, 1980); Figure 8, "The Manager's Roles," p. 59. Used by permission.

tion. Within this constellation the manager plays three distinct roles: figurehead, leader, and liaison.

In the *figurehead role* the manager acts as a symbol of the organization. Because of the manager's formal position, he or she must undertake activities designed to promote the interests of the organization. Thus he or she attends formal dinners as a representative of the organization, gives speeches that espouse the organization's position on various issues, and makes public pronouncements if the organization is attacked in the newspaper or on television. As the manager's status and position in the organization rise, he or she spends more time in activities that cast him or her as a figurehead.

However, the manager must also energize the organization and motivate subordinates so they will help accomplish the overall objectives of the enterprise. In this sense the manager undertakes a *leader role* in the organization. As a leader, the manager's direct relationship with subordinates is his or her main focus, for he or she must influence subordinates and persuade them to follow commands. It is vital that managers at all levels in the organization perform the leader role effectively. Researchers have studied this role much more than any of the others, probably because it is essential for the success of the organization and it affects the performance of every employee.

The manager also plays a *liaison role* in the organization. That is, he or she develops horizontal relationships with peers or equals in other parts of the organization or outside of it in order to accomplish his or her objectives. This web of relationships is important for the manager's work, since he or she frequently needs information, resources, and other kinds of help that can only be obtained from peers. At the top levels in the organization the managers typically act as liaison with peers who work in both their own and other organizations. At lower organizational levels managers spend more time with peers in other parts of their own enterprise.

Informational Roles. The manager is also the focal point of information in an organization. To complete tasks effectively, the manager must transmit and receive information. In this area he or she plays three distinct roles: monitor, disseminator, and spokesperson.

As *monitor,* the manager is constantly trying to obtain information that enables him or her to comprehend what is taking place in the organization and outside it. For this purpose the manager reads reports, attends meetings, and scans business publications. More importantly, however, he or she seeks current information by talking to peers and subordinates who have a basic understanding of new developments that might affect the organization. At the top levels in the organization managers focus on internal factors that affect the organization's effectiveness. They also scan the external environment

to pinpoint factors outside the organization that may have an adverse influence, such as new governmental regulations and new products created by competitors. At lower organizational levels managers focus on the internal factors that may inhibit the productivity of their own subunits.

The manager also serves as a *disseminator* of information. Because of the key position he or she occupies, the manager can transmit information that will be of help to associates and, in turn, receives information that will aid in completing activities. Again, managers at various levels of the organization perform this role differently. At the top levels managers share information with peers in other organizations that will be of mutual benefit and perform a similar function within their own organization. At lower organizational levels managers emphasize the sharing of information with peers who are in their own enterprise.

The third informational role the manager plays is that of *spokesperson.* Top managers typically transmit information to the media and other individuals outside the organization about the goals, policies, and plans of the enterprise. Top managers generally reserve this role for themselves, since their figurehead role makes them the logical vehicle for transmitting information to the public.

Decisional Roles. The manager also plays four decisional roles in an organization. The first is that of the *entrepreneur.* By this Mintzberg means that the manager must initiate change by searching the organization and its external environment for new products, programs, and opportunities that will ensure the continued success of the enterprise. Naturally top managers perform this role. However, many other managers throughout the organization also focus on entrepreneurial activity. Production managers attempt to develop methods to decrease costs; research and development managers seek to develop new processes and products; marketing managers try to create new ways of attracting customers; and so on.

The manager also serves as a *disturbance handler* in the organization. If two organizational subunits whose activities overlap cannot work together smoothly, managers must correct the situation. In addition, managers must react to any externally generated disturbance. For instance, if the organization cannot produce its final good or service because a supplier curtails shipment of raw materials, the managers must alleviate this situation. Managers at all levels of the organization function as disturbance handlers.

The manager also serves as a *resource allocator* who apportions organizational resources of all types to various individuals and groups. In this role the manager frequently confronts difficulties and hostilities, since resources are usually limited and scarce. But even if the organization is affluent, managers inevitably must decide to give some individuals and groups more resources than others. Top managers usually make policy and long-range decisions in this area (for example, the decision to close a particular plant). However, the upper middle managers are frequently charged with short-range and operational activities in this area, for they allocate scarce resources to the divisions of the organization.

Finally, the manager acts as a *negotiator.* In this capacity he or she

THE IMPORTANCE OF LEADERSHIP

Human beings are our most precious part of civilization. What responsibility could be more important than the leadership and development of people? Without leadership, an organization is but a muddle of men and machines. Leadership is the ability to persuade others to seek defined objectives enthusiastically. It is the human factor which binds a group together and motivates it toward goals. Management activities such as planning, organizing, and decision making are dormant cocoons until the leader triggers the power of motivation in people and guides them toward their goals. The leader's act of motivation is similar in its effect to the secret chemical which turns the insect pupa into the resplendent butterfly with all the beauty that was the pupa's potential. *Leadership transforms potential into reality.* It is the ultimate act which brings to success all of the potent potential that is in an organization and its people.

Leadership is so important to group accomplishment that mankind has been concerned about it since the beginning of recorded history.

Source: Keith Davis, *Human Relations at Work: The Dynamics of Organizational Behavior,* 3rd ed. (New York: McGraw-Hill, 1967), p. 96. Used with permission of McGraw-Hill Book Company.

represents the organization at major negotiations. For example, the vice-president of industrial relations puts forth management's position during contract negotiations with the union. Or a top manager may represent the organization if a public interest group pickets it to obtain a major innovation such as the hiring of a significant number of racial minorities and women. Usually top managers perform the role of negotiator, since they have the power to commit the organization to a particular course of action.

THEORIES OF LEADERSHIP

As suggested by the profile of managerial leadership, managers influence organizational activities in a number of ways, such as motivating subordinates, allocating scarce resources, and serving as a vehicle of communication. Over the years researchers have primarily emphasized one aspect of the manager's role in their theories – the influence of leadership on the activities of subordinates. Quite a few research studies have been completed in this area, many of which have had contradictory results. In this section the significant theories of leadership are explored for the purposes of reconciling the contradictory research findings and pointing out the critical factors of leadership with which a manager should be familiar.

Trait Theory

For many years researchers focused attention on the traits that make leaders successful. This research is usually classified as the "Great Man" theory of leadership, because it assumes the leader is quite different from the average person in terms of personality traits such as intelligence, perseverance, and ambition. Unfortunately, research in this area tended to be obscure and contradictory. For example, several writers developed lists of leadership traits, but the lists were quite different from each other.

One problem in these studies was that researchers did not have any way in which to measure traits accurately. Recently, however, Edwin Ghiselli (1971) developed a short self-description inventory that has succeeded in measuring the traits of individuals. Comparing successful and unsuccessful managers, Ghiselli found that the most important trait for successful managers is supervisory ability, followed closely by the desire for occupational achievement. Other important traits are intelligence, self-actualization (the desire to reach one's potential), self-assurance, and decisiveness.

A more lasting problem with the research in this area is that trait theorists have not considered the situation or environment in which leadership takes place. Specific traits may be predictive of successful leadership in one type of organization but not in others (Fiedler 1967). For example, an autocratic individual may be successful as a director of a prison but not a welfare agency.

Still, the work of Ghiselli over the past twenty-five years does suggest that certain traits are critical to a manager's success as a leader. And in an overall profile of managerial success, one dimension must be the personality traits of the individual (Campbell et al. 1970). Thus trait theory is relevant in our study of managerial leadership, and it will probably become even more important as researchers identify the traits related to success within specific organizational settings.

Leader Behavior Theory

In 1941 the United States entered World War II. This country was not well prepared for this war and had great difficulty transforming its civilian economy into a war economy. In addition, the United States did not have many experienced leaders who could direct this transformation at home or lead the military into battle abroad. The problem was especially pronounced in the battlefield, for the American military was unfamiliar with modern warfare and the kinds of leaders it required. At least partially because of these problems, interest in the study of leadership increased immediately after the war was over. Two important and long-term independent studies, undertaken at the University of Michigan and Ohio State University, came up with findings that were highly similar (Likert 1961 and 1967; Stogdill and Coons 1957). Because the Ohio State studies were more intensive and more exhaustive than the Michigan studies, they have been selected for discussion here.

In the Ohio State studies, managers completed a questionnaire focused on the *behavior of leaders.* It contained lists of statements developed to cover all aspects of each job under investigation. One questionnaire item might be "He is capable of performing all the jobs of his subordinates." Initially the researchers worked with a questionnaire of 1800 items; the questionnaire was eventually reduced to 150 items and administered to managers in a variety of positions.

According to the Ohio State studies, leader behavior has two major dimensions: the initiation of structure, or task orientation, and consideration. *Task orientation* concerns the degree to which the leader gives structure to his or her subordinates' work by assigning them definite tasks, specifying the procedures they are to follow, clarifying his or her expectations of them, and scheduling their work. *Consideration* refers to whether the leader constructs a supportive environment for his or her subordinates by being friendly and approachable, showing concern about the personal welfare of the group and its members, and providing advance notice of any changes that are going to take place. Statistically, task orientation and consideration are independent of each other. However, an individual can be task-oriented and considerate simultaneously.

The early research on these two dimensions indicated that as a leader's consideration increased, employee turnover and absenteeism declined, and as task orientation increased, employee performance rose. These findings are intuitively logical, in view of the theories of motivation described in Chapter 13. However, some contradictory results began to emerge in later research. In some instances an increase in consideration was accompanied by an increase in turnover and absenteeism. In others, as task orientation increased, employee performance declined (see Weissenberg and Kavanagh 1972). Much of modern leadership research has focused on these contradictory findings about the two major dimensions of leader behavior. In fact, all the theories in this chapter except trait theory can be logically related to one another in terms of the concepts of task orientation and consideration.

Managerial Grid

In line with the Ohio State studies, Robert Blake and Jane Mouton (1964, 1969) developed a distinctive approach to the study of leadership: the *managerial Grid®*. They began their analysis by focusing on the two basic aspects of leader behavior: concern for production (task orientation) and concern for people (consideration). Each of these dimensions was measured on a scale that ranges from one (low) to 9 (high). Thus, for instance, the 1,1 leader is neither task-oriented nor considerate; the 1,9 leader is very considerate but not task-oriented; the 9,1 leader is highly task-oriented but not considerate; the 5,5 leader is somewhat task-oriented and somewhat considerate; and the 9,9 leader is both very task-oriented and very considerate (see Figure 14–2).

According to Blake and Mouton, the 1.1 leader avoids making decisions, is neutral when conflict occurs, creates an apathetic organizational climate, provides little motivation for subordinates, and rarely offers feedback on performance. The results are that creativity is stifled and subordinates want only to survive as best they can. The 9,9 leader operates in exactly the opposite fashion. The leader bases his or her decisions on a consensus among members of the group, confronts and resolves conflict and problems associated with it, creates an organizational climate based on trust and acceptance, motivates subordinates by means of job content factors rather than hygiene factors, and provides subordinates with ratings and criticisms that are specific, spontaneous, and candid. The results are that the subordinates share in the creative approaches to problems and integrate their work and goals with those of the leader and the organization.

Blake and Mouton describe the remaining three styles in terms of the same categories. For example, the 1,9 leader tends to abdicate his or her role as a decision maker, to smooth over difficulties and problems between individuals and subordinates, to create a pleasant organizational climate, to motivate subordinates primarily by means

FIGURE 14–2
The Managerial Grid

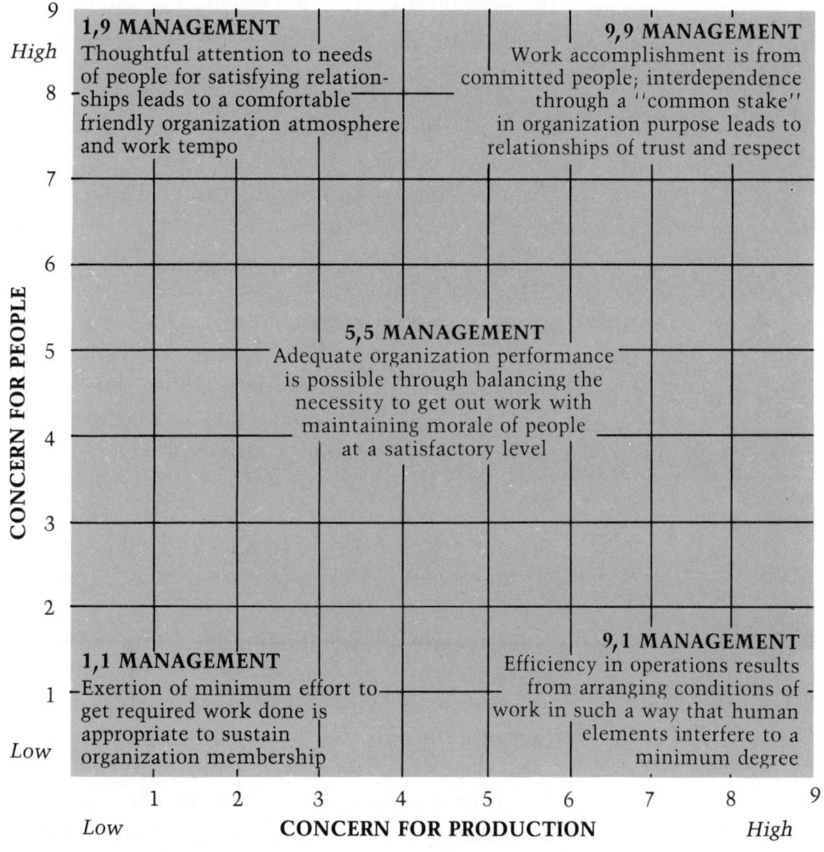

Source: From R. R. Blake and J. S. Mouton, *The New Managerial Grid,* p. 11. Copyright © 1978 by Gulf Publishing Company, Houston. Reprinted by permission.

of hygiene factors, and to provide praise as a substitute for a genuine rating of performance. Under these circumstances the employee's commitment to the organization is limited mainly to social activities, such as attending formal functions. The 9,1 leader railroads decisions, suppresses conflict, creates a win-lose organizational climate, relies on threats for motivating subordinates, and provides only negative feedback to the employees about their performance. The results are that the subordinates become antiorganizational and attempt to beat the system as often as possible. Finally, the 5,5 leader relies on traditional voting to make decisions, has difficulty making up his or her mind about whether conflict is acceptable, creates a manipulative organizational climate, uses a carrot and stick approach to motivating subordinates, and provides superficial feedback on performance. Under this leadership the subordinates' creativity is limited to providing ideas through the suggestion box and focused on maintaining the status quo.

Although there are exceptions, managers generally feel that the 9,9 leadership style is ideal. Thus in most organizations the major objective is to close the gap between the actual leadership style and the ideal leadership style through the use of the managerial Grid.

Leader Effectiveness: Fiedler

After the Ohio State studies were completed, researchers began to move beyond the concept of leader behavior to that of *leader effectiveness.* One of the major theories of leader effectiveness was developed by Fred Fiedler (1967), who added the organizational environment or situational favorableness as a key element in judging successful leadership. For his studies Fiedler asked a leader to answer a questionnaire in which he or she described the "least preferred" co-worker or subordinate in terms of a series of bipolar adjectives. From these data Fiedler developed the least preferred co-worker scale, which measures the degree of leniency with which the leader evaluates his or her most ineffective subordinate or co-worker. Originally Fiedler believed he was measuring the personality traits of the leader. However, his recent work suggests he was essentially measuring task orientation and consideration. A leader who describes his or her least preferred co-worker favorably tends to be considerate and employee-centered. A leader who describes his or her least preferred co-worker unfavorably tends to be task-oriented. Because Fiedler employed only one scale in his research, a leader could score high on either task orientation or consideration, but not both.

Fiedler then extended his analysis by focusing on three key situational factors:

1. *Leader-member relations:* the degree to which the employees accept the leader.
2. *Task structure:* the degree to which the subordinates' jobs are described in detail.
3. *Position power:* the amount of formal authority the leader possesses by virtue of his or her position in the organization.

Fiedler investigated eight possible combinations of these situations in terms of whether task orientation or consideration was a more appropriate leadership style. Task-oriented leadership was successful in five situations and consideration in three, as shown in Figure 14–3.

According to Fiedler, a task-oriented style of leadership is more effective than a considerate style under extreme situations; that is, when the situation is either very favorable (certain) or very unfavorable (uncertain). Thus task-oriented leadership would be advisable in a natural disaster, such as a flood or fire. In such a very uncertain situation the leader-member relations are moderately poor, the task is unstructured, and the position power of the leader is weak, for very few individuals know what to do and no one is typically appointed in any official way to be the leader. The individual who emerges as leader to direct the group's activity frequently does not know any of his or her subordinates intimately. Under such conditions the task-oriented leader who gets things accomplished proves to be most successful. If the leader is considerate, he or she may waste so much time that the disaster could get further out of control and lives might be lost.

A similar kind of leadership is required under very certain or favorable situations. For instance, blue-collar workers generally want to know exactly what they are supposed to do. Hence their task is usually highly structured. Moreover, the leader's position power is strong if management backs his or her decisions. Finally, even though the leader may not be considerate, since he or she cannot waste a lot of time, leader-member relations may be extremely strong if he or she

FIGURE 14–3
Fiedler's Contingency Theory of Leadership

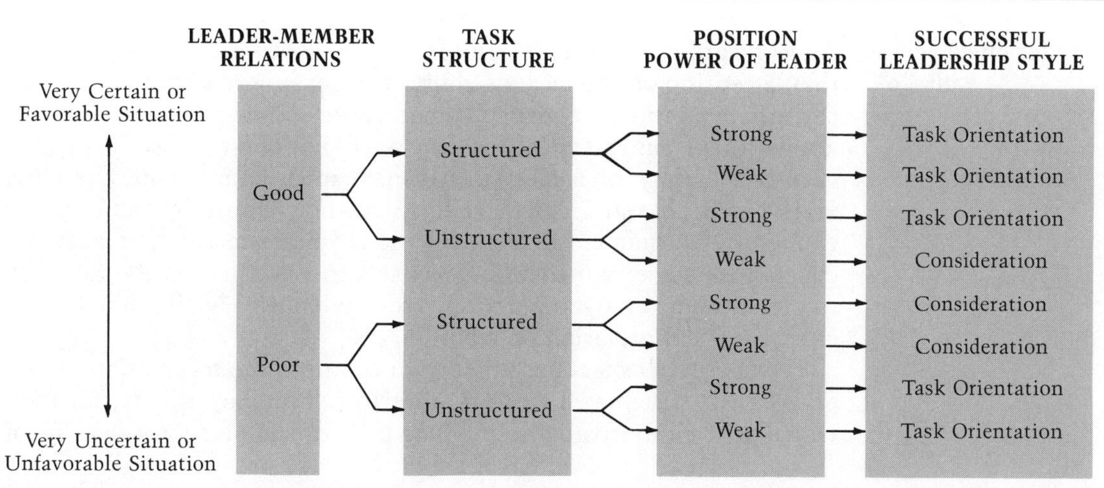

Source: Based on Fred Fiedler, *A Theory of Leadership Effectiveness* (New York: McGraw-Hill, 1967); and Fred Fiedler, "Validation and Extension of the Contingency Model of Leadership Effectiveness: A Review of Empirical Findings," *Psychological Bulletin* 76 (1971): 128–148.

is able to gain promotions and salary increases for subordinates. Under such conditions the task-oriented style of leadership is preferable to a considerate style.

The considerate style of leadership seems to be appropriate when the environment or situation is moderately favorable or certain, for example, when (1) leader-member relations are good, (2) the task is unstructured, and (3) position power is weak. For instance, research scientists do not like a strong superior who structures the task for them, for they must follow their own creative leads in order to solve their problems. Under such conditions a considerate style of leadership is preferable to a task-oriented style, for the leader's success depends partly on his or her good relations with subordinates.

In short, the task-oriented style is appropriate for very certain and very uncertain situations, whereas the considerate style is appropriate for moderately certain situations. Since the style of leadership that is effective is contingent upon the degree of situational favorableness, Fiedler's approach has been called the *contingency theory* of leadership.

There has been criticism of Fiedler's work because some researchers who have attempted to verify his conclusions in different organizational settings have been unable to do so (see, for example, Vecchio 1977). In addition, it can be argued that a leader can be considerate and task-oriented simultaneously. Despite these criticisms, though, Fiedler's approach has been instructive and important, since he introduced the situational or organizational environment into the study of leadership.

Leader Effectiveness: Path Goal

A second group of researchers interested in leader effectiveness focused their attention on the leader's ability to help subordinates identify the paths to attaining personal and organizational goals. Perhaps the best-known theory in this area was developed by Robert House (1971). His *path-goal theory* of leader effectiveness incorporates both the Ohio State approach and Fiedler's theory. Further, House introduced new elements that help clarify some of the problems researchers have uncovered in those two theories. House's theory changes the focus on the research by analyzing not only the style of leadership but also its effect on the motivation of subordinates.[1]

House uses expectancy theory to examine the motivation of employees (see Chapter 13). According to expectancy theory, an individual will be motivated to produce if he or she perceives that his or

[1] For other important articles and studies of the path-goal theory, see House and Mitchell (1974); Stinson and Johnson (1974); Schuler (1974); Schriesheim and von Glinow (1977); Dessler (1973); Downey, Sheridan, and Slocum (1975); and Schriesheim and Schriesheim (1980).

her efforts will result in successful performance, which, in turn, will lead to desired rewards.

House argues that the task-oriented and considerate styles of leadership are critical only if they help increase the subordinate's perception that his or her efforts will bring about successful performance, for which he or she will receive desired and equitable rewards. In other words, the style of leadership is important only when it can influence the motivational level of the subordinates. In House's opinion there are many situations in which the style of leadership cannot affect the motivation of subordinates.

Like Fiedler, House next concentrates on the situation or organizational environment. Previous research strongly suggests that individuals do not like to work in a situation where there is a high degree of job ambiguity, that is, where they do not know what they are supposed to do (Kahn et al. 1964). (The one major exception to this generalization occurs with professionals, who typically prefer to define their work for themselves. Thus they prefer a high degree of job ambiguity.) House concludes that a task-oriented style of leadership will be effective in an organizational environment where job ambiguity is high, since employees are seeking direction. (Again, this generalization does not apply to professionals.) In general, task-oriented leadership, by reducing job ambiguity, increases employees' perceptions that they can be successful and will be rewarded for their efforts, for they now know what they must do.

House also treats job satisfaction as a critical part of the organizational environment. If employees are unhappy, the leader may be able to change their expectancies by being considerate. In particular, a considerate leader who is patient with subordinates can encourage them to believe they are capable of performing successfully and can point out instances where successful performance has resulted in desired rewards. Hence the expectations of employees change and job satisfaction in the work force (group morale) increases.

House also argues that a particular style of leadership may have some indirect consequences. Because a considerate style of leadership may increase job satisfaction and group morale in the short run, employee performance in the long run will probably rise. For example, it is usually the most capable individuals who quit when dissatisfied; and if they do not quit, their performance will suffer.

House shows that a leader can combine task orientation and consideration. Such a combination can improve employee performance and group morale simultaneously. For Fiedler this combination does not occur, for a leader who scores high on the least preferred coworker scale is, by definition, task-oriented; if the leader receives a low score, he or she is considerate.

While House's theory will undoubtedly be refined as evidence is accumulated, he has constructed an approach that is extremely valuable for both the theory and the practice of management. To summarize, some important implications of House's theory follow:

1. A style of leadership cannot be evaluated without taking the motivation of subordinates into consideration. In this sense House has combined leadership theory and motivation theory.

2. The effectiveness of a particular leadership style is related to its impact on two situational factors, job ambiguity and job satisfaction.

3. In many situations the leader cannot significantly influence the level of employee performance or group morale. For example, the leader cannot influence performance among clerical workers if there is already a low degree of job ambiguity.

4. The leader can simultaneously influence group morale and employee performance; that is, he or she can be both considerate and task-oriented.

Reciprocal Causation Theory

A major theory of leadership, the *reciprocal causation theory,* focuses on the activities in a work group; this theory was developed by David Bowers and Stanley Seashore (1966). They expand on the concept of consideration by subdividing it into *support,* which reflects leader behavior that enhances the subordinates' belief of personal worth, and *interaction facilitation,* which encourages subordinates to develop close relationships with one another. They also subdivide task orientation into *goal emphasis,* which stimulates enthusiasm for attaining objectives and achieving a high level of performance, and *work facilitation,* which clarifies subordinates' duties and coordinates activities.

Bowers and Seashore argue that these four factors must be present in a work group if it is to be effective. However, they show that the presence of these factors reflects reciprocal causation: The leader can create an atmosphere in which these four factors are present, and so can the subordinates. In fact, there are some situations in which leadership may be superfluous, since the work group is so cohesive that these factors are either present or completely absent.

Bowers and Seashore tested their theory in forty agencies of a leading insurance company. Their research indicates that support by the leader is related to employees' satisfaction with both the job and the leader. In addition, interaction facilitation is positively related to employees' satisfaction with the firm and fellow employees and to a high level of performance in terms of cost savings and good interpersonal relations. Goal emphasis is associated with a large volume of business, and strong managerial work facilitation seems to lead to high levels of performance that subsequently are associated with favorable interpersonal relations.

Similar to the path-goal theory, this approach suggests that there are situations in which the leader can really do nothing to influence behavior. In addition, it provides a distinctive focus, that of the work group, to leadership studies and expands on the aspects of leader consideration and task orientation.

Vertical Dyadic Theory

Thus far all the theories of leadership we have examined can be logically related to one another in terms of the two major aspects of leader behavior, task orientation and consideration. However, there are alternative approaches, the most promising of which is the theory developed by George Graen and his associates (see Liden and Graen 1980; Graen and Cashman 1975; Dansereau, Graen, and Haga 1975).

These researchers question two of the basic assumptions used by other theorists. First, other researchers assume that subordinates as a group are relatively homogeneous in terms of perceptions, interpretations, and their reactions to orders issued by the leader. Second, other researchers generally assume that the superior behaves in essentially the same manner toward all members of his or her work group. But Graen and his associates believe that there are significant differences among subordinates and that the superior interacts with them in various ways. Thus Graen's research focuses on a *dyad,* that is, the relationship between a superior and *each* subordinate considered independently. Hence this approach is called the *vertical dyadic theory* of leadership.

Graen's research involves the study of new vertical dyadic relationships that occur in a new organization or in an established group after a reorganization. His research indicates that the superior identifies a cadre of in-group members whom he or she trusts. The types of role relationships that the leader negotiates with the cadre can be described in terms of pure leadership or Barnard's concept of leadership: The leader attempts to influence and persuade subordinates without excessive reliance on legitimate authority. This cadre is small and consists only of trusted lieutenants. The leader also identifies a larger number of hired hands who become members of the out-group. Over time the leader negotiates role relationships with these subordinates that are based purely on Max Weber's concept of power or legitimate authority: The leader gives commands that must be accepted by subordinates purely because of the legitimate authority vested in the superior's office.

As you can see, Graen's approach is radically different from that of other researchers. For instance, one implication of his research is that the superior is generally more considerate when dealing with members of the in-group than with members of the out-group. Thus Graen's theory provides a unique method for studying leadership.

CONTINGENCY FACTORS INFLUENCING LEADERSHIP

Thus far our discussion has centered primarily on describing the relationship between managerial leadership style and effectiveness. However, there are many contingency factors that influence this relationship; and in this section we discuss some of them.

Influence of Subordinates

Obviously the goal of leadership is to have the leader influence the behavior of subordinates. However, research has shown that subordinates' behavior often affects the style of leadership a manager uses.

For example, one experimental study investigated the way that the level of competence among clerical workers affected the style of their supervisor (Lowin and Craig 1968). The researchers instructed some of the clerical workers to perform competently and others to make a lot of errors. However, their supervisors were not informed of these instructions. Over time the leaders became task-oriented and inconsiderate in their relations with incompetent subordinates.

As this study indicates, subordinate behavior can influence the way a manager leads a group. In particular, it suggests that a manager, even if he or she wants to be considerate, will tend to deemphasize this style of leadership and stress a task-oriented style if subordinates are incompetent.

Short-Term Versus Long-Term Effects

In 1955 two University of Michigan researchers, Nancy Morse and Everett Reimer, conducted a year-long field experiment on leadership among the clerical employees of an insurance agency. One group of employees was managed in an autocratic fashion; that is, the superior did not allow his or her subordinates to participate in making any decisions that directly related to their own work. The other group's leadership was the exact opposite and stressed employee participation in decision making. At the end of the year absenteeism and turnover were significantly greater and job satisfaction significantly lower in the autocratic group than in the democratic group. While productivity of both groups increased over time, it was significantly higher in the autocratic group than in the democratic group.

These results were perplexing, since they suggested that autocratic leadership created a higher level of productivity than democratic leadership, in spite of the negative consequences such as decreased job satisfaction. However, other researchers at the University of Michigan, notably Rensis Likert, hypothesized that time was the key factor (Likert 1967; Marrow, Bowers, and Seashore 1967). These researchers suspected that autocratic leadership generates short-run increases in the rate of productivity, just because workers are intimidated. However, productivity probably will decline in the long run, since many of the most effective employees will either quit and obtain work elsewhere or become so dissatisfied that their productivity will decline.

THE SCARCITY OF EFFECTIVE LEADERS

The successful organization has one major attribute that sets it apart from unsuccessful organizations: dynamic and effective leadership. Peter F. Drucker . . . points out that managers (business leaders) are the basic and scarcest resource of any business enterprise. Statistics from recent years make this point more evident: "Of every 100 new business establishments started, approximately 50, or one-half, go out of business within two years. By the end of five years, only one-third of the original 100 will still be in business." . . . Most of the failures can be attributed to ineffective leadership.

On all sides there is a continual search for persons who have the necessary ability to enable them to lead effectively. This shortage of able administrators is not confined to business but is evident in the lack of able administrators in government, education, foundations, churches, and every other form of organization. Thus, when we decry the scarcity of leadership talent in our society, we are not talking about a lack of people to fill administrative or executive positions; we have plenty of administrative "bodies." What we are agonizing over is a scarcity of people who are willing to assume significant leadership roles in our society and can get the job done effectively.

Source: Paul Hersey and Kenneth Blanchard, *Management of Organizational Behavior: Utilizing Human Resources,* 3rd ed., © 1977, p. 83. Reprinted by permission of Prentice-Hall, Inc., Englewood Cliffs, N.J.

To test this theory, the Michigan researchers conducted a fifteen-year study of participative management in a factory. When the researchers introduced participative management, productivity did not increase immediately. However, productivity began to rise gradually after the first year and continued to do so over the fifteen-year period. The Michigan researchers then confirmed these findings in a later study at General Motors. And once again they found that after participative management was introduced, productivity increased over time (Dowling 1975). Both studies strongly suggest that participative leadership will not create a short-term increase in productivity but it will result in a long-term increase, since the effective employees will tend to stay with the organization and the less effective employees will be motivated to become more efficient (Likert 1967).

Personality Sometimes a leader is successful because there is a comfortable fit between his or her personality and those of his or her subordinates. James Mullen (1966) has investigated this fit between the personalities of leaders and subordinates in a study of three sales managers in a large insurance company. These managers' offices were all consistently superior in performance and sales, but their personalities were very different. Using a standard psychological test, Mullen found that one of the managers tended to be autocratic, another democratic, and the third had a mixture of both elements.

Mullen decided to examine the personalities of the subordinates by using the same standard psychological test. Generally, the subordinates of the democratic manager were highly independent. Hence they worked effectively for a manager who allowed them to define their own work. The subordinates of the autocratic manager tended to be highly dependent, so they responded well to the dictates of their leader. Finally, the subordinates of the manager who had a mixture of both elements wanted some direction but also some independence. Their needs consequently fitted a managerial style that was both autocratic and participative.

Locals and Cosmopolitans

Leadership theories have yet to incorporate adequately into their frameworks the social and economic backgrounds of individuals. The economic position of the leaders' parents, the schools they attended, the career patterns they follow—these and related factors are important for understanding leadership, especially the degrees of task orientation and consideration that the individual manifests.

In the late 1940s sociologists at Columbia University, under the direction of Robert Merton, studied the backgrounds of leaders in a small town (Merton 1957). When researchers asked the members of the community to identify their leaders, two profiles gradually began to emerge, the local and the cosmopolitan.

The *local leaders* usually had been members of the community since birth. In addition, they were more provincial than the cosmopolitan leaders in that they read only local newspapers and were mainly interested in the affairs of the community. Moreover, they usually worked within the community. The *cosmopolitans* tended to work outside the community. In addition, they were usually born and raised in another part of the country. These leaders also read several magazines and newspapers that were national and international in scope. While they were interested in community affairs and participated actively in them, they also were involved in many activities outside town.

Gouldner's Study. One of the Columbia University researchers, Alvin Gouldner (1957), went on to confirm that organizations are frequently directed by these two types of leaders. Gouldner showed that the two types of leaders serve different functions in the organization. Gouldner's analysis, which focused on university life, indicated that two kinds of professors tend to emerge as campus leaders. The first, the local leader, is a long-service professor who is usually an excellent teacher not interested in either publishing or a national reputation. The local leader is very considerate to students and fellow faculty members, and he or she spends a large portion of time helping them. The cosmopolitan leader is research-oriented and very interested in his or her national reputation. He or she is essentially task-oriented and does not like to waste time. Thus this leader typically meets with students and faculty members only to accomplish specific objectives.

Carlson's Research. In any organization usually one individual eventually becomes the leader. To find out what kind of individual this is, Richard Carlson (1961, 1972) studied a group of school superintendents. In some districts Carlson discovered that the school superintendents tended to be cosmopolitans: that is, they had served as superintendents elsewhere, had changed jobs and geographical locations several times during their careers, and had developed national reputations because of their work and publications. Other districts were headed by locals; that is, they had been promoted from within the system, had not changed jobs or locations during their careers, and did not have national reputations.

Carlson discovered that the critical factor determining the type of superintendent a school board appointed was whether the school system wanted change. If the members of a school board felt their district needed change and innovation, they generally hired a cosmopolitan. As indicated above, this type of leader is task-oriented, and he or she is hired to bring about major changes. In a school district where no major change was desired, board members preferred to promote from within the organization and appoint locals as superintendents. In such cases the superintendents tended to be considerate and interested in satisfying the needs of the subordinates.

Carlson's research also suggests that a cosmopolitan leader frequently appoints a local leader as his or her second-in-command. This course of action is logical, for it allows the cosmopolitan to concentrate on making the changes desired by the school district, while the local leader can attend to the social and emotional needs of the other people in the organization as innovations are introduced.

Pitfalls of the Cosmopolitan Type. The efficiency and task orientation of cosmopolitan leaders, although appropriate for initiating change, may offend people who are more accustomed to the consideration of local leaders. For instance, financial leaders in an eastern community decided to upgrade the quality of a private college located there and make it competitive with Ivy League schools. They hired a cosmopolitan leader who was given virtually unlimited financial resources. This leader hired outstanding academics throughout the United States.

He forced out many of the long-term and tenured professors by giving them unpleasant teaching and committee assignments and freezing their salaries. Within five years the leader brought about some of the desired change. However, many of the community leaders felt he was rude and offensive. They also wanted to change the name of the university to honor a major family in the community. When the cosmopolitan leader did not lend his support to this effort, the financial backers of the university withdrew their support and bestowed it on another university in the same geographical area. The leader's position was undermined so much that he resigned before he completed his goal of transforming the university from a minor into a major school.

Organizational Position

A major contingency factor influencing the relationship between style of leadership and a leader's effectiveness is the organizational position the manager occupies (Kanter 1979). The manager's power is circumscribed significantly if he must follow many rules, if he needs approval for nonroutine decisions, or if he must follow established routines (for additional factors, see Table 14–1). Even if managers appear to be doing similar work, their power and style of leadership may be radically different because of the specific organizational positions they occupy.

Type of Industry

Another major factor that influences the relationship between style of leadership and leader effectiveness is the type of industry in which a manager works. Michael Maccoby (1976) has focused on this factor in depth while studying the behavior of 250 managers over a period of years. From his analysis he has developed a typology of managerial styles that are successful in various types of industries or industrial situations.

According to Maccoby, some managers are *craftsmen:* they want to manufacture the best possible product. Their source of motivation is their intrinsic interest in work and their desire to do an excellent job. Such a manager is successful in an organization or organizational subsystem whose goal is to produce a high-quality product.

A second managerial type is the *jungle fighter.* This manager possesses a Machiavellian personality (see Chapter 12). Devious and untrustworthy, the manager believes he or she either must dominate or will be dominated. This manager is motivated by the desire to be the only one on top. He or she will be successful in an organization or a society in which there is great amount of uncertainty and few controls. Such a society existed in nineteenth-century America, as we shall see in Chapter 16.

Maccoby also portrays a third type, the *company man.* He or she is competitive but feels that competition is the price he or she must

TABLE 14–1

Ways Organizational Factors Contribute to Power or Powerlessness

Factor	*Generates power when factor is*	*Generates powerlessness when factor is*
Rules inherent in the job	Few	Many
Predecessors in the job	Few	Many
Established routines	Few	Many
Task variety	High	Low
Rewards for reliability/ predictability	Few	Many
Rewards for unusual performance/ innovation	Many	Few
Flexibility around use of people	High	Low
Approvals needed for nonroutine decisions	Few	Many
Physical location	Central	Distant
Publicity about job activities	High	Low
Relations of tasks to current problem areas	Central	Peripheral
Focus of tasks	Outside work unit	Inside work unit
Interpersonal contact in the job	High	Low
Contact with senior officials	High	Low
Participation in programs, conferences, meetings	High	Low
Participation in problem-solving task forces	High	Low
Advancement prospects of subordinates	High	Low

Source: Reprinted by permission of the Harvard Business Review. Exhibit from "Power Failure in Management Circuits" by Rosabeth Moss Kanter (July–August 1979).

pay for possessing a secure position in the organization. Such a manager is motivated by the desire for approval from authority and will be successful in an organization that does not value innovation or change.

Finally, there is the *gamesman*, the manager who approaches the managerial job as if it were a game: He or she either wins or loses, is either triumphant or humiliated. This type of manager is successful if the organization exists in a highly competitive or turbulent environment. For example, Maccoby points out that such managers can be found in high-technology firms that rely heavily on government contracts for their existence. For such a manager the source of motivation is the contest itself. Competing for contracts, developing new ploys, and controlling the play and timing are the major sources of motivation for the gamesman, who frequently becomes bored if there is no challenge.

TABLE 14–2

Substitutes for Leadership

Contingency variables	Will tend to neutralize: Consideration	Task orientation
Subordinates		
1. Ability		X
2. Work experience		X
3. Training		X
4. Knowledge		X
5. Indifferent toward organizational rewards	X	X
Task		
6. Unambiguous and routine		X
7. Simple, machine-paced, highly standardized methods		X
8. Provides its own feedback concerning accomplishment		X
9. Intrinsically interesting	X	
Organization		
10. Formalization (explicit plans, goals, and areas of responsibility)		X
11. Rigid (unbending rules and regulations)		X
12. Closely knit work groups	X	X
13. Organizational rewards not within the leader's control	X	X
14. Spatial distance between leader and superior	X	X

Source: Adapted from S. Kerr, "Substitutes for Leadership: Their Meaning and Measurement" (Paper presented at Eighth Annual Conference of the American Institute for Decision Sciences, San Francisco, November 1976). Used by permission.

Substitutes for Leadership

There are many additional contingency factors influencing the relationship between leadership style and leader effectiveness. Steven Kerr and John Jermier (1978) describe these factors as "substitutes for leadership," because they tend to neutralize consideration or task orientation. According to Kerr and Jermier, these substitutes relate to the characteristics of the subordinate, the task, and the organization. For example, if the subordinate is indifferent toward organizational rewards, then the leader cannot influence his or her behavior by being considerate or task-oriented, as the expectancy theory of motivation postulates (see Chapter 13). Similarly, an unambiguous and routine task will tend to neutralize the influence of task-oriented leadership. Also a large number of organizational rules will tend to neutralize the influence of task-oriented leadership. Other substitutes for leadership are shown in Table 14–2.

SUBORDINATE PARTICIPATION IN DECISION MAKING

A major managerial issue is the degree to which a manager should allow subordinates to participate in making decisions. Robert Tannenbaum and Warren Schmidt (1973) conceptualize this issue in terms of a continuum extending from manager-centered leadership to subordinate-centered leadership. Along this continuum are the various leadership styles that a manager can use (see Figure 14–4). If the manager merely wants to use the legitimate authority of his or her office in making decisions, he or she makes the decision and announces it to subordinates. However, as the manager begins to give subordinates freedom and delegate tasks to them, he or she should start to emphasize participative decision making.

Victor Vroom and Philip Yetton (1973) have expanded on this continuum. They identified two major conditions under which a manager should allow subordinates to participate in decisions: when the

FIGURE 14–4
Continuum of Leadership Behavior

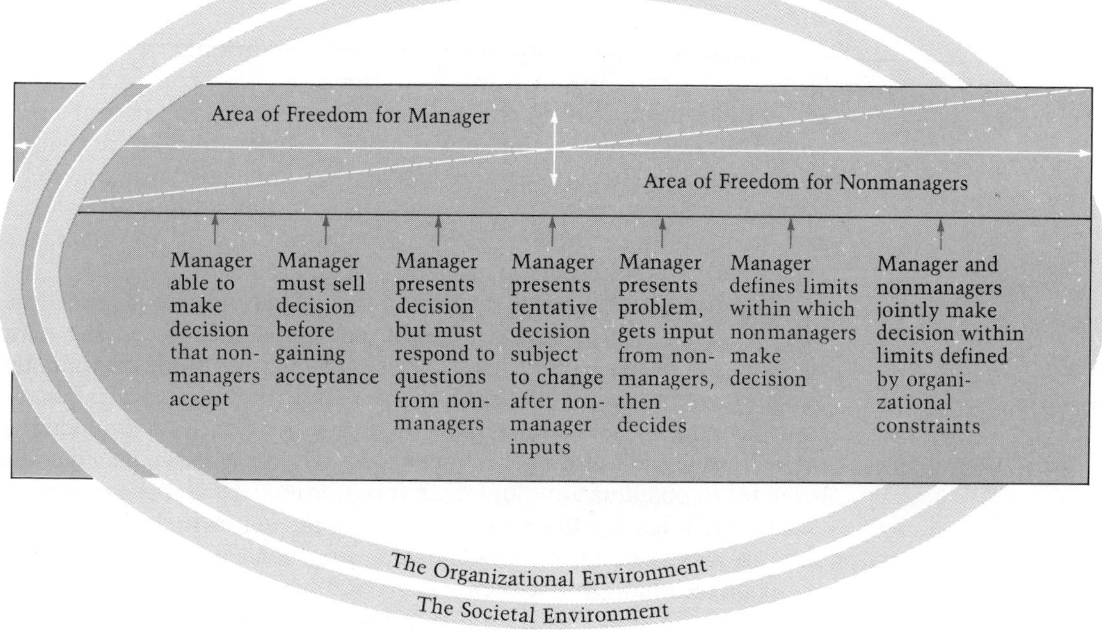

Source: Reprinted by permission of the Harvard Business Review. Exhibit from "How to Choose a Leadership Pattern" by Robert Tannenbaum and Warren H. Schmidt (May–June 1973).

level of technical effectiveness among the subordinates is high, and when the subordinates' level of motivation and acceptance is high. As shown in Figure 14–5, when the level of both conditions is low, the manager should make the decision. If, however, the level of subordinate motivation is high while technical effectiveness is low, then the manager should make the decision and delegate responsibility to subordinates to carry it out. A consultative decision-making style is appropriate when the level of technical effectiveness is high but the level of motivation among subordinates is low. Finally, when the level of both conditions is high, decision making should be shared. Research on this model in actual organizational settings indicates that a manager will be effective if he or she acts in accordance with it (Margerison and Glube 1979; Vroom and Jago 1978).

SUMMARY

In this chapter we pointed out the difference between leadership and managerial leadership. Leadership is the ability of a superior to influence the behavior of subordinates and persuade them to complete a particular course of action. To accomplish this objective, the leader has recourse to five major types of power: legitimate power, which the leader holds by virtue of his or her position, reward power, expert power, referent power, or the willingness of subordinates to identify with the leader, and coercive power.

Managerial leadership includes many additional roles besides leadership. According to Mintzberg, three of these are interpersonal roles: figurehead, leader, and liaison. Three are informational roles: monitor, disseminator, and spokesperson. Finally, four are decisional roles: entrepreneur, disturbance handler, resource allocator, and negotiator. The most important influence determining which roles a manager plays is organizational level. For example, only top managers usually act as spokespersons for the organization.

Theorists and researchers have emphasized one managerial role, that of leader, which focuses on the relationship between the manager and his or her subordinates. Ghiselli's research suggests that successful leaders possess distinctive traits, and the two most important traits are supervisory ability and the desire for occupational achievement. Leader behavior theory focuses on two dimensions of a leader's behavior, consideration and task orientation. Leader effectiveness theory includes Fiedler's contingency approach, which focuses not only on task orientation and consideration but also on the situation or organizational environment. A second leader effectiveness theory is that of path goal: A leader is effective when he or she identifies the paths subordinates may use to achieve personal and organizational goals. Reciprocal causation theory argues that the leader and the work group mutually influence one another. Vertical dyadic theory looks at the relationship between the leader and *each* of his or her subordinates independently.

There are also several contingency factors that influence the relationship between leadership style and leader effectiveness. These include the influence of subordinates, the leader's personality, background, and organizational position, and the type of industry. By focusing on the type of industry, Maccoby has profiled four managerial types: the craftsman, the jungle fighter, the company man, and the gamesman. These and related factors can be considered substitutes for leadership, since their presence tends to neutralize the impact of consideration and task orientation.

Finally, researchers have identified a continuum of leadership behavior based on the amount of subordinate participation in the decision-making process. The Vroom and Yetton model specifies two conditions that a manager should examine before allowing subordinates to participate in decisions: the level of technical effectiveness among subordinates and their level of motivation and acceptance. The degree to which each condition is present determines the style of leadership that the manager should employ.

FIGURE 14–5
Simplified Vroom-Yetton Model

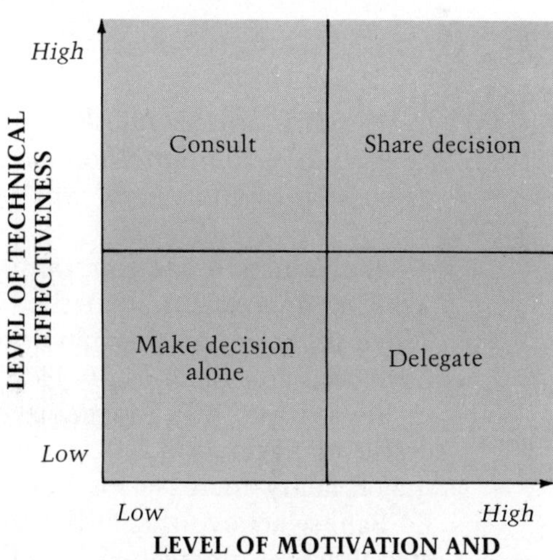

Source: Reprinted with permission from Michael Driver, "Individual Decision Making and Creativity," in *Organizational Behavior,* ed. Steven Kerr (Columbus: Grid, 1979), p. 85. Based on Victor Vroom and Philip Yetton, *Leadership and Decision Making* (Pittsburgh: University of Pittsburgh Press, 1973).

DISCUSSION QUESTIONS

1. From the research discussed in this chapter, what leadership style do you think is likely to characterize a politician? A religious leader? A film director?
2. Discuss the two definitions of leadership put forth by Max Weber and Chester Barnard. Which definition do you prefer? Why? How do these definitions relate to Theory X and Theory Y (see Chapter 2)?
3. What elements do motivation theory and leadership theory have in common? Would it be possible to formulate a theory of leadership without considering motivation?
4. Of the ten roles that Mintzberg discusses, theorists have emphasized one—the leader or the relationship between the leader and his or her subordinates. Do you feel this is the key role of a manager? Of Mintzberg's ten roles, which three are most important for a president of a company? For a middle manager?
5. Researchers have argued that the two major dimensions of leader behavior are task orientation and consideration. What are some other dimensions of leadership?
6. Why does House argue that a leader frequently cannot influence the behavior of subordinates? In House's theory why is it important that a leader can be simultaneously task-oriented and considerate?
7. In the Vroom and Yetton model how is leadership related to decision making?

CRITICAL INCIDENT

NOTE: This critical incident can be used by the whole class with the case observational method (see Appendix A) or used for thought and discussion by individual class members.

Joe Feinstein has a pressing problem. He is a long-term employee working as a scientist in the research section of a large R&D firm. Three years ago he was appointed supervisor of his section and things have been going smoothly. However, one of the outstanding scientists in his section, Bill Gracer, is furious because Mike Dodds, an autocratic manager two levels above Joe, does not want to authorize a major salary increase for him. Both Joe and his immediate superior, Ed Banks, believe that Bill deserves this increase because of his outstanding performance. Bill, who has a very good reputation throughout the organization, has made it clear both to Joe and Ed that he will jump organizational levels and go over Mike Dodds's head if he does not receive a salary increase. Ed told Joe that he would take the matter up with Mike Dodds.

QUESTIONS: What should Ed say to Mike? Should Ed take Joe along with him when he talks to Mike? Why or why not? If Mike Dodds refuses to budge, what should Joe and Ed do?

SUGGESTED READINGS

Hersey, Paul, and Blanchard, Kenneth. *Management of Organizational Behavior.* 2nd ed. Englewood Cliffs, N.J.: Prentice-Hall, 1972, 209 pages, paperback.

The authors present a "life cycle theory of leadership," which fits into the framework developed in this chapter.

Likert, Rensis. *The Human Organization.* New York: McGraw-Hill, 1967, 258 pages, hardback.

Likert's basic thesis is that a participative style of leadership is superior to others. This book is somewhat oversimplified, but students consistently enjoy it, especially if they have had limited exposure to behavioral applications in management. Two important ideas in this book are the following: While tight supervision may produce immediate results and increase productivity, in the long run morale will decline and the best individuals will seek work elsewhere, thus causing a downturn in productivity; and employees are assets, just as physical objects are, and they should be represented on the balance sheet.

15 Group Behavior

GROUP FORMATION AND DEVELOPMENT
TYPES OF GROUPS IN ORGANIZATIONS
FACTORS INFLUENCING BEHAVIOR IN GROUPS
CONTINGENCY VIEW OF GROUPS
SUMMARY
DISCUSSION QUESTIONS
CRITICAL INCIDENT
SUGGESTED READINGS

PERFORMANCE OBJECTIVES

1. To describe the major reasons individuals join groups, to describe how groups operate, and to illustrate the various stages through which groups evolve.
2. To outline and describe the various types of groups in organizations.
3. To examine the major factors influencing behavior in groups, including the physical environment in which group activity takes place, the personal characteristics of group members, group structure, and group composition.
4. To develop a contingency view of group behavior by analyzing the relationship between technology and group behavior.

From the point of view of management, an organization is a group of two or more individuals working together or interacting to accomplish a common purpose or purposes (Barnard 1938). If an organization consists only of one individual, relying solely on his or her work for its existence, it has no need to analyze group behavior. In this vein James Thompson (1967) has argued that an individual is indispensable in an organization only when he or she performs all its critical functions. This happens only infrequently. In fact, it is rare even for an organization to consist of a single group. Most organizations are composed of interrelated groups striving to accomplish the overall objectives of the enterprise. Many of these groups are formal; that is, the organization has designed them for specific reasons. In addition, a large number of informal groups spontaneously arise in organizations for a variety of reasons, such as members' common backgrounds and interests, their interest in sharing information that is mutually advantageous, and even their need to resist managerial pressure and demands.

Typically, group behavior is very complex and difficult to understand. The tone of a leader's voice at a meeting may result in activities among subordinates that he or she did not openly command; individuals will privately champion a particular point of view but oppose it vociferously in a group meeting; some individuals try to dominate others in groups; and one group may simply refuse to work with another group, even though its members cannot articulate all the reasons for this stance.

However, effective interaction between individuals and groups is critical to an organization's success. When misunderstandings or disagreements arise among organizational members, they are bound to interfere with the organization's overall efforts to achieve its goals.

This chapter begins with an introductory discussion of group formation and development. Then various types of groups that are found in organizations are described. Next the chapter examines some of the major factors determining behavior in groups. The chapter concludes with a description of a contingency perspective that emphasizes the influence of technology on group behavior.

GROUP FORMATION AND DEVELOPMENT

Groups constitute the critical building blocks in organizations and societies. For instance, the average person belongs to five or six groups at any given time (Mills 1967). Groups tend to be relatively small. One study indicated that approximately ninety-two percent of all group memberships are in groups of five persons or less (James 1951).

For our purposes a group can be defined as two or more individuals engaged in social interaction (Shaw 1976). There are many ways in which these interactions occur, as we shall see. In this section we describe Homans's theory of group formation, the reasons why individuals join groups, developmental processes in groups, and the concept of the ideal group.

Homans's System Theory

George Homans is a sociologist who has developed a system theory of group behavior that integrates many research studies. Homans's theory is built around three concepts: *activities, interactions,* and *sentiments.* When members of a group perform activities, they interact with one another. Through these interactions they develop feelings or sentiments toward one another. Hence these three variables are dynamically related—a change in one leads to a change in the others.

Homans argues that a social system is the state of relations among interaction, activity, and sentiment in a collection of two or more persons identifiable as a separate entity, such as a work group or a clique. He feels that this social system consists of two parts, the external system and the internal system. The *external system* reflects the relations among interaction, activity, and sentiment imposed on a group by forces external to it. The *internal system* focuses on the relations among interaction, activity, and sentiment that are spontaneously elaborated and standardized by members of the group.

According to Homans, any group tends to develop at least a rudimentary internal system in which three modes of behavior occur: elaboration, differentiation, and standardization. *Elaboration* refers to the manner in which individuals take part in activities beyond those required by the external system. For instance, a private in the army may be required to salute an officer, but he does not need to smile when doing so. *Differentiation* is the recognition of differences among members of the group. As a group elaborates and differentiates its behavior, *standardization* of certain activities, interactions, and sentiments occurs.

Using these three modes of behavior, Homans then introduces three related concepts: rank, norms, and role. A group differentiates usually in terms of *rank,* that is, a person's position in the group relative to other members. *Norms* are the expectations regarding the behavior of members; they regulate the interactions, activities, and sentiments of members both in the external and the internal system. *Role* is the characteristic pattern of a member's activities, interactions, and sentiments, along with his rank and the degree to which he or she conforms to the norms.

From this theory Homans proposes some hypotheses about group behavior. For example, the higher a person's rank in a group, the more closely he or she generally conforms to its norms; the more freedom he or she has in conforming to the norms, even to the extent that nonconformity is frequently overlooked or viewed as in the interests of the group; and the more interaction he or she will have as a group representative with members of other groups. And members of the group force other members to maintain their established degree of conformity to the norms but not to increase their conformity, since this might threaten the rank hierarchy.

Homans's theory is important for two reasons. First, he uses only a few essential concepts in developing his theory but is able to derive several hypotheses about the way people behave in groups. Second, his theory reflects everyday life and activities (see Homans 1950, 1961).

Evolution of Groups

Other researchers have also focused on the evolution of group processes. In particular, Robert Bales (1950) has examined the emergence of leadership in small groups whose members were not previously acquainted with one another. According to Bales, two distinct types of leaders emerge, often at the same time: the task-oriented and the socioemotional or considerate (see Chapter 14). The task-oriented leader directs the activity of the group; the considerate leader attempts to develop a feeling of group cohesion and to satisfy the social and emotional needs of the members. Typically one individual cannot satisfy both leadership roles.

Similarly, research suggests that groups do evolve in an orderly process and that stages of group evolution are reasonably consistent in groups of a specific type. For example, task-oriented groups typically proceed through three stages: an orientation phase during which members become acquainted with one another and the problem; an evaluation stage during which they examine various alternatives that might solve the problem; and a control phase during which they narrow the list of alternatives and limit the amount of interaction and conversation taking place in the group (Bales and Strodtbeck 1951). Similarly, discussion groups put together without assigning a formal leader are initially interested in authority relationships and then are preoccupied with personal concerns, such as discovering the needs and identity of others in the group (Bennis and Shepard 1956).

Joining Groups

It is difficult to specify all the reasons why individuals join groups. However, Shaw (1976) has identified five major ones.

The first reason is interpersonal attraction: The individual likes the members of a group and feels that interaction with them will be rewarding. If, for example, members of a group are considered beautiful or handsome, it is quite common for others to seek membership in that group (Schlosser 1969). Similarly, individuals tend to be attracted to a group if its members are similar to themselves, partially because such a group provides social support for a person's attitudes and beliefs.

"Naturally, Lyman, the company doesn't care whether its employees have little flags on their desks or not. It's purely a voluntary thing. We just wondered why you *happen to be the only person here who hasn't got one."*

Second, an individual may want to join a group because he or she feels that its goals are worthwhile. Ideally the group should develop superordinate goals that link the activities and interactions of group members into a meaningful whole (Sherif et al. 1961). Otherwise, it is easy for the group to splinter into subgroups seeking to achieve their own goals, and these goals may not be consistent with one another.

A third reason for joining a group is that the individual may enjoy the activities in which it engages. For example, boys interested in the same activities tend to form groups (Sherif and Sherif 1953).

Fourth, groups provide a channel through which individuals can fulfill their needs for social interaction. Such interaction tends to reduce anxiety. For example, as outside threats to members of a group increase, the attractiveness of group membership rises (Pepitone and Kleiner 1957).

Finally, there are instrumental reasons for joining groups. That is, the individual expects to derive benefits that are not ostensibly related to the group's goals. For instance, a businessman may join a country club not for socialization (its ostensible goals) but for making business contacts.

The Ideal Group

In the previous chapter we described the reciprocal causation theory of leadership (see pp. 364–365). According to this theory, four conditions must be present in a work group if it is to be effective: a high degree of support, interaction facilitation, goal emphasis, and work facilitation.

In a similar vein, Shepard (1964) argues that there are five features of an ideal small group. It must have clear goals that it seeks to attain, and its members must be characterized by personal objectives that are identical or compatible with them. Also, in the ideal group each person's role must be so clear that everyone in the group understands it. Members of the group must recognize who the unofficial and official leaders are, and roles must be graded in terms of status and prestige. In addition, members of the group must see a close relationship between values and norms; a value is something desired by an individual, while a norm is a rule governing behavior. Further, membership should be heterogeneous so that the group does not become closed and shortsighted. Finally, communication must be open and candid in an ideal group.

According to Shepard, these conditions increase the likelihood that cohesion and productivity will be high. However, if the external system does not allow the group to operate autonomously, it is probable that members of the group will become frustrated.

TYPES OF GROUPS IN ORGANIZATIONS

There are many ways to classify groups, such as formal and informal, or managerial and employee. Four types that are particularly relevant for understanding the behavior of individuals in organizations are primary and secondary groups, and problem-solving and creative groups.

Primary and Secondary Groups

If individuals interact face-to-face and their relationships are personal in nature, they constitute a *primary group.* Such groups have no formal written rules and procedures. Examples are the family and friendship groups.

The opposite of a primary group is the *secondary group,* which is usually larger and more impersonal than a primary group. Such groups follow formal rules, procedures, and policies. Typically, the work organization is a secondary group, as are professional associations and unions. However, work groups in the formal organization can sometimes become primary groups if the members' relationships become more personal. The informal work groups in the Hawthorne study, especially in the bank wiring observation room, represent primary groups (see Chapter 2). Similarly, printers working on a shift schedule tend to form primary groups and spend their leisure hours with one another, at least partially because of the shift nature of their work (Lipset, Trow, and Coleman 1956).

Primary groups are a necessary part of organizational life. Most people want allies, and one way to obtain them is to become an integral part of a primary work group. But the formation of primary groups in organizations can lead to some problems, for such groups do not exhibit a key characteristic of bureaucratic organizations, impersonality (Weber 1947). This characteristic is important since the ideal bureaucratic organization is one in which the individual's performance is judged without bias. As relationships become personal, biases begin to cloud judgments, especially when salary increases or promotions are involved.

An excellent example of such conflict is provided by the experience of a vice-president of personnel for a large brokerage house. A close friend of twenty years asked her for a job after the death of her husband. However, the friend began to use this friendship to her advantage in the organization and was not motivated to perform at a satisfactory level. The vice-president called her into the office and told her bluntly that although they were close friends, she would be forced to terminate her if her performance did not improve markedly.

Problem-solving Groups

Usually an organization establishes certain formal groups or departments that are responsible for solving particular sets of recurrent and routine problems. For example, the personnel department hires workers and attempts to eliminate sources of employee dissatisfaction that might lead to high turnover and low productivity. In addition, organizations often attempt to solve nonrecurring and nonroutine problems by creating special problem-solving groups. Temporary groups and task forces, as discussed in Chapter 9, are normally established to solve particular problems. After the problem has been solved, the temporary group or task force dissolves.

Normally a problem-solving group should not contain an even number of members, for in that event the decision can be deadlocked. In addition, the decision-making group should be small, so competitive subgroups do not emerge. Five members are often considered ideal; this allows members of the group to work closely together and still avoid a deadlock. Although there is some disagreement about the ideal size of a decision-making group, five seems to be the lower limit and ten the upper limit for effective groups (House and Miner 1969).

During the past thirty years researchers have analyzed the behavior of problem-solving groups in experimental situations. Typically the researchers present a problem to a group of individuals and ask them to develop a solution. For nonrecurring and nonroutine problem solving that takes place when individuals are very uncertain about the best course of action, research indicates that group decisions are superior to those offered by the average member of the group (Harrison 1975). This result is not surprising, for a group can filter out poor information and choices. When an individual is confronted with a problem, he or she is less able to obtain feedback that would help refine his or her approach to the solution. Also, the more possible solutions offered, the better the best of them is likely to be (Holloman and Hendrick 1972).

Research also indicates that group decisions are not superior to those offered by the best member of the group, at least in some situations (Harrison 1975). This result seems to occur because of the limitations and liabilities associated with problem-solving activities in a group. In some situations members of the group stop searching for a better alternative after most of them have agreed on an acceptable solution; in other situations, even though one solution is clearly superior to others, the members may accept an inferior alternative or compromise because of the resistance of a few individuals.

Creative Groups

Problem-solving groups are good at solving most of the difficulties an organization faces. However, when novel solutions are needed for unique problems, an organization may rely on the work of creative groups. We shall discuss various types of creative groups in Chapter 17; this section contains a brief description of the processes and dynamics of creative groups.

Creative groups frequently try to develop new products that will sustain the organization and compete effectively with those of other enterprises. These groups also are commonly used in advertising campaigns, which often seem to make or break a product or service. For example, Avis significantly increased its car rental profits by directing its advertising campaign against Hertz with the novel slogan, "We're only Number 2, so we try harder."

Usually the ideal size of the creative group is much larger than that of the problem-solving group, since the objective is to generate a large number of ideas. In general, a suitable size for a creative group would be ten to twenty members. A group of more than twenty individuals may become cumbersome and unmanageable, for the same reasons mentioned for problem-solving groups. In addition, the creative group should include individuals with diverse backgrounds. For instance, an organization that is trying to develop a new product may put together a creative group that consists of engineers, physicists, social scientists, advertising executives, and sales personnel. This heterogeneity provides the group with several perspectives in the analysis of the problem.

The most effective process that a creative group should use in generating ideas is still unknown. However, some research suggests that the group should meet for a warm-up period during which the general problem is presented (Dunnette, Campbell, and Jaastad 1963). After this short presentation the members of the group should work individually. Periodic group sessions might then be held to filter the information and narrow the range of acceptable solutions.

FACTORS INFLUENCING BEHAVIOR IN GROUPS

In this section we examine the key factors that influence the behavior of individuals in groups. Unfortunately, this is a murky area, since there are so many factors that can influence group behavior that it is difficult even to classify them. However, Marvin Shaw (1976) has attempted to provide a classification system, and it is his approach that we will follow. Shaw classifies the major factors as the physical environment in which the group activity takes place, the personal characteristics of group members, group structure, and group composition.

There is one aspect of the physical environment that seems to be of overwhelming importance: technology. As we have seen in Chapter 2, technology is a pivotal factor in the contingency theory of management. Since technology is so important, we devote a separate section at the end of this chapter to the subject.

Physical Environment

In Chapter 12 we analyzed the impact of various communication networks on the interpersonal communications that occur in different types of situations. Many aspects of the physical environment, including communication networks and the spatial arrangements of individuals, affect the behavior of individuals within groups. These include the color and attractiveness of the decor, the presence or absence of music, and the perceived attractiveness of the building in which the work is completed.

Physical Structure. One key aspect of the physical environment is the physical structure—the actual building—of the organization. It delimits the flow of work processes and interactions that can take place. For example, the conditions necessary for unionization can be created (or inhibited) in large part just by an organization's physical structure.

To explore this issue, Martin Estey compared the rise of unionism in food chain stores and department stores (Estey 1971). Historically, food stores were not unionized, because they were too small to justify the money it would take to organize them. In addition, workers in these stores were relatively unskilled. They did not have the necessary expertise or the skilled leaders available to unionize. But these conditions changed dramatically when food chains came into existence; then a large number of workers were housed under one roof. Additionally, leadership was provided by the highly skilled

GROUP INFLUENCES ON INDIVIDUALS

The most casual observation of groups indicates the existence of strong mechanisms for controlling the behavior of members. This capacity of groups to direct, limit, and influence what members do gives considerable power to the group setting and to individuals who are at the center of power in the group. The use of this power can have either positive or negative consequences for the individual and society. . . .

. . . The Chinese Communists have provided an example of systematic use of group pressures to win conversion to their doctrine. [Edgar] Schein reported these practices based on interviews with repatriated prisoners of war following the Korean War. The Chinese captors used their understanding of groups as controlling agents in an attempt to break down systems of belief and attitude. They prevented the formation of spontaneous primary groups which ordinarily serve as instruments for validating and sustaining beliefs of individuals through relationships with fellow group members. By segregating those who adamantly refused to cooperate and by exerting skills in the exposition of their tenets and in the use of group pressures, the Chinese Communists were able to induce a few of this isolated group to accept communist doctrine.

Source: Abraham Zalesnik and David Moment, *The Dynamics of Interpersonal Behavior* (New York: Wiley, 1964), pp. 96–97.

meat cutters, who served as the driving wedge when unionization was attempted.

In contrast, Estey found that department stores typically are not unionized, for each department is an organization unto itself, isolated in a separate part of the building. In effect, several organizations that are relatively unknown and foreign to one another exist within one structure. This lack of cohesion across departments inhibits the growth of unionism.

Personal Space. Another factor in the physical environment that managers often overlook in setting up work groups is each group member's sense of personal space. Some people simply dislike being forced to be too close to other people. According to Edward Hall (1968), Americans have established an intimate zone into which a few individuals are allowed; it extends from the surface of the skin to about 18 inches. In a second zone, from 1½ to 4 feet around the person, comfortable interactions that reflect friendship and closeness take place. The third zone extends from 4 to 12 feet from the person; most impersonal business is conducted in this range. Finally, there is the public zone of 12 feet and beyond in which individuals recognize one another and say hello but do not engage in comfortable interactions.

As Hall suggests, an individual who violates spacing rules will be disliked by members of the group. Sometimes members of the group will invoke sanctions to force the individual to conform. For example, they may simply walk away from the person or mention directly that he or she is out of order.

Characteristics of Group Members

The personal characteristics of the individual members in a group influence that group's behavior. These include the biographical characteristics of group members, their abilities, personality traits, and attitudes.

Biographical Characteristics. Factors such as the age distribution of a group and the degree to which the group members conform to social pressure are termed *biographical characteristics,* and they refer explicitly to the biography or life-cycle characteristics of a group. As individuals become older, they tend to change the manner in which they interact with others in group situations. They establish an increasing number of contacts with others in groups and become more selective in their relationships. Their behavior becomes more complex. In addition, the degree to which they will conform to peer group pressure increases until age 12, after which it declines (Shaw 1976).

There is also some evidence indicating that leaders of groups differ from nonleaders in terms of physical characteristics such as height, weight, and general physical condition. Although there are contradictory studies in this area, the general conclusion that can be drawn from them is that physically superior individuals have a slightly better chance of becoming leaders in groups (Shaw 1976).

Abilities. In Chapter 14 we described various types of power, one of which is expert power. An individual exerts expert power in a group if he or she is perceived to be knowledgeable about matters that are important to group members. Thus an individual's abilities are of major significance not only for leadership but also for general group behavior. Studies in this area suggest that as intelligence increases, individuals become more active and less willing to conform in groups. Also, the more intelligent members of a group are more effective than the less intelligent members (Shaw 1976).

Personality and Culture. We have already seen that personality is a contingency factor influencing leadership (see Chapter 14). It is also an important influence on behavior in groups. In general, group members look favorably on those personality traits that reflect cultural values. In the United States, for instance, such factors as sociability and independence are typically admired.

An excellent study of cultural influences on group behavior has been completed by Michel Crozier (1964). He examined two French organizations, a clerical agency and an industrial enterprise. Crozier argues that there are two contradictory cultural values that play a critical role in group behavior among the French: a high regard both for individualism and for sharp distinctions among social classes. Hence French organizations are structured in a highly formal manner in which there are clear demarcations of positions in the hierarchy. However, individuals are allowed to exercise a good amount of independence in completing their work. Thus the two contradictory cultural values are protected.

According to Crozier, this excessive emphasis on formality creates a vicious cycle. Typically it is very difficult to initiate any organizational change. In fact, organizational change usually occurs as a response to a crisis and it is mandated by top management.

Crozier also analyzed the Russian culture, which is characterized by friendliness and warmth. However, the government is highly autocratic. Hence members of each work group are warm and friendly toward one another but suspicious of outsiders who may be operating as spies.

In the United States, organizations and individuals tend to emphasize specialization according to function. However, a dominant value in America is the protection of individuals. Hence the American system is somewhat impersonal but reflects the cultural belief that the rights of individual workers must be protected.

Attitudes. Another characteristic of group members influencing their behavior is attitudinal orientation. An *attitude* may be defined as a predisposition to respond to something in a particular way. Attitudes are composed of three separate elements: cognitive, emotional, and behavioral. The *cognitive element* concerns the rational processes an individual uses before taking a particular course of action —his or her opinions. The *emotional element* refers to the nonrational commitment an individual makes to a particular course of action—his or her feelings. The *behavioral element* is the action the individual takes on the basis of his or her cognitive and emotional position.

A manager who understands the influence of attitudes on behavior is at a decided advantage when he or she attempts to motivate subordinates, either individually or in groups. The manager can appeal to the cognitive side of an attitude by telling subordinates they are making valuable contributions to the organization. Some companies extend this approach by giving visible recognition to outstanding work—for example, bonuses, vacation trips, and special programs or dinners during which individuals receive certificates of merit and other honors. A manager can appeal to the emotional side of an attitude by treating subordinates as personal friends, making sure that any special requests are honored, and showing a genuine interest in their career progression.

However, attitude changes may not persist if they are not reinforced on a regular basis. This problem has been highlighted by Edwin Fleishman (1953). He conducted a human relations training program for supervisors and, at the same time, also established a control group composed of supervisors who did not participate in the training. At the start of the program a standard human relations test indicated that the supervisors in the two groups were roughly equal

GROUP COHESION

In a discussion of difficulties arising in collective bargaining, [Benjamin] Selekman describes an incident which occurred in a men's clothing manufacturing plant. Five men joiners, who had worked together for years, carried through the complete process of sewing together the five sections of the coat. New methods were introduced by the management which required each man to sew only one section. Although they were all pieceworkers, with varying earning capacities, the five men arranged to pool their total earnings at the end of each week and to divide them into five equal parts. "They had always been friends, they explained, and so wanted to avoid any bad feelings different earnings might create among them." In this way, they resisted a program formulated by management which would serve to transform the close group into five competing individuals. Another group, including four women canvas basters, developed a comparable device for "defending their old work group integrity against the erosion of the new methods." They, like the joiners, differed from one another in speed, accuracy and earning capacity under a piecework wage plan. When there was a shortage of work, none would work unless each had a garment to sew on. "Time and again," says Selekman, "they had held up production because 'friends like us' could not let management give too much work to the speedier or better basters. So strong was their cohesiveness that when an arbitrator expressed the desire for interviews to get to the bottom of complaints, they refused to meet him unless they were interviewed as a group. None would talk except in the presence of all."

Source: Morris Viteles, *Motivation and Morale in Industry* (New York: Norton, 1953), p. 180.

in their sensitivity to the needs of others and their feelings toward others. After the program the trained supervisors scored significantly higher than the control group on the human relations test. However, six months later there were no significant differences between the two groups on this test. In fact, the trained supervisors proved to be *less* sensitive than they had been before the sessions. Many factors might account for this situation. But Fleishman's hypothesis was that the organizational climate to which these supervisors returned was autocratic, and thus it failed to reinforce their new attitude. He tested this hypothesis by examining the attitudes of the second-level supervisors to whom the first-level supervisors reported. As he suspected, the second-level supervisors were highly autocratic, and they pressured the first-level supervisors to act autocratically toward their subordinates.

Some of the ways a manager can reinforce desired employee attitudes have been discussed in Chapter 13. With regard to an individual's attitude toward other employees, one useful technique is *role playing.* If two individuals are antagonistic toward each other, it may be useful for them to switch roles during a training session. By being forced to represent each other's attitudes, they can learn more about each other's viewpoints and problems. In one organization management used this approach with white foremen who were harassing their black workers. When the white foremen were forced to take the insults and imperious commands of the black workers who were role playing as foremen, they began to dislike and change their own behavior. Group discussion sessions, in which participants are free to talk about their own and others' attitudes, are also valuable.

Group Composition

Group composition refers to the relationships among the personal characteristics of group members and the consequences of these relationships for group activities. Two important aspects of group composition are group cohesiveness and group compatibility.

As we might expect, as *cohesion*—the degree to which members of a group are attached to one another—increases in groups, favorable social interaction also rises, as does the number of interactions. Similarly, group cohesion is positively related to achieving goals and to satisfaction among the members of the group (Shaw 1976).

Group *compatibility* is the degree to which members of the group are at ease with one another. If the members of the group are compatible, some members will satisfy the needs of other members and vice versa. Individuals who like direction, for instance, would be reasonably satisfied in a group in which some strong leaders provide it. In general, as compatibility rises, so does group effectiveness in attaining goals.

Group Structure

The manner in which a group is structured is a powerful influence on the behavior of its members. Major factors of group structure include the style of leadership, the status of individuals, the organizational positions of the members and the degree of participation the members enjoy.

Leadership Style. Leaders have a strong influence on the manner in which groups are structured and behave. Alvin Gouldner (1954) has provided an extended case study on this topic. He analyzed the behavior of work groups in a gypsum plant in a midwestern city. For many years the manager of this plant, "Old Doug," guided it in a very loose and friendly fashion. While group cohesion and job satisfaction were high, the plant was becoming inefficient. Many employees arrived late for work and left early, and their jobs were not closely monitored. After Old Doug's death top management appointed a dynamic plant manager who imposed strict controls on the behavior of the workers in the plant. If they arrived late or left early, he punished them by docking their pay and giving them short layoffs. While most workers disliked the new system, they put up with it for fear of losing their jobs. The solidarity of the work groups in the plant weakened significantly, for most employees began to concern themselves only with their own careers and interests.[1]

The influence of a leader on a group is especially pronounced if he or she is *charismatic,* that is, if he or she has a special personal magnetism that convinces individuals to follow directives without question or criticism. Adolf Hitler was a charismatic leader, and millions of Germans obeyed his commands willingly. In some instances German citizens followed inhumane orders that conflicted with their own beliefs, largely because they completely accepted the legitimacy of Hitler's leadership.

Status. Groups typically develop structures in which there are marked status differences among members. Generally, people whose status is high tend to act differently in a group from those whose status is low. This proposition has received support from C. Northcote Parkinson (1957), who studied the behavior of individuals at parties. According to Parkinson, high-status individuals usually arrive late, but they immediately walk to the center of the room to be seen by their inferiors. At the end of the evening they leave earlier than the other guests, apparently so their exit can be duly noted.

[1] However, the miners who worked below the surface of the plant were able to resist the plant manager's rigid control system because of the flexible and dangerous nature of their work.

The status of individuals is frequently incorporated into their job titles. In one organization when the production manager's title was changed to vice-president of manufacturing, his status rose significantly, although his duties remained the same. The status of his subordinates also increased, even though there was no change whatsoever in their job duties (Harlow and Hanke 1975).

Individuals and groups try to maintain high status once it is attained, and in turn, they attempt to restrict the number of individuals who attain a position of high status. For example, in one large bank the people who kept the books had a low status until the organization hired computer specialists for this job. Because these specialists were highly educated and were critical factors in the bank's continued success, they demanded the same privileges that high-status officers had, such as access to the executive dining room. However, resistance was so great that it took several years for the computer specialists to attain a position of high status (Strauss and Sayles 1972).

Organizational Position. Like status, organizational position directly influences behavior in groups, since it dictates the specific role that an individual fulfills. An individual in a production position, for instance, can be expected to support people and ideas that reflect the production view. Even if the individual disagrees with some of the production department's policies, he or she is more likely to side with another production employee than with a member of the sales or marketing department.

The importance of organizational position was established in a study conducted by Seymour Lieberman (1956), who analyzed the attitudes of a group of workers over a period of three years. At the start of the study, as indicated on a standard test, all the workers were basically antimanagement and pro-union. Later some of these workers were promoted to supervisory positions; when retested, they were promanagement and antiunion. After a time, some of these workers were demoted because of an economic recession, and they became pro-union and antimanagement once again.

Participation. When groups or individuals are allowed to participate in decisions that bear directly on their own work, they typically react more favorably than they do if they feel decisions are imposed on them by management (Likert 1967; Coch and French 1948). (See Chapter 14.) This generalization is particularly true when management is introducing a major change in the organization. Even if the subordinates' participation is limited, they will be more supportive of the changes than they would be if they had not been consulted.

However, this approach may backfire if subordinates perceive it to be *pseudoparticipation,* that is, if management encourages them to express themselves freely but ignores their contributions. In this situation the subordinates justifiably feel they have been mistreated and manipulated by management. Some typical reactions are increased hostility toward management, lower productivity, and higher turnover. And even genuine participation may prove troublesome. Research demonstrates that employees desiring greater participation in decision making experience greater career dissatisfaction than the other employees (Alutto and Vredenburgh 1977). In some situations such workers may use participation as a weapon to attack management rather than as a vehicle for promoting rational change in the organization.

Participation can also be combined with public commitment. When an individual is required to make a public commitment that he or she will pursue a particular course of action after participating in a discussion of its merits, he or she is more likely to keep it than if the commitment is private. Kurt Lewin (1958) tested this hypothesis with research designed to increase the use of meats such as beef hearts, sweetbreads, and kidneys, all of which are usually disliked by consumers. Some groups of meat buyers heard a lecture on the values of unpopular meats; in other groups the lecture was supplemented by group discussion. Afterward the consumers were asked to raise their hands if they were willing to try these meats. In the follow-up study only three percent of the consumers in the lecture groups indicated they had served one of these meats; thirty-two percent of the consumers in the group that made a public commitment had served at least one of these meats.

In an organization it is not always feasible to obtain public commitment. Some individuals may be embarrassed; others may resent the technique; and some may even retaliate by following an opposite course of action. Still, the manager can use this approach in some situations. A manager who is contemplating a change from a five-day to a four-day workweek without reducing hours per week can discuss the proposed change with his or her employees and obtain a public commitment from them that they will not decrease their rates of productivity or increase their rates of absenteeism and lateness. Similarly, a manager may be able to give his or her subordinates more responsibilities and monitor them less frequently after they have participated in a discussion of the new program and made a public commitment to it.

In recent years researchers interested in participation have also focused on the *risky shift phenomenon,* which was first studied by Stoner (1961). His research indicated that individuals tend to advocate more risky positions as members of a group than they do as individuals. One possible explanation is that individuals are conservative in making decisions when the responsibility rests squarely on their own shoulders. When an individual makes a decision that is clearly his or her own, he or she is responsible for its success or failure. In a group situation the individual sometimes feels he or she can advocate a risky position because responsibility for the final decision is diffused throughout the group.

However, other research indicates that the shift can be reversed; that is, the individual will advocate a more conservative position in a group than he or she would independently. In this situation the individual may accede to the norms of the group, which are conservative.

Although the risky shift phenomenon does not seem to hold in all cases, it does indicate quite clearly that the behavior of an individual as an individual is quite different from his or her behavior in a group situation. One study that graphically supports this proposition is the "sexy picture" experiment. In this research undergraduate males as a group could not arrive at a consensus concerning the beauty of several women whose photographs were shown to them (March and Feigenbaum 1960). However, individual ratings of these photographs before the meeting indicated that each participant strongly favored one photograph in which a very attractive girl was in a provocative position. Apparently these males, during the meeting, suppressed their initial preferences because each believed his original choice would draw criticism from the group.

Admittedly individuals sometimes behave independently, regardless of the situation. However, the dynamics of a group can cause significant deviations in an individual's behavior. For this reason a manager must be aware that a commitment given privately may not be upheld in a group situation.

CONTINGENCY VIEW OF GROUPS

There are many contingencies that influence organizational factors such as design and leadership (see Chapters 11 and 14). Similarly, there are many contingencies affecting group behavior. Perhaps the most important contingency is technology. In this section we review three major studies demonstrating the influence of technology on group behavior.

Tavistock Coal-mining Study

In 1951 Eric Trist and K. W. Bamforth of the Tavistock Institute in London, a world-renowned social science institute, published an important study of work group behavior in coal mines. The study was undertaken because England faced a major problem: an aging and antiquated technology not only in coal mining but in many of its key industries. Because the Industrial Revolution originated in England, the country had an established technology that it found difficult to change. England faced the problem not only of developing new technology but also of winning the cooperation of labor unions in this endeavor. Normally the labor unions refuse to give up their traditional work privileges, such as *featherbedding* (using more workers than necessary to complete a job). In contrast, it is frequently argued that Japan and West Germany were lucky during World War II that their technologies were almost completely destroyed, because that forced them to create a new and efficient industrial order.

The Problem. In England, coal mining has traditionally been done by teams of two to eight men. Each team operates independently in a specific section of the mine. Because each team is small and operates under dangerous conditions, cohesion among members tends to be high. In fact, members come to see one another almost as brothers, and they even assume responsibility for one another's families if anyone dies.

After World War II the top management of large coal companies in England decided to modernize. To accomplish this objective, they introduced mass production techniques for mining coal. The mines in England have veins of coal of variable thickness. To modernize the process of extracting coal, the engineers in charge of the project installed a modified assembly line of approximately fifty workers and eliminated the use of the small, traditional work teams. This change gave each coal miner a cramped working space, only 2 yards by 1 yard. To complicate matters, some workers were not able to see the others in the tunnel and could converse with them only by shouting. Productivity declined dramatically.

The Solution. At this point Eric Trist and other behavioral science researchers from the Tavistock Institute conducted long interviews with some of the miners. Trist's researchers found that many workers had developed the symptoms of extreme psychological stress and had begun to lose their sense of identity and masculinity. This last finding was especially interesting, since a coal miner is typically a strong, independent, and masculine individual (Goldthorpe et al. 1968).

To eliminate these problems, the researchers modified the assembly line. They rearranged the work processes so the miners could interact comfortably with one another, placing them close enough to each other to converse freely. Most importantly, the workers were encouraged to participate in decisions that directly influenced their work. For instance, the workers constructed a set of rules that controlled their salaries and their assignments to the mine's three work shifts. Productivity increased significantly, and the symptoms of psychological stress disappeared.

Sociotechnical System. The researchers began to view any organization as a *sociotechnical system:* one in which the formal demands of the organization should mesh with the psychological and social needs of the workers. In effect, the coal miners had worked for centuries in an organic organization, for the use of the small work teams allowed them to define their jobs and the procedures for completing them in a flexible manner. Because of the traditional method, the jobs of the coal miners were enriched; each work team was solely responsible for extracting a specific amount of coal. In addition, there were several noneconomic sources of motivation, such as the cohesion of the work team.

When the engineers modernized the operations, they substituted a mechanistic organization (the assembly line) for the organic organization.[2] The extreme form of the mechanistic organization precipitated a loss of identity among the coal miners and a decline in job satisfaction, both of which appeared to have an adverse effect on the level of productivity. While Eric Trist and his research team did not advocate a return to the traditional organizational structure, they did attempt to alter the modernized structure by means of participative management and redesign of the assembly line so it would become less mechanistic.

The Tavistock coal-mining study does not propose that specialization per se is inefficient or evil. But it does argue that specialization or any other technology that disregards the needs of human beings will probably result in a significant decline in job satisfaction and productivity.

Industrial Work Groups

A related study of the influence of technology on group behavior has been completed by Leonard Sayles (1958). He analyzed the influence of skill level on behavior in several hundred American industrial work groups. His analysis indicated that these work groups were of four general types: apathetic, erratic, strategic, and conservative.

In *apathetic groups* the individuals were performing relatively unskilled, low-paid work. In addition, the work was frequently dangerous and unpleasant. Members of apathetic groups seemed to be dissatisfied, although they did not complain a great deal to management. In such groups there was considerable friction and ineffective, informal leadership.

Erratic groups could be identified when all the workers performed identical or nearly identical tasks. Usually this work was paced by machines. The feelings of such groups tended to fluctuate—at times

[2] For a description of mechanistic and organic organizations, see Chapter 2. Also, for recent studies in this area, see Susman (1976) and Hrebiniak (1974).

FIGURE 15–1
Summary of Work Group Differences

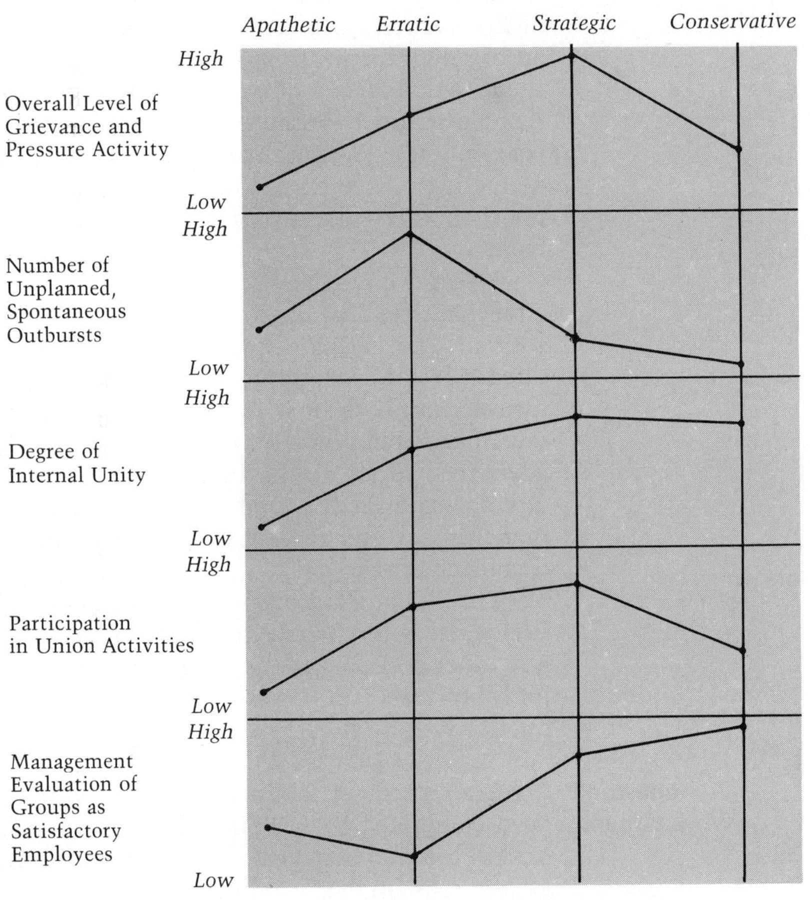

Source: From Leonard Sayles, *Behavior of Industrial Work Groups* (New York: Wiley, 1958), copyright © 1958 by Leonard Sayles. Reprinted by permission of the author.

they resisted management, but at other times they cooperated closely with it.

In *strategic groups* the work was skilled and the jobs were relatively important to the functioning of the organization. Still, the workers typically had no likelihood of promotion to more desirable jobs. These groups were highly cohesive and involved in union activities, and they consistently filed grievances with their union to settle disputes with management.

Finally, the members of *conservative groups* occupied the most esteemed positions in the plant. Their work was highly skilled and often individual, so they operated in an independent fashion. Members of conservative groups tended to be very satisfied and easily resolved their difficulties with management without the use of threats. (Figure 15–1 contains comparative profiles of the four types of work groups.)

Even on a worldwide basis, it appears that the nature of the work strongly affects group behavior. Clark Kerr and Abraham Siegel (1954) analyzed the strike rates of sixteen industries in eleven countries. Each industry was characterized by a definite strike rate that did not vary significantly from country to country (see Table 15–1). For example, miners everywhere tended to strike quite frequently. One reason for this outcome may be the miners' self-concept; that is, they see themselves as very masculine and aggressive (Goldthorpe et al. 1968). Or the nature of the work in this industry may create a climate favorable to strike activity. Miners tend to be close-knit because of the danger involved in their work; this may lead them to strike when they believe they are being treated unfairly. While the specific reason is not certain, it is clear that particular kinds of work are related to specific patterns of behavior.

Alienation and Work Group Behavior

Robert Blauner (1964) has also investigated the influence of technology on work group behavior. However, unlike Sayles, he examined the relationship between technology and *alienation* or lack of job satisfaction.

TABLE 15–1
General Patterns of Strike Propensities in Eleven Countries

Propensity to strike	*Industry*
High	Mining Maritime and longshore
Medium high	Lumber Textile
Medium	Chemical Printing Leather Manufacturing (general) Construction Food and kindred products
Medium low	Clothing Gas, water, and electricity Services (hotels, restaurants, etc.)
Low	Railroad Agriculture Trade

Source: From Clark Kerr and Abraham Siegel, "The Interindustry Propensity to Strike—An International Comparison," in *Industrial Conflict*, ed. Arthur Kornhauser et al., p. 107. Copyright © 1954 by McGraw-Hill Inc. Reprinted by permission of McGraw-Hill Book Company.

Types of Alienation. According to Blauner, a major form of alienation is the feeling of *powerlessness* that a person experiences when he or she has little freedom in his or her work and little control over it. An example of this form of alienation can be found on the assembly line, for the work is unskilled and machine-paced. Hence the worker must complete the job cycle within an allotted time. Usually the job is so simple that the entire cycle must be completed in seconds.

A second form of alienation is *meaninglessness.* In this case the individual does not understand how his or her work fits into the overall goals of the organization. Thus the assembly line employee whose job is highly specialized usually does not see the relationship between his work and all the other activities in the organization (for example, financial operations or marketing strategies).

Another form of alienation is *isolation;* this form occurs when the worker is not integrated into a work group. Consequently, he or she is not able to satisfy social needs through conversation and pleasant relationships with other workers.

The final form of alienation is *self-estrangement.* Under this type of alienation the individual does not understand the relationship between his work and his life's goals. In this sense the work is independent of those aspects of his life that he considers to be significant. Consequently, work is viewed merely as a vehicle for making money so that the individual can enjoy himself during leisure hours.

After defining these four types of alienation, Blauner then relates them to four kinds of work or technology: assembly line work, machine-tending textile work, the craft work of printers, and the continuous-process work that is found in oil refineries and chemical plants.

Assembly Line Worker. Although only about five percent of the U.S. work force works on assembly lines, this kind of work has been studied in depth. Blauner's analysis confirms the results of many other studies that have been completed in this area.

As suggested above, assembly line work is very difficult, for the individual must complete a task within a very short job cycle that may last only seconds. Hence the work becomes monotonous and dull.

Blauner argues that assembly line work creates the greatest amount of alienation. The worker feels powerless since the job is machine-paced. He or she has little freedom and no control whatsoever over the pace of the work. At the same time, the worker usually does not understand how his or her narrow job fits into the overall organizational goals that are determined by top management—that is, the work becomes meaningless. And since the pressure to produce is unrelenting, the employee is unable to form close relationships with fellow workers. Hence he or she feels isolated. In some circumstances the pace of the machine is increased to a point where the worker has great difficulty in completing the task. Under such conditions the worker becomes self-estranged, for he or she begins to view work as separate from the remainder of his or her life.

To eliminate or reduce feelings of alienation, the worker frequently builds a small workshop at home. In this setting the worker is challenged by his job, for he can become a skilled craftsman who controls the pace of his activities. The worker also reduces alienation by daydreaming on the job. One of the more popular daydreams among these workers is to send their children to college so they can avoid the misery of the assembly line. Another popular daydream is the creation of a small business in which the worker would be in total control. Ironically, few workers ever realize this objective, probably because they know that their lack of business experience increases dramatically their chances of failure.

Machine-tending Work. A special technology is used in small textile firms in which the machines complete the work while the individual merely tends it. Consequently the work is semiskilled. Like assembly line workers, the employees in a textile mill experience feelings of powerlessness and meaninglessness. These workers, a large proportion of whom are female, have little control over the pace of the work. At the same time, they have only a limited understanding of the overall operation of the firm, for their jobs are quite narrow.

However, textile mills are usually situated in small towns in which the mill is the only source of employment. Consequently, employment at the mill is considered to be important, especially if other workers cannot find jobs. In addition, the workers are able to converse freely while they tend the machines. Hence the mill becomes a mirror image of the town. Under such conditions feelings of isolation and self-estrangement are eliminated or reduced.

Craft Work. In recent years workers in the printing industry have been threatened with large-scale automation. If automation becomes widespread, the work of printers will become semiskilled. However, a printer is a highly skilled worker who must spend several years as an apprentice before becoming a full-fledged member of the profession. Because of their skills, printers receive excellent wages.

Overall, printers are proud of and enjoy their work. This conclusion has been confirmed by studies of labor unions. For example, one analysis has suggested that Michels' iron law of oligarchy, or one-party rule, holds almost universally in unions, primarily because the key leaders would lose status and money if forced to return to their regular jobs (Lipset, Trow, and Coleman 1956). The only major exception to this generalization is the International Typographical

Union (ITU) in which a two-party system flourishes. Apparently the transition from union official to the regular job is easy for printers since they have pride in their work.

Continuous-Process Work. The final type of technology investigated by Blauner is used in oil refineries and chemical plants. Here the employee never sees the product on which he or she is working. Rather, the worker sits before a machine that controls the travel of the product through the oil refinery or chemical plant. Hence the technology is called continuous process.

As in the case of textile mills, continuous-process work is semiskilled. Usually the workers are high school graduates who are trained for a short period of time to monitor the dials that control the flow of the product. And admittedly their work requires less skill than that of printers. However, continuous-process employees experience fewer feelings of alienation than do printers.

Apparently the major reason continuous-process workers are satisfied with their jobs is that they are able to exercise great responsibility. Although they work under the direction of highly skilled engineers, these workers must be able to react quickly as a team if a problem occurs, for millions of dollars can be lost in a short time. Hence the workers must thoroughly understand their own machines and dials. At the same time, they are made aware of how important their tasks are in the overall structure of the organization.

Since the workers must read their dials carefully in order to detect problems, management allows them much leisure to ensure that they are not tired. It is common practice for a worker to tend a machine only forty percent of the time while he or she is on duty. At other times the worker is free to relax and converse with fellow employees and the superior. This relaxed atmosphere breaks down any social distinction between the employees and their superior, even though he or she is much more educated and paid at a much higher rate. Frequently these conversations center around the complexity of the work. Hence the employees, who may appear to be relaxing completely, are actually familiarizing themselves with the intricacies of the work.

The most exciting moments of continuous-process work occur when a crisis materializes. At this time the workers and their superiors must react as a finely tuned team. If anyone fails to complete his or her tasks efficiently, the probability of large financial losses increases. Because the nature of the work is focused on crises and reactions to them as a team, the employees develop strong bonds of friendship. In fact, a frequent topic of conversation among these workers is their success as a team during crisis situations.

Table 15–2 contains a summary of all Blauner's major points and findings.

TABLE 15–2
Blauner's Analysis of Relationship Between Technology and Alienation

Technology and skill level (lowest to highest)	*Alienation experienced (highest to lowest)*	*Factors reducing alienation*
Assembly line workers (unskilled)	Assembly line workers	None
Textile workers (semiskilled)	Textile workers	The factory as an important part of the social fabric of a small town
Continuous-process workers (semi-skilled)	Printers	Skill
Printers (highly skilled)	Continuous-process workers	Responsibility

SUMMARY

Group behavior can be conceptualized in terms of George Homans's system theory, which proposes that a social system is the state of relations among three factors: interaction, activity, and sentiment. Other researchers have shown that groups evolve in predictable ways. For instance, Bales has shown that two distinct types of leaders emerge in a group whose members were not previously acquainted with one another: the task-oriented and the considerate leaders. Bales and others have also shown that different types of groups evolve through predictable stages and that these stages differ by group type.

There are at least five major reasons why individuals join groups: interpersonal attraction, the attractiveness of the group's goals, the attractiveness of its activities, social interaction, and instrumental reasons. There are many different types of groups in organizations, including primary and secondary groups, and problem-solving and creative groups.

Factors influencing behavior in groups include the physical environment in which the activity takes place, personal characteristics of group members, group structure, and group composition. Personal space and the actual structure of the organization are key aspects of the physical environment. Major personal characteristics of group members that influence group behavior include biographical characteristics such as age and physical condition, the members' abilities, individual personalities, and members' attitudes.

Group composition refers to the relationships among the personal characteristics of group members and the consequences of these relationships for group activities. Two aspects of composition are cohesiveness and group compatibility. As they increase, group effectiveness in achieving goals also rises.

The manner in which the group is structured or organized also influences behavior. Factors of importance in this area include leadership style, differential status of group members, organizational positions of members, and the degree to which individuals participate in decision making.

Finally, a contingency view of group behavior was developed by focusing principally on technology. According to the Tavistock coal-mining study, an organization is a sociotechnical system in which the formal demands of the organization should mesh with the psychological and social needs of the workers. Sayles's study indicates that there are four types of industrial work groups: apathetic, erratic, strategic, and conservative. The major factor predicting the formation of such groups is technology. Even on a worldwide basis, type of technology is related to propensity to strike among workers. And according to Robert Blauner, type of technology influences the degree of alienation or job satisfaction that workers and managers experience in various types of groups and work settings.

DISCUSSION QUESTIONS

1. Do you agree that the risky shift phenomenon exists? Why or why not? What are some organizational implications of this phenomenon for the effective functioning of individuals and organizations?
2. Can a problem-solving group operate effectively as a creative group? Explain. What are some of the factors that distinguish problem-solving and creative groups? Which type is more important to the functioning of an organization? Why?
3. The United States was long known as a melting pot of immigrants of various nationalities. How do you think this ethnic diversity affects the behavior of groups in a heterogeneous work force? How does the American pioneer spirit affect work groups?
4. Which factor seemed more important in bringing about unionization in food chains, the physical structure of the store or the skills of the employee? How were these two factors related? What are some other factors that might make a work group favorable toward unionizing?

CRITICAL INCIDENT

NOTE: This critical incident can be used by the whole class with the case observational method (see Appendix A) or used for thought and discussion by individual class members.

In the late 1960s the department of sociology at a major university experienced a sharp increase in student enrollment, but the resource base remained static. After three years the department was in a crisis;

several faculty members had quit and the entire program was in jeopardy because of their departure.

As in most universities, the faculty members believed in a system of democracy. Thus many major decisions were made in the faculty assembly, which consisted of the ninety faculty members in the department. But the chairperson of the department, Professor Gleesser, did not like to bring too many issues before the faculty assembly, since many of the members became emotional in this committee-of-the-whole setting and many really didn't understand the intricate problems the department faced. Hence he did not delegate many responsibilities and made most of the major and minor decisions by himself. Although faculty members liked Professor Gleesser personally, they perceived his style of leadership as autocratic.

Professor Gleesser discussed the issue with Professor Hart, a trusted colleague. She argued that a small decision-making and advisory group should be established that would be representative of the major factions within the department. This group would meet weekly for two hours and recommend courses of action that the department chairperson might follow. It would also publish minutes of its meeting indicating actions it had taken. Over time Professor Hart expected that the group members would begin to trust one another and try to work for the achievement of system goals. To ensure this outcome, Professor Hart recommended that Professor Gleesser not be present at most meetings of the group, since his presence might inhibit free discussion of issues. Professor Gleesser established a group of seven members and appointed Professor Hart as its chairperson. Its first task was to develop a strategy for obtaining additional resources from upper administration.

There were many advantages associated with the new structure of the department. Previously Professor Gleesser was the lightning rod for all complaints both from the faculty and from the upper administration. These complaints were now channeled through the small advisory group for discussion and resolution. This group also began to establish policies on such matters as teaching loads, student advisement, and allocation of teaching assistants. In addition, the group was proactive and tried to solve problems before they occurred. This behavior was much different from the reactive mode traditionally associated with the faculty assembly, which could only come to agreement on solutions to a few major problems and only after they had occurred. Finally, this advisory group could take quick actions as a whole against upper administration—such as voting to limit class sizes, thus forcing many students into other courses. Since the group had made these decisions, rather than the chairperson of the department, upper administration had difficulty in singling out faculty members for punishment (such as withholding salary increases).

However, one member of the group, Professor Porter, did not like the idea of group decision making. He was a powerful member of the faculty and for years had obtained a disproportionate share of the resources by various means, such as constantly nagging the chairperson, who eventually gave in just to get rid of him. In addition, he would agree to one course of action in the advisory group but would reverse his position in the Faculty Assembly. His behavior was detrimental to the group's activities, but Professor Hart did not know what to do in order to change it.

QUESTIONS: What types of decisions should be made by committees-of-the-whole? What types of decisions should be made by small decision-making groups similar to the one described above? If you were Professor Hart, how would you handle Professor Porter?

SUGGESTED READINGS

Crozier, Michel. *The Bureaucratic Phenomenon.* Chicago: University of Chicago Press, 1964, 320 pages, paperback.

This is a long and somewhat difficult book, but serious students enjoy it. Crozier focuses on the relationship among culture, bureaucracy, and group and individual behavior. An interesting aspect of this book is his comparative analysis of the kinds of bureaucracy that exist in France, Russia, and the United States (Chapter 10). He also presents an insightful treatment of French entrepreneurship.

Goldthorpe, John; Lockwood, David; Bechhofer, Frank; and Platt, Jennifer. *The Affluent Worker: Industrial Attitudes and Behavior.* New York: Oxford University Press, 1968, 206 pages, paperback.

Goldthorpe and his associates studied a group of workers in a prosperous industrial city in England, See the description in this chapter.

Sayles, Leonard. *Behavior of Industrial Work Groups.* New York: Wiley, 1958, 182 pages, hardback.

This is an excellent case study of different types of workers and the impact of technology on their behavior. It is one of the best anthropological studies of work groups and is very readable.

PART IV
EXPERIENTIAL EXERCISES

Assessing Motivation, Satisfaction, and Congruent Jobs

PURPOSE: 1. To diagnose your own need strength and need satisfaction. 2. To explore jobs and types of supervisors that would best fit your needs. 3. To help others explore their own needs.

ADVANCE PREPARATION: None required. However, it saves class time if participants fill out the questionnaire in this exercise and score it before class.

GROUP SIZE: Groups of 3, total of 100 participants.

TIME REQUIRED: Assessment exercise: 50 minutes; Career-planning option; 55 minutes; Leadership style option: 55 minutes.

SPECIAL MATERIALS: None.

SPECIAL PHYSICAL REQUIREMENTS: None.

RELATED TOPICS: Leadership; work, life, and career roles; applied motivation and job design.

INTRODUCTION

If you ask managers what is the most important problem or process in the management of people at work, chances are they will mention motivation. (Leadership and communication are other frequent responses to this question.) Motivation activates human energy; it is a force that leads people to attempt to satisfy their important needs. Furthermore, as many students of the subject have said, *all* human behavior is motivated. The critical factor is the *direction* of that motivation—is it to work hard, to do high-quality work, to spend time

Source: From Douglas Hall et al., *Experiences in Management and Organizational Behavior,* St. Claire Press, 1975; used by permission of John Wiley & Sons, Inc. Adapted from a questionaire by Lyman W. Porter, *Organizational Patterns of Managerial Job Attitudes* (New York: American Foundation for Management Research, 1964), pp. 1, 15 – 17. Published by American Management Assn., Inc.

with one's family, or to sleep as much as possible on the job without being caught by the foreman?

In this exercise we will focus not on assembly line workers or clerks or executives but on you and your own motivation. To do this, we will use a questionnaire developed by Lyman W. Porter originally to measure managerial motivation in national and worldwide samples. Since then it has been widely used to measure needs and satisfactions in all types of people. Porter sees the assessment of a person's motivation as a means of determining his or her psychological "fit" with various types of jobs:

> An understanding of the nature of job perceptions held by individuals in management positions would seem to be appropriate for the study of organizational problems. In many cases, for example, individuals are promoted within management on the basis of their technical qualifications for a job, while their performance may in large part depend on how well they are able to adjust to such psychological aspects of the job as the types of motivational rewards received, the various pressures encountered, and the perceived expectations of superiors and subordinates. In short, some individuals may be qualified technically for particular management jobs, but do not fit the psychological nature of the jobs. If management and the individuals themselves knew more about the psychological aspects of jobs, and of the differences between jobs at different levels and in different parts of the organization, promotional and other personnel errors might be reduced and organizational effectiveness thereby increased. *(Porter 1961, p. 1)*

Porter describes his measure of motivation as follows:

> . . . We have used a theoretical classification system that has been widely applied to the analysis of motivation in the work situation. This system, developed by A. H. Maslow, a psychologist, groups motives and needs according to a hierarchy of priority of prepotency (Maslow 1954). In the terms of Maslow's theory there are physiological – or primary – needs (water, food, and sleep) which are basic because the individual *must* satisfy them, at least to a minimal degree, before he can turn his attention to other, so-called "higher-order" needs. Next in priority after the physiological needs are the ones concerned with safety and security. Next, in order, come the social and esteem, or recognition, needs. Finally, the highest level need is "self-realization." It is defined by Maslow as "the desire for self-fulfillment, namely, . . . the tendency [for a person] to become actualized in what he is potentially . . . the desire to become more and more what one is, to become everything that one is capable of becoming. . . ." *(Maslow 1954, pp. 91–92; Porter 1964, pp. 15, 16)*

The Porter questionnaire measures all of the Maslow need levels, with the exception of the physiological needs, which we will assume to be relatively well satisfied for most participants. However, this assumption would not be valid for people who are ill (especially those with chronic illnesses), extremely poor people, people living in unsafe, high-crime areas, old people, and other groups whose physical well-being is unsatisfactory.

In this exercise you will be asked to assess your own motivation and satisfaction, either in your present job or in the kind of job you think you will be in when you finish this phase of your education. Then you may be asked to think about how these different levels of motivation might be linked to particular jobs or types of supervision.

PROCEDURE

Step 1: 10 minutes

Complete the questionnaire below. *If you are currently employed,* either part-time or full-time, respond in terms of your present job. *If you are not currently employed,* describe your *last job.* If you have never worked, respond in terms of the kind of job you *realistically think you will have* when you start working.

Questionnaire

Given below are several characteristics or qualities connected with your job. For each such characteristic, you will give three ratings:

a. *How much* of the characteristic *is there now* connected with your job?
b. *How much* of the characteristic do you think *should be* connected with your job?
c. *How important* is this characteristic *to you?*

Each rating will be on a seven-point scale, like this:

(minimum) 1 2 3 4 5 6 7 (maximum)

You are to *circle the number* on the scale that represents the amount of the characteristic being rated. Low numbers represent low or minimum amounts, and high numbers represent high or maximum amounts. If you think there is "very little" or "none" of the characteristic presently associated with your job, you would circle numeral 1. If you think there is "just a little," you would circle numeral 2, and so on. If you think there is a "great deal but not a maximum amount," you would circle numeral 6. For each scale, circle only one number. *Please do not omit any scales.*

1. The *feeling of self-esteem* a person gets from being in my job position:
   a. How much is there now? (min) 1 2 3 4 5 6 7 (max)
   b. How much should there be? 1 2 3 4 5 6 7
   c. How important is this to me? 1 2 3 4 5 6 7
2. The *opportunity for personal growth and development* in my job position:
   a. How much is there now? (min) 1 2 3 4 5 6 7 (max)
   b. How much should there be? 1 2 3 4 5 6 7
   c. How important is this to me? 1 2 3 4 5 6 7

3. The *prestige* of my job *inside* the company (that is, the regard received from others in the company):
   a. How much is there now? (min) 1 2 3 4 5 6 7 (max)
   b. How much should there be? 1 2 3 4 5 6 7
   c. How important is this to me? 1 2 3 4 5 6 7
4. The *opportunity for independent thought and action* in my position:
   a. How much is there now? (min) 1 2 3 4 5 6 7 (max)
   b. How much should there be? 1 2 3 4 5 6 7
   c. How important is this to me? 1 2 3 4 5 6 7
5. The *feeling of security* in my job position:
   a. How much is there now? (min) 1 2 3 4 5 6 7 (max)
   b. How much should there be? 1 2 3 4 5 6 7
   c. How important is this to me? 1 2 3 4 5 6 7
6. The *feeling of self-fulfillment* a person gets from being in my job position, that is, the feeling of being able to use one's own unique capabilities, realizing one's potentialities:
   a. How much is there now? (min) 1 2 3 4 5 6 7 (max)
   b. How much should there be? 1 2 3 4 5 6 7
   c. How important is this to me? 1 2 3 4 5 6 7
7. The *prestige* of my job position *outside* the company (that is, the regard received from others not in the company):
   a. How much is there now? (min) 1 2 3 4 5 6 7 (max)
   b. How much should there be? 1 2 3 4 5 6 7
   c. How important is this to me? 1 2 3 4 5 6 7
8. The *feeling of worthwhile accomplishment* in my job:
   a. How much is there now? (min) 1 2 3 4 5 6 7 (max)
   b. How much should there be? 1 2 3 4 5 6 7
   c. How important is this to me? 1 2 3 4 5 6 7
9. The *opportunity,* in my job, *to give help to other people:*
   a. How much is there now? (min) 1 2 3 4 5 6 7 (max)
   b. How much should there be? 1 2 3 4 5 6 7
   c. How important is this to me? 1 2 3 4 5 6 7
10. The *opportunity,* in my job, *for participation in the setting of goals:*
    a. How much is there now? (min) 1 2 3 4 5 6 7 (max)
    b. How much should there be? 1 2 3 4 5 6 7
    c. How important is this to me? 1 2 3 4 5 6 7
11. The *opportunity,* in my job, *for participation in the determination of methods and procedures:*
    a. How much is there now? (min) 1 2 3 4 5 6 7 (max)
    b. How much should there be? 1 2 3 4 5 6 7
    c. How important is this to me? 1 2 3 4 5 6 7
12. The *authority* connected with my job:
    a. How much is there now? (min) 1 2 3 4 5 6 7 (max)

b. How much should there be? 1 2 3 4 5 6 7
c. How important is this to me? 1 2 3 4 5 6 7

13. The *opportunity to develop close friendships* in my job:
a. How much is there now? (min) 1 2 3 4 5 6 7 (max)
b. How much should there be? 1 2 3 4 5 6 7
c. How important is this to me? 1 2 3 4 5 6 7

Step 2: 10 minutes Compute your need scores for each of the need categories, using the following scoring form. Remember that under each job characteristic you were asked to give three ratings, the third of which was "*How important* is this characteristic *to you*?" This question above measures the importance you attach to the various needs to be scored here.

1. Enter the number you circled in part c for each question in the space next to that number.
2. Next add up the numbers in each column to obtain your total score for each need.
3. Then divide by the number of questions used to measure that need, to obtain a raw score.
4. Finally, subtract the national mean from each raw score to obtain your adjusted score for each need. Be sure to retain the sign (+ or −).

	Security	*Social*	*Esteem*	*Autonomy*	*Self-realization*
	5c =	9c =	1c =	4c =	2c =
		13c =	3c =	10c =	6c =
			7c =	11c =	8c =
				12c =	
Total:	____	____	____	____	____
Divided by:	1	2	3	4	3
Equals raw score:	____	____	____	____	____
Minus national[1] mean:	5.33	5.36	5.28	5.92	6.35
Equals adjusted score:	____	____	____	____	____

[1] National means from Porter's sample of 1916 managers. These numbers are "grand means" for all levels of management combined.

TABLE 1

Dissatisfaction and Importance of Needs (by Level of Management)

Level	Needs: Security	Social	Esteem	Autonomy	Self-realization
Mean dissatisfaction[a]					
President	0.26	0.34	0.28	0.18	0.63
Vice-president	0.45	0.29	0.45	0.55	0.90
Upper middle	0.41	0.33	0.66	0.87	1.12
Lower middle	0.38	0.32	0.71	0.96	1.17
Lower	0.82	0.56	1.15	1.40	1.52
Mean importance[b]					
President	5.69	5.38	5.27	6.11	6.50
Vice-president	5.44	5.46	5.33	6.10	6.40
Upper middle	5.20	5.31	5.27	5.89	6.34
Lower middle	5.29	5.33	5.26	5.74	6.25
Lower	5.30	5.27	5.18	5.58	6.32

[a] Dissatisfaction score based on difference between obtained and expected fulfillment. Therefore, a difference score of 0 = complete satisfaction; a difference score of 6 = complete dissatisfaction.
[b] 1 = lowest degree of importance; 7 = highest degree of importance.

Source: Lyman W. Porter, *Organizational Patterns of Managerial Job Attitudes* (New York: American Foundation for Management Research, 1964), p. 17.

You are asked to subtract the national means from your own score to obtain an adjusted score for each category. This adjusted score tells you how strong your needs are in relation to each other. If you only looked at the raw scores, you would probably find that most people score highest on self-fulfillment and lowest on esteem or security. For comparative purposes, Table 1 gives Porter's means for managers at all levels.

Step 3: 5 minutes In a similar manner, compute your raw scores and adjusted scores for dissatisfaction. Dissatisfaction with each job characteristic is scored as the score for (b) minus the score for (a); that is, "How much there should be?" minus "How much there is now."

1. For each question, subtract part a's score from part b's score (that is, b − a).
2. Enter the (b − a) score for each question in the space next to the number of that question in the columns below. If b is greater than a, be sure to retain the minus sign for the difference.
3. Next, add up the numbers in each column to obtain a total for each need. Again, be sure to retain any minus signs.
4. Divide this total by the number of questions used to measure each need to obtain raw scores for each need.
5. Finally, subtract the national mean from each raw score to obtain your adjusted score for each need. Remember, this ad-

justed score is a measure of *dis*satisfaction. The lower it is, the more satisfied you are. The higher it is, the more dissatisfied you are.

	Security	*Social*	*Esteem*	*Autonomy*	*Self-realization*
	b − a =	b − a =	b − a =	b − a =	b − a =
	5b − 5a =	9b − 9a =	1b − 1a =	4b − 4a =	2b − 2a =
		13b − 13a =	3b − 3a =	10b − 10a =	6b − 6a =
			7b − 7a =	11b − 11a =	8b − 8a =
				12b − 12a =	
Total:	____	____	____	____	____
Divided by:	1	2	3	4	3
Equals raw score:	____	____	____	____	____
Minus national mean:[2]	0.43	0.33	0.61	0.78	1.05
Equals adjusted score:	____	____	____	____	____

Step 4: 15 minutes Meet in groups of three to discuss your need strength and satisfaction scores. If possible, meet with people who know you rather than with strangers. Figure the *rank order* of your adjusted need importance scores (highest number = most important; lowest number = least important). Ask the other two group members to guess the rank order of your adjusted needs. Ask them *what behaviors* you show that lead them to perceive you as having that pattern of needs. Then read the actual rank order of adjusted need importance you have computed. Discuss why there was or was not a difference between your view and their view of your needs. Repeat this process for each member of the group.

Step 5: 10 minutes NOTE: *If most of the participants have not had work experience, do not use step 5.*

Next discuss the rank order of each person's adjusted satisfaction scores. What *features of your job* were or are responsible for your areas of high and low satisfaction? How could the job be changed to remove the dissatisfaction? What different job would lead to greater satisfaction?

[2] National means from Porter's sample of 1916 managers. The numbers are "grand means" for all levels of management combined.

T-P Leadership Questionnaire: An Assessment of Style

GOAL: To evaluate oneself in terms of task orientation (T) and people orientation (P).

T-P LEADERSHIP QUESTIONNAIRE

Name ____________________ Group ____________________

The following items describe aspects of leadership behavior. Respond to each item according to the way you would most likely act if you were the leader of a work group. Circle whether you would most likely behave in the described way always (A), frequently (F), occasionally (O), seldom (S), or never (N).

A F O S N 1. I would most likely act as the spokesperson of the group.
A F O S N 2. I would encourage overtime work.
A F O S N 3. I would allow members complete freedom in their work.
A F O S N 4. I would encourage the use of uniform procedures.
A F O S N 5. I would permit the members to use their own judgment in solving problems.
A F O S N 6. I would stress being ahead of competing groups.
A F O S N 7. I would speak as a representative of the group.
A F O S N 8. I would needle members for greater effort.

Source: Reprinted from J. William Pfeiffer and John E. Jones, eds., *A Handbook of Structured Experiences for Human Relations Training,* vol. I (rev.), San Diego, Ca.: University Associates, 1974, pp. 7–12, as adapted from Sergiovanni, Metzcus, and Burden's revision of the Leadership Behavior Description Questionnaire, *American Educational Research Review* 6 (1969). Used with permission.

A F O S N 9. I would try out my ideas in the group.
A F O S N 10. I would let the members do their work the way they think best.
A F O S N 11. I would be working hard for a promotion.
A F O S N 12. I would tolerate postponement and uncertainty.
A F O S N 13. I would speak for the group if there were visitors present.
A F O S N 14. I would keep the work moving at a rapid pace.
A F O S N 15. I would turn the members loose on a job and let them go to it.
A F O S N 16. I would settle conflicts when they occur in the group.
A F O S N 17. I would get swamped by details.
A F O S N 18. I would represent the group at outside meetings.
A F O S N 19. I would be reluctant to allow the members any freedom of action.
A F O S N 20. I would decide what should be done and how it should be done.
A F O S N 21. I would push for increased production.
A F O S N 22. I would let some members have authority that I could keep.
A F O S N 23. Things would usually turn out as I had predicted.
A F O S N 24. I would allow the group a high degree of initiative.
A F O S N 25. I would assign group members to particular tasks.
A F O S N 26. I would be willing to make changes.

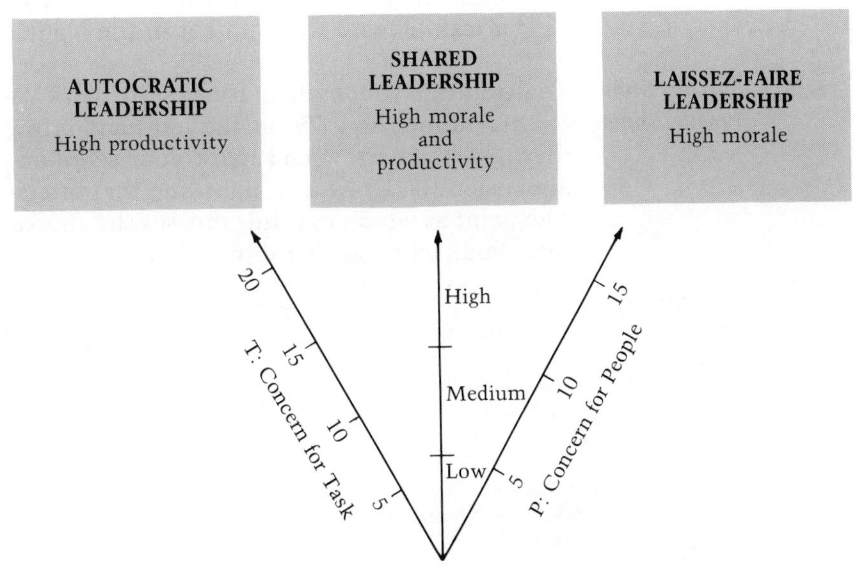

A F O S N 27. I would ask the members to work harder.
A F O S N 28. I would trust the group members to exercise good judgment.
A F O S N 29. I would schedule the work to be done.
A F O S N 30. I would refuse to explain my actions.
A F O S N 31. I would persuade others that my ideas are to their advantage.
A F O S N 32. I would permit the group to set its own pace.
A F O S N 33. I would urge the group to beat its previous record.
A F O S N 34. I would act without consulting the group.
A F O S N 35. I would ask that group members follow standard rules and regulations.

T_____ P_____

Scoring

1. Circle the item number for items 8, 12, 17, 18, 19, 30, 34, and 35.
2. Write the number 1 in front of a *circled item number* if you responded S (seldom) or N (never) to that item.
3. Also write a number 1 in front of *item numbers not circled* if you responded A (always) or F (frequently).
4. Circle the number 1s you have written in front of the following items: 3, 5, 8, 10, 15, 18, 19, 22, 24, 26, 28, 30, 32, 34, and 35.
5. *Count the circled number 1s.* This is your score for concern for people. Record the score in the blank following the letter P at the end of the questionnaire.
6. *Count the uncircled number 1s.* This is your score for concern for task. Record this number in the blank following the letter T.

T-P Leadership Style Profile Sheet

To determine your style of leadership, mark your score on the *concern for task* dimension (T) on the left-hand arrow below. Next move to the right-hand arrow and mark your score on the *concern for people* dimension (P). Draw a straight line that intersects the P and T scores. The point at which that line crosses the *shared leadership* arrow indicates your score on that dimension.

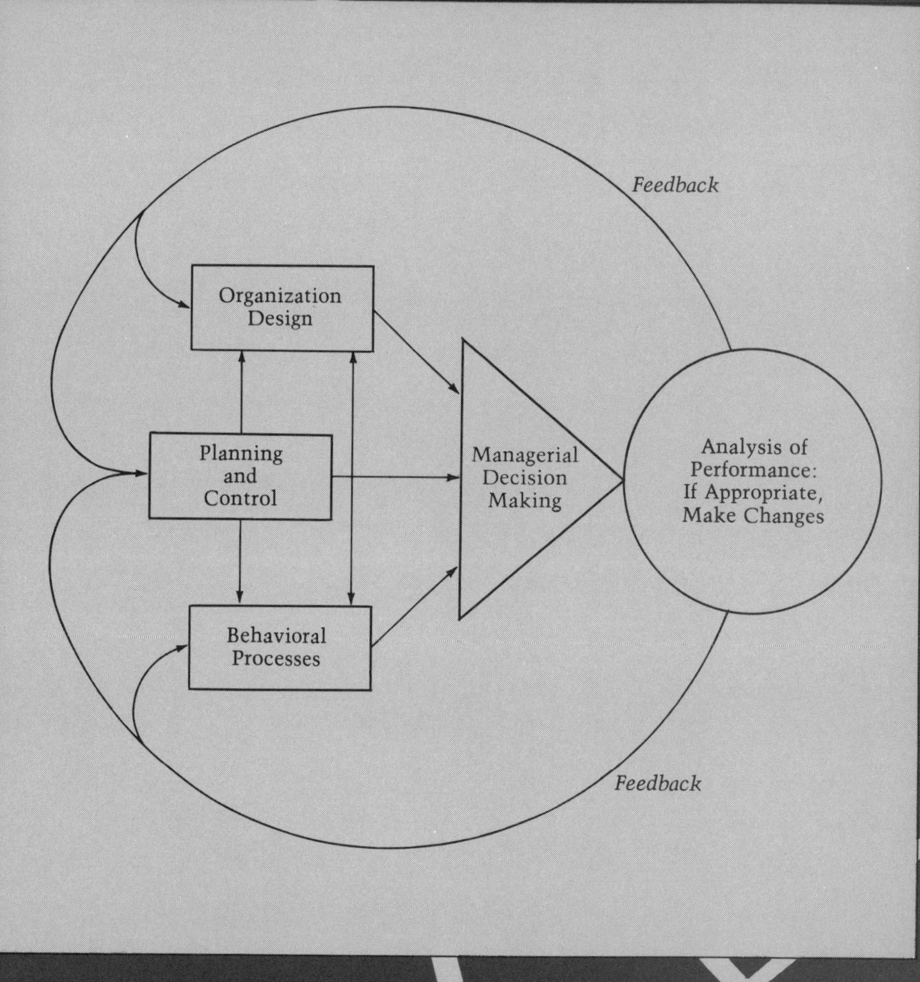
Feedback
Organization Design
Planning and Control
Behavioral Processes
Managerial Decision Making
Analysis of Performance: If Appropriate, Make Changes
Feedback

V SPECIFIC ORGANIZATIONAL ISSUES

Our integrated framework defines four organizational dimensions within which managerial activities take place: planning and control, organization design, behavioral processes, and managerial decision making. However, there are several organizational issues that cut across or encompass more than one of these dimensions. For example, conflict can easily take place between individuals, subgroups within one department, two or more departments, and organizations themselves.

In this part of the book we shall turn our attention to such specific organizational issues. In Chapter 16 we examine the issue of management's need to exercise social responsibility for the purposes of exercising good citizenry and of avoiding or minimizing governmental regulation. Chapter 17 focuses on the related problems of managing both conflict and creativity. Part V then concludes with a chapter on managing change and development within the organization.

The "Whiz Kids" (front row)—Ford's new managers—in 1946

CONTINUOUS CASE

The Ford Motor Company 1946 to Present

SUMMARY: Henry Ford was successful because of his strategic plan of manufacturing an all-purpose, inexpensive, and durable car, the Model T. To keep expenses down, he redesigned his company through the use of mass production. Although this change occurred in 1914, his personnel practices continued to be very farsighted during the period 1914–1920. However, the rise of General Motors in the twenties threatened Ford's financial stability. But rather than changing his strategic plan, Henry Ford kept the price of the Model T low by emphasizing tight control of the workers. This pattern continued between 1930 and 1945, and reflected a negative approach to our organizational dimension of behavioral processes.

After Henry Ford I stepped aside in 1946, Henry Ford II and a group of professional managers assumed control of the company. Their ability to make effective decisions led to the renascence of the company.

REORGANIZATION

At the end of World War II Henry Ford II's first major act was to reorganize the company. Actually the reorganization was suggested and carried out by a group of young executives that included Tex Thorton, Robert McNamara, R. J. Miller, and others well known in the history of American business. These men had worked together as systems analysts during World War II. Immediately after being discharged, they came as a group to Henry Ford and were hired to reorganize the company. Henry Ford II concerned himself with the external aspects of being company president while this group reorganized and modernized the company. The supreme irony of the reorganization is that it paralleled the policies General Motors had emphasized in 1920—federal decentralization, appealing to a cross section of customers, and annual changes in models. Because of this reorganization, the company has once again become very successful and it now ranks directly behind General Motors.

Since 1945 the Ford Motor Company has been very progressive in its relations with its workers and the UAW and has implemented some pioneering concepts, such as supplemental unemployment benefits. If a worker is laid off, he receives ninety-five percent of his salary for one year through a combination of unemployment benefits and supplemental funds provided by the company.

However, the Ford Motor Company has also experienced some major problems since 1946. For example, during the 1950s the company produced the ill-fated and unpopular Edsel, which resulted in a loss of $350 million. There were many reasons for this failure. Perhaps the major reason was that several years passed between the original engineering design of the car and its actual production. During these years the Korean War intervened, and consumer tastes moved away from a preference for large cars to one for small cars. Unfortunately, Ford's top management did not sufficiently appreciate this change in taste and went forward with the production of the Edsel, which today is a collector's item that is becoming more valuable every year.

In 1977, after the Ford Motor Company experienced the three best years in the company's history, it was ranked as the fourth largest industrial company in the United States in earnings: $1.7 billion. However, the company today is facing a challenging and uncertain future; to sustain its success, it must attack three major problems: governmental regulations and standards, increased competition, and managerial succession.

REGULATION AND COMPETITION

United States automotive companies must now meet new safety and pollution standards that require them to redesign their automobiles. For example, the National Highway Traffic Safety Administration has mandated that the gas consumption of an automobile be reduced to an average of 27.5 miles per gallon by 1985. To accomplish this task, Ford must reduce the size of its cars considerably. New designs must be developed and new materials used. General Motors has a larger financial base than Ford upon which to make such changes. Hence Ford must be more careful than General Motors to ensure that its engineering investments yield high profits when the new cars are actually produced and sold. The third largest American automotive company, Chrysler, is in even worse shape than Ford, and the fourth largest, American Motors, is now controlled by Renault, a French company.

Because of new governmental regulations, Ford must recall cars that have engineering defects. In addition, the company must respond to customer lawsuits that result from defective engineering.

Also, Ford faces new and increased competition. In particular, Japanese firms have positioned themselves well in the small-car market, and the combination of new safety standards and the fuel efficiency of small cars suggests that this market represents the wave of the future. To move strongly in this market, Ford must reduce the size of its cars but simultaneously make them attractive to Americans who had grown accustomed to larger cars.

MANAGERIAL SUCCESSION

Henry Ford II was chairman of the board for thirty-four years; he retired in 1980. During his chairmanship the company had a poor history of hiring and keeping top managerial talent. For example, since 1955 Henry Ford II had appointed six different top managers as president of the company, including Robert McNamara, former secretary of defense, and Arjay Miller, who became dean of the Graduate School of Business at Stanford University. This problem of hiring and keeping top managers may be exacerbated by the retirement of Henry Ford II. At the time of this writing it is too early to tell whether the Ford Motor Company can solve the problem.

QUESTIONS: Some analysts have argued that only two American companies, General Motors and Ford, will remain as American companies during the 1980s due to the increased competition in the international automotive market. Do you agree with this assessment? Also, in what ways are the managerial styles of Henry Ford I and Henry Ford II similar? How are they different? Do you feel, as Henry Ford I said, that a company is "just the lengthened shadow of a man"?

16 Social Responsibility in Management

EVOLUTION OF SOCIAL RESPONSIBILITY
ARGUMENTS FOR AND AGAINST SOCIAL RESPONSIBILITY
BUSINESS ETHICS
SOCIAL AUDITS
CURRENT ISSUES
SUMMARY
DISCUSSION QUESTIONS
CRITICAL INCIDENT
SUGGESTED READINGS

PERFORMANCE OBJECTIVES

1. To outline and describe how business has evolved as an institution in meeting the changing needs of society while reflecting the values of the larger social system.
2. To discuss the arguments for and against social responsibility.
3. To describe how social responsibility has emerged as a contemporary concern of management.
4. To discuss business ethics.
5. To examine proposals for the measurement of corporate social performance through various types of social audits.
6. To examine some of major current issues in the area of social responsibility.

To be effective, business must meet not only organizational objectives but also the needs and expectations of the larger society. Business operates as only one major component of a large social system. Within this system a process of interaction, interdependencies, and complex interrelationships occurs. The expectations and values of the society are reflected in this process, and these change over time. In earlier periods the role of business was primarily economic, with the principal responsibility being accorded to shareholders. The role of business has now evolved to include social as well as economic goals, and responsibilities have broadened to encompass customers, suppliers, employees, the community, and the general public.

The first part of this chapter describes the evolution of social responsibility as a business concern and analyzes the major arguments for and against social responsibility. Next the chapter examines the relationship between business ethics and social responsibility. There is then a brief description of the methods businesses use to assess corporate social performance. Finally, the chapter reviews major current issues.

EVOLUTION OF SOCIAL RESPONSIBILITY

The concept of social responsibility has evolved through several stages, although these stages overlap to a certain extent. To appreciate how social responsibility evolved as an important concern of management and business organizations, one must bear in mind that the activities of business are closely interrelated with the larger social system; this interrelationship has been termed *business and society.* During the development of business its role has changed in response to changes in expectations held by society. These expectations have been formulated and expressed by the major groups with which business interacts, including investors, customers, employees or labor unions, government, and the community. As we examine the stages of social responsibility in this section, we shall emphasize the interrelationship between business and society.

Early Views

The earliest concept of social responsibility was based on profit maximization. A firm was considered to be socially responsible if it used its resources optimally through efficient production, manufactured a product that consumers wanted, and sold it at a reasonable price. Social responsibility was not the objective of a business organization but coincided with the economic objective of profit maximization. By meeting its economic objective, the business firm was considered to be meeting the needs of society. There was little support for business involvement in social problems. Jacoby (1973) describes this approach as the classical market model of business enterprise.

Paternalism. Although business took no direct responsibility for social issues, indirectly it exercised some responsibility through *paternalism* (Davis and Blomstrom 1975). Paternalism was exemplified by the development of company towns in which businesses provided stores, housing, and social welfare for employees. The epitome of a company town was the industrial community on the outskirts of Chicago, Pullman, Illinois, founded during the 1880s by George M. Pullman of the Pullman Car Company. The community included tenements, parks, a church, a theater, a hotel, and an arcade. The community also had a Pullman band, which entertained the public and even went on nationwide tours. This community was regarded as an example of enlightened business policy and won several awards for its advanced housing standards. It is estimated that Pullman invested $8 million in the town (Heald 1970).

Paternalism did not always create goodwill; instead it often generated ill-will and hostility. In George Pullman's case, he saw no inconsistency between his community efforts and his determination to earn a profit in good or bad times. The company-built church on the town square remained unused unless a group could run the church at a six percent profit for Mr. Pullman. Company spies searched for evidence of union organizing attempts and disloyal employees. During the depression of 1894 workers were laid off and wages were cut almost twenty-five percent, while the rents workers paid remained the same (Heald 1970). These actions precipitated a railroad strike in Chicago that spread nationally and resulted in the jailing of Eugene Debs, president of the American Railway Union, for violation of a court injunction.

Philanthropy. As company towns disappeared and workers moved to the cities at the turn of the twentieth century, paternalism evolved into personal philanthropy, a sharing of the personal wealth of business owners with the less fortunate members of society. Davis and Blomstrom (1975) refer to this idea of social responsibility as *individual trusteeship.* Andrew Carnegie exemplified this approach; he believed that wealth was not for personal benefit but for the betterment of society. As the head of the Carnegie Steel Company, which later became a part of U.S. Steel, he amassed a fortune. But Carnegie made huge charitable contributions, estimated at $400 million, to a variety of social projects in his lifetime (Sturdivant 1977). At Carnegie's death, there was almost nothing left for his heirs, in accordance with his belief that wealth was to be used for the good of society.

Public Disclosures and Abuses. In the latter part of the nineteenth century and the early twentieth century, the growth of large-scale corporations was accompanied by public disclosures of business

*"It's not my factory that's polluting the lake. . . .
It's all those dead fish that're doing it."*

abuses, which resulted in mounting public criticism. Much of this criticism stemmed from the social problems created by business firms, which made only minimal efforts to alleviate them. Many of the business abuses occurred because of the competitive nature of business.

But the focal point of the criticism was the business trust. These trusts were huge business organizations formed from a combination of independent business units, generally in a single industry. For example, there were trusts in the oil, sugar, steel, tobacco, and railroad industries. The activities of trusts generally resulted in a lessening of competition and higher prices for consumers. For example, one common competitive abuse was *predatory pricing*, underpricing by large businesses to drive smaller businesses out of existence instead of simply to meet competition. Another type of unfair competition was practiced by the Standard Oil Trust headed by John D. Rockefeller. Because Standard Oil made huge shipments of crude and refined oil by railroad, it received a discount or rebate. In addition, part of the higher rates paid by other shippers was repaid to Standard Oil (Josephson 1934).

Critics of business at this time included consumers, labor unions, social welfare advocates, and the media. Their public outcry against business abuses resulted in government intervention and the passage of federal legislation such as the Interstate Commerce Commission Act in 1887, the Sherman Antitrust Act in 1890, the Pure Food and Drugs Act in 1906, and the Federal Trade Commission Act in 1914.

Gradually corporations began to be considered responsible for and representative of a variety of public concerns and the public interest instead of simply shareholders. This trend was manifested in the idea that social problems were a legitimate demand on corporate resources. Business responded by corporate donations to charitable groups, support for civic and public agencies, and publication of financial information (a departure for the time). Within businesses themselves management expended greater efforts and resources in attempting to improve employee welfare and working conditions.

Management as a Profession. Concurrently, management began to be recognized as an identifiable group of professionals, separate from the owners or shareholders of corporations. As a result, managers considered themselves responsible to many different social groups, not simply shareholders. This view of management's role became known as *management trusteeship* (Davis and Blomstrom 1975).

As we have seen, the corporate form of enterprise became pervasive in our economy during the twentieth century, and the trend toward professionalization of the manager's role was accentuated. These developments marked a major institutional change in the economy. From the 1930s until the 1950s a new view of American enterprise evolved that emphasized the central role of professional managers. The objectives of business organizations began to be largely determined by professional managers, with profit maximization for shareholders being replaced by security and growth objectives. Such changes provided a basis for justifying the use of corporate funds for social concerns.

It should again be noted that these early attitudes about social responsibility were evolutionary, and each phase did not necessarily replace a prior state. In fact, these different views of social responsibility help to explain why some managers are more socially responsible than others.

Beginning of the Modern Era

The modern era of social responsibility began in the early 1950s and was marked by the publication of Howard R. Bowen's book *Social Responsibilities of the Businessman* in 1953. Bowen traces the evolution of corporations and the outlook of managers. He describes the term *social responsibilities of businessmen* in this way: "It refers to the obligations of businessmen to pursue those policies, to make those decisions, or to follow those lines of action which are desirable in terms of the objectives and values of our society" (Bowen 1953, p. 6). According to Bowen, public responsibility, social obligations, and business morality are synonyms for social responsibility.

Bowen also uses the term *doctrine of social responsibility,* and he describes it in this way: It "refers to the idea, now widely expressed, that voluntary assumption of social responsibility by businessmen is, or might be, a practicable means toward ameliorating economic problems and attaining more fully the economic goals we seek" (Bowen 1953, p. 6).

Why did this concern for social responsibility develop? According to Bowen, there were three main reasons:

1. Businesses were forced to become more concerned because of the actions of the labor unions and federal government.
2. They were persuaded to become more concerned through education and interaction with other major groups. Business schools began to require a course in social responsibility, thus sensitizing managers to the needs of society.
3. Conditions were favorable for the development of this concern. Such conditions include the separation of ownership and control, with the managerial function vested in a professional group. These professional managers identify with the corporation and think in terms of the long-run welfare of the organization. They are susceptible to the views of a variety of groups rather than simply to those of shareholders.

Bowen's work was the first comprehensive approach to social responsibility. Afterward the issue of social responsibility received increased attention, both favorable and unfavorable. Murphy (1978) indicates that the ideas espoused by Bowen in 1953 marked the start of the "Awareness Era" of social responsibility, as corporations began to recognize explicitly their overall responsibilities to society. This period was characterized by corporations' active involvement in the community. According to Murphy, the period ended in the late 1960s when opposition to social responsibility began to emerge. We shall soon examine some of the arguments of proponents and opponents. At this point, however, we review the influential approach taken by the Committee for Economic Development.

CED and Social Responsibility

The Committee for Economic Development (CED) is a private, nonprofit group of businesspeople and educators involved in research on and the study of political, economic, and social issues. In 1971 the CED published a book called the *Social Responsibilities of Business Corporations.* In this book the CED provided a rational, philosophical background and perspective on the issue of social responsibility.

The book begins with a description of the evolution of the concern for social responsibility by treating the relationship between business and society as a social contract between the two groups. The parties to the contract are business and the larger society. As its major obligation, business provides those goods and services that society needs. In return, business functions by public consent, namely, in the form of a free enterprise economy. Traditionally societal needs have been economic, such as job opportunities, production of goods, a rising standard of living, and a higher gross national product. Business has met fully its economic responsibilities. However, the contract has changed because of the addition of a new responsibility, social values. These include social problems, human values, the quality of life, health care, equal employment opportunity, and the elimination of poverty.

Most people feel that business has a moral obligation to correct social problems. But according to the CED, business has not dealt adequately with these problems. The CED cites surveys in which business is criticized for its slow progress in many areas, such as improving relations with customers, providing adequate product information, removing deceptions in advertising, and dealing with pollution. In part these criticisms stem from social activism by various groups and from the disillusionment that the public feels with all major institutions in society, including business.

The evolution in concern for social values has been paralleled and to some extent facilitated by the evolution of the corporation and by changes in management outlook. Corporate growth has been accompanied by the realization that corporations are enormous and that their role in the economy is critical. Corporations have many constituencies, including employees, stockholders, consumers, suppliers, and community neighbors. In addition, there are corporate interrelationships with government, labor unions, public interest groups, and the press. The intermeshing of all these forces puts pressure on business to respond to a variety of emerging issues.

Corporate growth has also changed the outlook of managers. The permanency of the corporation forces management to focus on long-run instead of short-run profitability. Thus managers now view themselves as trustees for many interests and constituencies, not only shareholders. And for the ultimate survival of the corporation, managers realize that the corporation must be responsive to the environment.

The CED describes this change as the "doctrine of enlightened self-interest." Corporate well-being is an integral part of the well-being of society; to the extent that society is strengthened, the corporation benefits. Further, if business does not assume its fair share of responsibility, corporate interest may be jeopardized. By acting on its own, management preserves its flexibility and obviates government intervention and regulation. The CED applied this doctrine to the interests of shareholders also: Expenditures for social responsibility, while improving society, also improve the environment for investment. The CED then describes limits on corporate social activities, areas of business involvement, and ways to get business more involved.

The work by the Committee for Economic Development (1971) was written in a period that Murphy (1978) calls the "Issue Era," a period that began in 1967 and ended in 1973. According to Murphy, this era was characterized by the belief that corporations should play a significant role in alleviating social problems such as racial discrimination, pollution, and urban decay. It was marked by the creation of new programs, new positions, and the institutionalization of social responsibility in many corporations (Murphy 1978, pp. 21–22).

Current Era of Social Responsibility

There seems to be no uniformly accepted way to describe the contemporary period in terms of the evolution of social responsibility. Nevertheless, several writers (Hay and Gray in Luthans and Hodgetts 1976; Jacoby 1973; Murphy 1978) have made an attempt to do so.

Murphy (1978, p. 19) believes that "social responsiveness is a more positive and accurate term than social responsibility. . . . Many corporations have already recognized their responsibility (i.e., obligation) to society and now are reacting to these demands in diverse ways." He refers to the period beginning in 1974 as the "Era of Corporate Social Responsiveness," since "many corporations appear to be consciously responding, as opposed to reacting, to their constituencies" (Murphy 1978, p. 22). In this era corporations have responded to fundamental concerns about their role in society in three main areas—reforming boards of directors, improving business ethics, and reporting on social performance.

Jacoby (1973, p. 194) views the current period of corporate social involvement somewhat differently; he calls it a "Social Environment Model." He examines the responsiveness of business organizations to the total societal environment—namely, responsiveness to market as well as nonmarket forces. Thus Jacoby feels that the behavior of organizations in contemporary society may be explained in part by political forces such as public opinion, the urgings of legislators, and pressure from public interest groups in inducing corporations to allocate resources for social purposes. (For a summary of the various conceptualizations of social responsibility, see Table 16–1.)

Criticisms of Corporations

Jacoby (1973) has classified critics of corporations in terms of the depth of their criticisms of business. The three groups he cites are the reformist critics, the leftist critics, and the utopian critics. The *reformist critics* focus their criticisms on reforming the system, but they accept the basic institutional framework. They support reforms

TABLE 16–1
Evolution of Social Responsibility in the United States

Conceptualization	*Practices*	*Period*
Classical economic market	Profit maximization	Industrial Revolution to 1875
Individual trusteeship	Paternalism and personal philanthropy: the business-person shares wealth with less fortunate individuals	1875–1930
Management trusteeship	Corporate philanthropy: support for civic and public agencies, publication of financial information, and improvement of employee welfare	1930–1968
Issue-oriented management	Corporations play a significant role in alleviating *specific* problems, such as racial discrimination, pollution, and urban decay	1968–1973
Social environment model of management (social responsiveness)	Business must *actively* respond to both market and nonmarket forces	1973 to present

in business involvement in solving social problems such as pollution, urban decay, and hard-core unemployment. Most critics fit into this group. The *leftist critics* seek to substitute "authoritarian socialism for the capitalistic system of competitive private enterprise" (Jacoby 1973, p. 7). They seek to alter the institutional framework and they advocate state ownership and state operation of the economy.

The *utopian critics* want to establish a new social order based on different human values that would emphasize cooperative efforts instead of individual materialism. They reject capitalism and authoritarian socialism. Utopian critics believe the following (Jacoby 1973, p. 10):

1. Corporations exercise their economic power contrary to the public interest. Examples include the creation of monopoly, the stifling of free enterprise, and domination of the private sector.
2. Corporations exert political power contrary to the public interest. Examples are exploitation of poor countries by multinational corporations, control of public agencies designed to regulate them, and subversion and corruption of democratic government.

3. Corporations are controlled by a self-perpetuating, irresponsible power elite that makes boards of directors' duties largely ceremonial, with policies controlled by managers instead of shareholders.
4. Corporations exploit consumers, and they dehumanize workers by offering them little psychological satisfaction, caring little for their rights, and impairing the quality of life.
5. Corporations degrade the environment and the quality of life by overproducing and exhausting national resources, exploiting poor nations, and thrusting the costs for pollution, noise, and so on externally to the consumer.

Now that we have examined the evolution of social responsibility and some of the criticisms of corporations, we can profitably focus on the arguments both for and against social responsibility.

PROS AND CONS FOR SOCIAL RESPONSIBILITY

Probably the most comprehensive list of arguments for and against social responsibility is that provided by Davis (in Carroll 1977). We describe his list in detail.

Arguments for Social Responsibility

Long-Run Self-Interest of Business. If business improves society, it also improves the business environment in the long run. While spending on social programs may result in reducing short-run profits, these expenditures may increase long-run profits. For example, expenditures made to employ the hard-core unemployed may be beneficial by providing a pool of efficient and productive workers over time. In addition, society benefits through reduction in the costs of social welfare programs, which indirectly benefit business by reductions in taxes.

Public Image. By supporting social programs, business may improve its public image. In doing so, it may create favorable impressions in the minds of the public, which may generate greater sales and profits for an individual firm.

Business Viability. To improve the entire business system, organizations must assume social responsibilities. As a powerful institution in society, business is required to take actions commensurate with its resources. If it does not, the power and status of business may decline as other groups take on these obligations.

Avoidance of Government Regulation. If business works for the public good, it may accomplish a private good for itself and at the same time obviate government regulation. Thus business will not have to bear the implicit and explicit costs of government regulation, and in addition, managerial flexibility in decision making will be preserved.

Sociocultural Norms. As members of society, business executives are influenced by its broader norms. Presumably they reflect the values of the larger society, and since social responsibility is one of these values, business executives reflect it in their decision making. Also, managers pursue multiple goals. As each is accomplished, others become important. After satisfying goals like making a profit, managers turn to other goals, like social goals.

In the Stockholders' Interests. Profits generated through social programs may benefit shareholders, especially those with diversified portfolios. Benefits to a single shareholder in a single corporation may not be discernible, but those businesses with diversified portfolios benefit significantly by improvements in the investment environment.

Let Business Try. The fundamental premise of this argument is that since other institutions in society have failed to alleviate social problems, businesses should have an opportunity to provide solutions. Perhaps they can provide remedies, but even if they do not, at least the attempt will be worthwhile, for it will sensitize managers to the problems of society.

Business Has the Resources. Since business organizations are large and possess abundant material resources, they should use them to solve societal problems. Not only does business have financial and physical resources, but it also has managerial expertise, innovative abilities, and knowledge about efficient and productive use of resources. All these could be used to the benefit of society.

Problems Can Become Profits. This argument emphasizes the potential profit in dealing with social problems. For example, producers of metal beverage containers have found that the cost of collecting containers for recycling aluminum is more than offset by a reduction in energy use and other savings.

Prevention Is Better Than Curing. Identifiable social problems may be adroitly handled in their early stages before they become major and controversial issues. Once a problem becomes a major one and business is forced to react, it may consume inordinate amounts of management time, be very costly to solve, and divert business from efficient production of goods and services.

Arguments Against Social Responsibility

There are also several cogent arguments against social responsibility. In this section we describe them briefly.

Profit Maximization. Some argue that the primary mission of business is the efficient production of goods and services. Social responsibility and social goals are not relevant objectives of business; these objectives are better handled by noneconomic institutions in society.

Costs of Social Involvement. Minor social problems might feasibly be handled by business, but not major issues such as urban decay and the elimination of poverty. In the extreme, if business is forced to absorb social costs, business failures may result.

Lack of Social Skills. Business executives have neither the knowledge nor the expertise to deal with social problems since their primary concerns are related to economics. Managers simply are not equipped to deal with social problems, such as the hard-core unemployment, alcoholism and drug abuse, and the rehabilitation of handicapped workers.

Dilution of Businesses' Primary Purpose. By dividing the interests and objectives of corporations between economic ones and social ones, managers will serve neither aim usefully. The net result will be lower economic efficiency and increased costs of production.

Weakened International Balance of Payments. Socially responsible actions lead to increased costs, and these costs must be absorbed. If business is forced to absorb them, the prices of U.S. goods will be higher than those of foreign goods and may result in the loss of international markets. In the overall economy this loss will create trade imbalances and further exacerbate monetary problems for the United States. A decline in international sales may also produce a high level of unemployment.

Business Has Enough Power. Business is one of the most powerful institutions in society already. Providing business with additional responsibilities and power in the area of social actions may result in an undue concentration of power, which might threaten society.

Lack of Accountability. Activities that government undertakes in our society are subject to scrutiny and control through various means, such as voting. However, as yet there are no mechanisms to provide accountability to the public for business actions.

Lack of Broad Social Support. The final argument is that there is no consensus in our society that business should become involved in social problems. This lack of a broad base of support could create hostility toward business and could bring about chaotic conditions if business attempted to achieve social objectives.

Assessing the Arguments

Now that the arguments for and against social responsibility have been briefly described, let us make an assessment of the arguments. Each of the arguments we have examined is based on sound reasoning. To a large extent, the arguments concern the length to which business should go in *voluntarily* undertaking socially responsible actions. For example, an obvious limitation is that a firm should not undertake voluntary social actions that would jeopardize its survival or competitive position. But some governmentally legislated social programs, such as equal employment opportunity, are less susceptible to this limitation. However, current government regulation is a subject of intense debate, both with respect to the extent of regulation and with respect to the potential for further restrictions on business through additional legislation.

Which argument is most persuasive depends on many factors, such as an individual's values, attitudes, and beliefs. As far as the arguments against social responsibility are concerned, profit maximization is probably the one most frequently expressed. Milton Friedman (in Elkins and Callaghan 1975) is a well-known proponent of this view. The basic problems with this argument are the assumptions underlying it, particularly those of unbridled and unregulated competition (Andrews 1971). From a practical perspective, cost of social involvement is a more powerful argument, especially if the firm's existence is threatened by such outlays. As for the arguments for social responsibility, business viability and avoidance of government regulation are very persuasive.

BUSINESS ETHICS

In this section we examine the subject of business ethics. Initially, we explore the relationship between business ethics and social responsibility. Next, we review some of the major research studies on business ethics. Finally, we describe proposals for dealing with the problem of ethics.

There are many definitions of ethics; one describes ethics as a set of values or beliefs about the rightness or wrongness of conduct. Baumhart (1968, p. 15) defines ethics as "the study of the morality of human actions; hence, the standards of these actions." Ethics is rooted in religious, cultural, and philosophical beliefs. These beliefs become the bases for judging individual conduct as either ethical or unethical. These same standards apply to the behavior of managers.

Social Responsibility and Business Ethics

Business ethics is part of social responsibility. Frederick (1977, p. 13) asserts that the essence of the subject of social responsibility is considered by some business and society scholars as "a commitment to ethical decision making." In a study of practicing managers seventy-six percent of the respondents either agreed or somewhat agreed with the assertion that the subject of social responsibility is basically an ethical issue for the individual businessperson and a concern over "the role of the corporation" in society.

In recent years business ethics has been a subject of intense interest. A major catalyst for the examination of ethical business conduct was the direct involvement of business executives in the abuses of the 1972 presidential campaign. Many large corporations used corporate funds to make illegal political campaign contributions and were subsequently fined for doing so. Other activities exposed by the media include price fixing, dishonest or misleading advertisements, foreign bribery, misuse of insider information to purchase or sell company stock before others can act, and business scandals.

Ethical conduct is one of the principal issues facing business today; it has even been said we are in the midst of an "ethics crisis" (*Business Week* 1976). One writer (Boling 1978, p. 361) describing this crisis notes that the conflict between managerial practice and ethical ideals may have created an ethical lag. The main problem with unethical behavior in business or in other areas is that it poses a threat to the existence of institutions (Sturdivant and Robinson 1977).

Research on Business Ethics

Several major research studies of business executives have been conducted to gain insights into business ethics. In one of the most important studies Baumhart (1968) surveyed *Harvard Business Review* readers, a group that included top managers, middle- and lower-level managers, and professional and nonprofessional employees. Most of these were employed in medium-sized companies in the manufacturing industries. The most important findings were as follows:

1. Executives view themselves as more ethical than the average business executive.
2. Top management must lead the way to reduce unethical behavior.
3. Persons who behave ethically are those with a well-defined personal code.
4. Superiors have a strong influence on ethical behavior.
5. The vast majority of executives believe an ethical code for industry would be helpful.

In the Baumhart study executives were also asked to rank those qualities that most influence an executive to make ethical and unethical decisions. The results are shown in Table 16–2.

TABLE 16–2

Ranking of Influences Leading to Ethical and Unethical Decisions

	Unethical
1. A person's personal code of behavior	1. Behavior of superiors
2. Behavior of superiors	2. Ethical climate in the industry
3. Formal company policy	3. Behavior of company peers
4. Ethical climate in the industry	4. Lack of company policy
5. Behavior of company peers	5. Personal financial needs

Source: Adapted from R. Baumhart, *An Honest Profit: What Businessmen Say about Ethics,* p. 47. Copyright © 1968 by Holt, Rinehart and Winston. Used by permission of Holt, Rinehart and Winston.

An update of Baumhart's study was conducted in 1976 (Brenner and Molander 1977). The behavior of superiors was still the most important influence on unethical decisions. This follow-up also revealed that there was no clear indication among the respondents as to whether ethical standards had changed. It did find, though, that ethical dilemmas continue to exist in business.

Another study assessed the ethical beliefs and behavior of 121 managers who were participating in an executive development program (Newstrom and Ruch 1975). This research also dealt with their perceptions of the beliefs and behaviors of peers and top managers—for example, divulging confidential information, using company services for personal use, doing business on company time, and padding expense accounts. Some of the findings of this study were as follows:

1. Top managers serve as a key reference group for managers' ethical standards, and the beliefs of managers were congruent with their superiors.
2. Managers believe their peers to be far more unethical than they themselves are.
3. Ethical standards are highly individualized, and a personal code of ethics is hard to change.

In 1965 Schutte published a major study focusing on managerial views of the nature of business executives. He surveyed about 800 business executives, and he conducted personal interviews with leaders in business, government, and religion to gain insights into business ethics. Schutte's major findings were that business ethics is hard to define; businessmen were aware of the poor publicity they received because of poor ethical practices; there were differences in the practiced and the spoken ethic; and different functional areas were perceived as more unethical than others.

A related study was completed by Carroll (1975), who surveyed business executives representing three levels of management—lower, middle, and top—in a broad spectrum of industries including retailing, general manufacturing, petroleum, and data processing. His concerns were the state of business ethics and the relationship between business and political morality. In this study managers were asked questions focusing on whether they felt they were under pressure to compromise personal standards to achieve company goals and whether Watergate would influence public confidence in business. The most pertinent finding in the Carroll study was that pressure from top management to achieve results may cause a person lower in line management to compromise. These pressures may be real or perceived, but managers feel forced to compromise personal moral standards to satisfy organizational expectations, especially at lower- and middle-management levels. Additionally, fifty-three percent of the managers felt that current business ethics are superior to those of earlier periods, and sixty percent agreed that younger managers in business would have done what junior members of the Nixon reelection committee did in order to show loyalty.

Bowman (1976) used the same research approach as Carroll to compare the views of business executives with those of public sector administrators in the federal government. In general, the results of this study support the findings of Carroll. However, only forty percent of the public administrators indicated that they believed that current government ethics were superior to those of earlier periods.

Another study was completed by Hegarty and Sims (1978), who conducted a laboratory experiment with 120 graduate students "to empirically examine how the occurrence of unethical behavior would differ under different contingencies of rewards and punishments." The experiment was a simulated decision-making task by a sales manager and involved kickbacks by sales personnel to purchasing agents. The primary conclusions of this research were that a higher incidence of unethical behavior occurs when this behavior is reinforced by extrinsic rewards; unethical behavior decreases under the threat of punishment; and unethical behavior increases under competitive conditions.

Remedial Actions for Business Ethics

Concerned businesspeople have introduced many proposals to deal with the business ethics problem and, more broadly, to make corporations more accountable. These include tighter and more uniform financial controls, establishment of codes of conduct within organizations, increased penalties for unethical conduct, and more guidance and involvement by top management (*Business Week* 1976). Shareholder drives for more disclosure by corporations have also been mounted.

One example of remedial action is provided by the F. W. Woolworth Co. (*Business Ethics* 1977). Woolworth has developed a company code of conduct that each management employee must read and sign. Corporate conduct is monitored regularly through a yearly compliance review by an audit committee comprised of nonofficer directors. Employees are also encouraged to discuss problems with superiors rather than handling them alone.

Marcus and Walters (1978) have reviewed several proposals for reforming corporations, especially to attack the issue of the excessive control of boards of directors by chief executive officers. One proposal advocates the use of federal chartering of corporations; that is, the federal government rather than the states would issue corporate charters to corporations. Federal chartering would provide uniformity in accountability in areas such as financial reporting, disclosure, and representation of shareholder interests. The problem with this proposal is that it would create large regulatory costs and additional federal government bureaucracy.

The use of public directors has also been proposed. Under this proposal there would be mandatory appointment of a board member to represent the community-at-large. This member could be a general public director who would ensure that the corporation does a better job of obeying the law. Alternatively, he or she could be a special public director who would be appointed by a court to ensure that a corporation meets its legal responsibility to society. The problem with this proposal is the issue of conflict of loyalty between the corporation and the public.

A third proposal the authors reviewed argued for the use of independent outside directors who would not be officers of the corporation but would constrain and monitor management. The two problems with this proposal are the possibility of conflict and the relative composition of the board in terms of the number of outside and inside directors.

The last proposal is to use special-interest directors. They would be appointed to represent special-interest groups such as consumers, women, and minorities. However, here again the potential for conflict may exist, and a special-interest director would not meet the traditional role of a director in representing shareholders.

After reviewing the proposals, Marcus and Walters (1978) recommend using outside directors and special public directors in situations where corporations have repeatedly violated the law. In addition, they suggest that top management and boards of directors eliminate conflicts of interest, ensure that corporations obey the law, ask inquisitive questions, and speak out on whatever issues are confronting the corporation.

SOCIAL AUDITS

Business management functions in a new atmosphere of public scrutiny in which the traditional income statement and balance sheet are no longer adequate measures of performance or accountability, because they exclude social involvement. The *social audit* is a systematic attempt to assess the performance of a business in the area of social responsibility. The purposes of this section are to describe a social audit, to discuss some of the proposals or approaches to social audits, and to consider the current state of social audits.

Concept

Howard R. Bowen is generally regarded as the originator of the proposal for a social audit of business (Davis and Blomstrom 1975). Although there is no uniform definition of a social audit, the general objective is to assess corporate social performance (see, for example, Bower and Fenn 1973; Steiner 1975). Typically, reporting can be used for internal management purposes or external purposes.

No matter what definition is used for a social audit, it does not constitute an audit in the accounting sense—that is, an independent third party's verification of a firm's financial statements. Social audits need not be performed by third parties nor quantified in dollar or numerical terms. They usually represent qualitative judgments.

Approaches

Dilley and Weygandt (1973) have identified four specific approaches to social audits. These approaches are inventory, cost or outlay, program management, and benefit-cost.

When management relies on the *inventory approach,* it merely discloses all its socially responsible activities but does not try to quantify their cost or impact. When management utilizes the *cost* or *outlay approach,* it discloses not only the activities but the costs associated with each of them. The *program management approach* extends the inventory approach by not only disclosing social activities and their costs but also assessing whether program objectives are being met (see Butcher 1973). Finally, the *benefit-cost approach* involves the development of sophisticated quantitative measures of social responsibility in terms of the benefits derived from the investment.

Current Status

The importance of measuring social performance has been recognized at a national level by the former secretary of commerce, Juanita M. Kreps (1978) in testimony before a House subcommittee. The benefits of this effort to business would be (1) improvement in profitability, even in the short run; (2) building of long-term goodwill, consumer trust, and employee morale; and (3) curbing government regulation.

Indeed, the trend toward greater reporting on social responsibility disclosures has increased. Ernst and Ernst (now Ernst and Whinney), which began a survey of social responsibility disclosures of *Fortune* 500 companies beginning in 1971, confirms this trend. Between 1971 and 1975 disclosures had increased from about fifty-six percent to eighty-five percent in the annual reports of companies in the survey (Ernst and Ernst 1976).

However, according to *Business Week* (1978, p. 178), even though social accounting and social auditing have been discussed since the early 1970s, most companies devote very limited attention to them. *Business Week* states that a number of companies, such as Norton Company, General Motors, Atlantic Richfield, Equitable Life Assurance Society, and Bank of America, have expanded their efforts. But one company that was actively involved in social audits, Abt Associates, Inc., dropped its report in 1978 because of the cost and a decline in earnings. In Europe, however, there has been an increase in social reporting, especially in Germany. These reports include not only positive effects of corporate activities but also negative effects, so as to obviate criticisms of business.

CURRENT ISSUES

In this section we examine some of the most prominent contemporary issues in social responsibility and business ethics. In a broader sense these issues concern the complex relationship between business and society. There are countless issues in these areas, but we limit our attention to three – quality of the environment, government-business relations, and business ethics.

Quality of the Environment

The decade of the seventies was marked by increasing emphasis on the control of pollution and the improvement of the environment. Through the Environmental Protection Agency (EPA) the federal government has imposed restrictions on the levels of various pollutants, such as noise pollution, toxic substances seeping into water, and automobile emissions. The beneficial aspects of these controls have been apparent in the improved quality of the environment. Business executives probably do not dispute the necessity of some form of pollution control because of the benefits that result. However, many executives have criticized these regulations; they claim that the capital expenditures needed to meet the requirements of the law are too high, the standards are too stringent, the time to meet deadlines is too short, and the regulations sometimes conflict. For example, consider the question of costs. It is possible to clean up pollution to a given level, say, ninety-five percent, and have the costs versus benefits be proportional. But beyond that level the cost-benefit relationship may be disproportional; a small improvement may cost almost as much as the original investment. The question, then, is this: Is the marginal benefit worth the cost?

Nowhere is the complexity of pollution control more evident than in the steel industry. It is confronted with rising steel imports, outdated facilities, low profitability, inability to raise capital, and losses in jobs. In addition to these problems the steel industry is required to spend billions of dollars annually to clean up pollution. We now examine three case studies to illustrate how these problems in combination affect the decisions and activities of managers, employees, local communities, and even the entire society.

Mahoning Valley Steel Industries. In March 1976 the EPA granted an exemption from the 1977 federal water pollution control standards to eight steel plants located along the Mahoning River in the northeastern part of Ohio (Jaroslovsky 1976). This exemption was granted to the three steel companies—Republic Steel, U.S. Steel, and Youngstown Sheet and Tube Company, a Lykes Corporation subsidiary—after they threatened to close the plants because the plants were too old to justify costly pollution controls, which were estimated at between $140 million (Jaroslovsky 1976) and $300 million (La Rue 1977). The possibility of losing thousands of jobs had aroused community leaders, union officials, and politicians.

This ruling was protested by environmentalists because of the possibility of similar rulings spreading to other areas. The Pennsylvania Department of Environmental Resources was also upset over the ruling because the Mahoning River flowed into Pennsylvania communities that used its water for drinking purposes. Later a suit was filed and an appeals court overturned the EPA exemption in September 1977 (*Wall Street Journal,* September 19, 1977). Within a short time of the ruling, Lykes Corporation announced it was reducing steel operations at the Campbell Works of Youngstown Sheet and Tube Company. This action resulted in a permanent layoff of 5000 workers (*Wall Street Journal,* September 20, 1977). The company claimed that the closing was not directly attributable to invalidation of the exemption. Rather, the closing was a climax to many problems, including low-priced imported steel, government-mandated pollution controls, and government restrictions on steel prices. After the announcement Lykes was criticized by the Ecumenical Council, a group of religious leaders, for its neglect of its corporate social responsibility. Since the closing workers have attempted to get federal and other aid to reopen the plant but have been unsuccessful.

The problems in the Mahoning Valley did not end with this decision. Because of continuing financial losses, Lykes merged with LTV in late 1978, after receiving government approval. The merger brought together their steel subsidiaries of Youngstown Sheet and Tube Company and Jones and Laughlin Steel Corporation and made them into the third or fourth largest steel producer in the country. It was estimated that the consolidation would result in an estimated layoff of 1,200 by the end of 1979 in the Mahoning Valley (*Wall Street Journal*, December 4, 1978). In late 1979 U.S. Steel announced the closing of over a dozen steel plants for similar reasons; this closing would result in the loss of 13,000 jobs (Sease 1979), and about 3,500 of these jobs were in U.S. Steel facilities in the Mahoning Valley (Reiss 1980). The announcement by U.S. Steel resulted in a steelworker protest at U.S. Steel's corporate headquarters in Pittsburgh.

Oregon Bottle Bill. The preceding case illustrates the problems associated with the attempt to balance a clean environment, unemployment, and other economic loss. However, it does not suggest that job losses are directly caused by efforts at pollution control, for we are dealing with a complex problem. Still, the problem is not unique to the steel industry in the Mahoning Valley. For example, ever since the Oregon Bottle Bill was put into effect in 1972 to ban nonreturnable containers, environmentalists and others have been engaged in a dispute with opponents of bottle bills. Environmentalists claim that because of the ban, litter is reduced, energy is saved, and natural resources are preserved. Opponents, including unions and business executives in the steel and aluminum industries, claim that factory jobs will be lost, especially high-pay–high-skill jobs. So far at least six states have banned nonreturnables, and similar legislation has been proposed in other states and at the national level. In 1979 Ohio voters turned down a forced-deposit bottle bill because of the concern over potential job losses in Ohio manufacturing industries. These types of conflicts are likely to continue in the future.

Three Mile Island. The complexity of attempting to balance economic and environmental priorities is graphically illustrated by the 1979 incident at the Three Mile Island nuclear power plant in Harrisburg, Pennsylvania. Because of our energy demands and dependence on oil from the Middle East, nuclear power advocates and the nuclear industry pressed for the development of the Three Mile Island nuclear plant in spite of questions about its safety. As a result of a major accident at this plant, there has been a public questioning of the safety of nuclear plant operation and the problem of disposal of radioactive wastes. This protest has resulted in huge losses for utility companies because of delays in completing nuclear plants under construction and delays or termination of new licenses. In turn, these actions have created unemployment in the construction industry.

The issues we have examined in this section will undoubtedly continue in the future. And as we have seen, there is frequently a trade-off between economic and social concerns, and it is difficult to achieve a balance (see also Chapter 3).

TABLE 16–3

Major Federal Regulations of Business in the Area of Social Responsibility

Agency	*Created by*	*Purpose or functions*
Federal Trade Commission (FTC)	Federal Trade Commission Act (1914)	Enforces antitrust violations with the Justice Department; sets standards on unfair methods of competition and deceptive consumer practices including false advertising
Equal Employment Opportunity Commission (EEDC)	Title VII, Civil Rights Act (1964)	Investigates complaints and issues rulings on employment discrimination based on sex, age, race, color, religion, or national origin
Environmental Protection Agency (EPA)	Presidential Reorganization Plan No. 3	Sets standards and enforces federal laws on pollution control
Occupational Safety and Health Administration (OSHA)	Occupational Safety and Health Act (1970)	Responsible for regulating safety and health working conditions of employees
National Highway Traffic Safety Administration (NHTSA) (created in 1970)	Motor Vehicle Safety Standards Act (1966); Highway Safety Act (1966)	Regulates automobiles and other vehicle safety standards
Consumer Product Safety Commission (CPSC)	Consumer Product Safety Act (1972)	Sets safety standards in the production of consumer products
Federal Election Commission (FEC)	Campaign Finance Act (1974)	Supervises funding national election campaigns, including business contributions and political action

Government-Business Relations

The relations between business and government cover a vast spectrum of activities. One of the major areas in this relationship that has received increased emphasis recently has been government regulation. And much of the regulation involves government-mandated programs in the area of social responsibility. Presumably these laws reflect the needs of society as expressed in public policy. Table 16–3 summarizes the major forms of this regulation.

A main issue associated with government regulation is its cost. Butcher (1978) estimates that the total cost of government regulation at all levels was $100 billion in 1977, and $85 billion of it was for compliance costs by business and individuals. This outlay represents a diversion of funds from productive private investment.

Government regulation also has been criticized for sometimes imposing arbitrary and conflicting standards, heavy-handedness, and excessive interference in the economy. The Occupational Safety and Health Administration (OSHA) and the Federal Trade Commission are two agencies that have been the targets of substantial business criticism in recent years. Businesses have taken opposing action by lobbying Congress to change the regulations and by going to the courts. For instance, small businesses petitioned Congress for an exemption from the Occupational Safety and Health Act, and a suit was also filed with the Supreme Court, which responded by making a ruling that virtually eliminated OSHA's power to undertake warrantless inspections. In 1979 Congress attempted to restrict the authority of the Federal Trade Commission. The Equal Employment Opportunity Commission (EEOC) has also been a subject of mounting criticism.

Even though there is controversy over the intervention of government in the economy through regulations, business has not been loathe to seek government involvement in the economy through massive support of financially troubled firms. The case of Chrysler Corporation illustrates the point (see Chapter 6). If Chrysler had not received a $1.5 billion loan guarantee from the government, the firm would almost certainly have gone into bankruptcy. (This issue is still in doubt, though, since Chrysler lost almost $1.1 billion in 1979, is having difficulty in raising private capital, and is losing key personnel.) Chrysler's closing would have caused a loss of hundreds of thousands of jobs, with devastating effects on many communities. From a social viewpoint the socially responsible act was to provide the aid. But from the viewpoint of free enterprise advocates the case raises profound questions. For example, if a firm cannot compete effectively, should it survive?

The trend in the past has been for the government to pass legislation to deal with a problem relating to social responsibility when business has been unable or unwilling to respond to the issue. Even though businesses have reacted negatively to regulation, it appears that the trend toward greater involvement of government in business affairs will continue to accelerate.

Ethics and Managerial Practices

The question of business ethics is one of the most significant issues facing business today. And it has been complicated by the increase of business activity in multinational operations. There are major differences in ethical standards applied in the United States and abroad. For instance, payoffs in foreign countries are regarded by some American business executives as a requirement for doing business abroad, and they claim that bribery is a widely accepted practice in other countries. Many major United States corporations admitted to making payoffs abroad totaling hundreds of millions of dollars during the 1970s. Some of these payments were made to foreign government officials.

Governmental reaction—passing a law prohibiting this type of activity—was almost predictable. The Foreign Corrupt Practices Act was passed in 1977, and it prohibits businesses from making bribes to foreign political officials. But whether this act will significantly decrease payoffs is debatable.

Ethical problems are faced by managers almost daily in their business interactions with employees, customers, suppliers, competitors, and shareholders. Conflicts occur because the managers want to make decisions reflecting their own values, but they simultaneously try to balance these desires with the demands of the organization, their superiors, and clients.

Because of the size of corporations, unethical acts are subject to widespread public disclosure. Activities such as corporate payoffs overseas and business involvement in the Watergate scandal during the Nixon administration were widely publicized. In both instances, and in many others, the government passed legislation to deal with these ethical problems. More importantly, these activities created a poor public image of business and business executives. This image may result in more public pressure on Congress to place added controls on business activities. An example of this trend is the proposal that corporations be federally chartered. Another example is provided by the activities of Ralph Nader, the well-known consumer advocate, who has been an outspoken critic of corruption in executive suites. He led a coalition of groups in the first Big Business Day in April 1980; the focus of the event was corporate abuses. These types of action are likely to continue if the public perceives that business ethics are not improving.

The problem of business ethics is very likely to receive prominent attention in the future. The problem and the pressures associated with it will undoubtedly necessitate more positive responses from business.

SUMMARY

The concept of social responsibility evolved over time, and we can identify five stages in this evolution: (1) the classical economic market, with its emphasis on profit maximization; (2) individual trusteeship, emphasizing paternalism and personal philanthropy; (3) management trusteeship, stressing corporate philanthropy, support for civic and public agencies, publication of financial information, and improvement of employee welfare; (4) issue-oriented management, stressing corporations' role in alleviating specific problems such as racial discrimination; and (5) the social environment model of management, which emphasizes that business must actively respond to both market and nonmarket forces.

There are cogent arguments both for and against corporate social responsibility. However, the arguments for social responsibility are so overwhelming that many corporations now accept this goal, either in whole or in part, as one of their major objectives.

As we have seen, there is a direct relationship between business ethics and social responsibility. While managers view themselves as more ethical than the average manager, they feel a strong pressure to compromise personal standards to achieve company goals. Frequently, and perhaps inevitably, there will be tension between achieving company goals and being personally ethical. This tension is healthy when corporate goals do not overwhelm the personal ethics of the managers in the organizations.

In recent years corporations have introduced social audits, attempting to measure or assess their performance in social responsibility. There are four specific approaches: (1) inventory, which involves a listing of corporate social activities in qualitative terms; (2) cost or outlay, which attempts to calculate the costs of social activities in dollar terms; (3) program management, which focuses on assessing whether social program objectives are being met; and (4) benefit-cost, which involves sophisticated quantitative measures of the benefits of social programs.

We have examined three major contemporary business-society and social responsibility issues: quality of the environment, business-government relations, and ethics and managerial practices. These issues are likely to receive prominent attention in the future in the debate over social responsibility.

DISCUSSION QUESTIONS

1. Identify and describe the major early attitudes of business toward social responsibility. Are these attitudes still expressed in our society?
2. What is meant by corporate social responsibility?
3. What are the major arguments for and against social responsibility? What is your evaluation of these arguments?
4. What is a corporate social audit? Describe some of the specific approaches to social audits.
5. What is meant by business ethics? What are the major findings of research on business ethics? Do you believe that business ethics are better today than a decade ago?
6. How do you feel about the three major contemporary social responsibility issues? Can you identify others? What do you believe will occur in the future regarding social responsibility?

CRITICAL INCIDENT

NOTE: This critical incident can be used by the whole class with the class observational method (see Appendix A) or used for thought and discussion by individual class members.

During World War II most product prices, including those in the electrical equipment industry, were controlled by the federal government as part of the war effort. After World War II price controls were abolished. At that time, because of the growth in smaller companies that offered a broader product line, the electrical industry became very competitive. The quality and design of industry products, however, were very similar, so competition tended to be based on price. Buyers took advantage of the situation by introducing competitive bidding. These factors created great instability in the markets for the producers, and profit planning became extremely difficult. But instead of competing in factors such as quality, design, or service, producers continued to focus on price competition.

This competitive situation continued for several years. The response of the electrical industry to the competitive conditions was to begin engaging in a price conspiracy to set prices and divide up markets. The exact time at which the price-fixing arrangements began is not really known. When the pricing conspiracy was exposed in 1959, evidence indicated that a price-fixing conspiracy existed as early as 1945 in power transformers and about 1926 for circuit breakers. The two largest firms in the electrical conspiracy were General Electric (GE) and Westinghouse, but twenty-seven other companies were also involved. During the time when the price-fixing cartels existed, there were breakdowns in which one or more of the organizations left the cartel. In total, there were about nineteen cartel agreements, which in the case of GE represented over ten percent of sales. As part of the conspiracy, secret meetings were held in hotel rooms, special codes were used to rotate bid rigging, false entries were made in expense accounts, and numbers were used to disguise company names.

As a result of the government's antitrust case in 1960, seven executives were sent to prison for thirty days each; twenty-three were given suspended jail sentences and put on probation for five years; and fines were imposed on the companies and their executives totaling $2 million. Many suits were filed by buyers against the companies, and damages were awarded into the millions. However, no president or chief executive officer of any of the twenty-nine companies was ever convicted, and in only one situation was a charge brought and subsequently dropped. Most chief executives claimed that the lower-level executives acted unilaterally in violation of corporate policy or that in decentralized operations an individual manager had clear pricing powers. The lower-level executives claimed that while they had freedom, they were pressured to meet profit goals or they would lose their jobs.

Most of those who were either identified as part of the scandal or convicted returned to work for their respective companies. Their reemployment was justified on the basis that they had learned their lesson and corporate punishment would do no good. At GE, however, fourteen managers were either transferred, demoted, or given pay cuts (some chose to resign instead). Within about a month after the trial ended, those who had been retained were told to quit or resign.

QUESTIONS: What does this case illustrate to you? Was there any reasonable justification for the price conspiracy? How do you feel about the top managers getting off without any penalty? What is your opinion about the action GE took as opposed to others in the industry?

SUGGESTED READINGS

Carroll, Archie B., ed. *Managing Corporate Social Responsibility.* Boston: Little, Brown, 1977, paperback.

This book of readings is comprehensive in covering many of the major published works on social responsibility. The principal subject areas are the evolution of corporate social responsibility, the debate over it, management functions and social responsibility, and how corporations have responded to social responsibility.

Sethi, S. Prakash. *Up Against the Corporate Wall: Modern Corporations and Social Issues of the Seventies.* 3rd ed. Englewood Cliffs, N.J.: Prentice-Hall, 1977, paperback.

Sethi provides a very good selection of cases involving actual companies demonstrating the conflicts between large corporations and social institutions. The range of cases include those on the problems of pollution control, ethics of overseas operations, and corporate relationships with consumers, employees, shareholders, and government.

17 Managing Conflict and Creativity

CONFLICT IN ORGANIZATIONS
A CONTINGENCY APPROACH TO RESOLVING CONFLICT
THE CREATIVE PROCESS
CREATIVITY TECHNIQUES
SUMMARY
DISCUSSION QUESTIONS
CRITICAL INCIDENTS
SUGGESTED READINGS

PERFORMANCE OBJECTIVES

1. To define conflict and to identify the four major types of conflict: interpersonal, intergroup, interdepartmental, and organizational.
2. To describe the five major methods that managers can use to resolve conflict.
3. To explain why conflict has become increasingly important, and to describe its resolution from a contingency perspective.
4. To identify the steps in the creative process, the traits of creative individuals and organizations, the innovation process in organizations, and sources of creative ideas.
5. To describe two major types of group techniques used to generate creative ideas: nominal group technique and synectics.

When individuals and groups interact in an organization, they frequently come into conflict. Generally speaking, *conflict* includes all kinds of antagonistic behaviors, which can become prominent if one individual or group tries to control the behavior of another individual or group. A certain amount of conflict in organizations is healthy; it indicates that individuals and groups are vibrant. However, an excessive amount of conflict is distracting and may prevent the attainment of organizational goals.

Creativity, which is the ability to produce something new and original, is frequently associated with conflict, especially in large-scale organizations. In large organizations management establishes rules and procedures that may inhibit the creative endeavors of employees and managers. Hence conflict can easily occur between managers who try to impose rules and subordinates who attempt to circumvent them. Yet creativity is obviously important in any organization, for management needs to infuse new ideas and plans into the company if it is to remain competitive. Hence management must strike a fine balance between setting up rules and fostering creativity.

The first part of this chapter describes various types of conflict. Then a contingency approach to resolving conflict is discussed. The chapter also describes the creative process and various group techniques for generating creativity.

CONFLICT IN ORGANIZATIONS

Although we see many examples of conflict in organizations, it is not easy to define it precisely. In this section, there is a definition of conflict and a discussion of its increased importance in large-scale organizations. Two major types of conflict, interpersonal and interdepartmental, are then described.

Increased Importance of Conflict

As noted above, conflict represents all kinds of antagonistic behavior. More precisely, Kenneth Thomas (1976) defines conflict as "the process which begins when one party perceives that the other has frustrated, or is about to frustrate, some concern of his."

Kenneth Thomas and Warren Schmidt (1976) questioned 258 managers, including both chief executive officers and middle managers, about their concern with conflict. These managers indicated that they spend about twenty percent of their time attempting to resolve conflict. They also indicated that the ability to handle conflict has become increasingly important during the last ten years. This result is not surprising since many organizations are now designed as matrix structures, a format in which conflict seems inevitable (see Chapter 10). In addition, the managers in the survey rated conflict management as of equal or slightly higher importance than planning, motivating subordinates, and decision making and indicated the ability to handle conflict has become more important in the last ten years.

There is some evidence that the ability to handle conflict is related to managerial success. Graves (1978) obtained ratings on twenty-five skill and personality variables for managers participating in an assessment center (see Chapter 8). He also identified two independent measures of managerial success: effectiveness as perceived by superiors and career success (salary increases and promotions). Of the twenty-five measures, only one — the ability to handle conflict — was related positively to both effectiveness and career success.

Types of Conflict

In general, there are four major types of conflict: interpersonal, intergroup, interdepartmental, and organizational. *Interpersonal conflict* occurs between two or more individuals. When two or more groups within the same department are antagonistic toward one another, the conflict is called *intergroup. Interdepartmental conflict* takes place between two or more departments. Finally, *organizational conflict* occurs when two or more organizations are antagonistic toward one another.

We have already discussed some aspects of intergroup conflict in Chapter 2 (the bank-wiring observation room study). As for organizational conflict, it is less common than the other three types. Thus in this section we focus on interpersonal and interdepartmental conflict.

Interpersonal Conflict

An innovative approach to resolving interpersonal conflict has been developed by Robert Blake and Jane Mouton (1964). According to these researchers, there are five general ways to reduce interpersonal conflict (see Figure 17–1). If an individual wants to satisfy *only* his own needs and *not* the needs of others, he is pursuing a *win/lose strategy* of forcing; that is, he wants everything and does not want to give the

FIGURE 17–1
Strategies and Methods for Resolving Conflict

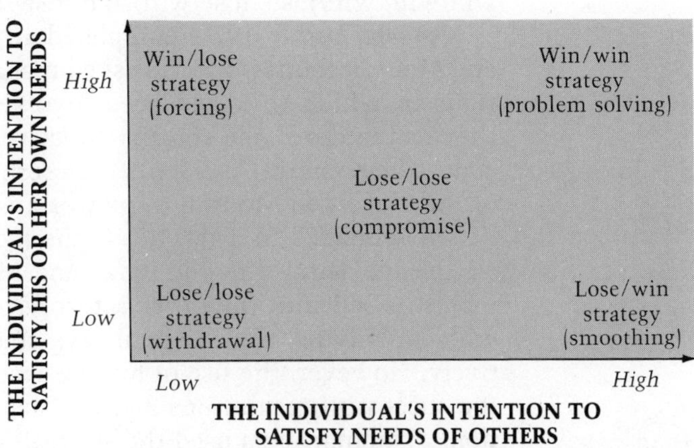

TABLE 17–1

Methods Associated with Effective and Ineffective Conflict Resolution

	Effective resolution	*Ineffective resolution*
Withdrawal	0.0%	9.4%
Smoothing	0.0	1.9
Compromise	11.3	5.7
Forcing	24.5	79.2
Problem solving	58.5	0.0
Other (still unresolved; unable to tell how resolved, etc.)	5.7	3.8

Source: Adapted from Ronald J. Burke, "Methods of Resolving Superior-Subordinate Conflict: The Constructive Use of Subordinate Differences and Disagreements," *Organizational Behavior and Human Performance* 5 (July 1970): 403. Reprinted by permission.

other person anything. If the individual wants to satisfy *only* the needs of others at the expense of his own needs, he is using a *lose/win strategy* of smoothing over difficulties. The remaining three methods are:

> *Win/win strategy:* the individual wants to satisfy both his own needs and the needs of others. This strategy represents problem solving, and it involves the integration of conflicting needs.
>
> *Lose/lose strategy:* the individual is willing to satisfy only *some* of the needs of others and *some* of his own needs. This is the style of compromise.
>
> *Lose/lose strategy:* the individual does not seek to satisfy his own needs or the needs of others; that is, he withdraws from the situation.

Thus there are five conflict resolution styles but only four strategies: win/win, win/lose, lose/win, and lose/lose.

Ronald Burke (1970) completed an interesting study of the Blake and Mouton framework. He asked managers to describe conflict situations in which they had been involved. He also identified whether they had resolved the conflict effectively or ineffectively. Judges then coded these critical incidents or descriptions independently by means of the Blake and Mouton framework.

As indicated in Table 17–1, the judges were able to place almost all the incidents into the Blake and Mouton framework; only a few incidents fell into the *other* category. Also, when the managers used problem solving, they were always able to resolve the conflict effectively. However, the use of forcing accounted for only 24.5 percent of the successful resolutions and 79.2 percent of the ineffective resolutions. The managers used the strategies of withdrawal and smoothing only infrequently, but these approaches always resulted in ineffective resolution. Compromise accounted for 11.3 percent of the effective resolutions and for 5.7 percent of the ineffective resolutions.

This study suggests that the Blake and Mouton framework is an appropriate way to categorize interpersonal conflict. It also suggests that problem solving is the best method for resolving conflict. And while forcing is sometimes successful, it frequently leads to ineffective resolution of conflict.

Interdepartmental Conflict

Frequently conflict involves groups or departments rather than individuals. As we saw in Chapter 7, organizations implement the related concepts of profit and cost centers to minimize the classic conflicts between such departments as sales and production. These conflicts can be so bitter that the entire organization may come to a complete halt until they are resolved.

Stuart Schmidt and Thomas Kochan (1972) have argued that interdepartmental conflict results when the units are interdependent, share resources, and perceive their respective goals as incompatible (see Figure 17–2). Shared resources and interdependent activities directly

FIGURE 17–2
A Model of Conflict

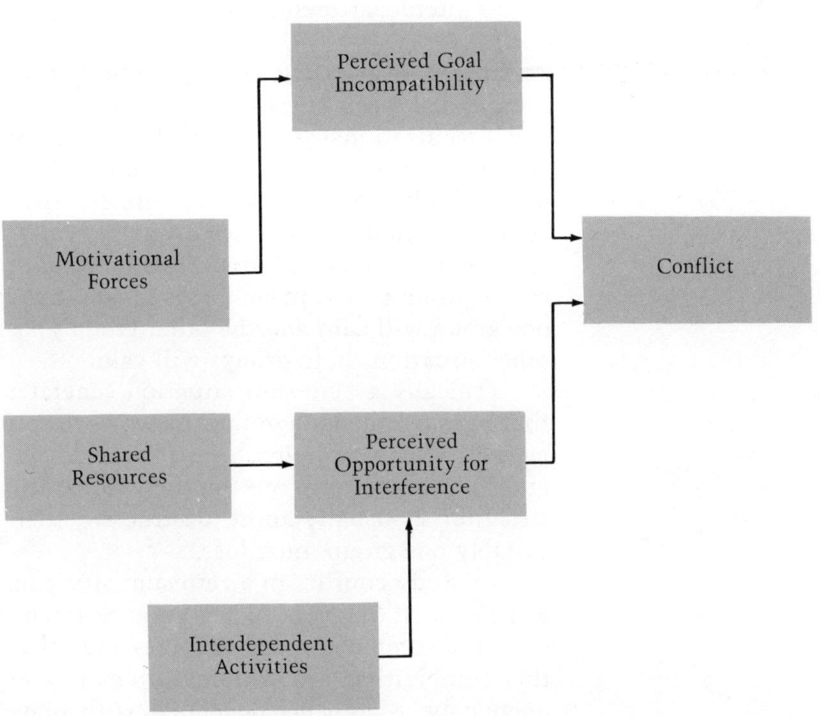

Source: Stuart Schmidt and Thomas Kochan, "Conflict: Toward Conceptual Clarity," *Administrative Science Quarterly* 17, no. 3 (September 1972): 363. Reprinted by permission.

affect the perceived opportunity for interference, while the motivational forces in the respective units affect perceived goal incompatibility. Under such conditions interdepartmental conflict occurs.

A related approach to interdepartmental conflict has been developed by John Seiler (1963), who argues that there are two dominant influences on interdepartmental relations: the points of view of interdependent departments and the relationship of authority and prestige between interdependent departments.

When the points of view of interdependent departments are closely allied and the authority-prestige relationship is consistent in the sense that everyone agrees about the relative status of each department, collaboration and productive conflict occur. However, the opposite occurs if the points of view of these departments are in conflict and there is an inconsistent relationship of authority and prestige between departments. In this case the groups initially attempt to reconcile their points of view and ideas about authority, but the task will be so patently fruitless that the groups will break off contact rather than expose themselves to further threats.

As suggested by this discussion, Seiler's typology consists of four types (see Figure 17–3). In combination with the Schmidt and Kochan model, Seiler's typology helps us to understand the major factors leading to interdepartmental conflict.

Zero-Sum Conflict

Another way to view conflict, either interpersonal or interdepartmental, has been suggested by game theorists interested in military and organizational strategies. They categorize situations as either zero-sum or nonzero-sum (Schelling 1960). In a *zero-sum situation* one individual or group wins at the expense of another group. For instance, a country that loses a war typically gives up many of its resources to the victor. A *nonzero-sum situation* exists when the gains of one group do not mean losses for another group. In some situations one group will gain and the other group's position will not change; in other situations both groups will gain.

Typically a zero-sum situation generates a great amount of conflict between the two groups. As we have seen, some conflict in an organization can be helpful, for it provides motivation for the various groups to outperform one another. However, conflict in the zero-sum situation is usually more destructive than constructive, since inevitably one group must lose.

To study conflict in a zero-sum situation, Muzafer Sherif and his associates (1961) constructed an experiment in which two groups of boys at a camp competed in sports and other activities. By the end of this competition the winning group was even more cohesive than previously. Members cooperated with one another and were complacent about the superiority of their group to the losing group. In the

FIGURE 17–3
Dominant Influences in Interdepartmental Relations

POINTS OF VIEW OF INTERDEPENDENT DEPARTMENTS	RELATIONSHIP OF AUTHORITY AND PRESTIGE BETWEEN INTERDEPENDENT DEPARTMENTS: *Consistent*	*Inconsistent*
Closely Allied	Collaboration and productive conflict	Energies devoted to regaining a "proper" authority relationship; relations will usually be distant and between low hierarchical levels of the two groups (e.g., messengers)
In Conflict	Energies absorbed by efforts to force points of view on other groups; relations between departments will be formal and often arbitrated by outsiders	Energies initially expended on forcing points of view and righting authority relations, but the task will be so patently fruitless that the groups will break contact rather than endure further threats

Source: Adapted from John Seiler, "Diagnosing Interdepartmental Conflict," *Harvard Business Review* 41, no. 5 (September-October, 1963): 129. Copyright © 1963 by the President and Fellows of Harvard College; all rights reserved. Reprinted by permission of the Harvard Business Review.

losing group, members began to deny or distort their situation with complaints such as "The judges were biased." Because their leader blamed group members for the losses, the group tended to splinter, fights broke out, and unresolved conflicts came to the fore. Although members of the losing group refused to consider themselves inferior to the winners, they were not supportive of one another.

To eliminate the conflict between the two groups, Sherif tried a number of tactics, such as lectures from counselors and even introducing a third group as a common enemy. Nothing worked. Apparently, once groups see each other as a source of frustration, a threat, and an obstacle to their goals, antagonism tends to be perpetuated by acts of renewed hostility. Neither group would give up its stereotyped view of the other. Finally, Sherif established a series of goals that could be attained only if both groups cooperated. In one instance all the boys had to work together to move a camp truck stuck in the mud. Gradually, as the two groups had to depend on each other for help in reaching their goals, the antagonism between them died down.

As this experiment indicates, it is preferable if groups within the organization view themselves as supportive of one another—that is, in a nonzero-sum situation. This proves to be true in management situations as well as in experiments. The top management of a major newspaper, the *Washington Star,* seriously considered bankruptcy in 1974 because of its shaky financial position. To help top management, all the groups within the organization went from a five-day to a four-day workweek, which reduced the wage bill by twenty percent. Top management, in turn, promised to return to the five-day workweek (which it has done) as soon as conditions improved. All groups felt they had interests in common, and thus they were in a nonzero-sum situation.

A CONTINGENCY APPROACH TO RESOLVING CONFLICT

The previous section contains a general description of conflict. In this section the discussion is more specific and revolves around a contingency approach to resolving conflict as practiced by project managers in matrix organizations and by chief executive officers. Additional techniques for resolving interpersonal and interdepartmental conflict are also discussed.

Conflict in Matrix Organizations

Matrix organizations are difficult to manage, because conflict is deliberately built into their structures. Hans Thamhain and David Wilemon (1977) have profiled the bases of influence that project managers in matrix organizations use to resolve conflict and the correct use of these bases if the organization is to be successful (see Chapter 10). These bases of influence are as follows:

Expertise: the manager influences subordinates and peers because of his or her knowledge and ability in a particular area.

Work challenge: the manager influences subordinates and peers by making the work challenging and exciting for subordinates.

Friendship: the manager influences subordinates and peers by establishing a long-standing friendship.

Fund allocation: the manager influences subordinates and peers by allocating funds in a particular way.

Promotion: the manager influences subordinates and peers because he or she has the ability to give promotions to subordinates.

Salary: the manager influences subordinates and peers because he or she has the authority to give salary increases.

Penalty: the manager influences subordinates and peers by punishing them in some way.

TABLE 17–2

Summary of the Most Significant Relationships Between Managerial Influence Style and Conflict Resolution Style

Managerial influence	*Conflict resolution*	
Project managers who rely on these influence bases	*Favor these conflict resolution modes*	*Avoid these conflict resolution modes*
Expertise	Problem solving	Withdrawal
Work challenge	Problem solving	Smoothing, withdrawal
Friendship	Compromise, smoothing, withdrawal	–
Fund allocation	–	Problem solving, withdrawal
Promotion	–	Compromise
Salary	Forcing	Problem solving
Penalty	Forcing	Problem solving

Source: Adapted from Hans Thamhain and David Wilemon, "Leadership, Conflict and Program Effectiveness," *Sloan Management Review* 19, no. 1 (Fall 1977): 69–89, by permission of the publisher.

Thamhain and Wilemon show that project managers favoring the use of particular bases of influence also favor the use of specific kinds of strategies to resolve conflict, as described by Blake and Mouton. As shown in Table 17–2, managers relying on expertise as a base of influence favor confrontation and avoid withdrawal; managers favoring work challenge as a base of influence prefer confrontation and avoid both smoothing and withdrawal; and so forth. In short, project managers behave in a reasonably predictable manner when attempting to resolve conflict in organizations.

Methods Used by Chief Executives

Kenneth Thomas (1977) has studied the methods chief executive officers use to resolve conflict. His research focuses on the five types of techniques for resolving conflict developed by Blake and Mouton. From his data Thomas argues that each of the five types is appropriate in certain situations. For example, forcing is appropriate when quick and decisive action is necessary. It is also appropriate when unpopular actions, such as cost cutting, are needed or on issues vital to the company welfare when the chief executive officer knows he or she is correct. In addition, forcing should be used against people who take advantage of noncompetitive behavior.

Table 17–3 describes the conditions under which each of the five types of conflict resolution techniques should be used. However, it is important to note that this table represents the viewpoints of only one group of chief executive officers. Also, Thomas did not study whether or not these conflict resolution techniques were effective. It may be that problem solving, as suggested by Burke's study cited earlier, is generally the best way to successfully handle a problem.

Additional Methods

There are several other methods that can be employed to reduce conflict. It is possible to use *advanced programming* and *planning* of the work schedules of interdependent units to avoid conflict entirely. For instance, many manufacturing organizations do not allow their maintenance crews to take care of the equipment whenever they wish, since this would interfere with the regular work flow. Rather, a predetermined time is established, such as the third day of the week, during which the maintenance crew completes its work.

Similarly, conflict can be reduced by providing *buffers or inventories* so that interrelated units always have goods on which to work and therefore whatever conflicts arise will not stop production. Both advanced planning and buffers represent the use of slack resources (discussed in Chapter 11).

It is also possible to reduce conflict by *implementing educational and training programs* that alter perceptions, expectations, and goals of interdependent units. The Blake and Mouton managerial grid is such a program, for its objective is to change leadership style and organizational climate, not only within individual departments but also within the entire organization (see pp. 358–360).

Some organizations resolve conflicts through the use of an *ombudsman,* an umpire for making the final decisions in conflicts. This approach, which originated in Sweden, is gradually taking hold in the United States. Others use *linking pins,* individuals who are members of two groups whose work overlaps, as a method for minimizing conflict (see Chapter 9). Typically the linking pins understand the viewpoints of both groups and can articulate them so that the groups begin to understand one another and work together harmoniously. Similarly, *integrators* can be used to encourage and help individuals and groups to work together (see Chapter 10); integrators are individuals not actually members of two or more interdependent groups whose job is to get these groups to interact effectively so that organizational goals can be achieved.

Redesigning the organization can also serve to reduce or eliminate conflict. We have already discussed Jay Galbraith's seven-step continuum that a manager can employ as a practical guide to redesigning an organization (see pp. 278–280). Under extreme circumstances top management may even *separate the groups* geographically. Joan Woodward (1965) reports that a British company moved its research and development department to a new location because it was always fighting with the production department. Alternatively, management might establish integrated *goal-oriented departments* so that different

TABLE 17–3
Uses of the Five Conflict Modes, as Reported by a Group of Chief Executives

Conflict-handling modes	*Appropriate situations*
Forcing	1. When quick, decisive action is vital—e.g., emergencies 2. On important issues where unpopular actions need implementing—e.g., cost cutting, enforcing unpopular rules, discipline 3. On issues vital to company welfare when you know you're right 4. Against people who take advantage of noncompetitive behavior
Problem solving	1. To find an integrative solution when both sets of concerns are too important to be compromised 2. When your objective is to learn 3. To merge insights from people with different perspectives 4. To gain commitment by incorporating concerns into a consensus 5. To work through feelings that have interfered with a relationship
Compromise	1. When goals are important, but not worth the effort or potential disruption of more assertive modes 2. When opponents with equal power are committed to mutually exclusive goals 3. To achieve temporary settlements to complex issues 4. To arrive at expedient solutions under time pressure 5. As a backup when collaboration or competition is unsuccessful
Withdrawal	1. When an issue is trivial, or more important issues are pressing 2. When you perceive no chance of satisfying your concerns 3. When potential disruption outweighs the benefits of resolution 4. To let people cool down and regain perspective 5. When gathering information supersedes immediate decision 6. When others can resolve the conflict more effectively 7. When issues seem tangential or symptomatic of other issues
Smoothing	1. When you find you are wrong—to allow a better position to be heard, to learn, and to show your reasonableness 2. When issues are more important to others than yourself—to satisfy others and maintain cooperation 3. To build social credits for later issues 4. To minimize loss when you are outmatched and losing 5. When harmony and stability are especially important 6. To allow subordinates to develop by learning from mistakes

Source: Kenneth W. Thomas, "Toward Multi-Dimensional Values in Teaching: The Example of Conflict Behaviors," *Academy of Management Review* 2 (1977), Table 1, p. 487. Reprinted by permission.

types of functional specialists would be forced to work together and thus begin to appreciate each other's views.

In addition, *joint decision making* that includes genuine participation by all involved parties is an effective way to reduce conflict. For example, organizations frequently set up ad hoc committees and task forces consisting of representatives from interdependent departments. These committees usually develop policies and procedures that guide the activities of the departments so that conflict is minimized.

Sometimes the conflict is so bitter that nothing seems to work. A *transfer of personnel* may then be appropriate. If the conflict persists, management can take advantage of its final recourse, *terminating* one or more individuals whose performance is being hindered because of conflict.

THE CREATIVE PROCESS

There seems to be an inevitable conflict between organizational rules and creativity. Organizations need rules, since they define the boundaries within which acceptable behavior can occur. However, too many rules can stifle the creative efforts of organizational members. Yet without creativity organizations may face the threat of extinction.

In this section we describe the stages that occur in an individual's creative process, give a profile of the creative individual and organization, outline some sources of creative ideas, and discuss the innovation process in organizations.

Steps in the Creative Process

Many researchers have studied the creative process and the steps through which an individual proceeds when he or she is seeking to develop a new idea or approach. For our purposes these stages can be identified as initial desire, saturation, incubation, illumination, and testing. Although these stages may overlap, they are sufficiently distinct that they can be treated separately.

The *initial motivation* for studying a problem is crucial. If an individual is not motivated, he or she can easily become discouraged, and the project will be terminated too early.

After deciding to study a problem fully, the individual must become *saturated* with information related to it. In short, he or she must become an expert in the problem area. This period can be quite long, especially if the individual possesses little knowledge in the area or if the subject is highly complex.

It is common for frustration to occur sometime during the creative process. The individual may then turn to other projects, but the original problem will still be on his or her mind. During this period the subconscious mind is playing with the problem. In other words, the individual is in a period of *incubation*; the problem is still alive but unsolved and unstudied in any formal manner.

Illumination—the solution itself—represents the next stage in the creative process. It frequently occurs at unusual times, such as in the middle of the night when the individual is half asleep. For this reason it is helpful for individuals to write down their thoughts immediately. Some individuals keep a pad of paper and a pen by the bed precisely for this purpose.

Finally, the individual must *test* the idea. Does it really work? Is it possible to manufacture the item? Is it practical? These and similar questions must be answered in the testing stage.

The Creative Individual

Although it is difficult to identify *all* the traits and abilities of creative individuals, Gary Steiner (1965) has summarized the research in this area and has found that creative individuals possess the following traits:

> *Conceptual fluency:* the individual can produce a large number of ideas quickly.
>
> *Originality:* the individual generates unusual and distinctive ideas.
>
> *Evaluating information:* the individual separates the source of the information from its content. He is motivated by his interest in the problem and follows wherever it leads.
>
> *Suspension of judgment:* the individual avoids early commitment and spends much time analyzing and exploring the various aspects of the problem.
>
> *World view:* the individual is antiauthoritarian and approaches life in a relativistic manner.
>
> *Personality:* the individual accepts his own impulses and explores problems in a playful, undisciplined manner. He is highly independent in his judgments and sees himself as different.
>
> *Fantasy life:* the individual has a rich, "bizarre" fantasy life.
>
> *Reality orientation:* the individual is oriented to reality and exercises superior control over his fantasy life, problems, and other aspects of his environment.

Creativity is an important factor in the success of most organizations; in some organizations, such as an advertising agency or a research and development firm, it is absolutely essential. But in many organizations there is a woefully inadequate supply of creative individuals. For this reason organizations should respect their creative individuals and safeguard them from attacks by individuals who do not understand creativity and its importance.

The Creative Organization

Steiner (1965) also provides a profile of creative organizations, which parallels in some ways his description of creative individuals. Steiner feels that the following characteristics are present in a creative organization:

> *Conceptual fluency:* the organization includes many employees who are given the opportunity for private thought; there are open channels of communication and little secrecy; and employees are encouraged to make contact with outside sources and experts.

Originality: the organization hires a wide variety of individuals with different skills and personalities, including marginal and unusual types; eccentricity is allowed; and nonspecialists as well as specialists are assigned to problems.

Organization design: the organization is decentralized and not run tightly, and there are separate units for creative and production employees so that creative individuals are able to work with one another.

Organizational climate: the organization both encourages and rewards risk taking and innovation, and employees do not have to worry about losing their jobs if mistakes are made.

Resources: there are ample resources to help the creative employees in their work and sufficient time to study a problem in depth and correct errors when they occur.

The Innovation Process

Michael Tushman (1977) has studied the innovation process in research and development firms. His research indicates that there are three phases of the innovation process: idea generation; problem solving, or testing the idea; and innovation, the successful realization of the idea.

An example of this three-stage process is provided by General Motors in the early 1920s. Alfred Sloan persuaded Charles Kettering, a close friend and world-renowned inventor, to become head of GM's research section. One of Kettering's first tasks was to develop a copper-cooled engine that would be less expensive but more durable than the available models. During the idea generation stage Kettering was very successful. However, he ran into problems during the problem-solving stage; some of the cars equipped with his engines ignited at high speeds. Kettering was convinced he could solve this problem, but he received little help from the top production managers, who viewed him as a competitor rather than a collaborator. The abortive project cost several million dollars. Defeated, Kettering tendered his resignation, which Durant refused to accept. Durant instead created a new research division that was completely independent of the production departments, dramatically increased its budget, and gave Kettering, its top manager, 500 miles of track to test cars before they were turned over to the production departments. This research department has been responsible for many innovations, which have been a major factor in GM's success. However, in the case of the copper-cooled engine, the third phase of the innovation process, the actual innovation, was not reached until the 1960s when GM introduced the Vega.

Tushman points out that organizations need individuals who can fill special "boundary" roles if innovation is to be successful. "Gate-

"Pleasant news, Dickerson. From now on it won't be necessary to wear a necktie. I'm moving you over to the creative department."

keepers" represent one major boundary role; they constitute the link between the research and development department and *outside* organizations. An example would be a researcher who attends professional meetings in order to keep up with the latest findings in his or her field. In addition, there are two other special boundary roles: organizational liaisons, individuals linking activities between the research and development department and other departments; and laboratory liaisons, individuals linking units within the research and development department.

Sources of Creative Ideas

There are many sources of creative ideas in organizations. Operating and lower-level employees frequently have ideas that, if implemented, could significantly enhance the effectiveness of the organization. Thus successful organizations will provide ways to tap the resources of these employees. Similarly, companies can strengthen creativity by rotating individuals through various jobs in the organization or by providing temporary assignments both within and outside the organization. In this way the individual's perspective is enlarged, and he or she may begin to view problems in a new and unusual way.

Some organizations, such as McCormick and Company in Baltimore, use junior boards of directors to generate ideas. At McCormick, managers are assigned to several junior boards during their careers.

These boards are temporary assignments lasting less than a year. Each board is directed to attack one major problem, and rotation through several board assignments provides the individual with an enlarged perspective and the organization with new ideas. At McCormick, work on the junior boards occurs outside the regular workday. During the depression of the 1930s, McCormick did not lay off one individual and managed to make a profit largely because of the ideas developed by its junior boards of directors.

Some organizations establish separate creative units so that their researchers will be able to generate ideas. William Whyte (1956) has argued that American Telephone and Telegraph has become very successful largely because of the innovations developed by Bell Laboratories, its research and development arm. Behavior that would not be tolerated in a bureaucratic organization, such as coming to work late or looking out of a window for hours, is common at Bell Labs.

It is also possible to generate creative ideas by providing organizational members with educational and training opportunities, either inside or outside the organization. James Hayes, president of the American Management Associations, estimates that over 500,000 managers receive training every year in the United States so that they will stay current and infuse organizations with new ideas and practices.

Finally, many organizations employ suggestion boxes and provide rewards for employees if their suggestions result in savings. However, if this technique is used, organizations should grant sizable rewards; otherwise members are not motivated to submit suggestions.

CREATIVITY TECHNIQUES

In Chapter 15 we described creative groups; we saw that such groups should be heterogeneous, should range from ten to twenty individuals, should engage in a short warm-up period during which they discuss the problem, and then should break up so that individuals may work by themselves. These groups are brainstorming groups, and they represent one approach to creativity. There are, however, alternative approaches. These include nominal group technique (NGT) and synectics.

Nominal Group Technique

Nominal group technique (NGT) represents a major alternative to brainstorming, and it is often used as an alternative to the delphi technique in forecasting (see Chapter 5). NGT is used in a structured group meeting (Delbecq, Van de Ven, and Gustafson 1975). Seven to ten individuals, who are not necessarily experts in an area, sit around a conference table, and each one writes ideas on the assigned topic on a pad of paper. NGT is used to attack a variety of problems, including forecasting. NGT forecasting can be either short-range or long-range.

For instance, a short-range forecast might focus on consumer demand for oil within the next six months. A long-range forecast might attack the issue of other fuels that could be developed as alternatives to oil within the next twenty years.

After a period that usually ranges from five to ten minutes, the participants share their ideas, one at a time, in a structured round robin manner. A secretary writes all the ideas on a flip chart or blackboard in full view of the participants. A period of structured discussion follows, during which all the ideas are analyzed by the participants. This period is structured to ensure that each idea receives an appropriate amount of attention. If the members of the group spend too much time on one idea, the secretary asks them to treat the other ideas. After the structured discussion participants rank each idea according to its relative probability of occurrence. The mathematically pooled results then become the group's decisions.

Research suggests that NGT is superior to brainstorming (see Burton, Pathak, and Burton 1978). In addition, NGT is enhanced if no one but the leader knows the real problem under consideration. That is, the leader should not identify all the details of the problem, since this action would tend to focus the participants' attention too early, and they might not examine all the alternatives available to them.

Finally, it can be noted that the delphi technique and NGT are very similar, since they both rely on the judgments of individuals to predict the future (see Chapter 5). However, there is a basic difference between them, anonymity. When the delphi technique is employed, the participants are anonymous; with NGT, of course, the participants are known to each other. However, NGT allows the participants to interact, while the delphi technique does not.

Synectics

A radically different approach, synectics, has been developed by William Gordon (1961). *Synectics* is an attempt to generate novel ideas and approaches by establishing a small group of individuals with heterogeneous backgrounds and abilities. Each group uses fantasy and analogies as techniques to broaden their perspectives on the problem at hand. One group established in this way consisted of an architect, an engineer, and an ichthyologist. This group designed a roof for a building in the tropics; the roof resembled a flounder—it could change color through inflating bubbles that absorbed or reflected heat. A second group came up with a design for a self-closing tube, which is now common in industry.

Synectics is very popular in industry today. Many small research and development firms specialize in synectics, and large corporations frequently subcontract their work to them. Many of these firms can be found in the research and development corridors surrounding both Boston and San Francisco.

SUMMARY

Conflict represents all kinds of antagonistic behaviors. It is of increasing importance in organizations, at all levels of management. On the average, managers spend twenty percent of their time resolving conflict.

Conflict can be defined as a process that begins when one party perceives that the other has frustrated, or is about to frustrate, some concern of his. There are four major types of conflict: interpersonal, intergroup, interdepartmental, and organizational.

According to Blake and Mouton, there are five general ways to resolve conflict: forcing, smoothing, problem solving, compromise, and withdrawal. Burke's research indicates that problem solving is by far the best approach. However, chief executive officers rely on all five types, and the final selection depends on the problems they face. Similarly, project managers in matrix organizations who rely on specific bases of influence such as expertise and punishment use some of the five types and avoid others.

Game theorists have created another way to conceptualize either personal or interdepartmental conflict: zero-sum and nonzero-sum situations. A zero-sum situation occurs when one individual or group wins at the expense of another individual or group. A nonzero-sum situation exists when the gains of one group do not mean losses for another group.

In addition to the five methods for resolving conflict described by Blake and Mouton, there are many other techniques that a manager can employ. These include advanced programming and planning, inventory buffers, education and training, the use of an ombudsman, a redesign of the organization, and joint decision making.

There are five stages in the creative process. These are initial motivation, saturation, incubation, illumination, and testing. Although in practice they overlap, they are sufficiently distinct that they can be discussed separately.

Steiner has described the creative individual as one possessing such traits as a high degree of conceptual fluency and originality. He or she is able to evaluate information efficiently, can suspend judgment until all the data have been analyzed, possesses an antiauthoritarian world view and independent personality, has a rich fantasy life, and is oriented to reality. Steiner also provides a profile of creative organizations, which tend to be decentralized. A wide variety of individuals with different skills and personalities is found in such organizations, and innovation and risk taking are both encouraged and rewarded.

Michael Tushman has profiled the innovation process as it takes place in research and development firms. He describes this process in terms of three stages: idea generation, problem solving, and innovation. He also describes various types of boundary roles that are necessary if innovation is to be successfully implemented. These include the gatekeeper, the organizational liaison, and the laboratory liaison.

There are many sources of creative ideas in organizations, including operating and lower-level employees, junior boards of directors, educational training opportunities for organizational members, and suggestion boxes. In some organizations management physically separates the creative unit from other units to facilitate the production of new ideas and approaches.

Finally, there are three prominent group techniques that can facilitate creativity. These are brainstorming, nominal group technique, and synectics.

DISCUSSION QUESTIONS

1. This chapter describes some techniques for resolving conflict. Describe at least three additional techniques.
2. Is it possible for individuals to experience a major conflict with one another and still like one another? Why or why not?
3. What are the major similarities and differences between the following: brainstorming, NGT, and synectics?
4. Among Blake and Mouton's five methods for resolving conflict, is problem solving the most effective? Why or why not?
5. Why is conflict increasing in organizations?
6. In a unionized firm would an ombudsman be necessary? Why or why not?
7. How is the creative process different from the innovative process?

CRITICAL INCIDENTS

NOTE: These critical incidents can be used by the whole class with the case observational method (see Appendix A) or used for thought and discussion by individual class members.

1. A major university offered an MBA program graduating over 1000 students each year. In the first year of the two-year program, there were several basic courses—Finance, Accounting, Management and Organizational Behavior, Marketing, and Statistics—that all students were required to take. Within each of the basic courses, there were several sections. Students began to complain about the variability in the different sections of each of the basic courses. Different professors ostensibly covering the same material were in many instances not doing so. For example, one professor in the basic course on Management and Organizational Behavior did not even include material on organizational design, motivation, and leadership.

The Dean decided that the basic courses should be rigidly structured, and that all professors teaching the section of a particular course would use the same syllabus and reading assignments. However, many professors complained about this new approach; they felt it was a violation of their academic freedom. They also felt that the students would be deprived of some interesting lectures that were the research specialties of the professors, but which could not be accommodated within a rigid curriculum.

QUESTIONS: Has the Dean created a conflict? Why or why not? What other approaches might the Dean have used to avoid resentment and still achieve his goal?

2. A personnel researcher in a large organization was asked to do a study based on the work of some other researchers in another part of the organization. This project was very important, since it concerned the development of a form rating the career potential of managers in the organization. However, when the researcher approached the managers and researchers in the other part of the organization for the information she needed, they were evasive. Finally, the manager who had been responsible for directing the first study told her to mind her own business. According to this manager, his researchers had completed an excellent study and it was not necessary to extend it.

QUESTION: If you were in this conflict situation, what are some alternatives you might pursue and what would you do?

SUGGESTED READINGS

Pondy, Louis. "Organizational Conflict: Concepts and Models." *Administrative Science Quarterly* 12 (1967), 296–320.

This scholarly article describes the various concepts and models that researchers interested in conflict have used in their research.

Thomas, Kenneth. "Organizational Conflict." In *Organizational Behavior,* edited by Steven Kerr, pp. 151–181. Columbus: Grid Publishing, 1979, 460 pages, hardback.

Thomas has written an excellent and current review of the conflict literature. He defines conflict, describes various types of conflict behaviors, delineates the conflict process, and discusses various types of interventions designed to resolve conflict.

18 Managing Change and Development

MANAGING TASK ASSIGNMENTS
MANAGING TECHNOLOGICAL CHANGE
MANAGING PEOPLE DURING CHANGE
MANAGING STRUCTURAL CHANGES
ORGANIZATION DEVELOPMENT
COMPLEX ISSUES FACING ORGANIZATION DEVELOPMENT
SUMMARY
DISCUSSION QUESTIONS
CRITICAL INCIDENT
SUGGESTED READINGS

PERFORMANCE OBJECTIVES

1. To summarize Harold Leavitt's model of change, and to outline and describe his four interrelated factors that management must consider when introducing change: The task to be completed, the organizational structure in which it is to be completed, the people completing it, and the technology by means of which it is to be completed.
2. To describe a specialized subfield of management, organization development (OD), which attempts to introduce planned and systematic changes into organizations in an orderly fashion.
3. To discuss some of the complex issues in the field of organization development.

Throughout this book the concept of change has been important. In Part II we described various ways to structure and restructure organizations to make them effective and efficient. In Part I we discussed planning as it relates to change. For example, managers use forecasting techniques to predict the future, to adjust their goals and plans, and to make appropriate changes in the design of the organization. Other chapters also highlighted the concept of change. For instance, managers sometimes alter their styles of leadership in order to influence the attitudes of subordinates and increase the level of productivity in the organization.

All this is to say that an organization is not static but dynamic. Even when it is successful, it is constantly changing in one way or another. But not all these changes are desired ones. Further, external environmental forces, such as the intensity of competition and the passage of laws, directly affect the activities of the organization. If the organization is to succeed, its managers must respond to such forces by introducing planned and systematic changes that will ensure its continued success.

As our organizational framework suggests, managers must evaluate the decisions they have made in terms of their consequences for individual and organizational performance. If appropriate, management should then introduce changes into any or all of our organizational dimensions of planning and control, organization design, and behavioral processes.

Our discussion of managing change and development is structured around the model of change developed by Harold Leavitt (1965). According to Leavitt, there are four interrelated factors that management must consider when introducing change: the task to be completed, the organizational structure in which it will be completed, the people completing it, and the technology by means of which it will be completed (see Figure 18–1). Finally we discuss organization development (OD), a specialized field of management focusing on the introduction of planned and systematic change in organizations.

MANAGING TASK ASSIGNMENTS

It is quite possible to introduce change into organizations simply by altering the tasks that employees and managers are required to complete. Throughout this book there has been a great emphasis on the management of task assignments. As we have seen in Chapter 11, if selection of organizational members is defective in the sense that they cannot effectively complete the tasks assigned to them, the organization suffers. Similarly, setting goals that are too hard usually results in failure to complete the task (see Chapter 13). In this section we treat three major approaches to task assignment: job enrichment, role negotiation, and MAPS.

FIGURE 18–1

Four Major and Interrelated Factors to Consider When Initiating Change in Organizations

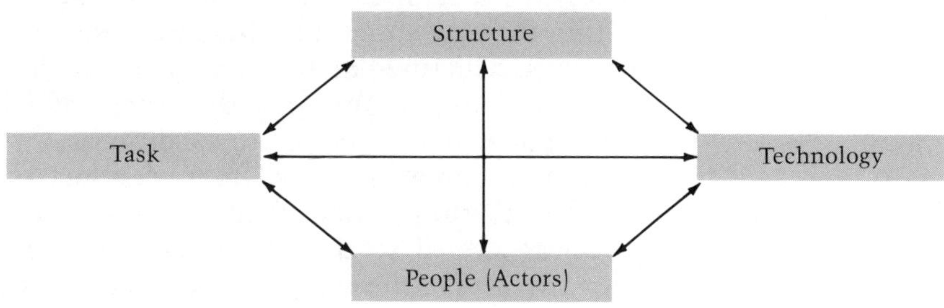

Source: Harold J. Leavitt, "Applied Organizational Change in Industry: Structural, Technological, and Humanistic Approaches," in *Handbook of Organizations* ed. James G. March (Chicago: Rand McNally, 1965), p. 1145. Used by permission.

Job Enrichment Revisited

Job enrichment refers to increasing the degree of responsibility an individual is able to exercise in completing his or her work. As we discussed in Chapter 13, it is possible to assess jobs in an organization by means of the job diagnostic survey. This questionnaire identifies the motivating potential score for each job and includes the following measures:

Skill variety: the number of skills required to complete a particular job.

Task identity: the degree to which an individual identifies with a job.

Task significance: the degree to which the individual perceives the task as being significant.

Autonomy: the degree to which an individual is able to exercise independent responsibility in completing the task.

Feedback: the amount of information that the superior provides the subordinate in terms of his or her performance in completing a job.

Once again, it is important to note that job enrichment is not a panacea for all problems. Only if employees are highly motivated will job enrichment work successfully. Among subordinates possessing only a low degree of need achievement, job enrichment frequently results in a decrease in performance.

Some programs of job enrichment have been well publicized. Gaines Foods, for instance, introduced job enrichment in its Topeka, Kansas, plant, which employs about 200 people. Under this program employees selected their supervisors, rotated tasks, and controlled the distribution of incentive pay. Although initially this program seemed to be working effectively, middle-management opposition to it let to its demise. Many middle managers had difficulty working within the new structure, which was much less bureaucratic than the previous structure. In the new program the middle managers possessed less formal authority than they had had previously, and they could not operate under these conditions.

Similar programs have been developed at Saab and Volvo in Sweden. In these small plants the traditional automotive assembly line was altered so that the workers experienced more variety and responsibility in the completion of their tasks. In addition, small work teams became responsible for producing a particular number of cars each day. Reportedly, productivity and job satisfaction were influenced positively by these changes.

However, American workers visiting these plants rejected the enriched jobs in favor of the traditional American assembly line. One reason for their stance may be that job enrichment actually increases management's control. Each work team signs every unit that it produces, and in the event that customers complain, it is easy to identify the work teams that were responsible for the product.

In short, there are both costs and benefits associated with the use of job enrichment, and it should be implemented only if the workers possess a high degree of achievement motivation.

Role Negotiation

A new and interesting approach to task assignment, role negotiation, has been used to alter the dimensions of the various tasks of all 2000 managers of the Diamond Shamrock Corporation, whose sales in 1975 topped $1 billion (Louis 1976). This approach requires training approximately 30 managers for three days in a lodge far removed from their everyday world of work. The basic premise of the approach is that nobody gets anything without promising something in return.

A superior and his or her immediate subordinates attend the training session as a group, thus constituting a "family team." Typically a family group consists of three to six members. Managers first complete questionnaires that provide them with insight into their own personalities. They are then requested to describe in writing what they are hiding from other members of their family team. Then each member describes in writing the work-related assets and liabilities of other members of his or her family group. He or she includes himself or herself in this analysis. These lists are subsequently used in group discussions.

After a lecture on role negotiation, each group presents a skit showing the impact of emotion in business. They re-create actual situations that took place in their own organizational settings. Some groups emphasize the favorable consequences of positive emotion, while other groups focus on the unfavorable consequences of negative emotion.

Finally, each family group convenes separately. A consultant is present at these meetings to handle any problems that may arise. Members list the kinds of decisions that they make and the individuals who contribute to them. They also critique one another's business behavior, using the lists of assets and liabilities developed previously.

Each member of the family group then negotiates with every other member on a one-to-one basis, but everyone is present. Each member must negotiate a contract with every other member: He or she must promise to correct two work-related attitudes or behaviors bothersome to the other party. In turn, the other party must make a similar promise. These promises are finalized in a written contract, which both parties sign. In effect, they are redefining the tasks and the manner in which they complete them in the organization.

The value of role negotiation at Diamond Shamrock has been assessed by means of a questionnaire, completed anonymously. Of the managers participating in the program, ninety-three percent felt that it led to improved teamwork and trust. The program has been so successful that the president of the company and the chairman of the board of directors have been trained in role negotiation.

MAPS A third approach to task design was developed by Bill McKelvey and Ralph Kilmann (1975). This approach is called MAPS (for multivariate analysis, participation, and structure). Two major objectives of this approach are to identify the independent clusters of tasks completed by the organization and to match the personal needs and work preferences of individuals with the tasks that must be completed.

By means of extensive interviews McKelvey and Kilmann identify a large number of tasks that the organization completes. Through various approaches, including judgmental analysis and a questionnaire survey, this large number is then reduced through a grouping process to a small number of tasks; within each group, the tasks are similar to one another. If a questionnaire is used, members of the organization are asked to indicate the degree to which each of these tasks is important to the organization. They respond on a 7-point scale of importance (1 is not important and 7 is very important). The questionnaire also contains a list of the members of the organization, and each respondent is asked to select the individuals with whom he or she would like to work in terms of a 7-point scale (1 is not interested in working with a particular individual and 7 is very interested). By means of a complex statistical analysis, individuals are matched to tasks according to their preferences both for specific types of work and for other organizational members with whom they would like to work. If they do not like their new assignments, they are typically allowed to change them.

MANAGING TECHNOLOGICAL CHANGE

While it is important to manage the tasks that organizational members perform, executives must also manage the rate at which technological change is introduced in the organization. This rate has accelerated dramatically since the turn of the twentieth century. For instance, in 1920, 46.7 percent of the American work force on nonagricultural payrolls was in the goods-producing sector; primarily because of technological changes, only 28.2 percent was in this sector in 1980 (U.S. Department of Labor, 1980). Also, fifty years ago only a handful of corporations maintained research and development departments; today such departments are the rule rather than the exception. These departments, small research and development firms, and universities have become the sources of innovations that have changed the complexion of American society.

In this section we discuss the impact of technological change in terms of the automated factory, the automated office, and telecommunications.

The Automated Factory

The major factor that has brought about the tremendous decrease in workers in the industrial or goods-producing sector of the economy is automation, a system in which the production processes are automatically controlled by self-operating machines. Typically automation is accompanied by a sharp decrease in the number of workers. For instance, if a plant of 10,000 workers goes to automation, only a few hundred workers may then be needed to produce an equivalent amount of work.

There are several types of automation, such as mass production and continuous-process production (see Chapter 15). Continuous-process production in particular leads to a drastic decrease in the number of employees necessary to operate an organization, for self-regulating control mechanisms are emphasized in the production of the final good, as is the case in an oil refinery or chemical plant. When mass production is introduced, it is possible to substitute unskilled workers for semiskilled and skilled workers. Similarly, continuous-process production allows the substitution of semiskilled workers for skilled workers.

Management, in introducing technological change, must be reasonably sure that the new equipment does not make the organization so inflexible that it eventually loses out to competitors. For instance, a steel-rolling producer decided to introduce single-process mills that would allow it to manufacture one product at an extremely low price. To accomplish this end, the company stopped producing other products. During the late fifties and early sixties the company was very successful against all competitors, both in the United States and elsewhere. However, the company now faces an uncertain future, primarily because Japanese and German firms have developed multiprocess mills allowing them to manufacture several related products rather than only one product. The firm has now lost many customers who need flexibility in their product lines.

Management must also be sure that the company does not spend money on equipment that is never used because of such factors as low demand for the products or resistance by employees to the new equipment. In view of the fact that industry spends approximately $25,000 to provide automated equipment for every first-line worker, management should take a cautious approach to the introduction of technological change in factories. Still, the investment can be worthwhile: Alan Purchase of the Stanford Research Institute estimates that from 1960 to 1969 productivity of factory workers increased eighty-three percent (*Dun's Review,* April 1978). Given the lag in the overall productivity of labor in the United States (about a one percent increase in 1979), we can fully expect such investments to continue, even to the extent that robots will replace workers on dull, repetitive jobs.

The Automated Office

The computer industry, which came into existence only after World War II, has shaped our organizations dramatically. It is now the third largest industry in the United States, behind oil and automotive. The word-processing industry, a related field, has also enjoyed tremendous growth during the past twenty years. This industry uses automated equipment to put words onto paper faster and more cheaply than workers can do it. Sales have increased from virtually zero in 1960 to $700 million in 1976, and it is estimated that this figure will rise to $1.5 billion by 1981 (*Dun's Review,* April 1978).

As we have seen, productivity of factory workers increased by 83 percent between 1960 and 1969. During the same period, productivity among office workers increased by only 4 percent (*Dun's Review,* April 1978). Alan Purchase estimates that partly as a result of this slow increase, office expenses have risen from 20 to 30 percent to 40 to 50 percent of the cost of running a company (*Dun's Review,* April 1978). As a result, the average investment per office employee will rise from $2,000 to $10,000 by 1985 (*Business Week,* June 30, 1975). Thus, just as the automated factory is a reality in many industries, we can expect to witness the growth of the automated office throughout the American workplace.

A major reason for the growth of the word-processing industry is the increase in employment in the service or non-goods-producing sector and the governmental sectors of the American economy. In 1920 43.8 percent of the American work force on nonagricultural payrolls was in the service sector; in 1980 the figure increased to 54.4

percent (*U.S. Department of Labor,* 1980). Similarly, the governmental sector increased from 9.5 percent of the nonagricultural work force in 1920 to 17.4 percent in 1980. Both sectors rely heavily on word-processing equipment.

All these changes have led to the concept of the automated office, already partially implemented in many organizations. For example, firms such as Xerox and IBM aggressively market such office machines as self-correcting typewriters and automatic copiers, which were not produced until after World War II.

It is difficult to assess the impact of the automated office on employee attitudes and behavior. But as Blauner's research has shown, the introduction of mass production is much more injurious to the employee than is continuous-process production, even though continuous-process production involves a much greater degree of automation (see Chapter 15). For the most part, office automation is more similar to continuous-process production than to mass production. Whatever the eventual influence turns out to be, it seems clear that the automated office is becoming a reality not only in the United States but in many other parts of the Western world.

Telecommunications

Even more striking changes than those in the automated factory or the automated office have been brought about by telecommunications, a system that uses sophisticated audiovisual equipment to transmit work from localized work centers to a central headquarters in a major city. The field of telecommunications is currently in an experimental state, but to a large extent the automated equipment necessary to expand it into a full-fledged industry already exists.

At a 1978 conference on the urban crisis sponsored by the Edison Electric Institute, the consensus of the experts was that telecommunications would increase in importance. In fact, telecommunications is likely to change the way cities develop and grow. Some large cities as we know them, such as New York and Chicago, will still exist. However, we are not likely to see additional cities of that size. These cities came into existence when workers needed to walk to their work in factories and offices, a situation that simply does not exist today. In addition, the growth of suburbs suggests that many individuals in our society do not want to live in large cities—and in any event they cannot do so because of the limits of growth. Hence the experts at the conference argued that most large cities would shrink to an average size of about 100,000 and that the work centers of these smaller cities would be linked to the larger cities by means of telecommunications.

As telecommunications becomes more widespread, managers in organizations in which it is used will be confronted with new and challenging problems. Supervising employees who work at local sites, ensuring that automated equipment is sufficiently powerful and flexible to meet organizational needs, and motivating both managers and workers are only some of the issues that will become dominant in the near future.

MANAGING PEOPLE DURING CHANGE

One of the truisms in the psychological literature is that the introduction of too much change into a person's life causes the individual to change his or her behavior radically; he or she may begin to feel insecure, have difficulties relating to others, have high blood pressure, and so on. Similarly, organizations frequently suffer if they manage people incorrectly during periods of change. For example, American corporations in Taiwan experienced no difficulty at all in recruiting Chinese workers because of the high rates of pay they were offering. However, when an economic recession occurred, the American corporations laid off the Chinese workers, as is the custom in America. This action violated the Chinese concept of lifetime employment in which the corporation is seen as an extension of the family and must be responsible for its employees during periods of austerity. Thus when the Taiwan economy later became robust, the American corporations experienced great difficulty obtaining workers, because they feared that a similar layoff would take place in the future.

Conversely, some American corporations have developed stable and highly efficient work forces because of enlightened personnel policies during periods of change. Both the Upjohn Company in Kalamazoo, Michigan, and the McCormick Company in Baltimore, Maryland, are noted for their loyal and productive work forces, a situation that has materialized partially because these corporations did not lay off any employees during the depression of the 1930s.

In this section we consider the management of people during periods of change and focus specifically on the issues of reductions in force, relocations, and directing employees during periods of technological and inevitable change.

Labor Force Reductions

A reduction in work force can be a traumatic experience for an individual, and many large companies attempt to minimize the negative impact of such reductions. For example, Westinghouse Corporation was forced to lay off several hundred of its engineers during the 1974 recession. Rather than simply laying them off, Westinghouse sponsored a career counseling program for the engineers and provided assistance so that they were able to obtain positions in other companies. A subsequent comparison of terminated and current engineers at Westinghouse indicated that there was no difference in the attitudes between these two groups (Gannon and Foreman 1974).

It is now generally realized that most terminations of middle managers occur because of limited organizational resources rather than ineffective performance (see Chapter 11). So many corporations use outplacement firms specializing in finding work for terminated executives. Some corporations even allow terminated executives to use their offices while job hunting so that prospective employers will not be aware that they have been terminated.

An enlightened personnel policy has been developed by IBM, which attempts to retrain rather than lay off employees during economic recessions. In 1969 IBM had to decide whether to lay off 8000 employees or to retrain them. The company set up a program asking for volunteers for retraining, a request that was enthusiastically received. Many of the IBM employees saw the retraining as a career opportunity, since they could learn new skills and, in some cases, could relocate to a geographically desirable location.

Relocations Organizations must also manage change that involves various types of relocation, including relocating plants, transferring executives to a new region of the country, and assigning new offices. Although all these relocations can be traumatic, wise management can minimize their deleterious effects.

A plant shutdown is a particularly troublesome change, because the entire community realizes it is losing a valuable economic resource. Thus when top management makes a decision to relocate, it should introduce the information in a slow and nonthreatening manner, both to the organization and to the community. Top management should guarantee jobs to any workers who will move to the new locality. And for those choosing not to move, management should set up career counseling centers and try to place these workers in new jobs. Also, management should try to provide the terminating workers with a suitable amount of separation pay.

Frequently it is necessary to transfer executives from one location to another, at least in part because upper-level executives in organizations need to understand the different subdivisions within the overall organization. In some companies refusal to accept such a transfer decreases the probability that an individual will be promoted. However, many corporations have developed farsighted policies in this area and provide training and counseling sessions for the transferred manager. The personnel office also tries to make the move easier by helping to find acceptable schooling for the executive's children, a suitable home, and so forth. In most cases the company makes sure that the executive does not suffer financially, especially if he or she is moving from a low-cost to a high-cost area.

Finally, research indicates that even an office move involving the transfer of individuals from an old to a new building is traumatic

(Quinn et al. 1978). People become tense during such moves, and rivalry develops over the selection of preferred offices. However, if management systematically explains the reasons for the move and for the assignment of offices, these feelings of tenseness and uncertainty will gradually evaporate. If at all possible, employees should be allowed to participate in some manner in the decisions about how offices will be assigned. In this way the social needs of individuals and the technical needs of the organization will be balanced, in line with the concept of a sociotechnical system (see Chapter 15).

Introducing Technological Change

Management faces a most difficult task when it introduces technological change into an organization on a large scale. Everyone must learn how to adapt to the new technology, which is not easy in many cases, especially if the managers and employees have become accustomed to the old technology and like it.

The experience of American Telephone and Telegraph when it eliminated the system of placing local telephone calls through operators and introduced the direct-dial system illustrates the correct introduction of technological change into an organization. Rather than abruptly forcing the change on its employees, AT&T spent over two years gradually introducing it into the entire organization. Mass meetings were held with employees indicating why the decision was made to introduce the dial system. Small discussion groups were then established in order to take the workers' viewpoints into consideration, receive suggestions from them, and allay their fears. The personnel office then conducted career counseling sessions with each employee, who was given several choices: a retraining in the new technology for the job the employee currently performed; a retraining in the new technology for a new type of job; early retirement that included generous financial benefits; or help in obtaining a new job in the event that the other choices proved unattractive.

In summary, top management must ensure that organizational members have enough time to absorb the change. The reasons for the change should be explained to them, and they should be allowed to make career choices within a feasible range of alternatives.

Introducing Inevitable Change

Sometimes an organization is faced with inevitable change: All or most managers and employees realize that various types of change—technological, task, personnel, and so forth—must be made if the organization is to survive. It is during these times that employees should be involved in the decision-making process since this will cement their feelings of allegiance to the organization (see Chapter 13). Also, if possible, top management should give organizational members time to absorb the realization that a major change will occur.

The recent experiences of the Graduate School of Fordham University, which is located in New York City, illustrate the proper introduction of inevitable change into an organization. The number of graduate students in the thirteen graduate departments of Fordham began to decrease dramatically, partially because of population changes and competition from other universities. So the president of Fordham established a five-person faculty task force to come up with alternatives to solve the problem of department changes due to decreasing enrollments. The task force spent a year studying the problem. It sent out questionnaires to all faculty members and met with all the thirteen departments to discuss the problem. Over time the task force identified four possible courses of action:

1. Close down the graduate school. The task force rejected this alternative, since some of the departments were prosperous.
2. Eliminate the financially weak departments, such as classics. The task force also rejected this alternative after studying it because some of the financially weak departments were academically superior and accounted for a large part of Fordham's reputation. Also, the elimination of these departments would not save much money; in the case of classics, a highly regarded department, only $75,000 would be saved on a one-time basis.
3. Eliminate the academically weak departments. The task force rejected this alternative, since it would be difficult to sponsor a graduate school if a large range of departments was not included within it. Rather, the task force felt that these departments should be strengthened.
4. Continue all departments as long as each department could attract a critical mass of students. However, this alternative would necessitate the elimination of courses in which there were only a few students. This alternative was selected and was generally accepted by the faculty, since it was clear that change was inevitable.

In many ways introducing technological and inevitable change are similar, since they both should involve a long period of time, should include employees in the decision-making process whenever feasible, and should be explained carefully to all affected parties.

MANAGING STRUCTURAL CHANGES

Periodically management introduces structural changes into the organization. It may create a new department, combine two departments into one, or set up a new division. We have already examined some aspects of structural change, such as Jay Galbraith's information-processing approach to organization design (see Chapter 7). In this section we focus on three issues, work processes, work scheduling, and shift work.

Work Processes Management may wish to change the processes by which work is completed. Workers whose jobs are closely related to one another can be brought into closer proximity so that they can help one another; activities necessary to produce the final good or service can be sequenced in a more efficient manner; and the machinery can be cleaned more often to avoid frequent breakdowns. Generally speaking, it is not necessary to change the entire design of the organization, but merely the manner in which the work is being processed.

A well-known structural change involving work processes took place in a large restaurant chain (Whyte 1948). The problem that initiated the change was excessive waitress turnover and absenteeism. Moreover, many waitresses were antagonistic toward one another, since they were competing for tips from customers. In some instances waitresses argued openly with each other and even broke down crying because of the pressures and tensions.

William Whyte solved this problem by changing the work processes in the restaurant. The problem actually involved the relationships between the short-order cooks (who were male) and the waitresses. In the restaurant the waitresses gave their orders verbally to the cooks, who unconsciously resented taking demands from women. To reestablish their own authority, the cooks began to play favorites. Only waitresses who were properly respectful were given good service. Naturally, the favored waitresses received better tips from the customers, for the food they served was well prepared and hot.

The problem was eliminated by means of one small structural change: A spindle on which written orders were placed was positioned between the waitresses and cooks. The time at which each order was placed was noted on the order slip; the cooks had to take the slips in order and so could not play favorites. Over time the problems in the restaurant began to fade away, for the status of the cooks was no longer a factor in their work.

Work Scheduling Management sometimes introduces structural changes in work scheduling to overcome problems that managers and employees experience. For example, many of the managers and workers in a German company were annoyed by the traffic jams they experienced coming to and going home from work. To combat the problem, the company introduced *flexitime.* Under flexitime all employees must be present during a core period—for example, from 9:00 A.M. to 3:00 P.M. However, the employees can begin work any time before 9:00 A.M., and their starting time determines their quitting time. For instance, an employee who starts work at 6:00 A.M. can quit at 3:00 P.M. Employees seem to like having this measure of control over their work life and the flexibility to schedule their outside activities more conveniently.

In recent years several firms and government agencies have begun to experiment with variants of the 5-day, 40-hour workweek. As early as 1972, it was estimated that one out of every 840 employees in the United States was on some form of the 4-day week; of these 60 percent were working on the 4–40 schedule, that is, 10 hours a day for 4 days a week (Wheeler, Gurman, and Tarnowieski 1972). Research on the 4–40 schedule has indicated that job satisfaction does seem to increase when the new approach is introduced (Nord and Costigan 1973). However, over time workers in low-level and routine jobs report that fatigue increases. In addition, the job satisfaction of these workers declines after about a year, especially if they have no outside interests to fill their long weekends. This result indicates that the Hawthorne effect (see p. 34) may be responsible for the initial positive effects of the 4–40 workweek: Workers may simply enjoy being part of an experiment or they may be refreshed by having a change. Later the fatigue associated with the longer hours of work overcomes the benefits of the switch.

In 1977 William Glueck reviewed the studies on the four-day workweek and flexitime. Generally speaking, the studies on the four-day workweek were mixed. In some instances this work schedule was highly successful, but in others it was unsuccessful as measured by such factors as turnover, absenteeism, and productivity. However, the studies on flexitime indicated that these experiments in work scheduling were typically very successful. Such results parallel the theoretical arguments favoring flexitime over the four-day workweek (Gannon 1974b). Among these arguments is the proposition that flexitime allows the worker to make his own decisions about the use of his own time. At the same time, the worker is better able to balance his work and familial activities.

Shift Work

Many organizations are beginning to increase their use of shift work. This form of work scheduling typically involves two or three groups of full-time workers who periodically rotate their hours of work so that everyone must work during the traditional nonbusiness hours for some space of time, such as a month. In some cases employees are assigned to shifts on a permanent basis.

There are at least two major reasons for this structural change in work scheduling: the economic need to employ equipment and machines during all hours of the day, and peak-time pricing, in which corporations are charged more for using energy during peak times of the day than during other times. This structural shift, however, creates some management problems. Moonlighting (holding a second job) is more common on the second and third shifts than on the regular shifts. This situation increases the probability of accidents, since such workers are generally more tired than regular workers (Gannon et al., in press). In addition, management pays a premium to shift workers, a practice that may attract workers who are only motivated by the desire to make money (and moonlight also).

Research suggests that shift workers experience conflict in fulfilling role expectations (Mott et al. 1965). For example, workers on the 6-P.M.-to-2-A.M. shift experience more difficulties with teenage children than do other workers, most probably because they rarely see them. If these role conflicts become too great, the individual can become physically ill, less productive, and more prone to accidents.

In introducing shift work, top management should attempt to avoid the establishment of permanent shifts, since some workers would never be able to work during regular business hours. Rather, the shifts should rotate. However, there is some debate about the frequency of rotation. If the rotation is too quick, the workers' bodily rhythms are in a constant state of change and they become more susceptible to illness. On the other hand, frequent rotation of shifts allows the workers to fulfill, at least partially, major role expectations.

Finally, research indicates that shift workers are as satisfied as regular workers if there is a sufficient number of them in the community (Mott et al. 1965). In this case shift workers can find companions when not working, and the community does not view them as abnormal if they engage in leisure activities during regular business hours. Thus if top management wants to introduce shift work, it might try to persuade other organizations in the community to follow its lead.

ORGANIZATION DEVELOPMENT

As our discussion thus far indicates, management can be very successful if it introduces major changes gradually and properly. This realization has led to the growth of a specialized subfield of management, *organization development* (OD). According to Wendell French, Cecil Bell, and Robert Zawicki (1978), OD is a program for introducing planned and systematic changes into an organization. OD specialists rely heavily on behavioral science techniques, such as questionnaire surveys and interviews, when they introduce changes. Typically members of the organization must actively collaborate with one another in the introduction of changes. However, they usually rely on the advice and direction of a professional change agent, the OD consultant.

In introducing changes, the OD consultant places special emphasis on the activities of work groups and the interactions among them. This emphasis is logical, for the OD consultant normally redesigns the organization so work groups can coordinate their efforts more effectively. He or she also attempts to change the behavioral processes within and among work groups so the overall level of productivity in the organization increases. As these descriptions imply,

OD is frequently a long-term program that may require several months or even years before the changes are successfully completed. For instance, an OD consultant might have to work with two departments that are having difficulty coordinating their work for several months or years before he or she irons out the problems to management's satisfaction.

Steps in OD

Organization development has three steps: diagnosis, intervention, and maintenance. Management must first recognize that a problem exists, at which time it will normally use an OD consultant to *diagnose* it. To do so, the consultant may examine standard management reports and use techniques such as the unstructured interview, the questionnaire survey, and group discussions.

Once the OD consultant and members of the organization diagnose the problem, the actual *intervention* takes place. That is, the consultant and members of the organization introduce the changes. For example, two departments such as sales and production may decide they can coordinate their work better if they establish a permanent task force to monitor relations between them and straighten out any problems before they get out of hand. The consultant assists in reaching this decision and in setting up the task force.

After the intervention takes place, the OD consultant must ensure that the organization does not slip back to its original position. Hence he or she focuses on the *maintenance* of these changes. The consultant may meet periodically with members of the task force and help them iron out any difficulties that could hinder their effectiveness, such as a halfhearted commitment to the recommendations of the task force by members of the sales department.

Specific Techniques

OD consultants usually rely on behavioral science techniques both to diagnose problems and to bring about changes in an organization. Three of the most important techniques are the unstructured interview, the questionnaire survey, and the conference or group discussion.

Interviews. An OD consultant's first task is to seek information that will provide him or her with an understanding of the organization and its problems. For this purpose he or she normally conducts private, unstructured interviews that allow an individual manager or employee to express himself or herself freely. In the *unstructured interview* the OD consultant merely provides the manager or employee with general questions designed to elicit information. Hence the manager rather than the consultant controls the pace of the interview.

Such interviews are extremely helpful, for the OD consultant learns a great deal about the organizational problems in a relaxed manner. He or she can then use this information in helping management decide on and implement changes. In one instance an OD consultant examining the causes of excessive turnover among keypunch operators in a large organization conducted several unstructured interviews with the employees, during which he discovered that they had an inaccurate idea of how their performance was being measured. Management was using a somewhat complicated formula that took into consideration both the number of cards punched and the number of errors per card. Some of the keypunch operators even said they were thinking of quitting because of the "unfair" method used to measure their performance. The OD consultant brought these facts to the attention of the managers, who scheduled a meeting with the employees to discuss and correct the problem. Because of these discussions, management changed its method of measuring employee performance, and the turnover rate declined significantly.

Questionnaire Surveys. Questionnaires are a popular technique for obtaining information. Like the unstructured interview, an anonymous and confidential questionnaire survey can provide the OD consultant with a wealth of information that cannot be obtained easily in a group situation where individuals may be somewhat afraid to speak out openly and honestly. In organization development the questionnaire survey is a valuable instrument, for it allows members of the organization to express themselves on a large number of job-related issues such as salaries, supervision, and working conditions. Management can use the data from the questionnaire survey to pinpoint problems.

OD consultants frequently employ the questionnaire survey in combination with the interview and group discussions. The consultant thus obtains information from three different sources. If he or she identifies the same or similar problems with each of these three methods, the consultant is on firm ground when recommending changes.

Group Discussion Sessions. Once the consultant has become familiar with the nature and problems of the organization, he or she will often use group discussion sessions or conferences as part of the actual intervention. Group discussions are an outgrowth of *sensitivity training,* an approach created by psychologists to help individuals increase their self-awareness and improve their ability to relate to other people. All members of a sensitivity group contribute to each other's development. Although a psychologist is present as group leader, he or she plays a passive role most of the time. The purpose of a sensitivity group is to have all members express themselves freely on a variety of issues having to do with interpersonal relations. Gradu-

"This is Willis Dunwoodie. His department is corporate feelings."

Source: *New Yorker,* April 14, 1980, p. 47. Drawing by Weber; © 1980 The New Yorker Magazine, Inc.

ally the psychologist intervenes in the group discussion to nudge its members toward insights that should prove helpful to them. Each member thus becomes sensitized to his or her own strengths and weaknesses. Members gain insight into themselves and change any attitudes that negatively affect the way they relate to others.

In recent years sensitivity groups have become popular as a training forum for managers; such groups are known as *training groups* (T-groups). However, there are several disadvantages to the use of T-groups in management. If a group leader is inexperienced and lacks adequate training, he or she may be unable to control the often highly emotional climate in the group. In addition, T-groups have been attacked on the ground that they encourage too much freedom of expression. Some members may severely criticize others, with destructive rather than constructive results. Perhaps the most serious accusation against T-groups, though, is that their positive effects often end when the group disbands. A manager who has learned to be sensitive to the other managers in a T-group does not necessarily carry this over to his or her own work situation.

OD consultants consequently have moved away from T-groups toward the conference approach. A *conference group* is brought together only for the purpose of attaining organizational objectives, not for personal insights. While the group members are encouraged to be open and frank, the OD consultant normally does not allow them to attack one another. For example, an OD consultant may bring together two departments that are not able to coordinate their work effectively. After some general discussion the consultant may ask the members of each department to go into a separate room and develop a list of major problems blocking cooperation and coordination. He or she may also request each department to develop another list of the feelings its members possess about the other department. After a few hours the two groups meet and share their lists, which then become the basis for discussion. Through these discussions, guided and controlled by the OD consultant, the two departments normally can solve their own problems.

The U.S. Postal Service sponsors a highly successful OD program that relies heavily on a conference method that is purposely nonthreatening. In the group sessions the OD consultant asks individuals to attack the problem at hand rather than one another. The Postal Service attempts to bring about planned and systematic change in the fifty largest post offices by means of this approach. During a series of conferences in a major post office, the middle and top managers decided they could dramatically increase productivity if they could only increase the speed of the stamp-processing machine. These managers then reengineered this machine, a change that now saves the Postal Service $4 million a year in all its post offices.

General Types of Intervention

Organization development usually attacks organizational problems of two general types: structural and process. A *structural intervention* involves altering the actual structure of the organization so that individuals relate to one another in a new and different way. For instance, the organization may decide to collapse ten departments into five. A *process intervention* changes the attitudes and the behavioral processes in organizational life without altering the structure in any way. Group discussions are a process intervention: If they indicate that the head of a particular department is too insensitive to the feelings of others, he or she should react by becoming more considerate.

Structural Interventions. Some examples of structural interventions are the introduction of a new technology, changing the work schedule from eight hours a day for five days a week to ten hours a day for four days a week, and developing a new system for communicating information among departments in an organization. Typically a structural intervention directly affects the behavior of organizational members, since they must relate to one another in a new and different fashion. Ideally these new behavioral relations will create more favorable attitudes among members of the organization and a higher level of employee performance.

Process Interventions. In a process intervention the OD consultant does not attempt to change the structure of the organization. Rather, the focus is on the dynamics of organizational life or the attitudes of members of the organization. The consultant attempts to change these attitudes so organizational objectives can be accomplished more successfully. For example, he or she may ask each member of a work group that is performing at a substandard level to write a narrative profile of the group's behavior. These profiles become the basis of extended discussions. Through these discussions the consultant seeks to change the attitudes of members of the work group who are inhibiting performance.

Normally a process intervention is accompanied by some structural changes or a structural intervention. Management might try a process intervention to deal with a work group that is producing at a substandard level. During the intervention the work group members may decide that some structural changes must be made: adding an integrator to coordinate their work with other work groups, introducing new machinery, redesigning the existing machinery, or placing workers closer together so they can communicate more effectively. Thus an organization often uses structural and process interventions simultaneously.

Specific Types of Intervention

Among OD consultants, process intervention has received much more attention than structural intervention. Usually it is difficult to change the structure of an organization. More importantly, a process intervention frequently results in a structural intervention, as in the case of the process intervention in the Postal Service that resulted in the improvement of the stamp-processing machine. Prominent types of process interventions are team building, intergroup interventions, and total organizational interventions. However, these techniques also represent structural interventions, as will be described shortly.

Team Building. This technique focuses on the operations of only one group. When members of a group are unfamiliar with one another or are having difficulty coordinating their work, an appropriate process intervention involves meetings of the members to strengthen their identity as a group. The goal is to build the group into a team. The group or unit should hold its meetings away from the work site if possible, to avoid outside interferences.

At the initial meetings group members diagnose the problems they face. One popular strategy is for the OD consultant to ask all members to write down five problems they consider detrimental to the functioning of the group. Each member then reads his or her list aloud, after which each problem is discussed in detail. Members then develop a final list of problems that all of them wish to attack.

After diagnosis, the group typically goes through several sessions during which they discuss possible solutions to these problems. Members also attempt to define their relationships to one another as they apply to the solution of these problems. The discussions should not become personal or vindictive, since only job-related factors are covered. After the major problems of the group have been ironed out, members may meet periodically to ensure that they do not arise again.

If the OD consultant decides the group is too large to interact and work effectively, he or she may recommend that it be split into two groups that function independently in the organization, even though he or she has not conducted group discussion sessions. In this instance the team-building intervention is structural.

Intergroup Interventions. When there is a great amount of tension and friction between two or more groups, an intergroup process intervention is appropriate. Many of the techniques employed in team building can also be used in intergroup interventions; the major difference is that more than one group is involved. Sometimes each group is asked to develop a list of strengths and weaknesses of the other group or groups. These lists become the basis for the diagnosis of problems.

Another popular intergroup approach is the *organizational mirror.* In this approach one group sits in an inside circle and is surrounded by the other group or groups. Members of the outside group discuss their general feelings about the strengths and weaknesses of the inside group, which is not allowed to participate in the discussion. Positions are then changed, and the inside group moves to the outside, where the exercise is repeated. After all groups understand how they are perceived by one another, they attempt to diagnose their problems and develop solutions.

Like team building, a structural intergroup intervention can be used as an alternative to a process intergroup intervention. For example, if two departments are unable to work together effectively because of the antagonistic relations between their two superiors, top management may put one individual in charge of both departments.

The Managerial Grid. We have already described Robert Blake and Jane Mouton's managerial Grid within the context of leadership styles and methods for resolving conflict (see Chapter 14). The managerial Grid is also an excellent example of a total organizational intervention, an attempt to change not only teams and groups but the entire organization and the climate in it.

Blake and Mouton begin their change efforts by focusing on the

WHY EFFORTS AT CHANGE FAIL

. . . I reviewed my notes from thirty-two major reorganizations in large organizations in which I played some consulting and research role. I did not find one that could be labeled as fully completed and integrated three years after the change had been announced (and in many cases had gone through several revisions). That is, after three years there were still many people fighting, ignoring, questioning, resisting, blaming the reorganization without feeling a strong obligation personally to correct the situation.

. . . I believe the reasons for this long delay are embedded in the change strategy typically used by management. . . . The basic strategy has been for the top management to take the responsibility to overcome and outguess the resistance to change. This strategy does tend to succeed because management works very hard, applies pressure, and, if necessary, knocks a few heads together (or eliminates some). However, as we have seen, the strategy creates resisting forces that are costly to the organization's effectiveness, to its long run viability and flexibility, as well as to the people at all levels.

Source: Chris Argyris, "Today's Problems with Tomorrow's Organizations," *Journal of Management Studies* 4, no. 1 (February 1967): 53.

two basic aspects of leader behavior, concern for production, or task orientation, and concern for people, or consideration. Each of these aspects is measured on a 9-point scale (see Chapter 14). Although there are exceptions, managers generally feel that the 9,9 leadership style is ideal—that is, when the leader is very strong in the two areas of task orientation and consideration. The major objective, then, is to close the gap between the actual leadership style and the ideal leadership style through the use of the managerial Grid. To accomplish this objective, Blake and Mouton use team building and intergroup process interventions. When all the managers in the organization pattern their behavior after the ideal style for their situation, total organizational intervention is completed.

COMPLEX ISSUES FACING OD

It is relatively easy to highlight the advantages and strengths of OD, for its goal of bringing about planned and systematic changes within the dimensions of organization design and behavioral processes is almost necessarily a desirable one. However, the field of OD is faced with many significant problems and complex issues in implementing this goal. While these problems can usually be overcome, they require constant attention if OD is to be successful.

Familiarity and Dependency

In OD a consultant who is experienced with the process must design and guide the intervention that takes place. But sometimes the consultant is not an employee of the organization; the organization only uses the individual as a consultant. This situation has the advantage of providing the organization with a fresh outlook on its problems. However, it also means the changes are being implemented by someone who probably is not familiar with the distinctive problems of the organization. Thus before the consultant can effectively guide the intervention, he or she must spend a significant amount of time becoming familiar with its unique characteristics.

An organization may also set up a separate division that lends its services to the various operating divisions that request its help. General Motors recently established an OD division that employs 140 professionals. The major advantage of this approach is that the OD consultant is familiar with the distinctive problems of the organization even before he or she visits the operating division that has requested help. The major disadvantage is that the consultant, as a member of the organization, may avoid recommending courses of action that seem risky and might harm his or her chances for promotion.

A related problem is that members of the organization may become too dependent upon the OD consultant. They may even reach a point where they will not undertake any changes without his or her advice. Moreover, the consultant may encourage this dependency, especially if he or she is an outsider whose fee will be terminated when the specific problem has been solved. Thus the management of an organization should closely monitor both the effectiveness of the intervention and the activities of the OD consultant.

Time and Measurement

A major problem sometimes associated with organization development is time. Blake and Mouton argue that three to five years is required to complete a total organizational intervention. Even team building takes time, for the group must meet several times before it can diagnose and solve its problems. But in recent years OD consultants have directed their attention to this problem, and they have made some progress. For instance, if an organization employs questionnaire surveys as part of a total organizational intervention, it can use them on an annual or biannual basis to monitor attitudes and to identify emerging problems. Such surveys are relatively inexpensive and can serve to integrate the other activities during the intervention, such as periodic team-building sessions.

Another problem is that it is very difficult to measure the success of an OD intervention precisely. Organizations are not scientific laboratories in which it is possible to control all factors in the study and identify the causal relations among them. This problem is particularly acute if the intervention requires several months or years, during which the consultant introduces many changes in the organization. In this case it may not even be possible to pinpoint the specific change or changes that seem to be creating the improved performance in the organization. Moreover, it is always possible that performance would have improved as a natural course of events even if the OD intervention had not taken place. Still, performance usually can be measured in a general but convincing manner. For example, a large industrial organization sponsored a total organizational intervention that lasted five years, during which net income increased 100 percent. Just this relationship convinced top management that the intervention had been very successful and well worth the investment.

Ethics Typically an OD intervention requires members of the organization to be candid with one another, for problems need to be identified. In addition, members must actively participate in defining and solving problems. However, it is often difficult for them to be open with one another, for they fear their remarks will come back to haunt them. One OD consultant who conducted fifty interviews with employees in an insurance company was normally greeted with hostility and remarks like "Are you a management spy?" Further, even though the OD consultant promises to treat the information confidentially, the employee still has reason to be wary. An OD consultant may obtain information during an unstructured and confidential interview that he or she then uses during a group session. Even if the consultant does not mention the source, the individuals in the group may recognize it purely on the basis of the specific information presented.

Unfortunately, a small number of OD consultants have engaged in unprofessional behavior. In one celebrated instance an OD consultant who was involved in redesigning a critical government agency supposedly began to leak information to the press because he became so frustrated in his attempts to change it. His effectiveness was seriously impaired by this action, as members of the organization could no longer trust him to keep the information they supplied in confidence. Another OD consultant introduced a job enrichment program into a large government agency, after which he made several speeches openly deploring the agency's managerial practices.

The problems of trust, participation, and confidentiality are difficult to resolve. Perhaps the only solution lies in the patience and skill of the consultant as he or she slowly tries to win the trust and confidence of organizational members. While such trust is sometimes difficult to win, it is essential to an effective job.

Some OD consultants are attacking these problems by suggesting that professional standards be established for individuals who want to practice in this area. They recommend that a certificate in OD be awarded to qualified individuals, as is the case in many professions (such as the CPA in accounting). Although licensing might restrict the range and type of service OD consultants could offer, it should eliminate marginal and unprofessional individuals.

SUMMARY

According to Harold Leavitt, there are four interrelated factors that management must consider when introducing change: the task to be completed, the organizational structure in which it is to be completed, the people completing it, and the technology by means of which it will be completed. Major approaches to changing task assignments include job enrichment, role negotiation, and MAPS.

Managing technological change is a major managerial responsibility, as demonstrated by the rapid rise in importance of the automated factory and the automated office. With automation the production processes are automatically controlled by self-operating machines. In recent years management has focused its attention on constructing the automated office in which machine equipment puts words onto paper faster and more cheaply than employees could do it. In addition, management is now interested in introducing technological change via telecommunications, using sophisticated audiovisual equipment to transmit work from localized work centers in small communities to a central headquarters in a major city.

Another important managerial responsibility is managing people efficiently and effectively during periods of change. Major issues of change impacting on individuals include reductions in force, relocations, technological change, and inevitable change.

Management also has the responsibility of introducing structural changes into the organization. Such changes can take place in many areas, including work processes, work scheduling, and the assignment of shifts.

Because of the importance of change and development, a specialized subfield of management, organization development, has come into existence. Its basic objective is to introduce planned and systematic change into an organization so that it will continue to grow and prosper. To accomplish this objective, OD consultants follow three steps: they identify problems (diagnosis), make changes (intervention), and ensure that the effects of the changes will last (maintenance). To gather information, the consultant typically employs behavioral science techniques such as questionnaire surveys, unstructured interviews, and group discussion sessions or conferences. OD consultants attempt to involve the members of the organization actively in the change process, and they focus on the interactions that take place within and among groups.

There are two major types of interventions: structural and process. The structural intervention actually changes the organization's design so that individuals relate to one another in a new and different fashion. The process intervention attempts to change the attitudes of organizational members. Typically a process intervention results in some structural changes in the organization.

There are three specific types of intervention, each of which can be either structural or process. Team building focuses only on cohesiveness within a single group; intergroup interventions strive to bring about changes in relations between two or more groups; and a total organizational intervention seeks to effect changes throughout the organization. The managerial grid represents a total organizational intervention.

Typically an intervention is guided by a professional OD consultant, who brings objectivity as well as expertise to the task. However, because an OD consultant needs to be familiar with the distinctive characteristics of the organization before he or she can guide and monitor an intervention, many large companies and government agencies have created their own OD departments.

OD involves several potential problems. Sometimes members of an organization become too dependent on their consultant. Also, an organization must invest a great amount of time and money in OD, even though it is sometimes difficult to measure the impact of changes on the performance of the organization. Finally, there are some ethical problems in this area, for the consultant must treat information he or she obtains from organizational members confidentially, and he or she should be qualified to undertake this kind of work.

DISCUSSION QUESTIONS

1. Why is it difficult to measure the success or failure of an OD program? How would you try to overcome this difficulty?
2. Is there a relationship between the declining level of worker productivity in the United States and increased interest in the automated office? Why or why not? Why is management seemingly less interested now in the concept of the automatic factory than it was in previous years?
3. Suppose you were in charge of a task force set up to develop a program to certify OD consultants. What kind of educational and professional background would a person need to obtain a certificate in OD? Would you establish a training program that an individual would have to take to obtain this certificate? If so, what topics would be treated in it? If not, why not?
4. Is it necessary to use an OD consultant when major changes such as those described in this chapter are introduced into an organiza-

tion? Is it always necessary for management and other organizational members to take part in an OD intervention? Explain.

5. What is the major difference between T-groups and the conference approach? Which would you expect to be more effective in bringing about organizational changes? Why?

CRITICAL INCIDENT

NOTE: This critical incident can be used by the whole class with the case observational method (see Appendix A) or used for thought and discussion by individual class members.

The *Washington Post,* one of the country's distinguished newspapers, faced a major financial problem in the early 1970s. Its profit margins were shrinking, in part because of the increased competition from other media such as magazines, radio, and TV. Management felt that only a significant decrease in its total labor costs could save the situation.

To decrease these labor costs, management proposed that many of its high-salaried printers be replaced by automated printing equipment. However, the printers were members of a strong craft union, the International Typographical Union, which had negotiated several very favorable contracts with the *Post* on behalf of its members. To ensure job security, the union persuaded the *Post* to accept the practice of "make-work," allowing a printer to destroy a page of set type and another printer to reset it solely for the purpose of making more work. The union even negotiated an agreement whereby *Post* management was not allowed into the composing room in which the printers worked.

The *Post* had access to the new automated equipment. It could also obtain many nonunion printers trained in the use of this equipment. In effect, the printers would move from a skilled to a semiskilled job classification, and the savings to the *Post* would be enormous.

Post management did not want to fire any of its printers or decrease their salaries. Rather, it proposed that the *Post* printers be retrained in the use of the new equipment. The *Post* management also proposed that as its printers retired, there would be a gradual reduction in the number of printers used to produce the paper, and that new employees would receive sharply lower salaries. Further, *Post* management wanted complete access to the composing room, for it felt that many of the printers were performing at a substandard level. The *Post* had justification for this belief, for several of its highly paid and full-time printers were also employed on a full-time basis at a crosstown newspaper, the *Washington Star. Post* management was adamant in its position because it felt that only the lowering of total labor costs and improved employee performance would save the newspaper from bankruptcy.

QUESTIONS: If you were in *Post* management, how would you approach the union and the printers about the proposed changes? If you were a union negotiator, how would you respond to *Post* management? From our discussion of introducing technological change, can you see an ideal way of implementing these management proposals?

SUGGESTED READINGS

Beckhard, Richard. *Organization Development: Strategies and Models.* Reading, Mass.: Addison-Wesley, 1969, 119 pages, paperback.
Beckhard outlines various methods of organization development. He then describes five organizational situations in which these methods were successfully used.

Blake, Robert, and Mouton, Jane. *Building a Dynamic Corporation Through Grid Organization Development.* Reading, Mass.: Addison-Wesley, 1969, 120 pages, paperback.
Blake and Mouton provide a full description of the managerial grid.

French, Wendell; Bell, Cecil; and Zawacki, Robert, eds. *Organization Development.* Dallas: Business Publications, 1978, paperback.
This excellent set of readings provides a thorough overview of the field of organization development.

PART V
EXPERIENTIAL EXERCISES

Conflict Styles: Organizational Decision Making

GOALS: (1) To identify ways of dealing with organizational or group conflict. (2) To discuss when and why different methods of resolving conflict are appropriate to different situations. (3) To provide an experience in group decision making.

GROUP SIZE: An unlimited number of groups of five to seven participants each.

TIME REQUIRED: Approximately one and one-half hours.

MATERIALS: (1) A Conflict Styles Worksheet for each participant and an extra copy for each team. (2) A pencil for each participant. (3) Newsprint and a felt-tipped marker.

PHYSICAL SETTING: A room large enough to accommodate all participants, with adequate tables and chairs available for each team.

PROCESS

1. The facilitator introduces the experience on the inevitability of conflict in groups and how conflict can be used as a constructive force.

2. He or she then gives the participants copies of the Conflict Styles Worksheet and instructs them to complete the worksheet in 15 minutes.

3. At the end of this time the facilitator divides the participants into groups of five to seven members each and appoints one observer for each group. Observers are briefed on what to look for.

4. A copy of the Conflict Styles sheet is given to each group, and the groups are instructed to complete the worksheet *as groups.* They

Source: Reprinted from John E. Jones and J. William Pfeiffer, eds., *The 1977 Annual Handbook for Group Facilitators.* (San Diego, Ca.: University Associates, 1977), pp. 15–19. Used with permission.

are advised to avoid conflict-reducing techniques such as the use of majority power (voting), minority (persuasion based on pressure), or compromise (giving in to keep the peace). The facilitator also urges them to view differences of opinion as constructive and to make their ranking decisions as a group, based on logic as well as mutual understanding. He or she tells them that they will have 45 minutes in which to complete the worksheet.

5. Each group observer reports to his or her group on how it handled the ranking task and any conflict that arose. Specific incidents are described to provide the group members with pertinent feedback.

6. When the observers have made their reports to the subgroups, the total group is reassembled, and each group's decision is posted on newsprint. If any groups' decisions differ widely (a "1" and "5" choice for the same problem), the facilitator may focus on *intergroup* conflict by having each of the small groups explain the rationale for each of its responses.

7. The facilitator discusses the five styles of handling organizational conflict. He or she gives an example of each style, when it might be appropriate, and so on. Participants may be urged to discuss these styles in terms of what they have just experienced. The participants then identify by style the ways of dealing with conflict listed for each case on the Conflict Styles Worksheet. (Usually they are able to identify the responses correctly.)

8. The facilitator processes the activity with the group by considering the learnings gained from the experience and their application to real life situations. He or she lists major points on newsprint.

Variations

1. The facilitator can increase the pressure on the small groups by reducing the time allotted for the ranking task to 30 minutes.

2. The situations described on the Conflict Styles Worksheet can be rewritten to reflect the interests or needs of the participants or groups involved (supervisors, sales personnel, governmental or clerical staffs, educators, etc.).

CONFLICT STYLES WORKSHEET

INSTRUCTIONS: Your task is to rank the five alternative courses of action under each of the four cases below, from the most desirable or appropriate way of dealing with the conflict situation to the least desirable. Rank the *most* desirable course of action "1," the next most desirable "2," and so on, ranking the *least* desirable or least appropriate action "5." Enter your rank for each item next to each choice.

Case One

Pete is lead operator of a production molding machine. Recently he has noticed that one of the men from another machine has been coming over to his machine and talking to one of his men (not on break time). The efficiency of Pete's operator seems to be falling off, and there have been some rejects due to his inattention. Pete thinks he detects some resentment among the rest of the crew. *If you were Pete, you would:*

____ A. Talk to your man and tell him to limit his conversations during on-the-job time.
____ B. Ask the foreman to tell the lead operator of the other machine to keep his operators in line.
____ C. Confront both men the next time you see them together (as well as the other lead operator, if necessary), find out what they are up to, and tell them what you expect of your operators.
____ D. Say nothing now; it would be silly to make something big out of something so insignificant.
____ E. Try to put the rest of the crew at ease; it is important that they all work well together.

Case Two Sally is the senior quality control (QC) inspector and has been appointed group leader of the QC people on her crew. On separate occasions two of her people have come to her with different suggestions for reporting test results to the machine operators. Paul wants to send the test results to the foreman and then to the machine, since the foreman is the person ultimately responsible for production output. Jim thinks the results should go directly to the lead operator on the machine in question, since he is the one who must take corrective action as soon as possible. Both ideas seem good, and Sally can find no ironclad procedures in the department on how to route the reports. *If you were Sally, you would:*

____ A. Decide who is right and ask the other person to go along with the decision (perhaps establish it as a written procedure).
____ B. Wait and see; the best solution will become apparent.
____ C. Tell both Paul and Jim not to get uptight about their disagreement; it is not that important.
____ D. Get Paul and Jim together and examine both of their ideas closcly.
____ E. Send the report to the foreman, with a copy to the lead operator (even though it might mean a little more copy work for QC).

Case Three Ralph is a module leader; his module consists of four very complex and expensive machines and five crewmen. The work is exacting, and inattention or improper procedures could cause a costly mistake or serious injury. Ralph suspects that one of his men is taking drugs on the job or at least is showing up for work under the influence of drugs.

Ralph feels that he has some strong indications, but he knows he does not have a "case." *If you were Ralph, you would:*

____ A. Confront the man outright, tell him what you suspect and why and that you are concerned for him and for the safety of the rest of the crew.
____ B. Ask the suspected offender to keep his habit off the job; what he does *on* the job is part of your business.
____ C. Not confront the individual right now; it might either "turn him off" or drive him underground.
____ D. Give the man the "facts of life"; tell him it is illegal and unsafe and that if he gets caught, you will do everything you can to see that the man is fired.
____ E. Keep a close eye on the man to see that he is not endangering others.

Case Four Gene is a foreman of a production crew. From time to time in the past the Product Development section has "tapped" the production crews for operators to augment their own operator personnel to run test products on special machines. This has put very little strain on the production crews, since the demands have been small, temporary, and infrequent. Lately, however, there seems to have been an almost constand demand for four production operators. The rest of the production crew must fill in for these missing people, usually by working harder and taking shorter breaks. *If you were Gene, you would:*

____ A. Let it go for now; the "crisis" will probably be over soon.
____ B. Try to smooth things over with your own crew and with the development foreman; we all have jobs to do and cannot afford a conflict.
____ C. Let development have two of the four operators they requested.
____ D. Go to the development supervisor or his foreman and talk about how these demands for additional operators could best be met without placing production in a bind.
____ E. Go to the supervisor of production (Gene's boss) and get him to "call off" the development people.

Conflict Styles Solution

Case One	*Case Two*	*Case Three*	*Case Four*
A. Compromise	A. Power	A. Integration	A. Denial
B. Power*	B. Denial	B. Compromise	B. Suppression
C. Integration†	C. Suppression	C. Denial	C. Compromise
D. Denial	D. Integration	D. Power	D. Integration
E. Suppression	E. Compromise	E. Suppression	E. Power

* = forcing.
† = problem solving.

Group Decision Making

GOALS: (1) To demonstrate the forms of conflict-resolving behavior. (2) To compare and contrast the effects of individual and group decision making. (3) To demonstrate the effect of consensus methods on group problem solving.

GROUP SIZE: Any number of people divided into small groups of four or five.

TIME REQUIRED: 15 minutes for individual responses, 30 minutes for group consensus.

MATERIALS NEEDED: worksheet for each individual, worksheet for each group, pencils, flip chart (newsprint or blackboard), marker pens or chalk.

PHYSICAL SETTING: flexible seating in one large room so that small groups may work together.

PROCESS

A. Each individual has 15 minutes to read the story and answer the 11 questions about the story. Each person may refer to the story as often as needed but may not confer with anyone else. Each person should circle "T" if the answer is clearly true; "F" if the answer is clearly false; or, "?" if he or she cannot tell from the story whether the answer is true or false.
B. After 15 minutes each small group makes the same decisions by using group consensus. No one should change his or her answers on the individual worksheet.

Source: From Alan Filley, *Interpersonal Conflict Resolution* (Glenview, Ill.: Scott, Foresman and Company, 1975), pp. 139–143, as adapted from William H. Haney, *Communication and Organizational Behavior* (Homewood, Ill.: Richard D. Irwin, 1967), pp. 319–320.

The ground rules for group decisions are as follows:

1. Group decisions should be made by consensus. It is illegal to vote, trade, average, flip a coin, and so on.
2. No individual group member should give in only to reach agreement.
3. No individual should argue for his or her own decision. Instead, he or she should approach the task by using logic and reason.
4. Every group member should be aware that disagreements may be resolved by facts. Conflict can lead to understanding and creativity if it does not make group members feel threatened or defensive.

C. After 30 minutes of group work, the exercise leader should announce the correct answers. Scoring is based on the number of correct answers out of a possible total of 11. Each individual is to score his or her own individual worksheet, and someone should score the group decision worksheet. The exercise leader should then call for the following:

1. The group decision score in each group.
2. The average individual score in each group.
3. The highest individual score in each group.

D. Responses should be posted on the tally sheet. Note should be taken of those groups in which the group score was higher than the average individual score and higher than the best individual score. Groups should discuss the way in which individual members resolved disagreements and the effect of the ground rules on such behavior. They may consider the obstacles experienced in arriving at consensus agreements and the possible reasons for the difference between individual and group decisions.

WORKSHEET

A businessman had just turned off the lights in the store when a man appeared and demanded money. The owner opened a cash register. The contents of the cash register were scooped up, and the man sped away. A member of the police force was notified promptly.

Statements About the Story

1. A man appeared after the owner had turned off his store lights. T F ?
2. The robber was a *man.* T F ?
3. A man did not demand money. T F ?
4. The man who opened the cash register was the owner. T F ?
5. The store owner scooped up the contents of the cash register and ran away. T F ?

TALLY SHEET

Group Number	Group Score	Average Individual Score	Best Individual Score	Group Score Better Than Average Individual?	Group Score Better Than Best Individual?

6. Someone opened a cash register. T F ?
7. After the man who demanded the money scooped up the contents of the register, he ran away. T F ?
8. While the cash register contained money, the story does *not* state *how much.* T F ?
9. The robber demanded money of the owner. T F ?
10. The story concerns a series of events in which only three persons are referred to: the owner of the store, a man who demanded money, and a member of the police force. T F ?
11. The following events in the story are true: someone demanded money, a cash register was opened, its contents were scooped up, and a man dashed out of the store. T F ?

PART V
CASE STUDY

Acme Markets, Inc.

NOTE: This case can be used by the whole class with the case observational method (see Appendix A) or used for thought and discussion by individual class members.

Acme Markets, Inc., is a large, national, retail food chain. The corporate headquarters, including the office of the president and chief executive officer, John R. Park, were located in Philadelphia in 1974. During late 1974 both the corporation and Park were charged with violations of the federal Food, Drug and Cosmetic Act of 1938 for storing food, which had been shipped in interstate commerce, in a Baltimore warehouse that was accessible to rodents and exposed to other unsanitary conditions. The charges were brought following two Food and Drug Administration (FDA) inspection tours in early 1972 and an inspection tour in late 1974.

Prior to the initial trial in a U.S. district court in Maryland, Acme pleaded guilty to a five-count charge. Park asked for an acquittal in his case, arguing that all the company's employees were under his general direction but that different phases of the operation were assigned to employees based on defined duties and responsibilities in the organizational structure. Upon receipt of a letter from the FDA after the initial inspection in 1972, Park conferred with the legal affairs department and was advised that a divisional vice-president in the Baltimore division was investigating immediately and corrective action would be taken. Park believed this was the most constructive action that could be taken.

In the initial trial the jury was told by the judge that, although Park did nothing consciously wrong nor personally participated in the situation, the critical issue was one of authority. If Park had a responsible relationship in terms of his authority and responsibility, he could be found guilty. The jury ruled that he was guilty on all counts, and a $50 fine was imposed for each offense.

The case was appealed and the judgment was reversed. The appeals court ruled that there was no proof Park had engaged in any wrongful action. A previous U.S. Supreme Court case was cited in the appeal in which the Court had held that individuals as well as corporations were liable under the act, and that awareness of actual wrongdoing or conscious fraud need not be proven for a violation to exist.

Afterward the case was appealed to the U.S. Supreme Court. The Court ruled against Park, saying that he had the power and authority to prevent violations of the law or to seek steps to correct them once discovered. The Court emphasized that it was not his position in the hierarchy, his title, or his closeness to the situation that constituted a criminal liability. Rather, his power and authority to obtain compliance with the law required an affirmative duty to do so. When corporate officers fail by omission to prevent or correct violations when they have the power and authority to do so, they may be liable.

QUESTIONS: Do you believe corporate officers should be held personally accountable for liability for the action or nonaction of their subordinates? Why or why not? Should the liability be that of the corporation instead of the officer? Do you see any issues in this case involving questions of social responsibility or business ethics?

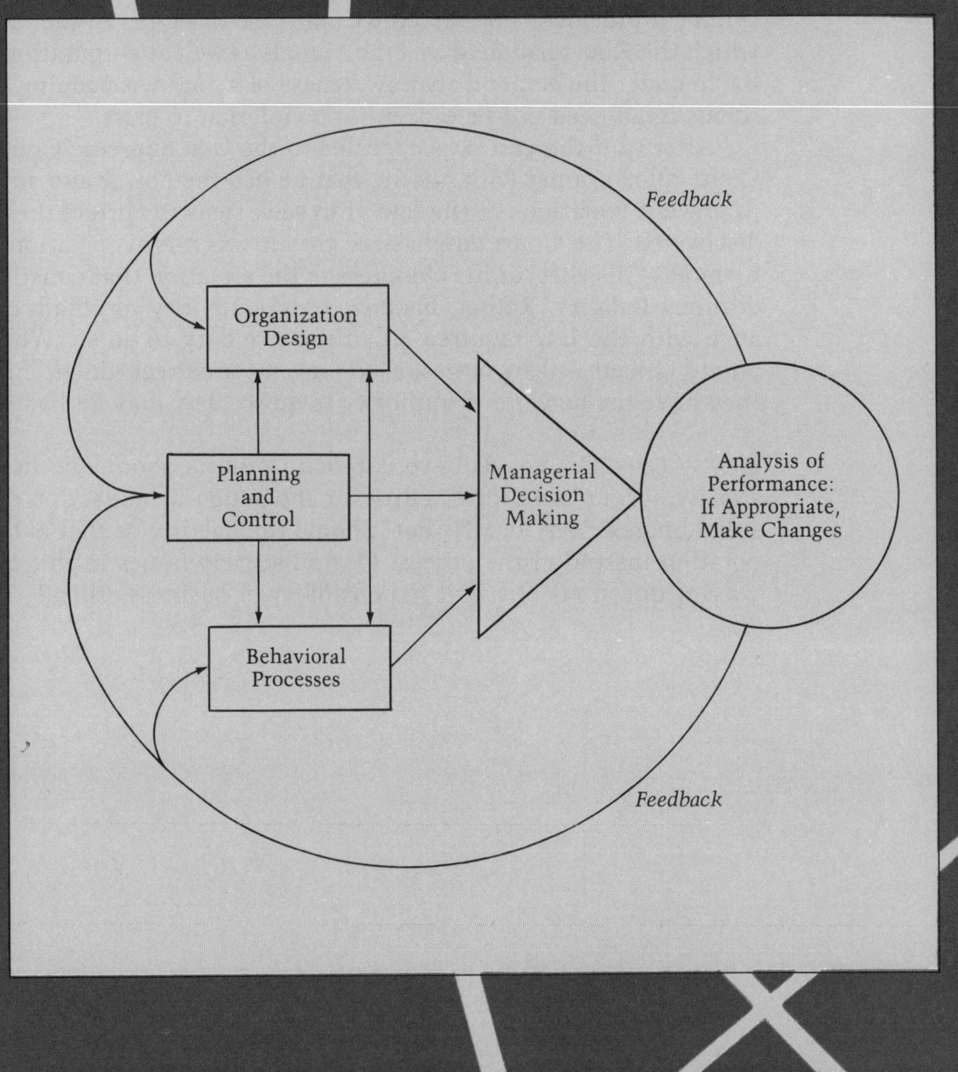
Feedback
Organization Design
Planning and Control
Behavioral Processes
Managerial Decision Making
Analysis of Performance: If Appropriate, Make Changes
Feedback

VI MANAGERIAL CAREERS AND ORIENTATIONS

Our organizational framework posits four dimensions within which managerial activities take place. How these four dimensions fit together in actual organizations, the implications they have for the manager's performance and success, and their importance for current and future practices and orientations of management are the topics in Part VI. In Chapter 19 the focus is on managerial performance and career success. Chapter 20 describes the current and future state of management.

19 Managerial Performance and Career Success

MODELS OF MANAGERIAL SUCCESS
CAREER PREPARATION
CAREER STRATEGIES
TIME MANAGEMENT
PERIODIC ASSESSMENT
ENTREPRENEURIAL MANAGEMENT
SUMMARY
DISCUSSION QUESTIONS
CRITICAL INCIDENTS
SUGGESTED READINGS

PERFORMANCE OBJECTIVES

1. To identify the predictors of managerial success by describing a specific model and a general model.
2. To describe how to prepare for a successful career as a manager, and to identify the career strategies an individual should follow to become a successful manager.
3. To demonstrate how time management can enhance one's career.
4. To discuss the techniques an individual can use to assess periodically the progress of his or her career.
5. To describe the personal traits of the typical entrepreneur, to discuss the similarities and differences between corporate executives and entrepreneurs, and to identify the most common reasons for failure among entrepreneurs.

Organizations rely heavily on managers for direction, since they complete the essential functions of planning, organizing, directing, and controlling. If managers are ineffective in completing these functions, the organization suffers and in many cases goes out of existence. Thus managerial performance is of major importance. And closely related to managerial performance is career success. What makes a manager successful? How can a manager simultaneously advance his or her career and complete organizational objectives effectively? These questions represent the starting point of this chapter.

This chapter discusses two models of managerial performance and career success as well as successful career preparation. The chapter then focuses on strategies that an individual can use to enhance his or her career, including the use of time management. In addition, a description is given of the techniques an individual can employ to periodically assess his or her career progress. The final part of the chapter discusses entrepreneurial management, or the management of small business. Senator Gaylord Nelson (1978) points out that independent small businesses with local ownership and control provide 52 percent of all employment, 48 percent of all business output, and 43 percent of the gross national product. As we shall see in the final section of the chapter, entrepreneurial management differs significantly from corporate management, and so it deserves separate treatment.

MODELS OF MANAGERIAL SUCCESS

Many writers have attempted to develop models of managerial performance and managerial career success, which, as indicated above, overlap one another. In this section we examine two of the major models in this area.

General Model

From numerous research studies Douglas Hall and Francine Hall (1976) have constructed a general model that effectively encompasses both managerial performance and career success. As shown in Figure 19–1, their model is a variant of the expectancy theory of motivation, which holds that (1) an individual must perceive that when he or she makes an effort, he or she will be able to perform successfully; (2) when an individual performs successfully, he or she will be rewarded; and (3) an individual desires these rewards (see Chapter 13).

The starting point of the model is the setting of challenging job goals. As we have seen, individuals will tend to achieve hard but attainable goals (see Chapter 13). However, the individual must perceive that he or she is being supported in his or her efforts. This support should come from the immediate superior and the organization. It can also come from other individuals, such as spouses and family members.

FIGURE 19–1
The Career Growth Cycle

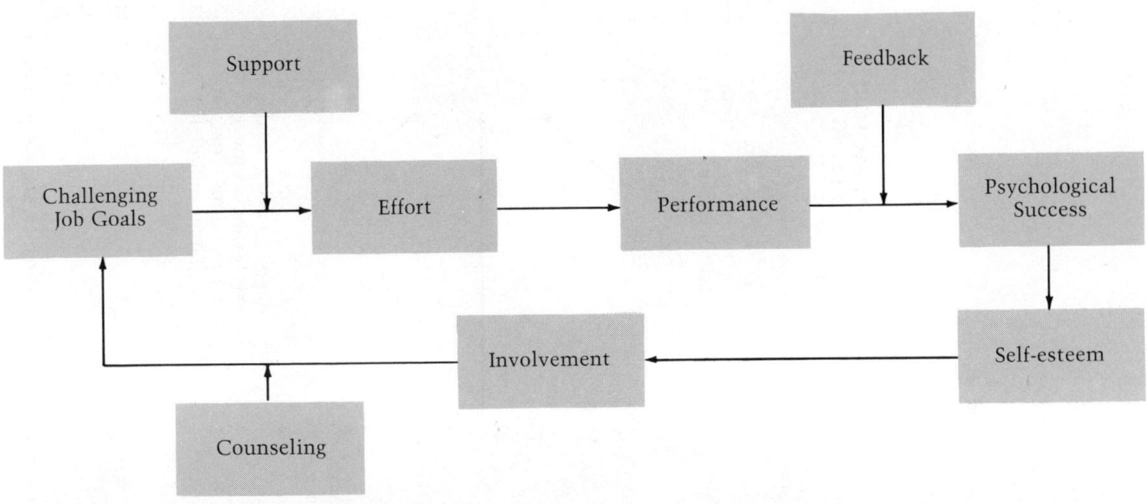

Source: Reprinted by permission of the publisher from "What's New in Career Management," by Douglas Hall and Francine Hall, *Organizational Dynamics*, Summer 1976, © 1976 by AMACOM, a division of American Management Associations, p. 31. All rights reserved.

Once the individual performs successfully, his or her superior and other members of the organization should provide positive verbal feedback. Such feedback leads to feelings of psychological success and self-esteem. In turn, a heightened sense of self-esteem leads to a high degree of involvement in the job. The immediate superior should then counsel the individual, pointing out both areas of strength and areas of weakness that need correction. This counseling is then followed by the setting of additional goals that are challenging.

Specific Model

John Aplin (1979) has intensively studied managerial success within the headquarters of a large United States corporation employing over 10,000 individuals. It is listed among the top 100 of *Fortune*'s list of the 500 largest corporations. Aplin's model generally parallels other models in this area, some of which are based on hundreds of studies (see Campbell et al. 1970).

According to Aplin, there are three major sets of factors predicting a manager's level of success: individualistic, environmental, and modifying or random factors (see Figure 19–2).

Individualistic Factors. To be successful, the individual should possess several personal skills and attributes. His or her educational background should include a solid technical preparation in the specialized

FIGURE 19–2

Factors Associated with Managerial Success

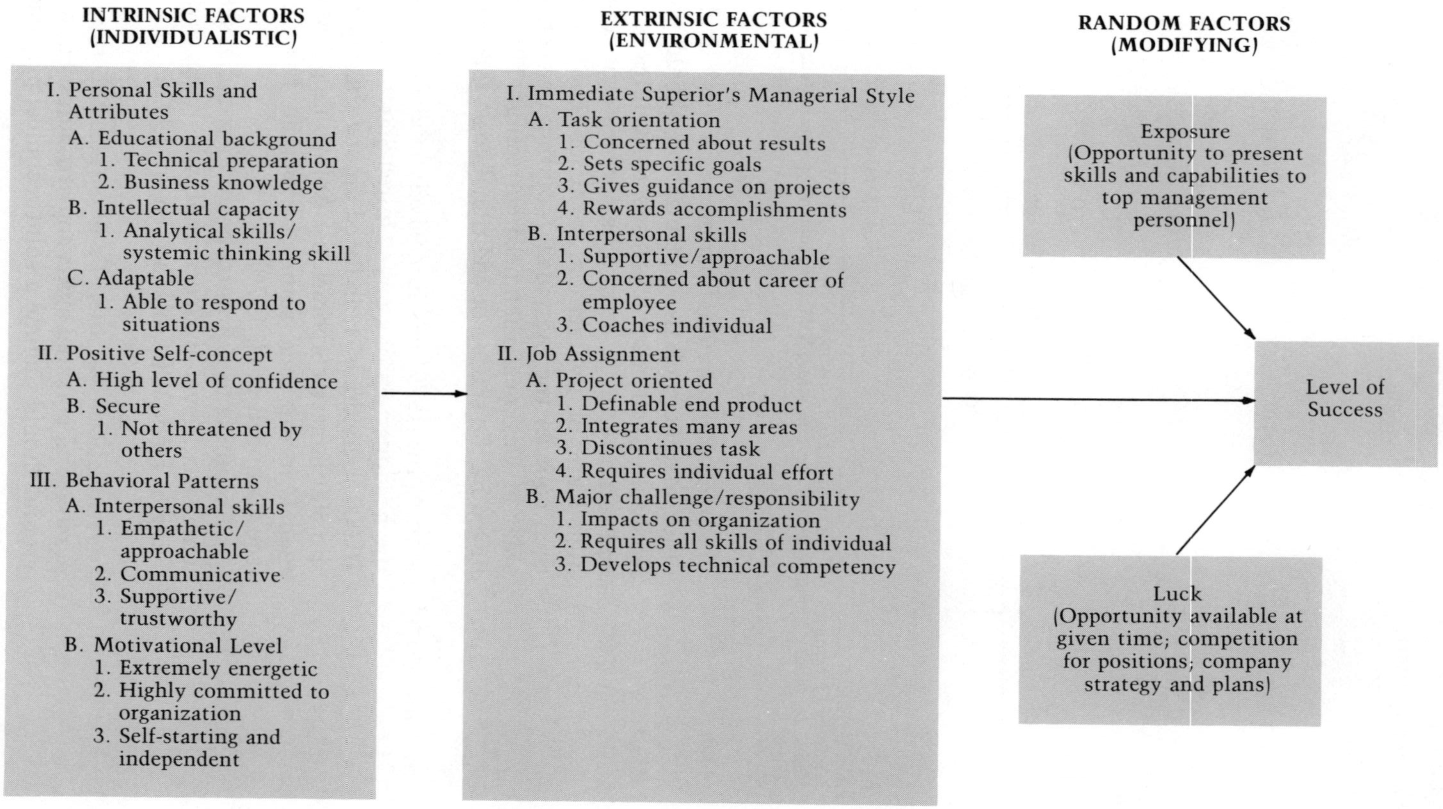

Source: John Aplin, "Issues and Problems in Developing Managerial Careers and Potential," *The Business Quarterly* 43 (1978): 28. Used by permission.

areas of business and a thorough knowledge of current business practices and activities. Intellectually, the individual should be systematic and analytic in approaching problems (see Chapter 4). He or she must also be adaptable and must respond flexibly to new and ill-structured situations in which there may be a great deal of uncertainty. In addition, the individual must possess a positive self-concept, being confident in his or her abilities to complete the tasks set for him or her and secure in the sense that he or she is not threatened by others. In terms of behavioral patterns the individual should possess such interpersonal skills as being approachable, articulate, supportive of other's efforts, and trustworthy. Finally, the individual should be highly motivated, energetic, committed to the organization, and self-starting.

Environmental Factors. Even if the individual possesses all these personal characteristics, he or she will not be successful unless environmental factors are favorable. In particular, the immediate superior's managerial style should be task-oriented. The superior should be concerned about results, should set specific goals, provide guidance, and reward the subordinate for performing successfully. Also, the immediate supervisor's interpersonal skills should tend toward consideration; that is, he or she should be supportive and approachable, concerned about the subordinate's career, and willing to coach him or her and offer advice.

Job assignment is a critical environmental factor. Ideally it should be project-oriented with a definable end product. The project should integrate the activities within many different areas of specialization, thus providing the individual with a comprehensive understanding of the organization.

Other major aspects of the external environment are challenge and responsibility. If the individual is challenged by the job and is allowed to exercise a good amount of responsibility, there is a greater probability that he or she will be successful in completing it. The individual should be able to see how the task will influence the organization. The task should also require the use of all the individual's skills, so that he or she becomes more accustomed to using them and develops more confidence in them. This situation also allows the individual to continually develop his or her technical and nontechnical skills.

Random Factors. Even if the individualistic and environmental factors are favorable, it is still possible that random factors over which the manager has little control will preclude success. A major random factor is the opportunity to present skills and capabilities to top management. Also, luck plays a key role in managerial success; this factor includes the opportunities available both within the company and outside it at a given time, competition for positions, and company strategies and plans.

CAREER PREPARATION

In Chapter 11 we saw that the hiring interview is of major importance. Inadequate preparation for it sharply limits the possibility that the individual will be offered a job. Similarly, many organizations have excellent training programs, and an individual who completes such a program in a particular industry becomes highly desirable to other organizations in that industry. These illustrations suggest that career preparation is of major importance.

However, many individuals prepare for their careers in a haphazard fashion. Peter Drucker, for instance, reports the following conversation: "Peter, I'm 59 years old, and I still don't know what I want to be when I grow up" (in Hall 1976).

Douglas Hall, after reviewing the literature on the subject of careers, concludes with the following observation:

> In the management of our lives and careers, most of us act more like Alice than we would care to admit. . . . Indeed, in a study of business executives who had changed jobs, Roe and Baruch (1967) found that these stereotypically "high-powered" people were remarkably passive and reactive in letting the work environment determine the course of their careers. However, a person's goals (Locke 1968), intentions (Holland 1973), and expectations (Livingston 1969) have a strong influence on the direction and success of his activities. In short, people tend to get where they want to go; if you know where you want to go, you're more likely to end up there. *(Hall 1976, p. 179)*

In this section we describe these major aspects of career preparation: past performance, academic training, and the possession of a unique feature.

Past Performance

The best predictor of future performance is past performance. John Campbell and his associates, after reviewing numerous studies on managerial performance, conclude with the following observation:

> Men rating high in overall success report backgrounds suggesting a kind of "life-style" of success—excellent health, scholastic and extracurricular leadership in high school and college, assumption of important responsibilities rather early in life, high ambition, and active participation in religious, charitable, or civic groups. *(Campbell 1970, p. 197)*

This observation should cause us to reflect on the importance of developing our skills and abilities. Many of us allow opportunities to fall by the wayside—at school, at work, and elsewhere. In the long run such haphazard career preparation will doom the individual to low-level jobs in which it is difficult to exercise autonomy and creativity.

Academic Training

It is difficult to say what kinds of academic training are most helpful for career advancement, since only limited research has been conducted in this area. Although researchers have been able to show that certain schools produce a disproportionately high number of successful managers, this result does not necessarily imply a causative relationship. For example, even though a significant number of successful managers have come out of the Harvard Business School, it is possible that the ability and motivation of these individuals rather than their Harvard degree explain their subsequent success (Swinyard and Bond 1980). That is, it may be that people with high ability and strong motivation tend to apply to certain schools.

Still, research studies have consistently indicated a strong relationship between the quality of the educational institution and subsequent success. It may be that the quality of the educational institution is related to the quality of the first job that the individual obtains once out of school. And research has shown that the occupational level of the first job is a good predictor of the occupational level the individual will eventually attain in his or her career (Lipset and Malm 1955). Thus the individual is wise to go to the best institution to which he or she is admitted, even if it involves financial sacrifice.

In today's world it is also sensible for an aspiring manager to obtain an advanced degree that will set him or her apart from other job applicants. The master of business administration program (MBA) is a good choice. An MBA degree gives the type of preparation that will help the individual obtain a responsible job and perform effectively. And some types of academic majors are better than others if an individual wants to become a successful line manager. For example, with an MBA in finance an individual can aspire to the top line positions in many organizations.

Having a Unique Feature

The competition for managerial positions is intense. A candidate can improve his or her chances for success by developing some unique feature that only a few other candidates possess. Stephen Carroll (1966) has shown that some prior experience in the work under consideration is related to success in the job hunt. For example, accounting majors who had worked for a semester as accounting interns obtained jobs more easily than accounting majors lacking this experience. Similarly, a PhD candidate can more easily obtain a position at a desirable university if he or she has published one or two significant articles. Even MBA students who have published one or two articles are in a desirable position in the job market.

The job applicant should include on his or her resume any significant achievements while in college: working on the college newspaper, being a member of the debating club, and so on. The applicant should also list all jobs he or she has held, both while attending school and during summer vacations. Any of these items may turn out to be a unique feature that will ensure a job offer.

CAREER STRATEGIES

Once working, the individual has recourse to various strategies that should serve to enhance his or her career. John Aplin's model, described earlier in this chapter, effectively delineates some of the significant strategies. In this section we describe in detail some of these major career strategies.

Job Challenge

Although the proper educational credentials are usually sufficient to obtain a job, the way the individual carries out this job determines whether he or she keeps it and is promoted to a better one. The first year in particular is very important. For example, in the AT&T study of its assessment center, the progress of the trainees was assessed after five and ten years. If the trainees were given responsible and challenging assignments in their first year, assignments that allowed them to mature as managers, they subsequently progressed in their careers significantly faster than the rest of the sample (Berlew and Hall 1966).

Even the outside professional activities of managers during the first years of employment are related to success. For instance, accountants in large CPA firms tend to be successful if they read several professional and trade journals in their area of expertise and regularly attend professional meetings during their first few years with a firm (Loeb and Gannon 1976). At least among accountants, such professional activities were more predictive of success than educational factors like grades in college and number of extracurricular activities.

The major implication of these studies is that the individual must be very aggressive and hardworking during the early stages of his or her career. Sometimes an individual can be stymied in a career because he or she is pigeonholed in a dull job at an early date. To combat this problem, the individual should request a major change in his or her position within the organization or actively seek work elsewhere.

Personal Responsibility

Even the individual who obtains a challenging job may be unsuccessful if he or she is not personally responsible for projects. If the individual is always a subordinate for projects, it is difficult for others to assess his or her potential as a leader, and he or she may be bypassed when promotions are handed out.

In one case a staff specialist in a large organization became the informal leader in his department because he was highly knowledgeable.

"Here's a thought: Instead of kicking old J.B. upstairs, why don't we just kick him out?"

He spent a great deal of time on group projects, but his contributions, although of obvious importance, could not be pinpointed with accuracy. To obtain a promotion, his superiors informed him, he needed to direct personally several projects. In the long run the top management of this organization probably damaged its effectiveness by this stance, which encouraged managers to work only on projects for which they were personally responsible.

Specialist Versus Generalist

A common pattern among managers is that they begin their careers as specialists but transfer to general management as they grow older. A classic example of this pattern is found among engineers and scientists, many of whom begin their careers in technical positions and end them in managerial positions. One of the major reasons for this shift is that an ambitious individual frequently winds up in a dead-end technical position from which the only promotion is into managerial responsibility.

However, as managerial responsibility increases, the individual usually begins to lose his or her technical competence. Hence there is a trade-off between the technical specialty and general managerial responsibility. Once a technical specialist has decided to accept a general management position, he or she normally cannot return to the former work, for technical knowledge becomes outdated within a few years. Thus someone who decides to make a career move in this direction should be fully aware of this trade-off.

The Protégé

When the individual is new in an organization, he or she can benefit by learning as much about the firm and the industry as possible. One way to accomplish this is to become the protégé of an older and successful executive in the organization who can teach the new employee about the organization and managerial responsibilities. However, a protégé relationship can be dangerous, for the individual can become too dependent on the senior executive. If the senior executive leaves or is displaced, his or her protégé may be left in a powerless position.

Although there are obvious dangers in the role of the protégé, the advantages are considerable. Friendship, a situation in which learning the ropes is made easy, and support when promotions are given out are but a few of the reasons why many individuals become protégés of executives who help them to advance their careers.

Special Factors

There are some special factors that, although difficult to identify with precision, must be considered in a career since they represent a unique fit between the individual and the organization. For example, a Catholic executive may find it difficult to advance in a company dominated by Protestant executives. Or an executive may not be advanced to a high position in the organization until he or she is admitted to an exclusive yacht club frequented by the top management of the firm (Dalton 1959).

A study of two Mexican firms (Andrews 1967) supports the proposition that the congruence between the organization and the individual is important. Andrews found that in the power-oriented firm those high on power needs were promoted; in the achievement-oriented firm those high on achievement needs were promoted.

Frequently the individual has a difficult time assessing the importance of special factors, especially when he or she is new to the organization. But if the individual discovers that some subtle standards are critical for advancement, he or she must attempt to meet them or forego advancement within a particular organization.

TIME MANAGEMENT

As we have seen, Henry Mintzberg (1973) describes managerial work in the following way: Managers work long hours at an unremitting pace; their tasks are varied, fragmented, and brief; and they rely primarily on verbal communication. If this profile is indeed correct, then it is essential that executives learn to manage their time efficiently, for otherwise their performance and career success will be impeded. In this section we describe the benefits of effective time management, the establishment of priorities, and some techniques that the manager can use to efficiently manage his or her time.

Benefits There are many benefits associated with managing time properly. A major benefit is good health. Since the manager knows how much time should be spent on each activity, he or she minimizes the pressure and stress that are typically associated with managerial work. Performance and effectiveness are also enhanced. The manager establishes priorities, which then determine the amount of time allocated to each activity. In this way the manager identifies the major activities and spends the greatest amount of time in completing them.

As the manager gains control over time and activities, he or she should improve his or her relations with others in the organization. Subject to less stress, the manager should be more approachable. In addition, others in the organization should begin to realize how the manager is allocating his or her time.

Finally, the manager's sense of personal satisfaction should rise. He or she now knows how to budget time and will complete major activities before attacking minor ones. Thus the manager may reduce the pressures and anxieties accompanying a heavy schedule, and satisfaction should be enhanced.

Priorities The key to time management is establishing priorities and sticking to them. One good way to accomplish this objective is to develop a "to do" list that is reviewed for a few minutes each day, either early in the morning or in the evening. Beside each activity the manager should identify priorities in terms of a 3-point scale: 3, essential to complete as soon as possible; 2, essential but completion can be delayed; and 1, important but not nearly as important as the essential activities.

The establishment of priorities forces the executive to identify major and minor activities. If the manager does not establish such priorities, he or she will tend to complete the easiest activities first, thus jeopardizing the completion of essential activities.

These priorities can change over time. At one point an activity may receive a 1. After one month this activity may be reclassified as a 3. The important point is to keep the activity on the "to do" list until it is completed.

In establishing priorities, the manager should consider the relationship of each activity to long-run goals. He or she should also compare the benefits of completing each activity and the costs associated with completing it. In addition, the manager should examine activities in terms of those that *must* be completed and those that the manager would *like* to complete if time permits.

Techniques To manage time effectively, the manager should set specific goals to complete and assign deadlines to them. If the manager is having a difficult time starting a major task, he or she can set a time limit for completing the introductory activity associated with the task. In this way the manager will at least begin to attack the project; then he or she may find that the project can be completed very quickly. Alternatively, the manager may establish several deadlines for completing various phases of the project.

If a task is boring or difficult to begin, the manager can establish a personal reward system. He can promise himself that completion of the first phase of the project will be followed by a leisurely walk. Using such a reward system is particularly helpful when there is no intrinsic motivation to complete a task.

A manager should allocate specific times of the day during which he or she can work alone. Coming to work early or staying late frequently provides executives with this time. In addition, the manager can limit access to himself by delegating activities, having a secretary screen individuals desiring an appointment, or making it known in the organization that he or she will be unavailable for a specific period each day.

Frequently a manager spends a great amount of time on a project that he or she gradually recognizes is only of marginal value. When this happens many managers have a tendency to complete the project, since they have sunk so much time and effort into it. But to manage time effectively, the manager should disregard time already spent and evaluate projects in terms of opportunity costs, that is, potential benefits to be derived from the completion of the marginal project and from the completion of new projects if the original project were to be shelved.

Many executives enhance their time management by organizing their work spaces efficiently. For example, TRW, a major conglomerate, trains their managers to handle paper only once; that is, they look at it, make a decision about what should be done with it, and get it off the desk. Otherwise, the desk becomes cluttered and disorganized, and it is difficult for the manager to complete the work that is there.

Similarly, it is helpful for an executive to develop his or her own filing system, since the executive is the one who must retrieve information when it is needed. Many executives keep the most important data in their offices for immediate retrieval and have their secretaries file away other data that may become important later.

Periodically an executive should analyze the amount of time he or she spends on various types of activities to see if he or she can decrease the amount of time spent on minor projects. One executive, for instance, discovered that he spent 12 hours a week watching sports events. He increased his efficiency by limiting this activity to 3 hours, increasing his time for active sports by 4 hours, and increasing his time for major business activities by 5 hours. Keeping a diary for one week is a good way to reexamine time allotments.

Some executives increase their effectiveness by carrying work with them that they can complete while waiting for an appointment or while traveling, periods when there is often much dead time. However, the executive should balance this approach by emphasizing relaxation away from work. Otherwise work becomes an overwhelming presence in a manager's life, and he or she may begin to feel stressed and nervous.

Finally, the executive must learn to say no to requests that have low priority. Otherwise the executive will find that he or she is burdened with so many tasks that the high-priority projects cannot even be identified, much less completed.

PERIODIC ASSESSMENT

A wise manager will periodically monitor his or her advancement. However, a periodic reassessment of a career is not always easy to accomplish, for it can involve many factors, such as a person's preference for staying in a particular part of the country, family pressures, and even the individual's state of health. Moreover, sometimes a manager or his or her superiors do not know exactly where the individual stands. In one instance the director of a university management development program was asked by the top management of a company to assess the capabilities of a participant being considered for a major promotion. The candidate's superiors were so unsure of his capabilities, even after twenty-five years, that they wanted the advice of an outside expert. Nevertheless, though it is difficult to reassess a career objectively, there are some standards by which such a judgment can be made. In this section we discuss three of them.

Age-Salary Ratio

There is a definite relationship among a manager's age, salary, and success. Korn/Ferry International, a management consulting firm that specializes in finding and placing qualified managers in top positions in industry, has shown that good performers should be making approximately $40,000 per year at age 40, superior performers approximately $63,000, and best performers $95,000 (see Figure 19–3). Although these figures, from a 1975 study, relate only to the top management positions, they do suggest that the individual should identify any gap between his or her current salary and potential salary. If the manager feels the gap is too wide, he or she should attempt to change the situation by either demanding a higher salary or moving to another company. If the manager accepts the status quo, his or her rate of advancement will probably slow down considerably.

FIGURE 19–3
What Top Executives Under 40 Can Expect to Earn

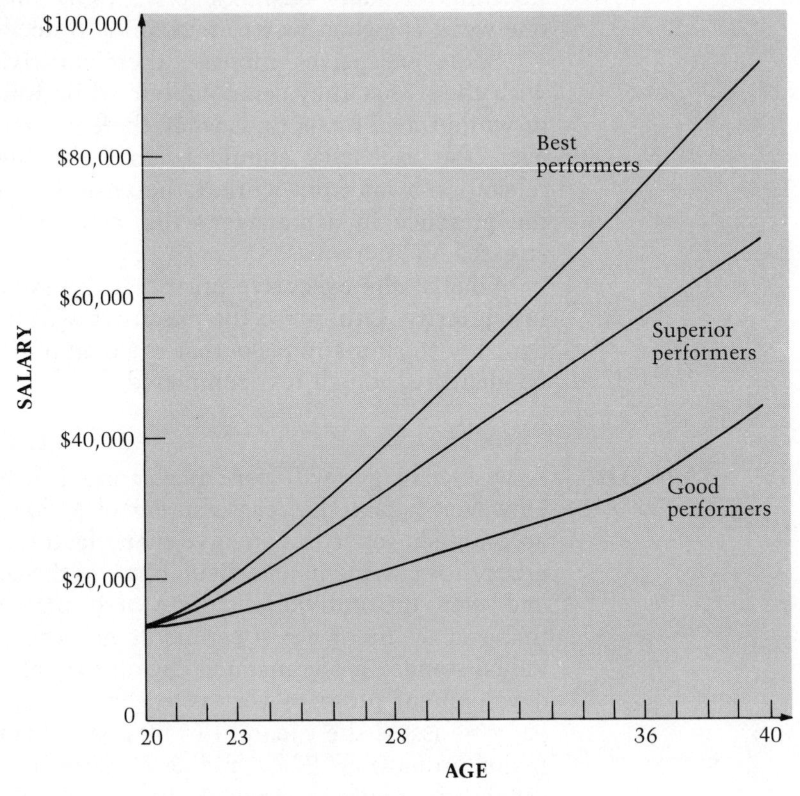

Note: Data from Korn/Ferry International, based on salaries of candidates placed.

Source: Reprinted from the October 6, 1975 issue of *Business Week* by special permission,

Further, the relationship between age and the number of promotions a person receives is important, even when salary is not considered. As indicated previously, the first few years on the job are critical. If the individual performs well, he or she usually advances at a rapid rate. But organizations sometimes bypass an individual later because he seems too old for a promotion, even though the law forbids discrimination against older people. Thus the young person who has already received several promotions is in an advantageous position when other opportunities arise. Hence it is important for the aspiring manager to obtain several promotions early in his or her career so as to be relatively assured of subsequent ones.

The Fast Track

Although very little has been written about the fast track, knowledgeable observers are aware that it exists in many organizations. In a company that uses a fast track for promotions, certain individuals are picked for rapid advancement while the rest of the managerial work force is essentially bypassed.

Usually an individual will receive some warning signals if he or she is not on the fast track. For example, one New York bank fed its management interns into a two-track system at the end of their six-month training course. If an individual performed well on the examination in finance and accounting, he or she became a high-status loan officer. Otherwise, the individual became a low-status operations officer and, as long as he or she stayed with this bank, had little chance of becoming a loan officer. When the slow-track individual receives such warning signals, he or she must decide how important managerial success is. If the individual is determined to become a top manager, he or she must either arrange to move to the fast track or consider changing jobs.

Job Satisfaction

The final standard by which an individual can evaluate his or her career is the level of job satisfaction. To many people job satisfaction is the main criterion of success—which is why there are so many stories of successful or promising managers giving up their careers to become novelists, artists, or even storekeepers.

Frequently individuals are unhappy with their jobs but are reluctant to make a change, perhaps because they fear the insecurity of unemployment. This reluctance is unwise, for job satisfaction is very important to health and success. In this regard Erdman Palmore (1969) conducted a long-term study of longevity. At the beginning of the study he measured the overall physical health of the subjects. Over a period of years job satisfaction was more predictive of longevity than either use of tobacco or health at the initial examination.

If an individual is deeply dissatisfied, he or she should seek work elsewhere or change careers. In today's world it is common to change careers during middle age. Often, however, such a change is made without the proper preparation and thought. For example, some executives decide to return to school for a few years, only to find their money has run out at the end of one year.

There are now programs tailor-made for the middle-aged individual who decides to change his or her career. Columbia University sponsors a highly successful program designed specifically for individuals contemplating a career change. Throughout this program counselors discuss any problems the student confronts, such as what courses to take, career possibilities, and personal problems. From all indications a well-run career program like Columbia's can be highly successful (Entine 1972).

ENTREPRENEURIAL MANAGEMENT

Founding or managing a small business is radically different from managing a large corporation. And many Americans do found their own businesses—approximately 400,000 every year. Unfortunately, the probability of failure for a small business is high—approximately 400,000 enterprises are liquidated each year. Although no precise figures are available, the conventional estimate is that two-thirds of new businesses fail by their fifth year.

In this section we give a profile of the personal traits of the entrepreneur, a comparison of entrepreneurs and managers, and an explanation of why small businesses fail. All discussions in this section are based on the following definition of *entrepreneur:* an entrepreneur is anyone who builds a small business with at least eight employees (Hornaday and Aboud 1971). In other words, the entrepreneur is someone who creates an organization characterized by an elementary form of the bureaucratic hierarchy.

Personal Traits

While some entrepreneurs seem to be born to running their own business—starting a lemonade stand in grade school and working up from there—many others learn it as the protégés of older and experienced executives. In recent years several important psychological studies of entrepreneurship have been completed. In this section we examine the results of some of this research.

Need for Achievement. David McClelland's studies which extended over a twenty-five-year period through 1976, indicate that entrepreneurs are characterized by their high need to achieve and accomplish (see p. 335). Because of their need to achieve, they prefer to work with experts rather than friends when faced with a problem. Also, they tend to be long-range thinkers and planners, focusing on an overall vision of the enterprise rather than immediate practical problems.

McClelland found that entrepreneurs prefer to undertake tasks that are accompanied by some risks. According to his findings, the entrepreneur is neither a low nor high risk taker but, rather, an intermediate risk taker. For example, individuals who score high on a test measuring need for achievement usually play a ring toss game from an intermediate distance, neither so close to the ring that they never miss nor so far away that they never hit.

In a related study of sixty male entrepreneurs, John Hornaday and John Aboud (1971) generally confirmed the results of McClelland. Compared to men in general, these entrepreneurs scored significantly higher on scales measuring their need to achieve, their independence, and the effectiveness of their leadership. They were significantly lower than men in general on scales that measured their need for supportive relationships with others. Hence the entrepreneur seems to be a self-confident loner who can withstand the criticisms of associates.

An individual's achievement motivation appears to be set at an early age. Marian Winterbottom's analysis (1958) indicates that children who are urged to be successful outside their home when they are between six and eight demonstrate higher achievement motivation than those who are encouraged to be successful only in their later years. Bernard Rosen and Roy D'Andrade (1959) have also shown that parental expectations are important. In general, the parents of high-achieving children establish goals for them that are higher than those set by parents of low-achieving children. These parents also involve themselves in their children's problems and concerns.

One's Own Master. Research suggests that entrepreneurs also have a firm belief in their skills and abilities (Shapero 1975). They feel their actions can change events. An entrepreneur is the master of his or her own life and refuses to believe that outside forces can decisively influence his or her success. For instance, a study of 375 college students indicated that those who planned to found their own enterprises strongly believed they were masters of their own destinies (Shapero 1975). This feeling was not evident among other students.

Few Emotional Attachments. Another important psychological study of entrepreneurship was conducted by Orvis Collins and David Moore (1964). In this study the authors suggest that entrepreneurs frequently have difficulty forming close emotional attachments—a finding similar to that of Hornaday and Aboud. However, Collins and Moore's research indicates this may result from the poor psychological relationships they developed with their parents and, in particular, with their fathers. Because of the entrepreneur's difficulty in forming close relationships, he or she becomes deeply involved in work and transfers all hopes and feelings from human beings to his or her business. Thus the entrepreneur treats the business almost as a living, breathing creature and is emotionally involved with it. The long hours of work are not burdensome but exciting and enjoyable.

Collins and Moore also suggest that the entrepreneur cannot maintain a close emotional attachment over an extended period, even with a business firm. Hence the entrepreneur unconsciously wants the business to fail, after which he or she can begin to structure another enterprise. Although this idea seems preposterous, a definite pattern of behavior among some entrepreneurs is to found a business that is highly successful, drive it into bankruptcy, and begin again (Collins and Moore 1964). Some entrepreneurs have achieved five or more gigantic successes during their lifetimes, each followed by the failure that Collins and Moore would predict.

Since the entrepreneur is only minimally concerned about relationships with others, he or she tends to treat subordinates in an autocratic fashion. The entrepreneur's word is law, and he or she will typically brook no opposition (Filley, House, and Kerr 1976).

Further, many entrepreneurs are not loyal or trustworthy. In the histories of various entrepreneurs it is common to come across stories of industrious and loyal subordinates who, after years of hard work for an entrepreneur, were fired for unjustified reasons. Such behavior fits well with the research findings that entrepreneurs are not influenced by the reactions and criticisms of their peers and their relationships with other human beings.

Lack of Attention to Details. Since entrepreneurs are moved by a need for personal achievement, they often have little interest in the organizational structure of the firm (Filley, House, and Kerr 1976). Organizing, staffing, motivating—the entrepreneur treats these and other key managerial activities with disdain.

William Durant, the founder of General Motors, aptly illustrates this pattern of behavior. He created GM essentially by buying other companies. However, he was so unconcerned about the daily organizational activities that he did not even know how many companies GM owned in 1920. When the company's financial backers forced Durant out in 1920, it took the accountants several months just to identify all of the holdings. Durant once remarked, supposedly in jest, that he loved to set policies—every time his door opened and closed, he had made and broken another policy. Durant even developed a novel motivational strategy when Walter Chrysler, his key production subordinate, constantly complained to him about his lack of attention to details—Durant merely raised Chrysler's salary each time he complained until Chrysler was making $500,000 a year, at which time he quit in disgust and formed his own company.

In sum, entrepreneurs are achievement-oriented and believe they are masters of their own destiny. They are not dependent on others for emotional support and are usually highly dictatorial and unconcerned about the daily organizational problems that plague most firms. A profile of the entrepreneur is shown in Figure 19–4.

Manager Versus Entrepreneur

Obviously some of the qualities necessary for a successful entrepreneur are also required of a successful manager. Why, then, do some people choose to start their own businesses while others prefer to work within existing firms?

Need for Independence. One hypothesis is that the type of individual who becomes a manager within a modern corporation is radically different from the entrepreneur in that he or she has much less need for independence. David Riesman (1950) holds that this attitude (among others) is related to the social patterns of the society at large. Traditionally social institutions such as the school, the family, and the

FIGURE 19–4
Relationship Between Personal Traits and Actions of Entrepreneur

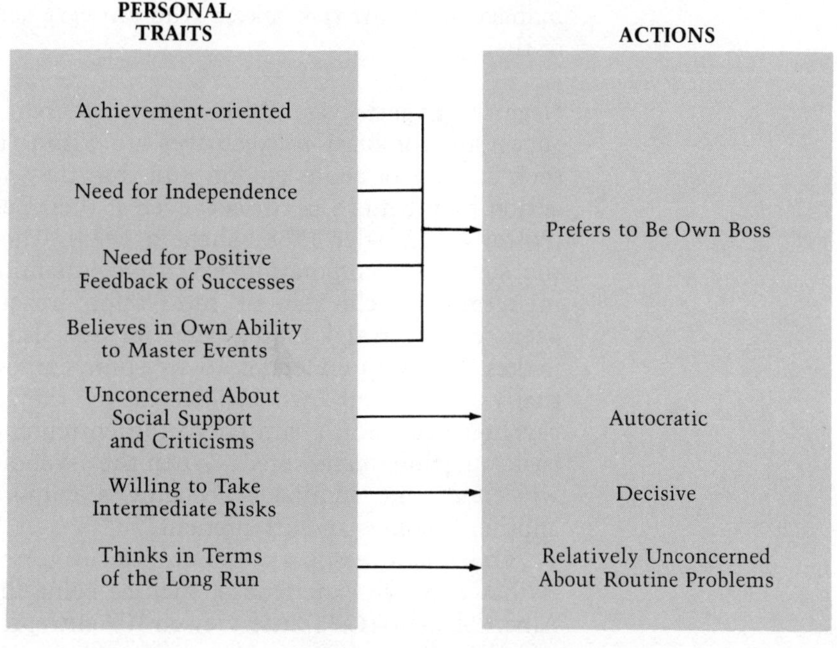

church teach children the values of the society so that they recognize right from wrong according to preestablished standards. Riesman compares these standards to the gyroscope that pilots a submarine. Even though the crew in the submarine cannot see water or land, they ascertain the proper direction by means of a gyroscope. Similarly, the primary institutions in a society give the individual a set of internal standards that guide him or her throughout life. But as society has become more complex, especially in cities, institutions no longer can maintain social control. The individual's value system becomes flexible, dependent on the peer group in which he or she operates.

Some writers, such as William H. Whyte, Jr. (1956), have used Riesman's theory to argue that entrepreneurship has declined in the United States since the 1800s. To found a business, an individual must be able to take risks and be relatively unconcerned about the feelings and reactions of peers. In a small but traditional society, such as the agriculturally based society of nineteenth-century America, the individual learns the values of society and therefore is prepared to become independent and self-reliant. In modern society, however, the individual, who is dependent on the peer group for his or her value system, must work under the protection of the corporation. Today's giant corporations typically protect their managers through handsome salaries and fringe benefits. Even the manager's old age is free of worry because of pension benefits. In such a setting Whyte believes managers are low risk takers who are very sensitive to the reactions of their peers.

Negative Experiences. More recent research, though, suggests that successful corporation executives are willing to take risks, that they seek a sense of achievement, and that they will pursue a course of action they believe is correct, even if their peers are critical of them (Porter and Lawler 1968; Shapero 1975). These findings imply that the successful corporation executive is similar to the entrepreneur in terms of achievement motivation, reactions to criticisms of peers, and even risk-taking behavior (see also Brockhaus 1980). This makes it easy to understand why some corporation executives eventually found their own businesses, for they are characterized by a psychological profile similar to the entrepreneur's. But it leaves the basic question unanswered—When the psychological factors are equal, why does one individual become a corporation executive while another becomes an entrepreneur?

One major reason a corporate executive becomes an entrepreneur is that negative experiences, such as being fired, propel him into it. Albert Shapero (1975) interviewed 109 entrepreneurs in Austin, Texas, and sixty-five percent indicated that their sole or primary influence was negative.

Although entrepreneurs and corporation executives are similar psychologically, they do differ on one dimension—entrepreneurs believe more strongly than do corporation executives that they are masters of their own destinies, and they do not like to be controlled by forces outside themselves (Shapero 1975). Many entrepreneurs have been fired from their jobs, and they insist that this will never happen again. So they form their own enterprises. But other corporation executives who have undergone the same experience are willing to put up with this lack of control. Hence they seek a similar job within another large corporation.

Environment. Although psychological factors are important in the explanation of entrepreneurship, the external environment in which the individual operates is also relevant. This is particularly true for the technical entrepreneur. A large-scale study of technical entrepreneurship was completed by Arnold Cooper (1970), who sought to discover why some engineers and scientists become entrepreneurs while others do not. His research was based in an area around Palo Alto, California, which is known for its large concentration of entrepreneurial firms. Cooper found that firms with less than 500 employees had a spin-off rate eight times as high as firms with more than 500 employees. Thus according to Cooper, an engineer or scientist in a small firm was attracted to entrepreneurial activity because he or she could see how it was carried out successfully. In the larger organizations such insights were difficult to obtain. Cooper also discovered that an individual who was thinking about founding his or her own firm learned a great deal through interactions with others in the organization who did eventually strike out on their own. Exposure to their experiences sensitized the potential entrepreneur to many of the problems he or she would encounter.

In a related paper Albert Shapero (1975) reports that his graduate students, after interviewing entrepreneurs, were attracted to this way of life, at least in part because they began to realize that entrepreneurs were not supermen. Some of the students were amazed to find out that the entrepreneurs were frequently no more—and in some cases much less—intelligent than they were.

The home environment also can be a decisive influence. Although only 7 percent of the nonagricultural work force in the United States claims to be self-employed, 58 percent of the American entrepreneurs who have been studied originated in families in which one or both parents were self-employed (Shapero 1975). These entrepreneurs saw the career independence of their parents, and they modeled their behavior accordingly. Similarly, particular ethnic groups such as the Chinese and the Jews produce a disproportionate number of entrepreneurs, at least in part because the children see visible and successful examples of entrepreneurship early in life.

Reasons for Failure

Stories about entrepreneurship tend to focus on success rather than failure. However, the failure rate is high, as indicated at the beginning of this section. According to Maury Delman (1971), there are nine major reasons why entrepreneurial businesses fail. Although his list is subject to question, it does describe most of the problems that entrepreneurs face.

The most important reason Delman cites for an entrepreneur's failure is a lack of balanced managerial experience. Many entrepreneurs do not fully understand the intricacies of running a business. For instance, an entrepreneurial engineer may be skilled enough to create a valuable product, but the business can easily fail if he or she knows nothing about accounting, finance, marketing, personnel, and so forth. Moreover, some entrepreneurs enter lines of business with which they are not familiar. Then when problems specific to the particular industry arise, they are not able to solve them.

Some entrepreneurs underestimate the capital they need to start a new business. They believe they have enough capital to see them through the first difficult years, but then they discover it is gone within the first few months. When the business fails, entrepreneurs are frequently embarrassed, since almost all of them borrow money from friends and relatives to start the enterprise. Venture capital firms, or organizations that exist solely to invest in other enterprises, average only 2.6 investments per year, and less than 15 percent of this capital goes to new ventures. These firms usually wait until a company proves itself before they provide expansion money (Shapero 1975).

Some entrepreneurs attempt to save money by picking an inexpensive location, only to find that the clientele they are seeking is not attracted to the organization because its location is unappealing or inconvenient. When location is critical, the entrepreneur is wise to spend the money for a suitable one.

Another reason many entrepreneurs fail once they have started a firm is that they use ineffective standard control procedures, such as inventory control systems and accounting systems. Frequently the entrepreneur will not even know the number of items in stock. Such poor practices keep the entrepreneur from planning effectively for the future, and he or she can eventually face financial losses that may lead to bankruptcy.

Some entrepreneurs put too much of their capital into fixed assets, such as furniture and office machines. This limits the working capital they have available. Hence when opportunities arise, the entrepreneur is unable to take advantage of them. For example, a client may wish to double his regular orders, but the entrepreneur has too little free cash to fulfill the request. A similar—and major—source of failure is poor credit-granting practices. If customers do not pay their bills, the entrepreneur is forced to operate with reduced working capital. Eventually this problem can become so great that the entrepreneur may have to liquidate the firm.

When the entrepreneur creates an organization, he or she frequently must exist on the salary allocated to himself or herself. At least initially the entrepreneur should draw only a small salary, for it is essential to put money into the company if it is to expand.

The entrepreneur also must be aware of the dedication to hard work that an owner-run business requires, especially in its formative years. He or she often will need to work long and irregular hours, will sometimes have to sacrifice family life, and must be willing to endure these difficulties until the business becomes sound. If the prospective entrepreneur is unwilling to make these sacrifices, he or she should not start a business.

Finally, even when the entrepreneur is successful, he or she may create major problems through overexpansion. When the business expands, the quality of service may decline, at least temporarily, and some of the entrepreneur's clients are likely to react negatively. Also, he or she may be unable to generate enough new business to pay off the price of the expansion.

In short, there are definite and clearly identifiable reasons why entrepreneurs fail. If an individual thinks about becoming an entrepreneur, he should be very sensitive to the pitfalls that he may encounter, many of which can be avoided or minimized through careful planning and effective control of resources.

SUMMARY

The related issues of managerial performance and career success significantly overlap. The Hall and Hall model, based on expectancy theory, gives a general approach to these related topics, while John Aplin's model gives a specific approach.

In preparing for a managerial career, the individual should attempt to obtain appropriate academic training for the position he or she seeks. Because competition for managerial positions is fierce, he or she should also strive to develop some unique feature that distinguishes the individual from other candidates. Finally, the individual should realize that successful past performance is essential to his or her career.

Once the individual begins to work on a regular basis, he or she should guide his or her career by means of strategies or general plans of action. To this end, the individual should try to obtain a challenging job and attempt to complete some tasks for which he or she is totally or primarily responsible. He or she may benefit by becoming the protégé of a powerful sponsor. The aspiring manager must also attempt to meet any special but unwritten standards the organization sets for promotion.

A major influence on managerial performance and career success is time management. If the individual is able to set priorities and stick to them, the probability of success increases. There are many techniques of time management, including delegation of work, refusal of low-priority requests, and organizing work spaces efficiently.

Periodically the manager should reassess his or her career and the rate of progress in it. In doing so, the individual should keep these points in mind: (1) generally there is a definite relationship among a person's age, salary, and success, and (2) there is often a fast track of promotion in an organization. If an individual finds that his or her career is progressing poorly, he or she should strive to change the situation by demanding a promotion or seeking work elsewhere. Further, the manager should think about changing jobs if his or her degree of job satisfaction is very low.

Entrepreneurial management differs significantly from corporate management. Both corporate executives and entrepreneurs are achievement-oriented. However, the entrepreneur has a stronger belief than does the corporate executive that he or she is the master of his or her own destiny. Many individuals become entrepreneurs because of a negative experience in an established organization—for example, losing a job. Individuals also learn to become entrepreneurs because they see examples, either at home or elsewhere, of other individuals who have successfully started their own enterprises. However, one should remember that the failure rate of new businesses is quite high. According to Maury Delman, the most important reason for failure is a lack of balanced managerial experience: Entrepreneurs frequently do not know how to run a business.

DISCUSSION QUESTIONS

1. What is the age-salary ratio? Why is it important? When would this ratio not be important? Can you measure this ratio in an organization in which salary information is secret?
2. What seems to be the major problem when an individual changes careers? How can it be corrected?
3. What are some unique features an individual applying for a managerial job should possess?
4. Shapero (1975) has put forth a theory that the entrepreneur is a misplaced person. What do you think Shapero means?
5. Suppose you would like to found your own business, but you don't have sufficient capital. Hence although you plan to found your own business eventually, you must obtain a middle-management job in industry or government after college. Would you choose industry or government? Why? Would you try to obtain a job in a large or small organization? Why?
6. If you decided to found your own business, what are some of the major problems you might face, and how would you solve them?

CRITICAL INCIDENTS

NOTE: These critical incidents can be used by the whole class with the case observational method (see Appendix A) or used for thought and discussion by individual class members.

1. Jane Garven, a business student with a major in marketing, is feeling low. It is the fall semester of her senior year in college at a state university. Her grades are only average, slightly below B, partly because she had to work 20 hours a week to support herself while attending school. She is feeling low for two major reasons: She does not know what to do with her life, and she feels her average grades will be too low for admission into a major MBA program.

Jane believes that the MBA degree is a good vehicle for entry into a managerial career. However, her undergraduate counselor tells her that her grades are probably too low for admission into the MBA program at her own university. Jane is unsure what she should do. She is 21 years old but feels she is going on 60.

QUESTIONS: What are some alternative career strategies that Jane could pursue? How should she go about making her decision? If she decides to apply for an MBA program, what narrative data should she provide on her application form that might help her gain admission?

2. Ed Matthews is feeling low. He is 40 years old and not too much of a success. On the other hand, he is certainly not a failure. He holds a middle-management position as a marketing manager in a medium-sized corporation of 5000 employees. It just seems that he is stuck in this position. Top management seems to have decided to pigeonhole him in it for the rest of his career.

Ed is thinking about changing careers. He would like to open a sporting goods store, since sports have always been one of his major interests. But he begins to worry. He was only an average student while in school; he has already changed jobs five times, because he always seems to become bored after working in an organization for a few years; and although he has saved some money, his financial position is not the best. His wife is working part time as an elementary schoolteacher, but he has two teenage children who will be going to college in a few years. If he fails at making the sporting goods store successful, his financial position will become precarious.

QUESTIONS: What are some alternatives that Ed might pursue? How should he go about making his decision? If you were Ed, what would you do? Why?

SUGGESTED READINGS

Baumback, Clifford, and Mancuso, Joseph, eds. *Entrepreneurship and Venture Management.* Englewood Cliffs, N.J.: Prentice-Hall, 1975, 335 pages, paperback.

Baumback and Mancuso have compiled an excellent set of readings on entrepreneurship, many of which are based on research findings.

Collins, Orvis, and Moore, David. *The Organization Makers.* New York: Appleton-Century-Crofts, 1970 (originally published in 1964), 237 pages, hardback.

These researchers conducted in-depth interviews with 150 entrepreneurs. They provide many fascinating case studies in this book, which is heavily psychological in orientation.

Hall, Douglas. *Careers in Organizations.* Pacific Palisades, Calif.: Goodyear, 1976, 236 pages, paperback.

This book summarizes research findings on career advancement and focuses on such topics as career choice, career stages, and methods of advancement.

20 The Current and Future State of Management

CHANGES IN THE WORK FORCE
CHANGING EXPECTATIONS OF WORK
INTERNATIONAL MANAGEMENT
MANAGEMENT OF DECLINING RESOURCES
COMPLEX ROLE OF THE MANAGER
SUMMARY
DISCUSSION QUESTIONS
SUGGESTED READINGS

PERFORMANCE OBJECTIVES

1. To describe the major changes in the work force, and to show how they are related to changing expectations of work.
2. To discuss the different management styles used throughout the world, and to show how these differences influence American managers who are sent on assignment to foreign countries.
3. To review the manner in which American corporations make their decisions to invest in foreign countries.
4. To describe the major factors influencing management during the current era of declining resources.
5. To discuss the complexities of the modern manager's role and the variations of it that will become more important in the future.

Throughout this book we have seen that many changes have gradually transformed the theory and practice of management. Planning systems, virtually nonexistent at the turn of the twentieth century, are now a major part of corporate enterprises. Various methods of structuring organizations, such as the matrix organization, have allowed management to develop complex responses to environmental pressures. Also, many technological changes, such as the introduction of the computer and word-processing equipment, have altered the way we do business. These changes have been accompanied by a shift in the composition of the work force from industrial to service orientation. And, as we have seen, the growth of the concept of social responsibility has allowed the federal government to take a much more active role in the activities of business.

In this final chapter of the book we analyze additional changes in the composition of the American work force that influence the manner in which managers direct organizations. We also examine changing expectations of work, which are related to the composition of the work force. In the third section of the chapter we focus on international management and the role the American manager plays in this arena. Finally, we close the chapter by describing the problems that managers face in the present era of declining resources and the complex roles that managers must now fulfill.

CHANGES IN THE WORK FORCE

In just the short span of eighty years the United States progressed through three stages. At the turn of the twentieth century approximately half the work force was employed in agriculture. By 1920 the industrial sector had become dominant. And today well over sixty percent of our workers are employed in the service sector.

In this section we discuss the rise of the white-collar work force, the educational composition of the work force, additional demographic changes, and occupational choices of workers.

White-Collar Work Force

Because the American work force has become increasingly better educated and has shifted more and more into service jobs, it is logical to expect that the blue-collar work force will shrink. And, in fact, such a dramatic shift has already occurred. In 1956 the number of white-collar workers surpassed the number of blue-collar workers for the first time in the history of the United States; by 1980 there were about 48 million white-collar workers and 31 million blue-collar workers (U.S. Bureau of Labor Statistics 1978–1979). Indeed, the entire occupational structure of the United States has visibly changed. Although total employment is expected to rise by 24 percent between 1974 and

1985, the number of professional and technical workers should increase by 50 percent, and the number of clerical workers by 33 percent (see Figure 20–1).

Education As the job mix of American workers has changed in recent years, their educational level has increased significantly. In 1952 the average number of years of education for a worker in the civilian labor force was 10.9. By 1976 this figure had risen to 12.6 (U.S. Bureau of Labor Statistics 1978–1979, p. 26). These figures indicate that the manager's job has become much more complex. He or she must now direct the work of subordinates who are better educated than their predecessors and who thus must be led and motivated differently.

In general, today's highly educated workers tend to prefer challenging jobs (Ford 1969; Miner 1974). At the same time, they would like a great amount of independence in the fulfillment of their responsibilities. Because of these preferences, management cannot expect to give orders and have them carried out without question or criticism. Rather, the modern manager must motivate members of this highly educated work force by a variety of techniques, most of which are more democratic than autocratic.

Additional Demographic Changes Other changes have affected employment, too. At the turn of the twentieth century the American wife normally did not work after marriage, and the American household included several children. Today the typical household includes only two children. Simultaneously, women have become a dominant part of the American work force; more than half the women over 18 are now employed in business and industry, and this figure will probably increase dramatically.

Also, as medical advances have progressed, the work force has aged considerably. Employees are now encouraged by federal law to continue working until the age of 70 rather than 65. Nearly 25 million Americans, or 11.2 percent of the population, are now over 65, up from 20 million, or 9.8 percent, a decade ago (Bronson 1979).

Changing Careers In previous eras it was quite common for an individual to work for only one organization during his or her lifetime. Today, however, workers are changing not only jobs but also careers at a relatively fast pace. Census data indicate that almost a third of all workers in 1965 transferred to a different occupation by 1970; changing occupations was twice as common as leaving the labor force (Sommers and Eck 1977).

This change, and the others described above, suggest that management today faces a much more difficult time motivating workers than their predecessors did. The work force is no longer homogeneous, consisting only of males possessing a relatively low degree of educa-

FIGURE 20–1
Projected Change in Employment, 1974–1985

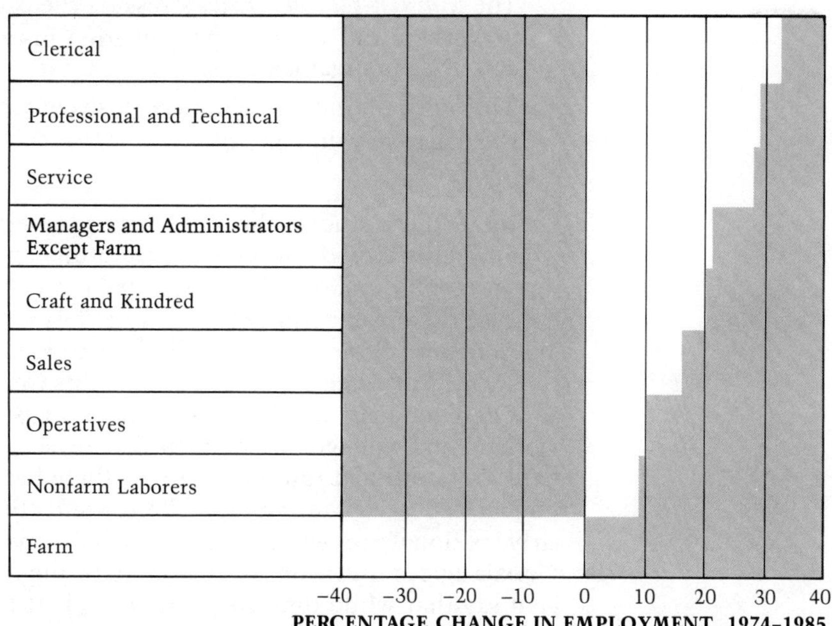

Source: Occupational Outlook Handbook, 1976–1977, p. 17.

tion. The modern work force is heterogeneous and includes many highly educated workers and a large proportion of females. Under such conditions management must develop a new understanding of the motivational frameworks of workers, a topic we shall now treat.

CHANGING EXPECTATIONS OF WORK

In this section we examine the changing expectations of the American worker and manager. We then describe some specific types of workers who exhibit different motivational profiles and needs.

The Humanistic Ethic

The major studies of changing expectations have been completed by Rogene Buchholz. He analyzed five independent motivational profiles among various types of workers:

The *work ethic,* stressing individualism, independence, and hard work.

The *organization ethic,* stressing the importance of group activity and the need to satisfy organizational goals.

The *humanistic ethic,* stressing fulfillment, growth, and satisfaction, in line with Maslow's theory of motivation.

The *Marxist-related ethic,* stressing the capitalistic exploitation of workers and workers' participation in major decision-making activities in organizations.

The *leisure ethic,* stressing the positive aspects of leisure and the negative value of work.

In all these studies the same results emerged: Respondents overwhelmingly favored the humanistic ethic, and they tended to reject the work ethic and the Marxist-related ethic. There was some support both for the organization ethic and the leisure ethic, but this support did not come close to that for the humanistic ethic.

Related research seems to confirm this trend. A longitudinal study of college students conducted over fifteen years suggests that younger workers and younger executives do not accept the idea of working hard for traditional rewards and that there has been a decline in their unqualified acceptance of the Protestant ethic (Miner 1974). Similarly, national surveys indicate that only one out of every five individuals agrees that work means more to them than leisure; sixty percent say that while they enjoy their work, it is not their major source of satisfaction.

It is possible that the decline in the acceptance of the Protestant ethic reflects a decline in the need to achieve. If this is confirmed, managers will have to develop more programs, like McClelland's, designed to increase achievement motivation (see Chapter 13). As indicated previously, job enrichment is effective only if the individual has a high need to achieve. Probably, however, it is not the need for achievement that has changed as much as the types of goals people are interested in pursuing. It may be that workers and managers are no longer willing to devote their lives to obtaining money and status and helping an organization make a profit.

If the belief in the work ethic continues to decline in the United States, it is quite possible that traditionally oriented organizations will find themselves less and less able to attract capable managers. In the long run the organizations that can convince job candidates that they are interested in social goals like decreasing pollution or supporting art and education may be the only ones able to attract the leadership necessary to fulfill organizational objectives.

Now that we have developed an overall profile of the motivational needs of modern workers, we can focus our attention on the specific needs of different types of workers. These include racial minorities, women, part-time workers, two-career families, and military and government employees.

Racial Minorities

For many years racial minorities were excluded from the mainstream of American life. However, equal employment opportunity laws now require organizations to hire a significant number of minority group members. These laws were dramatically upheld in 1973 when AT&T agreed to provide 6000 jobs for minority group males, 800 of which were at the management level. Other organizations are following the same pattern. Thus racial minorities have become an increasingly important force in American organizations.

Job satisfaction of nonwhites is significantly and consistently lower than that of other employees (Weaver 1974a). However, occupational level seems to be more important than race in the explanation of job satisfaction for all types of employees: Individuals in the lowest occupations are the most dissatisfied workers. So one major problem may be the extent to which members of racial minorities are treated inequitably in their search for satisfying jobs. Until this situation is corrected, managers must be sensitive to the needs of these employees, especially their feelings of deprivation and inequity.

SOURCES OF MOTIVATION

"Charley, how'd you like to join the millwright gang?" the foreman called to me. He appeared to think he was offering a distinguished honor—in spite of his explanation that it paid only 2 cents an hour more. The change was accepted with indifference; surely so slight an increase in pay could not mean much of a promotion. Half an hour sufficed to prove my error. As I came by my former companions, carrying oil can and wrench, I made a veritable sensation! Every one of these old friends leaned upon his shovel and wiped the sweat and dirt out of his eyes while he exclaimed: "Hey Boodie! Where you catch-em job? Meelwright gang? Oil can and wr-rench! No more . . . shovel! My Ga-wd."

From that moment it was possible to talk familiarly with the first and second helpers, those experts who peer through their colored spectacles into the changing conditions of the furnace's "bath" or "hot metal" up to the instant of the "tapping." For three weeks I had puzzled why these men would have nothing to do with me. Now we were suddenly become pals! But this was not all. My elevation brought honor not only inside but outside the plant. Without doubt, if my wife had lived nearby, she would have received the congratulations of the wives of the unskilled laborers: "Your man he catch-em fine job!" And not one of them but would have observed closely, the next day, to see whether she continued to speak to them!

Source: Whiting Williams, *Mainsprings of Men* (New York: Scribner, 1925), p. 56.

Women A great amount of literature recently has focused on working women, for women clearly are going to play an increasingly significant role in American society and management. In previous generations only a few women became managers. Today, however, many women are seeking advanced degrees in schools of management and competing with men for the prestigious and lucrative management training positions that organizations offer. The change has been dramatic in the past few years. For instance, in 1971 there were only 9,075 women enrolled in law schools; by 1975 the number had risen to 26,403. Similarly, there were only 5,819 females enrolled in graduate business schools in 1971; by 1975 the figure was 24,057 (U.S. Department of Health, Education and Welfare, Fall 1975). About 27 percent of the MBA students enrolled in accredited business schools in 1979 were female, compared to 10 percent in 1971–1972 (American Assembly of Collegiate Schools of Business, 1979). In addition equal employment opportunity laws have required organizations to hire more women. In the 1973 AT&T settlement the company agreed to provide 50,000 higher-paying jobs for women, 5,000 of which were at the management level.

In general, studies in this area suggest that the factors motivating men and women are identical. When men and women have interesting and challenging work that allows them to exercise authority and responsibility, both sexes tend to respond in a positive and similar fashion (Gannon and Hendrickson 1973). However, women frequently report lower job satisfaction than men (Weaver 1974b). This is especially true for working mothers who have children under the age of six (Quinn et al. 1974). Like racial minorities, women have generally been excluded from the mainstream of American working life. Thus, their lower level of job satisfaction probably relates to the fact that they are still treated inequitably. To minimize this problem, managers must try to distribute rewards as fairly as possible, regardless of the sex of the employee. And working women, especially those in managerial positions, must emphasize their professional standards and abilities.

Part-Time Workers If an individual works less than 35 hours per week, he or she is classified as part time. And in the United States the segment of the labor force increasing at the most rapid rate is the part-time work force. Since 1954 the number of part-time employees in nonagricultural industries has increased at an average annual rate of nearly 4 percent, more than double the rate of increase for full-time workers (Deutermann and Campbell 1978). Between 1967 and 1977 the percentage of workers in the civilian labor force classified as part time rose from 16.1 to 18.4 (*Employment and Earnings,* June 1967, p. 22; June 1977, p. 27).

Only a small amount of research has been conducted in this area. But in general, the research indicates that part-time employees seem to have more limited job satisfaction needs than full-time employees. One study suggests that part-time employees define their job satisfaction in terms of their relationships with fellow workers, whereas full-time employees emphasize such factors as the work itself, pay, promotion, and supervision (Logan, O'Reilly, and Roberts 1973).

Thus the critical factor explaining job satisfaction among part-time workers may be the reference groups to which they compare themselves. If a part-time worker compares himself to a full-time worker, he may feel he is being treated unfairly if he does not receive the same fringe benefits that the full-time worker obtains, but on a reduced or prorated basis. Conversely, if a part-time worker compares himself only to other part-time workers, the lack of prorated fringe benefits may not be bothersome (see Rotchford and Glick 1979).

If this approach is correct, management must identify the various reference groups to which its part-time workers—and even its full-time workers—compare themselves and develop different motivational schemes that would be appropriate for each group. Such reasoning underlies the "cafeteria" method of providing fringe benefits in which the organization offers a range of fringe benefits and the employee or manager is free to choose those that are personally appealing.

Two-Career Families

As we have seen, women are changing the American occupational structure. Although only a few women worked at the turn of the twentieth century, the labor force participation rate for women is now over fifty percent. In addition, today the typical American family includes only one or two children.

Because of such patterns, it is now common to find both parents working, either on a full-time or part-time basis. This change has influenced the satisfaction and career decisions of many individuals, for husbands and wives generally try to view their work in relation to the total family constellation. For example, today one might see a husband changing jobs and geographical locations to be with his wife if she obtains a high-paying and important position elsewhere. However, surveys indicate that spouses typically put the husband's career ahead of the wife's career in making decisions about job and geographical relocations. Also, working wives still do most of the household-related tasks, although this situation is changing among younger couples (Renwick 1978).

Such larger changes in the American society have critical implications for motivating individuals at work. For instance, recent surveys indicate that some husbands and wives want to decrease their hours of work in order to spend more time with their families (Sawyer

1977). To them, job satisfaction is much more than money, fringe benefits, and even interesting and challenging work. For such individuals job satisfaction also includes discretionary time that the individual can use for leisure and family activities. As such patterns spread, it is conceivable that managers will need to devise new motivational packages to offer the contemporary worker. Such strategies might include variants of flexitime. For example, a worker might choose to work full time for seven months of the year and part time the rest of the year. But whatever is done, it seems evident that managers must address the issue of the two-career family when they hire workers and potential managers.

Military and Government Employees

In the early 1970s the draft was ended, and the United States established an all-volunteer army. This change was predicated on many solid arguments, including the belief that volunteers would benefit through the training opportunities available in the army and the belief that job satisfaction would be increased. However, a comparison of job satisfaction of enlisted men in 1943 and of the volunteers in the 1970s indicates quite clearly that job satisfaction has declined dramatically (Segal, Lynch, and Blair 1979). In fact, there are some similarities in job satisfaction between World War II AWOLs and the volunteers.

It is difficult to identify all the sources of this dissatisfaction. It may be that the volunteers espouse a humanistic ethic, while their enlisted counterparts in 1943 believed in the work ethic. Also, the negative attitudes may reflect a Vietnam postwar demoralization similar to the one observed after the end of World War II. Whatever the reasons, it seems clear that the army faces many of the same motivational problems that afflict private organizations.

However, federal government employees exhibit a different motivational profile. A national survey indicates that they are at least as satisfied as private-sector employees and, in some areas, are more satisfied (U.S. Office of Personnel Management 1979). As in the private sector, satisfaction increases as occupational or organization level rises (Porter and Mitchell 1967).

INTERNATIONAL MANAGEMENT

We live in a highly integrated world economy. What happens in one country influences events in other countries, as we have seen from our recent experiences with oil crises. In addition, there are many large multinational corporations; some international firms employ over half a million workers, and many others employ at least 100,000. Thus international management is becoming increasingly important.

In this section we analyze international management styles, the manner in which American corporations make decisions to invest abroad, and the experience of working in another country.

Management Styles

When an American goes abroad, he or she should be sensitive to the unique needs, customs, and values of the host nation. This dictum is particularly true for the manager, who must direct the activities of subordinates with radically different orientations than his or her own. Some of these values and beliefs may be immediately apparent, but it is important for the American manager to identify and respect even the implicit and subtle customs. Otherwise he or she may encounter resistance that subsequently will be difficult to overcome and may seriously hinder the organization.

In 1966 three social scientists published a major study analyzing the management styles of 3600 managers in fourteen countries (Haire, Ghiselli, and Porter 1966). Five major studies completed since that time have arrived at the same general conclusions (see Griffeth et al. 1980). In this section we review the original study, since it focuses specifically on Douglas McGregor's profile of Theory X and Theory Y managers (see Chapter 2).

In general, a Theory X manager is highly autocratic and holds the following beliefs:

Subordinates possess a limited and perhaps nonexistent capacity for leadership and initiative.

It is not advisable to share information with subordinates or allow subordinates to help develop the objectives they must accomplish.

Employee participation in decision making is to be avoided at all costs.

The way to motivate subordinates is by means of internal control (e.g., promotion or punishment).

A Theory Y manager is exactly the opposite and believes that all these propositions are invalid. Obviously, there is a continuum ranging from an extreme form of Theory X to an extreme form of Theory Y. The researchers developed a questionnaire measuring the value systems of the 3600 managers in the fourteen countries along this continuum. To compare the fourteen countries, the researchers converted the raw data into standardized scores, which ranked the countries on the various items. The average standard score for all 3600 managers was considered to be 0.00. Any score above 0.00 would suggest an orientation toward democratic values.

The analysis of the questionnaire data indicated that the fourteen countries clustered into five major groups on the basis of similar re-

TABLE 20–1
Attitudes Toward Management Practices of 3600 Managers in Fourteen Countries

	Individual's capacity for leadership and initiative	*Advisability of sharing information and objectives*	*Value of employee participation*	*Desirability of internal control (e.g., promotion or punishment)*
Nordic-European countries (Denmark, Germany, Norway, Sweden)	−0.24	0.04	−0.04	0.16
Latin-European countries (Belgium, France, Italy, Spain)	−0.25	0.22	0.09	0.03
Anglo-American countries (England, United States)	0.45	0.36	−0.02	−0.16
Developing countries (Argentina, Chile, India)	0.21	−0.59	−0.21	−0.18
Japan	0.39	0.04	0.44	0.04

Note: Positive mean values indicate attitudes that are more democratic than those of managers from other countries; negative values indicate attitudes that are more autocratic than those of managers from other countries. For a description of five major studies that have confirmed the original findings of this study, see Rodger Griffeth, Peter Hom, Angelo DeNisi, and Wayne Kirchner, "A Multivariate Multinational Comparison of Managerial Attitudes," in *Proceedings of the 40th Annual Meeting of the Academy of Management, Detroit, Michigan, August 9–13, 1980,* ed. Richard Huseman (Detroit: Academy of Management, 1980), pp. 63–67.

Source: From Mason Haire, Edwin Ghiselli, and Lyman Porter, *Managerial Thinking: An International Study,* p. 28. Copyright 1966 by John Wiley & Sons, Inc. Reprinted by permission.

sponses: the Nordic-European countries, the Latin-European countries, the developing countries, the Anglo-American countries, and Japan. The five clusters of countries differed significantly from one another, as shown in Table 20–1. For example, the Nordic-European managers were less positive than other managers about the capacity of the average person to exercise leadership and initiative. However, the Nordic-European managers were about equal to other managers in their feelings about the sharing of information and the value of employee participation (0.04 and −0.04).

An interesting finding in this study was that the managers from the Anglo-American countries were more democratic than autocratic in orientation. However, except for believing that the individual has an adequate capacity for leadership and initiative, the managers from the developing countries were more autocratic than democratic. These findings suggest that American managers will experience some culture shock when they become managers in developing countries, for their styles of management seem to be opposed to those currently most common there.

By means of a complex statistical analysis, the researchers were also able to show that about thirty percent of the differences in managerial attitudes can be explained by variations in culture. This relationship is strong and suggests that the American manager who works outside the United States should be very sensitive to cultural differences and attempt to adapt to the distinctive characteristics of the country in which he or she works.

Japanese Management

As our analysis of international management styles indicates, Japan is unique among nations (see Table 20–1). Given the phenomenal economic success that Japan has achieved since the end of World War II, many writers and researchers have attempted to describe and explain why she has outshone the United States and other nations now facing serious declines in productivity.

Japan is a very small country with few natural resources and a large population. To survive and prosper, Japanese society has created a situation in which the individual, the family, the business corporation, and the state are closely aligned with one another. After World War II, Japan became an advocate of state-backed corporations, so that her business corporations were advantageously placed against companies in other societies that did not receive financial support from the state. Thus there is a close relationship between business executives and governmental leaders.

Concomitantly, there is a closer relationship between management and the worker in Japan than in many other countries. Approximately 35 percent of Japanese workers in the larger and more prosperous corporations are guaranteed lifetime employment to age 55, after which they accept lesser-paying jobs with subcontractors. This managerial sense of responsibility allows Japan to emphasize the use of group or consensus decision making (see Table 20–1). Given this organizational climate, it is also possible to emphasize the use of *quality circles,* discussion groups of workers and their immediate superiors that attempt to come up with new methods for increasing productivity. Productivity gains achieved through the ideas of such quality circles do not result in the awarding of individual bonuses. Rather, bonuses are awarded to all managers and workers at the end of the year based on the total increase in productivity. Thus the group is emphasized more than the individual, and all benefit.

Similarly, Japanese managers receive significantly fewer rewards than American managers, thus narrowing the gap between management and employees and allowing them to perceive a commonality of interests. For example, the president of SONY, one of the largest Japanese companies, makes approximately $200,000 a year in salary and bonuses which, after taxes, is only five or six times the amount of money that a highly-skilled worker receives. By contrast, American top executives make fifty to sixty times more than the most highly-skilled worker after taxes. There are now some American executives whose total compensation before taxes is over 3 million dollars per year.

Competition among corporations is intense in Japan. While the government is very supportive of successful organizations, such as computer firms, that are important for Japan's future (*sunrise industries*), it will not move to save a dying corporation that is losing its markets because of changes in society and consumer tastes (*sunset industries*). Also, there is a great emphasis on not only the quantity but the quality of production. Ironically, it was an American industrial engineer, Edward Deming, who introduced the concept of quality control to Japan after World War II, and Japan's highest business award is named in his honor.

Another widely-cited reason for Japan's success is that, while she has not been very creative in developing innovations, she has borrowed many innovations that have subsequently made her industries highly productive. For example, most of the robots that have revolutionized the automotive assembly line were developed in the United States, but Japan borrowed them from the United States and achieved unparalleled success. It is only in recent years that American industry has begun to introduce the use of robots to increase productivity.

Additionally, as the above discussion implies, Japanese management takes a long-run view of operations, and emphasis is put on long-term growth rather than short-term profitability. By contrast, many American corporate executives take only a short-run view of the future because their salaries and even the stability of their jobs are frequently determined by short-run profits and the rapid changes in the value of their company's stock, over which they often have little if any control.

In short, although it is difficult to identify all the reasons why Japan has been so successful since the end of World War II, the following reasons are important:

1. The close relationship among the individual, the family, the business corporation, and the state. As a consequence, the Japanese government backs its sunrise corporations financially, and consensus decision making occurs within the corporation.
2. Fierce business competition.
3. An emphasis on quality of production.
4. The use of existing innovations to improve productivity.
5. A long-term outlook.

There are, however, some emerging problems. The Japanese workforce is aging, and it is becoming increasingly difficult to guarantee lifetime employment to workers until age 55. Similarly, other countries such as the United States are beginning to emphasize the use of state-backed corporations, as the situation of Chrysler Corporation indicates (see Chapter 16). Still, Japanese management has been phenomenally successful, and it is important for us to learn from its success so that American productivity can increase.

"Mergers, mergers, mergers! The way it's going, one of these days EVERYBODY will be working for the SAME COMPANY."

Working Abroad Because of the growth of international corporations, it is now quite common for American managers to work abroad during some periods of their careers. As suggested in the previous section, these managers face a difficult task acclimatizing themselves to the prevailing values and beliefs in their new environments. For example, in one study 9 out of 10 American managers working in Japan were significantly less successful than in the previous assignment in their home countries (Seward 1975). A related study indicated that top management considered 4 out of 5 managers working in Japan to be failures (Adams and Kobayoski 1969).

There are, of course, many possible reasons for these failures. For instance, spouses frequently experience difficulty adjusting to the new country, making the home life of the executive more difficult to manage. Children also may have difficulty adjusting to the new country and new schools. However, there seems to be one major cause that can be controlled: preparation and training. Until recent years corporations provided only a minimal amount of preparation and training for the executive going abroad. Today, however, the situation has changed radically, for corporations now realize the importance of these factors. Training in the native language has been supplemented

TABLE 20–2
Ranking of Factors That Affect Investment Decisions in Foreign Countries

	Percentage of companies assigning each rank					
Factor	*1*	*2*	*3*	*4*	*5*	*6*
Sales (27)[a]	19	22	15	30	7	7
Profitability (32)	72	12	16			
Economic conditions (28)	21	39	36	4		
Political conditions (27)		22	44	30	4	
Sociological factors (24)	4	4	4	25	55	8
Cultural factors (23)		4	4		26	66

[a] The number of firms ranking each factor is indicated in parentheses.

Source: Randolph Pohlman, James Ang, and Syed Ali, "Policies of Multinational Firms: A Survey," *Business Horizons* 19, no. 6 (December 1976): 15. Used by permission.

by educational courses in the culture and history of the foreign country. Spouses and children of the executive also receive the same preparation in many instances. In this way culture shock is minimized for the entire family.

Investments in Foreign Countries

American corporations building plants in other countries must invest wisely. However, they face a major problem: obtaining accurate information. R. J. Rummel and David Heenan (1978) point out that they rely on four major techniques:

1. A grand tour, during which top managers visit the country and interview government officials and potential native managers and workers.
2. Information provided by old hands who have lived in the native country for many years.
3. The Delphi technique, which uses the pooled judgments of several experts (see Chapter 5).
4. Quantitative forecasting techniques, such as those described in Chapter 5.

Rummel and Heenan suggest that no one method is perfect. Rather, the corporation should use all four methods before making a decision to invest.

Bernard Bass and his associates (1977) have studied 118 decisions of American corporations that eventually resulted in the building of plant sites in Latin America, Europe, and Asia. Their study indicated that the major considerations, in order of importance, are increasing sales growth, local demand for the product, the host government's cooperativeness, governmental stability, honesty, a favorable labor relations climate, and a plentiful supply of workers and local managers. A related study of thirty-five corporations requested that they rank six factors in order of importance in terms of their influence on the decision to invest abroad. This study indicates that profitability is ranked first in importance by most corporations, followed by economic conditions (see Table 20–2).

In short, corporations use many criteria in deciding whether or not to invest abroad. Forecasting, which is an inherently imperfect art, becomes even more imperfect when corporations are faced with such a complex task, and hence they must supplement forecasting with other techniques.

MANAGEMENT OF DECLINING RESOURCES

The practice of management becomes especially critical in an era of declining resources. In prosperous times, while efficient management is important, organizations can tolerate costly mistakes since capital and resources are plentiful. But when resources become scarce, organizations cannot afford to make costly mistakes or waste valuable assets that they may not be able to replace.

The United States is now in an era of declining resources. Thus in this section we focus attention on the relative economic position of the United States, the energy crisis, and the potential dangers associated with increased worldwide population growth.

Relative Economic Position of the United States

At the end of World War II the United States was the most powerful country in the world. However, while its level of industrial productivity has increased in recent years, it has risen at a decreasing rate. In 1970 the index of labor productivity stood at 78.8 (output of manufacturing workers, the base year being 1967 with a score of 100); by 1977 the index had risen to 126.9. However, Japan increased from 52.6 to 206.6 during the same period, and West Germany from 68.7 to 169.6. Other countries, such as France and Italy, also outpaced the United States (McConnell 1979).

Similarly, Lawrence Franko (1978) points out that while the United States still possessed 68, or 44 percent, of the 156 largest companies in 13 industry groups in 1976, it had possessed 111, or 71 percent, in 1959. These and related changes suggest that the United States faces challenges that are much greater than those experienced immediately after World War II.

The Energy Crisis

The energy crisis is a major topic not only in the United States but in all countries. The U.S. Department of Energy estimates that at present rates of consumption America's oil and gas will be gone within a decade (*Newsweek* 1979). While the United States possesses an abundant supply of coal, estimated to be sufficient for 666 years, environmental and safety problems limit its use. At the same time, the Organization of Petroleum Exporting Countries, a cartel of several countries, has forced the price of a barrel of crude oil from less than $5 in 1972 to over $20 by 1979 (*Newsweek* 1979). To complicate matters, the United States has increased its dependence on foreign imported oil. In 1966 the United States imported less than 3 million barrels a day; by 1979 this figure had risen above 8 million barrels a day.

If the United States is to survive the energy crisis, it must develop a unified policy that will decrease its dependence on foreign oil and increase its use of newer forms of energy, such as solar energy. And to ensure this outcome, governmental and business leaders must act as managers, defining goals precisely and identifying means to their attainment.

Limits to Growth

A major danger facing the United States and other countries is the population explosion. It was only in 1800 that the world population reached 1 billion people. But by 1930 the population had grown to 2 billion. It is now over 4 billion people and rising rapidly.

These data suggest that many countries face a period of political and economic instability, for worldwide resources are not adequate to handle such a large number of human beings. This situation makes the role of the international corporations even more difficult, for they will operate in many countries during this period of instability. Unfortunately, there seem to be very few good solutions to the problems. Consequently, management will become even more important in future years as corporations and nations cope with the limits to growth.

COMPLEX ROLE OF THE MANAGER

Because of the growth of corporations and the changing composition of the work force, the managerial role has become very complex in recent years. This section describes some variations of the managerial role that are likely to become more important in the future.

Polyspecialist

The old view of a manager as a generalist, more concerned with making decisions than in becoming an expert in any specialized area, is no longer valid. Today the successful manager must be a polyspecialist knowledgeable in several areas: organizational behavior, computer science, and finance, for example. Modern management education encourages this background. In addition, managers frequently rotate through a variety of positions in an organization in order to increase their understanding of all its operations. Although the manager obviously will be stronger in some areas than others, he or she must not be completely ignorant in any area.

Integrator Another managerial role that is becoming very common is that of the integrator (see Chapter 11). An integrator is neither line nor staff. Rather, he or she is the manager of a decision process that involves two or more departments, although the integrator does not make the actual decisions. In the matrix organization, which is also becoming quite common, the integrator is an absolute necessity. Jay Galbraith (1977) points out that the integrating role is a general phenomenon, but titles vary from organization to organization. For instance, in business firms with diverse product lines subject to rapid change, the integrator is a product manager. In aerospace firms he or she is called a project or program manager; in hospitals the term is unit manager.

While coordinating the activities of two or more groups, the integrator is outside of, or marginal to, them. Hence the integrator must be recognized as an expert or polyspecialist by the groups. Also, he or she must not be absorbed into or identified with one of the groups, since this would severely curtail his or her effectiveness. Studies on integrators suggest that some individuals perform the linking, conflict-laden roles quite well and are satisfied completing such activities (Ziller, Stark, and Pruden 1969). Integrators must also be able to handle uncertainty, and they typically score high on affiliation needs (Galbraith 1977; see pp. 82–86).

Edgar Schein (1977) argues that the integrating role will increase in importance, since organizations are becoming more complex, and the integrator can provide a mechanism for balancing differentiation and integration (see Chapter 11). It is quite possible that more and more organizations will promote integrators to top managerial positions, since they have such a broad understanding of the organization and its problems (Galbraith 1977).

Manager Pairs One possibility that might materialize in the future—manager pairs—has arisen in direct response to the problems managers face. According to Henry Mintzberg (1973, 1975), the manager is constantly under pressure, so he or she can devote only limited attention to any specific problem. In Mintzberg's study the managers devoted an average of nine minutes to each specific problem they faced. To compensate for this lack of time, a manager usually relies on the instant information he or she can obtain through personal conversations and contacts.

Since managers are not able to devote much time to researching the details of their problems, Mintzberg suggests they work in pairs. Specifically, a manager would work with a specialist who would analyze problems. In effect the specialist would act as an organizational doctor, digging more deeply into the problems his or her partner diagnoses. The two individuals would need to work together over a period of years, since the relationship would require considerable mutual trust and understanding.

Although organizations have not yet implemented this system on a wide-scale basis, it seems to be a good way to make the role of the manager in an organization easier and more effective. It could help to eliminate some of the problems that have arisen from the complexity of the managerial job.

Specialized Managers for Specialized Jobs

As the structure of our economy has shifted away from industrial organizations toward service and governmental organizations, many new specialized managerial opportunities have developed. For instance, most hospitals are now run by administrators who are not doctors but were trained in schools of hospital administration. Professional managers also have a role to play in educational institutions and government agencies.

If an individual aspires to be a manager in a nontraditional setting, he or she might specialize in school so as to be eligible for positions that require particular qualifications. UCLA and Indiana conduct a graduate program in the management of the arts; several universities such as Cornell and Minnesota provide graduate degrees in industrial relations; and some universities now award advanced degrees in the management of specialized institutions such as prisons and churches.

Another type of specialist who may arise is the *transformation agent,* a person whose basic function would be to manage the vast amount of information generated by the computer (McGuire 1974). According to Mintzberg (1973, 1975), managers frequently are overwhelmed by the multitude of reports the computer generates, supposedly to help them in their work. However, the opposite seems to occur, for managers tend to disregard these reports, at least in part because they do not have the time to read or decipher them. One of the chief roles of the transformation agent would be to decipher and simplify these reports so they would be useful for the practicing manager.

Because of the expanded scope of American business, it is also possible for an individual to become an international manager. Today it is quite common for an American manager to spent at least part of his or her career directing a corporation's activity abroad. In fact, the demand for international managers is so great that several schools of management and business now offer specialized programs in international subjects. Many of these programs require the student to spend an internship in a foreign country before he or she is granted an MBA.

SUMMARY

The composition of the American work force has changed dramatically since the turn of the twentieth century. It is now quite heterogeneous and includes many women, older workers, and racial minorities. Accompanying the change in composition has been a decided shift in an individual's expectations from work. The traditional ideology of the Protestant or work ethic is no longer dominant and has been replaced by the humanistic ethic.

As the world economy has become integrated, international management has assumed greater importance. The analysis of international management styles suggests that American managers may experience difficulty when they work in other countries. For example, American managers tend to have a democratic orientation toward subordinates, but managers in developing countries treat their employees more autocratically. This conflict between autocratic and democratic orientations will have to be resolved by any manager sent to work in a developing country.

There are many criteria that American corporations use in deciding whether or not to invest in foreign countries. These include profitability and governmental stability of the host country. Because of the declining rate of productivity in the United States and worldwide problems such as the energy crisis, American corporations must make such decisions wisely. At this time it appears that the management of declining resources is our major problem.

Finally, the role of the modern manager has become extremely complex. But at the same time, this complexity has helped to expand the opportunities available to an individual who wants to be a manager. A manager can be a polyspecialist, an integrator, a member of a management pair, a specialist in a particular area such as hospital administration, a transformation agent, or a member of an international team, to name only a few. As the complexity of the managerial role continues to increase in the future, the variety of managerial opportunities probably will increase as well.

DISCUSSION QUESTIONS

1. Describe the United States as you expect it to be in the year 2050. What kinds of training and education will be appropriate for the individual who wants to become a manager? Why?
2. Mintzberg has advanced the concept of paired managers. That is, a manager would work closely with a specialist who would analyze problems from the manager's perspective. Is this concept practical? Why or why not?
3. Several kinds of managers were described in this chapter, such as the transformation agent and the polyspecialist. What other roles or kinds of managers do you know of that have developed in recent years? What other roles might you expect to see in the future?
4. Women and minorities are entering managerial positions in increasing numbers, as this chapter indicates. Do you feel this trend will create any problems? Why or why not? What are some problems that might occur?

5. Haire, Ghiselli, and Porter's study suggests that American managers are more democratic toward their subordinates than managers in developing countries. How do you think employees in these countries will react when American managers become their superiors? Why do you feel this way?

SUGGESTED READINGS

Dunnette, Marvin, ed. *Work and Nonwork in the Year 2001.* Monterey, Calif.: Brooks/Cole, 1973, 212 pages, paperback.

These predictions of the future society are put forth by social scientists. The chapters by Triandis and Bond are particularly rewarding.

Toffler, Alvin. *Future Shock.* New York: Bantam Books, 1970, 561 pages, paperback.

Toffler makes several fascinating predictions about the future. Following Bennis's ideas, he predicts that the predominant organizational structure will be "adhocracy," a temporary grouping of individuals assigned to a project until it is completed, after which the organization uncouples.

Walton, Clarence. *Corporate Social Responsibilities.* Belmont, Calif.: Wadsworth, 1967, 177 pages, paperback.

Walton provides a succinct overview of corporate social responsibility and describes its historical foundations.

PART VI
EXPERIENTIAL EXERCISE

Role Playing: The Promotion Interview

NOTE: Students are asked not to read the case materials on the next few pages before participating in the laboratory exercise.

A. Preparation for role playing.
   1. The instructor will select two players and give them their assignments at least a day ahead of time.
   2. One person is to play the role of Trudy Pearce and should study carefully "Background Information" and become thoroughly acquainted with "Special Instructions for Trudy Pearce."
   3. The other is to play the role of Jim Smith and should study carefully the "Background Information" and become thoroughly acquainted with "Special Instructions for Jim Smith."

B. Role-playing procedure.
   1. The instructor will read the "Background Information" aloud to the class and copy the schedule of jobs held by Smith on the chalkboard.
   2. All persons not assigned a role are to act as observers.
   3. The instructor will introduce Trudy Pearce to the class and seat her at desk in front of class, indicate that Pearce has an appointment with Jim Smith, and signal Smith to arrive for his appointment with Pearce.
   4. The interview is then to be allowed to proceed to a solution or conclusion as in a real life situation.

Source: From Norman R. F. Maier, *Psychology in Industrial Organizations,* 4th ed., pp. 501–505.

C. Discussion analysis with observers. (Pearce and Smith may enter discussion to evaluate correctness of conclusions reached.)
   1. Determine the degree to which Pearce established a mutual interest.
   2. What use did Pearce make of various types of questions?
   3. List the feelings expressed by Smith.
   4. Which feeling areas were thoroughly explored? Which were not?
   5. Obtain opinions on the degree to which Pearce understood Smith and vice versa.
   6. List the cues that indicate there was failure to communicate.
   7. Did Pearce change as a result of the interview or was she justified in maintaining her original estimation? List the reasons.
   8. How was Smith's attitude changed by the interview?

D. Repeat role playing of interview if time permits.
   1. The class is to divide into groups of three.
   2. The instructor will assign the role of Pearce to one member of each group, the role of Smith to a second member, and ask the third member to act as group leader and supervise the role playing.
   3. Role playing should be terminated 10 minutes before the end of the class period.
   4. Group leaders will hold a discussion with the role players and evaluate the progress made.

BACKGROUND INFORMATION

The American Consolidated Chemical Company has chemical plants located in various sections of the country. The main plant is in Detroit. Important branches are at Houston, St. Louis, St. Paul, and Cleveland. All the products are manufactured in Detroit, but each of the branches specializes in making chemicals that either utilize local raw materials available in the locality or have a concentration of outlets. Thus the Cleveland plant manufactures products needed in the Cleveland area, and the Houston plant manufactures products that utilize petroleum derivatives.

Since the Detroit plant makes all the products, an experienced person can be moved from Detroit to any of the other plants. When a vacancy opens up in a particular department in Detroit, it is possible to fill the vacancy by choosing someone local or by bringing in an employee from a branch that produces the product corresponding to the one made by a particular department in Detroit. Thus there has been a great deal of movement within the organization, and since the company has been expanding, opportunities for promotion have been good. Generally speaking, morale has been quite satisfactory.

Trudy Pearce is the assistant to the works manager of the Detroit plant. One of her duties is to keep track of the college recruits and plan their development. The company hires several college recruits each year and from these selects the employees for promotion and development in higher management positions. Pearce is about to have an interview with James Smith, a college graduate who was brought into the company ten years ago. The following schedule shows the positions Smith has held during his ten years with the company:

Detroit	Dept. A	1 year	Regular employee
St. Paul	Depts. A, B, C	2 years	Regular employee
Detroit	Dept. A	1 year	Foreman
St. Louis	Depts. B, F	2 years	Foreman
Cleveland	Depts. D, E	1½ years	Foreman
Houston	Dept. G	1½ years	Foreman
Detroit	Dept. H	1 year	Foreman

ROLE INSTRUCTIONS FOR TRUDY PEARCE

Ever since Jim Smith graduated from college and joined the company as a college recruit ten years ago, you have kept an eye on him. During his first year in the company you were impressed by his technical ability and even more by his leadership. After he'd had one year in Department A you sent him to St. Paul where they needed an employee with his training. He made a good showing and worked in Departments A, B, and C. After two years you brought him back to Detroit and made him a foreman in Department A. He did very well on this job, so you considered making some long-range plans for him. Here was a man you thought you could groom for an executive position. This meant giving him experience with all operations in all plants. To do this with the greatest ease, you decided to make him a foreman in each of the eight departments for a short period of time and to get him assignments in each of the branches.

During the past two years you have had some disturbing reports. Jim didn't impress Bill Jones, the department head at Houston, who reported that he had ideas but was always on the defensive. Since his return to Detroit he has shown a lack of job interest, and the employees who work for him don't back him up the way they used to. You feel you have made quite a mistake in this man and that he has let you down after you've given him good buildups with various department heads. Maybe the confidence you have shown in him and the praise you have given him during the several progress interviews have gone to his head. If so, he hasn't the stature it takes to make the top grade. Therefore, you have abandoned your plans of moving him up to superintendent at St. Paul (a two-step promotion) and think it may be best to send him to Houston where there is a job as general foreman in Department C. (Note that this is not the department in which Jones is the head.) This won't mean much of a promotion because you have moved his pay up as high as you could while he was a sort of roving foreman. However, you feel that he has earned some promotion even if he hasn't lived up to your expectations. This St. Paul position is still open, but unless you are convinced to the contrary he doesn't seem up to it.

Of course, it's possible that Jim is having marital trouble. At a recent company party you found his wife to be quite dissatisfied and unhappy. Maybe she is giving Jim a rough time.

While you are waiting for Jim to arrive you have his folder in front of you showing the positions he has held.

ROLE INSTRUCTIONS FOR JIM SMITH

You have been with the American Consolidated Chemical Company for ten years now. You joined the company on graduating from college with a major in chemistry. At the time you joined the company you were interviewed by Trudy Pearce and were told that a good employee could get ahead in the company. On the strength of the position you married your college sweetheart and moved to Detroit. You preferred the Houston and St. Paul branches, but Pearce thought Detroit was the place to start. So you took your chance along with other college recruits. Because you were a good student in college and were active in college affairs, you had reason to believe you possessed leadership ability.

During your first few years you thought you were getting someplace. You got moved to Minnesota and felt Pearce was doing you a favor by sending you there. After the first year you bought a home and got started on a family. During two years in Minnesota you gained considerable experience in Departments A, B, and C. Then you were offered a foremanship in Detroit, and since this meant a promotion and you had a second child on the way, you decided to return to Detroit. When you came to Detroit, Pearce again saw you and told you how pleased she was with your progress.

Since this time, however, you have been given a royal runaround. They tell you they like your work, but all you get are a lot of lateral transfers. You have been foreman in practically every department and have been moved from one branch to another. Other people that came to the company, even after you joined, have been made general foremen. They stick in a given department and are working up while you get moved from place to place. Although the company pays for your moves, both you and your wife want to settle down and have a permament home for your children. Why can't people be honest with you? First they tell you what a good job you are doing and then the next thing they do is get rid of you. Take, for example, Bill Jones, the department head at Houston. He acted as if you had done him a favor to go there, but you can tell he isn't sincere. Since you've gotten to know him you can see through him. From little remarks he has dropped you know he's been saying some nasty things about you to the home office. It's obvious that the Houston man is incompetent, and you feel he got rid of you because he considered you a threat to his job.

Your wife realizes that you are unhappy. She has told you she is willing to live on less just to get you out of the company. You know you could hold a superintendent's job, such as George Wilson got, who joined the company when you did, and he was just an average student in college. As a matter of fact, if the company was on the ball, it should realize that you have the ability to be a department head if George is superintendent material.

Pearce has asked you to come up and see her. You are a bit nervous about this interview because the news may not be so good. You've felt her to be less friendly lately and have no desire to listen to any smooth manipulations. Last night you and your wife had a good talk about things, and she's willing that you should look around for another job. Certainly you've reached the end of your patience, and you're fed up with any more of her attempts to move you around just because someone is jealous of your ideas.

APPENDIX A

The Case Observational Method

The case observational method is a means by which an entire class can be involved in a small-group discussion of a case or critical incident. A five-member group chosen from the class carries out the actual discussion; the rest of the class observes and evaluates the group's performance. In this fashion a large class can benefit from the type of analysis and give-and-take that ordinarily is possible only in small discussion sections.

To discuss a case, five members of the group sit in front of the class in a semicircle and carry on the discussion. (If the class is very large or the acoustics in the classroom are very poor, the group can sit in the middle of the class.) While the group is discussing the assigned critical incidents or cases, the other class members are judging its performance in terms of the criteria listed in Table 1 and Figure 1. Class members who are not included in the five-person group do not participate in the discussion of the critical incidents or cases, nor does the professor. However, everyone participates in the feedback discussion that takes place immediately after the group has disbanded.

INDIVIDUAL SCORES

Before the discussion starts, specific instructions and role assignments need to be given. An odd number of class members is assigned to each of the criteria shown in Table 1 and Figure 1. Usually three class members judge the performance of the individuals in the group on each

Source: From Martin J. Gannon, "The Case Observational Method: A New Training Technique." Reproduced by special permission from the September 1970 *Training and Development Journal,* vol. 24, pp. 39–41. Copyright 1970 by the American Society for Training and Development Inc.

criterion on a scale ranging from 1 (very poor) to 9 (very good). The median of these scores (not the mean) for each criterion is written on the blackboard immediately after the discussion has ended. For example, if three class members feel that Adams should be rated 1, 3, and 8 in terms of consideration, his score is 3, not 4 (see Table 1).

The criteria used in this exercise are as follows:

1. *Consideration:* how well the individual genuinely takes into account the attitudes and feelings of others, does not interrupt when someone else is speaking, and shows an awareness of the importance of human needs and aspirations.
2. *Task leadership:* the individual's leadership of the group in its attempt to find solutions for the cases or critical incidents under discussion.
3. *Disruption:* the extent to which the individual inhibits the solution of cases or critical incidents by interrupting, paying too little attention to details, and behaving in ways that are bothersome to the group.
4. *Hiring:* how inclined you are to hire this individual as a middle-management trainee based on his or her overall performance in the group.
5. *Promotion:* whether you would be confident enough to promote this individual, once hired, to a responsible middle-management position based on his or her performance in the group.
6. *Logic:* how logical the individual is in examining factors that should be taken into consideration if the case or critical incident is to be solved optimally.
7. *Frequency of remarks:* the number of remarks the individual makes during the discussion.
8. *Duration of remarks:* the total time (in seconds) the individual speaks during the discussion period.

TABLE 1
A Sample Scoring for Individuals

	Thomas	*Davis*	*Jones*	*Adams*	*Smith*
1. Consideration	2	6	6	3	2
2. Task leadership	7	5	5	8	2
3. Disruption (1 = high, 9 = low)	6	1	2	8	2
4. Hiring (1 = 0)	3	7	7	2	1
5. Promotion (1 = no)	2	5	5	2	1
6. Logic	1	6	6	1	2
7. Frequency of remarks	30	15	19	35	5
8. Duration of remarks (in seconds)	380	220	240	560	90

Note: All criteria are judged in terms of a scale ranging from 1 (very poor) to 9 (very good), except for items 7 and 8. Three class members are assigned to each criterion. The median rather than the mean is used in the scoring.

SCORING FOR THE GROUP

The eight criteria are used to measure how effectively each individual takes part in the group. To measure the group's characteristics as a whole, three class members are assigned to evaluate the overall productivity of the group, and another three judge its cohesion in terms of the 9-point scale. *Cohesion* refers to how well the group works smoothly together as a team. *Productivity* refers to whether the group solved the cases or critical incidents in an optimal manner by examining alternatives and then selecting the one that appeared best. After the group disbands, its members are also asked to assess its productivity and cohesion on the 9-point scale so that a comparison of the group's and class's feelings can be compared. Finally, three class members evaluate the group's productivity for each case or critical incident to compare its effectiveness at different times; they also evaluate cohesion for each case or critical incident.

The case observational method thus uses 12 criteria altogether, each requiring separate measurement by at least 3 class members. The theoretical class size is consequently 36, with 3 class members assigned to each of the 12 criteria. However, criteria can be dropped if the class is too small, or each class member can be assigned 2 or 3 criteria. The number of members assigned to a criterion should be odd, for the ratings are medians rather than means or averages.

A final measurement that can easily be taken is to ask each member of the group to select the individual he or she believes is the task leader. These selections can then be placed on the blackboard in order to determine the opinions of the group members on this matter.

FIGURE 1

A Sample Scoring for Group Characteristics

	Group	*Class*
Cohesion	8	4
Productivity	8	3

Critical Incidents or Cases

	1	2	3
Cohesion	2	2	2
Productivity	1	5	2

Note: Each criterion is judged in terms of a scale ranging from 1 (very poor) to 9 (very good). Class members judge cohesion and productivity in terms of both the overall discussion and each case or critical incident. The median rather than the mean is used in the scoring.

APPENDIX B

Theoretical Case Analysis

GOALS: (1) To identify the importance of applying theory to the solution of cases. (2) To apply our organizational model of management to the solution of cases. (3) To analyze an organizational situation or problem for which you have firsthand experience.

GROUP SIZE: The number of students that can be involved in this exercise varies considerably, from three to several hundred. Several groups can be directed simultaneously in a large room.

TIME REQUIRED: There is no ideal time required for this exercise; it can vary from 50 minutes to 3 hours.

MATERIALS: Each student should receive a three-page copy of the case problem, as explained below. However, it is also possible for the case problem to be presented verbally, thus eliminating the need for the handout.

PHYSICAL SETTING: This exercise can take place in a typical college classroom or large lecture hall.

PROCESS At the beginning of the semester the facilitator (professor) informs the students that they will be completing a unique project. Each student should think about an organizational problem of which he or she has firsthand knowledge, such as an organization experiencing a high rate of employee turnover or a low rate of productivity. Many students have had part-time jobs, so this should not present much of a problem to them. However, the student can use any organizational situation, such as a church, fraternity, army, college newspaper, and so forth. The important point is that the organization has experienced a definite problem.

Each student will then write a ten-page, double-spaced paper that consists of three parts. The first part, *case problem,* describes the organizational situation; it should be approximately three or four pages in length. The second part, *application of theory,* examines this problem in terms of our integrated organizational framework (Chapter 3) and the specific chapters in the textbook appropriate for its solution. The student should emphasize the *relationships* between the dimensions of management that seem to be accounting for the difficulties that this organization faced. This part of the paper should also be about three or four pages in length. The third part, *solution,* focuses on the approaches that the student would use to attack this problem. These approaches should logically follow from the second part of the paper, the application of our integrated framework. This part should also be about three or four pages in length.

The students should be allowed one month to write the paper. The facilitator should then select the best papers for class presentation. If there are a sufficient number of high-quality papers, more than one class period can be devoted to this exercise. Preferably, every member of the class should receive a copy of the first part of the paper, case problem. However, as explained above, the student presenter can describe the case problem verbally, thus eliminating the need for copies. After the student presenter describes the case problem, he or she then asks members of the class to express their own ideas on the second and third parts of the exercise, application of theory and solution. A class discussion then follows, its length depending on the length of the class. The student presenter does not volunteer any ideas during this period.

The student presenter then describes verbally the second and third parts of the paper. Class members then analyze the case problem in terms of the student presenter's ideas. The facilitator should encourage the class members to be highly critical in their analysis. The student presenter does not normally mind this criticism, since it is obvious that he or she has written a high-quality paper. The facilitator should reserve at least 20 minutes for this part of the exercise.

In a 50-minute class the times allocated to each segment should be approximately 10 minutes for the description of the case problem; 10 minutes for class reaction to the problem; 10 minutes for the student presenter's description of the second and third parts of his or her paper; and 20 minutes for class discussion of the student presenter's ideas. If the class meets for a longer period of time, the facilitator can adjust these estimates.

Variations If the room is large, it is possible to break the class into five-member groups for this exercise, with the exception that everyone can become a student presenter. However, previous experience with this exercise indicates that it is preferable to use only high-quality papers, even if five-member groups are used.

In a large lecture hall that contains hundreds of students, the facilitator can also use this exercise if there are suitable audio arrangements. Students who have written the best papers are placed in a group in front of the room. Each person serves as a student presenter when his or her case is analyzed; the other members of the group then play the role of critic. The facilitator can also assign some feedback time from class members who are not members of the group.

Glossary

Age-salary ratio. The relationship between an individual's age and the salary he or she receives.

Analysis of performance. The last phase of decision making; a manager's assessment, once a decision is made, of how well organizational members, organizational subsystems, and the entire organization are functioning as a result.

Aptitude. A potential talent for a particular type of work.

Assessment centers. Workshops in some large companies for new managerial trainees, designed to assess a candidate's managerial potential and counsel him or her on ways to become successful in the organization. Typically, candidates are put through a series of simulated exercises, group discussion sessions, and extended psychological interviews for a few days. Their performance is normally evaluated by both psychologists and successful line managers in the organization.

Assets. The total property owned by an organization.

Attitude. A predisposition to respond to a certain type of stimulus.

Attitude survey. A set of questionnaires or interviews an organization uses, usually periodically, to pinpoint problems and dissatisfactions among employees.

Authority, charismatic. A gift of leadership that motivates others to follow the commands of the leader without question.

Authority, rational-legal. In a bureaucracy, the authority an individual possesses purely because of his or her position or office.

Authority, traditional. That type of authority that individuals obey because tradition dictates they must do so.

Balance sheet. A detailed list of an organization's assets and liabilities.

Barnard's unit concept. Chester Barnard's idea that an organization should be composed of small units, each consisting of ten or fewer members.

Behavioral processes. Perception and interpersonal communication; motivation; leadership; and group behavior—the interactions between and among organizational members that enable the organization to move toward its goals. One of the four organizational dimensions of our integrated framework.

Behavioral science stream of management. One of the two major streams of modern management. It includes human relations, human resources, and systems and contingency theories. See *traditional management.*

Behavior modification. Increasing desired patterns of behavior, or decreasing undesirable behavior, by using scientifically determined rewards or punishments.

Bolstering the alternative. A decision-making technique in which the individual searches for information to support only the alternative he or she prefers in advance.

Bounded discretion. The area within which managers are free to make decisions by social norms, rules, and policies within the organization; legal restrictions; and moral and ethical norms.

Break-even analysis. A decision-making technique based on determining the point at which the income a product brings in equals the cost of producing it, at varying prices and levels of demand.

Bridge. In Henri Fayol's theory, the path by which someone in one part of a hierarchy can communicate with his or her equals in other sections without going through supervisors.

Budget. An allocation of specific amounts of money to various departments or groups for the purpose of controlling expenditures and monitoring activities.

Bureaucracy. A hierarchical organization characterized by specialized functions, adherence to fixed rules, impersonality, career orientation, separation of line and staff, record keeping, and rigid lines of authority.

Capital. The accumulated goods an organization possesses.

Capital budgeting. A decision-making technique in which a manager evaluates the relative attractiveness of various projects in which an initial lump payment generates a stream of earnings over a future period.

Capitalism. An economic system of private ownership of capital with competition in a free marketplace determining price, supply, and demand.

Centralization. The extent to which responsibility and authority in an organization are vested in a core executive group or office. (Contrast *decentralization.*)

Closed system. A system in which the organization is considered to be sealed off from external environmental influences. (See *open system.*)

Cognitive dissonance. An uncomfortable feeling that arises when an individual perceives a conflict between two of his or her ideas or cognitions, leading the person to abandon one of the ideas.

Committee, standing. A permanent group of organizational members who meet periodically and provide the organization with a stable structure by which routine or recurring activities can be handled efficiently.

Committee, temporary or ad hoc. A temporary group of organizational members formed to complete a particular objective, after which it disbands. (See *task force.*)

Communication. An exchange of information; one of an organization's behavioral processes. The intrapersonal perspective stresses communication within one person, such as neurological processes; the interpersonal perspective focuses on the interactions among individuals and within groups; the organizational perspective looks at the flow of information through various formal or informal organizational channels; and the technical perspective centers on the design and operation of management information systems.

Communication, horizontal. Exchange of information between peers or individuals at the same organizational levels; it tends to predominate at the lower levels in the organization.

Communication network. An arrangement by which a small number of individuals transmit information only in a set and defined pattern for the purpose of solving a problem. Types include the wheel, circle, chain, and completely connected.

Communication, one-way. A process by which one individual sends a message to another individual, with no response or feedback.

Communication, two-step. The flow of communication in two stages: (1) from the original communicator to the opinion leader or leaders in a group; and (2) from the opinion leader or leaders to the rest of the group.

Communication, two-way. An exchange of information between two individuals.

Communication, vertical. Transmission of information between individuals at different organizational levels; predominant at higher organizational levels.

Company union. A workers' organization existing only within one company, not affiliated with any other union, and generally under the control of management.

Conference approach. A group-discussion session similar to T-groups, focused on the solution of a specific organizational problem. (See *organization development.*)

Conflict. The process that begins when one party perceives that the other has frustrated, or is about to frustrate, some concern important to him or her.

Conglomerate. An organization comprising two or more companies that produce unrelated products.

Consideration. One of the two key dimensions of leader behavior—being supportive of subordinates and constructing a friendly organizational climate.

Consultative. Sharing opinions with no obligation to act on them. (Contrast *directive.*)

Contingency theory of leadership. Fred Fiedler's theory that a task-oriented style of leadership is successful when the environment or situation is either very uncertain or very certain, and that a considerate style is successful under moderate certainty.

Contingency theory of management. An approach that assumes the type of management that is successful depends on such factors as the kind of technology used to create the final product or service and the degree of external environmental uncertainty the organization faces.

Continuous process or automated technology. The process of transforming raw goods into finished products through the use of machine-controlled mechanisms so that the worker does not actually touch the raw goods but rather monitors the machines. The organization invests heavily in capital equipment but does not spend much money on labor. (See *unit technology* and *mass production.*)

Control. The monitoring of plans and the pinpointing of significant deviations from them. In some situations, the control system contains an action device that automatically corrects these deviations; in others, managers must determine what corrective action is appropriate. Both organizational subsystems and organization members must be controlled for plans to be accomplished.

Control, feedback. Diagnosis and correction of an error after it has occurred.

Control, feedforward. Diagnosis and correction of an error before it occurs.

Co-optation. A method an organization uses to reduce the uncertainty it faces: Management attempts to influence its external environment by seeking out representatives from the community to become members of the organization.

Coordination. The development of cooperative relationships between individuals and groups whose work overlaps.

Cosmopolitan leaders. Managers who move from organization to organization throughout their careers and have visibility outside the organization or community. (Contrast *local leaders.*)

Creative group. An informal committee formed to generate a large number of ideas for a nonroutine and distinctive problem. (See *problem-solving group.*)

Creativity. The ability to produce something new or original.

Critical path method. The specification of a series of interrelated steps necessary to complete a specific project in which the time estimates for completing each step are certain. (See *program evaluation and review technique (PERT).*)

Decentralization. The extent to which responsibility and authority are delegated to lower levels in the organization. (Contrast *centralization.*)

Decision environments. The conditions or constraints under which decision making occurs.

Decision heuristics. Rules that simplify the decision process enormously.

Decision making. A process of choice leading to the selection of one alternative rather than others. More generally, it involves problem-solving activity that comes into play when the manager realizes that a significant gap—either in performance or opportunity—exists between what is and what should be.

Decision strategy, incremental. Managers muddle their way through the deicision process by examining only a very small range of alternatives that differ to only a small degree from existing policy. (See *decision strategy, rational comprehensive.*)

Decision strategy, rational comprehensive. The manager examines a very large number of alternatives, and attempts to choose the most desirable one. (See *decision strategy, incremental.*)

Decision tree. A decision-making technique appropriate when a series of decisions must be made but their outcomes are unknown. (See *expected value.*)

Delphi technique. A forecasting technique in which the organization polls at periodic intervals a small number of experts who make predictions about long-run technological and market changes that eventually will affect the organization. (See *nominal group technique.*)

Departmentalization. Division or grouping of organizational jobs and subunits on the basis of a common characteristic, such as product or goal, function or area of specialization, place or clientele.

Descriptive. Based on actual practice rather than theory or ideals; as, a descriptive model of decision making. (Contrast *normative.*)

Deterministic model. A model in which the law of chance plays no part. (See probabilistic model.)

Differential piece rate. In scientific management, after a worker manufactures a specified number of units, he or she is paid a higher rate per unit for any additional units produced, and the rate per piece increases after each succeeding plateau reached.

Differentiation The process of increasing both the number of complex units and of differing points of view in an organization. As differentiation increases, the organization's need for integrating these units and viewpoints also rises.

Dimensions of management. Four organizational areas or dimensions within which managerial activities take place. These are planning and control; organization design; behavioral processes; and managerial decision making.

Directive. Involving orders that are to be followed. (Contrast *consultative.*)

Econometric model. A complex computer simulation of the entire economy used to forecast future levels of economic activity.

Economic man. A normative model of decision making, developed by Adam Smith, in which the manager is assumed to understand all the alternatives he can pursue to accomplish particular goals, from which he chooses the most desirable alternative. (See *satisficing.*)

Employee-owned companies. Private companies in which the employees are the stockholders.

Entrepreneur. An individual who starts a new enterprise consisting of eight or more employees. According to Joseph Schumpeter, one who combines given resources so as to radically alter the consumption and production patterns of a society.

EOP (economic order point) model. The management of inventories when an order is placed for two or more items or products simultaneously. (See *EOQ* and *MRP*).

EOQ (economic order quantity) model. The management of inventories of each individual product or item as usage occurs. (See *EOP* and *MRP.*)

Equity theory. A motivational theory that assumes an individual must see a relationship between the rewards he or she obtains (outcomes) and the amount of work he or she performs (inputs).

Expectancy theory. A theory that assumes an individual's motivation is a function of two expectancies: that effort will result in successful performance, and that successful performance will lead to desired outcomes.

Expected value. A decision-making technique that indicates probable profit by multiplying possible future outcomes and the probabilities of their occurrence, and summing the totals.

Fast track. A term for the path taken by certain individuals who are picked for rapid advancement while the remainder of the managerial workforce is essentially bypassed.

Federal decentralization. A combination of departmentalization by product or goal at the operating level and by function at the top level of an organization. Operating units that are largely self-contained draw personnel from functional departments as needed.

Feedback. Information on the outcome of an action or process.

First level. The lowest level in an organization.

Fixed costs. Expenses (such as rent) that are unaffected by changes in volume of business. (Contrast *variable costs.*)

Flexitime. A way of scheduling work under which employees must be present during a "core" period, but can begin work any time before the core period; their starting time determines their quitting time.

Forecasting. The prediction of occurrences that may affect the organization. Forecasts can be long-range, short-range, or rolling (integrating long- and short-range).

Forecasting techniques. There are three basic types. Qualitative techniques primarily involve subjective estimates of the future. Time series analysis focuses on past activities and their extrapolation statistically into the future. Mathematical models identify the underlying variables that actually influence and predict the changes the forecast describes.

Functional foremanship. In scientific management, a system whereby each aspect of an employee's job is examined by a specialized foreman. The worker thus reports to several functional foremen.

Functions of management. According to Fayol and other writers in the classical management school, the specific activities that a manager must perform (such as planning) to be successful.

Grapevine. An informal system of communication in an organization.

Group behavior. Interactions within and among work groups; one of the behavioral processes in an organization.

Groupthink. A concurrence-seeking tendency in small decision-making groups.

Hawthorne effect. The change in workers' behavior that automatically occurs when they are studied.

Hierarchy. The set of levels of power in an organization that makes some individuals subordinate to others in authority, earnings, and/or status.

Horizontal integration. A company's attempt to dominate a market at one particular stage of the production process by monopolizing resources at that stage. (Contrast *vertical integration.*)

Humanistic ethic. A motivational profile of individuals stressing fulfillment, growth, and satisfaction, in line with Maslow's theory of motivation. Supposedly the most popular ethic today.

Human relations. A school of management whose basic proposition is that the attitudes individuals develop in informal groups within an organization critically influence their commitment and level of productivity.

Human resource accounting system. A means of assessing an organization's employees in terms of replacement costs, selection costs, and the like.

Human resources. A school of management within the behavioral science stream that argues that managers frequently create their own problems by vastly underestimating the potential of individuals to assume responsibility in the work setting.

Hygiene factors. In two-factor theory, extrinsic sources of motivation, that do not relate directly to the nature of the work (for example, working conditions) and that affect rates of absenteeism and turnover.

Ideology. A system of beliefs used to justify a particular position.

Income statement. A detailed list of an organization's sources of revenues and expenses for a given year.

Integrator. An employee who is neither line nor staff, but has informal power to integrate the efforts of overlapping work groups or units.

Intervention. The process in organization development by which planned changes are implemented. (See *process intervention; structural intervention.*)

Interview, structured. An interview in which the interviewer controls the pace and subject matter. (Contrast *interview, unstructured.*)

Interview, unstructured. An interview in which the interviewee controls the pace and subject matter. (Contrast *interview, structured.*)

Inventory control. Monitoring the number of goods in stock. There are three prominent techniques of inventory management: the economic order quantity (EOQ) model, the economic order point (EOP) model, and the material requirements planning (MRP) model. (See *EOQ, EOP,* and *MRP.*)

Iron Law of Oligarchy. See *Michels' Iron Law.*

Job Diagnostic Survey. A questionnaire designed to measure the degree to which a job is enriched.

Job enlargement. Increasing the number of operations an individual performs in a job cycle.

Job enrichment. Increasing the amount of responsibility an individual can exercise in his or her job.

Leader behavior theory. Developed at Ohio State University, the theory that the two major dimensions of leader behavior are consideration and the initiation of structure or task orientation.

Leadership. The ability of a superior to influence the behavior of subordinates; one of the behavioral processes in an organization.

Leadership theory, reciprocal causation. The theory of leadership that argues that the leader and the members of his or her workgroup reciprocally influence one another.

Leadership theory, vertical dyad linkage. The theory of leadership focusing on the relationship between a superior and *each* subordinate.

Liabilities. An organization's total outstanding financial obligations.

Line. An employee or officer whose work contributes directly to the accomplishment of organizational goals and objectives.

Linear programming. The use of linear equations to solve a problem in which the goal is to maximize an objective function, such as profits, or minimize an objective function, such as costs. Linear programming is appropriate when scarce resources need to be allocated to competing projects, objectives, or product lines.

Linking pin. Rensis Likert's term for a member of two work groups whose work overlaps; this member is responsible for coordinating the work of the two groups.

Local leaders. Managers who normally stay with an organization or community their entire life, and who do not seek visibility outside the organization or community. (Contrast *cosmopolitan leaders.*)

Machine-controlled systems. Technology in which machines rather than human beings control or monitor the work processes, as in an oil refinery.

Management. That activity that performs certain functions in order to effectively acquire, allocate, and utilize human efforts and physical resources to accomplish some goal.

Management audit. A control technique that assesses the overall quality of management by means of methods such as questionnaires, interviews, and analysis of "hard" data elements (turnover, productivity, and so forth).

Management by objectives (MBO). An organization-wide planning system in which top management typically defines four or five general objectives it wishes to achieve within a given period. Managers throughout the hierarchy refine these objectives into subobjectives for their own units. Each employee's performance is then evaluated in terms of individual objectives that relate directly to the unit's objectives.

Management information system (MIS). Any system of data collection and analysis that will help the manager perform his or her job more effectively.

Managerial grid. An approach to leadership and organizational change that is based on the two major dimensions of leader behavior theory, consideration and task orientation or the initiation of structures.

Managerial team. A group of managers who successfully coordinate their efforts so that they and their respective organizational units benefit.

Manager pair. Two managers, a specialist and a generalist, who work together, the specialist digging more deeply into the problems the generalist diagnoses.

MAPS (Multivariate analysis, participation, and structure). An approach to organization development design that allows the members of the organization to define the major task groups or units and to select the individuals most suitable for working in them.

Mass production. The process of transforming raw goods into finished products through the use of an assembly line so that all the products are basically the same. The organization spends a great amount of money on both labor and capital equipment. (See *unit technology* and *continuous process or automated technology.*)

Matrix organization. An organization design that combines at least two different types of departments and openly violates the principle of unity of command. For example, functional managers exercise technical authority over projects, while the product managers have responsibility for budgets and the final completion of projects. The functional managers lend employees to product managers as needed.

Mechanistic structure. An organization having a high degree of functional specialization of jobs, a centralized hierarchy, formal and standardized jobs and procedures, economic sources of motivation, an authoritarian leadership style, formal and impersonal relations between individuals and groups, and vertical and directive communication. (Contrast *organic structure.*)

Michels' Iron Law. Michels' statement that whoever says organization, says oligarchy, or rule by the few.

Model. A simplified or concrete representation of a complex or abstract process or idea.

Motion study. Scientific management's analysis of the specific motions of workers at a given job, through the use of films and other devices, so as to determine what motions are necessary for the job's completion. (See *time study.*)

Motivation. The physical and mental state that propels an individual to act in a particular manner, or the deliberate creation of such a state; one of the behavioral processes in an organization.

Motivation, conditioning theories. Those theories of motivation focusing upon the cues and stimuli that elicit a particular type of behavior.

Motivation, content theories. Those theories of motivation describing the actual factors or needs motivating an individual.

Motivation, process theories. Those theories of motivation that seek to explain the manner or process in which an individual is motivated.

Motivators. In two-factor theory, intrinsic sources of motivation, relating directly to the nature of the work (for example, interesting and challenging assignments), which affect rates of productivity.

MRP (material requirements planning) model. The management of inventories when there is a commonality among products so that a subcomponent is used in more than one product. (See *EOQ* and *EOP.*)

Multi-national corporations. Corporations that, although based in one country for legal purposes, operate divisions in two or more countries.

Need hierarchy. Abraham Maslow's theory of motivation, which holds that human needs are arranged in a hierarchy; the individual seeks to satisfy basic and elementary needs first, and then higher-order needs.

Nominal group technique (NGT). A technique for developing a creative solution to a problem. Seven to ten experts meet to share their ideas in a highly structured manner. NGT can also be used for forecasting.

Nonprogrammed decision. A solution to a problem that cannot be found by using a standard routine or program, but demands a creative response.

Nonzero-sum situation. A competitive situation in which when one group wins, the other group also wins or its position remains unchanged. (Contrast *zero-sum situation.*)

Norm. A standard or ideal pattern, e.g., of behavior.

Normative. Reflecting a norm; as, a normative model of decision making. (Contrast *descriptive.*)

Office of the president. A system by which two or three co-equal chief executives in an organization divide the work and coordinate their respective efforts.

Open system. A system in which the organization and the environment in which it operates mutually influence one another. (See *closed system.*)

Organic structure. An organization design having enriched jobs, a decentralized hierarchy, flexible jobs and procedures, economic and non-economic sources of motivation, democratic leadership, informal and personal relations between individuals, and both vertical and lateral consultative communications. (See *mechanistic structure.*)

Organization design. The structure of an organization, which provides a framework for its activities and delineates lines of authority and responsibility.

Organization development (OD). The introduction of planned and systematic change into an organization through the application of behavioral science principles and techniques.

Overhead costs. Expenses that cannot be conveniently assigned as either fixed or variable; for example, electricity and the salaries of clerical personnel.

Parity principle. The idea that the amount of authority an individual possesses should be equal to his or her responsibility.

Participative management. A system by which employees are allowed to have a voice in decisions that bear directly on their work.

Payback period. The length of time required for the net revenues of an investment to cover its initial cost.

Perception. The manner in which an individual selects and organizes sensations or stimuli into a meaningful whole.

Performance appraisal. Evaluation of a person's performance. Four well-known methods of evaluating performance are trait rating, global ratings, behaviorally anchored rating scales, and goal-oriented evaluation.

Personal space. The physical area around an individual within which other people generally do not trespass.

Planning. Through environmental forecasting, selecting the basic mission or missions of the organization, the business or businesses the organization is in; developing desired outcomes (long-term goals and short-term objectives) for the organization in light of the mission; developing means (overall strategies and tactics related directly to these strategies) to achieve these goals and objectives; updating forecasts periodically to take account of environmental changes; possibly changing missions, goals, and objectives in light of these revised forecasts; and implementing policies, procedures, and rules.

Policy. A general guide management employs to direct organizational activities.

Polyspecialist. A manager who is neither a generalist nor a specialist, but rather is very knowledgeable in several areas.

Power. The source of a superior's ability to persuade subordinates to follow a particular course of action. There are five types of power: legitimate, reward, expert, coercive, and referent.

Principles of management. Certain guidelines that Fayol and other members of the classical management school held that a manager should follow to achieve success. (See, for example, *span of control.*)

Probabilistic model. A model that takes account of chance or random factors that exist under conditions of uncertainty or risk. (See *deterministic model.*)

Problem factoring. Breaking a large problem into smaller parts or stages.

Problem-solving group. A task-oriented informal committee brought together for the purpose of solving a specific problem. (See *creative group.*)

Procedures. Plans that establish a customary method of handling future activities. They normally accompany policies.

Process intervention. In organization development, an attempt to change the attitudes of organizational members so that organizational objectives can be accomplished more successfully. (See *structural intervention.*)

Program evaluation and review technique (PERT). The specification of a series of interrelated steps necessary to complete a specific project in which the time estimates for completing each step are probabilistic. (See *critical path method.*)

Programmed decision. A solution to a problem found by using a program, routine, or procedure that has been successful for similar problems in the past.

Project management. An organization design in which each subordinate is employed only for the life of a project; when the project is completed, the subordinate is either assigned to another project or let go.

Protégé. An individual whose career is advanced by the help of an older and successful executive.

Protestant ethic. The idea that worldly success is a necessary but not sufficient condition for salvation.

Quality control. Monitoring the grade and consistency in characteristics of the product that the organization produces.

Questionnaire data banks. Computer stores of information collected from a large number of questionnaires, used to pinpoint problems in an organization. Normally each organizational unit is compared to the norm or average on each questionnaire item.

Reliability, test. The degree to which individuals taking the same test at two different times, or groups similar in background characteristics, receive similar scores on the test.

Responsibility centers. Organizational subunits in which accountability is aligned with authority.

Risky shift phenomenon. The finding that the behavior of individuals as individuals often is radically different from their group behavior. In some situations, individuals take a riskier position; in others, a more conservative position.

Rules. Specific procedures that individuals and operating divisions of an organization should follow to conform with organizational policies. However, some rules are not related to policies.

Satisficing. Choosing a solution to a problem by examining only four or five alternatives that are minimally acceptable, and picking one that will be adequate, rather than taking additional time and effort to find the best possible solution. (See *economic man.*)

Scalar principle. The classical management principle holding that the hierarchy should be arranged in a chain ranging from the ultimate authority to the lowest ranks, graded in terms of specific responsibilities and rights.

Scientific management. A school within the traditional stream of management whose proponents argue that there is an ideal way of performing any job, which can be pinpointed scientifically through time and motion study.

Sensitivity training. A group-discussion method used to give individuals insight into their strengths and weaknesses. Although a psychologist is present, the group starts off its discussions in an unstructured and "leaderless" fashion; gradually the psychologist intervenes to help members understand their attitudes and behavior.

Simulation. Building and testing models that use mathematical relationships between critical, "real-world" factors to create a facsimile of real conditions; normally done on a computer.

Social audits. A systematic attempt to assess the performance of a business in the area of social responsibility.

Social responsibility. The obligation of a business to fulfill not only economic goals but also noneconomic goals encompassing responsibilities to customers, suppliers, employees, and the general public.

Span of control. The number of subordinates a manager supervises or should supervise.

Staff. Employees and managers who advise and assist line managers and employees. They are not directly involved in achieving organizational objectives.

Standard cost system. A control technique that estimates anticipated costs for a particular product or level of volume.

State-backed corporations. Corporations that receive financial support from the state.

Stereotypes. Preconceived notions about people, often based on superficial characteristics, which can distort communication between individuals.

Streams of management. The major divisions of management thought: the traditional management stream and the behavioral science stream.

Structural intervention. In organization development, altering the structure of an organization so that individuals relate to one another in a new and different way. (See *process intervention.*)

Structures, tall versus flat. An organization is tall if there are many levels, and flat if there are few.

Synectics. An attempt to generate novel ideas and approaches by establishing a small group of individuals with heterogeneous backgrounds and abilities.

Systems theory. An approach to management that assumes: (1) an organization is a system consisting of subunits that interact with one another and depend on one another; and (2) an organization is an open system interacting with its external environment and dependent on it.

Task force. A group set up within an organization to accomplish a specific objective, after which it disbands. It differs from a temporary committee in that its members are drawn from various departments in the organization interested in the outcome of the task force's work.

Task management. The use of time and motion study to analyze a specific job and develop the optimum method of performing it.

Task orientation. One of the two key dimensions of leader behavior, involving focusing on initiation of structure, assignment of tasks, specification of the manner in which tasks are to be completed, and clarification of schedules.

Team building. In organization development, an intervention focused on improving the effectiveness and efficiency of one group or unit.

Technology. The means an organization uses to produce its good or service.

Temporary committee. See *committee, temporary or ad hoc.*

Theory X. The managerial assumption that human beings are lazy, avoid responsibility, need direction, and must be coerced.

Theory Y. The managerial assumption that human beings seek responsibility and want to use their abilities.

Time study. Scientific management's method of determining, by the use of the stop watch, the time a worker needs to complete a given job cycle. (See *motion study.*)

Total organizational intervention. In organization development, an intervention focused on improving the efficiency and effectiveness of an entire organization.

Traditional management. One of the two major streams of modern management. It includes bureaucracy, the management process school, scientific management, and the quantitative school. See *behavioral science stream of management.*

Training groups (T-groups). Sensitivity training groups, which can be used to train managers in interpersonal insight and relations.

Trait theory. A view of leadership that assumes leaders differ from average people in traits like intelligence, perseverance, and ambition.

Two-factor theory. Frederick Herzberg's idea that job motivation has two independent sources: hygiene factors and motivators.

Unit technology. The process of transforming raw goods into finished products that are custom made on an individual basis by skilled workers. With unit technology, an organization spends a great deal of money on labor relative to capital investment in equipment. (See *continuous process or automated technology* and *mass production.*)

Unity of command. The principle in classical management that a subordinate should be responsible only to one superior.

Unity of direction. The classical management principle holding that there should be one head and one plan for a group of activities having the same objective.

Validity. The degree to which a test actually measures what it is supposed to measure.

Variable costs. Expenses that change with the level of output and that normally change each time they occur, such as materials and labor. (Contrast *fixed costs.*)

Vertical integration. A company's attempt to dominate a market by controlling all steps in the production process, from the extraction of raw materials through the manufacture and sale of the final product. (Contrast *horizontal integration.*)

Weighted application blank. An application blank that rates an individual's background characteristics relative to those of previous successful and unsuccessful performers.

Work group. The formal group of individuals assigned to perform a particular task or function in an organization.

Zero-based budgeting (ZBB). Budgeting that begins every year at zero and requires that every item be justified each year.

Zero-sum situation. A competitive situation in which resources are finite, so that what one group wins, the other necessarily loses. (Contrast *nonzero-sum situation.*)

Bibliography

Abelson, H., and Karlins, M. *Persuasion: How Opinions and Attitudes Are Changed.* 2nd rev. ed. New York: Springer-Verlag, 1970.

Adams, J. "Toward an Understanding of Inequity." *Journal of Abnormal and Social Psychology* 67 (1963): 422–436.

———. "Inequity in Social Exchange." In *Advances in Experimental Social Psychology,* vol. 2, edited by L. Berkowitz, pp. 267–299. New York: Academic Press, 1965.

Albaum, G. "Horizontal Information Flow: An Exploratory Study." *Academy of Management Journal* 7 (1964): 21–33.

Alderfer, C. *Existence, Relatedness, and Growth: Human Needs in Organizational Settings.* New York: Free Press, 1972.

Alutto, J., and Vredenburgh, D. "Characteristics of Decisional Participation by Nurses." *Academy of Management Journal* 20 (1977): 341–347.

American Assembly of Collegiate Schools of Business, *Newsline* 10, no. 1 (October 1979): 1–8.

Anderson, C. "Locus of Control, Coping Behaviors, and Performance in a Stress Setting: A Longitudinal Study." *Journal of Applied Psychology* 62 (1977): 446–451.

Anderson, C., and Paine, F. "PIMS: A Reexamination." *Academy of Management Journal* 3 (1978): 602–612.

Andrews, J. "The Achievement Motive and Advancement in Two Types of Organizations." *Journal of Personality and Social Psychology* 6 (1967): 163–169.

Andrews, K. *The Concept of Corporate Strategy.* Homewood, Ill.: Irwin, 1971.

Andrisani, P., and Nestel, G. "Internal-External Outcome as a Contributor to and Outcome of Work Experience." *Journal of Applied Psychology* 61 (1976): 156–165.

Andrisani, P., and Shapiro, M. "Women's Attitudes Toward Their Jobs: Some Longitudinal Data on a National Sample." *Personnel Psychology* 31 (1978): 15–34.

Annett, J. "The Role of Knowledge of Results in Learning: A Survey." In *Industrial Psychology,* edited by M. Blum and J. Nayler. New York: Harper & Row, 1968.

Aplin, J. "Issues and Problems in Developing Managerial Careers and Potential." *Business Quarterly* 43 (1978): 22–29.

Argyris, C. *Personality and Organization: The Conflict Between System and the Individual.* New York: Harper & Row, 1957.

———. "Today's Problems with Tomorrow's Organizations." *Journal of Management Studies* 4 (1967): 31–55.

Arvey, R.; Dewhirst, H.; and Boling, J. "Relationships Between Goal Clarity, Participation in Goal Setting, and Personality Characteristics on Job Satisfaction in a Scientific Organization." *Journal of Applied Psychology* 61 (1976): 103–105.

Asch, S. "Forming Impressions of Personality." *Journal of Abnormal and Social Psychology* 41 (1946): 258–290.

———. "Effects of Group Pressure upon the Modification and Distortion of Judgment." In *Groups, Leadership and Men,* edited by H. Guetzkow, pp. 177–190. Pittsburgh: Carnegie Press, 1951.

———. *Social Psychology.* Englewood Cliffs, N.J.: Prentice-Hall, 1952.

Athanassiades, J. "The Distortion of Upward Communication in Hierarchical Organizations." *Academy of Management Journal* 16 (1973): 207–226.

Atkinson, J., and Reitman, W. "Performance as a Function of Motive Strength and Expectancy of Goal Attainment." *Journal of Abnormal and Social Psychology* 53 (1956): 361–366.

Bales, R. *Interaction Process Analysis.* Reading, Mass.: Addison-Wesley, 1950.

Bales, R., and Strodtbeck, F. "Phases in Group Problem Solving." *Journal of Abnormal and Social Psychology* 46 (1951): 485–495.

Barad, C. "Flexitime Under Scrutiny: Research on Work Adjustment and Organizational Performance." *Personnel Administrator* 25 (1980): 69–74.

Barlund, D., and Harland, C. "Propinquity and Prestige as Determinants of Communication Networks." *Sociometry* 26 (1963): 467–479.

Barmash, I. *Welcome to the Conglomerate—You're Fired.* New York: Delacorte, 1971.

Barmash, I., ed. *Great Business Disasters.* New York: Ballantine Books 1973.

Barnard, C. *The Functions of the Executive.* Cambridge, Mass.: Harvard University Press, 1966. Originally published in 1938.

Bartol, K., and Butterfield, D. "Sex Effects in Evaluating Leaders." *Journal of Applied Psychology* 61 (1976): 446–454.

Bass, B. "Interface Between Personnel and Organizational Psychology." *Journal of Applied Psychology* 52 (1968): 81–88.

Bass, B.; McGregor, D.; and Walters, J. "Selecting Foreign Plant Sites: Economic, Social and Political Considerations." *Academy of Management Journal* 20 (1977): 535–551.

Bass, B., and Vaughan, J. *Training in Industry: The Management of Learning.* Belmont, Calif.: Wadsworth, 1966.

Bauer, R., and Fenn, D. "What Is a Corporate Social Audit?" *Harvard Business Review* 57 (1973): 37–48.

Baumback, C., and Mancuso, J., eds. *Entrepreneurship and Venture Management.* Englewood Cliffs, N.J.: Prentice-Hall, 1975.

Baumhart, R. *An Honest Profit: What Businessmen Say About Ethics in Business.* New York: Holt, Rinehart and Winston, 1968.

Beatty, R., and Schneier, C. "Training the Hard Core Unemployed Through Positive Reinforcement." *Human Resource Management* 11 (1972): 11–17.

Beckhard, R. *Organization Development: Strategies and Models.* Reading, Mass.: Addison-Wesley, 1969.

Beer, M., and Gerry, G. "Pay Systems Preferences and Their Correlates." Paper presented at the American Psychological Association Convention, August 1968, at San Francisco.

Behling, O.; Schriescheim, C.; and Tolliver, J. "Present Theories and New Directions in Theories of Work Effort." *Journal Supplement Abstract Service* of the American Psychological Corporation, 1976.

Bennis, W., and Shepard, H. "A Theory of Group Development." *Human Relations* 9 (1956): 415–437.

Berelson, B., and Steiner, G. *Human Behavior.* 1964. Shorter ed. New York: Harcourt, Brace & World, 1967.

Berlew, D., and Hall, D. "The Socialization of Managers: Effects of Expectations on Performance." *Administrative Science Quarterly* 11 (1966): 207–233.

Best, F. "Preferences on Worklife Scheduling and Work-Leisure Tradeoffs." *Monthly Labor Review* 101, no. 6 (1978): 22–30.

Bigoness, W. "Effect of Applicant's Sex, Race and Performance on Employers' Performance Ratings: Some Additional Findings." *Journal of Applied Psychology* 61 (1976): 80–84.

Blake, R., and Mouton, J. *The Managerial Grid.* Houston: Gulf Publishing, 1964.

———. *Building a Dynamic Corporation Through Grid Organization Development.* Reading, Mass.: Addison-Wesley, 1969.

Blau, P.; Falbe, C.; McKinley, W.; and Tracy, P. "Technology and Organization in Manufacturing." *Administrative Science Quarterly* 21 (1976): 20–39.

Blauner, R. *Alienation and Freedom.* Chicago: University of Chicago Press, 1964.

Boling, T. "The Management Ethics 'Crisis': An Organizational Perspective." *Academy of Management Review* 3 (1978): 360–365.

Boulton, W. "The Evolving Board: A Look at the Board's Changing Roles and Information Needs." *Academy of Management Journal* 3 (1978): 827–836.

Bowen, H. *Social Responsibilities of the Businessman.* New York: Harper & Brothers, 1953.

Bowers, D., and Seashore, S. "Predicting Organizational Effectiveness with a Four-Factor Theory of Leadership." *Administrative Science Quarterly* 11 (1966): 238–263.

Bowman, J. "Managerial Ethics in Business and Government." *Business Horizons* 19 (1976): 48–54.

Brenner, S., and Molander, E. "Is the Ethics of Business Changing?" *Harvard Business Review* 55, no. 1 (1977): 57–71.

Brockhaus, R. "Risk-Taking Propensity of Entrepreneurs." *Academy of Management Journal* 23 (1980): 509–520.

Bronfenbrenner, U. "Nobody Home: The Erosion of the American Family." *Psychology Today* 11 (1977): 41–47.

Browne, P., and Golembiewski, R. "The Line-Staff Concept Revisited: An Empirical Study of Organizational Images." *Academy of Management Journal* 17 (1974): 406–417.

Buchholz, R. "The Belief Structure of Managers Relative to Work Concepts Measured by a Factor Analytic Model." *Personnel Psychology* 30 (1977): 567–588.

———. "The Work Ethic Reconsidered." *Industrial and Labor Relations Review* 31 (1978): 450–459.

Burke, R. "Methods of Resolving Superior-Subordinate Conflict: The Constructive Use of Subordinate Differences and Disagreements." *Organizational Behavior and Human Performance* 5 (July 1970): 403.

Burke, R.; Weitzel, W.; and Weir, T. "Characteristics of Effective Employee Performance Review and Development Interviews: Replication and Extension." *Personnel Psychology* 31 (1978): 903–919.

Burns, T. "The Directions of Activity and Communication in a Departmental Executive Group." *Human Relations* 7 (1954): 73–97.

Burns, T., and Stalker, G. *The Management of Innovation.* London: Tavistock, 1961.

Burr, A. *Russell H. Conwell and His Work.* Philadelphia: Winston, 1917.

Burton, G.; Pathak, D.; and Burton, D. "The Gordon Effect in Nominal Grouping." *University of Michigan Business Review* XXX (1978): 7–10.

Business Ethics: Highlights of Bentley College's First Annual Conference on Business Ethics. Waltham, Mass.: Bentley College, 1977.

Business Week. "The Office of the Future," June 30, 1975, pp. 48–84.

———. "Young Top Management: The New Goals, Rewards, Lifestyles," October 6, 1975, pp. 56–68.

———. "How Companies React to the Ethics Crisis," February 9, 1976, pp. 78–79.

———. "When Businessmen Confess Their Social Sins," November 6, 1978, pp. 175–178.

Butcher, B. "The Program Management Approach to the Corporate Social Audit." *California Management Review* 16 (1973): 11–16.

Butcher, W. "The Stifling Costs of Regulations." *Business Week,* November 6, 1978, pp. 22–24.

Campbell, D. *Manual for the Strong-Campbell Interest Inventory.* Stanford: Stanford University Press, 1974.

Campbell, J.; Dunnette, M.; Lawler, E.; and Weick, K. *Managerial Behavior, Performance, and Effectiveness.* New York: McGraw-Hill, 1970.

Carlson, R. "Succession and Performance Among School Superintendents." *Administrative Science Quarterly* 6 (1961): 210–227.

———. *School Superintendents: Careers and Performance.* Columbus: Merrill, 1972.

Carlson, R.; Thayer, P.; Mayfield, E.; and Peterson, D. "Improvements in the Selection Interview." *Personnel Journal* 50 (1971): 268–275.

Carroll, A. "Managerial Ethics: A Post-Watergate View." *Business Horizons* 18 (1975): 75–80.

Carroll, S. "Relationships of Various College Graduate Characteristics to

Recruiting Decisions." *Journal of Applied Psychology* 50 (1966): 421–423.

Carroll, S., and Tosi, H. "Goal Characteristics and Personality Factors in a Management by Objectives Program." *Administrative Science Quarterly* 15 (1970): 295–305.

———. *Management by Objectives.* New York: Macmillan, 1973.

———. *Organizational Behavior.* Chicago: St. Clair Press, 1977.

Carzo, R., and Yanouzas, J. "Effects of Flat and Tall Organization Structures." *Administrative Science Quarterly* 14 (1969): 178–191.

Cecil, E.; Cummings, L.; and Chertkoff, J. "Group Composition and Choice Shift: Implications for Administration." *Academy of Management Journal* 16 (1973): 412–422.

Chambers, J.; Mullik, S.; and Smith, D. "How to Choose the Right Forecasting Technique." *Harvard Business Review* 49 (1971): 45–74.

Chandler, A. *Strategy and Structure.* Cambridge, Mass.: M.I.T. Press, 1962.

Chase, R., and Aquilano, N. *Production and Operations Management: A Life Cycle Approach.* 1973. Rev. ed. Homewood, Ill.: Irwin, 1977.

Child, J. "Organizational Structure, Environment and Performance: The Role of Strategic Choice." *Administrative Science Quarterly* 6 (1973): 168–185.

Child, J., and Mansfield, R. "Technology, Size and Organization Structure." *Sociology* 6 (1972): 369–393.

Coch, L., and French, J. "Overcoming Resistance to Change." *Human Relations* 1 (1948): 512–532.

Cofer, C., and Appley, M. *Motivation: Theory and Research.* New York: Wiley, 1964.

Cohen, A. "Changing Small-Group Communication Networks." *Administrative Science Quarterly* 6 (1962): 443–462.

Collins, O., and Moore, D. *The Enterprising Man.* East Lansing, Mich.: Michigan State University Business Studies, Bureau of Business and Economic Research, 1964.

———. *The Organization Makers.* New York: Appleton-Century-Crofts, 1970.

Committee for Economic Development. *Social Responsibilities of Business Corporations.* New York: 1971.

Commons, J. *Legal Foundations of Capitalism.* Madison, Wis.: University of Wisconsin Press, 1957. Originally published in 1935.

Cooper, A. "Entrepreneurial Environment." *Industrial Research* 12 (1970): 74–76.

Cosier, R. "The Effects of Three Potential Aids for Making Strategic Decisions on Prediction Accuracy." *Organizational Behavior and Human Performance* 22 (1978): 295–306.

Costello, T., and Zalkind, S., eds. *Psychology in Administration.* Englewood Cliffs, N.J.: Prentice-Hall, 1963.

Crozier, M. *The Bureaucratic Phenomenon.* Chicago: University of Chicago Press, 1964.

Cummings, L., and Schwab, D. *Performance in Organizations.* Glenview, Ill.: Scott, Foresman, 1973.

Daft, R., and MacIntosh, N. "A New Approach to the Design and Use of Management Information." *California Management Review* XXI (1978): 82–92.

Dahle, T. "An Objective and Comparative Study of Five Methods of Transmitting Information to Business and Industrial Employees." *Speech Monographs* 21 (1954): 21–28.

Dale, E. *Planning and Developing the Company Organization Structure.* New York: American Management Association, Research Report no. 20, 1952.

———. *The Great Organizers.* New York: McGraw-Hill, 1960.

Dalton, M. "Conflicts Between Staff and Line Managerial Officers." *American Sociological Review* 15 (1950): 342–351.

———. *Men Who Manage.* New York: Wiley, 1959.

———. "Changing Line-Staff Relationships." *Personnel Administration* 28 (1966): 3–5.

Dansereau, F.; Graen, G.; and Haga, W. "A Vertical Dyad Linkage Approach to Leadership with Formal Organizations." *Organizational Behavior and Human Performance* 13 (1975): 46–78.

Davis, K. "A Method of Studying Communication Patterns in Organizations." *Personnel Psychology* 6 (1953): 301–312.

———. *Human Relations at Work.* 3rd ed. New York: McGraw-Hill, 1967.

———. "Social Responsibility Is Inevitable." *California Management Review* XIX (1976): 14–20.

———. "The Case for and Against Business Assumption of Social Responsibility." In *Managing Corporate Social Responsibility,* edited by A. Carroll, pp. 35–45. Boston: Little, Brown, 1977.

Davis, K., and Blomstrom, R. *Business and Society: Environment and Responsibility.* 3rd ed. New York: McGraw-Hill, 1975.

Davis, S., and Lawrence, P. *Matrix.* Reading, Mass.: Addison-Wesley, 1977.

Dearborn, D., and Simon, H. "Selective Perception: A Note on the Departmental Identification of Executives." *Sociometry* 21 (1958): 140–144.

Delbecq, A.; Van de Ven, A.; and Gustafson, D. *Group Techniques for Program Planning.* Glenview, Ill.: Scott, Foresman, 1975.

Delman, M. "Pitfalls to Avoid in Starting Your Own Business." *American Legion Magazine* 90 (1971): 24–27, 41–44, 46.

Dessler, G. "An Investigation of the Path-Goal Theory of Leadership." PhD dissertation, City University of New York, 1973.

Deutermann, W., and Campbell, S. "Voluntary Part-Time Workers: A Growing Part of the Labor Force." *Monthly Labor Review* 101, no. 6 (1978): 3–10.

Digman, L. "How Well-Managed Organizations Develop Their Executives." *Organizational Dynamics* 7 (1978): 63–80.

Dilley, S., and Weygandt, J. "Measuring Social Responsibility: An Empirical Test." *Journal of Accountancy* 136 (1973): 62–70.

Dowling, W. "At GM: System 4 Builds Performance and Profits." *Organizational Dynamics* 3 (1975): 23–38.

Downey, H.; Sheridan, J.; and Slocum, J. "Analysis of Relationships Among Leader Behavior, Subordinate Job Performance and Satisfaction: A Path-Goal Approach." *Academy of Management Journal* 18 (1975): 253–262.

Downey, H., and Slocum, J. "Uncertainty: Measures, Research and Sources of Variation." *Academy of Management Journal* 18 (1975): 562–578.

Driscoll, J.; Carroll, D.; and Sprecher, T. "The First-Line Supervisor: Still the Man in the Middle." *Sloan Management Review* 19 (1978): 25–38.

Driscoll, J.; Cowger, G.; and Egan, R. "Private Managers and Public Myths—Public Managers and Private Myths." *Sloan Management Review* 21 (1979): 53–57.

Driver, M. "Individual Decision Making and Creativity." In *Organizational Behavior,* edited by S. Kerr. Columbus: Grid, 1979.

Drucker, P. *The Concept of Corporation.* New York: New American Library, 1964. Originally published in 1946.

———. "New Templates for Today's Organizations." *Harvard Business Review* 52 (1974): 45–53.

Dulz, T. "The Concept of Environmental Uncertainty: Lawrence and Lorsch Revisited." In *Proceedings of the 14th Annual Meeting of the Eastern Academy of Management,* edited by W. Allen and P. Weissenberg, pp. 72–75. Hartford, Conn., May 12-14, 1977.

Duncan, R. "Characteristics of Organizational Environments and Perceived Environmental Uncertainty." *Administrative Science Quarterly* 17 (1972): 313–327.

Dunham, R. "The Measurement and Dimensionality of Job Characteristics." *Journal of Applied Psychology* 61 (1976): 404–409.

Dunham, R.; Aldag, R.; and Brief, A. "Dimensionality of Task Design as Measured by the Job Diagnostic Survey." *Academy of Management Journal* 20 (1977): 209–233.

Dunnette, M., ed. *Work and Nonwork in the Year 2001.* Monterey, Calif.: Brooks/Cole, 1973.

Dunnette, M.; Campbell, J.; and Jaastad, K. "The Effect of Group Participation on Brainstorming Effectiveness for Two Industrial Samples." *Journal of Applied Psychology* 47 (1963): 30–37.

Dunnette, M.; Campbell, J.; and Lelevik, L. *Job Behavior Scales for Penney Co. Department Managers.* Minneapolis: Personnel Decisions, 1968.

Dun's Review. "The Boom in Word Processing," April 1978, pp. 24–25.

Elkins, A. "Toward a Positive Theory of Corporate Social Involvement." *Academy of Management Review* 2 (1977): 128–133.

Elkins, A., and Callaghan, P., eds. *A Managerial Odyssey: Problems in Business and Its Environment.* Reading, Mass.: Addison-Wesley, 1975.

English, J., and Marchione, A. "Nine Steps in Management Development." *Business Horizons* 20, no. 3 (1977): 88–94.

Entine, A. "Second Careers: Experience and Expectations." In *Where Have All the Robots Gone?: Worker Dissatisfaction in the 70s,* edited by H. Sheppard and N. Herrick, pp. 161–165. New York: Free Press, 1972.

Ernst and Ernst. *Social Responsibility Disclosure: 1976 Survey of Fortune 500 Annual Reports.* New York: 1976.

Estey, M. "The Retail Clerks." In *White-Collar Workers,* edited by A. Blum, M. Estey, J. Kuhn, W. Wildman, and L. Troy, pp. 47–82. New York: Random House, 1971.

Etzioni, A. *A Comparative Analysis of Complex Organizations,* 1960. 2nd ed. New York: Free Press, 1975.

Farr, J., and Joyce, W. "Outcome Usefulness in Expectancy Predictions of Work Efforts and Performance." In *Proceedings of the 14th Annual Meeting of the Eastern Academy of Management,* edited by W. Allen and P. Weissenberg, pp. 51–56. Hartford, Conn. May 12-14, 1977.

Fayol, H. *General and Industrial Management.* 1916. Translated by Constance Storrs. London: Pitman, 1949.

Federal Trade Commission, *Report on Motor Vehicle Industry,* House Document #468. Washington, D.C.: Government Printing Office, 1939.

Feeney, E. "Performance Audit, Feedback and Positive Reinforcement." *Training and Developmental Journal* 26 (1972): 8–13.

Ferster, C., and Skinner, B. *Schedules of Reinforcement.* New York: Appleton-Century-Crofts, 1957.

Festinger, L. *A Theory of Cognitive Dissonance.* Stanford, Calif.: Stanford University Press, 1957.

Fiedler, F. *A Theory of Leadership Effectiveness.* New York: McGraw-Hill, 1967.

———. "Validation and Extension of the Contingency Model of Leadership Effectiveness: A Review of Empirical Findings." *Psychological Bulletin* 76 (1971): 128–148.

Filley, A. *Interpersonal Conflict Resolution.* Glenview, Ill.: Scott, Foresman, 1975.

Filley, A.; House, R.; and Kerr, S. *Managerial Process and Organizational Behavior.* 2nd ed. Glenview, Ill.: Scott, Foresman, 1976.

Fisher, B. *Small Group Decision Making: Communication and the Group Process.* New York: McGraw-Hill, 1974.

Fleishman, E. "Leadership Climate, Human Relations Training and Supervisory Behavior." *Personnel Psychology* 6 (1953): 205–222.

Ford, H., with S. Crowther. *My Life and Work.* New York: Doubleday, Page, 1922.

———. *Today and Tomorrow.* New York: Doubleday, Page, 1926.

Ford, R. *Motivation Through the Work Itself.* New York: American Management Association, 1969.

Frederick, W. "Education for Social Responsibility: What the Business Schools Are Doing about It," *Working Paper Series.* Pittsburgh: Graduate School of Business, University of Pittsburgh, 1977.

French, J., and Raven, B. "The Bases of Social Power." In *Studies in Social Power,* edited by D. Cartwright, pp. 150–167. Ann Arbor: University of Michigan, Institute for Social Research, 1959.

French, W.; Bell, C.; and Zawacki, R., eds. *Organization Development.* Dallas: Business Publications, 1978.

Galbraith, J. *Designing Complex Organizations.* Reading, Mass.: Addison-Wesley, 1973.

———. *Organization Design.* Reading, Mass.: Addison-Wesley, 1977.

Gannon, M. "The Case Observational Method: A New Training Technique." *Training and Development Journal* 24 (1970): 39–41.

———. "Sources of Referral and Employee Turnover." *Journal of Applied Psychology* 55 (1971a): 226–228.

———. "Employee Perceptions of Promotion." *Personnel Journal* 50 (1971b): 213–215.

———. "Entrepreneurship and Labor Relations at the Ford Motor Co." *Marquette Business Review* XVI (1972): 63–75.

———. "Four Days, Forty Hours: A Case Study." *California Management Review* 17 (1974a): 74–81.

———. "A Profile of the Temporary Help Industry and Its Workers." *Monthly Labor Review* 97 (1974b): 44–49.

———. "Attitudes of Government Executives Toward Management Training." *Public Personnel Management* 4 (1975): 63–68.

———. "An Analysis of the Temporary Help Industry." In *Proceedings of a Conference on Labor Market Intermediaries, Sponsored by the National Commission for Manpower Policy,* Eli Ginzberg, Chairperson, pp. 195–225. Washington, D.C., November 16–17, 1977.

Gannon, M.; Pugh, K.; and Foreman, C. "The Influence of a Reduction in Force on the Attitudes of Engineers." *Academy of Management Journal* 16 (1973): 330–334.

Gannon, M., and Hendrickson, B. "Career Orientation and Job Satisfaction Among Working Wives." *Journal of Applied Psychology* 57 (1973): 339–340.

Gannon, M., and Paine, F. "Sources of Referral, Job Orientation, and Employee Effectiveness," In *Proceedings of the 32nd Annual Meeting of the Academy of Management,* edited by V. Mitchell, R. Barth, and F. Mitchell, pp. 36–38. Minneapolis, Minnesota, 1972.

———. "Unity of Command and Job Attitudes of Managers in a Bureaucratic Organization." *Journal of Applied Psychology* 59 (1974): 392–394.

Gannon, M.; Robeson, B.; and Norland, D. "A Behavioral Analysis of Shift Work." *Personnel Administrator,* in press.

Gemmill, G., and Heisler, W. "Machiavellianism as a Factor in Managerial Job Strain, Job Satisfaction and Upward Mobility." *Academy of Management Journal* 15 (1972): 51–64.

George, C. *The History of Management Thought.* 2nd ed. Englewood Cliffs, N.J.: Prentice-Hall, 1972.

Georgopoulos, B.; Mahoney, G.; and Jones, N. "A Path-Goal Approach to Productivity." *Journal of Applied Psychology* 41 (1957): 345–353.

Ghiselli, E. *Explorations in Managerial Talent.* Pacific Palisades, Calif.: Goodyear, 1971.

Gibb, J. "Communication and Productivity." *Personnel Administration* 27 (1964): 8–13, 45.

Gilbreth, F. *Primer of Scientific Management.* New York: Harper & Brothers, 1912.

Glueck, W. "Changing Hours of Work: A Review and Analysis of the Research." Paper presented at the Annual Meeting of the Academy of Management, August 15, 1977, at Orlando, Florida.

Goldner, F. "Demotion in Industrial Management." *American Sociological Review* 30 (1965): 714–725.

Goldthorpe, J.; Lockwood, D.; Bechhofer, F.; and Platt, J. *The Affluent Worker: Industrial Attitudes and Behavior.* London: Cambridge University Press, 1968.

Golembiewski, R., and Proehl, C. "A Survey of the Empirical Literature on Flexible Workhours: Character and Consequences of a Major Innovation." *Academy of Management Review* 3 (1978): 837–853.

Goleman, D. "Secrets of a Modern Mesmer." *Psychology Today* 11 (1977): 62, 63–65.

Gomersall, E., and Myers, S. "Breakthrough in On-the-Job Training." *Harvard Business Review* 44 (1966): 62–71.

Gordon, W. *Synectics.* New York: Harper & Brothers, 1961.

Gouldner, A. *Patterns of Industrial Bureaucracy.* New York: Free Press of Glencoe, 1954.

———. "Cosmopolitans and Locals: Toward an Analysis of Social Roles I and II." *Administrative Science Quarterly* 2 (1957): 281–306.

Graen, G.; Alvares, K.; and Orris, J. "Contingency Model of Leadership Effectiveness: Antecedent and Evidential Results." *Psychological Bulletin* 74 (1970): 285–296.

Graen, G., and Cashman, J. "A Role Making Model of Leadership in Formal Organizations: A Developmental Approach." In *Leadership Frontiers,* edited by J. Hunt and L. Larson. Kent, Ohio: Kent State University Press, 1975.

Graves, J. "Successful Management and Organizational Mugging." In *New Directions in Human Resource Management,* edited by J. Papp. Englewood Cliffs, N.J.: Prentice-Hall, 1978.

Greene, C. "Questions of Causation in the Path-Goal Theory of Leadership." *Academy of Management Journal* 22 (1977): 22–41.

Griffeth, R.; Hom, P.; DeNisi, A.; and Kirchner, W. "A Multinational Comparison of Managerial Attitudes." In the *Proceedings of the 40th Annual Meeting of the Academy of Management,* edited by R. Huseman, pp. 63–67. Detroit, Mich., Summer 1980.

Griffin, R., and Chonko, L. "Employee Preferences for Job Characteristics." In *Proceedings of the 37th Annual Meeting of the Academy of Management,* edited by R. Taylor, M. O'Connell, R. Zawicki, and P. Warrick, pp. 57–61. Orlando, Florida, 1977.

Griffin, R.; Moorhead, G.; Johnson, B.; and Chonko, L. "The Empirical Dimensionality of the Job Characteristic Survey." *Academy of Management Journal* 23 (1980): 772–777.

Guest, R. "Of Time and the Foreman." *Personnel* 32 (1956): 478–486.

Hackman, J., and Lawler, E. "Employee Reactions to Job Characteristics." *Journal of Applied Psychology* 55 (1971): 259–286.

Hackman, J., and Oldham, G. "Development of the Job Diagnostic Survey." *Journal of Applied Psychology* 60 (1975): 159–170.

———. "Motivation Through the Design of Work: Test of a Theory." *Organizational Behavior and Human Performance* 16 (1976): 250–279.

Haire, M. "Role-Perception in Labor-Management Relations: An Experimental Approach." *Industrial and Labor Relations Review* 8 (1955): 204–216.

Haire, M.; Ghiselli, E.; and Porter, L. *Managerial Thinking; An International Study.* New York: Wiley, 1966.

Haire, M., and Grunes, W. "Perceptual Defenses: Processes Protecting an Organized Perception of Another Personality." *Human Relations* 3 (1950): 403–412.

Hall, D. *Careers in Organizations.* Pacific Palisades, Calif.: Goodyear, 1976.

Hall, D., and Foster, L. "A Psychological Success Cycle and Goal Setting: Goals, Performance and Attitudes." *Academy of Management Journal* 20 (1977): 282–290.

Hall, D., and Hall, F. "What's New in Career Management." *Organizational Dynamics* 5 (1976): 3–16.

Hall, D., and Lawler, E. "Unused Potential in Research and Development Organizations." *Research Management* 12 (1969): 339–354.

Hall, D., and Morgan, M. "Career Development and Planning." In *Contemporary Problems in Personnel,* rev. ed., edited by W. Hammer and F. Schmidt. Chicago: St. Clair Press, 1977.

Hall, E. *The Hidden Dimension.* New York: Doubleday, 1968.

Hamner, C., and Organ, D. *Organizational Behavior.* Dallas: Business Publications, 1978.

Hamner, W., and Hamner, E. "Behavior Modification on the Bottom Line." *Organizational Dynamics* 21 (1976): 2–21.

Hampton, D. *Contemporary Management.* New York: McGraw-Hill, 1977.

Haney, W. *Communication and Organizational Behavior: Text and Cases.* 3rd ed. Homewood, Ill.: Irwin, 1973.

Harlow, D., and Hanke, J. *Behavior in Organizations.* Boston: Little, Brown, 1975.

Harris, H. *American Labor.* New Haven: Yale University Press, 1939.

Harrison, E. F. *The Managerial Decision Making Process.* Boston: Houghton Mifflin, 1975.

Harvey, E. "Technology and Structure of Organizations." *American Sociological Review* 33 (1968): 249–259.

Hay, R., and Gray, E. "Social Responsibilities of Business Managers." In *Social Issues in Business,* edited by F. Luthans and R. Hodgetts, pp. 104–113. New York: Macmillan, 1976.

Heald, M. *The Social Responsibilities of Business.* Cleveland: Case Western Reserve University Press, 1970.

Hedges, J. "New Patterns of Working Time." *Monthly Labor Review* 96 (1973): 3–8.

Hegarty, W., and Sims, H. "Some Determinants of Unethical Decision Behavior: An Experiment." *Journal of Applied Psychology* 63 (1978): 451–457.

Henderson, J. and Nutt, P. "On the Design of Planning Information Systems." *Academy of Management Review* 3 (1978): 774–785.

Hershey, R. "The Grapevine . . . Here to Stay But Not Beyond Control." *Personnel* 43 (1966): 62–66.

Herzberg, F. "One More Time: How Do you Motivate Employees?" *Harvard Business Review* 46 (1968): 53–62.

Herzberg, F.; Mausner, B.; and Snyderman, B. *The Motivation to Work.* New York: Wiley, 1959.

Hickson, D.; Pugh, D.; and Pheysey, D. "Operations Management and Organization Structure: An Empirical Reappraisal." *Administrative Science Quarterly* 14 (1969): 378–397.

Hill, R. "Managing Interpersonal Conflict in Project Teams." *Sloan Management Review* 18 (1977): 45–62.

Hinings, C.; Hickson, D.; Pennings, J.; and Schneck, R. "Structural Conditions of Intraorganizational Power." *Administrative Science Quarterly* 19 (1974): 22–44.

Hinrichs, J. "Communications Activity of Industrial Research Personnel." *Personnel Psychology* 17 (1964): 193–204.

Hlavacek, J., and Thompson, V. "Bureaucracy and New Product Innovation." *Academy of Management Journal* 16 (1973): 361–372.

Hollan, C., and Chesser, R. "The Relationship of Personal Influence Dissonance to Job Tension, Satisfaction and Involvement." *Academy of Management Journal* 19 (1976): 308–314.

Holloman, C., and Hendrick, H. "Adequacy of Group Decisions as a Function of the Decision-Making Process." *Academy of Management Journal* 15 (1972): 175–184.

Holmes, S. "Executive Perceptions of Corporate Social Responsibility." *Business Horizons* 19 (1976): 34–40.

Homans, G. *The Human Group.* New York: Harcourt, Brace & World, 1950.

———. *Social Behavior: Its Elementary Forms.* New York: Harcourt, Brace & World, 1961.

Hornaday, J., and Aboud, J. "Characteristics of Successful Entrepreneurs." *Personnel Psychology* 24 (1971): 141–153.

House, R. "A Path-Goal Theory of Leadership Effectiveness." *Administrative Science Quarterly* 16 (1971): 321–340.

House, R., and Miner, J. "Merging Management and Behavioral Theory: The Interaction Between Span of Control and Group Size." *Administrative Science Quarterly* 14 (1969): 451–466.

House, R., and Mitchell, T. "Path-Goal Theory of Leadership: A Theoretical and Empirical Analysis." *Contemporary Business* 3 (1974): 81–98.

Hovland, C.; Janis, I.; and Kelley, H. *Communication and Persuasion.* New Haven: Yale University Press, 1953.

Howard, A. "An Assessment of Assessment Centers." *Academy of Management Journal* 17 (1974): 115–134.

Hrebiniak, L. "Job Technology, Supervision, and Work-Group Structure." *Administrative Science Quarterly* 19 (1974): 395–410.

Huber, G. *Managerial Decision Making.* Glenview, Ill.: Scott, Foresman, 1980.

Hulin, C., and Blood, R. "Job Enlargement, Individual Differences, and Worker Responses." *Psychological Bulletin* 69 (1968): 41–55.

Hutchinson, J. *Organizations: Theory and Classical Concepts.* New York: Holt, Rinehart and Winston, 1967.

Ingham, G. *Size of Industrial Organization and Work Behaviour.* Cambridge, England: Cambridge University Press, 1970.

Jacoby, N. *Corporate Power and Social Responsibility.* New York: Macmillan, 1973.

James, J. "A Preliminary Study of the Size Determinant in Small Group Interaction." *American Sociological Review* 16 (1951): 474–477.

Janger, A. "Analyzing the Span of Control." *Management Record* 22 (1960): 7–10.

Janis, I. *Victims of Groupthink.* Boston: Houghton-Mifflin, 1972.

Janis, I., and Mann, L. "Effectiveness of Emotional Role-Playing on Opinion Change." *Journal of Abnormal and Social Psychology* 49 (1954): 84–90.

———. *Decision Making.* New York: Free Press, 1977.

Jaques, E. *Measurement of Responsibility.* New York: John Wiley and Sons, 1972.

Jaroslovsky, R. "Ohio's Mahoning Case Shows Rising Dilemma of Jobs vs. Pollution." *Wall Street Journal,* July 27, 1976, p. 1.

Johnson, M. "The Role of Help Wanted Ads." In *Labor Market Intermediaries,*

Special Report no. 82, edited by E. Ginzberg. Washington: National Commission for Manpower Policy, 1978.

Jolson, M., and Gannon, M. "The Influence of Wives on the Career Decisions of Businessmen." *Business Horizons* XV (1972): 83–88.

Josephson, M. *The Robber Barons.* New York: Harcourt, Brace & World, 1934.

Jurkus, A. "The Multiple Executive Office: Panacea or Selective Cure." *University of Michigan Business Review* XXX (1978): 15–19.

Kahn, R.; Wolfe, D.; Quinn, R.; and Snoek, J. *Organizational Stress: Studies in Role Conflict and Ambiguity.* New York: Wiley, 1964.

Kanter, R. "Power Failure in Management Circuits." *Harvard Business Review* 57, no. 4 (July-August 1979): 65–75.

Kast, F., and Rosenzweig, J. *Organization and Management: A Systems Approach.* 2nd ed. New York: McGraw-Hill, 1974.

Katz, D., and Kahn, R. *The Social Psychology of Organizations.* 1966. 2nd ed. New York: Wiley, 1978.

Katz, E., and Lazarsfeld, P. *Personal Influence.* Glencoe, Ill.: Free Press, 1955.

Keim, G. "Corporate Social Responsibility: An Assessment of the Enlightened Self-Interest Model." *Academy of Management Review* 3 (1978): 32–39.

Kepner, C., and Tregoe, B. *The Rational Manager.* New York: McGraw-Hill, 1965.

Kerr, C., and Siegel, A. "The Interindustry Propensity to Strike: An International Comparison." In *Industrial Conflict,* edited by A. Kornhauser, R. Dubin, and A. Ross, pp. 189–212. New York: McGraw-Hill, 1954.

Kerr, S. "Some Modifications in MBO as an OD Strategy." In the *Proceedings of the 32nd Annual Meeting of the Academy of Management,* edited by Vance Mitchell, R. Barth, and F. Mitchell, pp. 39–42. Minneapolis, Minn., 1972.

Kerr, S., and Jermier, J. "Substitutes for Leadership: Their Meaning and Measurement." *Organizational Behavior and Human Performance* 22 (1978): 375–403.

Khandwalla, P. *The Design of Organizations.* New York: Harcourt Brace Jovanovich, 1977.

Kilmann, R. "A Quasi-Experimental Paradigm for Organizational Development: Intervention Strategies vs. Environmental Conditions." In *Proceedings of the 12th Annual Conference of the Eastern Academy of Management,* edited by B. Kolasa, unpaginated, University Park, Penn., 1975.

Kilmann, R., and McKelvey, B. "The MAPS Route to Better Organization Design." *California Management Review* XVII (1975): 23–31.

Kim, J., and Hamner, W. "The Effect of Goal Setting, Feedback, and Praise on Productivity and Satisfaction in an Organizational Setting." *Journal of Applied Psychology* 61 (1976): 48–57.

Kreps, J. *Statement of the Secretary of Commerce before the State, Justice, Commerce, and Judiciary Subcommittee of the House Committee on Appropriations.* Washington, D.C.: U. S. Department of Commerce, January 23, 1978.

La Rue, D. "Court Decision on River Cleanup Surprises Valley Steel Executives." *Youngstown Vindicator,* September 18, 1977, p. 1.

Latham, G., and Baldes, J. "The Practical Significance of Locke's Theory of Goal Setting." *Journal of Applied Psychology* 60 (1975): 122–124.

Latham, G., and Kinne, S. "Improving Job Performance Through Training in Goal Setting." *Journal of Applied Psychology* 59 (1974): 20–24.

Latham, G., and Yukl, G. "A Review of Research on the Application of Goal Setting in Organizations." *Academy of Management Journal* 18 (1975): 824–845.

Lawler, E. *Pay and Organizational Effectiveness.* New York: McGraw-Hill, 1971.

Lawler, E., and Hackman, J. "Impact of Employee Participation in the Development of Pay Incentive Plans: A Field Experiment." *Journal of Applied Psychology* 53 (1969): 467–471.

Lawler, E., and Suttle, J. "A Causal Correlation Test of the Need Hierarchy Concept." *Organizational Behavior and Human Performance* 7 (1972): 265–287.

Lawrence, P.; Kolodny, H.; and Davis, S. "The Human Side of Matrix." *Organizational Dynamics* 6 (1977): 43–61.

Lawrence, P., and Lorsch, J. *Organization and Environment: Managing Differentiation and Integration.* Boston: Division of Research, Harvard Graduate School of Business, 1967.

Leadership. "What Is an Association?" May 1979, pp. 51–52.

Leavitt, H. "Applied Organizational Change in Industry: Structural Technological and Humanistic Approaches." In *Handbook of Organizations,* edited by J. March. Chicago: Rand McNally, 1965.

Leavitt, J., and Mueller, R. "Some Effects of Feedback on Communication." *Human Relations* 4 (1951): 401–410.

Leone, R., and Burke, D. *Women Returning to Work and Their Interaction with a Temporary Help Service.* Springfield, Va.: National Technical Information Service, 1976.

Lewin, K. "Group Decision and Social Change." In *Readings in Social Psychology,* 3rd ed., edited by E. Maccoby, T. Newcomb, and E. Hartley, pp. 330–344. New York: Holt, Rinehart and Winston, 1958.

Liden, R., and Graen, G. "Generalizability of the Vertical Dyad Linkage Model of Leadership." *Academy of Management Journal* 23 (1980): 451–465.

Lieberman, S. "The Effects of Changes in Roles on the Attitudes of Role Occupants." *Human Relations* 9 (1956): 385–402.

Likert, R. *New Patterns of Management.* New York: McGraw-Hill, 1961.

———. *The Human Organization.* New York: McGraw-Hill, 1967.

Lindblom, C. "The Science of Muddling Through." *Public Administration Review* 19 (1959): 79–88.

Lindsay, W., and Rue, L. "Impact of the Organization Environment on the Long-Range Planning Process: A Contingency View." *Academy of Management Journal* 23 (1980): 385–404.

Lippman, W. *Drift and Mastery.* Englewood Cliffs, N.J.: Prentice-Hall, 1961.

Lipset, S., and Malm, F. "First Jobs and Career Patterns." *American Journal of Economics and Sociology* 14 (1955): 247–261.

Lipset, S.; Trow, M.; and Coleman, J. *Union Democracy.* New York: Doubleday (Anchor Books), 1956.

Livingston, J. "Pygmalion in Management." *Harvard Business Review* 47 (1969): 81.

Locke, E. "Toward a Theory of Task Motivation and Incentives." *Organizational Behavior and Human Performance* 3 (1968): 157–189.

———. "The Nature and Causes of Job Satisfaction." In *Handbook of Industrial and Organizational Psychology,* edited by M. Dunnette, pp. 1297–1349. Chicago: Rand McNally, 1976.

Locke, E.; Feren, D.; McCaleb, V.; Shaw, K.; and Denny, A. "The Relative Effectiveness of Four Methods of Motivating Employee Performance." Paper presented at the N.A.T.O. International Conference on Changes in the Nature and Quality of Working Life, August 1979, at Thessaloniki, Greece.

Loeb, S., and Gannon, M. "Educational Factors, Professional Activity and Job Tenure Among Public Accountants." *Journal of Accountancy* 141, no. 4 (April 1976): 88–89.

Logan, N.; O'Reilly, C.; and Roberts, K. "Job Satisfaction Among Part-Time and Full-Time Employees." *Journal of Vocational Behavior* 3 (1973): 33–41.

Long, R. "Job Attitudes and Organizational Performance Under Employee Ownership." *Academy of Management Journal* 23 (1980): 726–737.

Louis, A. "They're Striking Some Strange Bargains at Diamond Shamrock." *Fortune* 93 (1976): 144–146, 148–153, 156.

Lowin, A., and Craig, J. "The Influence of Level of Performance on Managerial Style: An Experimental Object-Lesson in the Ambiguity of Correlational Data." *Organizational Behavior and Human Performance* (1968): 440–458.

Luthans, F., and Kreitner, R. *Organizational Behavior Modification.* Glenview, Ill.: Scott, Foresman, 1975.

Luthans, F., and White, D. "Behavior Modification: Application to Manpower Management." *Personnel Administrator* 17 (1971): 41–47.

McCarthy, C. "The Benefits of Bureaucratic Sin." *Washington Post,* November 11, 1979, p. K4.

McCaskey, M. "A Contingency Approach to Planning: Planning with Goals and Planning without Goals." *Academy of Management Journal* 17 (1974): 281–291.

McClelland, D. *The Achieving Society.* New York: Van Nostrand, 1961.

———. "Love and Power: The Psychological Signals of War." *Psychology Today* 8 (1975): 44–48.

McClelland, D., and Burnham, D. "Power Is the Great Motivator." *Harvard Business Review* 54 (1976): 100–110.

McClelland, D., and Winter, D. *Motivating Economic Achievement.* New York: Free Press, 1969.

Maccoby, M. *The Gamesman: The New Corporate Leaders.* New York: Simon & Schuster, 1977.

McConnell, C. "Why Is U.S. Productivity Slowing Down?" *Harvard Business Review* 57 (1979): 36–61.

McCormick, E., and Tiffin, J. *Industrial Psychology.* 6th ed. Englewood Cliffs, N.J.: Prentice-Hall, 1974.

MacCrimmon, K. "Managerial Decision Making." In *Contemporary Management,* edited by J. McGuire, pp. 445–494. Englewood Cliffs, N.J.: Prentice-Hall, 1974.

McGregor, D. *The Human Side of Enterprise.* New York: McGraw-Hill, 1960.

McGuire, J. "Management in the Future." In *Contemporary Management,* edited by J. McGuire, pp. 639–653. Englewood Cliffs, N.J.: Prentice-Hall, 1974.

McKelvey, B., and Kilmann, R. "Organization Design: A Participative Multivariate Approach." *Administrative Science Quarterly* 20 (1975): 24–36.

McKenney, J., and Keen, P. "How Managers' Minds Work." *Harvard Business Review* 52 (1974): 79–90.

Mahoney, T.; Jerdee, T.; and Carroll, S. "The Job(s) of Management." *Industrial Relations* 4 (1965): 97–110.

Maier, N. *Psychology in Industry.* 2nd ed. Boston: Houghton Mifflin, 1955.

———. *Psychology in Industrial Organizations.* 4th ed. Boston: Houghton Mifflin, 1973.

Maier, N., and Hoffman, L. "Quality of First and Second Solutions in Group Problem Solving." *Journal of Applied Psychology* 44 (1960): 278–283.

Maier, N.; Hoffman, L.; and Read, W. "Superior-Subordinate Communication: The Relative Effectiveness of Managers Who Held Their Subordinates' Positions." *Personnel Psychology* 16 (1963): 1–11.

March, J., and Feigenbaum, E. "Latent Motives, Group Discussion, and the 'Quality' of Group Decisions in a Non-Objective Decision Problem." *Sociometry* 23 (1960): 50–56.

March, J., and Simon, H. *Organizations.* New York: Wiley, 1958.

Marcus, S., and Walters, K. "Assault on Managerial Autonomy." *Harvard Business Review* 56 (1978): 57–66.

Margerison, C., and Glube, R. "Leadership Decision-Making: An Empirical Test of the Vroom and Yetton Model." *Journal of Management Studies* 16 (1979): 45–55.

Marion, B., and Trieb, S. "Job Orientation: A Factor in Employee Performance and Turnover." *Personnel Journal* 48 (1969): 779–804, 831.

Marrow, A.; Bowers, D.; and Seashore, S. *Management by Participation.* New York: Harper & Row, 1967.

Martin, N. "Differential Decisions in the Management of an Industrial Plant." *Journal of Business* 28 (1956): 249–260.

Maslow, A. "A Theory of Human Motivation." *Psychological Review* 50 (1943): 370–396.

———. *Motivation and Personality.* 1954. 2nd ed. New York: Harper & Row, 1970.

Mawhinney, T. "Operant Terms and Concepts in the Description of Individual Work Behavior: Some Problems of Interpretation, Application and Evaluation." *Journal of Applied Psychology* 60 (1975): 704–712.

Mechanic, D. "Sources of Power of Lower Participants in Complex Organizations." *Administrative Science Quarterly* 7 (1962): 349–364.

Merton, R. *Social Theory and Social Structure.* Rev. ed. Glencoe, Ill.: Free Press, 1957.

Michels, R. *Political Parties.* New York: Dover, 1959. Originally published in 1915.

Miles, R. *Theories of Management.* New York: McGraw-Hill, 1975.

Miles, R., and Snow, C. *Organizational Strategy, Structure, and Process.* New York: McGraw-Hill, 1978.

Miller, D., and Starr, M. *The Structure of Human Decisions.* Englewood Cliffs, N.J.: Prentice-Hall, 1967.

Mills, T. *The Sociology of Small Groups.* Englewood Cliffs, N.J.: Prentice-Hall, 1967.

Miner, J. *The Management Process: Theory, Research, and Practice.* New York: Macmillan, 1973.

———. *The Human Constraint.* Washington, D.C.: Bureau of National Affairs, 1974.

———. *The Challenge of Managing.* Philadelphia: Saunders, 1975.

Miner, J., and Heaton, E. "Company Orientation as a Factor in the Readership of Employee Publications." *Personnel Psychology* 12 (1959): 607–618.

Mintzberg, H. "The Manager's Job: Folklore and Fact." *Harvard Business Review* 53 (1975): 49–61.

Mintzberg, H. *The Nature of Managerial Work.* Englewood Cliffs, N.J.: Prentice-Hall, 1980. Originally published in 1973.

Mobley, W., and Meglino, B. "A Behavioral Choice Model Analysis of the Budget Allocation Behavior of Academic Deans." *Academy of Management Journal* 20 (1977): 564–572.

Morasky, R. "Self-Shaping Training Systems and Flexible-Model Behavior, i.e., Sales Interviewing." *Educational Technology* 11 (1971): 57–59.

Morrison, E. *Developing Computer-Based Employee Information Systems.* New York: American Management Association, 1969.

Morse, N., and Reimer, E. "The Experimental Change of a Major Organization Variable." *Journal of Abnormal and Social Psychology* 52 (1956): 120–129.

Mott, P.; Mann, F.; McLoughlin, Q.; and Warwick, D. *Shift Work: The Social, Psychological and Physical Consequences.* Ann Arbor: The University of Michigan Press, 1965.

Muczyk, J. "Dynamics and Hazards of MBO Application." *Personnel Administrator* 24 (1979): 51–61.

Mullen, J. "Personality Polarization as an Equilibrating Force in a Large Organization." *Human Organization* 25 (1966a): 330–338.

———. *Personality and Productivity in Management.* New York: Columbia University Press, 1966b.

Murphy, P. "An Evolution: Corporate Social Responsiveness." *University of Michigan Business Review* XXX (1978): 19–25.

Murray, H. "The Effect of Fear upon Estimates of the Maliciousness of Other Personalities." *Journal of Social Psychology* 4 (1933): 310–329.

Nash, A. "Vocational Interests of Effective Managers: A Review of the Literature." *Personnel Psychology* 25 (1965): 21–37.

Nash, A., and Carroll, S. *The Management of Compensation.* Belmont, Calif.: Wadsworth, 1975.

Nash, A.; Muczyk, J.; and Vettori, F. "The Relative Practical Effectiveness of Programmed Instruction." *Personnel Psychology* 24 (1971): 397–418.

National Association of Manufacturers. *Effectively Employing the Hard Core.* New York: 1968.

Nealey, S. "Pay and Benefit Preference." *Industrial Relations* 3 (1964): 7–12.

Nelson, G. "Let a Thousand Small Businesses Bloom." *Business and Society Review* 25 (1978): 50–54.

Nevins, A., and Hill, F. *Ford: The Times, the Man, the Company,* vol. 1. New York: Scribner, 1954.

———. *Ford: Expansion and Challenge, 1915–1933,* vol. 2. New York: Scribner, 1957.

———. *Ford: Decline and Rebirth, 1933–1962,* vol. 3. New York: Scribner, 1963.

Newstrom, J. "Evaluating the Effectiveness of Training Methods." *Personnel Administrator* 25 (1980): 55–60.

Newstrom, J., and Ruch, W. "The Ethics of Management and the Management of Ethics." *Michigan State University Business Topics* 23 (Winter 1975): 29–37.

Newsweek. "Special Report: The Energy Crisis," July 16, 1979, pp. 23–26, 31–33.

Nord, W. "Beyond the Teaching Machine: The Neglected Area of Operant Conditioning in the Theory and Practice of Management." *Organizational Behavior and Human Performance* 4 (1969): 375–401.

Nord, W., and Costigan, R. "Worker Adjustment to the Four-Day Week: A Longitudinal Study." *Journal of Applied Psychology* 58 (1973): 60–66.

Oldham, G.; Hackman, J.; and Pearce, J. "Conditions Under Which Employees Respond Positively to Enriched Work." *Journal of Applied Psychology* 61 (1976): 395–403.

Opshal, R., and Dunnette, M. "The Role of Financial Compensation in Industrial Motivation." *Psychological Bulletin* 66 (1966): 94–118.

O'Reilly, C. "The Intentional Distortion of Information in Organizational Communication: A Laboratory and Field Experiment." *Human Relations* 31 (1978): 173–193.

Ostlund, L. "Attitudes of Managers Toward Corporate Social Responsibility." *California Management Review* XIX (1977): 35–49.

Ouchi, W., and Maguire, M. "Organizational Control: Two Functions." *Administrative Science Quarterly* 4 (1975): 559–569.

Paine, F.; Carroll, S.; and Leete, B. "A Study of Need Satisfactions in Managerial Level Personnel in a Government Agency." *Journal of Applied Psychology* 50 (1966): 247–249.

Palmore, E. "Predicting Longevity: A Follow-up Controlling for Age." *Gerontologist* 9 (1969): 247–250.

Parkinson, C. *Parkinson's Law.* Boston: Houghton Mifflin, 1957.

Parsons, H. M. "What Happened at Hawthorne?" *Science* 183 (1974): 922–932.

Parsons, T. *Structure and Process in Modern Society.* New York: Free Press, 1960.

Patton, A. "Government's Revolving Door." *Business Week,* September 22, 1974, pp. 12–13.

Pepitone, A., and Kleiner, R. "The Effects of Threat and Frustration on Group Cohesiveness." *Journal of Abnormal and Social Psychology* 54 (1957): 192–199.

Perrow, C. *Complex Organizations: A Critical Essay.* Glenview, Ill.: Scott, Foresman, 1972.

Petty, M., and Gordon, L. "Moderating Effects of Sex of Supervisor and Subordinate on Relationships Between Supervising Behavior and Subordinate Satisfaction." *Journal of Applied Psychology* 60 (1975): 624–628.

Pondy, L. "Organizational Conflict: Concepts and Models." *Administrative Science Quarterly* 12 (1967): 296–320.

Porter, L. *Organizational Patterns of Managerial Job Attitudes.* New York: American Foundation for Management Research, 1964.

Porter, L., and Lawler, E. *Managerial Attitudes and Performance.* Homewood, Ill.: Irwin-Dorsey, 1968.

Porter, L.; Lawler, E.; and Hackman, J. *Behavior in Organizations.* New York: McGraw-Hill, 1975.

Porter, L., and Mitchell, V. "Comparative Study of Need Satisfactions in Military and Business Hierarchies." *Journal of Applied Psychology* 51 (1967): 139–144.

Quinn, J. *Logical Incrementalism.* Homewood, Ill.: Irwin, 1980.

Quinn, R.; Feldt, J.; and Kinney, T. "Sparse Space and Flying Files: An Exploratory Study of Organizational Relocations." In *Proceedings of the 16th Annual Conference of the Eastern Academy of Management,* edited by John Sheridan and Joseph Alutto, pp. 116–120. Newport, R.I., 1979.

Quinn, R.; Staines, G.; and McCullough, M. *Job Satisfaction: Is There a Trend?* U.S. Department of Labor, Manpower Research Monograph no. 30, Manpower Administration, 1974.

Rafey, D. "Computers and Management Structure: Some Empirical Findings Reexamined." *Human Relations* 30 (1977): 963–971.

Raia, A., and Rossy, G. *The Future of Management by Objectives.* Los Angeles: Graduate School of Management, University of California at Los Angeles, 1979.

Rauschenberger, J.; Schmitt, N.; and Hunter, J. "A Test of the Need Hierarchy Concept by a Markov Model of Change in Need Strength." *Administrative Science Quarterly* 25 (1980): 654–670.

Read, W. "Upward Communication in Industrial Hierarchies." *Human Relations* 15 (1962): 3–15.

Reed-Mendenhall, D., and Willard, C. "Orientation: A Training and Development Tool." *Personnel Administrator* 25 (1980): 40–44.

Reid, G. "Job Search and the Effectiveness of Job-Finding Methods." *Industrial and Labor Relations Review* 25 (1972): 479–495.

Reif, W. *Computer Technology and Management Organization.* Iowa City: University of Iowa Press, Bureau of Business and Economic Research, 1968.

Reilly, R.; Tenopyr, M.; and Sperling, S. "Effects of Job Previews on Job Acceptance and Survival of Telephone Operator Candidates." *Journal of Applied Psychology* 64 (1979): 218–220.

Reimann, B., and Inzerilli, G. "A Comparative Analysis of Empirical Research on Technology and Structure." *Journal of Management* 5 (1979): 167–192.

Reiss, G. "Steel Recession Foiled Kirwan in Attempt to Keep Mills Open." *Youngstown Vindicator,* January 6, 1980, p. A1.

Reitz, H. "Managerial Attitudes and Perceived Contingencies Between Performance and Organizational Response." In *Proceedings of the 31st Annual Meeting of the Academy of Management,* edited by R. Higgins, P. Croke, and J. Veiga, pp. 227–238. Atlanta, Georgia, 1971.

Renwick, P.; Lawler, E.; and the staff of *Psychology Today.* "What You Really Want from Your Job." *Psychology Today* 11 (May 1978): 53–65.

Reynolds, L. *The Structure of Labor Markets.* Westport, Conn.: Greenwood Press, 1971.

Rice, B. "Measuring Executive Muscle." *Psychology Today* 12, no. 7 (1978): 95–96, 99–100, 105–106, 109–110.

Ricklefs, R. "More Executives Take Work-Related Courses to Keep Up, Advance." *Wall Street Journal,* March 3, 1980, pp. 1, 25.

Riesman, D. *The Lonely Crowd.* New Haven: Yale University Press, 1950.

Rizzo, J.; House, R.; and Lirtzman, S. "Role Conflict and Ambiguity in Complex Organizations." *Administrative Science Quarterly* 15 (1970): 150–163.

Robinson, J.; Athanasiou, R.; and Head, K. *Measures of Occupational Attitudes and Occupational Characteristics.* Ann Arbor: University of Michigan, Survey Research Center, 1969.

Roe, A., and Baruch, R. "Occupational Changes in the Adult Years." *Personnel Administration* 30 (1967): 26–32.

Roethlisberger, F., and Dickson, W. *Management and the Worker.* Cambridge, Mass.: Harvard University Press, 1939.

Rollins, S., and Charters, W. "The Diffusion of Information Within Secondary School Staffs." *Journal of Social Psychology* 65 (1965): 167–178.

Rosen, B., and D'Andrade, R. "The Psychological Origins of Achievement Motivation." *Sociometry* 22 (1959): 185–218.

Rosen, B., and Jerdee, T. "Sex Stereotyping in the Executive Suite." *Harvard Business Review* 52 (1974): 133–142.

———. "The Nature of Job-Related Stereotypes." *Journal of Applied Psychology* 61 (1976): 180–183.

Rosenthal, R. *Experimenter Effects in Behavioral Research.* New York: Appleton-Century-Crofts, 1966.

Rosnow, R., and Kimmel, A. "Lives of a Rumor." *Psychology Today* 13 (1979): 88–92.

Rotchford, N., and Glick, W. "Comparative Model of Job Responses Across Work Schedules." Paper delivered at the 1979 Annual Meeting of the American Psychological Association at New York City.

Rummel, R., and Heenan, D. "How Multinationals Analyze Political Risk." *Harvard Business Review* 56 (1978): 67–76.

Sales, S. "Supervisory Style and Productivity: Review and Theory." *Personnel Psychology* 19 (1966): 275–294.

Sawyer, K. "Unpaid Time Off Studied." *Washington Post,* December 28, 1977, pp. A1, A5.

Sayles, L. *Behavior of Industrial Work Groups.* New York: Wiley, 1958.

———. "Matrix Management: The Structure with a Future." *Organizational Dynamics* 5 (Autumn 1976): 2–17.

Schein, E. "Management Development as a Process of Influence." *Industrial Management Review* 2 (1961): 149–172.

———. "Increasing Organizational Effectiveness Through Better Human Resource Planning and Development." *Sloan Management Review* 19 (1977): 1–20.

———. *Organizational Psychology.* 3rd ed. Englewood Cliffs, N.J.: Prentice-Hall, 1979.

Schelling, T. *The Strategy of Conflict.* Cambridge, Mass.: Harvard University Press, 1960.

Schermerhorn, J.; Snelson, A.; and Leader, G. "Women in Management: The MBA Student Perspective." In *Proceedings of the 35th Annual Meeting of the Academy of Management,* edited by A. Bedeian, A. Armenakis, W. Holley, and H. Field, pp. 451–453. New Orleans, Louisiana, August 10–13, 1975.

Schlosser, M. "Liking as a Function of Physical Attractiveness and Task Performance." Master's thesis, University of Florida, 1969.

Schmidt, S., and Kochan, T. "Conflict: Toward Conceptual Clarity." *Administrative Science Quarterly* 17 (1972): 359–370.

Schneider, B., and Locke, E. "A Critique of Herzberg's Classification System and a Suggested Revision." *Organizational Behavior and Human Performance* 6 (1971): 441–458.

Schneier, C. "Behavior Modification in Management: A Review and Critique." *Academy of Management Journal* 17 (1974): 528–548.

———. "Behavior Modification in Organizations." Paper presented at the 13th Annual Meeting of the Eastern Academy of Management, Washington, D.C., May 13–15, 1976.

Schriesheim, C., and von Glinow, M. "The Path Goal Theory of Leadership: A Theoretical and Empirical Analysis." *Academy of Management Journal* 20 (1977): 398–405.

Schriesheim, J., and Schriesheim, C. "A Test of the Path-Goal Theory of Leadership and Some Suggestions for Future Research." *Personnel Psychology* 33 (1980): 349–370.

Schuh, A. "The Predictability of Employee Tenure: A Review of the Literature." *Personnel Psychology* 20 (1967): 133–152.

Schuler, R. "A Path-Goal Theory of Leadership: An Empirical Investigation." PhD dissertation, Michigan State University, 1974.

Schumpeter, J. *The Theory of Economic Development.* Cambridge, Mass.: Harvard University Press, 1934.

Schutte, T. "Executives' Perception of Business Ethics." *Journal of Purchasing* 1 (1965): 38–52.

Schwenk, C., and Cosier, R. "Effects of the Expert, Devil's Advocate, and Dialectical Inquiry Methods on Prediction Performance." *Organizational Behavior and Human Performance* 26 (1980): 409–424.

Sease, D. R. "U.S. Steel Slates Several Closings, Operating Costs." *Wall Street Journal,* November 12, 1979, p. 2.

Segal, D.; Lynch, B.; and Blair, J. "The Changing American Soldier: Work-related Attitudes of U.S. Army Personnel in World War II and the 1970s." *American Journal of Sociology* 85 (1979): 95–108.

Seiler, J. "Diagnosing Interdepartmental Conflict." *Harvard Business Review* 41 (1963): 121–132.

Serbein, O. *Educational Activities of Business.* Washington, D.C.: American Council on Education, 1961.

Shannon, C., and Weaver, W. *The Mathematical Theory of Communication.* Urbana, Ill.: University of Illinois Press, 1949.

Shapero, A. "Who Starts New Businesses? The Displaced, Uncomfortable Entrepreneur." *Psychology Today* 9 (1975): 83–86, 88, 133.

Shaw, M. "An Overview of Small Group Behavior." In *Contemporary Topics in Social Psychology,* pp. 335–368. Morristown, N.J.: General Learning Press, 1976.

Shepard, C. *Small Groups.* San Francisco: Chandler, 1964.

Sheridan, J.; Slocum, J.; and Min, B. "Motivational Determinants of Job Performance." *Journal of Applied Psychology* 66 (1975): 119–121.

Sherif, M.; Harvey, O.; White, B.; Hood, W.; and Sherif, C. *Intergroup Conflict and Cooperation: The Robbers Cave Experiment.* Norman: University of Oklahoma Book Exchange, 1961.

Sherif, M., and Sherif, C. *Groups in Harmony and Tension.* New York: Harper & Row, 1953.

Shull, F.; Delbecq, A.; and Cummings, L. *Organizational Decision Making.* New York: McGraw-Hill, 1970.

Shultz, G., and Coleman, J., eds. *Labor Problems: Cases and Readings.* New York: McGraw-Hill, 1959.

Siegel, J. "Machiavellianism, MBA's and Managers: Leadership Correlates and Socializational Effects." *Academy of Management Journal* 16 (1973): 404–412.

Simon, H. *The Shape of Automation for Men and Management.* New York: Harper & Row, 1965.

———. Administrative Behavior. 1947. 3rd ed. New York: Free Press, 1976.

Simonds, R. "Is Organization Structure Reflecting New Techniques and Theory?" *Michigan State University Business Topics* 17 (1969): 65–71.

Simpson, R. "Vertical and Horizontal Communication in Formal Organizations." *Administrative Science Quarterly* 4 (1959): 188–196.

Sims, H.; Szilagyi, A.; and McKeney, D. "Antecedents of Work Related Experiences." *Academy of Management Journal* 19 (1976): 547–559.

Skinner, B. *Science and Human Behavior.* New York: Macmillan, 1953.

Sloan, A. *My Years with General Motors.* Edited by J. McDonald and C. Stevens. New York: Doubleday, 1963.

Slusher, A.; Van Dyke, J.; and Rose, G. "Technical Competence of Group Leaders, Managerial Role, and Productivity in Engineering Design Groups." *Academy of Management Journal* 15 (1972): 197–204.

Soelberg, P. "Unprogrammed Decision Making." *Industrial Management Review* 8 (1967): 19–29.

Sommers, D. and Eck, A. "Occupational Mobility in the American Labor Force." *Monthly Labor Review* 100, no. 1 (1977): 3–19.

Sorcher, M., and Goldstein, A. "A Behavior Modeling Approach to Training." *Personnel Administration* 35 (1972): 35–41.

Staines, G., and Quinn, R. "American Workers Evaluate the Quality of Their Jobs." *Monthly Labor Review* 102 (1979): 3–12.

Steele, F. *Physical Settings and Organization Development.* Reading, Mass.: Addison-Wesley, 1973.

Steinberg, H. "Your Wardrobe Is Your Weapon." *MBA* 9 (1975): 45–49.

Steiner, G. *Business and Society.* 2nd ed. New York: Random House, 1975.

Steiner, G., ed. *Creative Organization.* Chicago: University of Chicago Press, 1965.

Stewart, R. *Managers and Their Jobs.* London: Macmillan, 1967.

Stinson, J., and Johnson, T. "The Path-Goal Theory of Leadership: A Partial Test and Suggested Refinement." In *Proceedings of the 17th Annual Meeting of the Mid-West Division of the Academy of Management,* edited by K. Rowland, pp. 18–36. Kent, Ohio, April 1974.

Stogdill, R., and Coons, A., eds. *Leader Behavior: Its Description and Measurement.* Columbus: Ohio State University, Bureau of Business Research, Research Monograph no. 88, 1957.

Stoner, J. "A Comparison of Individual and Group Decisions Involving Risk." Master's thesis, Massachusetts Institute of Technology, School of Industrial Management, 1961. As reported in M. Wallach; N. Kogan; and D. Bem. "Group Influences on Individual Risk Taking." *Journal of Abnormal and Social Psychology* 65 (1962): 75–86.

Straub, A.; Sorensen, P.; and Babcock, R. "Organizational Variables and the Success of MBO: A Research Note." *Journal of Management Studies* 13 (1976): 84–86.

Strauss, G., and Sayles, L. *Personnel.* 3rd ed. Englewood Cliffs, N.J.: Prentice-Hall, 1972.

Sturdivant, F. *Business and Society: A Managerial Approach.* Homewood, Ill.: Irwin, 1977.

Sturdivant, F., and Ginter, J. "Corporate Social Responsiveness: Management Attitudes and Economic Performance." *California Management Review* XIX (1977): 30–39.

Sturdivant, F., and Robinson, L. *The Corporate Social Challenge: Cases and Commentaries.* Homewood, Ill.: Irwin, 1977.

Summer, C. *Strategic Behavior in Business and Government.* Boston: Little, Brown, 1980.

Susman, G. *Autonomy at Work.* New York: Praeger, 1976.

Sutton, H., and Porter, L. "A Study of the Grapevine in a Governmental Organization." *Personnel Psychology* 21 (1968): 223–230.

Sward, K. *The Legend of Henry Ford.* New York: Rinehart, 1948.

Swinyard, A., and Bond, F. "Who Gets Promoted?" *Harvard Business Review* 58 (1980): 6–8, 12, 14, 18.

Tannenbaum, A. *Control in Organizations.* New York: McGraw-Hill, 1968.

Tannenbaum, R., and Schmidt, W. "How to Choose a Leadership Pattern." *Harvard Business Review* 51 (1973): 162–180.

Taylor, F. *The Principles of Scientific Management.* New York: Harper & Brothers, 1911.

Thayer, L. *Communication and Communication Systems.* Homewood, Ill.: Irwin, 1968.

Thamhain, H., and Wilemon, D. "Leadership Conflict and Program Management Effectiveness." *Sloan Management Review* 19 (1977): 69–90.

Thibaut, J. "An Experimental Study of the Cohesiveness of Underprivileged Groups." *Human Relations* 3 (1950): 251–278.

Thomas, K. "Conflict and Conflict Management." In *Handbook of Industrial and Organizational Psychology,* edited by M. Dunnette, pp. 889–935. Chicago: Rand McNally, 1976.

———. "Toward Multi-Dimensional Values in Teaching: The Example of Conflict Behaviors." *Academy of Management Review* 2 (1977): 484–490.

Thomas, K., and Schmidt, W. "A Survey of Managerial Interests with Respect to Conflict." *Academy of Management Journal* 19 (1976): 315–318.

Thompson, J. *Organizations in Action.* New York: McGraw-Hill, 1967.

Thune, S., and House, R. "Where Long-Range Planning Pays Off." *Business Horizons* 13 (1970): 81–87.

Tillman, R. "Problems in Review: Committees on Trial." *Harvard Business Review* 38 (1960): 6–8.

Tosi, H.; Aldag, R.; and Storey, R. "On the Measurement of the Environment: An Assessment of the Lawrence and Lorsch Environmental Uncertainty Questionnaire." *Administrative Science Quarterly* 18 (1973): 27–36.

Trist, E., and Bamforth, K. "Some Social and Psychological Consequences of the Longwall Method of Coal-Getting." *Human Relations* 4 (1951): 3–38.

Tushman, M. "Special Boundary Roles in the Innovation Process." *Administrative Science Quarterly* 22 (1977): 587–605.

Ullman, J. "Employee Referrals: Prime Tools for Recruiting Workers." *Personnel* 43 (1966): 30–35.

U.S. Bureau of Labor Statistics. *Occupational Outlook Handbook, 1978–1979.* Washington, D.C.: Government Printing Office, 1978.

U.S. Bureau of Labor Statistics. *Occupational Outlook Handbook.* Washington, D.C.: Government Printing Office, 1976–1977.

U.S. Bureau of Labor Statistics. *Occupational Outlook Handbook.* Washington, D.C.: Government Printing Office, 1974–1975.

U.S. Department of Health, Education and Welfare. *Students Enrolled for Advanced Degrees, Fall 1975.* Washington, D.C.: Government Printing Office, 1977.

U.S. Department of Labor, *Employment and Earnings* 13, no. 6 (1967): 22.

U.S. Department of Labor. *Employment and Earnings* 20, no. 12 (1974): 24.

U.S. Department of Labor. *Employment and Earnings* 21, no. 9 (1975): 19–21.

U.S. Department of Labor. *Employment and Earnings* 23, no. 6 (1977): 27.

U.S. Department of Labor. *Employment and Earnings* 27, no. 8 (1980): 49.

U.S. Office of Personnel Management. "OPM Releases Attitude Survey Results." *News,* November 9, 1979, pp. 1–15.

Utterback, J. "Environmental Analysis and Forecasting." In *Strategic Management,* edited by D. Schendel and C. Hofer, pp. 134–144. Boston: Little, Brown, 1979.

Vancil, R. "The Accuracy of Long-Range Planning." *Harvard Business Review* 48 (1970): 98–101.

Vecchio, R. "An Empirical Examination of the Validity of Fiedler's Model of Leadership Effectiveness." *Organizational Behavior and Human Performance* 19 (1977): 180–206.

Viteles, M. *Motivation and Morale in Industry.* New York: Norton, 1953.

Vroom, V. *Work and Motivation.* New York: Wiley, 1964.

———. "Organizational Choice: A Study of Pre- and Post-Decision Processes." *Organizational Behavior and Human Performance* 1 (1966): 212–225.

Vroom, V., and Jago, A. "On the Validity of the Vroom-Yetton Model." *Journal of Applied Psychology* 63 (1978): 151–162.

Vroom, V., and Yetton, P. *Leadership and Decision Making.* Pittsburgh: University of Pittsburgh Press, 1973.

Walker, C., and Guest, R. *The Man on the Assembly Line.* Cambridge, Mass.: Harvard University Press, 1952.

Wall Street Journal. "EPA Exemption for Eight Steel Plants is Ruled Invalid." September 19, 1977, p. 14.

———. "Lykes to Slash Steel Operations at Youngstown." September 20, 1977, p. 2.

———. "LTV, Lykes Arrange $275 Million in Credit for Steelmaking Units." December 4, 1978, p. 37.

———. "Labor Letter." August 28, 1979, p. 1.

Walton, C., and Cleveland, F. *Corporations on Trial: The Electric Cases.* Belmont, Calif.: Wadsworth, 1964.

Weaver, C. "Negro-White Differences in Job Satisfaction." *Business Horizons* XVII (1974a): 67–78.

———. "Sex Differences in Job Satisfaction." *Business Horizons* XVII (1974b): 42–49.

———. "Job Satisfaction in the United States in the 1970's." *Journal of Applied Psychology* 65 (1980): 364–367.

Weber, M. *The Protestant Ethic and the Spirit of Capitalism.* Translated by T. Parsons. New York: Scribner, 1930.

———. *The Theory of Social and Economic Organization.* Translated by A. Henderson and T. Parsons. New York: Free Press, 1947.

Webster, E. *Decision Making in the Employment Interview.* Montreal: McGill University, Applied Psychology Centre, 1964.

Weimer, A. "Corporate Boards: Improving Their Job Performance." *Business Horizons* 22 (1979): 28–31.

Weissenberg, P., and Kavanagh, M. "The Independence of Initiating Structure and Consideration: A Review of the Literature." *Personnel Psychology* 25 (1972): 119–130.

Weitz, J. "Job Expectancy and Survival." *Journal of Applied Psychology* 40 (1956): 294–300.

Wheeler, K.; Gurman, R.; and Tarnowieski, D. *The Four-Day Week.* New York: American Management Association, 1972.

Whisler, T. *Information Technology and Organizational Change.* Belmont, Calif.: Wadsworth, 1970.

Whyte, W. F. *Human Relations in the Restaurant Industry.* New York: McGraw-Hill, 1948.

Whyte, W. H. *The Organization Man.* New York: Simon & Schuster, 1956.

Wickesberg, A. "Communications Network in the Business Organization Structure." *Academy of Management Journal* 11 (1968): 253–262.

Williams, W. *Mainsprings of Men.* New York: Scribner, 1925.

Winterbottom, M. "The Relation of Need for Achievement to Learning Experiences in Independence and Mastery." In *Motives in Fantasy, Action and Society,* edited by J. W. Atkinson, pp. 468–471. New York: Van Nostrand, 1958.

Woodward, J. *Industrial Organization: Theory and Practice.* New York: Oxford University Press, 1965.

Worthy, J. "Organization Structure and Employee Morale." *American Sociological Review* 15 (1950): 169–179.

Wren, D. *The Evolution of Management Thought.* 2nd ed. New York: Wiley, 1979.

Yankelovich, D. "The New Psychological Contracts at Work." *Psychology Today* 11 (1978): 46–50.

Yukl, G.; Wexley, K.; and Seymour, J. "Effectiveness of Pay Incentives Under Variable Ratio and Continuous Reinforcement Schedules." *Journal of Applied Psychology* 56 (1972): 19–23.

Zalesnik, A., and Moment, D. *The Dynamics of Interpersonal Behavior.* New York: Wiley, 1964.

Ziller, R.; Stark, B.; and Pruden, H. "Marginality and Integrative Management Positions." *Academy of Management Journal* 12 (1969): 487–495.

Zimbardo, P., and Ebbesen, E. *Influencing Attitudes and Changing Behavior.* 1969. 2nd ed. Reading, Mass.: Addison-Wesley, 1977.

Name Index

Abelson, H., 312
Aboud, John, 526, 527
Adams, J. Stacy, 328
Alderfer, C., 330
Alutto, J., 394
Anderson, C., 121, 346
Andrews, J., 520
Andrews, K., 436
Andrisani, Paul, 346
Annett, J., 186
Aplin, John, 513, 518
Appley, M., 330
Argyris, Chris, 42–43, 44
  Personality and Organization, 42
Arthur, Chester, 74
Arvey, R., 326
Asch, Solomon, 305
Athanasiou, R., 343, 344
Atkinson, J., 201
Avery, Clarence, 107

Babcock, R., 126
Baldes, J., 327
Bales, Robert, 381
Bamforth, K. W., 395
Barlund, D., 235
Barmash, I., 261
Barnard, Chester, 37, 38, 236, 351, 379
  The Functions of the Executive, 38
  on leadership, 352, 365
  systems theory of, 38–40
Barth, Carl, 28
Bass, B., 172, 187, 338, 550
Baumhart, R., 436, 437–438
Beatty, Richard, 340, 341
Beer, M., 202
Behling, O., 338
Bell, Cecil, 485
Bennett, Harry, 213, 295, 296–297
Bennis, W., 381
Berlew, D., 518
Blackett, P. M. S., 28
Blair, J., 544
Blake, Robert, 358, 453–455, 459, 460, 491–492
Blau, Peter, 169, 269–270, 271, 276
Blauner, Robert, 399–402, 478
Blomstrom, R., 426, 428, 441
Boling, J., 326
Boling, T., 437
Bond, F., 517
Boulton, W., 228
Bowen, Howard R., 441
  Social Responsibilities of the Businessman, 428–429
Bowers, David, 364, 366
Bowman, J., 439
Brenner, S., 438
Brockhaus, R., 530
Bronfenbrenner, U., 300
Browne, Philip, 232
Brownell, William, 214
Buchholz, Rogene, 539
Bugas, John, 296
Burke, Ronald, 192, 454
Burnham, D., 336
Burns, Tom, 46, 117, 306–307, 315
Burton, D., 467

Burton, G., 467
Butcher, B., 441
Butcher, W., 445

Callaghan, P., 436
Calvin, John, 16
Campbell, J., 181, 332, 357, 386, 516
Campbell, S., 542
Carlson, R., 183, 369
Carnegie, Andrew, 426
Carroll, A., 433, 439
Carroll, Daniel, 230
Carroll, Stephen, 22, 50, 183, 188, 257, 517
  contingency perspective of, 48–49
  and job satisfaction, 345
  and Locke's goal-setting theory, 326
  and Management by Objectives, 126–127
  motivational framework of, 199–201
Carter, Jimmy, 164, 190, 193, 235, 258
  and civil service reform, 75, 76
Carzo, R., 220
Cashman, J., 365
Chambers, John, 119
Chandler, Alfred, Jr., 275, 276
Charters, W., 236
Chesser, R., 327
Child, John, 271, 276
Chrysler, Walter, 246, 528
Churchill, Winston, 12
Clark, W. F., 87
Coch, L., 393
Cofer, C., 330
Cohen, A., 235
Coleman, J., 384, 401
Collins, Orvis, 527
Commons, J., 109
Conwell, Russell H., 16
Coons, A., 357
Cooper, Arnold, 530–531
Cosier, R., 96
Costello, T., 309
Costigan, R., 484
Couzens, James, 5, 6
Cowger, G., 302
Craig, J., 366
Crowther, S., 107, 108
Crozier, Michel, 389
Cummings, L., 87, 325

Dahle, T., 310–311
Dale, E., 219
Dalton, M., 232, 520
D'Andrade, Roy, 527
Dansereau, F., 365
Davis, K., 235, 236, 426, 428, 441
  on social responsibility, 433–436
Davis, S., 249, 250
Dearborn, D., 93
Debs, Eugene, 426
de Gaulle, Charles, 12
Delbecq, A., 87, 466
Delman, Maury, 531
Deming, Edward, 548
Deutermann, W., 542
Dewhirst, H., 326
Dickson, W., 33–34, 36
Digman, Lester, 188
Dilley, S., 441
Dowling, W., 367
Driscoll, J., 230, 302
Drucker, P., 250, 264
Duke, James, 131–132
Duncan, Robert, 117
Dunnette, M., 196, 201, 386
Durant, William, 245–246, 464, 528

Ebbesen, E., 327
Eck, A., 538
Egan, R., 302
Elkins, A., 436
English, Jon, 192
Entine, A., 525
Erickson, Milton, 300
Erlang, A. K., 149
Estey, Martin, 386–387
Etzioni, Amitai, 256, 259–260

Falbe, C., 169
Fayol, Henri, 11, 218, 221
  bridge of, 21–22, 236
  General and Industrial Management, 17
  and management process school, 17–22
Feigenbaum, E., 395
Ferster, C., 338
Festinger, Leon, 327
Fiedler, F., 356, 360–362, 363
Filley, A., 159, 187, 219, 221, 232, 333
  on entrepreneurs, 528
Fleishman, Edwin, 390–391
Ford, Henry, 5–6, 214–216, 421
  death of, 296
  and Hunger March, 293–294
  labor problems of, 294–295
  personnel reforms of, 107–109
  and union organization, 295–296
Ford, Henry, II, 297, 421, 423
Ford, R., 333, 538
Foreman, C., 479

Franko, Lawrence, 551
Fraser, Douglas, 263
Frederick, W., 437
French, John R. P., 352, 393
French, Wendell, 485
Friedman, Milton, 436

Galbraith, Jay, 274, 460, 553
  information-processing approach of, 276–280, 299, 482
Gannon, M., 179, 183, 184, 344, 479, 484
  and success of accountants, 518
  and women in work force, 542
Gantt, Henry, 144
Gemmill, Gary, 304
Georgopoulos, B., 325
Gerry, G., 202
Ghiselli, Edwin, 87, 356–357, 545
Gibb, J., 307
Gilbreth, Frank, 24
Gilbreth, Lillian, 24
Glick, W., 543
Glube, R., 374
Glueck, William, 484
Goldstein, A., 341
Goldthorpe, John, 345, 396, 399
Goleman, D., 300
Golembiewski, Robert, 232
Gomersall, E., 184
Gordon, William, 467
Gouldner, Alvin, 368–369, 392
Graen, George, 365
Graham, Billy, 317
Graves, J., 453
Gray, E., 431
Griffeth, R., 545
Grunes, W., 303
Guest, R., 314, 332
Gurman, R., 484
Gustafson, D., 466

Hackman, J. Richard, 159, 334–335, 342, 344
Haga, W., 365
Haire, M., 87, 302, 303, 545
Hall, D., 195, 512, 518
Hall, Edward, 387–388
Hall, Francine, 512
Hammond, Paul F., 341
Hamner, C., 340
Hamner, E., 341, 342
Hamner, W., 326, 341, 342
Hanke, J., 393
Harland, C., 235
Harlow, D., 393
Harris, H., 87
Harrison, E. F., 97, 98, 120, 385
Harvey, E., 270
Hay, R., 431
Hayes, James, 466
Head, K., 343, 344
Heald, M., 426
Heaton, E., 184
Heenan, David, 550
Hegarty, W., 439
Heisler, William, 304
Henderson, J., 170, 171
Henderson, L. J., 37
Hendrick, H., 385
Hendrickson, B., 542
Hershey, Robert, 236
Herzberg, Frederick, 328, 331–334
Hickson, D., 271
Hill, Frank, 294–295
Hill, Raymond, 254
Hinrichs, John, 299
Hitler, Adolf, 12, 392
Hlavacek, J., 262
Hodgetts, R., 431
Hoffman, L., 188, 235
Hollan, C., 327
Holloman, C., 385
Homans, George, 380–381
Hornaday, John, 526, 527
House, Robert, 219, 221, 232, 333, 528
  on control, 159
  his path-goal theory of leader effectiveness, 362–364
  on planning, 111
  and problem-solving groups, 384
  on training rules, 187
Hovland, C., 312
Huber, G., 97, 98
Hunter, J., 330

Ingham, G., 344
Inzerilli, G., 271

Jaastad, K., 386
Jacoby, N., 425, 431–433
Jago, A., 374
James, J., 379
Janger, A., 219
Janis, Irving, 85, 92, 93, 188, 312
  on decision making, 94, 95, 97, 98–99
Jaques, E., 198
Jaroslovsky, R., 443
Jerdee, T., 22
Jermier, John, 372
Johnson, M., 180

Jolson, M., 183
Jones, N., 325
Jordan, Hamilton, 193, 235
Josephson, M., 427

Kahn, R., 220, 252, 363
Kanter, R., 370
Karlins, M., 312
Katz, Elihu, 309–310
Kavanagh, M., 358
Keen, Peter, 316–317
Kelley, H., 312
Kepner, Charles, 94
Kerr, Clark, 399
Kerr, Steven, 159, 187, 219, 221, 232, 333
  on entrepreneurs, 528
  on Management by Objectives, 126, 127–128
  on substitutes for leadership, 372
Kettering, Charles, 464
Khandwalla, P., 303
Kilmann, Ralph, 475
Kim, J., 326
Kimmel, Allan, 235
Kinne, S., 326
Klann, William, 107
Kleiner, R., 382
Kochan, Thomas, 455, 456
Kolodny, H., 250
Kreps, Juanita M., 441

La Rue, D., 443
Latham, Gary, 326–327
Lawler, E., 159, 195, 201, 330, 332, 335
  and entrepreneurs, 530
  and job satisfaction, 342, 344
Lawrence, P., 233, 249, 250
  study of, on external environmental uncertainty, 272–274
Lazarsfeld, Paul, 309–310
Leavitt, Harold, 471, 472
Leavitt, J., 307
Leete, B., 345
Lewin, Kurt, 394
Liden, R., 365
Lieberman, Seymour, 393
Likert, Rensis, 236–237, 342, 357, 366, 367, 393
Lindblom, Charles, 88
Lindsay, William, 111
Lippman, W., 109
Lipset, S., 384, 401, 517
Locke, Edwin, 196, 332, 343
  goal-setting theory of, 326–327
Loeb, S., 518
Logan, N., 543
Long, R., 260
Lorsch, J., 233
  study of, on external environmental uncertainty, 272–274
Louis, A., 474
Lowin, A., 366
Luthans, F., 340, 431
Lynch, B., 544

McCarthy, C., 261
McCaskey, Michael, 123
McClelland, David, 300, 526, 540
  need theory of, 328, 335–336
Maccoby, Michael, 370–371
McConnell, C., 551
McCormick, E., 187
MacCrimmon, K., 61
McGregor, Douglas, 43–44, 545
McGuire, J., 554
McKelvey, Bill, 475
McKenney, James, 316–317
McKinley, W., 169
McNamara, Robert, 421, 423
Maguire, M., 159
Mahoney, G., 325
Mahoney, T., 22
Maier, N., 187, 188, 235
Malcomson, Alexander, 5
Malm, F., 517
Mann, Leon, 85, 92, 93, 94, 95, 97
  and training techniques, 188
Mansfield, R., 271
March, J., 89, 395
Marchione, Anthony, 192
Marcus, S., 440
Margerison, C., 374
Marion, B., 184
Marquis, Dean, 214
Marrow, A., 366
Martin, Homer, 295
Martin, N., 22
Maslow, Abraham, need hierarchy of, 328–331, 332, 408
Mausner, B., 331
Mawhinney, T., 337
Mayo, Elton, 34, 35, 38
Mechanic, D., 221
Merton, Robert, 368
Michels, Robert, 222, 401
Miller, R. J. (Arjay), 421, 423
Mills, T., 379
Miner, J., 181, 219, 333, 384, 538, 540
  and job orientation, 184

Mintzberg, Henry, 22, 170, 313–315, 351, 354, 520
  on managers, 553, 554
Mises, Leopold von, 317
Mitchell, V., 544
Molander, E., 438
Moore, David, 527
Morasky, R., 341
Morrison, E., 171
Morse, Nancy, 366–367
Mott, P., 485
Mouton, Jane, 358, 453–455, 459, 460, 491–492
Muczyk, J., 126, 188
Mueller, R., 307
Mullick, Satinder, 119
Murphy, P., 429, 431
Murray, H., 304
Myers, S., 184

Nader, Ralph, 447
Nash, A., 188, 199–201
Nelson, Gaylord, 512
Nestel, Gilbert, 346
Nevins, Allan, 294–295
Newstrom, J., 188, 438
Nixon, Richard, 235, 447
Nord, W., 484
Nutt, P., 170, 171

Oldham, Greg, 334–335
Opshal, R., 201
O'Reilly, C., 235, 543
Organ, D., 340
Ouchi, W., 159

Paine, F., 121, 184, 344, 345
Palmore, Erdman, 525
Park, John R., 506–507
Parkinson, C. Northcote, 392
Parsons, Talcott, 86
Pathak, D., 467
Pavlov, Ivan, 336–337
Pearce, J., 335
Pepitone, A., 382
Pheysey, D., 271
Porter, Lyman W., 87, 159, 235, 330–331, 530, 544
  and international management, 545
  and job satisfaction, 342, 344
  his questionnaire on motivation, 408–413
Pruden, H., 553
Pugh, D., 271
Pullman, George M., 426
Purchase, Alan, 477

Quinn, James, 88
Quinn, R., 344, 481, 542

Raia, Anthony, 129
Rauschenberger, J., 330
Raven, Bertram, 352
Read, W., 235
Reed-Mendenhall, D., 184
Reid, G., 179
Reif, W., 172
Reilly, R., 183
Reimann, B., 271
Reimer, Everett, 366–367
Reiss, G., 444
Reitman, W., 201
Reitz, H., 337
Renwick, P., 543
Reuther, Walter, 295
Reynolds, L., 201
Riesman, David, 528–529
Roberts, K., 543
Robinson, J., 343, 344
Robinson, L., 437
Rockefeller, John D., 427
Roethlisberger, F., 33–34, 36
Rollins, S., 236
Rosen, Bernard, 527
Rosenthal, R., 304–305
Rosnow, Ralph, 235
Rossy, Gerard, 129
Rotchford, N., 543
Ruch, W., 438
Rue, Leslie, 111
Rummel, R. J., 550

Sarnoff, Robert, 129–130
Sawyer, K., 543–544
Sayles, Leonard, 64, 250, 345, 393, 397, 399
Schein, E., 185, 553
Schelling, T., 456
Schlosser, M., 381
Schmidt, Stuart, 455, 456
Schmidt, Warren, 373, 452
Schmitt, N., 330
Schneider, B., 332
Schneier, Craig, 340, 341, 342
Schriesheim, C., 338
Schuh, A., 342
Schutte, T., 438
Schwab, D., 325
Schwenk, C., 96
Sease, D. R., 444
Seashore, Stanley, 364, 366
Segal, D., 544

Seiler, John, 456
Seymour, J., 340
Shannon, C., 305
Shapero, Albert, 527, 530, 531, 532
Shaw, Marvin, 379, 381, 386, 388, 391
Shepard, H., 381, 383
Sherif, C., 382
Sherif, M., 382, 456–457
Shull, F., 87
Siegel, Abraham, 399
Siegel, Jacob, 304
Simon, Herbert, 22, 61, 89, 91, 92, 93
Simonds, R., 219
Sims, H., 439
Skinner, B. F., 337, 338
Sloan, Alfred, 245, 246, 313, 316
Smith, Donald, 119
Snyderman, B., 331
Soelberg, Peer, 91–92
Sommers, D., 538
Sorcher, M., 341
Sorensen, P., 126
Sorenson, Charles, 296
Sperling, S., 183
Sprecher, Timothy, 230
Stalker, G. M., 46, 117
Stark, B., 553
Steele, F., 307
Steinberg, H., 183
Steiner, G., 441, 463–464
Stewart, Rosemary, 314–315
Stogdill, R., 357
Stoner, J., 394
Straub, A., 126
Strauss, G., 345, 393
Strodtbeck, F., 381
Sturdivant, F., 426, 437
Summer, Charles, 67
Suttle, J., 330
Sutton, H., 235
Sward, K., 108, 294
Swinyard, A., 517

Tannenbaum, Robert, 373
Tarnowieski, D., 484
Taylor, Frederick, 33, 35, 37, 324
  and scientific management, 22–28
Tenopyr, M., 183
Thamhain, Hans, 252, 254, 458–459
Thayer, L., 299
Thomas, Kenneth, 452, 459–460
Thomas, R. J., 295
Thompson, James, 84–85, 90, 379
Thompson, V., 262
Thorton, Tex, 421
Thune, Stanely, 111
Tiffin, J., 187
Tillman, R., 238
Tolliver, J., 338
Tosi, Henry, 50, 188, 199, 201, 257
  contingency perspective of, 48–49
  and Locke's goal-setting theory, 326
  and Management by Objectives, 126–127
Tracy, P., 169
Tregoe, Benjamin, 94
Trieb, S., 184
Trist, Eric, 395–397
Trow, M., 384, 401
Tushman, Michael, 464–465

Ullman, J., 179
Utterback, James, 117, 118

Van de Ven, A., 466
Vaughn, J., 187, 338
Vecchio, R., 362
Vettori, F., 188
Viteles, M., 200
Vredenburgh, D., 394
Vroom, Victor, 94, 200, 324, 327, 373–374

Walker, C., 332
Walters, K., 440
Watt, James, 173
Weaver, C., 541, 542
Weaver, W., 305
Weber, Max, 68, 221, 351, 365, 384
  on authority, 12–13
  on bureaucracy, 10–17, 21
  on capitalism, 12
  his concept of power, 13, 40
Webster, E., 183, 302
Weir, Tamara, 192
Weissenberg, P., 358
Weitzel, William, 192
Wexley, K., 340
Weygandt, J., 441
Wheeler, K., 484
Whisler, T., 172
White, D., 340
Whyte, William F., 483
Whyte, William H., 466, 529
Wickesberg, A. K., 234, 316
Wilemon, David, 252, 254, 458–459
Willard, C., 184
Winter, D., 335

Winterbottom, Marian, 527
Woodward, Joan, 218, 219, 232, 344, 460
  study of, on technology, 218, 270–271
Wren, Daniel, 8–9, 10

Yanouzas, J., 220
Yetton, Philip, 94, 373–374
Yukl, Gary, 326, 340

Zalkind, S., 309
Zawicki, Robert, 485
Ziller, R., 553
Zimbardo, P., 327

Subject Index

Abilities, group behavior and, 388
Academic training, 517
Accounting, double-entry, 15-16
Accuracy, of communication, 310-312
Achievement, need for, 526-527
Acme Markets, Inc., 506
Action devices, 159
Agent
  of change, 12
  transformation, 554
Age-salary ratio, 523-524
Alienation, 399
  of assembly-line worker, 400-401
  in continuous-process work, 402
  in craft work, 401-402
  in machine-tending work, 401
  relationship between technology and, 400-402
  types of, 400
Alternatives/choice, evaluation of, in decision making, 62, 83
American Assembly of Collegiate Schools of Business, 542
American Federation of Labor, 109
American Institute of Management, 174
American Management Associations, 230, 466
American Telephone & Telegraph Company (AT&T), 191, 333-334, 466, 481, 541, 542
Analysis of performance, 65-67
Application blanks, 181-183
  weighted, 182
Appraisal. *See* Performance appraisal
Assessment, periodic, 523
  and age-salary ratio, 523-524
  and fast track, 525
  and job satisfaction, 525
Assessment centers, for employee development, 191-192
Association of Legal Administrators, 256
Attitudes
  behavioral element of, 389
  cognitive element of, 389
  defined, 389
  emotional element of, 389
  group behavior and, 389-391
  surveys of, 173-174
Audit, management, 174. *See also* Social audit
Authority
  charismatic leadership as, 12-13
  as principle of management, 20
  rational-legal, 13
  traditional, 12
Automated technology, 218, 270
  factories, 476-477
  offices, 477-478

Balance sheet, 172
Bank(ing)
  case study of branch, 76-78
  case study of overly successful, 284-286
  tellers, monitoring performance of, 206-208
Bank of America, 442
Barnard's unit concept, 40, 236
Barriers to integration, 233
  control systems as, 234
  design, 233
  grapevine as, 235-236
  hierarchical, 234-236
  organizational communication as, 234-235
  status differences as, 235
  voluntary, 233-234

Behavioral conditions, for training, 186
Behaviorally anchored rating scales, 195–196
Behavioral processes
  impact of, 64, 65
  as organizational dimension, 3, 56, 61, 291
Behavioral science stream of management, 3, 32–33
  organizational framework and, 69–70
  summarized, 51–52
Behavior modeling, 341
Behavior modification (BMod) programs, 337, 340–342
Big Business Day (April 1980), 447
Biographical characteristics, group behavior and, 388
Black and Decker Manufacturing Company, 126, 340
Boards of directors, 227–228
Bolstering the alternative, 92–93
Bounded discretion, 87
Brainstorming, 466, 467
Branch banking, case study of, 76–78
Break-even analysis, 138–139
  costs, 139
  demand, 139–141
  price, 139
Bridge, Fayol's, 21–22, 236
Briggs Company, 294
Budgets
  capital, 141–142
  control of, 162–165
  types of, 162
  zero-based (ZBB), 164–165
Bureaucracy, Weber's theory of, 10–17
Bureau of Labor Statistics, U.S., 537, 538
Business
  government relations, social responsibility and, 445–446
  and society, 425
Business ethics, 436
  organizational development and, 494–495
  remedial actions for, 439–440
  research on, 437–439
  social responsibility and, 437, 446–447
Business Week, 121–122, 437, 439, 442, 477

Capital budgeting, 141–142
Capitalism
  bureaucracy and, 13–15
  preconditions for, 15–17
  Weber's analysis of, 12
Career(s)
  changing, 538–539
  counseling, 189–190
  path, 190
  periodic assessment of, 523–525
  preparaion, 516–518
  strategies, 518–520
  summarized, 533–534
Carnegie Steel Company, 426
Centralization
  computerized MISs and, 168–169
  and decentralization, 222–223
  defined, 222
  degree of, as principle of management, 20
Certainty
  degrees of, 272–273
  and structure, 273–274
  -uncertainty decision-making strategies, 90–91
Change(s). *See also* Organization development (OD)
  agent of, 12
  failure of efforts at, 492
  introducing inevitable, 481–482
  introducing technological, 481
  managing people during, 479–482
  managing structural, 482–485
  managing technological, 476–479
  summarized, 495–496
Charisma, charismatic leadership, 12–13, 392
  routinization of, 13
Chase Manhattan Bank, 190–191
Chemical Bank of New York, 179, 185
Chief executive officer (CEO), 228–229
Chinese fast-food chain, 132–133
Chrysler Corporation, 246, 262–263, 422, 446, 548
Civil Service Commission, U.S., 74–75, 173
Civil Service Reform Act (1978), 75–76, 257
Classical conditioning, 336–337
Clientele, departmentalization by, 226
Codetermination, 262–263
Cognitive dissonance theory of motivation, 327–328
Columbia University, 368, 525
Commanding, as function of management, 18, 19
Commerce, U.S. Department of, 116, 260
Commitment, public, 394
Committee for Economic Development (CED), *Social Responsibilities of Business Corporations*, 429–431
Committees
  ad hoc or temporary, 238
  for improving integration, 238
  standing, 238
Communication, 298–299
  barriers to, 306–307
  basic model of, 305–306
  consultative, 48
  essence of, 306
  importance of, 314
  among individuals, 305–313
  interpersonal, 61, 299
    and managerial work, 313–317
  intrapersonal, 299

Communication *(continued)*
methods of, 310–312
networks, 307–309
oral, 314–315
organizational, 234–235, 299
perception and, 299–305
summarized, 318–319
technical, 299
two-step flow of, 309–310
Yale studies on, 312–313
Companies, employee-owned, 260–261
Company man, manager as, 370–371
Competition, motivational strategy of, 200–201
Complex man, 69
Compromise, decision-making strategy of, 90, 91
Computational decision-making strategy, 90, 91
Computer, impact of, on MISs, 171–172
Conditioning
classical, 336–337
operant, 337
theories of motivaion, 323, 336–342
Conference groups, 488–489
Conflict, 451–452. *See also* Creativity
advanced programming and planning to reduce, 460
buffers or inventories to reduce, 460
contingency approach to resolving, 458–462
educational and training programs to reduce, 460
goal-oriented departments to resolve, 460–461
increased importance of, 452–453
integrators to reduce, 460
interdepartmental, 453, 455–456
intergroup, 453
interpersonal, 453–455
joint decision making to reduce, 461
linking pins to minimize, 460
methods used by chief executives to resolve, 459–460
methods used to resolve, 460–462
ombudsman to resolve, 460
organizational, 453
in organizations, 452–458
perceived psychological, in decision making, 85
redesigning organization to reduce, 460
separating groups to reduce, 460
styles, 499–502
summarized, 468–469
transfer or termination of personnel to resolve, 461–462
types of, 453
zero-sum, 456–458
Conglomerates, 261
Consideration, as dimension of leader behavior, 357–358, 365, 381
Contact, direct, 278
Content (or needs) theories of motivation, 323, 328–336
Contingency contracting, 341
Contingency theory of leadership, 362
Contingency theory of management, 44
critique of, 50–51
and organic and mechanistic structures, 46–48
Tosi and Carroll's perspective on, 48–50
Contracting, contingency, 341
Control, 158–159. *See also* Planning
attitude survey for, 173–174
budgetary, 162–165
chart, 167
combinations of, 161
concept of, 159–161
feedback, 159–160
feedforward, 160
financial statements for, 172
as function of management, 18, 19
inventory and quality, 165–167
management audit for, 174
and management information systems, 167–172
of members and subsystems, 160
optimum span of, 60
and planning, impact of, 62–64
as organizational dimension, 3, 56, 59–60, 105
span of, 217–219
strategic, 60
summarized, 174–175
systems, as barrier to integration, 234
cybernetic, 173
tactical, 60
techniques, additional, 172–174
Cooperative system, 39–40
Coordinating, as function of management, 18, 19
Corporation(s)
criticisms of, 431–433
defined, 226
early concept of, 10
leftist critics of, 432
multinational, 263–264
reformist critics of, 431–432
state-backed, 262–263
utopian critics of, 432–433
Cosmopolitans, as leaders, 368–370
Costs
fixed (FC), 139
standard, 162–163
total (TC), 139
variable (VC), 139
CPM (critical path method), 144, 145–147, 171
Craftsmen, managers as, 370
Creativity, creative process, 451–452, 462. *See also* Conflict
and creative groups, 385–386, 466–467

in individuals, 463
innovation process in, 464–465
and nominal group technique (NGT), 466–467
in organizations, 463–464
sources of, 465–466
steps in, 462
summarized, 468–469
and synectics, 467
techniques, 466–467
Culture
effect of, on decision making, 87–88
group behavior and, 388–389
Cybernetic (machine-controlled) systems, 173

Decentralization
centralization and, 222–223
defined, 222
federal, 214, 245–247, 421–422
Decision making, 81–82
constrained environments for, 84–88
criteria for, 95
culture's effect on, 87–88
decision heuristics for, 96–97
evaluation of alternatives/choice in, 62, 83
goals and policies in, 85
group, 97–98, 503–505
and groupthink, 98–99
implementation in, 62, 84
improving, 93–99
information search in, 62, 82–83
intuitive, 317
leadership and subordinate participation in, 373–374
manager's role in, 354–356
normative models for, 93–94
as organizational dimension, 3, 56, 61–62
organizational level in, 86–87
perceived psychological conflict in, 85
preceptive, 316, 317
problem factoring in, 94–96
problem formulation in, 62, 83
receptive, 316, 317
setting for, 64–68
societal expectations in, 87
stages in, 82–84
stimulus event in, 61–62, 82
styles, 316–317
suboptimal, 91–93
summarized, 99–100
systematic, 316–317
uncertainty in, 84–85
Decision-making strategies, 88
certainty-uncertainty, 90–91
of compromise, 90, 91
computational, 90, 91
defective, 93
defensive avoidance, 93
hypervigilance, 93
incremental, 88
inspirational, 91
judgmental, 91
nonprogrammed, 89–90, 91
programmed, 89, 90, 91
rational comprehensive, 88
unconflicted adherence, 93
unconflicted change, 93
Decision trees, 150
Defective decision-making strategies, 93
Defensive avoidance decision-making strategy, 93
Delphi technique of forecasting, 119–120
Demand, 139–141
Departmentalization, 223, 245
by clientele, 226
by function, 223–224
by place, 225–226
by product, 224–225
Departmental planning, 124
Design barriers to integration, 233
Deterministic models, 138, 148, 150
Development, employee, 178, 185, 189
assessment centers for, 191–192
issues in, 192–193
programs, successful, 189–191, 192
summarized, 203
Diamond Shamrock Corporation, 474–475
Differential piece rate, 25
Differentiation, 233
in group behavior, 380
and integration, 272
Diffusion index, 121–122
Dimensions, organizational. *See also* Organizational framework
behavioral processes, 3, 56, 61
managerial decision making, 3, 56, 61–62
organization design, 3, 56, 60–61
planning and control, 3, 56, 57–60
relationships among, 62–68
Directors, boards of, 227–228
Discipline, as principle of management, 20
Disclosures and abuses, public, 426–428
Discretion, bounded, 87
Discussion, lectures vs., 188
Disseminator, manager as, 354
Disturbance handler, manager as, 355
Division of work, as principle of management, 20
Double-entry accounting, 15–16
Duke Tobacco Company, 131–132

Dun's Review, 188, 477
Dyad, vertical, 365

Economic man, model of, 37
Economic position, relative, of U.S., 551
Education, Department of, 257
Effectiveness, leader, 40, 360–362, 368
  path-goal theory of, 362–364
Effectuating devices, 159
Efficiency, 40
Effort-performance linkage, 325
Elaboration, 380
Emery Air Freight, 341–342
Employee
  -owned companies, 260–261
  preference, in reward systems, 201–202
Employment and Earnings, 258, 542
Energy, U.S. Department of, 257, 551
Energy crisis, 551–552
Engineers, case study of, 70–74
Entrepreneurs, 526
  defined, 526
  failure of, 531–533
  managers as, 354
  managers vs., 528–531
  personal traits of, 526–528
Environment
  constrained, for decision making, 84–88
  effect of physical, on group behavior, 386–388
  managing external, 278
  simple-complex dimension of, 117–118
  social responsibility and quality of, 442–444
  static-dynamic dimension of, 117–118
Environmental forecasting, 57–58
Environmental Protection Agency (EPA), 442, 443
Environmental uncertainty, external, studies on, 272–274, 275, 276
EOP (Economic Order Point) model, 165–166
EOQ (Economic Order Quality) model, 165
Equal Employment Opportunity Commission (EEOC), 446
Equity, as principle of management, 20
Equity theory of motivation, 328
Ernst and Ernst, 441–442
Esprit de corps, as principle of management, 21
Ehics. *See* Business ethics
Expectancy theory of motivation, 199, 323, 324–325
Expected value, 148–149
External social system, 380
Extrinsic rewards, 325

Factoring, problem, 94–96
Factory, automated, 476–477
Failures, case studies of strategic, 129–133
Fast track, 525
Fayol's bridge, 21–22, 236
Fear, as negative approach to motivation, 199
Featherbedding, 396
Federal decentralization, 214, 245–247, 421–422
Federal Trade Commission, 108, 445–446
Federal Trade Commission Act (1914), 428
Feedback
  control, 159–160
  of results, as behavioral determinant of learning, 186
  technique of, in behavior modification, 340–341
Feedforward control, 160
Figureheads, managers as, 353
Financial statements, as control mechanisms, 172
First-line supervision, 230–231
Fixed costs (FC), 139
Fixed-interval schedule, 339
Fixed-ratio schedule, 339
Flexitime, 483–484
Food, Drug, and Cosmetic Act (1938), 506
Food and Drug Administration (FDA), 506
Fordham University, Graduate School of, 482
Ford Motor Company, 66, 229
  Edsel production at, 62, 131, 422
  Hunger March at, 293–294
  labor costs of, 6
  labor problems at, 294–295
  managerial style of, 50
  managerial succession at, 423
  Model A of, 215
  Model T of, 5, 6, 107, 213, 246, 293, 421
  organization design at, 213–215
  personnel reforms at, 107–109
  regulation and competition at, 422–423
  reorganization of, by Henry Ford II, 421–422
  stratetic failure at, 131
  strategic planning by, 5–6
  transitional period at, 296–297
  union organization at, 295–296
Forecasting, 115
  Delphi technique, 119–120
  diffusion index, 121–122
  environmental, 57–58
  long-range, 116
  mathematical models, 121–122
  moving average, 120
  panel consensus, 120
  poor, 122
  purposes of, 115–116
  qualitative techniques, 119–122
  regression model, 121
  rolling, 117
  short-range, 116
  time series analysis and projection in, 120–121

trend projection, 121
types of, 116–117, 118–119
typology, 117–119
visionary, 120
Foreign Corrupt Practices Act (1977), 446–447
Formal job search methods, 178
Function, departmentalization by, 223–224
Functional foreman, 26

Gaines Foods, 473–474
Gamesman, manager as, 371
Gantt chart, 144–145
General Accounting Office, U.S., 174
General Electric, 121, 341
General Foods, 272
Generalist, specialist vs., 519–520
General Motors, 293, 313, 316, 367, 464, 493
domination of automobile industry by, 66, 215
federal decentralization at, 214, 245–247, 421–422
financial base of, 422
international division of, 264
managerial style at, 50, 528
social auditing at, 442
Giant Food, 111–114, 122, 123
Gillette Company, 58–59
Goal(s)
in decision making, 85
emphasis, 364
long-term, 58, 112
-oriented appraisal, 196–197
path approach to motivation, 201
planning with precise and imprecise, 122–124
-setting theory of motivation, 326–327
Government
-business relations, social responsibility and, 445–446
and military employees, 544
organizations, 257–258
Grapevine
as barrier to integration, 235–236
as method of communication, 311–312
Group(s). *See also* Group behavior
activities of, 380
apathetic, 397
cohesion, 390, 391
compatibility, 391
composition, 391
conference, 488–489
conservative, 398–399
contingency view of, 395–402
creative, 385–386, 466–467
decision-making, 97–98, 503–505
discussion sessions, 487–489
erratic, 397–398
evolution of, 381
formation and development of, 379–383
ideal, 383
industrial work, 397–399
influences on individuals, 387
interactions in, 380
primary, 383–384
problem-solving, 384–385
reasons for joining, 381–382
secondary, 383–384
sentiments of, 380
strategic, 398
structure, 392–395
technique, nominal (NGT), 466–467
training (T-), 488
types of, in organizations, 383–386
Group behavior, 378–379. *See also* Group(s)
alienation and work, 399–402
behavioral process of, 61
characteristics of group members, effect on, 388–391
factors influencing, 386–395
personal space and, 387–388
physical environment's effect on, 386–388
physical structure and, 386–387
summarized, 403–404
system thory of, 380–381
Tavistock coal-mining study on, 395–397
Groupthink, 98–99
Growth, limits to, 552
Guidance systems, 226
boards of directors, 227–228
chief executive officer (CEO), 228–229
first-line supervision, 230–231
line and staff, 231–233
middle management, 229–230
office of the president, 229
stockholders, 226–227

Halo effect, 303
Harvard Business Review, 437
Harvard Business School, 316, 517
Hawthorne effect, 34, 484
Hawthorne study, 33–36, 38
findings of, 37
Health, Education, and Welfare, U.S. Department of, 257, 542
Heuristics, decision, 96–97
Hierarchy and specialization, 13, 217
basis of departmentalization in, 223–226
boards of directors in, 227–228
building organization in, 217–223
centralization and decentralization in, 222–223
chief executive officer in, 228–229
constructing guidance systems in, 226–233

Hierarchy and specialization *(continued)*
first-line supervision in, 230–231
line and staff in, 231–233
middle management in, 229–230
office of the president in, 229
scalar principle in, 221–222
span of control in, 217–219
stockholders in, 226–227
tall vs. flat structures in, 219–220
unity of command in, 220
unity of direction in, 220–221
Hiring interview, 183
Horizontal integration, 261–262
Humanistic ethic, 539–540
Human relations school, 33
and Hawthorne study, 33–37
and interviewing program, 35–36
and observation room study, 36–37
and test room experiments, 34–35
Human resources file, 190
Human resources school, 42
Argyris's theory, 42–43
McGregor's theories, 43–44
Hygiene factors in motivation, 331–332
Hypervigilance decision-making strategy, 93

IBM, 129–130, 131, 168–169, 478, 480
Ideology, 16
Illumination, in creative process, 462
Implementation, in decision making, 62, 84
Implicit personality theory, 305
Income statement, 172
Incremental decision-making strategy, 88
Incubation, in creative process, 462
Individual interest, as principle of management, 20
Individual trusteeship, 426
Informal job search methods, 178
Informational roles, managerial, 353–354
Information evaluation, 316–317
Information gathering, 316, 317
Information-processing synthesis, 276–277
steps for creating lateral relations in, 278–280
strategies for, 277–278
Information search
biased, as cause of suboptimization, 92–93
in decision making, 62, 82–83
Initiative, as principle of management, 21
Innovation process, 464–465
Inspirational decision-making strategy, 91
Instruction, programmed, 187–188
Integration
defined, 233
differentiation and, 272
hierarchical barriers to, 234–236
horizontal, 261–262
personal methods for improving, 239
structural methods for improving, 236–239
vertical, 261
voluntary barriers to, 233–234
Integrators, 279
defined, 274
managers as, 553
to reduce conflict, 460
successful, 274–275
Intentions, defined, 326
Interaction facilitation, 364
Interdepartmental conflict, 453, 455–456
Internal Revenue Service, 118
Internal social system, 380
International management, 544–545
investments in foreign countries, 550–551
Japanese management, 547–548
styles of, 545–547
working abroad, 549–550
International Typographical Union (ITU), 401–402
International Workers of the World (IWW), 107
Intern program, 190–191
Interpersonal conflict, 453–455
Interpersonal roles, managerial, 352–353
Interstate Commerce Commission Act (1887), 428
Interval schedules, 338–339
Interventions, 489
intergroup, 491
managerial Grid®, 491–492
process, 489, 490
structural, 489–490
team building, 490–491
Interviews
advantages of, 173–174
hiring, 183
structured, 35
unstructured, 35–36, 486–487
Intrinsic rewards, 325
Inventory
models, 165–166
and quality control, 165–167
Investments, in foreign countries, 550–551
Involvement
alienative, 259
calculative, 259
moral, 259
Iron law of oligarchy, 222, 401
Isolation, 400
Itel Corporation, 130–131

Japanese management, 547–548
Job challenge, 518
Job Diagnostic Survey, 334–335

Job enlargement, 332–334
Job enrichment, 201, 332–334, 473–474
Job factors, in motivation, 332
Job orientation, 178, 184–185
Job rotation, 190
Job satisfaction, 342–343
  and career assessment, 525
  design factors in, 344–345
  and labor market, 345
  and occupational and organizational level, 343–344
  and orientation to work, 345–346
  and psychological characteristics, 346
Job search methods, 178–180
Joint ventures, 262
Jones and Laughlin Steel Corporation, 443–444
Judgmental decision-making strategy, 91
Jungle fighters, managers as, 370

Korn/Ferry International, 523

Labor, U.S. Department of, 116, 257, 476, 478
Labor force. *See* Work; Work force
Lateral decision processes (relations), 278
  steps for creating, 278–280
Leadership, 350–351
  autocratic, 366
  behavioral process of, 61
  charismatic, 12–13, 392
  and consideration, 357–358, 365, 381
  contingency factors influencing, 366–372
  contingency theory of, 362
  defined, 351, 352
  democratic, 366
  importance of, 355
  leader behavior theory of, 357–358
  and leader effectiveness, 360–362
  by locals vs. cosmopolitans, 368–370
  managerial Grid® approach to, 358–360
  managerial roles in, 352–356
  nature of, 351–352
  organizational position of, 370
  and path-goal theory of leader effectiveness, 362–364
  and personality, 367–368
  power, types of, 352
  profile of managerial, 351–356
  reciprocal causation theory of, 364–365
  scarcity of effective, 367
  short-term vs. long-term effects of, 366–367
  style, group structure and, 392
  subordinate influence on, 366
  and subordinate participation in decision making, 373–374
  substitutes for, 372
  summarized, 374–375
  and task orientation, 357–358, 365, 381
  theories of, 356–365
  T-P questionnaire on, 414–416
  trait theory of, 356–357
  and type of industry, 370–371
  vertical dyadic theory of, 365
Learning
  prior, 186
  uniqueness facilitating, 187
  whole vs. part, 187
Lectures, discussion vs., 188
Legal system, 16
Leisure ethic, 540
Liaison role of managers, 278, 353
Linear programming, 142–144
Line personnel, 14–15, 231–233
Linking pins
  for improving integration, 236–237
  to minimize conflict, 460
Lloyd's of London, 130–131
Locals, as leaders, 368–369
Logical incrementalism, 88
LTV, 443–444
Lykes Corporation, 443–444

McCormick and Company, 465–466, 479
Mahoning Valley Steel Industries (Ohio), 443–444
Management
  audit, 174
  behavioral science stream of, 3, 32–33, 69–70
  contingency theory of, 44–51
  of declining resources, 551–552
  defined, 8, 10
  early concepts of, 9–10
  entrepreneurial, 526–533
  functions of, 18–19
  general, 17–18
  human relations school of, 33–37
  human resources school of, 42–44
  information systems, 167–172
  international, 544–551
  Japanese, 547–548
  middle, 229–230
  by objectives (MBO), 124–129
  organizational dimensions of, 3, 56–62
  of people during change, 479–482
  in preindustrial societies, 8–10
  principles of, 20–21
  process school, 17–22
  as profession, 428
  project, 247–249
  quantitative school of, 28–29
  scientific, 22–28
  streams of, 3

Management *(continued)*
of structural changes, 482–485
style of, 50
system theory of, 37–42
task, 23–25
of task assignments, 472–476
of technological change, 476–479
time, 520–523
traditional stream of, 3, 7–8, 32–33, 68–69
trusteeship, 428
-worker relations, 23
Management by Objectives (MBO), 111, 124–126, 196, 326
advantages of, 128–129
future of, 129
limitations of, 127–128, 165
research on, 126–127
Management information systems (MIS), 167–168
completely integrated, 171
computerized, and centralization, 168–169
computer's impact on, 171–172
design of, 169–170
key attributes of, 170–171
networks and, 171
Management process school, 17
criticisms of, 22
and Fayol's bridge, 21–22
and functions of management, 18–19
and general management, 17–18
and principles of management, 20–21
Managerial Grid®, 358–360, 491–492
Managerial work, 313
decision-making styles in, 316–317
interpersonal communication and, 313–317
nature of, 313–316
Manager(s). *See also* Leadership
as company men, 370–371
complex role of, 552–554
as craftsmen, 370
decisional roles of, 354–356
as disseminators, 354
as disturbance handlers, 355
as entrepreneurs, 354
vs. entrepreneurs, 528–531
ethical problems faced by, 446–447
figurehead role of, 353
as gamesmen, 371
informational roles of, 353–354
as integrators, 553
interpersonal roles of, 352–353
as jungle fighters, 370
leader role of, 353
liaison role of, 278, 353
linking role of, 279
as monitors, 353–354
as negotiators, 355–356
pairs, 553–554
and planning techniques, 152–154
as polyspecialists, 552
as resource allocators, 355
roles of, 352–356
specialized, for specialized jobs, 554
as spokespersons, 354
success of, 512–516
successful project, in matrix organization, 254–255
types of, 370–371
MAPS (multivariate analysis, participation, and structure), 475–476
Marxist-related ethic, 540
Mass production, 218, 270
Mathematical models, 121–122
Matrix organization, 249–250, 279
conflict in, 252–254, 458–459
essential characteristics of, 250–252
successful project manager in, 254–255
Maximizing, 91
Meaninglessness, 400
Mechanistic structures, 46–48, 269. *See also* Organic structures
Merit System Protection Board, 75–76
Michigan, University of, 357, 366–367
Survey Research Center of, 342–343
Middle management, 229–230
Milestones, 146–147
Military and government employees, 544
Mirror, organizational, 491
MIS. *See* Management information systems
Mission, defining organization's, 58
Modeling, behavior, 341
Models
deterministic, 138, 148, 150
expected value, 148
inventory, 165–166
of managerial success, 512–516
mathematical, 121–122
normative, 93–94
probabilistic, 138, 148–152
quantitative, 119
regression, 121
transportation, 143
Monitor, manager as, 353–354
Monitoring, 118–119
Moonlighting, 484–485
Motion study, 24–25
Motivation, 186, 322–323
behavioral process of, 61
and behavior modification, 340–342
cognitive dissonance theory of, 327–328

conditioning theories of, 323, 336–342
content (or needs) theories of, 323, 328–336
defined, 323
equity theory of, 328
expectancy theory of, 199, 323, 324–325
goal-setting theory of, 326–327
hygiene factors in, 331–332
initial, in creative process, 462
and Job Diagnostic Survey, 334–335
job enlargement and enrichment in, 201, 332–334
job factors in, 332
and job satisfaction, 342–346
need hierarchy theory of, 328–331
need theory of, 335–336
noneconomic, 345
Porter questionnaire on, 407–413
process (or cognitive) theories of, 323, 324–328
and schedules of reinforcement, 338–340
sources of, 541
strategies of, 199–201
summarized, 346–347
two-factor theory of, 331–334
Moving average, 120
MRP (Material Requirements Planning) model, 165, 166
Multinational corporations (MNC), 263–264
Multiple correlation, 121

National Industrial Recovery Act (NIRA, 1933), 294
National Labor Relations Act, 230
Need hierarchy theory of motivation, 328–331
Need theory of motivation, 335–336
Negotiator, manager as, 355–356
Networks, 144
chain, 308–309
circle, 308, 309
communication, 307–309
completely connected, 308, 309
consequences of, 308–309
Gantt chart, 144–145
and MISs, 371
in organizations, 309
PERT and CPM, 145–147
wheel, 307, 308–309
Nominal group technique (NGT), 466–467
Nonprogrammed decision-making strategy, 89–90, 91
Normative models, 93–94
Norms, of group members, 380

Objectives, short-term, 59, 113
Occupational Safety and Health Act, 446
Occupational Safety and Health Administration (OSHA), 445–446
Office, automated, 477–478
Office of Management and Budget (OMB), U.S., 75
Office of Personnel Management (OPM), U.S., 74, 75–76, 118, 173, 544
Office of the president, 229
Ohio State University studies, 357, 358, 360, 362
Open system, 38
Operant conditioning, 337
Order, as principle of management, 20
Oregon Bottle Bill, 444
Organic structures, 46–48, 269. *See also* Mechanistic structures
Organizational framework. *See also* Dimensions, organizational
and behavioral science stream, 69–70
dynamics of, 70–78
relationships within, 62–68
summarized, 78–79
and traditional management, 68–69
Organization design. *See also* Hierarchy and specialization; Integration
impact of, 64, 65
and job satisfaction, 344–345
as organizational dimension, 3, 56, 60–61
summarized, 239–240
Organization development (OD), 485–486
complex issues facing, 492–495
and familiarity and dependency, 493
and group discussion sessions, 487–489
and interventions, 489–492
and interviews, 486–487
and questionnaire surveys, 487
steps in, 486
summarized, 495–496
techniques of, 486–489
and time and measurement, 493–494
Organizations
bureaucratic, 49
communication in, 234–235
conflict in, 452–458
creative, 463–464
ethic of, 539, 540
Etzioni's typology of, 259–260
flexible and dynamic, 50
government, 257–258
group structure and position in, 393
hierarchical, 49
institutional level of, 86
leadership and position in, 370
levels of, 86–87
managerial level of, 86
market-dominated, 49
matrix, 249–255, 279, 458–459
mechanistic, 46–48, 269
modern forms of, 245–255
networks in, 309

Organizations *(continued)*
organic, 46–48, 269
professional, 256
service, 258–259
size of, 269–270, 276
as sociotechnical systems, 397
specialized forms of, 256–260
summarized, 264–265
technical level of, 86
technology-dominated, 49
using schedules in, 340
Organization of Petroleum Exporting Countries, 552
Organizing, as function of management, 18, 19
Orientation
external, 346
internal, 346
job, 178, 184–185
to work, 345–346

Panel consensus forecasting technique, 120
Participation
group structure and, 393–395
of subordinates in decision making, 373–374
Part-time workers, 542–543
Paternalism, 426
Path-goal theory of leader effectiveness, 362–364
Payback period, 141–142
Perception, 299–300
behavioral process of, 61
biases in, 302–303
factors influencing, 300–302
organization of, 302–305
and personality, 303
techniques to organize, 304–305
Performance
analysis of, 65–67
past, 516–517
typology, 67–68
Performance appraisal, 178, 193
invalid data in, 198
issues in, 197–199
measuring activities and results in, 198
rating methods for, 193–197
sessions, frequency of, 198–199
single criterion in, 197–198
summarized, 203
Personality
defined, 303
group behavior and, 388–389
leadership and, 367–368
Machiavellian, 304
and perception, 303–304
theory, implicit, 305
Personal methods, for improving integration, 239
Personal space, group behavior and, 387–388
Personnel
remuneration of, as principle of management, 20
stability of tenure of, as principle of management, 21
PERT (program evaluation and review technique), 144, 145–147, 171
Philanthropy, 426
Physical environment, effect on group behavior of, 386–388
PIMS (Profit Impact of Market Strategies), 121
Place, departmentalization by, 225–226
Planning, 110–111. *See also* Control
and control, impact of, 62–64
as organizational dimension, 3, 56, 57–59, 105
defining mission in, 111–112
departmental, 124
and forecasting, 115–122
as function of management, 18, 19
goals in, 112
horizon, 116
MBO (Management by Objectives), 124–129
objectives in, 113
policies, 114
with precise and imprecise goals, 122–124
procedures, 114–115
process, organizational, 111–115
rules, 115
strategies in, 112–113
summarized, 133–134
tactics in, 113
Planning techniques, 137–138
break-even analysis, 138–141
capital budgeting, 141–142
CPM, 144, 145–147
implications for managers of, 152–154
linear programming, 142–144
networks, 144–147
PERT, 144, 145–147
probabilistic models, 148–152
summarized, 154–155
Polaris missile program, 145
Policies
in decision making, 85
developing, 59, 114
Polyspecialist, manager as, 552
Postal Service, U.S., 489, 490
Power
coercive, 259, 352
expert, 352, 388
legitimate, 352
normative, 259
referent, 352
reward, 352
types of, 352

utilitarian, 259
Weber's concept of, 13, 40
Powerlessness, 400
Predatory pricing, 427
Preindustrial societies, management in, 8–10
President, office of the, 229
Price, selling, 139
Pricing, predatory, 427
Primary groups, 383–384
Prior learning, 186
Probabilistic models, 138, 148
decision trees, 150
expected value, 148–149
simulation, 150–152
waiting line analysis (queuing), 149–150
Problem(s)
factoring, 94–96
formulation, in decision making, 62, 83
ill-structured, 89–90
structured, 89
Problem-solving groups, 384–385
Procedures, 59, 114–115
Process (or cognitive) theories of motivation, 323, 324–328
Process interventions, 489, 490
Process technology, 218, 270
Product, departmentalization by, 224–225
Professional organizations, 256
Profit maximizer, manager as, 67
Program evaluation and review technique (PERT), 144, 145–147, 171
Programmed decision-making strategy, 89, 90, 91
Programmed instruction, 187–188
Programming, linear, 142–144
Projection, 304
time series analysis and, 120–121
Project management, 247–249
Protégé, 520
Protestant ethic, 16, 540
Protestant theologians, 16
Pseudoparticipation, 394
Pullman Car Company, 426
Pure Food and Drugs Act (1906), 428

Qualitative forecasting techniques, 119–120
Delphi technique, 119–120
panel consensus, 120
visionary forecasts, 120
Quality
circles, 547
control, inventory and, 165–167
defining and monitoring, 167
Quantitative school, 28–29
Questionnaire(s)
of employee attitudes, 173–174
surveys, 487
Queuing (waiting line analysis), 149–150

Racial minorities, in work force, 541
Rank, of group member, 380
Rating(s), employee, 193
and goal-oriented appraisal, 196–197
scales, behaviorally anchored, 195–196
single global, 195
trait, 193–195
Rational comprehensive decision-making strategy, 88
Rationality, human limits to, as cause of suboptimization, 91–92
Ratio schedules, 339–340
RCA, 129–130, 229
Reciprocal causation theory of leadership, 364–365
Reciprocity, as approach to motivation, 199–200
Recitation, 187
Regression model, 121
Reinforcer, defined, 337. *See also* Schedules of reinforcement
Reliability, test, 181
Relocations, 480–481
Repetition, for learning
active, 187
distributed, 187
frequent, 187
massed, 187
Republic Steel, 443
Resource allocator, manager as, 355
Resources, management of declining, 551–552
Responsibility. *See also* Social responsibility
centers, 163–164
personal, 518–519
Rewards
extrinsic, 325
intrinsic, 325
Reward systems, 178, 199
employee preferences in, 201–202
motivational framework of, 199–201
summarized, 203
Risky shift phenomenon, 394–395
Role(s)
of group member, 380
managerial. *See* Manager(s)
negotiation, 200, 474–475
playing, 188, 391
Rules, 59, 115

Satisfaction, employee, with rewards, 201. *See also* Job satisfaction
Satisficing, 91
Saturation, in creative process, 462

Scalar principle, 20, 221–222
Schedules of reinforcement, 338
  fixed, 339
  interval, 338–339
  ratio, 339–340
  use of, in organizations, 340
  variable, 339–340
Scientific management, 22–23
  and motion study, 24–25
  problems of application of, 26–28
  resistance to, 25
  and task management, 23–25
  Taylor's four principles of, 25–26
  and worker-management relations, 23
SCM Corporation, 227
Sears, Roebuck and Company, 219
Secondary groups, 383–384
Selection, 178
  application blanks for, 181–183
  and hiring interview, 183
  job search methods for, 178–180
  summarized, 202
  tests for, 180–181
Self-contained tasks, 277–278
Self-estrangement, 400
Self-fulfilling prophecy, 304–305
Self-shaping, 341
Sensitivity training, 487–488
Sequence, 59, 96
Service organizations, specialized, 258–259
Shaping, 341
Sherman Antitrust Act (1890), 428
Shift work, 484–485
Simplex Method, 143
Simulation, 150–152
Single global ratings, 195
Situational theory of behavior, 44
Sleeper effect, 313
Social audit, 441
  approaches to, 441
  benefit-cost approach to, 441
  concept of, 441
  cost or outlay approach to, 441
  current status of, 441–442
  inventory approach to, 441
  program management approach to, 441
Social man, model of, 37
Social responsibility, 67, 87, 424–425
  arguments against, 435–436
  arguments for, 433–434
  assessing arguments about, 436
  and business ethics, 436–440, 446–447
  of businessmen, 428–429
  Committee for Economic Development (CED) and, 429–431
  current era of, 431
  doctrine of, 429
  early views of, 425–428
  environmental quality and, 442–444
  evolution of, 425–433
  government-business relations and, 445–446
  modern era of, 428–429
  social audit for, 441–442
  summarized, 447–448
Social system
  external, 380
  group as, 37
  internal, 380
Societal expectations, in decision making, 87
Society, business and, 425
Sociotechnical system, organization as, 397
Span of control, 217–219
Specialist, vs. generalist, 519–520
Spokesperson, manager as, 354
Staff personnel, 14–15, 231–233
Staff work, completed, 96
Standard costs, 162–163
Standardization, 380
Standard Oil Trust, 427
Stanford Research Institute, 477
State-backed corporations, 262–263
State University Medical Center, case study of, 287–289
Status
  differences, as barrier to integration, 235
  group structure and, 392–393
Stereotypes, 302–303
Stimulus event, in decision making, 61–62, 82
Stockholders, 226–227
Strategic failures, case studies of, 129–133
Strategic Management Institute, 121
Strategies. *See also* Decision-making strategies
  developing, 58–59, 112–113
  for processing information, 277–278
Streams of management. *See* Behavioral science stream of management; Traditional management stream
Structural changes, managing, 482
  and shift work, 484–485
  and work processes, 483
  and work scheduling, 483–484
Structural interventions, 489–490
Structural methods, for improving integration, 236–239
Structure(s)
  certainty and, 273–274
  group, 392–395
  mechanistic, 46–48, 269
  organic, 46–48, 269
  physical, and group behavior, 386–387
  tall vs. flat, 219–220
Suboptimization, 91
  biased information search as cause of, 92–93

human limits to rationality as cause of, 91–92
Subordinates
influence of, on leadership, 366
participation of, in decision making, 373–374
Subsystems, 38
Success, models of managerial, 512–516
Sunrise, sunset industries, 548
Supervision, first-line, 230–231
Support, 364
Synectics, 467
Systems forces, 37
System(s) theory, 37
assumptions of, 38
Barnard's, 38–40
evaluation of, 40–42
of group behavior, 380–381

Tactics, developing, 59, 113
Task assignments, managing, 472
and job enrichment, 473–474
and MAPS, 475–476
and role negotiation, 474–475
Task forces
for improving integration, 238–239
temporary, 279
Task management, 23–25
Task orientation, as dimension of leader behavior, 357–358, 365, 381
Tavistock coal-mining study, 395–397
Team(s)
building, 490–491
permanent, 279
Technological change, managing, 476, 481
and automated factory, 476–477
and automated office, 477–478
and telecommunications, 478–479
Technology, 276
alienation and, 400–402
automated, 218, 270
mass production, 218, 270
process, 218, 270
unit, 218, 270
Woodward study on, 218, 270–271
Telecommunications, 478–479
Testing, in creative process, 462
Tests, as selection devices, 180
concurrent validity of, 181
predictive validity of, 181
reliability of, 181
validity of, 180
Texas Instruments, 164, 184
Thematic Apperception Test (TAT), 335
Theory X, 43, 545
Theory Y, 43, 230, 545
Therbligs, 24
Three Mile Island, 444
Time management, 520–521
benefits of, 521
establishing priorities in, 521
techniques in, 522–523
Time series analysis and projection, 120
moving average, 120
trend projections, 121
Time span of discretion, 198–199
Total costs (TC), 139
Traditional management stream, 3, 7–8, 32–33
organizational framework and, 68–69
summarized, 29–30
Training, employee, 178, 185–186. *See also* Development, employee
behavioral conditions for, 186
programs, effective, 188–189
rules, 187
summarized, 203
techniques, 187–188
Training (T-) groups, 488
Trait ratings, traditional, 193–195
Trait theory of leadership, 356–357
Transformation agent, 554
Transportation Model, 143
Treasury, U.S. Department of the, 116
Trend
extrapolation, 119
projections, 121
Trusteeship
individual, 426
management, 428
Two-career families, 543–544

Uncertainty
amount of, in decision making, 84–85
studies on external environmental, 272–274, 275, 276
Unconflicted adherence decision-making strategy, 93
Unconflicted change decision-making strategy, 93
Unit concept, Barnard's, 40, 236
United Automobile Workers (UAW), 295–296, 422
Unit technology, 218, 270
Unity of command, 13, 20, 220
Unity of direction, 20, 220–221
U.S. Steel, 426, 443–444

Validity, of tests, 180
concurrent, 181
predictive, 181
Value
defined, 326
expected, 148–149
Variable costs (VC), 139
Variable-interval schedules, 339
Variable-ratio schedules, 339

Ventures, 262
  joint, 262
Vertical dyadic theory of leadership, 365
Vertical information systems, 278
Vertical integration, 261
Visionary forecasts, 120

Wagner Act (1935), 295
Waiting line analysis (queuing), 149–150
Wall Street Journal, 190, 443, 444
Washington Star, 458
Watergate scandal, 447
Weighted application blank, 182
Westinghouse Corporation, 223, 479
Women, working, 542
Woolworth, F. W., Co., 440
Work
  abroad, 549–550
  changing expectations of, 539–544
  ethic, 539, 540
  facilitation, 364
  and military and government employees, 544
  and part-time workers, 542–543
  processes, 483
  and racial minorities, 541
  scheduling, 483–484
  shift, 484–485
  and two-career families, 543–544
  women and, 542
Worker-management relations, 23
Work force
  changes in, 537–539
  growth of skilled, 15
  reductions in, 479–480
  white-collar, 537–538

Yale University studies on communication, 312–313
Youngstown Sheet and Tube Company, 443–444

Zero-based budgeting (ZBB), 164–165
Zero-sum conflict, 456–458